T0064981

THE ORIGINAL WHITE HOUSE COOK BOOK

COOKING, ETIQUETTE, MENUS, AND MORE
FROM THE EXECUTIVE ESTATE
1887 EDITION

F.L. GILLETTE AND
HUGO ZIEMANN STEWARD OF THE WHITE HOUSE

FOREWORD BY **JOHN MOELLER**
FORMER WHITE HOUSE CHEF

Racehorse Publishing

First published in 1887 by The Werner Company

First Racehorse Publishing Edition 2017

All rights to any and all materials in copyright owned by the publisher are strictly reserved by the publisher.

Foreword © 2017 Racehorse Publishing

Racehorse Publishing books may be purchased in bulk at special discounts for sales promotion, corporate gifts, fund-raising, or educational purposes. Special editions can also be created to specifications. For details, contact the Special Sales Department, Skyhorse Publishing, 307 West 36th Street, 11th Floor, New York, NY 10018 or info@skyhorsepublishing.com.

Racehorse Publishing™ is a pending trademark of Skyhorse Publishing, Inc.®, a Delaware corporation.

Visit our website at www.skyhorsepublishing.com.

10 9 8 7 6 5

Library of Congress Cataloging-in-Publication Data is available on file.

Cover artwork credit: iStockphoto
Cover photo credit: Harris & Ewing, Library of Congress

Print ISBN: 978-1-63158-131-1
Ebook ISBN: 978-1-63158-132-8

Printed in China

To the
Wives of Our Presidents,
Those Noble Women who have
Graced the White House,
And whose Names and Memories
Are dear to all Americans,
This Volume
Is affectionately dedicated

—BY THE AUTHOR.

Table of Contents

☙

Foreword

After spending nearly forty years cooking—thirteen of them as a chef at the White House, serving three first families and all of the official functions that we executed—I can say that a book like this not only celebrates the traditions of the White House from over a century ago, but also some grand dishes and cooking techniques that can be applied to the modern-day cook.

I started my culinary career in the late seventies working in a hotel in my hometown of Lancaster, Pennsylvania. I enrolled in the culinary program at the local vo-tech in high school and then went on to Johnson & Wales University for culinary arts. I watched *The Galloping Gourmet* on TV along with Julia Child. One of the highlights of my career was when Mrs. Child was invited to the White House for a ladies luncheon. I was preparing the menu for this event and was unaware that she was going to be there. She came into the kitchen after the luncheon, and thanked us all for a job well done. A week later, one of the ushers (management of the White House) showed me a letter that Mrs. Child wrote to Mrs. Clinton about how much she enjoyed the experience, from the service to how delicious the food was. It was an awesome experience. During my tenure at the White House, I served many notable people, but that was a particularly good day!

In the mid-eighties, I decided to follow a chef friend of mine to France to see if I could try and work there. Well, this trip lasted almost three years. I started at a small bistro in Dijon and worked my way up to a two-star Michelin restaurant, which was the changing point in my career. Watching what the chefs were doing in each of their kitchens, and seeing them use their great ingredients was just incredible. I returned to the United States and found a job at a resort in St. Croix USVI for a year. Then, while passing though Washington, DC, I quickly found work at a French style restaurant off of Dupont Circle. This began my relationship with other French chefs in the area, which eventually led me to one who started working at the White House as a sous chef.

Almost two years later, he contacted me to see if I would be interested in being his sous chef. He said that he was French-born but an American citizen, and informed me that being an American citizen was a prerequisite to being employed full-time in the White House. The pastry chef was in a similar situation. He said that he could bring in a French-born chef who is an American citizen, but he felt that would be too many French chefs on a team that consists of only five employees. What he was looking for was an American that knew something about French cooking. So that séjour in France is what separated me from the other candidates and got me into the White House. I started cooking for President George H.W. Bush, and remained there through the Clinton and Bush Jr. presidencies. This was an amazing experience: not just cooking for the first families, but also getting to know them on a personal basis.

The job as a White House chef has two major responsibilities. One, you are a private chef in the Executive Residence taking care of the First Family's needs for breakfast, lunch, and dinner as well as taking care of their guests. The White House is also a banquet house, and it's your job to organize meals for any of the entertaining that the First Family might need—from state dinners, First Lady Tea, or a picnic on the South Grounds. This book will help you with wide spectrum recipes and techniques to achieve this versatility on a daily basis.

During my time as a chef there, we would have a rotation of menu items for the daily meals to serve the First Family, but when it came to the official functions, we would never do the same menu twice. This was the hardest part of being a chef at the White House. I was always on the hunt looking for new menu ideas to present to the Social Secretary, and ultimately, the First Lady. I would always turn to what is in season and locally obtained before I reach outside the area.

I find that the parts of this book that explain basic cooking terminology and recipes are surprisingly accurate and can be applied to a novice or seasoned cook. I would use heavy cream instead of the milk of today (which was richer back then). I find it fun to read about all of the ingredients and animal products that were available during this time period. You do not see many of these nowadays, unless you are a hunter.

When using this cookbook, the one thing you have to keep in mind is that the ingredient list is in the body of the recipe. You will have to read the entire recipe in order to make a list of the things that you will need. This is not the conventional way that you see a recipe, but the steps are simple enough to follow.

The sections on canning and preserving your food might not be as useful in today's age. However, during the late 1800s, when the book was written, this was an important storage technique in most households. You may not want to do this, but I personally enjoy preserving summer fruit into jams and keep them for the year. The home chef will find this part interesting.

This book also educates the reader on how to run a home. With the busy schedule of a family in which both spouses are working, you will be able to use this book as a quick reference for getting ready for a dinner party or just managing your household. Entertaining can only be achieved successfully if you have a complete knowledge of the details of setting up an event. The chapters discussing health issues, table etiquette, and beverage service are extremely helpful, as are the measures and weights included in the recipes.

I hope that you will enjoy this cookbook because it is more than just that. The author really guides you through all sorts of cooking skills, and shows you how to prepare your meals from scratch. These techniques will help you enrich your culinary repertoire and take on new challenges so that you can experiment with new foods. Cooking is a life skill that everyone should have at least some basic knowledge of. It can be difficult to think of what you are going to do with a chicken breast when it's five-thirty in the evening, and you know your family will be looking for something special. What I always try to convey to my clients and students is to just start today with the basics and try not to take on too much in the beginning. As each week passes, and you begin to hone your cooking skills, you'll become more comfortable and confident in the kitchen. There is nothing more satisfying than preparing a meal for friends or family and breaking bread together. You feel good that you can nourish those that come to your table. It is an awesome feeling and a basic human need. Good luck and bon appétit!

Chef John Moeller
former White House chef,
author of *Dining at the White House*,
and teacher of the culinary profession

White House Cook Book.

CARVING.

Carving is one important acquisition in the routine of daily living, and all should try to attain a knowledge or ability to do it well, and withal gracefully.

When carving use a chair slightly higher than the ordinary size, as it gives a better purchase on the meat, and appears more graceful than when standing, as is often quite necessary when carving a turkey, or a very large joint. More depends on skill than strength. The platter should be placed opposite, and sufficiently near to give perfect command of the article to be carved, the knife of medium size, sharp with a keen edge. Commence by cutting the slices thin, laying them carefully to one side of the platter, then afterwards placing the desired amount on each guest's plate, to be served in turn by the servant.

In carving fish, care should be taken to help it in perfect flakes; for if these are broken the beauty of the fish is lost. The carver should acquaint himself with the choicest parts and morsels; and to give each guest an equal share of those *tidbits* should be his maxim. Steel knives and forks should on no account be used in helping fish, as these are liable to impart a *very* disagreeable flavor. A fish-trowel of silver or plated silver is the proper article to use.

Gravies should be sent to the table very *hot*, and in helping one to gravy or melted butter, place it on a vacant side of the plate; not *pour* it over their meat, fish or fowl, that they may use only as much as they like.

When serving fowls, or meat, accompanied with stuffing, the guests should be asked if they would have a portion, as it is not every one to whom the flavor of stuffing is agreeable; in filling their plates, avoid heaping one thing upon another, as it makes a bad appearance.

A word about the care of carving knives: a fine steel knife should not come in contact with intense heat, because it destroys its temper, and therefore impairs its cutting qualities. Table carving knives should not be used in the kitchen, either around the stove, or for cutting bread, meats, vegetables, etc.; a fine whetstone should be kept for sharpening, and the knife cleaned carefully to avoid dulling its edge, all of which is quite essential to successful carving.

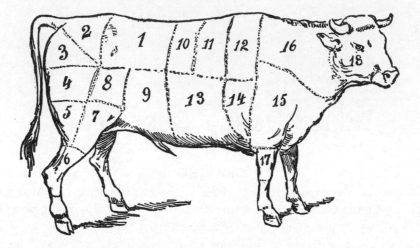

BEEF.

HIND-QUARTER.

No. 1. Used for choice roasts, the porter-house and sirloin steaks.

No. 2. Rump, used for steaks, stews and corned beef.

No. 3. Aitch-bone, used for boiling-pieces, stews and pot roasts.

No. 4. Buttock or round, used for steaks, pot roasts, beef *á la mode*; also a prime boiling-piece.

No. 5. Mouse round, used for boiling and stewing.

No. 6. Shin or leg, used for soups, hashes, etc.

No. 7. Thick flank, cut with under fat, is a prime boiling piece, good for stews and corned beef, pressed beef.

No. 8. Veiny piece, used for corned beef, dried beef.

No. 9. Thin flank, used for corned beef and boiling-pieces.

FORE-QUARTER.

No. 10. Five ribs called the fore-rib. This is considered the primest piece for roasting; also makes the finest steaks.

No. 11. Four ribs, called the middle ribs, used for roasting.

No. 12. Chuck ribs, used for second quality of roasts and steaks.

No. 13. Brisket, used for corned beef, stews, soups and spiced beef.

No. 14. Shoulder-piece, used for stews, soups, pot-roasts, mince-meat, and hashes.

Nos. 15, 16. Neck, clod or sticking-piece, used for stocks, gravies, soups, mince-pie meat, hashes, bologna sausages, etc.

No. 17. Shin or shank, used mostly for soups and stewing.

No. 18. Cheek.

The following is a classification of the qualities of meat, according to the several joints of beef, when cut up.

First Class.—Includes the sirloin with the kidney suet (1), the rump steak piece (2), the forerib (11).

Second Class.—The buttock or round (4), the thick flank (7), the middle ribs (11).

Third Class.—The aitch-bone (3), the mouse-round (5), the thin flank (8, 9), the chuck (12), the shoulder piece (14), the brisket (13).

Fourth Class.—The clod, neck and sticking piece (15, 16.)

Fifth Class.—Shin or shank (17).

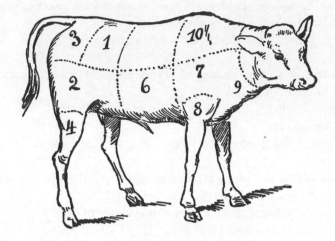

VEAL.

HIND-QUARTER.

No. 1. Loin, the choicest cuts used for roasts and chops.

No. 2. Fillet, used for roasts and cutlets.

No. 3. Loin, chump-end used for roasts and chops.

No. 4. The hind-knuckle or hock, used for stews, pot-pies, meat-pies.

FORE-QUARTER.

No. 5. Neck, best end used for roasts, stews and chops.

No. 6. Breast, best end used for roasting, stews and chops.

No. 7. Blade-bone, used for pot roasts and baked dishes.

No. 8. Fore-knuckle, used for soups and stews.

No. 9. Breast, brisket-end used for baking, stews and pot-pies.

No. 10. Neck, scrag-end used for stews, broth, meat-pies, etc.

In cutting up veal, generally, the hind-quarter is divided in loin and leg, and the fore-quarter into breast, neck and shoulder.

The Several Parts of a Moderately-sized, well-fed Calf, about eight weeks old, are nearly of the following weights:—Loin and chump, 18 lbs.; fillet, 12½ lbs.; hind knuckle, 5½ lbs.; shoulder, 11 lbs.; neck, 11 lbs.; breast, 9 lbs.; and fore knuckle, 5 lbs.; making a total of 144 lbs. weight.

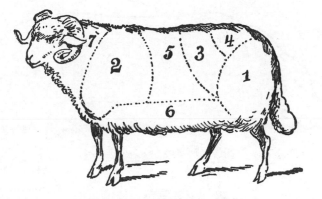

MUTTON.

No. 1. Leg, used for roasts and for boiling.

No. 2. Shoulder, used for baked dishes and roasts.

No. 3. Loin, best end used for roasts, chops.

No. 4. Loin, chump end used for roasts and chops.

No. 5. Rack, or rib chops, used for French chops, rib chops, either for frying or broiling; also used for choice stews.

No. 6. Breast, used for roast, baked dishes, stews, chops.

No. 7. Neck or scrag end, used for cutlets and stews and meat pies.

NOTE.—A saddle of mutton or double loin is two loins cut off before the carcase is split open down the back. French chops are a small rib chop, the end of the bone trimmed off and the meat and fat cut away from the thin end, leaving the round piece of meat attached to the larger end, which leaves the small rib-bone bare. Very tender and sweet.

Mutton is *prime* when cut from a carcase which has been fed out of doors, and allowed to run upon the hillside; they are best when about three years old. The fat will then be abundant, white and hard, the flesh juicy and firm, and of a clear red color.

For mutton roasts, choose the shoulder, the saddle, or the loin or haunch. The leg should be boiled. Almost any part will do for broth.

Lamb born in the middle of the winter, reared under shelter, and fed in a great measure upon milk, then killed in the spring, is considered a great delicacy, though lamb is good at a year old. Like all young animals, lamb ought to be thoroughly cooked, or it is most unwholesome.

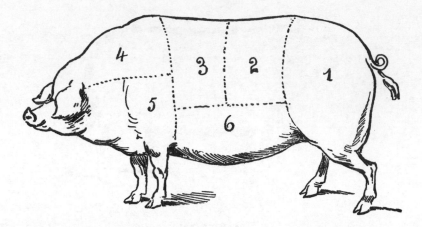

PORK.

No. 1. Leg, used for smoked hams, roasts and corned pork.

No. 2. Hind-loin, used for roasts, chops and baked dishes.

No. 3. Fore-loin or ribs, used for roasts, baked dishes or chops.

No. 4. Spare-rib, used for roasts, chops, stews.

No. 5. Shoulder, used for smoked shoulder, roasts and corned pork.

No. 6. Brisket and flank, used for pickling in salt, and smoked bacon.

The cheek is used for pickling in salt, also the shank or shin. The feet and usually used for souse and jelly.

For family use, the leg is the most economical, that is when fresh, and the loin the richest. The best pork is from carcases weighing from fifty to about one hundred and twenty-five pounds. Pork is a white and close meat, and it is almost impossible to over-roast pork or cook it too much; when underdone it is exceedingly unwholesome.

VENISON.

No. 1. Shoulder, used for roasting; it may be boned and stuffed, then afterwards baked or roasted.

No. 2. Fore-loin, used for roasts and steaks.

No. 3. Haunch or loin, used for roasts, steaks, stews.   The ribs cut close may be used for soups.   Good for pickling and making into smoked venison.

No. 4. Breast, used for baking dishes, stewing.

No. 5. Scrag or neck, used for soups.

The choice of venison should be judged by the fat, which, when the venison is young, should be thick, clear and close, and the meat a very dark red.   The flesh of a female deer, about four years old, is the sweetest and best of venison.

Buck venison, which is in season from June to the end of September, is finer than doe venison, which is in season from October to December.   Neither should be dressed at any other time of year, and no meat requires so much care as venison in killing, preserving, and dressing.

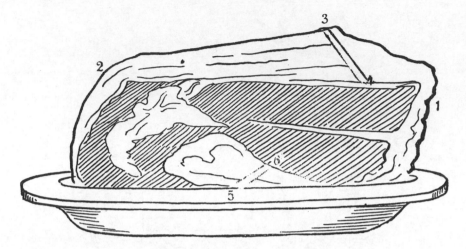

SIRLOIN OF BEEF.

This choice roasting-piece should be cut with one good firm stroke from end to end of the joint, at the upper part, in thin, long, even slices in the direction of the line from 1 to 2, cutting across the grain, serving each guest with some of the fat with the lean; this may be done by cutting a small thin slice from underneath the bone from 5 to 6, through the tenderloin.

Another way of carving this piece, and which will be of great assistance in doing it well, is to insert the knife just above the bone at the bottom, and run sharply along, dividing the meat from the bone at the bottom and end, thus leaving it perfectly flat; then carve in long, thin slices the usual way. When the bone has been removed and the sirloin rolled before it is cooked, it is laid upon the platter on one end, and an even, thin slice is carved across the grain of the upper surface.

Roast ribs should be carved in thin, even slices from the thick end towards the thin in the same manner as the sirloin; this can be more easily and cleanly done if the carving knife is first run along between the meat and the end and rib-bones, thus leaving it free from bone to be cut into slices.

Tongue.—To carve this, it should be cut crosswise, the middle being the best; cut in very *thin* slices. thereby improving its delicacy, making it more tempting; as is the case of all well-carved meats. The root of the tongue is usually left on the platter.

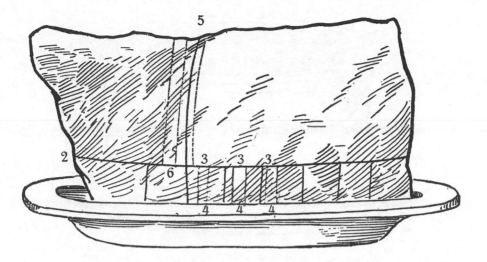

BREAST OF VEAL.

This piece is quite similar to a fore-quarter of lamb after the shoulder has been taken off. A breast of veal consists of two parts, the rib-bones and the gristly brisket. These parts may be separated by sharply passing the carving knife in the direction of the line from 1 to 2; and when they are entirely divided, the rib bones should be carved in the direction of the line from 5 to 6, and the brisket can be helped by cutting slices from 3 to 4.

The carver should ask the guests whether they have a preference for the brisket or ribs; and if there be a sweetbread served with the dish, as is frequently with this roast of veal, each person should receive a piece.

Though veal and lamb contain less nutrition than beef and mutton, in proportion to their weight, they are often preferred to these latter meats on account of their delicacy of texture and flavor. A whole breast of veal weighs from nine to twelve pounds.

A FILLET OF VEAL.

A fillet of veal is one of the prime roasts of veal; it is taken from the leg above the knuckle; a piece weighing from ten to twelve pounds is a good size and requires about four hours for roasting. Before roasting, it is dressed with a force meat or stuffing placed in the cavity from where the bone was taken out and the flap tightly secured together with skewers; many bind it together with tape.

To carve it, cut in even thin slices off from the whole of the upper part or top, in the same manner as from a rolled roast of beef, as in the direction of the figures 1 and 2; this gives the person served some of the dressing with each slice of meat.

Veal is very unwholesome unless it is cooked thoroughly, and when roasted should be of a rich brown color. Bacon, fried pork, sausage-balls, with greens are among the accompaniments of roasted veal, also a cut lemon.

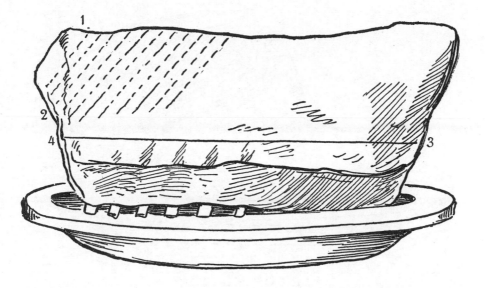

NECK OF VEAL.

The best end of a neck of veal makes a very good roasting-piece; it however is composed of bone and ribs that make it quite difficult to carve, unless it is done properly. To attempt to carve each chop and serve it, you would not only place *too* large a piece upon the plate of the person you intend to serve; but you would waste much time, and should the vertebræ have not been removed by the butcher, you would be compelled to exercise such a degree of strength that would make one's appearance very ungraceful, and possibly, too, throwing gravy over your neighbor sitting next to you. The correct way to carve this roast is to cut diagonally from figure 1 to 2, and help in slices of moderate thickness; then it may be cut from 3 to 4, in order to separate the small bones; divide and serve them, having first inquired if they are desired.

This joint is usually sent to the table accompanied by bacon, ham, tongue, or pickled pork on a separate dish and with a cut lemon on a plate. There are also a number of sauces that are suitable with this roast.

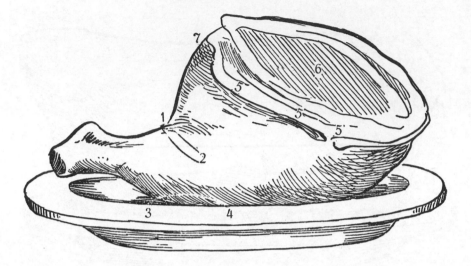

LEG OF MUTTON.

The best mutton, and that from which most nourishment is obtained, is that of sheep from three to six years old, and which have been fed on dry sweet pastures; then mutton is in its *prime*, the flesh being firm, juicy, dark colored, and full of the richest gravy. When mutton is two years old, the meat is flabby, pale and savorless.

In carving a roasted leg, the best slices are found by cutting quite down to the bone, in the direction from 1 to 2, and slices may be taken from either side.

Some very good cuts are taken from the broad end from 5 to 6, and the fat on this ridge is very much liked by many. The cramp-bone is a delicacy, and is obtained by cutting down to the bone at 4, and running the knife under it in a semicircular direction to 3. The nearer the knuckle the drier the meat, but the under side contains the most finely grained meat, from which slices may be cut lengthwise. When sent to the table a frill of paper around the knuckle will improve its appearance.

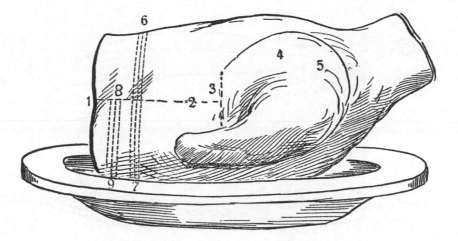

FORE-QUARTER OF LAMB.

The first cut to be made in carving a fore-quarter of lamb is to separate the shoulder from the breast and ribs; this is done by passing a sharp carving knife lightly around the dotted line as shown by the figures 3, 4, and 5, so as to cut through the skin, and then, by raising with a little force the shoulder, into which the fork should be firmly fixed, it will easily separate with just a little more cutting with the knife; care should be taken not to cut away too much of the meat from the breast when dividing the shoulder from it, as that would mar its appearance. The shoulder may be placed upon a separate dish for convenience. The next process is to divide the ribs from the brisket by cutting through the meat in the line from 1 to 2; then the ribs may be carved in the direction of the line 6 to 7, and the brisket from 8 to 9. The carver should always ascertain whether the guest prefers ribs, brisket or a piece of the shoulder.

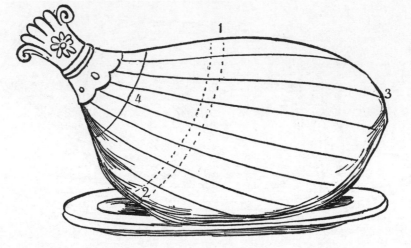

HAM.

The carver in cutting a ham must be guided according as he desires to prac-
tise economy, or have at once fine slices out of the prime part.   Under the first
supposition, he will commence at the knuckle end, and cut off thin slices towards
the thick and upper part of the ham.

To reach the choicer portion of the ham, the knife, which must be very sharp
and thin, should be carried quite down to the bone through the thick fat in the
direction of the line, from 1 to 2.   The slices should be even and thin, cutting
both lean and fat together, always cutting down to the bone.   Some cut a circular hole in the middle of a ham gradually enlarging it outwardly.   Then again
many carve a ham by first cutting from 1 to 2, then across the other way from
3 to 4.   Remove the skin after the ham is cooked and send to the table with
dots of dry pepper or dry mustard on the top, a tuft of fringed paper twisted
about the knuckle, and plenty of fresh parsley around the dish.   This will always
ensure an inviting appearance.

Roast Pig.—The modern way of serving a pig is not to send it to the table
whole, but have it carved partially by the cook; first, by dividing the shoulder
from the body; then the leg in the same manner; also separating the ribs into
convenient portions.   The head may be divided and placed on the same platter.   To be served as hot as possible.

A Spare Rib of Pork is carved by cutting slices from the fleshy part, after
which the bones should be disjointed and separated.

A leg of pork may be carved in the same manner as a ham.

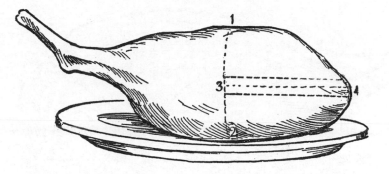

HAUNCH OF VENISON.

A haunch of venison is the *prime* joint, and is carved very similar to almost any roasted or boiled leg; it should be first cut crosswise down to the bone following the line from 1 to 2; then turn the platter with the knuckle farthest from you, put in the point of the knife, and cut down as far as you can, in the directions shown by the dotted lines from 3 to 4 then there can; be taken out as many slices as is required on the right and left of this. Slices of venison should be cut thin, and gravy given with them, but as there is a special sauce made with red wine and currant jelly to accompany this meat, do not serve gravy before asking the guest if he pleases to have any.

The fat of this meat is like mutton, apt to cool soon, and become hard and disagreeable to the palate; it should therefore be served always on warm plates, and the platter kept over a hot-water dish, or spirit lamp. Many cooks dish it up with a white paper frill pined around the knuckle-bone.

A haunch of mutton is carved the same as a haunch of venison.

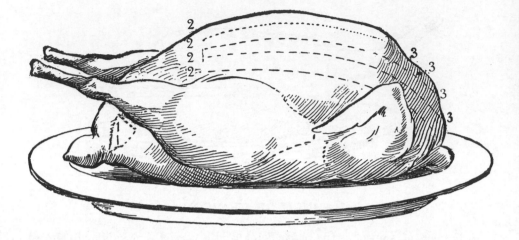

TURKEY.

A turkey having been relieved from strings and skewers used in trussing should be placed on the table with the head or neck at the carver's right hand. An expert carver places the fork in the turkey, and does not remove it until the whole is divided. First insert the fork firmly in the lower part of the breast, just forward of fig. 2, then sever the legs and wings on both sides, if the whole is to be carved, cutting neatly through the joint next to the body, letting these parts lie on the platter. Next, cut downward from the breast from 2 to 3, as many even slices of the white meat as may be desired, placing the pieces neatly on one side of the platter. Now unjoint the legs and wings at the middle joint, which can be done very skillfully by a little practice. Make an opening into the cavity of the turkey for dipping out the inside dressing, by cutting a piece from the rear part 1, 1, called the apron. Consult the tastes of the guests as to which part is preferred; if no choice is expressed, serve a portion of both light and dark meat. One of the most delicate parts of the turkey, are two little muscles, lying in small dish-like cavities on each side of the back, a little behind the leg attachments; the next most delicate meat fills the cavities in the neck bone, and next to this, that on the second joints. The lower part of the leg (or drumstick, as it is called) being hard, tough, and stringy is rarely ever helped to any one, but allowed to remain on the dish.

ROAST GOOSE.

To carve a goose, first begin by separating the leg from the body, by putting the fork into the small end of the limb, pressing it closely to the body, then passing the knife under at 2, and turning the leg back as you cut through the joint. To take off the wing, insert the fork in the small end of the pinion, and press it close to the body; put the knife in at figure 1, and divide the joint. When the legs and wings are off, the breast may be carved in long even slices, as represented in the lines from 1 to 2. The back and lower side bones, as well as the two lower side bones by the wing, may be cut off; but the best pieces of the goose are the breast and thighs, after being separated from the drum-sticks. Serve a little of the dressing from the inside, by making a circular slice in the apron at figure 3. A goose should never be over a year old; a tough goose is very difficult to carve, and certainly most difficult to eat.

FOWLS.

First insert the knife between the leg and the body, and cut to the bone; then turn the leg back with the fork, and if the fowl is tender the joint will give away easily. The wing is broken off the same way, only dividing the joint with the knife, in the direction from 1 to 2. The four quarters having been removed in this way, take off the merry-thought and the neck-bones; these last are to be removed by putting the knife in at figure 3 and 4, pressing it hard, when they will break off from the part that sticks to the breast. To separate the breast from the body of the fowl, cut through the tender ribs close to the breast, quite down to the tail. Now turn the fowl over, back upwards; put the knife into the bone midway between the neck and the rump, and on raising the lower end it will separate readily. Turn now the rump from you, and take off very neatly the two side-bones and the fowl is carved. In separating the thigh from the drum-stick, the knife must be inserted exactly at the joint, for if not accurately hit, some difficulty will be experienced to get them apart; this is easily acquired by practice. There is no difference in carving roast and boiled fowls if full grown; but in very young fowls, the breast is usually served whole; the wings and breast are considered the best part, but in young ones the legs are the most juicy. In the case of a capon or large fowl, slices may be cut off at the breast, the same as carving a pheasant.

ROAST DUCK.

A young duckling may be carved in the same manner as a fowl, the legs and wings being taken off first on either side.   When the duck is full size, carve it like a goose; first cutting it in slices from the breast, beginning close to the wing and proceeding upward towards the breast bone, as is represented by the lines 1 to 2. An opening may be made, by cutting out a circular slice as shown by the dotted lines at number 3.

Some are fond of the feet, and when dressing the duck, these should be neatly skinned and never removed.   Wild duck is highly esteemed by epicures; it is trussed like a tame duck, and carved in the same manner, the breast being the choicest part.

PARTRIDGES.

Partridges are generally cleaned and trussed the same way as a pheasant, but the custom of cooking them with the heads on is going into disuse somewhat. The usual way of carving them is similar to a pigeon, dividing it into two equal parts.   Another method is to cut it into three pieces, by severing a wing and leg on either side from the body, by following the lines 1 to 2, thus making two servings of those parts, leaving the breast for a third plate.   The third method is to thrust back the body from the legs, and cut through the middle of the breast, thus making four portions that may be served.   Grouse and prairie-chicken are carved from the breast when they are large, and quartered or halved when of medium size.

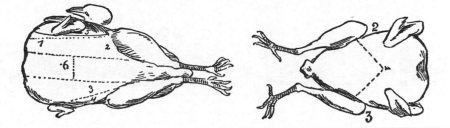

PHEASANT.

Place your fork firmly in the centre of the breast of this large game bird and cut deep slices to the bone at figures 1 and 2; then take off the leg in the line from 3 and 4 and the wing 3 and 5, severing both sides the same. In taking off the wings, be careful not to cut too near the neck; if you do you will hit upon the neck-bone, from which the wing must be separated. Pass the knife through the line 6, and under the merry-thought towards the neck, which will detach it. Cut the other parts as in a fowl. The breast, wings, and merry-thought of a pheasant, are the most highly prized, although the legs are considered very finely flavored. Pheasants are frequently roasted with the head left on; in that case, when dressing them, bring the head round under the wing, and fix it on the point of a skewer.

PIGEONS.

A very good way of carving these birds is to insert the knife at figure 1, and cut both ways to 2 and 3, when each portion may be divided into two pieces, then served. Pigeons, if not too large, may be cut in halves, either across or down the middle, cutting them into two equal parts; if young and small they may be served entirely whole.

Tame pigeons should be cooked as soon as possible after they are killed, as they very quickly lose their flavor. Wild pigeons, on the contrary, should hang a day or two in a cool place before they are dressed. Oranges cut into halves are used as a garnish for dishes of small birds, such as pigeons, quails, woodcock, squabs, snipe, etc. These small birds are either served whole or split down the back, making two servings.

MACKEREL.

The mackerel is one of the most beautiful of fish, being known by their silvery whiteness. It sometimes attains to the length of twenty inches, but usually, when fully grown, is about fourteen or sixteen inches long, and about two pounds in weight. To carve a baked mackerel, first remove the head and tail by cutting downward at 1 and 2; then split them down the back, so as to serve each person a part of each side piece. The roe should be divided in small pieces and served with each piece of fish. Other whole fish may be carved in the same manner. The fish is laid upon a little sauce or folded napkin, on a hot dish, and garnished with parsley.

BOILED SALMON.

This fish is seldom sent to the table whole, being *too* large for any ordinary sized family; the middle cut is considered the choicest to boil. To carve it, first run the knife down and along the upper side of the fish from 1 to 2, then again on the lower side from 3 to 4. Serve the thick part, cutting it lengthwise in slices in the direction of the line from 1 to 2, and the thin part breadthwise, or in the direction from 5 to 6. A slice of the thick with one of the thin, where lies the fat, should be served to each guest. Care should be taken when carving not to break the flakes of the fish, as that impairs its appearance. The flesh of the salmon is rich and delicious in flavor. Salmon is in season from the first of February to the end of August.

Soups.

Consommé, or Stock, forms the basis of all meat soups, and also of all princi pal sauces. It is, therefore, essential to the success of these culinary operations to know the most complete and economical method of extracting from a certain quantity of meat the best possible stock or broth. Fresh uncooked beef makes the best stock, with the addition of cracked bones, as the glutinous matter contained in them renders it important that they should be boiled with the meat, which adds to the strength and thickness of the soup. They are composed of an earthy substance—to which they owe their solidity—of gelatine, and a fatty fluid, something like marrow. *Two ounces* of them contain as much gelatine as *one pound* of meat; but in them, this is so encased in the earthy substance, that boiling water can dissolve only the surface of the whole bones, but by breaking them they can be dissolved more. When there is an abundance of it, it causes the stock, when cold, to become a jelly. The flesh of old animals contains more flavor than the flesh of young ones. Brown meats contain more flavor than white.

Mutton is too strong in flavor for good stock, while veal, although quite glutinous, furnishes very little nutriment.

Some cooks use meat that has once been cooked; this renders little nourishment and destroys the flavor. It might answer for ready soup, but for stock to keep it is not as good, unless it should be roasted meats. Those contain higher fragrant properties; so by putting the remains of roast meats in the stock-pot you obtain a better flavor.

The shin bone is generally used, but the neck or "sticking piece," as the butchers call it, contains more of the substance that you want to extract, makes a stronger and more nutritious soup, than any other part of the animal. Meats for soup should always be put on to cook in *cold* water, in a covered pot, and allowed to simmer slowly for several hours, in order that the essence of the meat may be drawn out thoroughly, and should be carefully skimmed to prevent it from becoming turbid, never allowed to *boil fast* at any time, and if more water is needed, use boiling water from the tea-kettle; cold or lukewarm water spoils the flavor. Never salt it before the meat is tender (as that hardens and toughens the meat), especially if the meat is to be eaten. Take off every particle of scum as it rises, and before the vegetables are put in.

Allow a little less than a quart of water to a pound of meat and bone, and a teaspoonful of salt. When done, strain through a colander. If for clear soups strain again through a hair sieve, or fold a clean towel in a colander set over an earthen bowl, or any dish large enough to hold the stock. As stated before, stock is not as good when made entirely from cooked meats, but in a family where it requires a large joint roasted every day, the bones and bits and underdone pieces of beef, or the bony structure of turkey or chicken that has been left from carving, bones of roasted poultry, these all assist in imparting a rich dark color to soup, and would be sufficient, if stewed as above, to furnish a family, without buying fresh meat for the purpose; still, with the addition of a little fresh meat it would be more nutritious. In cold weather you can gather them up for several days and put them to cook in cold water, and when done, strain, and put aside until needed.

Soup will be as good the second day as the first if heated to the boiling point. It should never be left in the pot, but should be turned into a dish or shallow pan, and set aside to get cold. Never cover it up, as that will cause it to turn sour very quickly.

Before heating a second time, remove all the fat from the top. If this be melted in, the flavor of the soup will certainly be spoiled.

Thickened soups require nearly double the seasoning used for thin soups or broth.

Coloring is used in some brown soups, the chief of which is brown burnt sugar, which is known as caramel by French cooks.

Pounded spinach leaves give a fine green color to soup. Parsley, or the green leaves of celery, put in soup will serve instead of spinach.

Pound a large handful of spinach in a mortar, then tie it in a cloth, and wring out all the juice; put this in the soup you wish to color green, five minutes before taking it up.

Mock turtle, and sometimes veal and lamb soups, should be this color.

Ochras gives a green color to soup.

To color soup red, skin six red tomatoes, squeeze out the seeds and put them into the soup with the other vegetables—or take the juice only as directed for spinach.

For white soups, which are of veal, lamb or chicken, none but white vegetables are used; rice, pearl barley, vermicelli, or macaroni for thickening.

Grated carrot gives a fine amber color to soup; it must be put in as soon as the soup is free from scum.

Hotel and private-house stock is quite different.

Hotels use meat in such large quantities, that there is always more or less trimmings and bones of meat to add to fresh meats; that makes very strong stock, which they use in most all soups and gravies and other made dishes.

The meat from which soup has been made is good to serve cold thus: take out all the bones, season with pepper and salt, and catsup, if liked, then chop it small, tie it in a cloth, and lay it between two plates, with a weight on the upper one: slice it thin for luncheon or supper; or make sandwiches of it; or make a hash for breakfast; or make it into balls, with the addition of a little wheat flour and an egg, and serve them fried in fat, or boil in the soup.

An agreeable flavor is sometimes imparted to soup by sticking some cloves into the meat used for making stock; a few slices of onions fried very brown in butter are nice; also flour browned by simply putting it into a saucepan over the fire and stirring it constantly until it is a dark brown.

Clear soups must be perfectly transparent and thickened soups about the consistence of cream. When soups and gravies are kept from day to day in hot weather, they should be warmed up every day, and put into fresh-scalded pans or tureens, and placed in a cool cellar. In temperate weather, every other day may be sufficient.

HERBS AND VEGETABLES USED IN SOUPS.

Of vegetables the principal ones are carrots, tomatoes, asparagus, green peas, okra, macaroni, green corn, beans, rice, vermicelli, Scotch barley, pearl barley, wheat flour, mushroom or mushroom catsup, parsnips, beet-root, turnips, leeks, garlic, shalots and onions; sliced onions fried with butter and flour until they are browned, then rubbed through a sieve, are excellent to heighten the color and flavor of brown sauces and soups. The herbs usually used in soups are parsley, common thyme, summer savory, knotted marjoram, and other seasonings such as bay-leaves, tarragon, allspice, cinnamon, nutmeg, cloves, mace, black and white pepper, red pepper, lemon-peel and juice, orange peel and juice. The latter imparts a finer flavor and the acid much milder. These materials, with wine, and the various catsups, combined in various proportions, are, with other ingredients, made into almost an endless variety of excellent soups and gravies.

Soups that are intended for the principal part of a meal certainly ought not to be flavored like sauces. which are only intended to give relish to some particular dish.

STOCK.

Six pounds of shin of beef, or six pounds of knuckle of veal; any bones, trimmings of poultry, or fresh meat; one-quarter pound of lean bacon or ham, two ounces of butter, two large onions, each stuck with cloves; one turnip, three carrots, one head of celery, two ounces of salt, one-half teaspoonful of whole pepper, one large blade of mace, one bunch of savory herbs except sage, four quarts and one-half pint of cold water.

Cut up the meat and bacon, or ham, into pieces of about three inches square; break the bones into small pieces, rub the butter on the bottom of the stewpan; put in one-half a pint of water, the broken bones, then meat and all other ingredients. Cover the stewpan, and place it on a sharp fire, occasionally stirring its contents. When the bottom of the pan becomes covered with a pale, jelly-like substance, add the four quarts of cold water, and simmer very gently for five or six hours. As we have said before, do not let it boil quickly. When nearly cooked, throw in a tablespoonful of salt to assist the scum to rise. Remove every particle of scum whilst it is doing, and strain it through a fine hair sieve; when cool remove all grease. This stock will keep for many days in cold weather.

Stock is the basis of many of the soups afterwards mentioned, and this will be found quite strong enough for ordinary purposes. Keep it in small jars, in a cool place. It makes a good gravy for hash meats; one tablespoonful of it is sufficient to impart a fine flavor to a dish of macaroni and various other dishes. Good soups of various kinds are made from it at short notice; slice off a portion of the jelly, add water, and whatever vegetables and thickening preferred. It is best to partly cook the vegetables before adding to the stock, as much boiling injures the flavoring of the soup. Season and boil a few moments and serve hot.

WHITE STOCK.

White stock is used in the preparation of white soups, and is made by boiling six pounds of a knuckle of veal, cut up in small pieces, poultry trimmings, and four slices of lean ham. Proceed according to directions given in "Stock," above.

TO CLARIFY STOCK.

Place the stock in a clean saucepan, set it over a brisk fire. When boiling, add the white of one egg to each quart of stock, proceeding as follows: beat the whites of the eggs up well in a little water; then add a little hot stock; beat to a froth, and pour gradually into the pot; then beat the whole hard and long; allow it to boil up once, and immediately remove and strain through a thin flannel cloth.

BEEF SOUP.

Select a small shin of beef of moderate size, crack the bone in small pieces, wash and place it in a kettle to boil, with five or six quarts of *cold* water. Let it boil about two hours, or until it begins to get tender, then season it with a tablespoonful of salt, and a teaspoonful of pepper; boil it one hour longer, then add to it one carrot, two turnips, two tablespoonfuls of rice or pearl barley, one head of celery and a teaspoonful of summer savory powdered fine; the vegetables to be minced up in small pieces like dice. After these ingredients have boiled a quarter of an hour, put in two potatoes cut up in small pieces; let it boil half an hour longer, take the meat from the soup, and if intended to be served with it, take out the bones and lay it closely and neatly on a dish, and garnish with sprigs of parsley.

Serve made mustard and catsup with it. It is very nice pressed and eaten cold with mustard and vinegar, or catsup. Four hours are required for making this soup. Should any remain over the first day, it may be heated, with the addition of a little boiling water, and served again. Some fancy a glass of brown sherry added just before being served. Serve very hot.

VEAL SOUP. (Excellent.)

Put a knuckle of veal into three quarts of cold water, with a small quantity of salt, and one small tablespoonful of uncooked rice. Boil slowly, hardly above simmering, four hours, when the liquor should be reduced to half the usual quantity; remove from the fire. Into the tureen put the yolk of one egg, and stir well into it a teacupful of cream, or, in hot weather, new milk; add a piece of butter the size of a hickory-nut; on this strain the soup, boiling hot, stirring all the time. Just at the last, beat it well for a minute.

SCOTCH MUTTON BROTH.

Six pounds neck of mutton, three quarts water, five carrots, five turnips, two onions, four tablespoonfuls barley, a little salt. Soak mutton in water for an hour, cut off scrag, and put it in stewpan with three quarts of water. As soon as it boils, skim well, and then simmer for one and one-half hours Cut best end of mutton into cutlets, dividing it with two bones in each; take off nearly all fat before you put it into broth; skim the moment the meat boils, and every ten minutes afterwards; add carrots, turnips and onions, all cut into two or three pieces, then put them into soup soon enough to be thoroughly done; stir in barley; add salt to taste; let all stew together for three and one-half hours: about one-half hour before sending it to table, put in little chopped parsley and serve.

Cut the meat off the scrag into small pieces, and send it to table in the tureen with the soup. The other half of the mutton should be served on a separate dish, with whole turnips boiled and laid round it. Many persons are fond of mutton that has been boiled in soup.

You may thicken the soup with rice or barley that has first been soaked in cold water; or with green peas; or with young corn, cut down from the cob; or with tomatoes scalded, peeled and cut into pieces.

GAME SOUP.

Two grouse or partridges, or, if you have neither, use a pair of rabbits; half a pound of lean ham; two medium-sized onions; one pound of lean beef; fried bread; butter for frying; pepper, salt, and two stalks of white celery cut into inch lengths; three quarts of water.

Joint your game neatly; cut the ham and onions into small pieces, and fry all in butter to a light brown. Put into a soup-pot with the beef, cut into strips, and a little pepper. Pour on the water; heat slowly, and stew gently two hours. Take out the pieces of bird, and cover in a bowl; cook the soup an hour longer; strain; cool; drop in the celery, and simmer ten minutes. Pour upon fried bread in the tureen.

Venison soup made the same, with the addition of a tablespoonful of brown flour wet into a paste with cold water, adding a tablespoonful of catsup, Worcestershire, or other pungent sauce, and a glass of Madeira or brown sherry.

CONSOMME SOUP.

Take good strong stock (see pages 21 and 24), remove all fat from the surface, and for each quart of the stock allow the white and shell of one egg and a tablespoonful of water, well whipped together. Pour this mixture into a saucepan containing the stock; place it over the fire and heat the contents gradually, stirring often to prevent the egg from sticking to the bottom of the saucepan. Allow it to boil gently until the stock looks perfectly clear under the egg, which will rise and float upon the surface in the form of a thick white scum. Now remove it and pour it into a folded towel laid in a colander set over an earthen bowl, allowing it to run through without moving or squeezing it. Season with more salt if needed, and quickly serve very hot. This should be a clear amber color.

JULIENNE SOUP.

Cut carrots and turnips into quarter inch pieces the shape of dice; also celery into thin slices. Cover them with boiling water; add a teaspoonful of salt, half a teaspoonful pepper, and cook until soft. In another saucepan have two quarts of boiling stock (see pages 21 and 24), to which add the cooked vegetables, the water and more seasoning if necessary. Serve hot.

In the spring and summer season use asparagus, peas and string beans — all cut into small uniform thickness.

CREAM OF SPINACH.

Pick, wash and boil enough spinach to measure a pint, when cooked, chopped and pounded into a soft paste. Put it into a stewpan with four ounces of fresh butter, a little grated nutmeg, a teaspoonful of salt. Cook and stir it about ten minutes. Add to this two quarts of strong stock (see pages 21 and 24); let boil up, then rub it through a strainer. Set it over the fire again, and, when on the point of boiling, mix with it a tablespoonful of butter, and a teaspoonful of granulated sugar.

CHICKEN CREAM SOUP.

An old chicken for soup is much the best. Cut it up into quarters, put it into a soup kettle with half a pound of corned ham, and an onion; add four quarts of cold water. Bring slowly to a gentle boil, and keep this up until the liquid has diminished one-third, and the meat drops from the bones; then add half a cup of rice. Season with salt, pepper, and a bunch of chopped parsley.

Cook slowly until the rice is tender, then the meat should be taken out. Now, stir in two cups of rich milk thickened with a little flour. The chicken could be fried in a spoonful of butter and a gravy made, reserving some of the white part of the meat, chopping it and adding it to the soup.

PLAIN ECONOMICAL SOUP.

Take a cold-roast-beef bone, pieces of beef-steak, the rack of a cold turkey or chicken. Put them into a pot with three or four quarts of water, two carrots, three turnips, one onion, a few cloves, pepper and salt. Boil the whole gently four hours; then strain it through a colander, mashing the vegetables so that they will all pass through. Skim off the fat, and return the soup to the pot. Mix one tablespoonful of flour with two of water, stir it into the soup and boil the whole ten minutes. Serve this soup with sippets of toast.

Sippets are bits of dry toast cut into a triangular form.

A seasonable dish about the holidays.

OX-TAIL SOUP.

Two ox-tails, two slices of ham, one ounce of butter, two carrots, two turnips, three onions, one leek, one head of celery, one bunch of savory herbs, pepper, a tablespoonful of salt, two tablespoonfuls of catsup, one-half glass of port wine, three quarts of water.

Cut up the tails, separating them at the joints; wash them, and put them in a stewpan with the butter. Cut the vegetables in slices and add them with the herbs. Put in one-half pint of water, and stir it over a quick fire till the juices are drawn. Fill up the stewpan with water, and when boiling, add the salt. Skim well, and simmer very gently for four hours, or until the tails are tender. Take them out, skim and strain the soup, thicken with flour, and flavor with the catsup and port wine. Put back the tails, simmer for five minutes and serve.

Another way to make an appetizing ox-tail soup. You should begin to make it the day before you wish to eat the soup. Take two tails, wash clean, and put in a kettle with nearly a gallon of cold water; add a small handful of salt; when the meat is well cooked, take out the bones. Let this stand in a cool room, covered, and next day, about an hour and a half before dinner, skim off the crust or cake of fat which has risen to the top. Add a little onion, carrot, or any vegetables you choose, chopping them fine first; summer savory may also be added.

CORN SOUP.

Cut the corn from the cob, and boil the cobs in water for at least an hour, then add the grains, and boil until they are thoroughly done; put one dozen ears of corn to a gallon of water, which will be reduced to three quarts by the time the soup is done; then pour on a pint of new milk, two well-beaten eggs, salt and pepper to your taste; continue the boiling a while longer, and stir in, to season and thicken it a little, a tablespoonful of good butter rubbed up with two tablespoonfuls of flour. Corn soup may also be made nicely with water in which a pair of grown fowls have been boiled or parboiled, instead of having plain water for the foundation.

SPLIT PEA SOUP. No. 1.

Wash well a pint of split peas and cover them well with cold water, adding a third of a teaspoonful of soda; let them remain in it over night to swell. In the morning put them in a kettle with a close fitting cover. Pour over them three quarts of cold water, adding half a pound of lean ham or bacon cut into slices or pieces; also a teaspoonful of salt and a little pepper, and some celery chopped fine. When the soup begins to boil, skim the froth from the surface. Cook slowly from three to four hours, stirring occasionally till the peas are all dissolved, adding a little more boiling water to keep up the quantity as it boils away. Strain through a colander, and leave out the meat. It should be quite thick. Serve with small squares of toasted bread, cut up and added. If not rich enough, add a small piece of butter.

CREAM OF ASPARAGUS.

For making two quarts of soup, use two bundles of fresh asparagus. Cut the tops from one of the bunches and cook them twenty minutes in salted water, enough to cover them. Cook the remainder of the asparagus about twenty minutes in a quart of stock or water. Cut an onion into thin slices and fry in three tablespoonfuls of butter ten minutes, being careful not to scorch it; then add the asparagus that has been boiled in the stock; cook this five minutes, stirring constantly; then add three tablespoonfuls of dissolved flour, cook five minutes longer. Turn this mixture into the boiling stock and boil twenty minutes. Rub through a sieve; add the milk and cream and the asparagus heads. If water is used in place of stock, use all cream.

GREEN PEA SOUP.

Wash a small quarter of lamb in cold water, and put it into a soup-pot with six quarts of cold water; add to it two tablespoonfuls of salt, and set it over a moderate fire—let it boil gently for two hours, then skim it clear: add a quart of shelled peas, and a teaspoonful of pepper; cover it, and let it boil for half an hour; then having scraped the skins from a quart of small young potatoes, add them to the soup; cover the pot and let it boil for half an hour longer; work quarter of a pound of butter and a dessert spoonful of flour together, and add them to the soup ten or twelve minutes before taking it off the fire.

Serve the meat on a dish with parsley sauce over, and the soup in a tureen.

DRIED BEAN SOUP.

Put two quarts of dried white beans to soak the night before you make the soup, which should be put on as early in the day as possible.

Take two pounds of the lean of fresh beef—the coarse pieces will do.   Cut them up, and put them into your soup-pot with the bones belonging to them, (which should be broken in pieces,) and a pound of lean bacon, cut very small. If you have the remains of a piece of beef that has been roasted the day before, and so much under-done that the juices remain in it, you may put it into the pot and its bones along with it.   Season the meat with pepper only, and pour on it six quarts of water.   As soon as it boils, take off the scum, and put in the beans (having first drained them) and a head of celery cut small, or a table-spoonful of pounded celery seed.   Boil it slowly till the meat is done to shreds, and the beans all dissolved.   Then strain it through a colander into the tureen, and put into it small squares of toasted bread with the crust cut off.

TURTLE SOUP FROM BEANS.

Soak over night one quart of black beans; next day boil them in the proper quantity of water, say a gallon, then dip the beans out of the pot and strain them through a colander.   Then return the flour of the beans, thus pressed, into the pot in which they were boiled.   Tie up in a thin cloth some thyme, a tea-spoonful of summer savory and parsley, and let it boil in the mixture.   Add a tablespoonful of cold butter, salt and·pepper.   Have ready four hard-boiled yolks of eggs quartered, and a few force meat balls; add this to the soup with a sliced lemon, and half a glass of wine just before serving the soup.

This approaches so near in flavor to the real turtle soup that few are able to distinguish the difference.

PHILADELPHIA PEPPER POT.

Put two pounds of tripe and four calves' feet into the soup-pot and cover them with cold water; add a red pepper, and boil closely until the calves' feet are boiled very tender; take out the meat, skim the liquid, stir it, cut the tripe into small pieces, and put it back into the liquid; if there is not enough liquid, add boiling water; add half a teaspoonful of sweet marjoràm, sweet basil, and thyme, two sliced onions, sliced potatoes, salt.   When the vegetables have boiled until almost tender, add a piece of butter rolled in flour, drop in some egg balls, and boil fifteen minutes more.   Take up and serve hot.

SQUIRREL SOUP.

Wash and quarter three or four good sized squirrels; put them on, with a small tablespoonful of salt, directly after breakfast, in a gallon of cold water.

Cover the pot close, and set it on the back part of the stove to simmer gently, *not* boil. Add vegetables just the same as you do in case of other meat soups in the summer season, but especially good will you find corn, Irish potatoes, tomatoes and Lima beans. Strain the soup through a coarse colander when the meat has boiled to shreds, so as to get rid of the squirrel's troublesome little bones. Then return to the pot, and after boiling a while longer, thicken with a piece of butter rubbed in flour. Celery and parsley leaves chopped up are also considered an improvement by many. Toast two slices of bread, cut them into dice one half inch square, fry them in butter, put them into the bottom of your tureen, and then pour the soup boiling hot upon them. Very good.

TOMATO SOUP. No. 1.

Place in a kettle four pounds of beef. Pour over it one gallon of cold water. Let the meat and water boil slowly for three hours, or until the liquid is reduced to about one-half. Remove the meat and put into the broth a quart of tomatoes, and one chopped onion; salt and pepper to taste. A teaspoonful of flour should be dissolved and stirred in, then allowed to boil half an hour longer. Strain and serve hot. Canned tomatoes, in place of fresh ones, may be used.

TOMATO SOUP. No. 2.

Place over the fire a quart of peeled tomatoes, stew them soft with a pinch of soda. Strain it so that no seeds remain, set it over the fire again, and add a quart of hot boiled milk; season with salt and pepper, a piece of butter the size of an egg, add three tablespoonfuls of rolled cracker, and serve hot. Canned tomatoes may be used in place of fresh ones.

TOMATO SOUP. No. 3.

Peel two quarts of tomatoes, boil them in a sauce-pan with an onion, and other soup vegetables; strain and add a level tablespoonful of flour dissolved in a third of a cup of melted butter; add pepper and salt. Serve very hot over little squares of bread fried brown and crisp in butter.

An excellent addition to a cold meat lunch.

MULLAGATAWNY SOUP. (As made in India.)

Cut four onions, one carrot, two turnips, and one head of celery into three quarts of liquor, in which one or two fowls have been boiled; keep it over a brisk

fire, till it boils, then place it on a corner of the fire, and let it simmer twenty minutes; add one tablespoonful of currie powder, and one tablespoonful of flour; mix
the whole well together, and let it boil three minutes; pass it through a colander;
serve with pieces of roast chicken in it; add boiled rice in a separate dish. It
must be of good yellow color, and not too thick. If you find it too thick, add a
little boiling water and a teaspoonful of sugar. Half veal and half chicken answers as well.

A dish of rice, to be served separately with this soup, must be thus prepared:
put three pints of water in a sauce-pan and one tablespoonful of salt; let this
boil. Wash well, in three waters, half a pound of rice; strain it, and put it into
the boiling water in sauce-pan. After it has come to the boil—which it will do
in about two minutes—let it boil twenty minutes; strain it through a colander,
and pour over it two quarts of cold water. This will separate the grains of rice.
Put it back in the sauce-pan, and place it near the fire until hot enough to send
to the table. This is also the proper way to boil rice for curries. If these directions are strictly carried out every grain of the rice will separate, and be thoroughly cooked.

MOCK TURTLE SOUP, OF CALF'S HEAD.

Scald a well-cleansed calf's head, remove the brain, tie it up in a cloth, and
boil an hour, or until the meat will easily slip from the bone; take out, save the
broth; cut it in small, square pieces, and throw them into cold water; when
cool, put it in a stewpan, and cover with some of the broth; let it boil until
quite tender, and set aside.

In another stewpan melt some butter, and in it put a quarter of a pound of
lean ham, cut small, with fine herbs to taste; also parsley and one onion; add
about a pint of the broth; let it simmer for two hours, and then dredge in a
small quantity of flour; now add the remainder of the broth, and a quarter bottle of Madeira or sherry; let all stew quietly for ten minutes and rub it through
a medium sieve; add the calf's head, season with a very little cayenne pepper, a
little salt, the juice of one lemon, and if desired, a quarter teaspoonful pounded
mace and a dessert-spoon sugar.

Having previously prepared force-meat balls, add them to the soup, and five
minutes after serve hot.

GREEN TURTLE SOUP.

One turtle, two onions, a bunch of sweet herbs, juice of one lemon, five quarts
of water, a glass of Madeira.

After removing the entrails, cut up the coarser parts of the turtle meat and bones. Add four quarts of water, and stew four hours with the herbs, onions, pepper and salt. Stew very slowly, do not let it cease boiling during this time. At the end of four hours strain the soup, and add the finer parts of the turtle and the green fat, which has been simmered one hour in two quarts of water. Thicken with brown flour; return to the soup-pot, and simmer gently for an hour longer. If there are eggs in the turtle, boil them in a separate vessel for four hours, and throw into the soup before taking up. If not, put in force-meat balls; then the juice of the lemon, and the wine; beat up at once and pour out.

Some cooks add the finer meat before straining, boiling all together five hours; then strain, thicken, and put in the green fat, cut into lumps an inch long. This makes a handsomer soup than if the meat is left in.

Green turtle can now be purchased preserved in air-tight cans.

Force Meat Balls for the Above.—Six tablespoonfuls of turtle-meat chopped very fine. Rub to a paste, with the yolk of two hard-boiled eggs, a tablespoonful of butter, and, if convenient a little oyster liquor. Season with cayenne, mace, and half a teaspoonful of white sugar and a pinch of salt. Bind all with a well-beaten egg; shape into small balls; dip in egg, then powdered cracker; fry in butter, and drop into the soup when it is served.

MACARONI SOUP.

To a rich beef or other soup, in which there is no seasoning other than pepper or salt, take half a pound of small pipe macaroni, boil it in clear water until it is tender, then drain it and cut it in pieces of an inch length; boil it for fifteen minutes in the soup and serve.

TURKEY SOUP.

Take the turkey bones and boil three-quarters of an hour in water enough to cover them; add a little summer savory and celery chopped fine. Just before serving, thicken with a little flour (browned), and season with pepper, salt, and a small piece of butter. This is a cheap but good soup, using the remains of cold turkey which might otherwise be thrown away.

GUMBO OR OKRA SOUP.

Fry out the fat of a slice of bacon or fat ham, drain it off, and in it fry the slices of a large onion brown; scald, peel, and cut up two quarts fresh tomatoes, when in season, (use canned tomatoes otherwise), and cut thin one quart okra;

put them, together with a little chopped parsley, in a stew-kettle with about three quarts of hot broth of any kind; cook slowly for three hours, season with salt and pepper. Serve hot.

In chicken broth the same quantity of okra pods, used for thickening instead of tomatoes, forms a chicken gumbo soup.

TAPIOCA CREAM SOUP.

One quart of white stock; one pint of cream or milk; one onion; two stalks celery; one-third of a cupful of tapioca; two cupfuls of cold water; one tablespoonful of butter; a small piece of mace; salt, pepper. Wash the tapioca and soak over night in cold water. Cook it and the stock together very gently for one hour. Cut the onion and celery into small pieces, and put on to cook for twenty minutes with the milk and mace. Strain on the tapioca and stock. Season with salt and pepper, add butter, and serve.

Soups Without Meat.

ONION SOUP.

One quart of milk, six large onions, yolks of four eggs, three tablespoonfuls of butter, a large one of flour, one cupful of cream, salt, pepper. Put the butter in a frying pan. Cut the onions into thin slices and drop in the butter. Stir until they begin to cook; then cover tight and set back where they will simmer, but not burn, for half an hour. Now put the milk on to boil, and then add the dry flour to the onions and stir constantly for three minutes over the fire; then turn the mixture into the milk and cook fifteen minutes. Rub the soup through a strainer, return to the fire, season with salt and pepper. Beat the yolks of the eggs well, add the cream to them and stir into the soup. Cook three minutes, stirring constantly. If you have no cream, use milk, in which case add a tablespoonful of butter at the same time. Pour over fried croutons in a soup tureen.

This is a refreshing dish when one is fatigued.

WINTER VEGETABLE SOUP.

Scrape and slice three turnips and three carrots, and peel three onions, and fry all with a little butter until a light yellow; add a bunch of celery and three or four leeks cut in pieces; stir and fry all the ingredients for six minutes;

when fried, add one clove of garlic, two stalks of parsley, two cloves, salt, pepper and a little grated nutmeg; cover with three quarts of water and simmer for three hours, taking off the scum carefully. Strain and use. Croutons, vermicelli, Italian pastes, or rice may be added.

VERMICELLI SOUP.

Swell quarter of a pound of vermicelli in a quart of warm water, then add it to a good beef, veal, lamb, or chicken soup or broth, with quarter of a pound of sweet butter; let the soup boil for fifteen minutes after it is added.

SWISS WHITE SOUP.

A sufficient quantity of broth for six people; boil it; beat up three eggs well, two spoonfuls of flour, one cup milk; pour these gradually through a sieve into the boiling; soup salt and pepper.

SPRING VEGETABLE SOUP.

Half pint green peas, two shredded lettuces, one onion, a small bunch of parsley, two ounces butter, the yolks of three eggs, one pint of water, one and a half quarts of soup stock. Put in a stewpan the lettuce, onion, parsley and butter, with one pint of water, and let them simmer till tender. Season with salt and pepper. When done strain off the vegetables, and put two-thirds of the liquor with the stock. Beat up the yolks of the eggs with the other third, toss it over the fire, and at the moment of serving add this with the vegetables to the strained-off soup.

CELERY SOUP.

Celery soup may be made with *white stock*. Cut down the white of half a dozen heads of celery into little pieces and boil it in four pints of white stock, with a quarter of a pound of lean ham and two ounces of butter. Simmer gently for a full hour, then strain through a sieve, return the liquor to the pan, and stir in a few spoonfuls of cream with great care. Serve with toasted bread and, if liked, thicken with a little flour. Season to taste.

IRISH POTATO SOUP.

Peel and boil eight medium-sized potatoes with a large onion, sliced, some herbs, salt and pepper; press all through a colander; then thin it with rich milk and add a lump of butter, more seasoning, if necessary; let it heat well and serve hot.

PEA SOUP.

Put a quart of dried peas into five quarts of water; boil for four hours; then add three or four large onions, two heads of celery, a carrot, two turnips, all cut up rather fine. Season with pepper and salt. Boil two hours longer, and if the soup becomes too thick add more water. Strain through a colander and stir in a tablespoonful of cold butter. Serve hot, with small pieces of toasted bread placed in the bottom of the tureen.

NOODLES FOR SOUP.

Beat up one egg light, add a pinch of salt, and flour enough to make a *very stiff* dough; roll out very thin, like thin pie crust, dredge with flour to keep from sticking. Let it remain on the bread board to dry for an hour or more; then roll it up into a tight scroll, like a sheet of music. Begin at the end and slice it into slips as thin as straws. After all are cut, mix them lightly together, and to prevent them sticking, keep them floured a little until you are ready to drop them into your soup, which should be done shortly before dinner, for if boiled *too long* they will go to pieces.

FORCE MEAT BALLS FOR SOUP.

One cupful of cooked veal or fowl meat, minced; mix with this a handful of fine bread-crumbs, the yolks of four hard-boiled eggs rubbed smooth together with a tablespoon of milk; season with pepper and salt; add a half teaspoon of flour, and bind all together with two beaten eggs; the hands to be well floured, and the mixture to be made into little balls the size of a nutmeg, drop into the soup about twenty minutes before serving.

EGG BALLS FOR SOUP.

Take the yolks of six hard-boiled eggs and half a tablespoonful of wheat flour, rub them smooth with the yolks of two raw eggs and a teaspoonful of salt; mix all well together; make it in balls, and drop them into the boiling soup a few minutes before taking it up.

Used in green turtle soup.

EGG DUMPLINGS FOR SOUP.

To half a pint of milk put two well-beaten eggs, and as much wheat flour as will make a smooth, rather *thick* batter free from lumps; drop this batter, a tablespoonful at a time, into boiling soup.

Another mode.—One cupful of sour cream and one cupful of sour milk, three eggs, well beaten, whites and yolks separately; one teaspoonful of salt, one level teaspoonful of soda, dissolved in a spoonful of water, and enough flour added to make a *very stiff* batter. To be dropped by spoonfuls into the broth and boiled twenty minutes, or until no raw dough shows on the outside.

SUET DUMPLINGS FOR SOUP.

Three cups of sifted flour in which three teaspoonfuls of baking powder have been sifted; one cup of finely chopped suet, well rubbed into the flour, with a teaspoonful of salt. Wet all with sweet milk to make a dough as stiff as biscuit. Make into small balls as large as peaches, well floured. Drop into the soup three-quarters of an hour before being served. This requires steady boiling, being closely covered, and the cover not to be removed until taken up to serve. A very good form of pot-pie.

SOYER'S RECIPE FOR FORCE MEATS.

Take 1½ lbs. of lean veal from the fillet, and cut it in long thin slices; scrape with a knife till nothing but the fibre remains; put it in a mortar, pound it 10 minutes, or until in a purée; pass it through a wire sieve (use the remainder in stock); then take 1 lb. of good fresh beef suet, which skin, shred, and chop very fine; put it in a mortar and pound it; then add 6 oz. of panada (that is, bread soaked in milk, and boiled till nearly dry) with the suet; pound them well together, and add the veal; season with 1 teaspoonful of salt, ¼ teaspoonful of pepper, ½ that of nutmeg; work all well together; then add 4 eggs by degrees, continually pounding the contents of the mortar. When well mixed, take a small piece in a spoon, and poach it in some boiling water; and if it is delicate, firm, and of a good flavor, it is ready for use.

CROUTONS FOR SOUP.

In a frying pan have the depth of an inch of boiling fat; also have prepared slices of stale bread cut up into little half-inch squares; drop into the frying pan enough of these bits of bread to cover the surface of the fat. When browned, remove with a skimmer and drain; add to the hot soup and serve.

Some prefer them prepared in this manner:

Take very thin slices of bread, butter them well; cut them up into little squares three fourths of an inch thick, place them in a baking pan, buttered side up, and brown in a quick oven.

FISH STOCK.

Place a saucepan over the fire with a good sized piece of sweet butter, and a sliced onion; put into that some sliced tomatoes, then add as many different kinds of small fish as you can get—oysters, clams, smelts, pawns, crabs, shrimps, and all kinds of pan-fish; cook all together, until the onions are well browned; then add a bunch of sweet herbs, salt and pepper, and sufficient water to make the required amount of stock. After this has cooked for half an hour pound it with a wooden pestle, then strain and cook again until it jellies.

FISH SOUP.

Select a large, fine fish, clean it thoroughly, put it over the fire with a sufficient quantity of water, allowing for each pound of fish one quart of water; add an onion cut fine, and a bunch of sweet herbs. When the fish is cooked, and is quite tasteless, strain all through a colander, return to the fire, add some butter, salt and pepper to taste. A small tablespoonful of Worcestershire sauce may be added if liked. Served with small squares of fried bread and thin slices of lemon.

LOBSTER SOUP, OR BISQUE.

Have ready a good broth made of three pounds of veal boiled slowly in as much water as will cover it, till the meat is reduced to shreds. It must then be well strained.

Having boiled one fine middle-sized lobster, extract all the meat from the body and claws. Bruise part of the coral in a mortar, and also an equal quantity of the meat. Mix them well together. Add mace, cayenne, salt and pepper, and make them up into force-meat balls, binding the mixture with the yolk of an egg slightly beaten.

Take three quarts of the veal broth, and put into it the meat of the lobster cut into mouthfuls. Boil it together about twenty minutes. Then thicken it with the remaining coral (which you must first rub through a sieve), and add the force-meat balls and a little butter rolled in flour. Simmer it gently for ten minutes but do not let it come to a boil, as that will injure the color. Serve with small dice of bread fried brown in butter.

OYSTER SOUP. No. 1.

Two quarts of oysters, one quart of milk, two tablespoonfuls of butter, one teacupful of hot water; pepper, salt.

Strain all the liquor from the oysters; add the water, and heat. When near the boil, add the seasoning, then the oysters. Cook about five minutes from the time they begin to simmer, until they "ruffle." Stir in the butter, cook one minute, and pour into the tureen. Stir in the boiling milk, and send to table. Some prefer all water in place of milk.

OYSTER SOUP. No. 2.

Scald one gallon of oysters in their own liquor. Add one quart of rich milk to the liquor, and when it comes to a boil, skim out the oysters and set aside. Add the yolks of four eggs, two good tablespoonfuls of butter, and one of flour, all mixed well together, but in this order—first, the milk, then, after beating the eggs, add a little of the hot liquor to them gradually, and stir them rapidly into the soup. Lastly, add the butter and whatever seasoning you fancy besides plain pepper and salt, which must both be put in to taste with caution. Celery salt most persons like extremely; others would prefer a little marjoram and thyme; others, again, mace and a bit of onion. Use your own discretion in this regard.

CLAM SOUP. (French Style.)

Mince two dozen hard-shell clams very fine. Fry half a minced onion in an ounce of butter; add to it a pint of hot water, a pinch of mace, four cloves, one allspice and six whole pepper corns. Boil fifteen minutes and strain into a sauce-pan; add the chopped clams and a pint of clam-juice or hot water; simmer slowly two hours; strain and rub the pulp through a sieve into the liquid. Return it to the sauce-pan and keep it lukewarm. Boil three half-pints of milk in a sauce-pan (previously wet with cold water, which prevents burning) and whisk it into the soup. Dissolve a teaspoonful of flour in cold milk, add it to the soup, taste for seasoning; heat it gently to near the boiling point; pour it into a tureen previously heated with hot water, and serve with or without pieces of fried bread—called *croutons* in kitchen French.

CLAM SOUP.

Twenty-five clams chopped fine. Put over the fire the liquor that was drained from them, and a cup of water; add the chopped clams, and boil half an hour; then season to taste with pepper and salt and a piece of butter as large as an egg; boil up again and add one quart of milk boiling hot, stir in a table-spoon of flour made to a cream with a little cold milk, or two crackers rolled fine. Some like a little mace and lemon juice in the seasoning.

MODES OF FRYING.

The usual custom among professional cooks is to entirely immerse the article to be cooked in boiling fat, but from inconvenience most households use the half-frying method of frying in a small amount of fat in a frying-pan. For the first method a shallow iron frying-kettle, large at the top and small at the bottom, is best to use. The fat should half fill the kettle, or an amount sufficient to float whatever is to be fried; the heat of the fat should get to such a degree that, when a piece of bread or a teaspoonful of the batter is dropped in it, it will become brown almost instantly, but should not be so hot as to burn the fat. Some cooks say that the fat should be smoking, but my experience is, that is a mistake, as that soon ruins the fat. As soon as it begins to smoke it should be removed a little to one side, and still be kept at the boiling point. If fritters, crullers, croquettes, etc., are dropped into fat that is too hot, it crusts over the outside before the inside has fully risen, making a heavy hard article, and also ruining the fat; giving it a burnt flavor.

Many French cooks prefer beef fat or suet to lard for frying purposes, considering it more wholesome and digestible, does not impart as much flavor, or adhere or soak into the article cooked as pork fat.

In families of any size, where there is much cooking required, there are enough drippings and fat remnants from roasts of beef, skimmings from the soup-kettle, with the addition of occasionally a pound of suet from the market, to amply supply the need. All such remnants and skimmings should be clarified about twice a week, by boiling them all together in water. When the fat is all melted, it should be strained with the water and set aside to cool. After the fat on the top has hardened, lift the cake from the water on which it lies, scrape off all the dark particles from the bottom, then melt over again the fat; while hot strain into a small clean stone jar or bright tin pail, and then it is ready for use. Always after frying anything, the fat should stand until it settles and has cooled somewhat; then turn off carefully so as to leave it clear from the sediment that settles at the bottom.

Refined cotton-seed oil is now being adopted by most professional cooks in hotels, restaurants, and many private households for culinary purposes, and will doubtless in future supersede animal fats, especially for frying, it being quite as delicate a medium as frying with olive oil. It is now sold by leading grocers, put up in packages of two and four quarts.

The second mode of frying, using a frying-pan with a small quantity of fat or grease, to be done properly, should in the first place have the frying-pan hot over the fire, and the fat in it *actually boiling* before the article to be cooked is placed in it, the intense heat quickly searing up the pores of the article and forming a brown crust on the lower side, then turning over and browning the other the same way.

Still, there is another mode of frying; the process is somewhat similar to broiling, the hot frying-pan or spider replacing the hot fire. To do this correctly, a thick bottom frying-pan should be used. Place it over the fire, and when it is so hot that it will siss, oil over the bottom of the pan with a piece of suet, that is if the meat is all lean; if not, it is not necessary to grease the bottom of the pan. Lay in the meat quite flat, and brown it quickly, first on one side then on the other; when sufficiently cooked, dish on a *hot* platter and season the same as broiled meats.

Fish

In selecting fish, choose those only in which the eye is full and prominent, the flesh thick and firm, the scales bright and fins stiff. They should be thoroughly cleaned before cooking.

The usual modes of cooking fish are boiled, baked, broiled, fried and occasionally stewed. Steaming fish is much superior to boiling, but the ordinary conveniences in private houses do not admit of the possibility of enjoying this delicate way of cooking it. Large fish are generally boiled, medium-sized ones baked or boiled, the smaller kinds fried or broiled. Very large fish, such as cod, halibut, etc., are cut in steaks or slices for frying or broiling. The heads of some fish, as the cod, halibut, etc., are considered tidbits by many. Small fish, or pan fish, as they are usually called, are served without the heads, with the exception of brook-trouts and smelts; these are usually cooked whole, with the head on. Bake fish slowly, basting often with butter and water. Salmon is considered the most nutritious of all fish. When boiling fish, by adding a little vinegar and salt to the water, it seasons and prevents the nutriment from being drawn out; the vinegar acting on the water hardens the water.

Carrie Scott Harrison

Fill the fish with a nicely prepared stuffing of rolled cracker or stale bread crumbs, seasoned with butter, pepper, salt, sage, and any other aromatic herbs fancied; sew up; wrap in a well-floured cloth, tied closely with twine, and boil or steam. The garnishes for boiled fish are: For turbot, fried smelts; for other boiled fish, parsley, sliced beets, lemon or sliced boiled egg. Do not use the knives, spoons, etc., that are used in cooking fish, for other food, or they will be apt to impart a fishy flavor.

Fish to be boiled should be put into *cold water* and set on the fire to cook very gently, or the outside will break before the inner part is done. Unless the fish are small, they should never be put into warm water; nor should water, either hot or cold, be poured *on* to the fish, as it is liable to break the skin: if it should be necessary to add a little water while the fish is cooking, it ought to be poured in gently at the side of the vessel.

Fish to be broiled should lie, after they are dressed, for two or three hours, with their inside well sprinkled with salt and pepper.

Salt fish should be soaked in water before boiling, according to the time it has been in salt. When it is hard and dry, it will require thirty-six hours soaking before it is dressed, and the water must be changed three or four times. When fish is not very salt, twenty-four hours, or even one night, will suffice.

When frying fish the fire must be hot enough to bring the fat to such a degree of heat as to sear the surface and make it impervious to the fat, and at the same time seal up the rich juices. As soon as the fish is browned by this sudden application of heat, the pan may be moved to a cooler place on the stove, that the process may be finished more slowly.

Fat in which fish has been fried is just as good to use again for the same purpose, but it should be kept by itself and not be put to any other use.

TO FRY FISH.

Most of the smaller fish (generally termed pan-fish) are usually fried. Clean well, cut off the head, and, if quite large, cut out the backbone, and slice the body crosswise into five or six pieces; season with salt and pepper. Dip in Indian meal or wheat flour, or in beaten egg, and roll in bread or fine cracker crumbs—trout and perch should not be dipped in meal; put into a thick bottomed iron frying-pan, the flesh side down, with hot lard or drippings; fry slowly, turning when lightly browned. The following method may be deemed preferable: Dredge the pieces with flour; brush them over with beaten egg; roll in bread crumbs, and fry in hot lard or drippings sufficient to cover, the same as frying crullers. If the fat is very hot, the fish will fry without absorbing it, and it will be palatably cooked. When browned on one side, turn it over in the fat and brown the other, draining when done. This is a particularly good way to fry slices of large fish. Serve with tomato sauce; garnish with slices of lemon.

PAN FISH.

Place them in a thick bottom frying-pan with heads all one way. Fill the spaces with smaller fish. When they are fried quite brown and ready to turn, put a dinner plate over them, drain off the fat; then invert the pan, and they will be left unbroken on the plate. Put the lard back into the pan, and when *hot* slip back the fish. When the other side is brown, drain, turn on a plate as before, and slip them on a warm platter, to be sent to the table. Leaving the heads on and the fish a crispy-brown, in perfect shape, improves the appearance if not the flavor. Garnish with slices of lemon.

—Hotel Lafayette, Philadelphia.

BAKED PICKEREL.

Carefully clean and wipe the fish, and lay in a dripping-pan with enough hot water to prevent scorching. A perforated sheet of tin, fitting loosely, or several muffin rings may be used to keep it off the bottom. Lay it in a circle on its belly, head and tail touching, and tied, or as directed in note on fish; bake slowly, basting often with butter and water. When done, have ready a cup of sweet cream or rich milk to which a few spoons of hot water has been added; stir in two large spoons of melted butter and a little chopped parsley; heat all by setting the cup in boiling water; add the gravy from the dripping-pan, and let it boil up once; place the fish in a hot dish, and pour over it the sauce. Or an egg sauce may be made with drawn butter; stir in the yolk of an egg quickly, and then a teaspoon of chopped parsley. It can be stuffed or not, just as you please.

BOILED SALMON.

The middle slice of salmon is the best. Sew up neatly in a mosquito-net bag, and boil a quarter of an hour to the pound in hot salted water. When done, unwrap with care, and lay upon a hot dish, taking care not to break it. Have ready a large cupful of drawn butter, very rich, in which has been stirred a tablespoonful of minced parsley and the juice of a lemon. Pour half upon the salmon, and serve the rest in a boat. Garnish with parsley and sliced eggs.

BROILED SALMON.

Cut slices from an inch to an inch and a half thick, dry them in a cloth, season with salt and pepper, dredge them in sifted flour, and broil on a gridiron rubbed with suet.

Another mode.—Cut the slices one inch thick, and season them with pepper and salt; butter a sheet of white paper, lay each slice on a separate piece, envelope them in it with their ends twisted; broil gently over a clear fire, and serve with anchovy or caper sauce. When higher seasoning is required, add a few chopped herbs and a little spice.

FRESH SALMON FRIED.

Cut the slices three-quarters of an inch thick, dredge them with flour, or dip them in egg and crumbs,—fry a light brown. This mode answers for all fish cut into steaks. Season well with salt and pepper.

SALMON AND CAPER SAUCE.

Two slices of salmon, one-quarter pound butter, one-half teaspoonful of chopped parsley, one shalot; salt and pepper to taste.

Lay the salmon in a baking-dish, place pieces of butter over it and add the other ingredients, rubbing a little of the seasoning into the fish; place it in the oven and baste it frequently; when done, take it out and drain for a minute or two; lay it in a dish, pour caper sauce over it, and serve. Salmon dressed in this way, with tomato sauce, is very delicious.

BROILED SALT SALMON OR OTHER SALT FISH.

Soak salmon in tepid or cold water twenty-four hours, changing water several times, or let stand under faucet of running water. If in a hurry or desiring a very salt relish, it may do to soak a short time, having water warm, and changing, parboiling slightly. At the hour wanted, broil sharply. Season to suit taste, covering with butter. This recipe will answer for all kinds of salt fish.

PICKLED SALMON.

Take a fine, fresh salmon, and having cleaned it, cut it into large pieces, and boil it in salted water as if for eating. Then drain it, wrap it in a dry cloth, and set it in a cold place till next day. Then make the pickle, which must be in proportion to the quantity of fish. To one quart of the water in which the salmon was boiled, allow two quarts of the best vinegar, one ounce of whole black pepper, one nutmeg grated and a dozen blades of mace. Boil all these together in a kettle closely covered to prevent the flavor from evaporating. When the vinegar thus prepared is quite cold, pour it over the salmon, and put on the top a tablespoonful of sweet oil, which will make it keep the longer.

Cover it closely, put it in a dry, cool place, and it will be good for many months. This is the nicest way of preserving salmon, and is approved by all who have tried it.

SMOKED SALMON.

Smoked salmon to be broiled should be put upon the gridiron first, with the flesh side to the fire.

Smoked salmon is very nice when shaved like smoked beef, and served with coffee or tea.

FRICASSEE SALMON.

This way of cooking fresh salmon is a pleasant change from the ordinary modes of cooking it: Cut one and one-half pounds of salmon into pieces one inch square; put the pieces in a stewpan with half a cupful of water, a little salt, a little white pepper, one clove, one blade of mace, three pieces of sugar, one shalot and a heaping teaspoonful of mustard mixed smoothly with half a teacupful of vinegar. Let this boil up once and add six tomatoes peeled and cut into tiny pieces, a few sprigs of parsley finely minced, and one wineglassful of sherry. Let all simmer gently for three-quarters of an hour. Serve very hot, and garnish with dry toast cut in triangular pieces. This dish is good, very cold, for luncheon or breakfast.

SALMON PATTIES.

Cut cold cooked salmon into dice. Heat about a pint of the dice in half a pint of cream. Season to taste with cayenne pepper and salt. Fill the shells and serve. Cold cooked fish of any kind may be made into patties in this way. Use any fish sauce you choose—all are equally good.

FISH AND OYSTER PIE.

Any remains of cold fish, such as cod or haddock, 2 dozen oysters, pepper and salt to taste, bread-crumbs sufficient for the quantity of fish; ½ teaspoonful of grated nutmeg, 1 teaspoonful of finely chopped parsley.

Clear the fish from the bones, and put a layer of it in a pie-dish, which sprinkle with pepper and salt; then a layer of bread-crumbs, oysters, nutmeg, and chopped parsley. Repeat this till the dish is quite full. You may form a covering either of bread-crumbs, which should be browned, or puff-paste, which should be cut off into long strips, and laid in cross-bars over the fish, with a line of the paste first laid round the edge. Before putting on the top, pour in some made melted butter, or a little thin white sauce, and the oyster-liquor, and bake.

Time.—If of cooked fish, $\frac{1}{4}$ hour; if made of fresh fish and puff-paste, $\frac{3}{4}$ hour.

STEAMED FISH.

Secure the tail of the fish in its mouth, the body in a circle; pour over it half a pint of vinegar, seasoned with pepper and salt; let it stand an hour in a cool place; pour off the vinegar, and put it in a steamer over boiling water, and steam twenty minutes, or longer for large fish. When the meat easily separates from the bone it is done. Drain well, and serve on a very clean white napkin, neatly folded and placed on the platter; decorate the napkin around the fish with sprigs of curled parsley, or with fanciful beet cuttings, or alternately with both.

TO BROIL A SHAD.

Split and wash the shad, and afterwards dry it in a cloth. Season it with salt and pepper. Have ready a bed of clear, bright coals. Grease your gridiron well, and as soon as it is hot, lay the shad upon it, the flesh side down; cover with a dripping-pan and broil it for about a quarter of an hour, or more, according to the thickness. Butter it well, and send it to the table. Covering it while broiling gives it a more delicious flavor.

BAKED SHAD.

Many people are of the opinion that the very best method of cooking a shad is to bake it. Stuff it with bread-crumbs, salt, pepper, butter and parsley, and mix this up with the beaten yolk of egg; fill the fish with it, and sew it up or fasten a string around it. Pour over it a little water and some butter, and bake as you would a fowl. A shad will require from an hour to an hour and a quarter to bake. Garnish with slices of lemon, water cresses, etc.

Dressing for Baked Shad.—Boil up the gravy in which the shad was baked, put in a large tablespoonful of catsup, a tablespoonful of brown flour which has been wet with cold water, the juice of a lemon, and a glass of sherry or Madeira wine. Serve in a sauce boat.

TO COOK A SHAD ROE.

Drop into boiling water, and cook gently for twenty minutes; then take from the fire, and drain. Butter a tin plate, and lay the drained roe upon it. Dredge well with salt and pepper, and spread soft butter over it; then dredge thickly with flour. Cook in the oven for half an hour, basting frequently with salt, pepper, flour, butter and water.

TO COOK SHAD ROE. (Another Way.)

First partly boil them in a small covered pan, take out and season them with salt, a little pepper, dredge with flour and fry as any fish.

BOILED BASS.

After thoroughly cleaning it place in a saucepan with enough water to cover it; add two tablespoonfuls of salt; set the saucepan over the fire, and when it has boiled about five minutes try to pull out one of the fins; if it loosens easily from the body carefully take the fish out of the water, lay it on a platter, surround it with half a dozen hard-boiled eggs, and serve it with a sauce.

BOILED BLUEFISH.

Boiled the same as Bass.

BAKED BLUEFISH.

Baked the same as Baked Shad—see page 46.

FRIED EELS.

After cleaning the eels well, cut them in pieces two inches long; wash them and wipe them dry; roll them in wheat flour or rolled cracker, and fry as directed for other fish, in hot lard or beef dripping, salted. They should be browned all over and thoroughly done.

Eels are sometimes dipped in batter and then fried, or into egg and bread crumbs. Serve with crisped parsley.

SHEEPSHEAD WITH DRAWN BUTTER.

Select a medium-sized fish, clean it thoroughly, and rub a little salt over it; wrap it in a cloth and put it in a steamer; place this over a pot of fast-boiling water and steam one hour; then lay it whole upon a hot side-dish, garnish with tufts of parsley and slices of lemon, and serve with drawn butter, prepared as follows: Take two ounces of butter and roll it into small balls, dredge these with flour; put one-fourth of them in a sauce-pan, and as they begin to melt, whisk them; add the remainder, one at a time, until thoroughly smooth; while stirring, add a tablespoonful of lemon juice, half a tablespoonful of chopped parsley; pour into a hot sauce boat, and serve.

BAKED WHITE FISH.

Thoroughly clean the fish; cut off the head or not, as preferred; cut out the backbone from the head to within two inches of the tail, and stuff with the following: Soak stale bread in water, squeeze dry; cut in pieces a large onion, fry in butter, chop fine; add the bread, two ounces of butter, salt, pepper and a little parsley or sage; heat through, and when taken off the fire, add the yolks of two well-beaten eggs; stuff the fish rather full, sew up with fine twine, and wrap with several coils of white tape. Rub the fish over slightly with butter; just cover the bottom of a baking pan with hot water, and place the fish in it, standing back upward, and bent in the form of an S. Serve with the following dressing: Reduce the yolks of two hard-boiled eggs to a smooth paste with two tablespoonfuls good salad oil; stir in half a teaspoon English mustard, and add pepper and vinegar to taste.

HALIBUT BOILED.

The cut next to the tail-piece is the best to boil. Rub a little salt over it, soak it for fifteen minutes in vinegar and cold water, then wash it and scrape it until quite clean; tie it in a cloth, and boil slowly over a moderate fire, allowing seven minutes boiling to each pound of fish; when it is half cooked, turn it over in the pot; serve with drawn butter or egg sauce.

Boiled halibut minced with boiled potatoes, and a little butter and milk, makes an excellent breakfast dish.

STEAMED HALIBUT.

Select a three-pound piece of white halibut, cover it with a cloth and place it in a steamer; set the steamer over a pot of fast-boiling water and steam two hours; place it on a hot dish surrounded with a border of parsley, and serve with egg-sauce.

FRIED HALIBUT. No. 1.

Select choice, firm slices from this large and delicate-looking fish, and, after carefully washing and drying with a soft towel, with a sharp knife take off the skin. Beat up two eggs, and roll out some brittle crackers upon the kneading board until they are as fine as dust. Dip each slice into the beaten egg, then into the cracker crumbs, (after you have salted and peppered the fish), and place them in a hot frying-pan half full of boiling lard, in which a little butter has been added to make the fish brown nicely; turn and brown both sides, remove from the frying-pan and drain. Serve hot.

FRIED HALIBUT. No. 2.

First fry a few thin slices of salt pork until brown in an iron frying-pan; then take it up on a hot platter, and keep it warm until the halibut is fried. After washing and drying two pounds of sliced halibut, sprinkle it with salt and pepper, dredge it well with flour, put it into the hot pork-drippings and fry brown on both sides; then serve the pork with the fish.

Halibut broiled in slices is a very good way of cooking it, broiled the same as Spanish mackerel.

BAKED HALIBUT.

Take a nice piece of halibut weighing five or six pounds, and lay it in salt water for two hours. Wipe it dry and score the outer skin. Set it in a dripping-pan in a moderate hot oven, and bake an hour, basting often with butter and water heated together in a sauce-pan or tin cup. When a fork will penetrate it easily, it is done. It should be a fine, brown color. Take the gravy in the dripping-pan, add a little boiling water should there not be enough, stir in a tablespoonful of walnut catsup, a teaspoonful of Worcestershire sauce, the juice of a lemon, and thicken with brown flour, previously wet with cold water. Boil up once and put in a sauce boat.

HALIBUT BROILED.

Broil the same as other fish, upon a buttered gridiron, over a clear fire, first seasoning with salt and pepper, placed on a hot dish when done, buttered well and cover closely.

FRIED BROOK TROUT.

These delicate fish are usually fried, and form a delightful breakfast or supper dish. Clean wash and dry the fish, split them to the tail, salt and pepper them, and flour them nicely. If you use lard instead of the fat of fried salt pork, put in a piece of butter to prevent their sticking, and which causes them to brown nicely. Let the fat be hot, fry quickly to a delicate brown. They should be sufficiently browned on one side before turning on the other side. They are nice served with slices of fried pork, fried crisp. Lay them side by side on a heated platter, garnish and send hot to the table. They are often cooked and served with their heads on.

FRIED SMELTS.

Fried with their heads on the same as brook trout. Many think that they make a much better appearance as a dish when cooked whole with the heads on, and nicely garnished for the table.

BOILED WHITE FISH.

Taken from Mrs. A. W. Ferry's Cook Book, Mackinac, 1824. The most delicate mode of cooking white fish. Prepare the fish as for broiling, laying it open; put it into a dripping-pan with the back down; nearly cover with water; to one fish two tablespoonfuls of salt; cover tightly and simmer (not boil) one-half hour. Dress with gravy, a little butter and pepper, and garnish with hard-boiled eggs.

BAKED WHITE FISH. (Bordeaux Sauce.)

Clean and stuff the fish. Put it in a baking-pan and add a liberal quantity of butter, previously rolled in flour, to the fish. Put in the pan half a pint of claret, and bake for an hour and a quarter. Remove the fish and strain the gravy; add to the latter a gill more of claret, a teaspoonful of brown flour and a pinch of cayenne, and serve with the fish.

—Plankington House, Milwaukee.

BAKED SALMON TROUT.

This deliciously flavored game-fish is baked precisely as shad or white fish, but should be accompanied with cream gravy to make it perfect. It should be baked slowly, basting often with butter and water. When done, have ready in a sauce-pan a cup of cream, diluted with a few spoonfuls of hot water, for fear it might clot in heating, in which have been stirred cautiously two tablespoonfuls of melted butter, a scant tablespoonful of flour, and a little chopped parsley. Heat this in a vessel set within another of boiling water, add the gravy from the dripping-pan, boil up once to thicken, and when the trout is laid on a suitable hot dish, pour this sauce around it. Garnish with sprigs of parsley.

This same fish boiled, served with the same cream gravy, (with the exception of the fish gravy,) is the proper way to cook it.

TO BAKE SMELTS.

Wash and dry them thoroughly in a cloth, and arrange them nicely in a flat baking-dish; the pan should be buttered, also the fish; season with salt and pepper, and cover with bread or cracker-crumbs. Place a piece of butter over each. Bake for fifteen or twenty minutes. Garnish with fried parsley and cut lemon.

BROILED SPANISH MACKEREL.

Split the fish down the back, take out the back bone, wash it in cold water, dry it with a clean dry cloth, sprinkle it lightly with salt and lay it on a buttered gridiron, over a clear fire, with the flesh side downward, until it begins to brown; then turn the other side. Have ready a mixture of two tablespoonfuls of butter melted, a tablespoonful of lemon juice, a teaspoonful of salt, some pepper. Dish up the fish hot from the gridiron on a hot dish, turn over the mixture and serve it while hot.

Broiled Spanish mackerel is excellent with other fish sauces. Boiled Spanish mackerel is also very fine with most of the fish sauces, more especially "Matre d'Hotel Sauce."

BOILED SALT MACKEREL.

Wash and clean off all the brine and salt; put it to soak with the meat side down, in cold water over night; in the morning rinse it in one or two waters. Wrap each up in a cloth and put it into a kettle with considerable water, which should be cold; cook about thirty minutes. Take it carefully from the cloth, take out the back bones and pour over a little melted butter and cream; add a light sprinkle of pepper. Or make a cream sauce like the following:

Heat a small cup of milk to scalding. Stir into it a teaspoonful of corn-starch wet up with a little water. When this thickens, add two tablespoonfuls of butter, pepper, salt, and chopped parsley, to taste. Beat an egg light, pour the sauce gradually over it, put the mixture again over the fire, and stir one minute, not more. Pour upon the fish, and serve it with some slices of lemon, or a few sprigs of parsley or water-cresses, on the dish as a garnish.

BAKED SALT MACKEREL.

When the mackerel have soaked over night, put them in a pan and pour on boiling water enough to cover. Let them stand a couple of minutes, then drain them off, and put them in the pan with a few lumps of butter; pour on a half teacupful of sweet cream, or rich milk, and a little pepper; set in the oven and let it bake a little until brown.

FRIED SALT MACKEREL.

Select as many salt mackerel as required; wash and cleanse them well, then put them to soak all day in *cold* water, changing them every two hours; then put them into fresh water just before retiring. In the morning drain off the water, wipe them dry, roll them in flour, and fry in a little butter on a hot thick-bottom frying-pan. Serve with a little melted butter poured over, and garnish with a little parsley.

BOILED FRESH MACKEREL.

Fresh mackerel are cooked in water salted, and a little vinegar added; with this exception they can be served in the same way as the salt mackerel. Broiled ones are very nice with the same cream sauce, or you can substitute egg sauce.

POTTED FRESH FISH.

After the fish has laid in salt water six hours, take it out, and to every six pounds of fish take one-quarter cupful each of salt, black pepper and cinnamon, one eighth cupful of allspice, and one teaspoonful of cloves.

Cut the fish in pieces and put into a half gallon stone baking-jar, first a layer of fish, then the spices, flour, and then spread a thin layer of butter on, and continue so until the dish is full. Fill the jar with equal parts of vinegar and water, cover with tightly fitting lid, so that the steam cannot escape; bake five hours, remove from the oven, and when it is cold, it is to be cut in slices and served. This is a tea or lunch dish.

SCALLOPED CRABS.

Put the crabs into a kettle of boiling water, and throw in a handful of salt. Boil from twenty minutes to half an hour. Take them from the water when done and pick out all the meat; be careful not to break the shell. To a pint of meat put a little salt and pepper; taste, and if not enough add more, a little at a time, till suited. Grate in a very little nutmeg, and add one spoonful of cracker or bread-crumbs, two eggs well beaten, and two tablespoonfuls of butter (even full): stir all well together; wash the shells clean, and fill each shell full of the mixture; sprinkle crumbs over the top and moisten with the liquor; set in the oven till of a nice brown; a few minutes will do it. Send to the table hot, arranged on large dishes. They are eaten at breakfast or supper.

FISH IN WHITE SAUCE.

Flake up cold boiled halibut and set the plate into the steamer, that the fish may heat without drying. Boil the bones and skin of the fish with a slice of onion and a *very* small piece of red pepper; a bit of this the size of a kernel of coffee will make the sauce quite as hot as most persons like it. Boil this stock down to half a pint; thicken with one teaspoonful of butter and one teaspoonful of flour, mixed together. Add one drop of extract of almond. Pour this sauce over your halibut and stick bits of parsley over it.

FRESH STURGEON STEAK MARINADE.

Take one slice of sturgeon two inches thick; let it stand in hot water five minutes; drain; put it in a bowl and add a gill of vinegar, two tablespoonfuls of melted butter, half a teaspoonful of salt, a saltspoonful of black pepper, and the juice of half a lemon; let it stand six hours, turning it occasionally; drain and dry on a napkin; dip it in egg; roll in bread-crumbs, and fry, or rather boil, in very hot fat. Beat up the yolks of two raw eggs, add a teaspoonful of French mustard, and, by degrees, half of the marinade, to make a smooth sauce, which serve with the fish.

POTTED FISH.

Take out the backbone of the fish; for one weighing two pounds take a tablespoonful of allspice and cloves mixed; these spices should be put into little bags of not too thick muslin; put sufficient salt directly upon each fish; then roll in a cloth, over which sprinkle a little cayenne pepper; put alternate layers of fish, spice and sage in an earthern jar; cover with the best cider vinegar; cover the jar closely with a plate, and over this put a covering of dough, rolled out to twice the thickness of pie crust. Make the edges of paste, to adhere closely to the sides of the jar, so as to make it air-tight. Put the jar into a pot of cold water and let it boil from three to five hours, according to quantity. Ready when cold.

MAYONNAISE FISH.

Take a pound or so of cold boiled fish (halibut, rock, or cod), not chop, but cut, into pieces an inch in length. Mix in a bowl a dressing as follows: The yolk of four boiled eggs rubbed to a smooth paste with salad oil or butter; add to these salt, pepper, mustard, two teaspoonfuls of white sugar, and, lastly, six tablespoonfuls of vinegar. Beat the mixture until light, and just before pouring it over the fish, stir in lightly the frothed white of a raw egg. Serve the fish in a glass dish, with half the dressing stirred in with it. Spread the remainder over the top, and lay lettuce leaves (from the core of the head of lettuce) around the edges, to be eaten with it.

FISH CHOWDER.　(Rhode Island.)

Fry five or six slices of fat pork crisp in the bottom of the pot you are to make your chowder in; take them out and chop them into small pieces, put them back into the bottom of the pot with their own gravy. (This is much better than having the slices whole.)

Cut four pounds of fresh cod or sea-bass into pieces two inches square, and lay enough of these on the pork to cover it. Follow with a layer of chopped onions, a little parsley; summer savory and pepper, either black or cayenne. Then a layer of split Boston, or butter, or whole cream crackers, which have been soaked in warm water until moistened through, but not ready to break. Above this put a layer of pork, and repeat the order given above—onions, seasoning, (not too much), crackers and pork, until your materials are exhausted. Let the topmost layer be buttered crackers well soaked. Pour in enough cold water to barely cover all. Cover the pot, stew gently for an hour, watching that the water does not sink too low. Should it leave the upper layer exposed, replenish cautiously from the boiling tea-kettle. When the chowder is thoroughly done, take out with a perforated skimmer and put into a tureen. Thicken the gravy with a tablespoonful of flour and about the same quantity of butter; boil up and pour over the chowder. Serve sliced lemon, pickles and stewed tomatoes with it, that the guests may add if they like.

CODFISH BALLS.

Take a pint bowl of codfish picked very fine, two pint bowls of whole raw peeled potatoes, sliced thickly; put them together in plenty of cold water and boil until the potatoes are thoroughly cooked; remove from the fire, and drain off all the water. Mash them with the potato masher, add a piece of butter the size of an egg, one well-beaten egg, and three spoonfuls of cream or rich milk. Flour your hands and make into balls or cakes. Put an ounce each of butter and lard into a frying pan; when hot, put in the balls and fry a nice brown. Do not freshen the fish before boiling with the potatoes. Many cooks fry them in a quantity of lard similar to boiled doughnuts.

STEWED CODFISH. (Salt.)

Take a thick, white piece of salt codfish, lay it in cold water for a few minutes to soften it a little, enough to render it more easily to be picked up. Shred it in very small bits, put it over the fire in a stew-pan with cold water; let it come to a boil, turn off this water carefully, and add a pint of milk to the fish, or more according to quantity. Set it over the fire again and let it boil slowly about three minutes, now add a good-sized piece of butter, a shake of pepper and a thickening of a tablespoonful of flour in enough cold milk to make a cream. Stew five minutes longer, and just before serving stir in two well-beaten eggs. The eggs are an addition that could be dispensed with, however, as it is very good without them. An excellent breakfast dish.

CODFISH Á LA MODE.

Pick up a teacupful of salt codfish very fine, and freshen—the dessicated is nice to use; two cups mashed potatoes, one pint cream or milk, two well-beaten eggs, half a cup butter, salt and pepper; mix; bake in an earthen baking dish from twenty to twenty-five minutes; serve in the same dish, placed on a small platter, covered with a fine napkin.

BOILED FRESH COD.

Sew up the piece of fish in thin cloth, fitted to shape; boil in salted water (boiling from the first), allowing about fifteen minutes to the pound. Carefully unwrap, and pour over it warm oyster sauce. A whole one boiled the same.

—*Hotel Brighton.*

SCALLOPED FISH.

Pick any cold fresh fish, or salt codfish, left from the dinner, into fine bits, carefully removing all the bones.

Take a pint of milk in a suitable dish, and place it in a sauce-pan of boiling water; put into it a few slices of onion, cut very fine, a sprig of parsley minced fine, add a piece of butter as large as an egg, a pinch of salt, a sprinkle of white pepper, then stir in two tablespoonfuls of corn-starch, or flour, rubbed in a little cold milk; let all boil up and remove from the fire. Take a dish you wish to serve it in, butter the sides and bottom. Put first a layer of the minced fish, then a layer of the cream, then sprinkle over that some cracker or bread-crumbs, then a layer of fish again, and so on, until the dish is full; spread cracker or bread-crumbs last on the top, to prevent the milk from scorching.

This is a very good way to use up cold fish, making a nice breakfast dish, or a side-dish for dinner.

FISH FRITTERS.

Take a piece of salt codfish, pick it up very fine, put it into a sauce-pan, with plenty of *cold* water; bring it to a boil, turn off the water, and add another of cold water; let this boil with the fish about fifteen minutes, very slowly; strain off this water, making the fish quite dry, and set aside to cool. In the meantime, stir up a batter of a pint of milk, four eggs, a pinch of salt, one large teaspoonful of baking powder in flour, enough to make thicker than batter cakes. Stir in the fish and fry like any fritters. Very fine accompaniment to a good breakfast.

BOILED SALT CODFISH. (New England Style).

Cut the fish into square pieces, cover with cold water, set on the back part of the stove; when hot, pour off water and cover again with cold water; let it stand about four hours and simmer, not boil; put the fish on a platter, then cover with a drawn-butter gravy, and serve. Many cooks prefer soaking the fish over night.

BOILED CODFISH AND OYSTER SAUCE.

Lay the fish in cold salted water half an hour before it is time to cook it, then roll it in a clean cloth dredged with flour; sew up the edges in such a manner as to envelope the fish entirely, yet have but *one* thickness of cloth over any part. Put the fish into boiling water, slightly salted; add a few whole cloves and peppers and a bit of lemon peel; pull gently on the fins, and when they come out easily the fish is done. Arrange neatly on a folded napkin, garnish and serve with oyster sauce. Take six oysters to every pound of fish and scald (blanch) them in a half-pint of hot oyster liquor; take out the oysters and add to the liquor, salt, pepper, a bit of mace and an ounce of butter; whip into it a gill of milk containing half of a teaspoonful of flour. Simmer a moment; add the oysters, and send to table in a sauce-boat. Egg sauce is good with this fish.

BAKED CODFISH.

If salt fish, soak, boil and pick the fish, the same as for fish-balls. Add an equal quantity of mashed potatoes, or cold, boiled, chopped potatoes, a large piece of butter, and warm milk enough to make it quite soft. Put it into a buttered dish, rub butter over the top, shake over a little sifted flour, and bake about thirty minutes, and until a rich brown. Make a sauce of drawn butter, with two hard-boiled eggs sliced, served in a gravy-boat.

CODFISH STEAK. (New England Style.)

Select a medium-sized fresh codfish, cut it in steaks cross-wise of the fish, about an inch and a half thick; sprinkle a little salt over them, and let them stand two hours. Cut into dice a pound of salt fat pork, fry out all the fat from them and remove the crisp bits of pork; put the codfish steaks in a pan of corn meal, dredge them with it, and when the pork fat is smoking hot, fry the steaks in it to a dark-brown color on both sides. Squeeze over them a little lemon juice, add a dash of freshly ground pepper, and serve with hot, old-fashioned, well-buttered Johnny Cake.

SALMON CROQUETTES.

One pound of cooked salmon (about one and a half pints when chopped), one cup of cream, two tablespoonfuls of butter, one tablespoonful of flour, three eggs, one pint of crumbs, pepper and salt; chop the salmon fine, mix the flour and butter together, let the cream come to a boil, and stir in the flour and butter, salmon and seasoning; boil one minute; stir in one well-beaten egg, and remove from the fire; when cold make into croquettes; dip in beaten egg, roll in crumbs and fry. Canned salmon can be used.

Shell=Fish.

STEWED WATER TURTLES, OR TERRAPINS.

Select the largest, thickest and fattest, the females being the best; they should be alive when brought from market. Wash and put them alive into boiling water, add a little salt, and boil them until thoroughly done, or from ten to fifteen minutes, after which take off the shell, extract the meat, and remove carefully the sand-bag and gall; also all the entrails; they are unfit to eat, and are no longer used in cooking terrapins for the best tables. Cut the meat into pieces, and put it into a stew-pan with its eggs, and sufficient fresh butter to stew it well. Let it stew till quite hot throughout, keeping the pan carefully covered, that none of the flavor may escape, but shake it over the fire while stewing. In another pan make a sauce of beaten yolk of egg, highly flavored with Madeira or sherry, and powdered nutmeg and mace, a gill of currant jelly, a pinch of cayenne pepper, and salt to taste, enriched with a large lump of fresh butter. Stir this sauce well over the fire, and when it has almost come to a boil, take it off. Send the terrapins to the table hot in a covered dish, and the sauce separately in a sauce-tureen, to be used by those who like it, and omitted by those who prefer the genuine flavor of the terrapins when simply stewed with butter. This is now the usual mode of dressing terrapins in Maryland, Virginia, and many other parts of the South, and will be found superior to any other. If there are no eggs in the terrapin, "egg balls" may be substituted. (See recipe).

STEWED TERRAPIN, WITH CREAM.

Place in a sauce-pan, two heaping tablespoonfuls of butter and one of dry flour; stir it over the fire until it bubbles; then gradually stir in a pint of cream, a teaspoonful of salt, a quarter of a teaspoonful of white pepper, the same of grated nutmeg, and a very small pinch of cayenne. Next, put in a pint of terrapin meat and stir all until it is scalding hot. Move the sauce-pan to the back part of the stove or range, where the contents will keep hot but not boil; then stir in four well-beaten yolks of eggs; do not allow the terrapin to boil after adding the eggs, but pour it immediately into a tureen containing a gill of good Madeira and a tablespoonful of lemon juice. Serve hot.

STEWED TERRAPIN.

Plunge the terrapins alive into boiling water, and let them remain until the sides and lower shell begin to crack—this will take less than an hour; then remove them and let them get cold; take off the shell and outer skin, being careful to save all the blood possible in opening them. If there are eggs in them put them aside in a dish; take all the inside out, and be very careful not to break the gall, which must be immediately removed or it will make the rest bitter. It lies within the liver. Then cut up the liver and all the rest of the terrapin into small pieces, adding the blood and juice that have flowed out in cutting up; add half a pint of water; sprinkle a little flour over them as you place them in the stew-pan; let them stew slowly ten minutes, adding salt, black and cayenne pepper, and a very small blade of mace; then add a gill of the best brandy and half a pint of the very best sherry wine; let it simmer over a slow fire very gently. About ten minutes or so, before you are ready to dish them, add half a pint of rich cream, and half a pound of sweet butter, with flour, to prevent boiling; two or three minutes before taking them off the fire, peel the eggs carefully and throw them in whole. If there should be no eggs use the yolk of hens' eggs, hard boiled. This receipt is for four terrapins.

—Rennert's Hotel, Baltimore.

BOILED LOBSTER.

Put a handful of salt into a large kettle or pot of boiling water. When the water boils very hard, put in the lobster, having first brushed it, and tied the claws together with a bit of twine. Keep it boiling from 20 minutes to half an hour in proportion to its size. If boiled too long the meat will be hard and stringy. When it is done take it out, lay it on its claws to drain, and then wipe it dry.

It is scarcely necessary to mention that the head of a lobster, and what are called the lady-fingers, are not to be eaten.

Very large lobsters are not the best, the meat being coarse and tough. The male is best for boiling; the flesh is firmer, and the shell a brighter red; it may readily be distinguished from the female; the tail is narrower, and the two up-per-most fins within the tail are stiff and hard. Those of the hen lobster are not so, and the tail is broader.

Hen lobsters are preferred for sauce or salad, on account of their coral. The head and small claws are never used.

They should be alive and freshly caught when put into the boiling kettle. After being cooked and cooled, split open the body and tail, and crack the claws, to extract the meat. The sand pouch found near the throat should be removed. Care should be exercised that none of the feathery, tough, gill-like particles found under the body shell get mixed with the meat, as they are indigestible, and have caused much trouble. They are supposed to be the cause of so-called poisoning from eating lobster.

Serve on a platter. Lettuce, and other concomitants of a salad, should also be placed on the table or platter.

SCALLOPED LOBSTER.

Butter a deep dish, and cover the bottom with fine bread-crumbs; put on this a layer of chopped lobster, with pepper and salt; so on alternately until the dish is filled, having crumbs on top. Put on bits of butter, moisten with milk, and bake about twenty minutes.

DEVILED LOBSTER.

Take out all the meat from a boiled lobster, reserving the coral; season highly with mustard, cayenne, salt and some kind of table sauce; stew until well mixed, and put it in a covered sauce-pan, with just enough hot water to keep from burning; rub the coral smooth, moistening with vinegar until it is thin enough to pour easily, then stir it into the sauce-pan. The dressing should be prepared before the meat is put on the fire, and which ought to boil but once before the coral is put in; stir in a heaping teaspoonful of butter, and when it boils again it is done, and should be taken up at once, as too much cooking toughens the meat.

LOBSTER CROQUETTES.

Take any of the lobster remaining from table, and pound it until the dark, light meat and coral are well mixed; put with it not quite as much fine bread-crumbs; season with pepper, salt and a very little cayenne pepper; add a little melted butter, about two tablespoonfuls if the bread is rather dry; form into egg-shaped or round balls; roll them in egg, then in fine crumbs, and fry in boil·ing lard.

LOBSTER PATTIES.

Cut some boiled lobster in small pieces; then take the small claws and the spawn, put them in a suitable dish, and jam them to a paste with a potato masher. Now add to them a ladleful of gravy or both, with a few bread-crumbs; set it over the fire and boil; strain it through a strainer, or sieve, to the thickness of a cream, and put half of it to your lobsters, and save the other half to sauce them with after they are baked. Put to the lobster the bigness of an egg of butter, a little pepper and salt; squeeze in a lemon, and warm these over the fire enough to melt the butter, set it to cool, and sheet your patty-pan or a plate or dish with good puff paste; then put in your lobster, and cover it with a paste; bake it within three-quarters of an hour before you want it; when it is baked, cut up your cover, and warm up the other half of your sauce above mentioned, with a little butter, to the thickness of cream, and pour it over your patty, with a little squeezed lemon; cut your cover in two, and lay it on the top, two inches distant, so that what is under may be seen. You may bake crawfish, shrimps or prawns the same way; and they are all proper for plates or little dishes for a second course.

LOBSTER A LA NEWBURG.

Take one whole lobster, cut up in pieces about as large as a hickory nut. Put in the same pan with a piece of butter size of a walnut, season with salt and pepper to taste, and thicken with heavy cream sauce; add the yolk of one egg and two oz. of sherry wine.

Cream Sauce for above is made as follows: 1 oz. butter, melted in sauce pan. 2 oz. flour, mixed with butter; thin down to proper consistency with boiling cream.

—*Rector's Oyster House, Chicago.*

BAKED CRABS.

Mix with the contents of a can of crabs, bread-crumbs or pounded crackers. Pepper and salt the whole to taste; mince some cold ham; have the baking-pan well buttered, place therein first a layer of the crab meat, prepared as above, then a layer of the minced ham, and so on, alternating until the pan is filled. Cover the top with bread-crumbs and bits of butter, and bake.

DEVILED CRABS.

Half a dozen fresh crabs, boiled and minced, two ounces of butter, one small teaspoonful of mustard powder; cayenne pepper and salt to taste. Put the meat into a bowl and mix carefully with it an equal quantity of fine bread-crumbs. Work the butter to a light cream, mix the mustard well with it, then stir in very carefully, a handful at a time, the mixed crabs, a tablespoonful of cream, and crumbs. Season to taste with cayenne pepper and salt: fill the crab shells with the mixture, sprinkle bread-crumbs over the tops, put three small pieces of butter upon the top of each, and brown them quickly in a hot oven. They will puff in baking and will be found very nice. Half the quantity can be made A crab-shell will hold the meat of two crabs.

CRAB CROQUETTES.

Pick the meat of boiled crabs and chop it fine. Season to taste with pepper, salt and melted butter. Moisten it well with rich milk or cream, then stiffen it slightly with bread or cracker-crumbs. Add two or three well-beaten eggs to bind the mixture. Form the croquettes, egg and bread-crumb them and fry them delicately in boiling lard. It is better to use a wire frying-basket for croquettes of all kinds.

TO MAKE A CRAB PIE.

Procure the crabs alive, and put them in boiling water, along with some salt. Boil them for a quarter of an hour or twenty minutes, according to the size. When cold, pick the meat from the claws and body. Chop all together, and mix it with crumbs of bread, pepper and salt, and a little butter. Put all this into the shell, and brown in a hot oven. A crab-shell will hold the meat of two crabs.

CRABS. (Soft Shell.)

Crabs may be boiled as lobsters. They make a fine dish when stewed. Take out the meat from the shell, put it into a sauce-pan with butter, pepper, salt, a pinch of mace, and a very little water; dredge with flour, and let simmer five minutes over a slow fire. Serve hot; garnish the dish with the claws laid around it.

The usual way of cooking them is frying them in plenty of butter and lard mixed; prepare them the same as frying fish. The spongy substance from the sides should be taken off, also the sand bag. Fry a nice brown, and garnish with parsley.

OYSTERS.

Oysters must be fresh and fat to be good. They are in season from September to May.

The small ones, such as are sold by the quart, are good for pies, fritters, or stews; the largest of this sort are nice for frying or pickling for family use.

FRIED OYSTERS.

Take large oysters from their own liquor into a thickly folded napkin to dry them; then make hot an ounce each of butter and lard, in a thick-bottom frying-pan. Season the oysters with pepper and salt, then dip each one into egg and cracker-crumbs rolled fine, until it will take up no more. Place them in the hot grease and fry them a delicate brown, turning them on both sides by sliding a broad-bladed knife under them. Serve them crisp and hot.

—Boston Oyster House.

Some prefer to roll oysters in corn-meal and others use flour, but they are much more crisp with egg and cracker-crumbs.

OYSTERS FRIED IN BATTER.

Ingredients.—½ pint of oysters, 2 eggs, ½ pint of milk, sufficient flour to make the batter; pepper and salt to taste; when liked, a little nutmeg; hot lard.

Scald the oysters in their own liquor, beard them, and lay them on a cloth to drain thoroughly. Break the eggs into a basin, mix the flour with them, add the milk gradually, with nutmeg and seasoning, and put the oysters in a batter. Make some lard hot in a deep frying-pan; put in the oysters, one at a time; when done, take them up with a sharp-pointed skewer, and dish them on a napkin. Fried oysters are frequently used for garnishing boiled fish, and then a few bread-crumbs should be added to the flour.

STEWED OYSTERS. (In Milk or Cream.)

Drain the liquor from two quarts of oysters; mix with it a small teacupful of hot water, add a little salt and pepper, and set it over the fire in a sauce-pan. Let it boil up once, put in the oysters, let them come to a boil, and when they "ruffle" add two tablespoonfuls of butter. The instant it is melted and well stirred in, put in a pint of boiling milk, and take the sauce-pan from the fire. Serve with oyster or cream crackers. Serve while hot.

If thickening is preferred, stir in a little flour or two tablespoonfuls of cracker-crumbs.

PLAIN OYSTER STEW.

Same as milk or cream stew, using only oyster liquor and water instead of milk or cream, adding more butter after taking up.

OYSTER SOUP.

For oyster soup, see Soups.

DRY OYSTER STEW.

Take six to twelve large oysters and cook them in half a pint of their own liquor; season with butter and white pepper; cook for five minutes, stirring constantly. Serve in hot soup-plates or bowls.

—Fulton Market, New York.

BOSTON FRY.

Prepare the oysters in egg batter and fine cracker meal; fry in butter over a slow fire for about ten minutes; cover the hollow of a hot platter with tomato sauce; place the oysters in it, but not covering; garnished with chopped parsley sprinkled over the oysters.

—Boston Oyster House.

BROILED OYSTERS.

Dry a quart of oysters in a cloth, dip each in melted butter well peppered; then in beaten egg, or not, then in bread or cracker-crumbs, also peppered. Broil on a wire broiler over live coals, three to five minutes. Dip over each a little melted butter. Serve hot.

ROAST OYSTERS IN THE SHELL.

Select the large ones, those usually termed "Saddle Rocks," formerly known as a distinct variety, but which are now but the large oysters selected from any beds; wash and wipe them, and place with the upper or deep shell down, to catch the juice, over or on live coals. When they open their shells, remove the shallow one, being careful to save all the juice in the other; place them, shells and all, on a hot platter, and send to table hot, to be seasoned by each person with butter and pepper to taste. If the oysters are fine, and they are just cooked enough and served all hot, this is, *par excellence*, the style.

OYSTER ROAST. No. 2.

Put one quart of oysters in a basin with their own liquor and let them boil three or four minutes; season with a little salt, pepper and a heaping spoonful of butter. Serve on buttered toast.

STEAMED OYSTERS.

Wash and drain a quart of counts or select oysters; put them in a shallow pan and place in a steamer over boiling water; cover and steam till they are plump, with the edges ruffled, but no longer. Place in a heated dish, with butter, pepper and salt, and serve.

—Baltimore Style.

STEAMED OYSTERS IN THE SHELL.

Wash and place them in an air-tight vessel, laying them the upper shell downward, so that the liquor will not run out when they open. Place this dish or vessel over a pot of boiling water where they will get the steam. Boil them rapidly until the shells open, about fifteen to twenty minutes. Serve at once while hot. seasoned with butter, salt and pepper.

PAN OYSTERS. No. 1.

Cut some stale bread in thin slices, taking off all the crust; round the slices to fit patty-pans, toast, butter, place them in the pans and moisten with three or four teaspoonfuls of oyster liquor; place on the toast a layer of oysters, sprinkle with pepper, and put a small piece of butter on top of each pan; place all the pans in a baking-pan, and place in the oven, covering tightly. They will cook in seven or eight minutes if the oven is hot; or, cook till the beards are ruffled; remove the cover, sprinkle lightly with salt, replace, and cook one minute longer. Serve in patty-pans. They are delicious.

—New York Style.

PAN OYSTERS. No. 2.

Lay in a thin pie-tin or dripping-pan half a pint of large oysters, or more if required; have the pan large enough so that each oyster will lie flat on the bottom; put in over them a little oyster liquor, but not enough to float; place them carefully in a hot oven and just heat them through thoroughly—do not bake them—which will be in three to five minutes, according to fire; take them up and place on toast; first moistened with the hot juice from the pan. Are a very good substitute for oysters roasted in the shell, the slow cooking bringing out the flavor.

—French Restaurant, New Orleans, La.

OYSTER FRITTERS.

Select plump, good-sized oysters; drain off the juice, and to a cup of this juice add a cup of milk, a little salt, four well-beaten eggs, and flour enough to make batter like griddle-cakes.

Envelop an oyster in a spoonful of this batter, (some cut them in halves or chop them fine,) then fry in butter and lard, mixed in a frying-pan the same as we fry eggs, turning to fry brown on both sides. Send to the table very hot.

—Delmonico.

Most cooks fry oyster fritters the same as crullers, in a quantity of hot lard, but this is not always convenient; either way they are excellent.

OYSTER PATTIES.

Line patty-pans with thin pastry, pressing it well to the tin. Put a piece of bread or a ball of paper in each. Cover them with paste and brush them over with the white of an egg. Cut an inch square of thin pastry, place on the centre of each, glaze this also with egg, and bake in a quick oven fifteen to twenty minutes. Remove the bread or paper when half cold.

Scald as many oysters as you require (allowing two for each patty, three if small) in their own liquor. Cut each in four and strain the liquor. Put two tablespoonfuls of butter and two of flour into a thick sauce-pan; stir them together over the fire till the flour smells cooked, and then pour half a pint of oyster liquor and half a pint of milk into the flour and butter. (If you have cream, use it instead of milk.) Stir till it is a thick, smooth sauce. Put the oysters into it and let them boil once. Beat the yolks of two eggs. Remove the oysters for one minute from the fire, then stir the eggs into them till the sauce looks like thick custard.

Fill the patties with this oyster fricassee, taking care to make it hot by standing in boiling water before dinner on the day required, and to make the patty cases hot before you fill them.

FULTON MARKET ROAST.

It is still known in New York from the place at which it was and is still served. Take nine large oysters in the shell; wash, dry and roast over a charcoal fire, on a broiler. Two minutes after the shells open they will be done. Take them up quickly, saving the juice in a small, shallow, tin pan; keep hot until all are done; butter them and sprinkle with pepper.

This is served for one person when calling for a roast of this kind. It is often poured over a slice of toast.

SCALLOPED OYSTERS.

Have ready about a pint bowl of fine cracker-crumbs. Butter a deep earthen dish; put a layer of the cracker-crumbs on the bottom; wet this with some of the oyster liquor; next have a layer of oysters; sprinkle with salt and pepper, and lay small bits of butter upon them; then another layer of cracker-crumbs and oyster juice; then oysters, pepper, salt and butter, and so on, until the dish is full; the top layer to be cracker-crumbs. Beat up an egg in a cup of milk and turn over all. Cover the dish and set it in the oven for thirty or forty-five minutes. When baked through, uncover the top, set on the upper grate and brown.

OYSTER POT-PIE.

Scald a quart can of oysters in their own liquor; when it boils, skim out the oysters and set aside in a warm place. To the liquor add a pint of hot water; season well with salt and pepper, a generous piece of butter, thicken with flour and cold milk. Have ready nice light biscuit dough, rolled twice as thick as pie-crust; cut out into inch squares, drop them into the boiling stew, cover closely, and cook forty minutes. When taken up, stir the oysters into the juice and serve all together in one dish. A nice side *entrée.*

—Prince's Bay, S.I.

BOSTON OYSTER PIE.

Having buttered the inside of a *deep* pie-plate, line it with puff-paste, or common pie-crust, and prepare another sheet of paste for the lid; put a clean towel into the dish (folded so as to support the lid), set it into the oven and bake the paste well; when done, remove the lid and take out the towel. While the paste is baking prepare the oysters. Having picked off carefully every bit of shell that may be found about them, drain off the liquor into a pan and put the oysters into a stew-pan with barely enough of the liquor to keep them from burning; season them with pepper, salt and butter; add a little sweet cream or milk, and one or two crackers rolled fine; let the oysters simmer, but *not boil,* as that will shrivel them. Remove the upper crust of pastry and fill the dish with the oysters and gravy; replace the cover and serve hot.

Some prefer baking the upper crust on a pie-plate, the same size as the pie, then slipping it off on top of the pie after the same is filled with the oysters.

MOCK OYSTERS.

Grate the corn, while green and tender, with a coarse grater, into a deep dish. To two ears of corn, allow one egg; beat the whites and yolks separately, and add them to the corn, with one tablespoonful of wheat flour and one of butter, a teaspoonful of salt and pepper to taste. Drop spoonfuls of this batter into a frying-pan with hot butter and lard mixed, and fry a light brown on both sides.

In taste, they have a singular resemblance to fried oysters. The corn *must* be *young.*

FRICASSEED OYSTERS.

Take a slice of raw ham, which has been pickled, but not smoked, and soak in boiling water for half an hour; cut it in quite small pieces, and put in a sauce-pan with two-thirds of a pint of veal or chicken broth, well strained; the liquor from a quart of oysters, one small onion, minced fine, and a little chopped parsley, sweet marjoram, and pepper; let them simmer for twenty minutes, and then boil rapidly two or three minutes; skim well, and add one scant table-spoonful of corn-starch, mixed smoothly in one-third cup of milk; stir constantly, and when it boils add the oysters and one ounce of butter; after which, just let it come to a boil. and remove the oysters to a deep dish; beat one egg, and add to it gradually some f the hot broth, and, when cooked, stir it into the pan; season with salt, and pour the whole over the oysters. When placed upon the table, squeeze the juice of a lemon over it.

SMALL OYSTER PIES.

For each pie take a tin plate half the size of an ordinary dinner plate; butter it, and cover the bottom with a puff paste, as for pies; lay on it five or six select oysters, or enough to cover the bottom; butter them and season with a little salt and plenty of pepper; spread over this an egg batter, and cover with a crust of the paste, making small openings in it with a fork. Bake in a hot oven fifteen to twenty minutes, or until the top is nicely browned.

—Boston Oyster House.

STEWED CLAMS.

Wash clean as many round clams as required; pile them in a large iron pot, with half a cupful of hot water in the bottom, and put over the fire; as soon as the shells open, take out the clams, cut off the hard, uneatable "fringe" from each, with strong, clean scissors, put them into a stew-pan with the broth from the pot, and boil slowly till they are quite tender; pepper well, and thicken the gravy with flour, stirred into melted butter.

Or, you may get two dozen freshly opened *very* small clams. Boil a pint of milk, a dash of white pepper and a small pat of butter. Now add the clams. Let them come to a boil, and serve. Longer boiling will make the clams almost indigestible.

ROAST CLAMS IN THE SHELL.

Roast in a pan over a hot fire, or in a hot oven, or, at a "Clam Bake," on hot stones; when they open, empty the juice into a sauce-pan; add the clams with butter, pepper and a very little salt.

—Rye Beach.

CLAM FRITTERS.

Take fifty small or twenty-five large sand clams from their shells; if large, cut each in two, lay them on a thickly folded napkin; put a pint bowl of wheat flour into a basin, add to it three well-beaten eggs, half a pint of sweet milk, and nearly as much of their own liquor; beat the batter until it is smooth and perfectly free from lumps; then stir in the clams. Put plenty of lard or beef fat into a thick-bottomed frying-pan, let it become boiling hot; put in the batter by the spoonful; let them fry gently; when one side is a delicate brown, turn the other.

CLAM CHOWDER.

The materials needed are fifty round clams (quahogs), a large bowl of salt pork, cut up fine, the same of onions, finely chopped, and the same (or more, if you desire,) of potatoes cut into eighths or sixteenths of original size; wash the clams very thoroughly, and put them in a pot with half a pint of water; when the shells are open they are done; then take them from the shells and chop fine, saving all the clam water for the chowder; fry out the pork very gently, and when the scraps are a good brown, take them out and put in the chopped onions to fry; they should be fried in a frying-pan, and the chowder-kettle be made very clean before they are put in it, or the chowder will burn. (The chief secret in chowder-making is to fry the onions so delicately that they will be missing in the chowder.)

Add a quart of hot water to the onions; put in the clams, clam-water and pork scraps. After it boils, add the potatoes, and when they are cooked, the chowder is finished. Just before it is taken up, thicken it with a cup of powdered crackers, and add a quart of fresh milk. If too rich, add more water. No seasoning is needed but good black pepper.

With the addition of six sliced tomatoes, or half a can of the canned ones, this is the best recipe of this kind, and is served in many of our best restaurants.

—New Bedford Recipe.

SCALLOPED CLAMS.

Purchase a dozen large soft clams in the shell and three dozen opened clams. Ask the dealer to open the first dozen, care being used not to injure the shells, which are to be used in cooking the clams. Clean the shells well, and put two soft clams on each half shell; add to each a dash of white pepper, and half a teaspoonful of minced celery. Cut a slice of fat bacon into the smallest dice, add four of these to each shell, strew over the top a thin layer of cracker-dust; place a piece of table butter on top, and bake in the oven until brown. They are delightful when properly prepared.

SCALLOPS.

If bought in the shell boil them and take out the hearts, which is the only part used. Dip them in beaten egg, and fry in the same manner as oysters.

Some prefer them stewed the same as oysters.

FROGS FRIED.

Frogs are usually fried, and are considered a great delicacy. Only the hind-legs and quarters are used. Clean them well, season, and fry in egg batter, or dipped in beaten egg and fine cracker-crumbs, the same as oysters.

FROGS STEWED.

Wash and skin the quarters, parboil them about three minutes, drain them. Now, put into a stew-pan two ounces of butter. When it is melted, lay in the frogs, and fry about two minutes, stirring them to prevent burning; shake over them a tablespoonful of sifted flour and stir it into them; add a sprig of parsley, a pinch of powdered summer savory, a bay leaf, three slices of onion, salt and pepper, a cup of hot water and one of cream. Boil gently until done; remove the legs, strain and mix into the gravy the yolks of two eggs, well beaten to a cream; put the legs in a suitable dish, pour over the gravy and serve.

POULTRY AND GAME.

In choosing poultry, select those that are fresh and fat, and the surest way to determine whether they are young, is to try the skin under the leg or wing. If it is easily broken, it is young; or, turn the wing backwards, if the joint yields readily, it is tender. When poultry is young the skin is thin and tender, the legs smooth, the feet moist and limber, and the eyes full and bright. The body should be thick and the breast fat. Old turkeys have long hairs, and the flesh is purplish where it shows under the skin on the legs and back. About March they deteriorate in quality.

Young ducks and geese are plump, with light, semi-transparent fat, soft breast-bone, tender flesh, leg-joints which will break by the weight of the bird, fresh-colored and brittle beaks, and wind-pipes that break when pressed between the thumb and forefinger. They are best in fall and winter.

Young pigeons have light red flesh upon the breast, and full, fresh-colored legs; when the legs are thin and the breast very dark the birds are old.

Fine game birds are always heavy for their size; the flesh of the breast is firm and plump, and the skin clear; and if a few feathers be plucked from the inside of the leg and around the vent, the flesh of freshly-killed birds will be fat and fresh-colored; if it is dark and discolored, the game has been hung a long time. The wings of good ducks, geese, pheasants, and woodcock are tender to the touch; the tips of the long wing feathers of partridges are pointed in young birds and round in old ones. Quail, snipe and small birds should have full, tender breasts. Poultry should never be cooked until six or eight hours after it has been killed, but it should be picked and drawn as soon as possible. Plunge it in a pot of scalding hot water; then pluck off the feathers, taking care not to tear the skin; when it is picked clean, roll up a piece of white paper, set fire to it, and singe off all the hairs. The head, neck and feet should be cut off, and the ends of the legs skewered to the body, and a string tied tightly around the body. When roasting a chicken or small fowl there is danger of the legs browning or becoming too hard to be eaten. To avoid this, take strips of cloth, dip them into a little melted lard, or even just rub them over with lard, and wind them around the legs. Remove them in time to allow the legs to brown delicately.

Fowls, and also various kinds of game, when bought at our city markets, require a more thorough cleansing than those sold in country places, where as a general thing the meat is wholly dressed. In large cities they lay for some length of time with the intestines undrawn, until the flavor of them diffuses itself all through the meat, rendering it distasteful. In this case, it is safe after taking out the intestines, to rinse out in several waters, and in next to the last water, add a teaspoonful of baking soda; say to a quart of water. This process neutralizes all sourness, and helps to destroy all unpleasant taste in the meat.

Poultry may be baked so that its wings and legs are soft and tender, by being placed in a deep roasting pan with close cover, thereby retaining the aroma and essences by absorption while confined. These pans are a recent innovation, and are made double with a small opening in the top for giving vent to the accumulation of steam and gases when required. Roast meats of any kind can also be cooked in the same manner, and it is a great improvement on the old plan.

ROAST TURKEY.

Select a young turkey; remove all the feathers carefully, singe it over a burning newspaper on the top of the stove; then "draw" it nicely, being very careful not to break any of the internal organs; remove the crop carefully; cut off the head, and tie the neck close to the body by drawing the skin over it. Now rinse the inside of the turkey out with several waters, and in the next to the last, mix a teaspoonful of baking soda; oftentimes the inside of a fowl is very sour, especially if it is not freshly killed. Soda, being cleansing, acts as a corrective, and destroys that unpleasant taste which we frequently experience in the dressing when fowls have been killed for some time. Now, after washing, wipe the turkey dry, inside and out, with a clean cloth, rub the inside with some salt, then stuff the breast and body with "Dressing for Fowls." Then sew up the turkey with a strong thread, tie the legs and wings to the body, rub it over with a little soft butter, sprinkle over some salt and pepper, dredge with a little flour; place it in a dripping pan, pour in a cup of boiling water, and set it in the oven. Baste the turkey often, turning it around occasionally so that every part will be uniformly baked. When pierced with a fork and the liquid runs out perfectly clear, the bird is done. If any part is likely to scorch, pin over it a piece of buttered white paper. A fifteen-pound turkey requires between three and four hours to bake. Serve with cranberry sauce.

Gravy for Turkey.—When you put the turkey in to roast, put the neck, heart, liver and gizzard into a stew-pan with a pint of water; boil until they become quite tender; take them out of the water, chop the heart and gizzard, mash the liver and throw away the neck; return the chopped heart, gizzard and liver to the liquor in which they were stewed; set it to one side, and when the turkey is done it should be added to the gravy that dripped from the turkey, having first skimmed off the fat from the surface of the dripping-pan; set it all over the fire, boil three minutes and thicken with flour. It will not need brown flour to color the gravy. The garnishes for turkey or chicken are fried oysters, thin slices of ham, slices of lemon, fried sausages, or force-meat balls, also parsley.

DRESSING OR STUFFING FOR FOWLS.

For an eight or ten pound turkey, cut the brown crust from slices or pieces of stale bread until you have as much as the inside of a pound loaf; put it into a suitable dish, and pour tepid water (not warm, for that makes it heavy) over it; let it stand one minute, as it soaks very quickly. Now take up a handful at a time and squeeze it hard and dry with both hands, placing it, as you go along, in another dish; this process makes it very light. When all is pressed dry, toss it all up lightly through your fingers; now add pepper, salt,—about a teaspoonful —also a teaspoonful of powdered summer savory, the same amount of sage, or the green herb minced fine; add half a cup of melted butter, and a beaten egg, or not. Work thoroughly all together, and it is ready for dressing either fowls, fish or meats. A little chopped sausage in turkey dressing is considered by some an improvement, when well incorporated with the other ingredients. For geese and ducks the stuffing may be made the same as for turkey with the addition of a few slices of onion chopped fine.

OYSTER DRESSING OR STUFFING.

This is made with the same ingredients as the above, with the exception of half a can of oysters drained, and slightly chopped and added to the rest. This is used mostly with boiled turkey and chicken, and the remainder of the can of oysters used to make an oyster sauce to be poured over the turkey when served; served generally in a separate dish, to be dipped out as a person desires.

These recipes were obtained from an old colored cook, who was famous for **his** fine dressings for fowls, fish and meats, and his advice was, *always* soak stale bread in *cold* liquid, either milk or water, when *used* for stuffing or for pud-dings, as they were much lighter. Hot liquid makes them heavy.

BOILED TURKEY.

Prepare as you would for baking or roasting; fill with an oyster stuffing, made as the above. Tie the legs and wings close to the body, place in salted boiling water with the breast downward; skim it often and boil about two hours, but not till the skin breaks. Serve with oyster or celery sauce. Boil a nicely pickled piece of salt pork, and serve at table a thin slice to each plate. Some prefer bacon or ham instead of pork.

Some roll the turkey in a cloth dipped in flour. If the liquor is to be used afterwards for soup, the cloth imparts an unpleasant flavor. The liquor can be saved and made into a nice soup for the next day's dinner, by adding the same seasonings as for chicken soup.

TURKEY SCALLOP.

Pick the meat from the bones of cold turkey, and chop it fine. Put a layer of bread-crumbs on the bottom of a buttered dish, moisten them with a little milk, then put in a layer of turkey with some of the filling, and cut small pieces of butter over the top; sprinkle with pepper and salt; then another layer of bread-crumbs, and so on until the dish is nearly full; add a little hot water to the gravy left from the turkey and pour over it; then take two eggs, two table-spoonfuls of milk, one of melted butter, a little salt and cracker-crumbs as much as will make it thick enough to spread on with a knife; put bits of butter over it, and cover with a plate. Bake three-quarters of an hour. Ten minutes before serving, remove the plate and let it brown.

TURKEY HASHED.

Cut the remnants of turkey from a previous dinner into pieces of equal size. Boil the bones in a quart of water, until the quart is reduced to a pint; then take out the bones, and to the liquor in which they were boiled add turkey gravy, if you have any, or white stock, or a small piece of butter with salt and pepper; let the liquor thus prepared boil up once; then put in the pieces of turkey, dredge in a little flour, give it one boil-up, and serve in a hot dish.

TURKEY WARMED OVER.

Pieces of cold turkey or chicken may be warmed up with a little butter in a frying-pan; place it on a warm platter, surround it with pieces of small thick slices of bread or biscuit halved, first dipping them in hot salted water; then place the platter in a warm oven with the door open. Have already made the following gravy to pour over all:

Into the frying-pan put a large spoonful of butter, one or two cupfuls of milk, and any gravy that may be left over. Bring it to a boil; then add sufficient flour, wet in a little cold milk or water, to make it the consistency of cream. Season with salt, pepper and add a little of the dark meat chopped *very* fine. Let the sauce cook a few moments; then pour over the biscuit and fowl. This will be found a really nice dish.

BONED TURKEY.

Clean the fowl as usual. With a sharp and pointed knife, begin at the extremity of the wing, and pass the knife down close to the bone, cutting all the flesh from the bone, and preserving the skin whole; run the knife down each side of the breast bone and up the legs, keeping close to the bone; then split the back half way up, and draw out the bones; fill the places whence the bones were taken with a stuffing, restoring the fowl to its natural form, and sew up all the incisions made in the skin. Lard with two or three rows of slips of fat bacon on the top, basting often with salt and water, and a little butter. Some like a glass of port wine in the gravy.

This is a difficult dish to attempt by any but skillful hands. Carve across in slices, and serve with tomato sauce.

ROAST GOOSE.

The goose should not be more than eight months old, and the fatter the more tender and juicy the meat. Stuff with the following mixture: Three pints of bread-crumbs, six ounces of butter, or part butter and part salt pork, one teaspoonful each of sage, black pepper and salt, one chopped onion. Do not stuff very full, and stitch openings firmly together to keep flavor in and fat out. Place in a baking pan with a little water, and baste frequently with salt and water (some add vinegar); turn often so that the sides and back may be nicely browned. Bake two hours or more; when done take from the pan, pour off the fat, and to the brown gravy left, add the chopped giblets which have previously been stewed until tender, together with the water they were boiled in; thicken with a little flour and butter rubbed together, bring to a boil and serve. English style.

ROAST CHICKEN.

Pick and draw them, wash out well in two or three waters, adding a little soda to the last but one to sweeten it. if there is doubt as to its being fresh. Dry it well with a clean cloth, and fill the crop and body with a stuffing the same as "Dressing for Fowls." Lay it in a dripping-pan; put a pint of hot water and a piece of butter in the dripping-pan, add to it a small tablespoonful of salt, and a small teaspoonful of pepper; baste frequently, and let it roast quickly, without scorching; when nearly done, put a piece of butter the size of a large egg to the water in the pan; when it melts, baste with it, dredge a little flour over, baste again, and let it finish; half an hour will roast a full-grown chicken, if the fire is right. When done, take it up.

Having stewed the necks, gizzards, livers and hearts in a very little water, strain it and mix it hot with the gravy that has dripped from the fowls, and which must be first skimmed. Thicken it with a little browned flour, add to it the livers, hearts and gizzards chopped small. Or, put the giblets in the pan with the chicken, and let them roast. Send the fowls to the table with the gravy in a boat. Cranberry sauce should accompany them, or any tart sauce.

BOILED CHICKEN.

Clean, wash and stuff, as for roasting. Baste a floured cloth around each, and put into a pot with enough boiling water to cover them well. The hot water cooks the skin at once and prevents the escape of the juice. The broth will not be so rich as if the fowls are put on in cold water, but this is a proof that the meat will be more nutritious and better flavored. Stew very slowly, for the first half hour especially. Boil an hour or more, guiding yourself by size and toughness. Serve with egg, bread, or oyster sauce. (See Sauces.)

STEAMED CHICKEN.

Rub the chicken on the inside with pepper and half a teaspoonful of salt; place in a steamer in a kettle that will keep it as near the water as possible, cover, and steam an hour and a half; when done, keep hot while dressing is prepared, then cut up, arrange on the platter, and serve with the dressing over them.

The dressing is made as follows: Boil one pint of gravy from the kettle without the fat, add cayenne pepper and half a teaspoonful of salt; stir a tablespoonful of flour into a quarter of a pint of cream until smooth, and add to the gravy. Corn starch may be used instead of the flour, and some cooks add nutmeg or celery salt.

FRICASSEE CHICKEN.

Cut up two young chickens, put them in a stew-pan with just enough cold water to cover them. Cover closely, and let them heat very slowly; then stew them over an hour, or until tender. If they are old chickens, they will require long, slow boiling, often from three to four hours. When tender, season with salt and pepper, a piece of butter as large as an egg, and a little celery, if liked. Stir up two tablespoonfuls of flour in a little water or milk, and add to the stew, also two well-beaten yolks of eggs; let all boil up one minute; arrange the chicken on a warm platter, pour some of the gravy over it, and send the rest to the table in a boat. The egg shou'd be added to a little of the cooled gravy, before putting with the hot gravy.

STEWED WHOLE SPRING CHICKEN.

Dress a full-grown spring chicken the same as for roasting, seasoning it with salt and pepper inside and out; then fill the body with oysters; place it in a tin pail with a close-fitting cover. Set the pail in a pot of fast-boiling water and cook until the chicken is tender. Dish up the chicken on a warm dish, then pour the gravy into a sauce-pan, put into it a tablespoonful of butter, half of a cupful of cream or rich milk, three hard-boiled eggs chopped fine; some minced herbs and a tablespoonful of flour. Let all boil up and then pour it over the chicken. Serve hot.

PICKLED CHICKEN.

Boil four chickens till tender enough for meat to fall from bones: put meat in a stone jar, and pour over it three pints of cold, good cider vinegar and a pint and a half of the water in which the chickens were boiled; add spices if preferred, and it will be ready for use in two days. This is a popular Sunday evening dish; it is good for luncheon at any time.

RISSOLES OF CHICKEN.

Mince up finely the remains of a cold chicken together with half the quantity of lean, cold ham. Mix them well, adding enough white sauce to moisten them. Now have light paste rolled out until about a quarter of an inch or a little more in thickness. Cut the paste into pieces, one inch by two in size, and lay a little of the mixture upon the centres of half of the pieces and cover them with the other halves, pressing the edges neatly together and forming them into little rolls. Have your frying-pan ready with plenty of boiling hot lard, or other frying medium, and fry until they become a golden-brown color. A minute or two will be sufficient for this. Then drain them well and serve immediately on a napkin.

CHICKEN PATTIES.

Mince up fine cold chicken, either roasted or boiled. Season it with pepper and salt, and a little minced parsley and onion. Moisten it with chicken gravy or cream sauce, fill scalloped shells that are lined with pastry with the mixture, and sprinkle bread-crumbs over the tops. Put two or three tiny pieces of butter over each, and bake brown in a hot oven.

TO BROIL CHICKEN.

After dressing and washing the chickens as previously directed, split them open through the back-bone; frog them by cutting the cords under the wings and laying the wings out flat; cut the sinews under the second joint of the leg and turn the leg down; press down the breast-bone without breaking it.

Season the chicken with salt and pepper, lay it upon the gridiron with the inside first to the fire; put the gridiron over a slow fire, and place a tin sheet and weight upon the chicken, to keep it flat; let it broil ten minutes, then turn and proceed in the same manner with the other side.

The chicken should be perfectly cooked, but not scorched. A broiled chicken brought to the table with its wings and legs burnt, and its breast half cooked, is very disagreeable. To avoid this, the chicken must be closely watched while broiling, and the fire must be arranged so that the heat shall be equally dispensed. When the fire is too hot under any one part of the chicken, put a little ashes on the fire under that part, that the heat may be reduced.

Dish a broiled chicken on a hot plate, putting a large lump of butter and a tablespoonful of hot water upon the plate, and turning the chicken two or three times that it may absorb as much of the butter as possible. Garnish with parsley. Serve with poached eggs on a separate dish. It takes from thirty to forty minutes to broil a chicken well.

CHICKEN PIE.

Prepare the chicken as for fricassee. When the chickens are stewed tender, seasoned, and the gravy thickened, take it from the fire; take out the largest bones, scrape the meat from the neck and back-bone, throw the bones away; line the sides of a four or six quart pudding-dish with a rich baking powder or soda biscuit-dough, a quarter of an inch thick; put in part of the chicken, a few lumps of butter, pepper and salt, if needed, some cold boiled eggs cut in slices. Add the rest of the chicken and season as before; a few new potatoes in their season might be added. Pour over the gravy, being sure to have enough to fill the dish, and cover with a crust a quarter of an inch thick, made with a hole in the centre the size of a teacup.

Brush over the top with beaten white of egg, and bake for half to three-quarters of an hour. Garnish the top with small bright celery leaves, neatly arranged in a circle.

FRIED CHICKEN.

Wash and cut up a young chicken, wipe it dry, season with salt and pepper, dredge it with flour, or dip each piece in beaten egg and then in cracker-crumbs. Have in a frying-pan, one ounce each of butter and sweet lard, made boiling hot. Lay in the chicken and fry brown on both sides. Take up, drain them, and set aside in a covered dish. Stir into the gravy left, if not too much, a large table-spoonful of flour, make it smooth, add a cup of cream or milk, season with salt and pepper, boil up and pour over the chicken. Some like chopped parsley added to the gravy. Serve hot.

If the chicken is old, put into a stew-pan with a little water, and simmer gently till tender; season with salt and pepper, dip in flour or cracker-crumb and egg, and fry as above. Use the broth the chicken was cooked in to make the gravy instead of the cream or milk, or use an equal quantity of both.

FRIED CHICKEN Á LA ITALIENNE.

Make common batter; mix into it a cupful of chopped tomatoes, one onion chopped, some minced parsley, salt and pepper. Cut up young tender chickens, dry them well and dip each piece in the batter; then fry brown in plenty of butter, in a thick bottom frying-pan. Serve with tomato sauce.

CHICKEN CROQUETTES. No. 1.

Put a cup of cream or milk in a sauce-pan, set it over the fire, and when it boils add a lump of butter as large as an egg, in which has been mixed a table-spoonful of flour. Let it boil up thick; remove from the fire, and when cool, mix into it a teaspoonful of salt, half a teaspoonful of pepper, a bit of minced onion or parsley, one cup of fine bread-crumbs, and a pint of finely-chopped cooked chicken, either roasted or boiled. Lastly, beat up two eggs and work in with the whole. Flour your hands and make into small, round, flat cakes; dip in egg and bread-crumbs, and fry like fish-cakes, in butter and good sweet lard mixed, or like fried cakes in plenty of hot lard. Take them up with a skimmer and lay them on brown paper to free them from the grease. Serve hot.

CHICKEN CROQUETTES. No. 2.

Take any kind of fresh meat or fowl, chop very fine, add an equal quantity of smoothly mashed potatoes, mix, and season with butter, salt, black pepper, a little prepared mustard, and a little cayenne pepper; make into cakes, dip in egg and bread-crumbs and fry a light brown. A nice relish for tea.

TO FRY CROQUETTES.

Beat up two eggs in a deep bowl; roll enough crackers until you have a cupful of crumbs, or the same of fine stale bread-crumbs; spread the crumbs on a large plate or pie-tin. Have over the fire a kettle containing two or three inches of boiling lard. As fast as the croquettes are formed, roll them in the crumbs, then dip them in the beaten egg, then again roll them in crumbs; drop them in the smoking hot fat and fry them a light golden brown.

PRESSED CHICKEN.

Clean and cut up your chickens. Stew in just enough water to cover them. When nearly cooked, season them well with salt and pepper. Let them stew down until the water is nearly all boiled out, and the meat drops easily from the bones. Remove the bones and gristle; chop the meat rather coarsely, then turn it back into the stew-kettle, where the broth was left (after skimming off all fat), and let it heat through again. Turn it into a square bread-pan, placing a platter on the top, and a heavy weight on the platter. This, if properly prepared, will turn out like a mold of jelly and may be sliced in smooth, even slices. The success of this depends upon not having too much water; it will not jelly if too weak, or if the water is allowed to boil away entirely while cooking. A good way to cook old fowls.

CHICKEN LUNCH FOR TRAVELLING.

Cut a young chicken down the back; wash and wipe dry; season with salt and pepper; put in a dripping pan and bake in a moderate oven three-quarters of an hour. This is much better for travelling lunch than when seasoned with butter.

All kinds of poultry and meat can be cooked quicker by adding to the water in which they are boiled a little vinegar or a piece of lemon. By the use of a little acid there will be a considerable saving of fuel, as well as shortening of time. Its action is beneficial on old tough meats, rendering them quite tender and easy of digestion. Tainted meats and fowls will lose their bad taste and odor if cooked in this way, and if not used too freely no taste of it will be acquired.

POTTED CHICKEN.

Strip the meat from the bones of a cold, roast fowl; to every pound of meat allow a quarter of a pound of butter, salt and cayenne pepper to taste; one tea-spoonful of pounded mace, half a small nutmeg. Cut the meat into small pieces, pound it well with the butter, sprinkle in the spices gradually, and keep pounding until reduced to a perfectly smooth paste. Pack it into small jars and cover with clarified butter, about a quarter of an inch in thickness. Two or three slices of ham, minced and pounded with the above, will be an improvement. Keep in a dry place. A luncheon or breakfast dish.

Old fowls can be made very tender by putting into them, while boiling, a piece of soda as large as a bean.

SCALLOPED CHICKEN.

Divide a fowl into joints and boil till the meat leaves the bone readily. Take out the bones and chop the meat as small as dice. Thicken the water in which the fowl was boiled with flour, and season to taste with butter and salt. Fill a deep dish with alternate layers of bread-crumbs and chicken and slices of cooked potatoes, having crumbs on top. Pour the gravy over the top, and add a few bits of butter and bake till nicely browned. There should be gravy enough to moisten the dish. Serve with a garnish of parsley. Tiny new potatoes are nice in place of sliced ones, when in season.

BREADED CHICKEN.

Prepare young chickens as for fricassee by cutting them into pieces. Dip each piece in beaten egg, then in grated bread-crumbs or rolled cracker; season them with pepper and salt, and a little minced parsley. Place them in a baking-pan, and put on the top of each piece a lump of butter, add half of a cupful of hot water; bake slowly, basting often. When sufficiently cooked take up on a warm platter. Into the pan pour a cup of cream or rich milk, a cupful of bread-crumbs. Stir it well until cooked then pour it over the chicken. Serve while hot.

BROILED CHICKEN ON TOAST.

Broil the usual way, and when thoroughly done take it up in a square tin or dripping-pan, butter it well, season with pepper and salt, and set it in the oven for a few minutes. Lay slices of moistened buttered toast on a platter; take the chicken up over it, add to the gravy in the pan part of a cupful of cream, if you have it; if not, use milk. Thicken with a little flour and pour over the chicken. This is considered most excellent.

CURRY CHICKEN.

Cut up a chicken weighing from a pound and a half to two pounds, as for fricassee, wash it well, and put it into a stew-pan with sufficient water to cover it; boil it closely covered, until tender; add a large teaspoonful of salt, and cook a few minutes longer; then remove from the fire, take out the chicken, pour the liquor into a bowl, and set it one side. Now cut up into the stew-pan two small onions, and fry them with a piece of butter as large as an egg; as soon as the onions are brown, skim them out and put in the chicken; fry for three or four minutes; next sprinkle over two teaspoonfuls of Curry Powder. Now pour over the liquor in which the chicken was stewed, stir all well together, and stew for five minutes longer, then stir into this a tablespoonful of sifted flour made thin with a little water; lastly, stir in a beaten yolk of egg, and it is done.

Serve with hot boiled rice laid round on the edge of a platter, and the chicken curry in the centre.

This makes a handsome side dish, and a fine relish accompanying a full dinner of roast beef or any roast.

All first-class grocers and druggists keep this "India Curry Powder," put up in bottles. Beef, veal, mutton, duck, pigeons, partridges, rabbits or fresh fish may be substituted for the chicken, if preferred, and sent to the table with or without a dish of rice.

To Boil Rice for Curry.—Pick over the rice, a cupful. Wash it thoroughly in two or three cold waters; then leave it about twenty minutes in cold water. Put into a stew-pan two quarts of water with a teaspoonful of salt in it, and when it boils, sprinkle in the rice. Boil it briskly for twenty minutes, keeping the pan covered. Take it from the fire, and drain off the water. Afterwards set the sauce-pan on the back of the stove, with the lid off, to allow the rice to dry and the grains to separate.

Rice, if properly boiled, should be soft and white, and every grain stand alone. Serve it hot in a separate dish or served as above, laid around the chicken curry.

CHICKEN POT-PIE. No. 1.

Cut and joint a large chicken, cover with cold water, and let it boil gently until tender. Season with salt and pepper, and thicken the gravy with two tablespoonfuls of flour, mixed smooth with a piece of butter the size of an egg. Have ready nice light bread-dough; cut with the top of a wineglass about half an inch thick; let them stand half an hour and rise, then drop these into the boiling gravy. Put the cover on the pot closely, wrap a cloth around it, in order that no steam shall escape; and by no means allow the pot to cease boiling. Boil three-quarters of an hour.

CHICKEN POT-PIE. No. 2.

This style of pot-pie was made more in our grandmother's day than now, as most cooks consider that cooking crust so long destroys its spongey lightness, and renders it too hard and dry.

Take a pair of fine fowls; cut them up, wash the pieces, and season with pepper only. Make a light biscuit dough, and plenty of it, as it is always much liked by the eaters of pot-pie. Roll out the dough not very thin, and cut most of it into long squares. Butter the sides of a pot, and line them with dough nearly to the top. Lay slices of cold ham at the bottom of the pot, and then the pieces of fowl, interspersed all through with squares of dough and potatoes, pared and quartered. Pour in a quart of water. Cover the whole with a lid of dough, having a slit in the centre, through which the gravy will bubble up. Boil it steadily for two hours. Half an hour before you take it up, put in through the hole in the centre of the crust some bits of butter rolled in flour, to thicken the gravy. When done, put the pie on a large dish, and pour the gravy over it.

You may intersperse it all through with cold ham.

A pot-pie may be made of ducks, rabbits, squirrels, or venison. Also of beef-steak. A beef-steak, or some pork-steaks (the lean only), greatly improve a chicken pot-pie. If you use no ham, season with salt.

CHICKEN STEWED, WITH BISCUIT.

Take chickens, and make a fricassee; just before you are ready to dish it up, have ready two baking-tins of rich soda or baking-powder biscuits; take them from the oven hot, split them apart by breaking them with your hands, lay them on a large meat platter, covering it, then pour the hot chicken stew over all. Send to the table hot. This is a much better way than boiling this kind of biscuit in the stew, as you are more sure of its being always light.

CHICKEN DRESSED AS TERRAPIN.

Select young chickens, clean and cut them into pieces; put them into a stew-pan with just *enough* water to cook them. When tender stir into it half of a cup of butter and one beaten egg. Season it with salt and pepper, a teaspoonful of powdered thyme; add two hard-boiled eggs coarsely minced and a small glass of wine. Boil up once and serve with jelly.

CHICKEN ROLY-POLY.

One quart of flour, two teaspoonfuls of cream tartar mixed with the flour, one teaspoonful of soda dissolved in a teacupful of milk; a teaspoonful of salt; do not use shortening of any kind, but roll out the mixture half an inch thick, and on it lay minced chicken, veal or mutton. The meat must be seasoned with pepper and salt, and be free from gristle. Roll the crust over and over, and put it on a buttered plate and place in a steamer for half an hour. Serve for breakfast or lunch, giving a slice to each person with gravy served with it.

CHICKEN TURNOVERS.

Chop cold roast chicken very fine. Put it into a sauce-pan, place it over the fire, moisten it with a little water and gravy, or a piece of butter. Season with salt and pepper; add a small tablespoonful of sifted flour, dissolved in a little water; heat all through, and remove from the fire to become cool. When cooled roll out some plain pie-crust quite thin, cut out in rounds as large as a saucer; wet the edge with cold water, and put a large spoonful of the minced meat on one-half of the round; fold the other half over, and pinch the edges well together, then fry them in hot drippings or fat, a nice brown. They may also be cooked in a moderate oven.

CHICKEN PUDDING.

Cut up two young chickens into good-sized pieces; put them in a sauce-pan with just enough water to cover them well. When boiled quite tender, season with salt and pepper; let them simmer ten or fifteen minutes longer; then take the chicken from the broth and remove all the large bones. Place the meat in a well-buttered pudding-dish, season again, if necessary, adding a few bits of butter. Pour over this the following batter:

Eight eggs beaten light and mixed with one quart of milk, three tablespoonfuls of melted butter, a teaspoonful of salt, and two large teaspoonfuls of baking powder, added to enough sifted flour to make a batter like griddle-cakes.

Bake one hour in a *moderate* oven.

Make a gravy of the broth that remained from the cooking of the chicken, adding a tablespoonful of flour, stirred into a third of a cup of melted butter; let it boil up, putting in more water, if necessary. Serve hot in a gravy boat, with the pudding.

CHICKEN AND MACCARONI.

Boil a chicken until very tender, take out all the bones, and pick up the meat quite fine. Boil half a pound of maccaroni until tender, first breaking it up to pieces an inch long. Butter a deep pudding-dish, put on the bottom a layer of the cooked maccaroni, then a layer of the minced chicken, bits of butter, pepper and salt, then some of the chicken liquor, over this put another layer of maccaroni, and so on, until the dish is filled. Pour a cup of cream over the whole, and bake half an hour. Serve on a platter.

ROAST DUCK. (Tame.)

Pick, draw, clean thoroughly, and wipe dry. Cut the neck close to the back, beat the breast-bone flat with a rolling-pin, tie the wings and legs securely, and stuff with the following:

Three pints bread-crumbs, six ounces butter, or part butter and salt pork, two chopped onions and one teaspoonful each of sage, black pepper and salt. Do not stuff very full, and sew up the openings firmly to keep the flavor in and the fat out. If not fat enough, it should be larded with salt pork, or tie a slice upon the breast. Place in a baking-pan, with a little water, and baste frequently with salt and water—some add onion, and some vinegar; turn often, so that the sides and back may all be nicely browned. When nearly done, baste with butter and a little flour. These directions will apply to tame geese as well as ducks. Young ducks should roast from twenty-five to thirty minutes, and full-grown ones for an hour or more, with frequent basting. Some prefer them underdone and served very hot; but, as a rule, thorough cooking will prove more palatable. Make a gravy out of the neck and gizzards by putting them in a quart of cold water, that must be reduced to a pint by boiling. The giblets, when done, may be chopped fine and added to the juice. The preferred seasonings are one table-spoonful of Madeira or sherry, a blade of mace, one small onion, and a little cayenne pepper; strain through a hair sieve; pour a little over the ducks and serve the remainder in a boat. Served with jellies or any tart sauce.

BRAISED DUCKS.

Prepare a pair of fine young ducks, the same as for roasting, place them in a stew-pan together with two or three slices of bacon, a carrot, an onion stuck with two cloves, and a little thyme and parsley. Season with pepper, and cover the whole with a broth, adding to the broth a gill of white wine. Place the pan over a gentle fire and allow the ducks to simmer until done, basting them frequently. When done remove them from the pan, and place them where they will keep hot. A turnip should then be cut up and fried in some butter. When nicely browned, drain the pieces and cook them until tender in the liquor in which the ducks were braised. Now strain and thicken the gravy, and after dishing up the ducks, pour it over them, garnishing with the pieces of turnip.

—Palmer House, Chicago.

STEWED DUCK.

Prepare them by cutting them up the same as chicken for fricassee. Lay two or three very thin slices of salt pork upon the bottom of a stew-pan; lay the pieces of duck upon the pork. Let them stew slowly for an hour, closely covered. Then season with salt and pepper, half a teaspoonful of powdered sage, or some green sage minced fine; one chopped onion. Stew another half hour until the duck is tender. Stir up a large tablespoonful of brown flour in a little water and add it to the stew. Let it boil up, and serve all together in one dish, accompanied with green peas.

—Palmer House, Chicago.

DUCK PIE.

Cut all the meat from cold roast ducks; put the bones and stuffing into cold water; cover them and let boil; put the meat into a deep dish; pour on enough of the stock made from the bones to moisten; cover with pastry slit in the centre with a knife, and bake a light brown.

WARMED UP DUCK.

A nice dish for breakfast, and very relishing, can be made from the remains of a roast of duck. Cut the meat from the bones, pick out all the little tidbits in the recesses, lay them in a frying-pan, and cover with water and the cold gravy left from the roast; add a piece of butter; let all boil up once and if not quite thick enough, stir in a little dissolved flour. Serve hot.

ROAST WILD DUCK.

Wild duck should not be dressed too soon after being killed. If the weather is cold it will be better for being kept several days. Bake in a hot oven, letting it remain for five or ten minutes without basting to keep in the gravy, then baste frequently with butter and water. If over-done it loses flavor, 30 to 40 minutes in the right kind of an oven being sufficient. Serve on a very hot dish, and send to table as hot as possible with a cut lemon and the following sauce:

Put in a tiny sauce-pan a tablespoonful each of Worcestershire sauce and mushroom catsup, a little salt and cayenne pepper, and the juice of half a lemon. Mix well, make it hot, remove from the fire, and stir in a teaspoonful of made mustard. Pour into a hot gravy boat.

—California Style, Lick House.

WILD DUCKS.

Most wild ducks are apt to have the flavor of fish, and when in the hands of inexperienced cooks are sometimes unpalatable on this account. Before roasting them, parboil them with a small peeled carrot put within each duck. This absorbs the unpleasant taste. An onion will have the same effect, but unless you use onions in the stuffing, the carrot is preferable. Roast the same as tame duck. Or put into the duck a whole onion peeled, plenty of salt and pepper and a glass of claret, bake in a hot oven 20 minutes. Serve hot with the gravy it yields in cooking and a dish of currant jelly.

CANVAS-BACK DUCK.

The epicurean taste declares that this special kind of bird requires no spices or flavors to make it perfect, as the meat partakes of the flavor of the food that the bird feeds upon, being mostly wild celery; and the delicious flavor is best preserved when roasted quickly with a hot fire. After dressing the duck in the usual way, by plucking, singing, drawing, wipe it with a wet towel, truss the head under the wing; place it in a dripping-pan, put it in the oven, basting often, and roast it half an hour. It is generally preferred a little underdone. Place it when done on a hot dish, season well with salt and pepper, pour over it the gravy it has yielded in baking and serve it immediately while hot.

—Delmonico.

ROAST PIGEONS.

Pigeons lose their flavor by being kept more than a day after they are killed. They may be prepared and roasted or broiled the same as chickens; they will require from twenty to thirty minutes cooking. Make a gravy of the giblets or not, season it with pepper and salt, and add a little flour and butter.

STEWED PIGEONS.

Clean and stuff with onion dressing, thyme, etc.,—do not sew up; take five or more slices of corned pork, let it fry a while in a pot so that the fat comes out and it begins to brown a little; then lay the pigeons all around in the fat, leaving the pork still in; add hot water enough to partially cover them; cover tightly and boil an hour or so until tender; then turn off some of the liquid, and keep turning them so they will brown nicely; then heat and add the liquor poured off; add extra thyme, pepper, and keep turning until the pigeons and gravy are nicely browned. Thicken with a little flour, and serve with the gravy poured over them; garnish with parsley.

PIGEON PIE.

Take half a dozen pigeons; stuff each one with a dressing the same as for turkey; loosen the joints with a knife, but do not separate them. Put them in a stew-pan with water enough to cover them, let them cook until nearly tender, then season them with salt and pepper and butter. Thicken the gravy with flour, remove and cool. Butter a pudding-dish, line the sides with a rich crust. Have ready some hard-boiled eggs cut in slices. Put in a layer of egg and birds and gravy until the dish is full. Cover with a crust and bake.

BROILED PIGEONS OR SQUABS.

Split them down the back and broil the same as chicken; seasoning well with salt, pepper and plenty of butter. Broil slices of salt pork, very thin; place a slice over each bird and serve.

SQUAB POT-PIE.

Cut into dice three ounces of salt pork; divide six wild squabs into pieces, at the joints; remove the skin. Cut up four potatoes into small squares, and prepare a dozen small dough balls.

Put into a yellow, deep baking-dish the pork, potatoes and squabs, and then the balls of dough; season with salt, white pepper, a dash of mace or nutmeg; add hot water enough to cover the ingredients, cover with a "short" pie-crust and bake in a moderate oven three-quarters of an hour.

—Palmer House, Chicago.

WOODCOCK, ROASTED.

Skin the head and neck of the bird, pluck the feathers, and truss it by bringing the beak of the bird under the wing, and fastening the pinion to the thigh; twist the legs at the knuckles and press the feet upon the thigh. Put a piece of bread under each bird to catch the drippings, baste with butter, dredge with flour, and roast fifteen or twenty minutes with a sharp fire. When done, cut the bread in diamond shape, each piece large enough to stand one bird upon, place them aslant on your dish, and serve with gravy enough to moisten the bread; serve some in the dish and some in the tureen; garnish with slices of lemon. Roast from twenty to twenty-five minutes.

SNIPE.

Snipe are similar to woodcock, and may be served in the same manner; they will require less time to roast.

REED BIRDS.

Pick and draw them very carefully, salt and dredge with flour, and roast with a quick fire ten or fifteen minutes. Serve on toast with butter and pepper. You can put in each one an oyster dipped in butter and then in bread-crumbs before roasting. They are also very nice broiled.

ROAST QUAIL.

Rinse well and steam over boiling water until tender, then dredge with flour, and smother in butter; season with salt and pepper and roast inside the stove; thicken the gravy; serve with green grape jelly, and garnish with parsley.

TO ROAST PARTRIDGES, PHEASANTS, QUAILS OR GROUSE.

Carefully cut out all the shot, wash thoroughly but quickly, using soda in the water; rinse again, and dry with a clean cloth. Stuff them and sew them up. Skewer the legs and wings to the body, larder the breast with very thin slices of fat salt pork, place them in the oven, and baste with butter and water before taking up, having seasoned them with salt and pepper; or you can leave out the pork and use only butter, or cook them without stuffing. Make a gravy of the drippings thickened with browned flour. Boil up and serve in a boat.

These are all very fine broiled, first splitting down the back, placing on the gridiron the inside down, cover with a baking tin, and broil slowly at first. Serve with cream gravy.

GAME PIE.

Clean well, inside and out, a dozen small birds, quail, snipe, woodcock, etc., and split them in half; put them in a sauce-pan with about two quarts of water; when it boils, skim off all scum that rises; then add salt and pepper, a bunch of minced parsley, one onion chopped fine, and three whole cloves. Cut up half a pound of salt pork into dice, and let all boil until tender, using care that there be enough water to cover the birds. Thicken this with two tablespoonfuls of browned flour and let it boil up. Stir in a piece of butter as large as an egg; remove from the fire and let it cool. Have ready a pint of potatoes cut as small as dice, and a rich crust made. Line the sides of a buttered pudding-dish with the crust; lay in the birds, then some of the potatoes, then birds and so on, until the dish is full. Pour over the gravy, put on the top crust, with a slit cut in the

Frances Folsom Cleveland

THE BRIDE OF THE WHITE HOUSE

centre, and bake. The top can be ornamented with pastry leaves in a wreath about the edge, with any fancy design placed in the centre across the slit.

—Rockaway Beach.

SNOW BIRDS.

One dozen thoroughly cleaned birds; stuff each with an oyster, put them into a yellow dish, and add two ounces of boiled salt pork and three raw potatoes cut into slices; add a pint of oyster liquor, an ounce of butter; salt and pepper; cover the dish with a crust and bake in a moderate oven.

SQUIRREL.

They are cooked similar to rabbits, are excellent when broiled or made into a stew, and, in fact, are very good in all the different styles of cooking similar to rabbit.

There are many species common to this country; among them the black, red, gray and fox. Gophers and chipmunks may also be classed as another but smaller variety

ROAST HARE OR RABBIT.

A very close relationship exists between the hare and the rabbit, the chief difference being in the smaller size and shorter legs and ears of the latter. The manner of dressing and preparing each for the table is, therefore, pretty nearly the same. To prepare them for roasting, first skin, wash well in cold water and rinse thoroughly in lukewarm water. If a little musty from being emptied before they were hung up, and afterward neglected, rub the insides with vinegar and afterward remove all taint of the acid by a thorough washing in lukewarm water. After being well wiped with a soft cloth put in a dressing as usual, sew the animal up, truss it, and roast for a half or three-quarters of an hour, until well-browned, basting it constantly with butter and dredging with flour, just before taking up.

To make a gravy, after the rabbits are roasted, pour nearly all the fat out of the pan, but do not pour the bottom or brown part of the drippings; put the pan over the fire, stir into it a heaping tablespoonful of flour, and stir until the flour browns. Then stir in a pint of boiling water. Season the gravy with salt and pepper; let it boil for a moment. Send hot to the table in a tureen with the hot rabbits. Serve with currant jelly.

FRICASSEE RABBIT.

Clean two young rabbits, cut into joints, and soak in salt and water half an hour. Put into a sauce-pan with a pint of cold water, a bunch of sweet herbs, an onion finely minced, a pinch of mace, half a nutmeg, a pinch of pepper and half a pound of ,salt pork cut in small thin slices. Cover and stew until tender. Take out the rabbits and set in a dish where they will keep warm. Add to the gravy a cup of cream (or milk), two well-beaten eggs, stirred in a little at a time, a tablespoonful of butter, and a thickening made of a tablespoonful of flour and a little milk. Boil up once; remove the sauce-pan from the fire, squeeze in the juice of a lemon, stirring all the while, and pour over the rabbits. Do not cook the head or neck.

FRIED RABBIT.

After the rabbit has been thoroughly cleaned and washed, put it into boiling water, and let it boil ten minutes; drain it, and when cold, cut it into joints, dip into beaten egg, and then in fine bread-crumbs; season with salt and pepper. When all are ready, fry them in butter and sweet lard, mixed over a moderate fire until brown on both sides. Take them out, thicken the gravy with a spoonful of flour, turn in a cup of milk or cream; let all boil up, and turn over the rabbits. Serve hot with onion sauce. (See Sauces.) Garnish with sliced lemon.

RABBIT PIE.

This pie can be made the same as "Game Pie," excepting you scatter through it four hard-boiled eggs cut in slices. Cover with puff paste, cut a slit in the middle, and bake one hour, laying paper over the top should it brown too fast.

BROILED RABBITS.

After skinning and cleaning the rabbits, wipe them dry, split them down the back lengthwise, pound them flat, then wrap them in letter paper well buttered, place them on a buttered gridiron, and broil over a clear, brisk fire, turning them often. When sufficiently cooked, remove the papers, lay them on a very hot platter, season with salt, pepper, and plenty of butter, turning them over and over to soak up the butter. Cover and keep hot in a warming oven until served.

SALMI OF GAME.

This is a nice mode of serving the remains of roasted game, but when a superlative salmi is desired, the birds must be scarcely more than half roasted for it. In either case, carve them very neatly, and strip every particle of skin and fat from the legs, wings and breasts; bruise the bodies well, and put them with the skin and other trimmings into a very clean stew-pan. If for a simple and inexpensive dinner, merely add to them two sliced onions, a bay-leaf, a small blade of mace and a few peppercorns; then pour in a pint or more of good veal gravy, or strong broth, and boil it briskly until reduced nearly half; strain the gravy, pressing the bones well to obtain all the flavor; skim off the fat, add a little cayenne and lemon juice, heat the game very gradually in it, but do not on any account allow it to boil; place pieces of fried bread round a dish, arrange the birds in good form in the centre, give the sauce a boil, and pour it on them.

ROAST HAUNCH OF VENISON.

To prepare a haunch of venison for roasting, wash it slightly in tepid water, and dry it thoroughly by rubbing it with a clean, soft cloth. Lay over the fat side a large sheet of thickly buttered paper, and next a paste of flour and water about three-quarters of an inch thick; cover this again with two or three sheets of stout paper, secure the whole well with twine, and put down to roast, with a little water, in the dripping-pan. Let the fire be clear and strong; baste the paper immediately with butter or clarified drippings, and roast the joint from three to four hours, according to its weight and quality. Doe venison will require half an hour less time than buck venison. About twenty minutes before the joint is done remove the paste and paper, baste the meat in every part with butter, and dredge it very lightly with flour; let it take a pale brown color, and serve hot with unflavored gravy made with a thickening, in a tureen and good currant jelly. Venison is much better when the deer has been killed in the autumn, when wild berries are plentiful, and it has had abundant opportunities to fatten upon this and other fresh food.

—Windsor Hotel, Montreal.

BROILED VENISON STEAK.

Venison steaks should be broiled over a clear fire, turning often. It requires more cooking than beef. When sufficiently done, season with salt and pepper, pour over two tablespoonfuls of currant jelly, melted with a piece of butter. Serve hot on hot plates.

Delicious steaks, corresponding to the shape of mutton chops, are cut from the loin.

BAKED SADDLE OF VENISON.

Wash the saddle carefully; see that no hairs are left dried on to the outside. Use a saddle of venison of about ten pounds. Cut some salt pork in strips about two inches long, and an eighth of an inch thick, with which lard the saddle with two rows on each side. In a large dripping-pan cut two carrots, one onion, and some salt pork in thin slices; add two bay leaves, two cloves, four kernels of allspice, half a lemon, sliced, and season with salt and pepper; place the saddle of venison in the pan, with a quart of good stock, boiling hot, and a small piece of butter, and let it boil about fifteen minutes on top of the stove; then put it in a hot oven and bake, basting well every five minutes, until it is medium rare, so that the blood runs when cut; serve with jelly or a wine sauce. If the venison is desired well done, cook much longer, and use a cream sauce with it, or stir cream into the venison gravy. (For cream sauce see Sauces.)

Venison should never be roasted unless very fat. The shoulder is a roasting piece, and may be done without the paper or paste.

In ordering the saddle request the butcher to cut the ribs off pretty close, as the only part that is of much account is the tenderloin and thick meat that lies along the backbone up to the neck. The ribs which extend from this have very little meat on them, but are always sold with the saddle. When neatly cut off they leave the saddle in a better shape, and the ribs can be put into your stock-pot to boil for soup.

—Windsor Hotel, Montreal.

VENISON PIE OR PASTRY.

The neck, breast and shoulder are the parts used for a venison pie or pastry. Cut the meat into pieces (fat and lean together) and put the bones and trimmings into the stew-pan with pepper and salt, and water or veal broth enough to cover it. Simmer it till you have drawn out a good gravy. Then strain it.

In the meantime make a good rich paste, and roll it rather thick. Cover the bottom and sides of a deep dish with one sheet of it, and put in your meat, having seasoned it with pepper, salt, nutmeg and mace. Pour in the gravy which you have prepared from the trimmings, and a glass of port wine. Lay on the top some bits of butter rolled in flour. Cover the pie with a thick lid of paste and ornament it handsomely with leaves and flowers formed with a tin cutter. Bake two or more hours according to the size. Just before it is done, pull it forward in the oven, and brush it over with beaten egg; push it back and let it slightly brown.

—Windsor Hotel, Montreal.

VENISON HASHED.

Cut the meat in nice small slices, and put the trimmings and bones into a sauce-pan with barely water enough to cover them. Let them stew for an hour. Then strain the liquid into a stew-pan; add to it some bits of butter, rolled in flour, and whatever gravy was left of the venison the day before. Stir in some currant jelly, and give it a boil up. Then put in the meat, and keep it over the fire just long enough to warm it through; but do not allow it to boil, as it has been once cooked already.

FRIED VENISON STEAK.

Cut a breast of venison into steaks; make a quarter of a pound of butter hot in a pan; rub the steaks over with a mixture of a little salt and pepper; dip them in wheat flour, or rolled crackers, and fry a rich brown; when both sides are done, take them up on a dish, and put a tin cover over; dredge a heaping teaspoonful of flour into the butter in the pan, stir it with a spoon until it is brown, without burning; put to it a small teacupful of boiling water, with a tablespoonful of currant jelly dissolved into it; stir it for a few minutes, then strain it over the meat, and serve. A glass of wine, with a tablespoonful of white sugar dissolved in it, may be used for the gravy, instead of the jelly and water. Venison may be boiled, and served with boiled vegetables, pickled beets, etc., and sauce.

MEATS.

In the selection of meat it is most essential that we understand how to choose it; in beef it should be a smooth, fine grain, of a clear bright red color, the fat white, and will feel tender when pinched with the fingers. Will also have abundant kidney fat or suet. The most choice pieces for roast are the sirloin, fore and middle ribs.

Veal, to be good, should have the flesh firm and dry, fine grained and of a delicate pinkish color, and plenty of kidney fat; the joints stiff.

Mutton is good when the flesh is a bright red, firm and juicy and a close grain, the fat firm and white.

Pork: if young, the lean will break on being pinched smooth when nipped with the fingers. also the skin will break and dent; if the rind is rough and hard it is old.

In roasting meat, allow from fifteen to twenty minutes to the pound, which will vary according to the thickness of the roast. A great deal of the success in roasting depends on the heat and goodness of the fire; if put into a cool oven it loses its juices, and the result is a tough, tasteless roast; whereas, if the oven is of the proper heat, it immediately sears up the pores of the meat and the juices are retained.

The oven should be the hottest when the meat is put into it, in order to quickly crisp the surface and close the pores of the meat, thereby confining its natural juices. If the oven is too hot to hold the hand in for only a moment, then the oven is right to receive the meat. The roast should first be washed in pure water, then wiped dry with a clean dry cloth, placed in a baking-pan, without any seasoning; some pieces of suet or cold drippings laid under it, but *no water* should be put into the pan, for this would have a tendency to soften the outside of the meat. The water can never get so hot as the hot fat upon the surface of the meat, and the generating of the steam prevents its crispness, so desirable in a roast.

It should be frequently basted with its own drippings which flow from the meat when partly cooked and well seasoned. Lamb, veal and pork should be cooked rather slower than beef, with a more *moderate* fire, covering the fat with a piece of paper, and *thoroughly* cooked till the flesh parts from the bone; and nicely browned, without being burned. An onion sliced and put on top of a roast while cooking, especially roast of pork, gives a nice flavor. Remove the onion before serving.

Larding meats is drawing ribbons of fat pork through the upper surface of the meat, leaving both ends protruding. This is accomplished by the use of a larding-needle, which may be procured at house-furnishing stores.

Boiling or stewing meat, if fresh, should be put into *boiling* water, closely covered, and boiled *slowly*, allowing twenty minutes to each pound, and when partly cooked, or when it begins to get tender, salted, adding spices and vegetables.

Salt meats should be covered with *cold* water, and require thirty minutes *very slow* boiling, from the time the water boils, for each pound; if it is very salt, pour off the first water, and put it in another of boiling water, or it may be soaked one night in cold water. After meat commences to boil, the pot should *never stop* simmering and always be replenished from the *boiling* tea-kettle.

Frying may be done in two ways: one method, which is most generally used, is by putting one ounce or more (as the case requires) of beef drippings, lard or butter, into a frying-pan, and when at the *boiling point*, laying in the meat, cooking both sides a nice brown. The other method is to *completely immerse* the article to be cooked in sufficient *hot* lard to cover it, similar to frying doughnuts.

Broiled meats should be placed over clear, red coals, free from smoke, giving out a good heat, but not too brisk or the meat will be hardened and scorched; but if the fire is dead, the gravy will escape, and drop upon the coals, creating a blaze, which will blacken and smoke the meat. Steaks and chops should be turned often, in order that every part should be evenly done—never sticking a fork into the lean part, as that lets the juices escape; it should be put into the outer skin or fat. When the meat is sufficiently broiled, it should be laid on a *hot* dish and seasoned. The best pieces for steak are the porter-house, sirloin, and rump.

THAWING FROZEN MEAT, Etc.

If meat, poultry, fish, vegetables, or any other article of food, when found frozen, is thawed by putting it into *warm water* or placing it before the fire, it will most certainly spoil by that process, and be rendered unfit to eat. The only

d

way to thaw these things is b ˙mmersing them in *cold* water. This should be done as soon as they are brou˷ ᵤ in from market, that they may have time to be well thawed before they are cooked. If meat that has been frozen is to be boiled, put it on in cold water. If to be roasted, begin by setting it at a distance from the fire; for if it should not chance to be thoroughly thawed all through to the centre, placing it at first too near the fire will cause it to spoil. If it is expedient to thaw the meat or poultry the night before cooking, lay it in cold water early in the evening, and change the water at bed-time. If found crusted with ice in the morning, remove the ice, and put the meat in fresh cold water, letting it lie in it till wanted for cooking.

Potatoes are injured by being frozen. Other vegetables are not the worse for it, provided they are always thawed in cold water.

TO KEEP MEAT FROM FLIES.

Put in sacks, with enough straw around it so the flies cannot reach through. Three-fourths of a yard of yard-wide muslin is the right size for the sack. Put a little straw in the bottom, then put in the ham and lay straw in all around it; tie it tightly, and hang it in a cool, dry place. Be sure the straw is all around the meat, so the flies cannot reach through to deposit the eggs. (The sacking must be done early in the season before the fly appears.) Muslin lets the air in and is much better than paper. Thin muslin is as good as thick, and will last for years if washed when laid away when emptied.

—National Stockman.

ROAST BEEF.

One very essential point in roasting beef is to have the oven well heated when the beef is first put in; this causes the pores to close up quickly, and prevents the escape of the juices.

Take a rib piece or loin roast of seven or eight pounds. Wipe it thoroughly all over with a clean wet towel. Lay it in a dripping-pan, and baste it well with butter or suet fat. Set it in the oven. Baste it frequently with its own drippings, which will make it brown and tender. When partly done, season with salt and pepper, as it hardens any meat to salt it when raw, and draws out its juices, then dredge with sifted flour to give it a frothy appearance. It will take a roast of this size about two hours time to be properly done, leaving the inside a little rare or red—half an hour less would make the inside quite rare. Remove the beef to a heated dish, set where it will keep hot; then skim the drippings from all fat, add a tablespoonful of sifted flour, a little pepper and a teacupful of boiling water. Boil up once and serve hot in a gravy boat.

Some prefer the clear gravy without the thickening. Serve with mustard or grated horse-radish and vinegar.

YORKSHIRE PUDDING.

This is a very nice accompaniment to a roast of beef; the ingredients are, one pint of milk, four eggs, white and yolks beaten separately, one teaspoonful of salt, and two teaspoonfuls of baking powder sifted through two cups of flour. It should be mixed very smooth, about the consistency of cream. Regulate your time when you put in your roast, so that it will be done half an hour or forty minutes before dishing up. Take it from the oven, set it where it will keep hot. In the meantime have this pudding prepared. Take two common biscuit tins, dip some of the drippings from the dripping-pan into these tins, pour half of the pudding into each, set them into the hot oven, and keep them in until the dinner is dished up; take these puddings out at the last moment and send to the table hot. This I consider much better than the old way of baking the pudding under the meat.

BEEFSTEAK. No. 1.

The first consideration in broiling is to have a clear, glowing bed of coals. The steak should be about three-quarters of an inch in thickness, and should be pounded only in extreme cases, *i.e.*, when it is cut *too* thick and is "stringy." Lay it on a buttered gridiron, turning it often, as it begins to drip, attempting nothing else while cooking it. Have everything else ready for the table; the potatoes and vegetables dished and in the warming closet. Do not season it until it is done, which will be in about ten to twelve minutes. Remove it to a warm platter, pepper and salt it on both sides and spread a liberal lump of butter over it. Serve at once while hot. No definite rule can be given as to the *time* of cooking steak, individual tastes differ so widely in regard to it, some only liking it when well done, others so rare that the blood runs out of it. The best pieces for broiling are the porter-house and sirloin.

BEEFSTEAK. No. 2.

Take a smooth, thick-bottomed frying-pan, scald it out with hot water, and wipe it dry; set it on the stove or range, and when *very* hot, rub it over the bottom with a rag dipped in butter; then place your steak or chops in it, turn often until cooked through, take up on a warm platter, and season both sides with salt, pepper and butter. Serve hot.

Many prefer this manner of cooking steak rather than broiling or frying in a quantity of grease.

BEEFSTEAK AND ONIONS.

Prepare the steak in the usual way. Have ready in a frying pan a dozen onions cut in slices and fried brown in a little beef drippings or butter. Dish your steak, and lay the onions thickly over the top. Cover and let stand five minutes, then send to the table hot.

BEEFSTEAK AND OYSTERS.

Broil the steak the usual way. Put one quart of oysters with very little of the liquor into a stew-pan upon the fire; when it comes to a boil, take off the scum that may rise, stir in three ounces of butter mixed with a tablespoonful of sifted flour, let it boil one minute until it thickens, pour it over the steak. Serve hot.

—Palace Hotel, San Francisco

TO FRY BEEFSTEAKS.

Beefsteak for frying should be cut much thinner than for broiling. Take from the ribs or sirloin and remove the bone. Put some butter or nice beef dripping into a frying-pan, and set it over the fire, and when it has boiled and become hot, lay in the steaks; when cooked quite enough, season with salt and pepper, turn and brown on both sides. Steaks when fried should be thoroughly done. Have ready a hot dish, and when they are done, take out the steaks and lay them on it, with another dish cover the top to keep them hot. The gravy in the pan can be turned over the steaks, first adding a few drops of boiling water, or a gravy to be served in a separate dish made by putting a large tablespoonful of flour into the hot gravy left in the pan, after taking up the steaks. Stir it smooth, then pour in a pint of cream or sweet rich milk, salt and pepper, let it boil up once until it thickens, pour hot into a gravy dish, and send to the table with the steaks.

POT ROAST. (Old Style.)

This is an old-fashioned dish, often cooked in our grandmothers' time. Take a piece of fresh beef weighing about five or six pounds. It must not be *too fat.* Wash it and put it into a pot with barely sufficient water to cover it. Set it over a slow fire, and after it has stewed an hour salt and pepper it Then stew it slowly until tender, adding a little onion if liked. Do not replenish the water at the last, but let all nearly boil away. When tender all through take the meat from the pot, and pour the gravy in a bowl. Put a large lump of butter in the bottom of the pot, then dredge the piece of meat with flour, and return it to the pot to brown, turning it often to prevent its burning. Take the gravy that you have poured from the meat into the bowl, and skim off all the fat; pour this gravy in with the meat and stir in a large spoonful of flour; wet with a little water; let it boil up ten or fifteen minutes and pour into a gravy dish. Serve both hot, the meat on a platter. Some are very fond of this way of cooking a piece of beef which has been previously placed in spiced pickle for two or three days.

SPICED BEEF. (Excellent.)

For a round of beef weighing twenty or twenty-four pounds, take one quarter of a pound of saltpetre, one quarter of a pound of coarse brown sugar, two pounds of salt, one ounce of cloves, one ounce of allspice, and half an ounce of mace; pulverize these materials, mix them well together, and with them rub the beef thoroughly on every part; let the beef lie for eight or ten days in the pickle thus made, turning and rubbing it every day; then tie it around with a broad tape, to keep it in shape; make a coarse paste of flour and water, lay a little suet finely chopped over and under the beef, inclose the beef entirely in the paste, and bake it six hours. When you take the beef from the oven, remove the paste, but do not remove the tape until you are ready to send it to the table. If you wish to eat the beef cold, keep it well covered that it may retain its moisture.

BEEF Á LA MODE.

Mix together three teaspoonfuls of salt, one of pepper, one of ginger, one of mace, one of cinnamon, and two of cloves. Rub this mixture into ten pounds of the upper part of a round of beef. Let this beef stand in this state over night. In the morning, make a dressing or stuffing of a pint of fine bread-crumbs, half a pound of fat salt pork cut in dice, a teaspoonful of ground thyme or summer savory, two teaspoonfuls sage, half a teaspoonful of pepper, one of nutmeg, a little cloves, an onion minced fine, moisten with a little milk or water. Stuff this mixture into the place from whence you took out the bone. With a long skewer fasten the two ends of the beef together, so that its form will be circular, and bind it around with tape, to prevent the skewers giving away. Make incisions in the beef with a sharp knife; fill these incisions very closely with the stuffing, and dredge the whole with flour.

Put it into a dripping-pan and pour over it a pint of hot water; turn a large pan over it to keep in the steam, and roast slowly from three to four hours, allowing a quarter of an hour to each pound of meat. If the meat should be tough, it may be stewed first in a pot with water enough to cover it, until tender, and then put into a dripping-pan and browned in the oven.

If the meat is to be eaten hot, skim off the fat from the gravy, into which, after it is taken off the fire, stir in the beaten yolks of two eggs. If onions are disliked you may omit them and substitute minced oysters.

TENDERLOIN OF BEEF.

To serve tenderloin as directed below, the whole piece must be extracted before the hind quarter of the animal is cut out. This must be particularly noted, because not commonly practised, the tenderloin being usually left attached to the roasting pieces, in order to furnish a tidbit for a few. To dress it whole, proceed as follows: Washing the piece well, put it in an oven; add about a pint of water, and chop up a good handful of each of the following vegetables as an ingredient of the dish, *viz.*, Irish potatoes, carrots, turnips, and a large bunch of celery. They must be washed, peeled, and chopped up raw, then added to the meat; blended with the juice, they form and flavor the gravy. Let the whole slowly simmer, and when nearly done, add a teaspoonful of pounded allspice. To give a richness to the gravy, put in a tablespoonful of butter. If the gravy should look too greasy, skim off some of the melted suet. Boil also a lean piece of beef, which, when perfectly done, chop fine, flavoring with a very small quantity of onion, besides pepper and salt to the taste. Make into small balls, wet them on the outside with eggs, roll in grated cracker or fine bread-crumbs. Fry these force-meat balls a light brown. When serving the dish, put these around the tenderloin, and pour over the whole the rich gravy. This dish is a very handsome one, and, altogether, fit for an epicurean palate. A sumptuous dish.

STEWED STEAK WITH OYSTERS.

Two pounds of rump steak, one pint of oysters, one tablespoonful of lemon juice, three of butter, one of flour, salt, pepper, one cupful of water. Wash the oysters in the water, and drain into a stew-pan. Put this liquor on to heat. As soon as it comes to a boil, skim and set back. Put the butter in a frying-pan, and when hot, put in a steak. Cook ten minutes. Take up the steak, and stir the flour into the butter remaining in the pan. Stir until a dark brown. Add the oyster liquor, and boil one minute. Season with salt and pepper. Put back the steak, cover the pan, and simmer half an hour or until the steak seems tender, then add the oysters and lemon juice. Boil one minute. Serve on a hot dish with points of toast for a garnish.

SMOTHERED BEEFSTEAK.

Take *thin* slices of steak from the upper part of the round or one large thin steak. Lay the meat out smoothly and wipe it dry. Prepare a dressing, using a cupful of fine bread-crumbs, half a teaspoonful of salt, some pepper, a table spoonful of butter, half a teaspoonful of sage, the same of powdered summer savory, and enough milk to moisten it all into a stiff mixture. Spread it over the meat, roll it up carefully, and tie with a string, securing the ends well. Now fry a few thin slices of salt pork in the bottom of a kettle or sauce-pan, and into the fat that has fried out of this pork, place this roll or rolls of beef, and brown it on all sides, turning it until a rich color all over, then add half a pint of water, and stew until tender. If the flavor of onion is liked, a slice may be chopped fine and added to the dressing. When cooked sufficiently, take out the meat, thicken the gravy, and turn over it. To be carved cutting crosswise, in slices, through beef and stuffing.

BEEFSTEAK ROLLS.

This mode is similar to the above recipe, but many might prefer it.

Prepare a good dressing, such as you like for turkey or duck; take a round steak, pound it, but not very hard, spread the dressing over it, sprinkle in a little salt, pepper, and a few bits of butter, lap over the ends, roll the steak up tightly and tie closely; spread two great spoonfuls of butter over the steak after rolling it up, then wash with a well-beaten egg, put water in the bake-pan, lay in the steak so as not to touch the water, and bake as you would a duck, basting often. A half hour in a brisk oven will bake. Make a brown gravy, and send to the table hot.

TO COLLAR A FLANK OF BEEF.

Procure a well-corned flank of beef,—say six pounds. Wash it, and remove the inner and outer skin with the gristle. Prepare a seasoning of one teaspoon-ful each of sage, parsley, thyme, pepper and cloves. Lay your meat upon a board and spread this mixture over the inside. Roll the beef up tight, fasten it with small skewers, put a cloth over it, bandage the cloth with tape, put the beef into the stew-pot, cover it with water to the depth of an inch, boil gently six hours; take it out of the water, place it on a board without undoing it; lay a board on top of the beef, put a fifty pound weight upon this board, and let it remain twenty-four hours. Take off the bandage, garnish with green pickles and curled parsley, and serve.

DRIED BEEF.

Buy the best of beef, or that part which will be the most lean and tender. The tender part of the round is a very good piece. For every twenty pounds of beef use one pint of salt, one teaspoonful of saltpetre, and a quarter of a pound of brown sugar. Mix them well together, and rub the beef well with one-third of the mixture for three successive days. Let it lie in the liquor it makes for six days, then hang up to dry.

A large crock or jar is a good vessel to prepare the meat in before drying it.

BEEF CORNED OR SALTED. (Red.)

Cut up a quarter of beef. For each hundred weight take half a peck of coarse salt, a quarter of a pound of saltpetre, the same weight of saleratus, and a quart of molasses, or two pounds of coarse brown sugar. Mace, cloves and allspice, may be added for spiced beef.

Strew some of the salt in the bottom of a pickle-tub or barrel; then put in a layer of meat, strew this with salt, then add another layer of meat, and salt and meat alternately, until all is used. Let it remain one night. Dissolve the saleratus and saltpetre in a little warm water, and put it to the molasses or sugar; then put it over the meat, add water enough to cover the meat, lay a board on it to keep it under the brine. The meat is fit for use after ten days. This receipt is for winter beef. Rather more salt may be used in warm weather.

Towards spring take the brine from the meat, make it boiling hot, skim it clear, and when it is cooled, return it to the meat.

Beef tongues and smoking pieces are fine pickled in this brine. Beef liver put in this brine for ten days, and then wiped dry and smoked, is very fine. Cut it in slices, and fry or broil it. The brisket of beef, after being corned, may be smoked, and is very good for boiling.

Lean pieces of beef, cut properly from the hind quarter, are the proper pieces for being smoked. There may be some fine pieces cut from the fore-quarter.

After the beef has been in brine ten days or more, wipe it dry, and hang it in a chimney where wood is burned, or make a smothered fire of sawdust or chips, and keep it smoking for ten days; then rub fine black pepper over every part to keep the flies from it, and hang it in a *dry, dark, cool place.* After a week it is fit for use. A strong, coarse brown paper, folded around the beef, and fastened with paste, keeps it nicely.

Tongues are smoked in the same manner. Hang them by a string put

through the root end. Spiced brine for smoked beef or tongues will be generally liked.

ROAST BEEF PIE WITH POTATO CRUST.

When you have a cold roast of beef, cut off as much as will half fill a baking-
dish suited to the size of your family; put this sliced beef into a stew-pan with
any gravy that you may have also saved, a lump of butter, a bit of sliced onion,
and a seasoning of pepper and salt, with enough water to make plenty of gravy;
thicken it, too, by dredging in a tablespoonful of flour; cover it up on the fire,
where it may stew gently, but not be in danger of burning. Meanwhile there
must be boiled a sufficient quantity of potatoes to fill up your baking-dish, after
the stewed meat has been transferred to it. The potatoes must be boiled done,
mashed smooth, and beaten up with milk and butter, as if they were to be
served alone, and placed in a thick layer on top of the meat. Brush it over with
egg, place the dish in an oven, and let it remain there long enough to be brown.
There should be a goodly quantity of gravy left with the beef, that the dish be
not dry and tasteless. Serve with it tomato sauce, Worcestershire sauce or any
other kind that you prefer. A good, plain dish.

ROAST BEEF PIE.

Cut up roast beef, or beef steak left from a previous meal, into thin slices,
lay some of the slices into a deep dish which you have lined *on the sides* with
rich biscuit dough, rolled very thin, (say a quarter of an inch thick); now
sprinkle over this layer a little pepper and salt; put in a small bit of butter, a
few slices of cold potatoes, a little of the cold gravy, if you have any left from
the roast. Make another layer of beef, another layer of seasoning, and so on,
until the dish is filled; cover the whole with paste. leaving a slit in the centre,
and bake half an hour.

BEEF STEAK PIE.

Cut up rump or flank steak into strips two inches long and about an inch
wide. Stew them with the bone in just enough water to cover them until partly
cooked; have half a dozen of cold boiled potatoes sliced. Line a baking-dish
with pie paste, put in a layer of the meat with salt, pepper, and a little of thinly
sliced onion, then one of the sliced potatoes, with bits of butter dotted over
them. Then the steak, alternated with layers of potato, until the dish is full.
Add the gravy or broth, having first thickened it with brown flour. Cover
with a top crust, making a slit in the middle; brush a little beaten egg over it,
and bake until quite brown.

FRIZZLED BEEF.

Shave off *very thin* slices of smoked or dried beef, put them in a frying-pan, cover with cold water, set it on the back of the range or stove, and let it come to a very slow heat, allowing it time to swell out to its natural size, but not to boil. Stir it up, then drain off the water. Melt one ounce of sweet butter in the frying-pan, and add the wafers of beef. When they begin to frizzle or turn up, break over them three eggs; stir until the eggs are cooked; add a little white pepper, and serve on slices of buttered toast.

FLANK STEAK.

This is cut from the boneless part of the flank and is secreted between an outside and inside layer of creamy fat. There are two ways for broiling it. One is to slice it diagonally across the grain; the other is to broil it whole. In either case brush butter over it and proceed as in broiling other steaks. It is considered by butchers the finest steak, which they frequently reserve for themselves.

TO BOIL CORNED BEEF.

The aitch-bone and the brisket are considered the best pieces for boiling. If you buy them in the market already corned, they will be fit to put over the fire without a previous soaking in water. If you corn them in the brine in which you keep your beef through the winter, they must be soaked in cold water over night. Put the beef into a pot, cover with sufficient *cold* water place over a brisk fire, let it come to a boil in half an hour; just before boiling remove all the scum from the pot, place the pot on the back of the fire, let it boil very slowly until quite tender.

A piece weighing eight pounds requires two and a half hours' boiling. If you do not wish to eat it hot, let it remain in the pot after you take it from the fire, until nearly cold, then lay it in a colander to drain, lay a cloth over it to retain its fresh appearance; serve with horse-radish and pickles.

If vegetables are to accompany this, making it the old-fashioned "boiled dinner," about three-quarters of an hour before dishing up skim the liquor free from fat and *turn part of it out into another kettle*, into which put a cabbage carefully prepared, cutting it into four quarters; also half a dozen peeled medium-sized white turnips, cut into halves; scrape four carrots and four parsnips each cut into four pieces. Into the kettle with the meat, about half an hour before serving, pour on more water from the boiling tea-kettle, and into this put peeled medium-sized potatoes. This dinner should also be accompanied by boiled beets, sliced hot, cooked separate from the rest, with vinegar over them. Cooking the cabbage separately from the meat prevents the meat from having the flavor of cabbage when cold. The carrots, parsnips and turnips will boil in about an hour. A piece of salt pork was usually boiled with a "New England boiled dinner."

SPICED BEEF RELISH.

Take two pounds of raw, tender beefsteak, chop it *very fine*, put into it salt, pepper and a little sage, two tablespoonfuls of melted butter; add two rolled crackers made very fine, also two well-beaten eggs. Make it up into the shape of a roll and bake it; baste with butter and water before baking. Cut in slices when cold.

FRIED BEEF LIVER.

Cut it in rather thin slices, say a quarter of an inch thick, pour over it *boiling* water, which closes the pores of the meat, makes it impervious to the fat, and at the same time seals up the rich juice of the meat. It may be rolled in flour or bread-crumbs, seasoned with salt and pepper, dipped in egg and fried in hot fat mixed with one-third butter.

PRESSED BEEF.

First have your beef nicely pickled: let it stay in pickle a week; then take the thin flanky pieces, such as will not make a handsome dish of themselves; put on a large potful, and let them boil until perfectly done; then pull to pieces, and season just as you do souse, with pepper, salt and allspice; only put it in a coarse cloth and press down upon it some very heavy weight.

The advantage of this recipe is that it makes a most acceptable, presentable dish out of a part of the beef that otherwise might be wasted.

FRENCH STEW.

Grease the bottom of an iron pot, and place in it three or four pounds of beef; be very careful that it does not burn, and turn it until it is nicely browned. Set a muffin ring under the beef to prevent its sticking. Add a few sliced carrots, one or two sliced onions, and a cupful of hot water; keep covered, and stew slowly until the vegetables are done. Add pepper and salt. If you wish more gravy, add hot water, and thicken with flour. Serve on a dish with the vegetables.

TO POT BEEF.

The round is the best piece for potting, and you may use both the upper and under part. Take ten pounds of beef, remove all the fat, cut the lean into square pieces, two inches thick. Mix together three teaspoonfuls of salt, one of pepper, one of cloves, one of mace, one of cinnamon, one of allspice, one of thyme, and one of sweet basil. Put a layer of the pieces of beef into an earthen pot, sprinkle some of this spice mixture over this layer, add a piece of fat salt pork, cut as thin as possible, sprinkle a little of the spice mixture over the pork, make another layer of the beef with spices and pork, and so on, until the pot is filled. Pour over the whole three tablespoonfuls of Tarragon vinegar, or, if you prefer it, half a pint of Madeira wine; cover the pot with a paste made of flour and water, so that no steam can escape. Put the pot into an oven, moderately heated, and let it stand there eight hours; then set it away to use when wanted.

Beef cooked in this manner will keep good a fortnight in moderate weather.

It is an excellent relish for breakfast, and may be eaten either warm or cold. When eaten warm, serve with slices of lemon.

STEWED BRISKET OF BEEF

Put the part that has the hard fat into a stew-pot, with a small quantity of water; let it boil up, and skim it thoroughly; then add carrots, turnips, onions, celery and a few pepper-corns. Stew till extremely tender; then take out all the flat bones and remove all the fat from the soup. Either serve that and the meat in a tureen, or the soup alone, and the meat on a dish, garnished with some vegetables. The following sauce is much admired served with the beef: Take half a pint of the soup, and mix it with a spoonful of catsup, a teaspoonful of made mustard, a little flour, a bit of butter and salt; boil all together a few minutes, then pour it round the meat.

DRIED BEEF, WITH CREAM.

Shave your beef *very* fine. Put it into a suitable dish on the back of the stove; cover with cold water and give it time to soak out to its original size before being dried. When it is quite soft and the water has become hot (it must not boil), take it off, turn off the water, pour on a cup of cream; if you do not have it use milk and butter, a pinch of pepper; let it come to a boil, thicken with a tablespoonful of flour, wet up in a little milk. Serve on dipped toast or not, just as one fancies. A nice breakfast dish.

BEEF CROQUETTES. No. 1.

Chop fine one cup of cold, cooked, lean beef, half a cup of fat, half a cup of cold boiled or fried ham; cold pork will do if you have not the ham. Also mince up a slice of onion. Season all with a teaspoonful of salt, half a teaspoonful of pepper, and a teaspoonful of powdered sage or parsley, if liked. Heat together with half a cup of stock or milk; when cool, add a beaten egg. Form the mixture into balls, slightly flattened, roll in egg and bread-crumbs, or flour and egg. Fry in hot lard or beef drippings. Serve on a platter and garnish with sprigs of parsley. Almost any cold meats can be used instead of beef.

BEEF CROQUETTES. No. 2.

Take cold roast or corned beef. Put it into a wooden bowl and chop it fine. Mix with it about twice the quantity of hot mashed potatoes well seasoned with butter and salt. Beat up an egg and work it into the potato and meat, then form the mixture into little cakes the size of fish balls. Flatten them a little, roll in flour or egg and cracker crumbs, fry in butter and lard mixed, browning on both sides. Serve piping hot.

MEAT AND POTATO CROQUETTES.

Put in a stew-pan an ounce of butter and a slice of onion minced fine; when this simmers, add a level tablespoonful of sifted flour; stir the mixture until it becomes smooth and frothy; then add half of a cupful of milk, some seasoning of salt and pepper; let all boil, stirring it all the while. Now add a cupful of cold meat chopped fine and a cupful of cold or hot mashed potato. Mix all thoroughly and spread on a plate to cool. When it is cool enough, shape it with your hands into balls or rolls. Dip them in beaten egg and roll in cracker or bread-crumbs. Drop them into hot lard and fry about two minutes a delicate brown; take them out with a skimmer and drain them on a piece of brown paper. Serve immediately while hot. These are very nice.

Cold rice or hominy may be used in place of the potato; or a cupful of cold fish minced fine in place of the meat.

COLD ROAST, WARMED.

Cut from the remains of a cold roast the lean meat from the bones into small, thin slices. Put over the fire a frying-pan containing a spoonful of butter or drippings. Cut up a quarter of an onion and fry it brown, then remove the onion, add the meat gravy left from the day before, and if not thick enough, add a little flour; salt and pepper.

Turn the pieces of meat into this, and let them *simmer* a few minutes. Serve hot.

COLD ROAST, WARMED. No. 2.

Cold rare roast beef may be made as good as when freshly cooked by slicing, seasoning with salt, pepper and bits of butter; put it in a plate or pan with a spoonful or two of water, covering closely, and set in the oven until hot, but no longer. Cold steak may be shaved very fine with a knife and used the same way.

Or, if the meat is in small pieces, cover them with buttered letter paper, twist each end tightly, and boil them on the gridiron, sprinkling them with finely chopped herbs.

Still another nice way of using cold meats is to mince the lean portions very fine, and add to a batter made of one pint of milk, one cup of flour and three eggs. Fry like fritters, and serve with drawn butter or sauce.

COLD MEAT AND POTATO, BAKED.

Put in a frying-pan a round tablespoonful of cold butter; when it becomes hot, stir into it a teaspoonful of chopped onion and a tablespoonful of flour, stirring it constantly until it is smooth and frothy; then add two-thirds of a cupful of cold milk or water. Season this with salt and pepper and allow it to come to a boil; then add a cupful of cold meat finely chopped and cleared from bone and skin; let this all heat thoroughly; then turn it into a shallow dish well buttered. Spread hot or cold mashed potatoes over the top, and cook for fifteen or twenty minutes in a moderate hot oven.

Cold hominy or rice may be used in place of mashed potatoes, and is equally as good.

BEEF HASH. No. 1.

Chop rather finely cold roast beef or pieces of beef steak, also chop twice as much cold boiled potatoes. Put over the fire a stew-pan or frying-pan, in which put a piece of butter as large as required to season it well, add pepper and salt, moisten with beef gravy if you have it, if not, with hot water; cover and let it steam and heat through thoroughly, stirring occasionally, so that the ingredients be evenly distributed, and to keep the hash from sticking to the bottom of the pan. When done it should not be at all watery, nor yet dry, but have sufficient adhesiveness to stand well on a dish, or buttered toast. Many like the flavor of onion; if so, fry two or three slices in the butter before adding the hash. Corned beef makes excellent hash.

BEEF HASH. No. 2.

Chop cold roast beef, or pieces of beefsteak; fry half an onion in a piece of butter; when the onion is brown, add the chopped beef; season with a little salt and pepper; moisten with the beef gravy, if you have any, if not, with sufficient water and a little butter; cook long enough to be hot, but no longer, as much cooking toughens the meat. An excellent breakfast dish.

—Prof. Blot.

Some prefer to let a crust form on the bottom and turn the hash brown side uppermost. Served with poached eggs on top.

HAMBURGER STEAK.

Take a pound of raw flank or round steak, without any fat, bone or stringy pieces. Chop it until a perfect mince; it cannot be chopped too fine. Also chop a small onion quite fine, and mix well with the meat. Season with salt and pepper; make into cakes as large as a biscuit, but quite flat, or into one large flat cake a little less than half an inch thick. Have ready a frying-pan, with butter and lard mixed; when boiling hot, put in the steak and fry brown. Garnish with celery top around the edge of the platter and two or three slices of lemon on the top of the meat.

A brown gravy made from the grease the steak was fried in, and poured over the meat, enriches it.

TO ROAST BEEF HEART.

Wash it carefully and open it sufficiently to remove the ventricles, then soak it in cold water until the blood is discharged; wipe it dry and stuff it nicely with dressing, as for turkey; roast it about an hour and a half. Serve it with the gravy, which should be thickened with some of the stuffing, and a glass of wine. It is very nice hashed. Served with currant jelly.

—Palmer House, Chicago.

STEWED BEEF KIDNEY.

Cut the kidney into slices, season highly with pepper and salt, fry it a light brown, take out the slices, then pour a little warm water into the pan, dredge in some flour, put in slices of kidney again; let them stew very gently; add some parsley if liked. Sheep's kidneys may be split open, broiled over a clear fire, and served with a piece of butter placed on each half.

BEEF'S HEART, STEWED.

After washing the heart thoroughly, cut it up into squares half an inch long; put them into a sauce-pan with water enough to cover them. If any scum rises, skim it off. Now take out the meat, strain the liquor, and put back the meat, also add a sliced onion, some parsley, a head of celery chopped fine, pepper and salt, and a piece of butter. Stew until the meat is very tender. Stir up a tablespoonful of brown flour with a small quantity of water, and thicken the whole. Boil up and serve.

BOILED BEEF TONGUE.

Wash a fresh tongue and just cover it with water in the pot; put in a pint of salt and a small red pepper; add more water as it evaporates, so as to keep the tongue nearly covered until done—when it can be easily pierced with a fork; take it out, and if wanted soon, take off the skin and set it away to cool. If wanted for future use, do not peel until it is required. A cupful of salt will do for three tongues, if you have that number to boil; but do not fail to keep water enough in the pot to keep them covered while boiling. If salt tongues are used, soak them over night, of course omitting the salt when boiling. Or, after peeling a tongue, place it in a sauce-pan with one cup of water, half a cup vinegar, four tablespoonfuls sugar, and cook until the liquor is evaporated.

SPICED BEEF TONGUE.

Rub into each tongue a mixture made of half a pound of brown sugar, a piece of saltpetre the size of a pea, and a tablespoonful of ground cloves; put it in a brine made of three-quarters of a pound of salt to two quarts of water and keep covered. Pickle two weeks, then wash well and dry with a cloth; roll out a thin paste made of flour and water, smear it all over the tongue and place in a pan to bake slowly; baste well with lard and hot water; when done scrape off the paste and skin.

TO BOIL TRIPE.

Wash it well in warm water, and trim it nicely, taking off all the fat. Cut into small pieces, and put it on to boil five hours before dinner in water enough to cover it very well. After it has boiled four hours, pour off the water, season the tripe with pepper and salt, and put it into a pot with milk and water mixed in equal quantities. Boil it an hour in the milk and water.

Boil in a sauce-pan ten or a dozen onions. When they are quite soft, drain them in a colander, and mash them. Wipe out your sauce-pan and put them on again, with a bit of butter rolled in flour and a wineglass of cream or milk. Let them boil up, and add them to the tripe just before you send it to table. Eat it with pepper, vinegar and mustard.

It is best to give tripe its first and longest boiling the day before it is wanted.

TO FRY TRIPE.

Boil the tripe the day before till it is quite tender, which it will not be in less than four or five hours. Then cover it and set it away. Next day cut it into long slips, and dip each piece into beaten yolk of egg, and afterwards roll them in grated bread-crumbs. Have ready in a frying-pan over the fire some good beef-dripping. When it is boiling hot put in the tripe, and fry it about ten minutes, till of a light brown.

You may serve it with onion sauce.

Boiled tripe that has been left from the dinner of the preceding day may be fried in this manner.

FRICASSEED TRIPE.

Cut a pound of tripe in narrow strips, put a small cup of water or milk to it, add a bit of butter the size of an egg, dredge in a large teaspoonful of flour, or work it with the butter; season with pepper and salt, let it simmer gently for half an hour, serve hot. A bunch of parsley cut small and put with it is an improvement.

Some put in oysters five minutes before dishing up.

TRIPE LYONNAISE.

Cut up half a pound of cold boiled tripe into neat squares. Put two ounces of butter and a tablespoonful of chopped onion in a frying-pan and fry to a delicate brown; add to the tripe a teaspoonful of chopped parsley and a little strong vinegar, salt, and cayenne; stir the pan to prevent burning. Cover the bottom of a platter with tomato-sauce, add the contents of the pan and serve.

TO CLARIFY BEEF DRIPPINGS.

Drippings accumulated from different cooked meats of beef or veal can be clarified by putting it into a basin and slicing into it a raw potato, allowing it to boil long enough for the potato to brown, which causes all impurities to disappear. Remove from the fire, and when cool drain it off from the sediment that settles at the bottom. Turn it into basins or small jars and set it in a cool place for future use. When mixed with an equal amount of butter it answers the same purpose as clear butter for frying and basting any meats excepting game and poultry.

Mutton drippings impart an unpleasant flavor to anything cooked outside of its kind.

ROAST LOIN OF VEAL.

Prepare it the same as any roast, leaving in the kidney, around which put considerable salt. Make a dressing the same as for fowls; unroll the loin, put the stuffing well around the kidney, fold and secure with several coils of white cotton twine wound around in all directions; place in a dripping-pan with the thick side down, and put in a rather hot oven, graduated after it commences to roast to moderate; in half an hour add a little hot water to the pan, and baste often; in another half hour turn over the roast, and when about done dredge lightly with flour and baste with melted butter. Before serving, carefully remove the twine. A roast of four to five pounds will bake in about two hours. For a gravy, skim off some of the fat if there is too much in the drippings; dredge in some flour, stir until brown, add some hot water if necessary, boil a few minutes, stir in such sweet herbs as fancied, and put in a gravy boat. Serve with green peas and lemon jelly. Is very nice sliced cold for lunch, and Worcestershire or Chili sauce forms a fine relish.

ROAST FILLET OF VEAL.

Select a nice fillet, take out the bone, fill up the space with stuffing, and also put a good layer under the fat. Truss it of a good shape by drawing the fat round, and tie it up with tape. Cook it rather moderately at first, and baste with butter. It should have careful attention and frequent basting, that the fat may not burn. Roast from three to four hours, according to the size. After it is dished, pour melted butter over it; serve with ham or bacon, and fresh cucumbers, if in season. Veal, like all other meat, should be well washed in cold water before cooking and wiped thoroughly dry with a clean cloth. Cold fillet of veal is very good-stewed with tomatoes and an onion or two.

In roasting veal, care must be taken that it is not at first placed in too hot an oven; the fat of a loin, one of the most delicate joints of veal, should be covered with greased paper; a fillet, also, should have on the caul until nearly done enough.

BOILED FILLET OF VEAL.

Choose a small, delicate fillet; prepare as for roasting, or stuff it with an oyster force-meat; after having washed it thoroughly, cover it with water and let it boil very gently three and a half or four hours, keeping it well skimmed. Send it to the table with a rich white sauce, or, if stuffed with oysters, a tureen of oyster sauce. Garnish with stewed celery and slices of bacon. A boiled tongue should be served with it.

VEAL PUDDING.

Cut about two pounds of lean veal into small collops a quarter of an inch in thickness; put a piece of butter the size of an egg into a very clean frying pan to melt; then lay in the veal and a few slices of bacon, a small sprig of thyme, and a seasoning of pepper and salt; place the pan over a slow fire for about ten minutes, then add two or three spoonfuls of warm water. Just boil it up, and then let it stand to cool. Line a pudding-dish with a good suet crust, lay in the veal and bacon, pour the gravy over it; roll out a piece of paste to form a lid, place it over, press it close with the thumb, tie the basin in a pudding cloth, and put it into a sauce-pan of boiling water, keeping continually boiling until done, or about one hour.

FRIED VEAL CUTLETS.

Put into a frying-pan two or three tablespoonfuls of lard or beef drippings. When boiling hot lay in the cutlets, well seasoned with salt and pepper, and dredged with flour. Brown nicely on both sides, then remove the meat, and if you have more grease than is necessary for the gravy, put it aside for further use. Reserve a tablespoonful or more, and rub into it a tablespoonful of flour, with the back of the spoon, until it is a smooth, rich brown color; then add gradually a cup of *cold water* and season with pepper and salt. When the gravy is boiled up well return the meat to the pan and gravy. Cover it closely and allow it to stew gently on the back of the range for fifteen minutes. This softens the meat, and with this gravy it makes a nice breakfast dish.

Another mode is to simply fry the cutlets, and afterwards turning off some of the grease they were fried in and then adding to that left in the pan a few drops of hot water, turning the whole over the fried chops.

FRIED VEAL CHOPS. (Plain.)

Sprinkle over them salt and pepper, then dip them in beaten egg and cracker-crumbs, and fry in drippings, or hot lard and butter mixed. If you wish a gravy with them, add a tablespoonful of flour to the gravy they were fried in and turn in cream or milk; season to taste with salt and pepper. Boil up and serve hot with the gravy in a separate dish. This dish is very fine accompanied with a few sound fresh tomatoes, sliced and fried in the same grease the cutlets were, and all dished on the same platter.

VEAL COLLOPS.

Cut veal from the leg or other lean part into pieces the size of an oyster. Season with pepper, salt and a little mace; rub some over each piece; dip in egg, then into cracker-crumbs, and fry. They both look and taste like oysters.

VEAL OLIVES.

Cut up a slice of a fillet of veal, about half an inch thick, into squares of three inches. Mix up a little salt pork, chopped with bread-crumbs, one onion, a little pepper, salt, sweet marjoram, and one egg well beaten; put this mixture upon the pieces of veal, fastening the four corners together with little bird skewers; lay them in a pan with a sufficient veal gravy or light stock to cover the bottom of the pan, dredge with flour, and set in a hot oven. When browned on top, put a small bit of butter on each, and let them remain until quite tender, which will take twenty minutes. Serve with horse-radish.

VEAL CHEESE.

Prepare equal quantities of boiled sliced veal and smoked tongue. Pound the slices separately in a mortar, moistening with butter as you proceed; then pack it in a jar or pail, mixing it in alternate layers; first, the tongue and then the veal, so that when cut it will look variegated. Press it down hard and pour melted butter over the top. Keep it well covered and in a dry place. Nice for sandwiches, or sliced cold for lunch.

VEAL CROQUETTES.

Mince a coffee cup of cold veal in a chopping bowl, adding a little cold ham, and two or three slices of onion, a pinch of mace, powdered parsley and pepper, some salt. Let a pint of milk or cream come to the boiling point, then add a tablespoonful of cold butter, then the above mixture. Beat up two eggs and mix with a teaspoonful of corn-starch or flour, and add to the rest; cook it all about ten minutes, stirring with care. Remove from the fire, and spread it on a platter, roll it into balls, when cooled flatten each; dip them in egg and bread-crumbs, and fry in a wire basket, dipped in hot lard.

BROILED VEAL CUTLETS. (Fine.)

Two or three pounds of veal cutlets, egg and bread-crumbs, two tablespoonfuls of minced savory herbs, salt and pepper to taste, a little grated nutmeg.

Cut the cutlets about three-quarters of an inch in thickness, flatten them, and brush them over with the yolk of an egg; dip them into bread-crumbs and minced herbs, season with pepper and salt, and fold each cutlet in a piece of white letter paper well buttered; twist the ends, and broil over a clear fire; when done remove the paper. Cooked this way, they retain all the flavor.

VEAL POT-PIE.

Procure a nice breast or brisket of veal, well jointed, put the pieces into the pot with one quart of water to every five pounds of meat; put the pot over a slow fire; just before it comes to a boil, skim it well and pour in a teacupful of cold water; then turn over the meat in order that all the scum may rise, remove all the scum, boil quite hard, season with pepper and salt to your taste, always remembering that the crust will take up part of the seasoning; when this is done cut off your crust in pieces of equal size, but do not roll or mould them; lay them on top of the meat, so as to cover it; put the lid on the pot closely, let the whole boil slowly one hour. If the lid does not fit the pot closely, wrap a cloth around it, in order that no steam shall escape; and by no means allow the pot to *stop boiling.*

The crust for pot-pie should be raised with yeast. To three pints of flour add two ounces of butter, a little salt, and wet with milk sufficient to make a soft dough; knead it well and set it away to rise; when quite light, mould and knead it again, and let it stand, in winter, one hour, in summer, one half hour, when it will be ready to cut.

In summer you had better add one-half a teaspoonful of soda when you knead it the second time, or you may wet it with water, and add another bit of butter.

VEAL PIE.

Cut the veal into rather small pieces or slices, put it in a stew-pan, with hot water to cover it; add to it a tablespoonful of salt, and set it over the fire; take off the scum as it rises; when the meat is tender turn it into a dish to cool; take out all the small bones, butter a tin or earthen basin or pudding-pan, line it with pie paste, lay some of the parboiled meat in to half fill it; put bits of butter in the size of a hickory nut all over the meat; shake pepper over, dredge wheat flour over, until it looks white, then fill it nearly to the top with some of the water in which the meat was boiled; roll a cover for the top of the crust, puff-paste it, giving it two or three turns, and roll it to nearly half an inch thickness; cut a slit in the centre, and make several small incisions on either side of it, put the crust on, trim the edges neatly with a knife; bake one hour in a quick oven. A breast of veal will make two two-quart basin pies; half a pound of nice corned pork, cut in thin slices, and parboiled with the meat, will make it very nice, and very little, if any, butter, will be required for the pie; when pork is used, no other salt will be necessary. Many are fond of thin slices of sweet ham cooked with the veal for pie.

VEAL STEW.

Cut up two or three pounds of veal into pieces three inches long and one thick. Wash it, put it in your stew-pan with two quarts of water, let it boil skim it well, and, when all the scum is removed, add pepper and salt to your taste, and a small piece of butter; pare and cut in halves twelve small Irish potatoes, put them into the stew-pan; when it boils, have ready a batter made with two eggs, two spoonfuls of cream or milk, a little salt and flour enough to make it a little thicker than for pan-cakes; drop this into the stew, a spoonful at a time, while it is boiling; when all is in, cover the pan closely so that no steam can escape; let it boil twenty minutes, and serve in a deep dish.

VEAL LOAF.

Three pounds of raw veal, chopped very fine, butter the size of an egg, three eggs, three tablespoonfuls of cream or milk; if milk use a small piece of butter; mix the eggs and cream together; mix with the veal four pounded crackers, one teaspoonful of black pepper, one large tablespoonful salt, one large tablespoonful of sage; mix well together and form into a loaf. Bake two and one-half hours, basting with butter and water while baking. Serve cut in thin slices.

VEAL FOR LUNCH.

Butter a good-sized bowl, and line it with thin slices of hard-boiled eggs; have veal and ham both in very thin slices; place in the bowl a layer of veal, with pepper and salt, then a layer of ham, omitting the salt, then a layer of veal, and so on, alternating with veal and ham, until the bowl is filled; make a paste of flour and water, as stiff as it can be rolled out; cover the contents of the bowl with the paste, and over this tie a double cotton cloth; put the bowl into a sauce-pan, or other vessel, with water just up to the rim of the bowl, and boil three hours; then take it from the fire, remove the cloth and paste, and let it stand until the next day, when it may be turned out and served in very thin slices. An excellent lunch in travelling.

VEAL PATTIES.

Cut portions of the neck or breast of veal into small pieces, and, with a little salt pork cut fine, stew gently for ten or fifteen minutes; season with pepper and salt, and a small piece of celery chopped coarsely, also of the yellow top, picked (not chopped) up; stir in a paste made of a tablespoonful of flour the yolk of one egg, and milk to form a thin batter; let all come to a boil, and it is ready for the patties. Make the patties of a light, flaky crust, as for tarts, cut round, the size of a small sauce-plate; the centre of each, for about three inches, cut half way through, to be raised and serve as a cover. Put a spoonful of the stew in each crust, lay on the top, and serve. Stewed oysters or lamb may be used in place of veal.

BRAISED VEAL.

Take a piece of the shoulder weighing about five pounds. Have the bone removed and tie up the meat to make it firm. Put a piece of butter the size of half an egg, together with a few shavings of onion, into a kettle or stone crock and let it get hot. Salt and pepper the veal and put it into the kettle, cover it tightly and put it over a medium fire until the meat is brown on both sides, turning it occasionally. Then set the kettle back on the stove, where it will simmer slowly for about two hours and a half. Before setting the meat back on the stove, see if the juice of the meat together with the butter do not make gravy enough, and if not, put in about two tablespoonfuls of hot water. When the gravy is cold it will be like jelly. It can be served hot with the hot meat, or cold with the cold meat.

BAKED CALF'S HEAD.

Boil a calf's head (after having cleaned it) until tender, then split it in two, and keep the best half; (bone it if you like); cut the meat from the other in uniform pieces; the size of an oyster; put bits of butter, the size of a nutmeg, all over the best half of the head; sprinkle pepper over it, and dredge on flour until it looks white, then set it on a trivet or muffin rings in a dripping-pan; put a cup of water into the pan, and set it in a hot oven; turn it that it may brown evenly; baste once or twice. Whilst this is doing, dip the prepared pieces of the head in wheat flour or batter, and fry in hot lard or beef dripping a delicate brown; season with pepper and salt and slices of lemon, if liked. When the roast is done put it on a hot dish, lay the fried pieces around it, and cover it with a tin cover; put the gravy from the dripping-pan into the pan in which the pieces were fried, with the slices of lemon, and a tablespoonful of browned flour, and, if necessary, a little hot water. Let it boil up once, and strain it into a gravy boat, and serve with the meat.

CALF'S HEAD CHEESE.

Boil a calf's head in water enough to cover it, until the meat leaves the bones; then take it with a skimmer into a wooden bowl or tray; take from it every particle of bone; chop it small; season with pepper and salt, a heaping tablespoonful of salt, and a teaspoonful of pepper will be sufficient; if liked, add a tablespoonful of finely chopped sweet herbs; lay in a cloth in a colander, put the minced meat into it, then fold the cloth closely over it, lay a plate over, and on it a gentle weight. When cold it may be sliced thin for supper or sandwiches. Spread each slice with made mustard.

BRAIN CUTLETS.

Well wash the brains and soak them in cold water till white. Parboil them till tender in a small sauce-pan for about a quarter of an hour; then thoroughly drain them, and place them on a board. Divide them into small pieces with a knife. Dip each piece into flour, and then roll them in egg and bread-crumbs, and fry them in butter or well-clarified dripping. Serve very hot with gravy. Another way of doing brains is to prepare them as above, and then stew them gently in rich stock, like stewed sweetbreads. They are also nice plainly boiled, and served with parsley and butter sauce.

CALF'S HEAD BOILED.

Put the head into boiling water and let it remain about five minutes; take it out, hold it by the ear, and with the back of the knife scrape off the hair, (should it not come off easily, dip the head again in boiling water). When perfectly clean, take the eyes out, cut off the ears, and remove the brain, which soak for an hour in warm water. Put the head to soak in hot water a few minutes to make it look white, and then have ready a stew-pan, into which lay the head; cover it with cold water, and bring it gradually to boil. Remove the scum, and add a little salt, which increases it and causes it to rise to the top. Simmer it very gently from two and a half to three hours, or until the bones will slip out easily, and when nearly done, boil the brains fifteen or twenty minutes; skin and chop them, (not too finely), and add a tablespoonful of minced parsley which has been previously scalded; also a pinch of pepper, salt; then stir into this four tablespoonfuls of melted butter, set it on the back of the range to keep it hot. When the head is done, take it up, and drain very dry. Score the top and rub it over with melted butter; dredge it with flour, and set it in the oven to brown.

When you serve the head, have it accompanied with a gravy boat of melted butter and minced parsley.

CALF'S LIVER AND BACON.

Slice the liver a quarter of an inch thick; pour hot water over it, and let it remain for a few minutes to clear it from blood; then dry it in a cloth. Take a pound of bacon, or as much as you require, and cut the same number of thin slices as you have of liver; fry the bacon to a nice crisp; take it out and keep it hot; then fry the liver in the same pan, having first seasoned it with pepper and salt and dredged in a little flour; lay it in the hot bacon fat and fry it a nice brown. Serve it with a slice of bacon on the top of each slice of liver.

If you wish a gravy with it, pour off most of the fat from the frying-pan, put in about two ounces of butter, a tablespoonful of flour well rubbed in, add a cup of water, salt and pepper, give it one boil and serve in a gravy boat.

Another way.—Cut the liver in nice thin slices, pour boiling water over it, and let it stand about five minutes; then drain and put in a dripping-pan with three or four thin slices of salt pork or bacon; pepper and salt, and put in the oven, letting it cook until thoroughly done, then serve with a cream or milk gravy poured over it.

Calf's liver and bacon are very good broiled after cutting each in thin slices Season with butter, pepper and salt.

CROQUETTES OF SWEETBREADS.

Take four veal sweetbreads, soak them for an hour in cold salted water, first remov ing the pipes and membranes; then put them into boiling salted water with a table-spoonful of vinegar, and cook them twenty minutes, then drop them again into cold water to harden. Now remove them, chop them very fine, almost to a paste. Season with salt, pepper and a teaspoonful of grated onion; add the beaten yolks of three raw eggs, one tablespoonful of butter, half a cupful of cream, and sufficient fine cracker crumbs to make stiff enough to roll out into little balls or cork-shaped cro-quettes. Have ready a frying-kettle half-full of fat over the fire, a dish containing three smoothly beaten eggs, a large platter of cracker dust; wet the hands with cold water and make the mixture in shape; afterwards rolling them in the cracker dust, then into the beaten egg, and again in the cracker dust; smooth them on the outside and drop them carefully in the hot fat. When the croquettes are fried a nice golden brown, put them on a brown paper a moment to free them from grease. Serve hot with sliced lemon or parsley.

SWEETBREADS.

There are two in a calf, which are considered delicacies. Select the largest. The color should be clear and a shade darker than the fat. Before cooking in any manner let them lie for half an hour in tepid water; then throw into hot water to whiten and harden, after which draw off the outer casing, remove the little pipes, and cut into thin slices. They should always be thoroughly cooked.

FRIED SWEETBREADS.

After preparing them as above they are put into hot fat and butter, and fried the same as lamb chop, also broiled the same, first rolling them in egg and cracker-crumbs.

BAKED SWEETBREADS.

Three sweetbreads, egg and bread-crumbs, oiled butter, three slices of toast, brown gravy.

Choose large, white sweetbreads; put them into warm water to draw out the blood, and to improve their color; let them remain for rather more than one hour; then put them into boiling water, and allow them to simmer for about ten minutes, which renders them firm.   Take them up, drain them, brush over the egg, sprinkle with bread-crumbs; dip them in egg again, and then into more bread-crumbs.   Drop on them a little oiled butter, and put the sweetbreads into a moderately heated oven, and let them bake for nearly three-quarters of an hour. Make three pieces of toast; place the sweetbreads on the toast, and pour round, but not over them, a good brown gravy.

FRICASSEED SWEETBREADS.

If they are uncooked, cut into thin slices, let them simmer in a rich gravy for three-quarters of an hour, add a well-beaten egg, two tablespoonfuls of cream and a tablespoonful of chopped parsley; stir all together for a few minutes and serve immediately.

Mutton and Lamb.

ROAST MUTTON.

The pieces mostly used for roasting are the hind quarter of the sheep, called the loin and leg, the fore-quarter, the shoulder, also the chine or saddle, which is the two loins together.   Every part should be trimmed off that cannot be eaten; then wash well and dry with a clean cloth; lay it in your dripping-pan and put in a little water to baste it with at first; then afterward with its own gravy. Allow, in roasting, about twelve minutes to the pound; that is, if your fire is strong, which it should be.   It should not be salted at first, as that tends to harden it, and draws out too much of the blood or juices; but salt soon after it begins to roast well.   If there is danger of its browning too fast, cover it with a sheet of white paper.   Baste it often, and about a quarter of an hour before you think it will be done dredge the meat very lightly with flour and baste it with butter.   Skim the gravy well and thicken very slightly with brown flour.   Serve with currant jelly or other tart sauce.

BONED LEG OF MUTTON ROASTED.

Take the bone out of a small leg of mutton, without spoiling the skin if possible, then cut off most of the fat.   In the hole whence the bone was taken, fill with a stuffing made the same as for fowls, adding to it part of an onion finely minced. Sew the leg up underneath to prevent the dressing or stuffing from falling out. Bind and tie it up compactly; put it in a roasting-pan, turn in a cupful of hot water and place it in a moderately hot oven, basting it occasionally. When partly cooked season with salt and pepper. When thoroughly cooked, remove and place the leg on a warm platter; skim the grease from the top of the drippings, add a cup of water and thicken with a spoonful of dissolved flour. Send the gravy to the table in a gravy dish, also a dish of currant jelly.

BOILED LEG OF MUTTON.

To prepare a leg of mutton for boiling, wash it clean, cut a small piece off the shank bone, and trim the knuckle. Put it into a pot with water enough to cover it, and boil gently from two to three hours, skimming well. Then take it from the fire, and keeping the pot well covered, let it finish by remaining in the steam for ten or fifteen minutes. Serve it up with a sauce-boat of melted butter, into which a teacupful of capers or nasturtiums, have been stirred. If the broth is to be used for soup, put in a little salt while boiling; if not, salt it well when partly done, and boil the meat in a cloth.

BRAISED LEG OF MUTTON.

This recipe can be varied either by preparing the leg with a stuffing, placed in the cavity after having the bone removed, or cooking it without. Having lined the bottom of a thick iron kettle or stew-pan with a few thin slices of bacon, put over the bacon four carrots, three onions, a bunch of savory herbs; then over these place the leg of mutton. Cover the whole with a few more slices of bacon, then pour over half of a pint of water. Cover with a tight cover and stew very gently for four hours, basting the leg occasionally with its own liquor, and seasoning it with salt and pepper as soon as it begins to be tender. When cooked strain the gravy, thicken with a spoonful of flour, (it should be quite brown), pour some of it over the meat and send the remainder to the table in a tureen, to be served with the mutton when carved. Garnish the dish around the leg with potatoes cut in the shape of olives and fried a light brown in butter.

LEG OF MUTTON A LA VENISON.

Remove all the rough fat from the mutton and lay it in a deep earthen dish; rub into it thoroughly the following: One tablespoonful of salt, one each of celery-salt, brown sugar, black pepper, English mustard, allspice, and some sweet herbs, all powdered and mixed; after which pour over it slowly a teacup of good vinegar, cover tightly, and set in a cool place four or five days, turning it and

basting often with the liquid each day.   To cook, put in a kettle a quart of boiling water, place over it an inverted shallow pan, and on it lay the meat just as
removed from the pickle; cover the kettle tightly and stew four hours.   Do not
let the water touch the meat.   Add a cup of hot water to the pickle remaining
and baste with it.   When done, thicken the liquid with flour and strain through
a fine sieve, to serve with the meat; also a relish of currant jelly, the same as for
venison.

This is a fine dish when the directions are faithfully followed.

STEAMED LEG OF MUTTON.

Wash and put the leg in a steamer and cook it until tender, then place in a
roasting pan, salt and dredge well with flour and set in a hot oven until nicely
browned; the water that remains in the bottom of the steamer may be used for
soup.   Serve with currant jelly.

HASHED MUTTON.

Cut into small pieces the lean of some cold mutton that has been underdone,
and season it with pepper and salt.   Take the bones and other trimmings, put
them into a sauce-pan with as much water as will cover them, and some sliced
onions, and let them stew till you have drawn from them a good gravy.   Having
skimmed it well, strain the gravy into a stew-pan, and put the mutton into it.
Have ready-boiled some carrots, turnips, potatoes and onions.   Slice them and
add to the meat and gravy.   Set the pan on the fire and let it simmer till the
meat is warmed through, but do not allow it to boil, as it has been once cooked
already.   Cover the bottom of a dish with slices of buttered toast.   Lay the meat
and vegetables upon it, and pour over them the gravy.

Tomatoes will be found an improvement.

If green peas or Lima beans are in season, you may boil them and put them
to the hashed mutton, leaving out the other vegetables, or serving them up
separately.

BROILED MUTTON CHOPS.

Loin of mutton, pepper and salt, a small piece of butter.   Cut the chops from
a tenderloin of mutton, remove a portion of the fat, and trim them into a nice
shape; slightly beat and level them; place the gridiron over a bright, clear fire,
rub the bars with a little fat, and lay on the chops.   While broiling frequently
turn them, and in about eight minutes they will be done.   Season with pepper
and salt, dish them on a very hot dish, rub a small piece of butter on each chop,
and serve very hot and expeditiously.   Nice with tomato sauce poured over them.

FRIED MUTTON CHOPS. No. 1.

Put into a frying-pan a tablespoonful of cold lard and butter mixed; have some fine mutton chops without much fat; trim off the skin. Dip each in wheat flour, or rolled cracker, and beaten egg, then lay them into the hot grease, sprinkle with salt and pepper, fry on both sides a fine brown. When done, take them up and place on a hot dish. If you wish a made gravy, turn off the superfluous grease, if any, stir into the hot gravy remaining a heaping spoonful of flour, stirring it until smooth and free from lumps, then turn into that a cup of cold water or milk; season with pepper and salt, let it boil up thick. You can serve it in a separate dish or pour it over the chops. Tomato sauce is considered fine, turned over a dish of hot fried or broiled chops.

FRIED MUTTON CHOPS. No. 2.

Prepare the chops by trimming off all extra fat and skin, season them with salt and pepper; dip each chop in beaten egg, then in rolled cracker or breadcrumbs; dip again in the egg and crumbs, and so on until they are well coated with the crumbs. Have ready a deep spider containing a pound or more of lard, hot enough to fry crullers. Drop into this hot lard the chops, frying only a few at one time, as too many cool the fat. Fry them brown, and serve up hot and dry, on a warm platter.

MUTTON CUTLETS. (Baked).

Prepare them the same as for frying, lay them in a dripping pan with a *very* little water at the bottom. Bake quickly, and baste often with butter and water. Make a little brown gravy and turn over them when they are served.

BAKED MUTTON CHOPS AND POTATOES.

Wash and peel some good potatoes and cut them into slices the thickness of a penny-piece. The quantity of potatoes must, of course, be decided according to the number of persons to whom they have to be served; but it is a safe plan to allow two, or even three, potatoes for each person. After the potatoes are sliced, wash them in two or three waters, to thoroughly cleanse them; then arrange them neatly (in layers) in a brown stone dish proper for baking purposes. Sprinkle a little salt and pepper between each layer, and add a sufficient quantity of cold water to prevent their burning. Place the dish in a very hot oven—on the top shelf—so as to brown the potatoes in a few minutes. Have ready some nice loin chops (say one for each person); trim off most of the fat; make them into a neat round shape by putting a small skewer through each. When the potatoes are nicely browned, remove the dish from the oven, and place the chops on the top. Add a little more salt and pepper, and water if required, and return the dish to a cooler part of the oven, where it may be allowed to remain until sufficiently cooked, which will be in about three-quarters of an hour. When the upper sides of the chops are a nice crisp brown, turn them over so as to brown the other side also. If, in the cooking, the potatoes appear to be getting too dry, a little more water may be gently poured in at one corner of the dish, only care must be taken to see that the water is hot this time—not cold, as at first. The dish in which the chops and potatoes are baked must be as neat-looking as possible, as it has to be sent to the table; turning the potatoes out would, of course, spoil their appearance. Those who have never tasted this dish have no idea how delightful it is. While the chops are baking the gravy drips from them among the potatoes, rendering the whole most delicious.

MUTTONETTES.

Cut from a leg of mutton slices about half an inch thick. On each slice lay a spoonful of stuffing made with bread-crumbs, beaten egg, butter, salt, pepper, sage and summer savory. Roll up the slices, pinning with little skewers or small wooden toothpicks to keep the dressing in. Put a little butter and water in a baking-pan with the muttonettes, and cook in hot oven three-quarters of an hour. Baste often, and when done thicken the gravy, pour over the meat, garnish with parsley, and serve on hot platter.

IRISH STEW.

Time about two hours. Two and a half pounds of chops, eight potatoes, four turnips, four small onions, nearly a quart of water. Take some chops from loin of mutton, place them in stew-pan in alternate layers of sliced potatoes and chops; add turnips and onions cut into pieces, pour in nearly a quart of cold water; cover stew-pan closely, let it stew gently till vegetables are ready to mash and the greater part of the gravy is absorbed; then place in a dish; serve it up hot.

MUTTON PUDDING.

Line a two-quart pudding-basin with some beef suet paste; fill the lining with thick mutton cutlets, slightly trimmed, or, if preferred, with steaks cut from the leg; season with pepper and salt, some parsley, a little thyme and two slices of onion chopped fine, and between each layer of meat, put some slices of potatoes. When the pudding is filled, wet the edges of the paste around the top of the basin, and cover with a piece of paste rolled out the size of the basin. Fasten down the edge by bearing all around with the thumb; and then with the thumb and forefinger twist the edges of the paste over and over so as to give it a corded appearance. This pudding can be set in a steamer and steamed, or boiled. The time required for cooking is about three hours. When done, turn it out carefully on a platter and serve with a rich gravy under it.

This is a very good recipe for cooking small birds.

SCRAMBLED MUTTON.

Two cups of chopped cold mutton, two tablespoonfuls of hot water, and a piece of butter as large as an English walnut. When the meat is hot, break in three eggs, and constantly stir until the eggs begin to stiffen. Season with pepper and salt.

SCALLOPED MUTTON AND TOMATOES.

Over the bottom of an earthen baking-dish place a layer of bread-crumbs, and over it alternate layers of cold roast mutton cut in thin slices, and tomatoes peeled and sliced; season each with salt, pepper and bits of butter, as laid in. The top layer should be of tomatoes, spread over with bread-crumbs. Bake three-quarters of an hour, and serve immediately.

LAMB SWEETBREADS AND TOMATO SAUCE.

Lamb sweetbreads are not always procurable, but a stroll through the markets occasionally reveals a small lot of them, which can invariably be had at a low price, owing to their excellence being recognized by but few buyers. Wash them well in salted water and parboil fifteen minutes; when cool, trim neatly and put them in a pan with just butter enough to prevent their burning; toss them about until a delicate color; season with salt and pepper and serve, surrounded with tomato sauce. See Sauces.

ROAST QUARTER OF LAMB.

Procure a nice hind-quarter, remove some of the fat that is around the kidney, skewer the lower joint up to the fillet, place it in a moderate oven, let it heat through slowly, then dredge it with salt and flour; quicken the fire, put half a pint of water into the dripping-pan, with a teaspoonful of salt. With this liquor baste the meat occasionally; serve with lettuce, green peas, and mint sauce.

A quarter of lamb weighing seven or eight pounds will require two hours to roast.

A breast of lamb roasted is very sweet, and is considered by many as preferable to hind-quarter. It requires nearly as long a time to roast as the quarter, and should be served in the same manner.

Make the gravy from the drippings, thickened with flour.

The mint sauce is made as follows: Take fresh, young spearmint leaves stripped from stems; wash and drain them or dry on a cloth, chop very fine, put in a gravy tureen, and to three tablespoonfuls of mint add two of finely powdered cut-loaf sugar; mix, and let it stand a few minutes; then pour over it six tablespoonfuls good cider or white-wine vinegar. The sauce should be made some time before dinner, so that the flavor of the mint may be well extracted.

TO BROIL THE FORE-QUARTER OF LAMB.

Take off the shoulder and lay it upon the gridiron with the breast; cut in two parts, to facilitate its cooking; put a tin sheet on top of the meat, and a weight upon that; turn the meat around frequently to prevent its burning; turn over as soon as cooked on one side; renew the coals occasionally, that all parts may cook alike; when done, season with butter, pepper, and salt,—exactly like beef-steak. It takes some time to broil it well; but when done it will be found to be equal to broiled chicken, the flavor being more delicate than when cooked otherwise. Serve with cream sauce, made as follows: Heat a tablespoonful of butter in a sauce-pan, add a teaspoonful of flour and stir until perfectly smooth; then add, slowly stirring in, a cup of cold milk; let it boil up once, and season to taste with salt and pepper and a teaspoonful of finely chopped fresh parsley. Serve in a gravy boat, all hot.

LAMB STEW.

Cut up the lamb into small pieces (after removing all the fat), say about two inches square. Wash it well and put it over the fire, with just enough cold water to cover it well, and let it heat gradually. It should stew gently until it is partly done; then add a few thin slices of salt pork, one or two onions sliced up fine, some pepper and salt if needed, and two or three raw potatoes cut up into inch pieces. Cover it closely and stew until the meat is tender. Drop in a few made dumplings, made like short biscuit, cut out *very* small. Cook fifteen minutes longer. Thicken the gravy with a little flour moistened with milk. Serve.

PRESSED LAMB.

The meat, either shoulder or leg, should be put to boil in the morning with water just enough to cover it; when tender, season with salt and pepper, then keep it over the fire until *very* tender and the juice nearly boiled out. Remove it from the fire-place in a wooden chopping-bowl, season more if necessary, chop it up like hash. Place it in a bread-pan, press out all the juice, and put it in a cool place to harden. The pressing is generally done by placing a dish over the meat and putting a flat-iron upon that. Nice cut up cold into thin slices, and the broth left from the meat would make a nice soup served with it, adding vegetables and spices.

CROQUETTES OF ODDS AND ENDS.

These are made of any scraps or bits of good food that happen to be left from one or more meals, and in such small quantities that they cannot be warmed up separately. As, for example, a couple of spoonfuls of frizzled beef and cream, the lean meat of one mutton chop, one spoonful of minced beef, two cold hard-boiled eggs, a little cold chopped potato, a little mashed potato, a chick's leg, all the gristle and hard outside taken from the meat. These things well chopped and seasoned, mixed with one raw egg, a little flour and butter, and boiling water; then made into round cakes, thick like fish-balls, and browned well with butter in a frying-pan or on a griddle.

Scraps of hash, cold rice, boiled oatmeal left from breakfast, every kind of fresh meat, bits of salt tongue, bacon, pork or ham, bits of poultry, and crumbs of bread, may be used. They should be put together with care, so as not to have them too dry to be palatable, or too moist to cook in shape. Most housekeepers would be surprised at the result, making an addition to the breakfast or lunch table. Serve on small squares of buttered toast, and with cold celery if in season.

Pork.

The best parts and those usually used for roasting are the loin, the leg, the shoulder, the spare-rib and chine. The hams, shoulders and middlings are usually salted, pickled and smoked. Pork requires more thorough cooking than most meats; if the least underdone it is unwholesome.

To choose pork: if the rind is thick and tough, and cannot be easily impressed with the finger, it is old; when fresh, it will look cool and smooth, and only corn-fed pork is good; swill or still-fed pork is unfit to cure. Fresh pork is in season from October to April. When dressing or stuffing is used, there are more or less herbs used for seasoning,—sage, summer savory, thyme, and sweet marjoram; these can be found (in the dried, pulverized form, put up in small, light packages) at most of the best druggists; still those raised and gathered at home are considered more fresh.

ROAST PIG.

Prepare your dressing as for "Dressing for Fowls," adding half an onion, chopped fine; set it inside. Take a young pig about six weeks old, wash it thoroughly inside and outside, and in another water put a teaspoonful of baking soda, and rinse out the inside again; wipe it dry with a fresh towel, salt the inside and stuff it with the prepared dressing; making it full and plump, giving it its original size and shape. Sew it up, place it in a kneeling posture in the dripping-pan, tying the legs in proper position. Pour a little hot salted water into the dripping-pan, baste with butter and water a few times as the pig warms; afterwards with gravy from the dripping-pan. When it begins to smoke all over rub it often with a rag dipped in melted butter. This will keep the skin from cracking and it still will be crisp. It will take from two to three hours to roast. Make the gravy by skimming off most of the grease; stir into that remaining in the pan a good tablespoon of flour, turn in water to make it the right consistency, season with pepper and let all boil up once. Strain, and if you like wine in it, add half a glass; turn it into a gravy boat. Place the pig upon a large, hot platter, surrounded with parsley or celery tops; place a green wreath around the neck, and a sprig of celery in its mouth. In carving, cut off its head first; split down the back, take off its hams and shoulders, and separate the ribs.

ROAST LOIN OF PORK.

Score the skin in strips about a quarter of an inch apart; place it in a dripping-pan with a *very little* water under it; cook it moderately at first, as a high heat hardens the rind before the meat is heated through. If it is very lean, it should be rubbed with fresh lard or butter when put into the pan. A stuffing might be made of bread-crumbs, chopped sage and onions, pepper and salt, and baked separately on a pie dish; this method is better than putting it in the meat, as many persons have a great aversion to its flavor. A loin weighing about six pounds will roast in two hours; allow more time if it should be very fat. Make a gravy with flour stirred into the pork drippings. Serve with apple sauce and pickles.

ROAST LEG OF PORK.

Choose a small leg of fine young pork; cut a slit in the knuckle with a sharp knife, and fill the space with sage and onion chopped, and a little pepper and salt. When half done, score the skin in slices, but do not cut deeper than the outer rind. Apple sauce and potatoes should be served with it. The gravy is to be made the same way as for beef roast, by turning off all the superfluous fat and adding a spoonful of flour stirred with a little water; add water to make the right consistency. Serve in a gravy boat.

BOILED LEG OF PORK.

For boiling, choose a small, compact, well-filled leg, and rub it well with salt; let it remain in pickle for a week or ten days, turning and rubbing it every day. An hour before dressing it put it into cold water for an hour, which improves the color. If the pork is purchased ready salted, ascertain how long the meat has been in pickle, and soak it accordingly. Put it into a boiling-pot, with sufficient cold water to cover it; let it gradually come to a boil, and remove the scum as it rises. Simmer it very gently until tender, and do not allow it to boil fast, or the knuckle will fall to pieces before the middle of the leg is done. Carrots, turnips or parsnips may be boiled with the pork, some of which should be laid around the dish as a garnish.

Time.—A leg of pork weighing eight pounds, three hours after the water boils, and to be simmered very gently.

FRESH PORK POT-PIE.

Boil a spare-rib, after removing all the fat and cracking the bones, until tender; remove the scum as it rises, and when tender season with salt and pepper; half an hour before time for serving the dinner thicken the gravy with a little flour. Have ready another kettle, into which remove all the bones and most of the gravy, leaving only sufficient to cover the pot half an inch above the rim that rests on the stove; put in the crust, cover tight, and boil steadily forty-five minutes. To prepare the crust, work into light dough a *small* bit of butter, roll it out thin, cut it in small square cakes, and lay them on the moulding-board until very light. No steam should possibly escape while the crust is cooking, and by no means allow the pot to cease boiling.

ROAST SPARE-RIB.

Trim off the rough ends neatly, crack the ribs across the middle, rub with salt and sprinkle with pepper, fold over, stuff with turkey dressing, sew up tightly, place in a dripping-pan with a pint of water, baste frequently, turning over once so as to bake both sides equally until a rich brown.

PORK TENDERLOINS.

The tenderloins are unlike any other part of the pork in flavor. They may be either fried or broiled; the latter being dryer, require to be well-buttered before serving, which should be done on a hot platter before the butter becomes oily. Fry them in a little lard, turning them to have them cooked through; when done, remove, and keep hot while making a gravy by dredging a little flour into the hot fat; if not enough add a little butter or lard, stir until browned, and add a little milk or cream, stir briskly, and pour over the dish. A little Worcestershire sauce may be added to the gravy if desired.

PORK CUTLETS.

Cut them from the leg, and remove the skin; trim them and beat them, and sprinkle on salt and pepper. Prepare some beaten egg in a pan; and on a flat dish a mixture of bread-crumbs, minced onion and sage. Put some lard or drippings into a frying pan over the fire, and when it boils put in the cutlets; having dipped every one first in the egg, and then in the seasoning. Fry them twenty or thirty minutes, turning them often. After you have taken them out of the frying-pan, skim the gravy, dredge in a little flour, give it one boil, and then pour it on the dish round the cutlets.

Have apple sauce to eat with them.

Pork cutlets prepared in this manner may be stewed instead of being fried. Add to them a little water, and stew them slowly till thoroughly done, keeping them closely covered, except when you remove the lid to skim them.

PORK CHOPS AND FRIED APPLES.

Season the chops with salt and pepper and a little powdered sage; dip them into bread-crumbs. Fry about twenty minutes, or until they are done. Put them on a hot dish; pour off part of the gravy into another pan to make a gravy to serve with them, if you choose. Then fry apples which you have sliced about two-thirds of an inch thick, cutting them around the apple so that the core is in the centre of each piece; then cut out the core. When they are browned on one side and partly cooked, turn them carefully with a pan-cake turner, and finish cooking; dish around the chops or on a separate dish.

FRIED PORK CHOPS.

Fry them the same as mutton chops. If a sausage flavor is liked, sprinkle over them a little powdered sage or summer savory, pepper and salt, and if a gravy is liked, skim off some of the fat in the pan and stir in a spoonful of flour; stir it until free from lumps, then season with pepper and salt and turn in a pint of sweet milk. Boil up and serve in a gravy boat.

PORK PIE.

Make a good plain paste. Take from two and a half to three pounds of the thick ends of a loin of pork, with very little fat on it; cut into very thin slices three inches long by two inches wide; put a layer at the bottom of a pie-dish.

Wash and chop finely a handful of parsley, also an onion. Sprinkle a small portion of these over the pork, and a little pepper and salt. Add another layer of pork, and over that some more of the seasoning, only be sparing of the nutmeg. Continue this till the dish is full. Now pour into the dish a cupful of stock or water, and a spoonful or two of catsup. Put a little paste around the edge of the dish; put on the cover, and place the pie in a rather hot oven. When the paste has risen and begins to take color, place the pie at the bottom of the oven, with some paper over it, as it will require to be baked at least two hours. Some prefer to cook the meat until partly done, before putting into the crust.

—Palmer House, Chicago.

PORK POT-PIE.

Take pieces of ribs of lean salt pork, also a slice or two of the fat of salt pork; scald it well with hot water so as to wash out the briny taste. Put it into a kettle and cover it with cold water, enough for the required want. Cover it and boil an hour, season with pepper; then add half a dozen potatoes cut into quarters. When it all commences to boil again, drop in dumplings made from this recipe:

One pint of sour or buttermilk, two eggs, well beaten, a teaspoonful of salt, a level teaspoonful of soda; dissolve in a spoonful of water as much flour as will make a very stiff batter. Drop this into the kettle or broth by spoonfuls, and cook forty minutes, closely covered.

PORK AND BEANS. (Baked).

Take two quarts of white beans, pick them over the night before, put to soak in cold water; in the morning put them in fresh water and let them scald, then turn off the water and put on more, hot; put to cook with them a piece of salt pork, gashed, as much as would make five or six slices; boil slowly till soft (not mashed), then add a tablespoonful of molasses, half a teaspoonful of soda, stir in well, put in a deep pan, and bake one hour and a half. If you do not like to use pork, salt the beans when boiling, and add a lump of butter when preparing them for the oven.

BOSTON PORK AND BEANS.

Pick over carefully a quart of small, white beans; let them soak over night in cold water; in the morning wash and drain in another water. Put on to boil in plenty of cold water with a piece of soda the size of a bean; let them come to a boil, then drain again, cover with water once more, and boil them fifteen minutes, or until the skin of the beans will crack when taken out and blown upon. Drain the beans again, put them into an earthen pot, adding a table-spoonful of salt; cover with hot water, place in the centre of a pound of salt pork, first scalding it with hot water, and scoring the rind across the top, a quarter of an inch apart to indicate where the slices are to be cut. Place the pot in the oven, and bake six hours or longer. Keep the oven a moderate heat; add hot water from the tea-kettle as needed, on account of evaporation, to keep the beans moist. When the meat becomes crisp and looks cooked, remove it, as too long baking the pork destroys its solidity.

FRIED SALT PORK.

Cut in thin slices, and freshen in cold water, roll in flour, and fry crisp. If required quickly, pour boiling water over the slices, let stand a few minutes, drain and roll in flour as before; drain off most of the grease from the frying-pan; stir in while hot one or two tablespoonfuls of flour, about half a pint of milk, a little pepper, and salt if over freshened; let it boil, and pour into a gravy dish. A teaspoonful of finely-chopped parsley will add pleasantly to the appearance of the gravy.

GRILLED SALT PORK.

Take quite thin slices of the thick part of side pork, of a clear white, and thinly streaked with lean; hold one on a toasting fork before a brisk fire to grill; have at hand a dish of cold water, in which immerse it frequently while cooking, to remove the superfluous fat and render it more delicate. Put each slice as cooked in a warm covered pan; when all are done, serve hot.

FRIED HAM AND EGGS.

Cut slices of ham quite thin, cut off the rind or skin, put them into a hot frying-pan, turning them often until crisp, taking care not to burn the slices; three minutes will cook them well. Dish them on a hot platter; then turn off the top of the grease, rinse out the pan, and put back the clear grease to fry the eggs. Break the eggs separately in a saucer, that in case a bad one should be among them it may not mix with the rest. Slip each egg gently into the frying-pan. Do not turn them while they are frying, but keep pouring some of the hot lard over them with a kitchen spoon; this will do them sufficiently on the upper side. They will be done enough in about three minutes; the white must retain its transparency so that the yolk will be seen through it. When done, take them up with a tin slice, drain off the lard, and if any part of the white is discolored or ragged, trim it off. Lay a fried egg upon each slice of the ham, and send to table hot.

COLD BACON AND EGGS.

An economical way of using bacon and eggs that have been left from a previous meal is to put them in a wooden bowl and chop them quite fine, adding a little mashed or cold chopped potato, and a little bacon gravy, if any was left. Mix and mould it into little balls, roll in raw egg and cracker-crumbs, and fry in a spider the same as frying eggs; fry a light brown on both sides. Serve hot. Very appetizing.

SCRAPPEL.

Scrappel is a most palatable dish. Take the head, heart and any lean scraps of pork, and boil until the flesh slips easily from the bones. Remove the fat, gristle and bones, then chop fine. Set the liquor in which the meat was boiled aside until cold, take the cake of fat from the surface and return to the fire. When it boils, put in the chopped meat and season well with pepper and salt. Let it boil again, then thicken with corn-meal as you would in making ordinary corn-meal mush, by letting it slip through the fingers slowly to prevent lumps. Cook an hour, stirring constantly at first, afterwards putting back on the range in a position to boil gently. When done, pour into a long, square pan, not too deep, and mold. In cold weather this can be kept several weeks. Cut into slices when cold, and fried brown, as you do mush, is a cheap and delicious breakfast dish.

TO BAKE A HAM. (Corned.)

Take a medium-sized ham and place it to soak for ten or twelve hours. Then cut away the rusty part from underneath, wipe it dry, and cover it rather thickly over with a paste made of flour and water. Put it into an earthen dish, and set it in a moderately heated oven. When done, take off the crust carefully, and peel off the skin, put a frill of cut paper around the knuckle, and raspings of bread over the fat of the ham, or serve it glazed and garnished with cut vegetables. It will take about four or five hours to bake it.

Cooked in this way the flavor is much finer than when boiled.

PIGS' FEET PICKLED.

Take twelve pigs' feet, scrape and wash them clean, put them into a sauce-pan with enough hot (not boiling) water to cover them. When partly done, salt them. It requires four to five hours to boil them soft. Pack them in a stone crock, and pour over them spiced vinegar made hot. They will be ready to use in a day or two. If you wish them for breakfast, split them, make a batter of two eggs, a cup of milk, salt, a teaspoonful of butter, with flour enough to make a thick batter; dip each piece in this and fry in hot lard. Or, dip them in beaten egg and flour and fry. Souse is good eaten cold or warm.

BOILED HAM.

First remove all dust and mold, by wiping with a coarse cloth; soak it for an hour in cold water, then wash it thoroughly. Cut with a sharp knife the hardened surface from the base and butt of the ham. Place it over the fire in *cold* water, and let it come to a moderate boil, keeping it steadily at this point, allowing it to cook twenty minutes for every pound of meat. A ham weighing twelve pounds will require four hours to cook properly, as underdone ham is very unwholesome. When the ham is to be served hot, remove the skin by peeling it off, place it on a platter, the fat side up, and dot the surface with spots of black pepper. Stick in also some whole cloves.

If the ham is to be served cold, allow it to remain in the pot until the water in which it was cooked becomes cold. This makes it more juicy. Serve it in the same manner as when served hot.

BROILED HAM.

Cut your ham into thin slices, which should be a little less than one quarter of an inch thick. Trim very closely the skin from the upper side of each slice, and also trim off the outer edge where the smoke has hardened the meat. If the ham is very salt lay it in *cold* water for one hour before cooking, then wipe with a dry cloth. Never soak ham in tepid or hot water, as it will toughen the meat.

Broil over a brisk fire, turning the slices constantly. It will require about five minutes, and should be served the last thing directly from the gridiron, placed on a warm platter, with a little butter and a sprinkle of pepper on the top of each slice. If ham or bacon is allowed to stand by the fire after it has been broiled or fried, it will speedily toughen, losing all its grateful juices.

Cold boiled ham is very nice for broiling, and many prefer it to using the raw ham.

POTTED HAM.

To two pounds of lean ham allow one pound of fat, two teaspoonfuls of powdered mace, half a nutmeg, grated, rather more than half a teaspoonful of cayenne.

Mode.—Mince the ham, fat and lean together, in the above proportion, and pound it well in a mortar, seasoning it with cayenne pepper, pounded mace and nutmeg; put the mixture into a deep baking dish, and bake for half an hour; then press it well into a stone jar, fill up the jar with clarified lard, cover it closely, and paste over it a piece of thick paper. If well seasoned, it will keep a long time in winter, and will be found very convenient for sandwiches, etc.

BOLOGNA SAUSAGE. (Cooked.)

Two pounds of lean pork, two pounds of lean veal, two pounds of fresh lean beef, two pounds of fat salt pork, one pound beef suet, ten tablespoonfuls of powdered sage, one ounce each of parsley, savory, marjoram and thyme, mixed. Two teaspoonfuls of cayenne pepper, the same of black, one grated nutmeg, one teaspoonful of cloves, one minced onion, salt to taste. Chop or grind the meat and suet; season, and stuff into beef skins; tie these up, prick each in several places to allow the escape of steam; put into hot, not boiling water, and heat gradually to the boiling point. Cook slowly for one hour; take out the skins and lay them to dry in the sun, upon clean, sweet straw or hay. Rub the outside of the skins with oil or melted butter, and place in a cool, dry cellar. If you wish to keep them more than a week, rub ginger or pepper on the outside, then wash it off before using. This is eaten without further cooking. Cut in round slices and lay sliced lemon around the edge of the dish, as many like to squeeze a few drops upon the sausage before eating. These are very nice smoked like hams.

COUNTRY PORK SAUSAGES.

Six pounds lean fresh pork, three pounds of chine fat, three tablespoonfuls of salt, two of black pepper, four tablespoonfuls of pounded and sifted sage, two of summer savory. Chop the lean and fat pork finely, mix the seasoning in with your hands, taste to see that it has the right flavor, then put them into cases, either the cleaned intestines of the hog, or make long, narrow bags of stout muslin, large enough to contain each enough sausage for a family dish. Fill these with the meat, dip in melted lard, and hang them in a cool, dry dark place. Some prefer to pack the meat in jars, pouring melted lard over it, covering the top, to be taken out as wanted and made into small round cakes with the hands, then fried brown. Many like spices added to the seasoning—cloves, mace and nutmeg. This is a matter of taste.

—Marion Harland.

TO FRY SAUSAGES.

Put a small piece of lard or butter into the frying-pan. Prick the sausages with a fork, lay them in the melted grease, keep moving them about, turning them frequently to prevent bursting; in ten or twelve minutes they will be sufficiently browned and cooked. Another sure way to prevent the cases from bursting is to cover them with cold water and let it come to the boiling point; turn off the water and fry them.   Sausages are nicely cooked by putting them in a baking-pan and browning them in the oven, turning them once or twice.   In this way you avoid all smoke and disagreeable odor.   A pound will cook brown in ten minutes in a hot oven.

HEAD CHEESE.

Boil the forehead, ears and feet, and nice scraps trimmed from the hams of a fresh pig, until the meat will almost drop from the bones.   Then separate the meat from the bones, put it in a large chopping-bowl, and season with pepper, salt, sage and summer savory.   Chop it rather coarsely; put it back into the same kettle it was boiled in, with just enough of the liquor in which it was boiled to prevent its burning; warm it through thoroughly, mixing it well together. Now pour it into a strong muslin bag, press the bag between two flat surfaces, with a heavy weight on top; when cold and solid it can be cut in slices.   Good cold, or warmed up in vinegar.

TO CURE HAMS AND BACON.   (A Prize Recipe.)

For each hundred pounds of hams, make a pickle of ten pounds of salt, two pounds of brown sugar, two ounces of saltpetre, and one ounce of red pepper, and from four to four and a half gallons of water, or just enough to cover the hams, after being packed in a water-tight vessel, or enough salt to make a brine to float a fresh egg high enough, that is to say, out of water.   First rub the hams with common salt, and lay them into a tub.   Take the above ingredients, put them into a vessel over the fire, and heat it hot, stirring it frequently; remove all the scum, allow it to boil ten minutes, let it cool and pour over the meat.   After laying in this brine five or six weeks, take out, drain and wipe, and smoke from two to three weeks.   Small pieces of bacon may remain in this pickle two weeks, which would be sufficient.

TO SMOKE HAMS AND FISH AT HOME.

Take an old hogshead, stop up all the crevices, and fix a place to put a cross-stick near the bottom, to hang the articles to be smoked on.   Next, in the side, cut a hole near the top, to introduce an iron pan filled with hickory wood sawdust and small pieces of green wood.   Having turned the hoshead upside down, hang the articles upon the cross-stick, introduce the iron pan in the opening, and place a piece of red-hot iron in the pan, cover it with sawdust, and all will be complete. Let a large ham remain ten days, and keep up a good smoke.   The best way for keeping hams is to sew them in coarse cloths, whitewashed on the outside. .

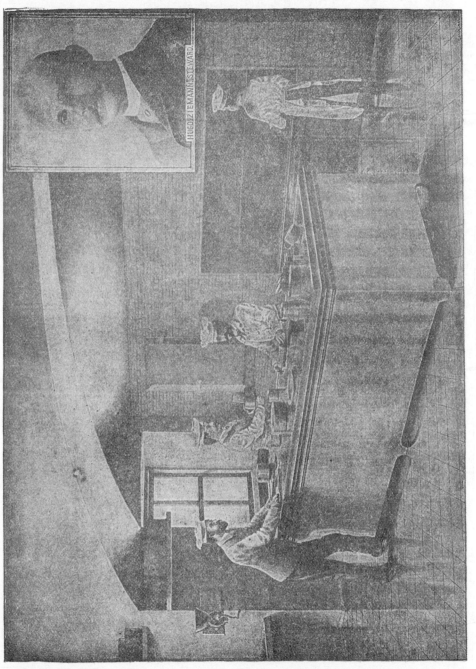

HUGO ZIEMANN STEWARD.

THE WHITE HOUSE KITCHEN.

TO CURE ENGLISH BACON.

This process is called the " dry cure, " and is considered far preferable to the New England or Yankee style of putting prepared brine or pickle over the meat. First the hog should not be too large or too fat, weighing not over two hundred pounds; then after it is dressed and cooled cut it up into proper pieces; allow to every hundred pounds a mixture of four quarts of common salt, one quarter of a pound of saltpetre and four pounds of sugar. Rub this preparation thoroughly over and into each piece, then place them into a tight tub or suitable cask; there will a brine form of itself, from the juices of the meat, enough at least to baste it with, which should be done two or three times a week; turning each piece every time.

In smoking this bacon, the sweetest flavor is derived from black birch chips, ·but if these are not to be had, the next best wood is hickory; the smoking with corn-cobs imparts a rank flavor to this bacon, which is very distasteful to English people visiting this country. It requires three weeks or a month to smoke this bacon properly.

—Berkshire Recipe.

TO TRY OUT LARD.

Skin the leaf lard carefully, cut it into small pieces, and put it into a kettle or sauce-pan; pour in a cupful of water to prevent burning; set it over the fire where it will melt slowly. Stir it frequently and let it simmer until nothing remains but brown scraps. Remove the scraps with a perforated skimmer, throw in a little salt to settle the fat, and, when clear, strain through a coarse cloth into jars. Remember to watch it constantly, stirring it from the bottom until the salt is thrown in to settle it; then set it back on the range until clear. If it scorches it gives it a very bad flavor.

Sauces and Dressings.

DRAWN BUTTER

Melted butter is the foundation of most of the common sauces. Have a covered sauce-pan for this purpose. One lined with porcelain will be best. Take a quarter of a pound of the best fresh butter, cut it up, and mix with it about one tablespoonful of flour. When it is thoroughly mixed, put it into the sauce-pan, and add to it half a teacupful of hot water. Cover the sauce-pan and set it in a large tin pan of boiling water. Shake it round continually (always moving it the same way) till it is entirely melted and begins to simmer. Then let it rest till it boils up.

If you set it on too hot a fire, it will be oily.

If the butter and flour are not well mixed, it will be lumpy.

If you put too much water, it will be thin and poor. All these defects are to be carefully avoided.

In melting butter for sweet or pudding sauce, you may use milk instead of water.

TARTARE SAUCE.

The raw yolks of two eggs, half a teacupful of pure olive oil, three tablespoonfuls of vinegar, one of made mustard, one teaspoonful of sugar, a quarter of a teaspoonful of pepper, one teaspoonful of salt, one of onion juice, one tablespoonful of chopped capers, one of chopped cucumber pickle. Put together the same as mayonnaise dressing, adding the chopped ingredients the last thing.

This sauce is good for fried or boiled fish, boiled tongue, fish salad, and may be used with fried and broiled meats.

EGG SAUCE, OR WHITE SAUCE.

Mix two tablespoonfuls of sifted flour with half a teacup of warm butter. Place over the fire a sauce-pan containing a pint of sweet milk and a salt-spoon of salt, and a dash of white pepper; when it reaches the boiling point, add the butter and flour, stirring briskly until it thickens and becomes like cream. Have ready three cold, hard-boiled eggs, sliced and chopped, add them to the sauce; let them heat through thoroughly, and serve in a boat. If you have plenty of cream, use it and omit the butter. By omitting the eggs, you have the same as "White Sauce."

OYSTER SAUCE.

Take a pint of oysters and heat them in their own liquor long enough to come to a boil, or until they begin to ruffle. Skim out the oysters into a warm dish, put into the liquor a teacup of milk or cream, two tablespoonfuls of cold butter, a pinch of cayenne and salt; thicken with a tablespoonful of flour stirred to a paste, boil up and then add the oysters.

Oyster sauce is used for fish, boiled turkey chickens and boiled white meats of most kinds.

LOBSTER SAUCE.

Put the coral and spawn of a boiled lobster into a mortar, with a tablespoonful of butter; pound it to a smooth mass, then rub it through a sieve; melt nearly a quarter of a pound of sweet butter, with a wineglass of water or vinegar; add a teaspoonful of made mustard, stir in the coral and spawn, and a little salt and pepper; stir it until it is smooth, and serve. Some of the meat of the lobster may be chopped fine, and stirred into it.

SAUCE FOR SALMON AND OTHER FISH.

One cupful of milk heated to a boil and thickened with a tablespoonful of corn-starch previously wet up with cold water, the liquor from the salmon, one great spoonful of butter, one raw egg beaten light, the juice of half a lemon, mace and cayenne pepper to taste. Add the egg to thickened milk when you have stirred in the butter and liquor; take from the fire, season and let it stand in hot water three minutes, covered. Lastly put in lemon juice and turn out immediately. Pour it all over and around the salmon.

SAUCE FOR BOILED COD.

To one gill of boiling water add as much milk; stir into this while boiling two tablespoonfuls of butter gradually, one tablespoonful of flour wet up with cold water; as it thickens, the chopped yolk of one boiled egg, and one raw egg beaten light. Take directly from the fire, season with pepper, salt, a little chopped parsley and the juice of one lemon, and set covered in boiling water (but not over fire) five minutes, stirring occasionally. Pour part of the sauce over fish when dished; the rest in a boat. Serve mashed potatoes with it.

FISH SAUCE. No. 2.

Make a pint of drawn butter, add one tablespoonful of pepper sauce or Worcestershire sauce, a little salt and six hard-boiled eggs, chopped fine. Pour over boiled fish and garnish with sliced lemon. Very nice.

FISH SAUCE. No. 3.

Half a cupful of melted butter, half a cupful of vinegar, two tablespoonfuls or tomato catsup, salt, and a tablespoonful of made mustard. Boil ten minutes.

CELERY SAUCE.

Mix two tablespoonfuls of flour with half a teacupful of butter; have ready a pint of boiling milk; stir the flour and butter into the milk; take three heads of celery, cut into small bits, and boil for a few minutes in water, which strain off; put the celery into the melted butter, and keep it stirred over the fire for five or ten minutes. This is very nice with boiled fowl or turkey. Another way to make celery sauce is: Boil a head of celery until quite tender, then put it through a sieve; put the yolk of an egg in a basin, and beat it well with the strained juice of a lemon; add the celery and a couple of spoonfuls of liquor in which the turkey was boiled; salt and pepper to taste.

CAPER SAUCE.

Chop the capers a very little, unless quite small; make half a pint of drawn butter, to which add the capers, with a large spoonful of the juice from the bottle in which they are sold; let it just simmer, and serve in a tureen. Nasturtiums much resemble capers in taste, though larger, and may be used, and, in fact, are preferred by many. They are grown on a climbing vine, and are cultivated for their blossom and for pickling. When used as capers they should be chopped more. If neither capers nor nasturtiums are at hand, some pickles chopped up form a very good substitute in the sauce.

BREAD SAUCE.

One cup of stale bread-crumbs, one onion, two ounces of butter, pepper and salt, a little mace. Cut the onion fine, and boil it in milk till quite soft; then strain the milk on to the stale bread-crumbs, and let it stand an hour. Put it in a sauce-pan with the boiled onion, pepper, salt and mace. Give it a boil, and serve in sauce tureen. This sauce can also be used for grouse, and is very nice. Roast partridges are nice served with bread-crumbs, fried brown in butter, with cranberry or currant jelly laid beside them in the platter.

TOMATO SAUCE.

Take a quart can of tomatoes, put it over the fire in a stew-pan, put in one slice of onion, and two cloves, a little pepper and salt; boil about twenty minutes; then remove from the fire and strain it through a sieve. Now melt in another pan an ounce of butter, and as it melts, sprinkle in a tablespoonful of flour; stir it until it browns and froths a little. Mix the tomato pulp with it, and it is ready for the table.

Excellent for mutton chops, roast beef, etc.

ONION SAUCE.

Work together until light a heaping tablespoonful of flour, and half a cupful of butter, and gradually add two cups of boiling milk; stir constantly until it comes to a boil; then stir into that four tender boiled onions that have been chopped fine. Salt and pepper to taste. Serve with boiled veal, poultry or mutton.

CHILI SAUCE.

Boil together two dozen ripe tomatoes, three small green peppers, or a half teaspoonful of cayenne pepper, one onion cut fine, half a cup of sugar. Boil until thick; then add two cups of vinegar; then strain the whole, set back on the fire and add a tablespoonful of salt, and a teaspoonful each of ginger, allspice, cloves and cinnamon; boil all five minutes, remove and seal in glass bottles. This is very nice.

MINT SAUCE.

Take fresh young spearmint leaves, stripped from the stems; wash and drain them, or dry on a cloth. Chop very fine, put in a gravy boat, and to three tablespoonfuls of mint put two of white sugar; mix and let it stand a few minutes, then pour over it six tablespoonfuls of good cider or white-wine vinegar. The sauce should be made some time before it is to be used, so that the flavor of the mint may be well extracted. Fine with roast lamb.

SHARP BROWN SAUCE.

Put in a sauce-pan one tablespoonful of chopped onion, three tablespoonfuls of good cider vinegar, six tablespoonfuls of water, three of tomato catsup, a little pepper and salt, half a cup of melted butter, in which stir a tablespoonful of sifted flour; put all together and boil until it thickens. This is most excellent with boiled meats, fish and poultry.

BECHAMEL SAUCE.

Put three tablespoonfuls of butter in a sauce-pan; add three tablespoonfuls of sifted flour, quarter of a teaspoonful of nutmeg, ten pepper-corns, a teaspoonful of salt; beat all well together; then add to this, three slices of onion, two slices of carrot, two sprigs of parsley, two of thyme, a bay leaf and half a dozen mushrooms cut up. Moisten the whole with a pint of stock or water and a cup of sweet cream. Set it on the stove and cook slowly for half of an hour, watching closely that it does not burn; then strain through a sieve. Most excellent with roast veal, meats and fish.   *—St. Charles Hotel, New Orleans.*

MAITRE D'HOTEL SAUCE.

Make a teacupful of drawn butter; add to it the juice of a lemon, two table-spoonfuls of minced onion, three tablespoonfuls of chopped parsley, a teaspoon-ful of powdered thyme or summer savory, a pinch of cayenne and salt. Simmer over the fire, and stir well. Excellent with all kinds of fish.

WINE SAUCE FOR GAME.

Half a glass of currant jelly, half a glass of port wine, half a glass of water, a tablespoonful of cold butter, a teaspoonful of salt, the juice of half a lemon, a pinch of cayenne pepper and three cloves. Simmer all together a few minutes, adding the wine after it is strained. A few spoonfuls of the gravy from the game may be added to it. This sauce is especially nice with venison.

—Tabor House, Denver.

HOLLANDAISE SAUCE.

Half a teacupful of butter, the juice of half a lemon, the yolk of two eggs, a speck of cayenne pepper, half a cupful of boiling water, half a teaspoonful of salt; beat the butter to a cream, add the yolks of eggs one by one; then the lemon-juice, pepper and salt, beating all thoroughly; place the bowl in which is the mixture in a sauce-pan of boiling water; beat with an egg-beater until it begins to thicken which will be in about a minute; then add the boiling water, beating all the time; stir until it begins to thicken like soft custard; stir a few minutes after taking from the fire; be careful not to cook it too long. This is very nice with baked fish.

—Miss Parloa.

CURRANT JELLY SAUCE.

Three tablespoonfuls of butter, one onion, one bay leaf, one sprig of celery, two tablespoonfuls of vinegar, half a cupful of currant jelly, one tablespoonful of flour, one pint of stock, salt, pepper. Cook the butter and onion until the latter begins to color. Add the flour and herbs. Stir until brown; add the stock, and simmer twenty minutes. Strain, and skim off all the fat. Add the jelly, and stir over the fire until it is melted. Serve with game.

BROWN SAUCE.

Delicious sauce for meats is made in this way: Slice a large onion, and fry in butter till it is brown; then cover the onion with rich brown gravy, which is left from roast beef; add mustard, salt and pepper, and if you choose a tablespoonful of Worcestershire sauce; let this boil up, and if too thick, thin it with a little stock or gravy, or even a little hot water with butter. Pour this when done through a fine sieve. Of course a larger quantity can be prepared at once than is mentioned here.

MUSHROOM SAUCE.

Wash a pint of small button mushrooms, remove the stems and outside skins, stew them slowly in veal gravy or milk or cream, adding an onion, and seasoning with pepper, salt and a little butter rolled in flour. Their flavor will be heightened by salting a few the night before, to extract the juice. In dressing mushrooms, only those of a dull pearl color on the outside and the under part tinged with pale pink should be selected. If there is a poisonous one among them, the onion in the sauce will turn black. In such a case throw the whole away. Used for poultry, beef or fish.

APPLE SAUCE.

When you wish to serve apple sauce with meat prepare it in this way: Cook the apples until they are very tender, then stir them thoroughly so there will be no lumps at all; add the sugar and a little gelatine dissolved in warm water, a tablespoonful in a pint of sauce; pour the sauce into bowls, and when cold it will be stiff like jelly, and can be turned out on a plate. Cranberry sauce can be treated in the same way. Many prefer this to plain stewing.

Apples cooked in the following way look very pretty on a tea-table, and are appreciated by the palate. Select firm, round greenings; pare neatly and cut in halves; place in a shallow stew-pan with sufficient boiling water to cover them, and a cupful of sugar to every six apples. Each half should cook on the bottom of the pan, and be removed from the others so as not to injure its shape. Stew slowly until the pieces are very tender; remove to a dish carefully; boil the syrup half an hour longer; pour it over the apples and eat cold. A few pieces of lemon boiled in the syrup adds to the flavor. These sauces are a fine accompaniment to roast pork or roast goose.

CIDER APPLE SAUCE.

Boil four quarts of new cider until it is reduced to two quarts, then put into it enough pared and quartered apples to fill the kettle; let the whole stew over a moderate fire four hours; add cinnamon if liked. This sauce is very fine with almost any kind of meat.

OLD-FASHIONED APPLE SAUCE.

Pare and chop a dozen medium-sized apples, put them in a deep pudding-dish; sprinkle over them a heaping coffee-cupful of sugar and one of water. Place them in the oven and bake slowly two hours or more, or until they are a deep red brown; quite as nice as preserves.

CRANBERRY SAUCE.

One quart of cranberries, two cupfuls of sugar, and a pint of water. Wash the cranberries, then put them on the fire with the water, but in a covered sauce-pan. Let them simmer until each cranberry bursts open; then remove the cover of the sauce-pan, add the sugar and let them all boil for twenty minutes without the cover. The cranberries must never be stirred from the time they are placed on the fire. This is an unfailing recipe for a most delicious preparation of cran-berries. Very fine with turkey and game.

APPLE OMELET.

Apple omelet, to be served with broiled spare-rib or roast pork, is very deli-cate. Take nine large, tart apples, four eggs, one cup of sugar, one tablespoon-ful of butter; add cinnamon or other spices to suit your taste; stew the apples till they are very soft; mash them so that there will be no lumps; add the butter and sugar while they are still warm; but let them cool before putting in the beaten eggs; bake this till it is brown; you may put it all in a shallow pudding-dish or in two tin plates to bake. Very good.

FLAVORED VINEGARS.

Almost all the flavorings used for meats and salads may be prepared in vinegar with little trouble and expense, and will be found useful to impart an acid to flavors when lemons are not at hand.

Tarragon, sweet basil, burnet, green mint, sage, thyme, sweet-marjoram, etc., may be prepared by putting three ounces of either of these herbs, when in blossom, into one gallon of sharp vinegar; let stand ten days, strain off clear, and bottle for use.

Celery and cayenne may be prepared, using three ounces of the seed as above.

CUCUMBER VINEGAR.

Ingredients.—Ten large cucumbers, or twelve smaller ones, one quart of vinegar, two onions, two shalots, one tablespoonful of salt, two tablespoonfuls of pepper, a quarter of a teaspoonful of cayenne.

Mode.—Pare and slice the cucumbers, put them in a stone jar, or wide-mouthed bottle, with the vinegar; slice the onions and shalots, and add them, with all the other ingredients, to the cucumbers. Let it stand four or five days; boil it all up, and when cold, strain the liquor through a piece of muslin, and store it away in small bottles well sealed. This vinegar is a very nice addition to gravies, hashes, etc., as well as a great improvement to salads, or to eat with cold meat.

CURRY POWDER.

To make curry powder, take one ounce of ginger, one ounce of mustard, one ounce of pepper, three ounces of coriander seed, three ounces of turmeric, half an ounce of cardamoms, one-quarter ounce of cayenne pepper, one-quarter ounce of cinnamon, and one-quarter ounce of cummin seed. Pound all these ingredients very fine in a mortar; sift them and cork tight in a bottle.

This can be had already prepared at most druggists, and it is much less trouble to purchase it than to make it at home.

CURRY SAUCE.

One tablespoonful of butter, one of flour, one teaspoonful of curry powder, one large slice of onion, one large cupful of stock, salt and pepper to taste. Cut the onion fine, and fry brown in the butter. Add the flour and curry powder. Stir for one minute, add the stock and season with the salt and pepper. Simmer five minutes; then strain and serve. This sauce can be served with a broil or *sauté* of meat or fish.

TO BROWN BUTTER.

Put a lump of butter into a hot frying-pan, and toss it about until it browns. Stir brown flour into it until it is smooth and begins to boil. Use it for coloring gravies, and sauces for meats.

TO BROWN FLOUR.

Spread flour upon a tin pie-plate, set it upon the stove or in a *very* hot oven, and stir continually after it begins to color, until it is brown all through.

Keep it always on hand; put away in glass jars covered closely. It is excellent for coloring and thickening many dishes.

TO MAKE MUSTARD.

Boil some vinegar; take four spoonfuls of mustard, half of a teaspoonful of sugar, a salt-spoonful of salt, a tablespoonful of melted butter; mix well.

FRENCH MUSTARD.

Three tablespoonfuls of mustard, one tablespoonful of granulated sugar, well worked together, then beat in an egg until it is smooth; add one teacupful of vinegar, a little at a time, working it all smooth; then set on the stove and cook three or four minutes, stirring all the time; when cool, add one tablespoonful of the best olive oil, taking care to get it all thoroughly worked in and smooth. You will find this very nice.

—*Mrs. D. Riegel.*

KITCHEN PEPPER.

Mix one ounce of ground ginger, half an ounce each of black pepper, ground cinnamon, nutmeg and allspice, one teaspoonful of ground cloves, and six ounces of salt. Keep in a tightly corked bottle.

—*The Caterer.*

PREPARED COCOANUT (For Pies, Puddings, &c.)

To prepare cocoanut for future use; first cut a hole through the meat at one of the holes in the end, draw off the milk, then loosen the meat by pounding the nut well on all sides. Crack the nut and take out the meat, and place the pieces of meat in a cool open oven over night, or for a few hours, to dry; then grate it. If there is more grated than is needed for present use, sprinkle it with sugar, and spread out in a cool dry place. When dry enough put away in dry cans or bottles. Will keep for weeks.

SPICES.

Ginger is the root of a shrub first known in Asia, and now cultivated in the West Indies and Sierra Leone. The stem grows three or four feet high, and dies every year. There are two varieties of ginger—the white and black—caused by taking more or less care in selecting and preparing the roots, which are always dug in winter, when the stems are withered. The white is the best.

Cinnamon is the inner bark of a beautiful tree, a native of Ceylon, that grows from twenty to thirty feet in height and lives to be centuries old.

Cloves.—Native to the Molucca Islands, and so called from resemblance to a nail (*clavis*). The East Indians call them "changkek," from the Chinese "te-chengkia" (fragrant nails). They grow on a strait, smooth-barked tree, about forty feet high. Cloves are not fruits, but blossoms. gathered before they are quite unfolded.

Allspice.—A berry so called because it combines the flavor of several spices grows abundantly on the allspice or bayberry tree; native of South America and the West Indies. A single tree has been known to produce one hundred and fifty pounds of berries. They are purple when ripe.

Black pepper is made by grinding the dried berry of a climbing vine, native to the East Indies. White pepper is obtained from the same berries, freed from their husk or rind. Red or cayenne pepper is obtained by grinding the scarlet pod or seed-vessel of a tropical plant that is now cultivated in all parts of the world.

Nutmeg is the kernel of a small, smooth, pear-shaped fruit that grows on a tree in the Molucca Islands, and other parts of the East. The trees commence bearing in the seventh year, and continue fruitful until they are seventy or eighty years old. Around the nutmeg or kernel is a bright, brown shell. This shell has a soft scarlet covering, which, when flattened out and dried, is known as mace. The best nutmegs are solid, and emit oil when pricked with a pin.

HERBS FOR WINTER.

To prepare herbs for winter use, such as sage, summer savory, thyme, mint or any of the sweet herbs, they should be gathered fresh in their season, or procure them from the market. Examine them well, throwing out all poor sprigs; then wash and shake them; tie into small bundles, and tie over the bundles a piece of netting or old lace, (to keep off the dust); hang up in a warm, dry place, the leaves downward. In a few days the herb will be thoroughly dry and brittle. Or you may place them in a cool oven, and let them remain in it until perfectly dry. Then pick off all the leaves, and the tender tops of the stems; put them in a clean, large-mouthed bottle that is perfectly dry. When wanted for use, rub fine, and sift through a sieve. It is much better to put them in bottles as soon as dried, as long exposure to the air causes them to lose strength and flavor.

MEATS AND THEIR ACCOMPANIMENTS.

With roast beef: tomato sauce, grated horse-radish, mustard, cranberry sauce, pickles.

With roast pork: apple sauce, cranberry sauce.

With roast veal: tomato sauce, mushroom sauce, onion sauce and cranberry sauce. Horse-radish and lemons are good.

With roast mutton: currant jelly, caper sauce.

With boiled mutton: onion sauce, caper sauce.

With boiled fowls: bread sauce, onion sauce, lemon sauce, cranberry sauce, jellies. Also cream sauce.

With roast lamb: mint sauce.

With roast turkey: cranberry sauce, currant jelly.

With boiled turkey: oyster sauce.

With venison or wild ducks: cranberry sauce, currant jelly, or currant jelly warmed with port wine.

With roast goose: apple sauce, cranberry sauce, grape or currant jelly.

With boiled fresh mackerel: stewed gooseberries.

With boiled blue fish: white cream sauce, lemon sauce.

With broiled shad: mushroom sauce, parsley or egg sauce.

With fresh salmon: green peas, cream sauce.

Pickles are good with all roast meats, and in fact are suitable accompaniments to all kinds of meats in general.

Spinach is the proper accompaniment to veal; green peas to lamb.

Lemon juice makes a very grateful addition to nearly all the insipid members of the fish kingdom. Slices of lemon cut into very small dice and stirred into drawn butter and allowed to come to the boiling point, served with fowls, is a fine accompaniment.

VEGETABLES APPROPRIATE TO DIFFERENT DISHES.

Potatoes are good with all meats. With fowls they are nicest mashed. Sweet potatoes are most appropriate with roast meats, as also are onions, winter squash, cucumbers and asparagus.

Carrots, parsnips, turnips, greens and cabbage are generally eaten with boiled meat, and corn, beets, peas and beans are appropriate to either boiled or roasted meat. Mashed turnip is good with roast pork and with boiled meats. Tomatoes are good with almost every kind of meats, especially with roasts.

WARM DISHES FOR BREAKFAST.

The following of hot breakfast dishes may be of assistance in knowing what to provide for the comfortable meal called breakfast.

Broiled beef steak, broiled chops, broiled chicken, broiled fish, broiled quail on toast, fried pork tenderloins, fried pig's feet, fried oysters, fried clams, fried liver and bacon, fried chops, fried pork, ham and eggs fried, veal cutlets breaded, sausages, fricasseed tripe, fricasseed kidneys, turkey or chicken hash, corn beef hash, beef croquettes, codfish balls, creamed codfish, stewed meats on toast, poached eggs on toast, omelettes, eggs boiled plain, and eggs cooked in any of the various styles.

VEGETABLES FOR BREAKFAST.

Potatoes in any of the various modes of cooking, also stewed tomatoes, stewed corn, raw radishes, cucumbers sliced, tomatoes sliced raw, water cress, lettuce.

To be included with the breakfast dishes: oatmeal mush, cracked wheat, hominy or corn-meal mush, these with cream, milk and sugar or syrup.

Then numberless varieties of bread can be selected, in form of rolls, fritters, muffins, waffles, corn-cakes, griddle-cakes, etc., etc.

For beverages, coffee, chocolate and cocoa, or tea if one prefers it; these are all suitable for the breakfast table.

When obtainable always have a vase of choice flowers on the breakfast table; also some fresh fruit, if convenient.

Salads.

Everything in the make-up of a salad should be of the freshest material, the vegetables crisp and fresh, the oil or butter the very best, meats, fowl and fish well cooked, pure cider or white-wine vinegar—in fact, every ingredient first-class, to insure success.

The vegetables used in salad are: Beet-root, onions, potatoes, cabbage, lettuce, celery, cucumbers, lentils, haricots, winter cress, peas, French beans, radish, cauliflower,—all these may be used judiciously in salad, if properly seasoned, according to the following directions:

Chervil is a delicious salad herb, invariably found in all salads prepared by a French *gourmet.* No man can be a true epicure who is unfamiliar with this excellent herb. It may be procured from the vegetable stands at Fulton and Washington markets the year round. Its leaves resemble parsley, but are more divided, and a few of them added to a breakfast salad give a delightful flavor.

Chervil vinegar.—A few drops of this vinegar added to fish sauces or salads is excellent, and well repays the little trouble taken in its preparation. Half fill a bottle with fresh or dry chervil leaves; fill the bottle with good vinegar and heat it gently by placing it in warm water, which bring to boiling point; remove from the fire; when cool cork, and in two weeks it will be ready for use.

MAYONNAISE DRESSING.

Put the yolks of four fresh raw eggs, with two hard-boiled ones, into a cold bowl. Rub these as smoooth as possible before introducing the oil; a good measure of oil is a tablespoonful to each yolk of raw egg. All the art consists in introducing the oil by degrees, a few drops at a time. You can never make a good salad without taking plenty of time. When the oil is well mixed, and assumes the appearance of jelly, put in two heaping teaspoonfuls of dry table salt, one of pepper, and one of made mustard. Never put in salt and pepper before this stage of the process, because the salt and pepper would coagulate the albumen of the eggs, and you could not get the dressing smooth. Two table-spoonfuls of vinegar added gradually.

The *Mayonnaise* should be the thickness of thick cream when finished, but if it looks like curdling when mixing it, set in the ice-box or in a *cold* place for about forty minutes or an hour, then mix it again. It is a good idea to place it in a pan of cracked ice while mixing.

For lobster salad, use the *coral*, mashed and pressed through a sieve, then add to the above.

Salad dressing should be kept in a separate bowl in a cold place, and not mixed with the salad until the moment it is to be served, or it may lose its crispness and freshness.

DRESSING FOR COLD SLAW. (Cabbage Salad.)

Beat up two eggs, with two tablespoonfuls of sugar add a piece of butter the size of half an egg, a teaspoonful of mustard, a little pepper, and lastly a teacup of vinegar. Put all these ingredients into a dish over the fire, and cook like a soft custard. Some think it improved by adding half a cupful of thick sweet cream to this dressing; in that case use less vinegar. Either way is very fine.

SALAD CREAM DRESSING. No. 1.

One cup fresh cream, one spoonful fine flour, the whites of two eggs beaten stiff, three spoonfuls of vinegar, two spoonfuls of salad oil or soft butter, two spoon-fuls of powdered sugar, one teaspoonful salt, one half teaspoonful pepper, one teaspoonful of made mustard. Heat cream almost to boiling; stir in the flour, previously wet with cold milk; boil two minutes, stirring all the time; add sugar and take from fire. When half cold, beat in whipped whites of egg; set aside to cool. When quite cold, whip in the oil or butter, pepper, mustard and salt; if the salad is ready, add vinegar, and pour at once over it.

CREAM DRESSING. No. 2.

Two tablespoonfuls of whipped sweet cream, two of sugar, and four of vine-gar; beat well and pour over the cabbage, previously cut very fine and seasoned with salt

FRENCH SALAD DRESSING.

Mix one saltspoon of pepper with one of salt; add three tablespoonfuls of olive oil, and one even tablespoonful of onion, scraped fine; then one tablespoonful of vinegar; when well mixed, pour the mixture over your salad, and stir all till well mingled.

The merit of a salad is that it should be cool, fresh and crisp. For vegetables, use only the delicate white stalks of celery, the small heart-leaves of lettuce, or tenderest stalks and leaves of the white cabbage. Keep the vegetable portions crisp and fresh, until the time for serving, when add the meat. For chicken and fish salads, use the Mayonnaise dressing. For simple vegetable salads, the French dressing is most appropriate, using onion rather than garlic.

MIXED SUMMER SALAD.

Three heads of lettuce, two teaspoonfuls of green mustard leaves; a handful of water-cresses; five tender radishes; one cucumber; three hard-boiled eggs; two teaspoonfuls of white sugar; one teaspoonful of salt; one teaspoonful of pepper; one teaspoonful of made mustard; one teacupful of vinegar; half a teacupful of oil.

Mix all well together, and serve with a lump of ice in the middle.

—"Common Sense in the Household."

CHICKEN SALAD.

Boil the fowls tender, and remove all the fat, gristle and skin; mince the meat in small pieces, but do not hash it. To one chicken put twice and a half its weight in celery, cut in pieces of about one-quarter of an inch; mix thoroughly, and set it in a cool place,—the ice chest.

In the meantime prepare a "Mayonnaise dressing," and when ready for the table pour this dressing over the chicken and celery, tossing and mixing it thoroughly. Set it in a cool place until ready to serve. Garnish with celery tips, or cold hard-boiled eggs, lettuce-leaves, from the heart, cold boiled beets or capers olives.

Crisp cabbage is a good substitute for celery; when celery is not to be had use celery vinegar in the dressing. Turkey makes a fine salad.

LOBSTER SALAD. No. 1.

Prepare a sauce with the *coral* of a fine, new lobster, boiled fresh for about half an hour. Pound and rub it smooth, and mix very gradually with a dressing made from the yolks of two hard-boiled eggs, a tablespoonful of made mustard, three of salad oil, two of vinegar, one of white powdered sugar, a small teaspoonful of salt, as much black pepper, a pinch of cayenne and two fresh yolks of eggs. Next fill your salad bowl with some shred lettuce, the better part of two, leaving the small curled centre to garnish your dish with. Mingle with this the flesh of your lobster, torn, broken or cut into bits seasoned with salt and pepper and a small portion of the dressing. Pour over the whole the rest of the dressing; put your lettuce-hearts down the centre and arrange upon the sides slices of hard-boiled eggs.

LOBSTER SALAD. No. 2.

Using canned lobsters, take a can, skim off all the oil on the surface, and chop the meat up coarsely on a flat dish. Prepare the same way six heads of celery; mix a teaspoonful of mustard into a smooth paste with a little vinegar; add two fresh yolks of eggs; a tablespoonful of butter, creamed, a small teaspoonful of salt, the same of pepper, a quarter of a teaspoonful of cayenne pepper, a gill of·vinegar, and the mashed yolks of two hard-boiled eggs. Mix a small portion of the dressing with the celery and meat, and turn the remainder over all. Garnish with the green tops of celery, and a hard-boiled egg, cut into thin rings.

FISH SALAD.

Take a fresh white fish or trout, boil and chop it, but not too fine; put with the same quantity of chopped cabbage, celery or lettuce; season the same as chicken salad. Garnish with the tender leaves of the heart of lettuce.

OYSTER SALAD.

Drain the liquor from a quart of fresh oysters. Put them in hot vinegar enough to cover them placed over the fire; let them remain until *plump*, but not cooked; then drop them immediately in cold water, drain off, and mix with them two pickled cucumbers cut fine, also a quart of celery cut in dice pieces, some seasoning of salt and pepper. Mix all well together, tossing up with a silver fork. Pour over the whole a "Mayonnaise dressing." Garnish with celery tips and slices of hard-boiled eggs arranged tastefully.

DUTCH SALAD.

Wash, split and bone a dozen anchovies, and roll each one up; wash, split and bone one herring, and cut it up into small pieces; cut up into dice an equal quantity of Bologna or Lyons sausage, or of smoked ham and sausages; also, an equal quantity of the breast of cold roast fowl, or veal; add likewise, always in the same quantity, and cut into dice, beet-roots, pickled cucumbers, cold boiled potatoes cut in larger dice, and in quantity according to taste, but at least thrice as much potato as anything else; add a tablespoonful of capers, the yolks and whites of some hard-boiled eggs, minced separately, and a dozen stoned olives;

mix all the ingredients well together, reserving the olives and anchovies to orna
ment the top of the bowl; beat up together oil and Tarragon vinegar with white
pepper and French mustard to taste; pour this over the salad and serve.

HAM SALAD.

Take cold boiled ham, fat and lean together, chop it until it is thoroughly
mixed, and the pieces are about the size of peas; then add to this an equal quantity of celery cut fine; if celery is out of season, lettuce may be substituted.
Line a dish thickly with lettuce-leaves and fill with the chopped ham and celery.
Make a dressing the same as for cold slaw and turn over the whole. Very
fine.

CRAB SALAD.

Boil three dozen hard-shell crabs twenty-five minutes; drain and let them
cool gradually; remove the upper shell and the tail, break the remainder apart
and pick out the meat carefully. The large claws should not be forgotten, for
they contain a dainty morsel, and the creamy fat attached to the upper shell
should not be overlooked. Line a salad-bowl with the small white leaves of two
heads of lettuce, add the crab meat, pour over it a Mayonnaise garnish with
crab claws, hard-boiled eggs, and little mounds of cress-leaves, which may be
mixed with the salad when served.

COLD SLAW.

Select the finest head of bleached cabbage—that is to say, one of the finest
and most compact of the more delicate varieties; cut up enough into shreds to
fill a large vegetable-dish or salad-bowl—that to be regulated by the size of the
cabbage and the quantity required; shave very fine, and after that chop up, the
more thoroughly the better. Put this into a dish in which it is to be served,
after seasoning it well with salt and pepper. Turn over it a dressing made as
for cold slaw; mix it well, and garnish with slices of hard-boiled eggs.

PLAIN COLD SLAW.

Slice cabbage very fine; season with salt, pepper and a little sugar; pour
over vinegar and mix thoroughly. It is nice served in the centre of a platter
with fried oysters around it.

HOT SLAW.

Cut the cabbage as for cold slaw; put it into a stew-pan, and set it on the top
of the stove for half an hour, or till hot all through; do not let it boil. Then
make a dressing the same as for cold slaw, and, while hot, pour it over the hot

cabbage. Stir it until well mixed and the cabbage looks coddled. Serve immediately.

TOMATO SALAD.

Peel and slice twelve good, sound, fresh tomatoes; the slices about a quarter of an inch thick. Set them on the ice or in a refrigerator while you make the dressing. Make the same as "Mayonnaise," or you may use "Cream dressing." Take one head of the broad-leaved variety of lettuce, wash, and arrange them neatly around the sides of a salad bowl. Place the cold, sliced tomatoes in the centre. Pour over the dressing and serve.

ENDIVE.

This ought to be nicely blanched and crisp, and is the most wholesome of all salads. Take two, cut away the root, remove the dark-green leaves, and pick off all the rest; wash and drain well, add a few chives. Dress with Mayonnaise dressing.

Endive is extensively cultivated for the adulteration of coffee; is also a fine relish, and has broad leaves. Endive is of the same nature as chiccory, the leaves being curly.

CELERY SALAD.

Prepare the dressing the same as for tomato salad; cut the celery into bits half an inch long, and season. Serve at once before the vinegar injures the crispness of the vegetable.

LETTUCE SALAD.

Take the yolks of three hard-boiled eggs, and salt and mustard to taste; mash it fine; make a paste by adding a dessertspoonful of olive oil or melted butter (use butter always when it is difficult to get *fresh* oil); mix thoroughly, and then dilute by adding *gradually* a teacupful of vinegar, and pour over the lettuce. Garnish by *slicing* another egg and laying over the lettuce. This is sufficient for a moderate-sized dish of lettuce.

POTATO SALAD, HOT.

Pare six or eight large potatoes, and boil till done, and slice thin while hot; peel and cut up three large onions, into small bits and mix with the potatoes; cut up some breakfast bacon into small bits, sufficient to fill a teacup; and fry it a light brown; remove the meat, and into the grease stir three tablespoonfuls of vinegar, making a sour gravy, which with the bacon pour over the potato and onion; mix lightly. To be eaten when hot.

POTATO SALAD, COLD.

Chop cold boiled potatoes fine, with enough raw onions to season nicely make a dressing as for lettuce salad, and pour over it.

BEAN SALAD.

String young beans; break into half-inch pieces or leave whole; wash and cook soft in salt water; drain well; add finely chopped onions, pepper, salt and vinegar; when cool, add olive oil or melted butter.

TO DRESS CUCUMBERS RAW.

They should be as fresh from the vine as possible, few vegetables being more unwholesome when long gathered. As soon as they are brought in, lay them in cold water. Just before they are to go to table take them out, pare them and slice them into a pan of fresh cold water. When they are all sliced, transfer them to a deep dish; season them with a little salt and black pepper, and pour over them some of the best vinegar. You may mix with them a small quantity of sliced onions, not to be eaten, but to communicate a slight flavor of onion to the vinegar.

CELERY UNDRESSED.

Celery is sometimes sent to the table without dressing. Scrape the outside stalks, and cut off the green tops and the roots; lay it in cold water until near the time to serve, then change the water, in which let it stand three or four minutes; split the stalks in three, with a sharp knife, being careful not to break them, and serve in goblet-shaped salad glasses.

To crisp celery, let it lie in ice-water two hours before serving; to fringe the stalks, stick several coarse needles into a cork, and draw the stalk half way from the top through the needles several times and lay in the refrigerator to curl and crisp.

RADISHES.

All the varieties are generally served in the same manner, by scraping and placing on the table in glasses containing some cold water to keep them fresh looking.

PEPPERGRASS AND CRESS.

These are used mostly as an appetizer, served simply with salt. Cresses are occasionally used in making salad.

HORSE-RADISH.

Horse-radish is an agreeable relish, and has a particularly fresh taste in the spring; is scraped fine or grated, and set on the table in a small covered cup; much that is bottled and sold as horse-radish is adulterated with grated turnip.

LETTUCE.

Wash each leaf separately, breaking them from the head; crisp in ice-water and serve the leaves whole, to be prepared at table, providing hard-boiled eggs cut in halves or slices, oil and other ingredients, to be mixed at table to individual taste.

Catsups.

TOMATO CATSUP. No. 1.

Put into two quarts of tomato-pulp (or two cans of canned tomatoes) one onion, cut fine, two tablespoonfuls of salt and three tablespoonfuls of brown sugar. Boil until quite thick; then take from the fire and strain it through a sieve, working it until it is all through but the seeds. Put it back on the stove, and add two tablespoonfuls of mustard, one of allspice, one of black pepper, and one of cinnamon, one teaspoonful of ground cloves, half a teaspoonful of cayenne pepper, one grated nutmeg, one pint of good vinegar; boil it until it will just run from the mouth of a bottle. It should be watched, stirred often, that it does not burn. If sealed tight while *hot*, in large-mouthed bottles it will keep good for years.

TOMATO CATSUP. No. 2.

Cook one gallon of choice ripe tomatoes; strain them, and cook again until they become quite thick. About fifteen minutes before taking up put into them a small level teaspoonful of cayenne pepper, one tablespoonful of mustard seed, half a tablespoonful of whole cloves, one tablespoonful of whole allspice, tied all in a thin muslin bag. At the same time, add one heaping tablespoonful of sugar, and one teacupful of best vinegar, and salt to suit the taste. Seal up air-tight, either in bottles or jugs. This is a valuable Southern recipe.

GREEN TOMATO CATSUP.

One peck of green tomatoes, and two large onions, sliced. Place them in layers, sprinkling salt between; let them stand twenty-four hours and then drain them. Add a quarter of a pound of mustard seed, one ounce allspice, one ounce cloves, one ounce ground mustard, one ounce ground ginger, two table-spoonfuls black pepper, two teaspoonfuls celery seed, a quarter of a pound of brown sugar. Put all in preserving-pan, cover with vinegar, and boil two hours; then strain through a sieve and bottle for use.

WALNUT CATSUP.

One hundred walnuts, six ounces of shalots, one head of garlic, half a pound of salt, two quarts of vinegar, two ounces of anchovies, two ounces of pepper, a quarter of an ounce of mace, half an ounce of cloves; beat in a large mortar a hundred green walnuts until they are thoroughly broken; then put them into a jar with six ounces of shalots cut into pieces, a head of garlic, two quarts of vinegar and the half pound of salt; let them stand for a fortnight, stirring them twice a day. Strain off the liquor, put into a stew-pan with the anchovies, whole pepper, half an ounce of cloves and a quarter of an ounce of mace; boil it half an hour, skimming it well. Strain it off, and when cold, pour it clear from any sediment into small bottles, cork it down closely and store it in a dry place. The sediment can be used for flavoring sauces.

OYSTER CATSUP.

One pint of oyster meats, one teacupful of sherry, a tablespoonful of salt, a teaspoonful of cayenne pepper, the same of powdered mace, a gill of cider vinegar.

Procure the oysters very fresh, and open sufficient to fill a pint measure; save the liquor, and scald the oysters in it with the sherry; strain the oysters, and chop them fine with the salt, cayenne and mace, until reduced to a pulp; then add it to the liquor in which they were scalded; boil it again five minutes, and skim well; rub the whole through a sieve, and when cold, bottle and cork closely. The corks should be sealed.

MUSHROOM CATSUP.

Use the larger kind, known as umbrellas or "flaps." They must be very fresh and not gathered in very wet weather, or the catsup will be less apt to keep. Wash and cut them in two to four pieces, and place them in a wide, flat jar or crock in layers, sprinkling each layer with salt, and let them stand for twenty-four hours; take them out and press out the juice, when bottle and cork; put the mushrooms back again, and in another twenty-four hours press them again; bottle and cork; repeat this for the third time, and then mix together all the juice extracted; add to it pepper, allspice, one or more cloves according to quantity, pounded together; boil the whole, and skim as long as any scum rises; bottle when cool; put in each bottle two cloves and a pepper-corn. Cork and seal, put in a dry place, and it will keep for years.

GOOSEBERRY CATSUP.

Ten pounds of fruit gathered just before ripening, five pounds of sugar, one quart of vinegar, two tablespoonfuls each of ground black pepper, allspice, and cinnamon. Boil the fruit in vinegar until reduced to a pulp, then add sugar and the other seasoning. Seal it hot.

Grape catsup is made in the same manner.

CUCUMBER CATSUP.

Take cucumbers suitable for the table; peel and grate them, salt a little, and put in a bag to drain over night; in the morning season to taste with salt, pepper and vinegar, put in small jars and seal tight for fall or winter use.

CURRANT CATSUP.

Four pounds of currants, two pounds of sugar, one pint of vinegar, one tea-spoonful of cloves, a tablespoonful of cinnamon, pepper and allspice. Boil in a porcelain sauce-pan until thoroughly cooked. Strain through a sieve, all but the skins; boil down until just thick enough to run freely from the mouth of a bottle when cold. Cork and set aside.

APPLE CATSUP.

Peel and quarter a dozen sound, tart apples; stew them until soft, in as little water as possible, then pass them through a sieve. To a quart of the sifted apple, add a teacupful of sugar, one teaspoonful of pepper, one of cloves, one of mustard, two of cinnamon, and two medium-sized onions, chopped *very* fine. Stir all together, adding a tablespoonful of salt and a pint of vinegar. Place over the fire and boil one hour, and bottle while hot; seal very tight. It should be about as thick as tomato catsup, so that it will just run from the bottle.

CELERY VINEGAR.

A quart of fresh celery, chopped fine, or a quarter of a pound of celery seed; one quart of best vinegar; one tablespoonful of salt, and one of white sugar. Put the celery or seed into a jar, heat the vinegar, sugar and salt; pour it boiling hot over the celery, let it cool, cover it tightly and set away. In two weeks strain and bottle.

SPICED VINEGAR.

Take one quart of cider vinegar, put into it half an ounce of celery seed, one-third of an ounce of dried mint, one-third of an ounce of dried parsley, one garlic, three small onions, three whole cloves, a teaspoonful of whole pepper-corns, a teaspoonful of grated nutmeg, salt to taste, and a tablespoonful of sugar; add a tablespoonful of good brandy. Put all into a jar, and cover it well; let it stand for three weeks, then strain and bottle it well. Useful for flavoring salad and other dishes.

Pickles.

Pickles should never be put into vessels of brass, copper or tin, as the action of the acid on such metals often results in poisoning the pickles. Porcelain or granite-ware is the best for such purposes.

Vinegar that is used for pickling should be the best cider or white-wine, and should never be boiled more than five or six minutes, as it reduces its strength. In putting away pickles, use stone or glass jars; the glazing on common earthen-ware is rendered injurious by the action of the vinegar. When the jar is nearly filled with the pickles, the vinegar should completely cover them, and if there is any appearance of their not doing well, turn off the vinegar, cover with fresh vinegar, and spices. Alum in small quantities is useful in making them firm and crisp. In using ground spices, tie them up in muslin bags.

To green pickles, put green grape-vine leaves or green cabbage leaves between them when heating. Another way is to heat them in strong ginger tea. Pickles should be kept closely covered, put into glass jars and sealed tightly.

"Turmeric" is India saffron, and is used very much in pickling as a coloring.

A piece of horse-radish put into a jar of pickles will keep the vinegar from losing its strength, and the pickles will keep sound much longer, especially tomato pickles.

CUCUMBER PICKLES.

Select the medium, small-sized cucumbers. For one bushel make a brine that will bear up an egg; heat it boiling hot and pour it over the cucumbers; let them stand twenty-four hours, then wipe them dry; heat some vinegar boiling hot, and pour over them, standing again twenty-four hours. Now change the vinegar, putting on fresh vinegar, adding one quart of brown sugar, a pint of white mustard seed, a small handful of whole cloves, the same of cinnamon sticks, a piece of alum the size of an egg, half a cup of celery seed; heat it all boiling hot and pour over the cucumbers.

SLICED CUCUMBER PICKLE.

Take one gallon of medium-sized cucumbers, put them into a jar or pail. Put into enough *boiling* water to cover them a small handful of salt, turn it over them and cover closely; repeat this three mornings, and the fourth morning scald enough cider vinegar to cover them, putting into it a piece of alum as large as a walnut, a teacup of horse-radish root cut up fine; then tie up in a small muslin bag, one teaspoonful of mustard, one of ground cloves, and one of cinnamon. Slice up the cucumbers half of an inch thick, place them in glass jars and pour the scalding vinegar over them. Seal tight and they will keep good a year or more.

—MRS. LYDIA C. WRIGHT, *South Vernon, Vermont.*

CUCUMBER PICKLES. (For Winter Use.)

A good way to put down cucumbers, a few at a time:

When gathered from the vines, wash, and put in a firkin or half barrel layers of cucumbers and rock-salt alternately, enough salt to make sufficient brine to cover them, no water; cover with a cloth; keep them under the brine with a heavy board; take off the cloth, and rinse it every time you put in fresh cucumbers, as a scum will rise and settle upon it. Use plenty of salt and it will keep a year. To prepare pickles for use, soak in hot water, and keep in a warm place until they are fresh enough, then pour spiced vinegar over them and let them stand over night, then pour that off and put on fresh.

GREEN TOMATO PICKLES. (Sweet.)

One peck of green tomatoes, sliced the day before you are ready for pickling, sprinkling them through and through with salt, not *too* heavily; in the morning drain off the liquor that will drain from them. Have a dozen good-sized onions rather coarsely sliced; take a suitable kettle and put in a layer of the sliced tomatoes, then of onions, and between each layer sprinkle the following spices: Six *red* peppers chopped coarsely, one cup of sugar, one tablespoonful of ground allspice, one tablespoonful of ground cinnamon, a teaspoonful of cloves, one tablespoonful of mustard. Turn over three pints of good vinegar, or enough to completely cover them; boil until tender. This is a choice recipe.

If the flavor of onions is objectionable, the pickle is equally as good without them.

GREEN TOMATO PICKLES. (Sour.)

Wash and slice, without peeling, one peck of sound green tomatoes, put them into a jar in layers with a slight sprinkling of salt between. This may be done over night; in the morning drain off the liquor that has accumulated. Have two dozen medium-sized onions peeled and sliced, also six red peppers chopped fine. Make some spiced vinegar by boiling for half an hour a quart of cider vinegar with whole spices in it. Now take a porcelain kettle and place in it some of the sliced tomatoes, then some of the sliced onions; shake in some black pepper and some of the chopped red peppers; pour over some of the spiced vinegar; then repeat with the tomatoes, onions, etc., until the kettle is full; cover with cold, pure, cider vinegar, and cook until tender, but not too soft. Turn into a jar well-covered, and set in a cool place.

PICKLED MUSHROOMS.

Sufficient vinegar to cover the mushrooms; to each quart of mushrooms two blades pounded mace, one ounce ground pepper, salt to taste. Choose some nice young button-mushrooms for pickling, and rub off the skin with a piece of flannel and salt, and cut off the stalks; if very large, take out the red inside, and reject the black ones, as they are too old. Put them in a stew-pan, sprinkle salt over them, with pounded mace and pepper in the above proportion; shake them well over a clear fire until the liquor flows, and keep them there until it is all dried up again; then add as much vinegar as will cover them; just let it simmer for one minute, and store it away in stone jars for use. When cold, tie down with bladder, and keep in a dry place; they will remain good for a length of time, and are generally considered excellent for flavoring stews and other dishes.

PICKLED CABBAGE. (Purple.)

Cut a sound cabbage into quarters, spread it on a large flat platter or dish and sprinkle thickly with salt; set it in a cool place for twenty-four hours; then drain off the brine, wipe it dry and lay it in the sun two hours, and cover with cold vinegar for twelve hours. Prepare a pickle by seasoning enough vinegar to cover the cabbage with equal quantities of mace, allspice, cinnamon and black pepper, a cup of sugar to every gallon of vinegar, and a teaspoonful of celery seed to every pint. Pack the cabbage in a stone jar; boil the vinegar and spices five minutes and pour on hot. Cover and set away in a cool, dry place. It will be good in a month. A few slices of beet-root improves the color.

PICKLED WHITE CABBAGE.

This recipe recommends itself as of a delightful flavor, yet easily made, and a convenient substitute for the old-fashioned, tedious method of pickling the same vegetable. Take a peck of quartered cabbage, put a layer of cabbage and one of salt, let it remain over night; in the morning squeeze them and put them on the fire, with four chopped onions covered with vinegar; boil for half an hour, then add one ounce of turmeric, one gill of black pepper, one gill of celery seed, a few cloves, one tablespoonful of allspice, a few pieces of ginger, half an ounce of mace, and two pounds of brown sugar. Let it boil half an hour longer, and when cold it is fit for use. Four tablespoonfuls of made mustard should be added with the other ingredients.

PICKLED CAULIFLOWER.

Break the heads into small pieces, and boil ten or fifteen minutes in salt and water; remove from the water and drain carefully. When cold, place in a jar, and pour over it hot vinegar, in which has been scalded a liberal supply of whole cloves, pepper, allspice and white mustard. Tie the spices in a bag, and, on removing the vinegar from the fire, stir into each quart of it two teaspoonfuls of French mustard, and half a cup of white sugar. Cover tightly and be sure to have the vinegar cover the pickle.

PICKLED GREEN PEPPERS.

Take two dozen large, green, bell peppers, extract the seeds by cutting a slit in the side (so as to leave them whole). Make a strong brine and pour over them; let them stand twenty-four hours. Take them out of the brine, and soak them in water for a day and a night; now turn off this water and scald some vinegar, in which put a small piece of alum, and pour over them, letting them stand three days. Prepare a stuffing of two hard heads of white cabbage, chopped fine, seasoned slightly with salt and a cup of white mustard seed; mix it well and stuff the peppers hard and full; stitch up, place them in a stone jar, and pour over spiced vinegar scalding hot. Cover tightly.

GREEN PEPPER MANGOES.

Select firm, sound, green peppers, and add a few red ones, as they are ornamental and look well upon the table. With a sharp knife remove the top, take out the seed, soak over night in salt water, then fill with chopped cabbage and green tomatoes, seasoned with salt, mustard seed and ground cloves. Sew on the top.   Boil vinegar sufficient to cover them, with a cup of brown sugar, and pour over the mangoes.   Do this three mornings, then seal.

CHOWCHOW.   (Superior English Recipe.)

This excellent pickle is seldom made at home, as we can get the imported article so much better than it can be made from the usual recipes.   This we vouch for as being as near the genuine article as can be made: One quart of young, tiny cucumbers, not over two inches long, two quarts of *very* small white onions, two quarts of tender string beans, each one cut in halves, three quarts of green tomatoes, sliced and chopped very coarsely, two fresh heads of cauliflower, cut into small pieces, or two heads of white, hard cabbage.

After preparing these articles, put them in a stone jar, mix them together, sprinkling salt between them sparingly.   Let them stand twenty-four hours, then drain off *all* the brine that has accumulated.   Now put these vegetables in a preserving kettle over the fire, sprinkling through them an ounce of turmeric for coloring, six red peppers, chopped coarsely, four tablespoonfuls of mustard seed, two of celery seed, two of whole allspice, two of whole cloves, a coffee cup of sugar, and two-thirds of a teacup of best ground mixed mustard.   Pour on enough of the best cider vinegar to cover the whole well; cover tightly and simmer all well until it is cooked all through and seems tender, watching and stirring it often.   Put in bottles or glass jars.   It grows better as it grows older, especially if sealed when hot.

PICKLED ONIONS.

Peel small onions until they are white.   Scald them in salt and water until tender, then take them up, put them into wide-mouthed bottles, and pour over them hot spiced vinegar; when cold, cork them close.   Keep in a dry, dark place.   A tablespoonful of sweet oil may be put in the bottles before the cork. The best sort of onions for pickling are the small white buttons.

PICKLED MANGOES.

Let the mangoes, or young musk-melons, lie in salt water strong enough to bear an egg, for two weeks; then soak them in pure water for two days, changing the water two or three times; then remove the seeds and put the mangoes in a kettle, first a layer of grape leaves, then mangoes, and so on until all are in, covering the top with leaves; add a lump of alum the size of a hickory nut; pour vinegar over them and boil them ten or fifteen minutes; remove the leaves and let the pickles stand in this vinegar for a week; then stuff them with the following mixture: One pound of ginger soaked in brine for a day or two, and cut in slices, one ounce of black pepper, one of mace, one of allspice, one of turmeric, half a pound of garlic, soaked for a day or two in brine, and then dried; one pint grated horse-radish, one of black mustard seed and one of white mustard seed; bruise all the spices and mix with a teacup of pure olive oil; to each mango add one teaspoonful of brown sugar; cut one solid head of cabbage fine; add one pint of small onions, a few small cucumbers and green tomatoes; lay them in brine a day and a night, then drain them well and add the imperfect mangoes chopped fine and the spices; mix thoroughly, stuff the mangoes and tie them; put them in a stone jar and pour over them the best cider vinegar; set them in a bright, dry place until they are canned. In a month add three pounds of brown sugar; if this is not sufficient, add more until agreeable to taste. This is for four dozen mangoes.

PICKLE OF RIPE CUCUMBERS.

This is a French recipe, and is the most excellent of all the high-flavored condiments; it is made by *sun-drying* thirty *old*, full-grown cucumbers, which have first been pared and split, had the seeds taken out, been salted, and let stand twenty-four hours. The sun should be permitted to *dry*, not simply drain them. When they are moderately dry, wash them with vinegar, and place them in layers in a jar, alternating them with a layer of horse-radish, mustard seed, garlic, and onions, for each layer of cucumbers. Boil in one quart of vine-gar, one ounce of race-ginger, half an ounce of allspice, and the same of turmeric; when cool pour this over the cucumbers, tie up tightly, and set away. This pickle requires several months to mature it, but is delicious when old, keeps admira-bly, and only a little is needed as a relish.

PICKLED OYSTERS.

One gallon of oysters; wash them well in their own liquor; carefully clear away the particles of shell,. then put them into a kettle, strain the liquor over them, add salt to your taste, let them just come to the boiling point, or until the edges curl up; then skim them out and lay in a dish to cool; put a sprig of mace and a little cold pepper; and allow the liquor to boil some time, skimming it now and then so long as any scum rises. Pour it into a pan and let it cool. When perfectly cool, add a half pint of strong vinegar, place the oysters in a jar and pour the liquor over them.

RIPE CUCUMBER PICKLES. (Sweet.)

Pare and seed ripe cucumbers. Slice each cucumber lengthwise into four pieces, or cut it into fancy shapes as preferred. Let them stand twenty-four hours covered with cold vinegar. Drain them; then put them into fresh vinegar, with two pounds of sugar and one ounce of cassia buds to one quart of vinegar, and a tablespoonful of salt. Boil all together twenty minutes. Cover them closely in a jar.

PICCALILI.

One peck of green tomatoes; eight large onions, chopped fine, with one cup of salt well stirred in. Let it stand over night; in the morning drain off all the liquor. Now take two quarts of water and one of vinegar, boil all together twenty minutes. Drain all through a sieve or colander. Put it back into the kettle again; turn over it two quarts of vinegar, one pound of sugar, half a pound of white mustard seed, two tablespoonfuls of ground pepper, two of cinnamon, one of cloves, two of ginger, one of allspice, and half a teaspoonful of cayenne pepper. Boil all together fifteen minutes, or until tender. Stir it often to prevent scorching. Seal in glass jars.

A most delicious accompaniment for any kind of meat or fish.

—Mrs. St. Johns.

PICKLED EGGS.

Pickled eggs are very easily prepared and most excellent as an accompaniment for cold meats. Boil quite hard three dozen eggs, drop in cold water and remove the shells, and pack them when entirely cold in a wide-mouthed jar, large enough to let them in or out without breaking. Take as much vinegar as you think will cover them entirely, and boil in it white pepper, allspice, a little root-ginger; pack them in stone or wide-mouthed glass jars, occasionally putting in a tablespoonful of white and black mustard seed mixed, a small piece of race ginger, garlic, if liked, horse-radish ungrated, whole cloves, and a very little allspice. Slice two or three green peppers, and add in very small quantities. They will be fit for use in eight or ten days.

AN ORNAMENTAL PICKLE.

Boil fresh eggs half an hour, then put them in cold water. Boil red beets until tender, peel and cut in dice form, and cover with vinegar, spiced; shell the eggs and drop into the pickle jar.

EAST INDIA PICKLE.

Lay in strong brine for two weeks, or until convenient to use them, small cucumbers, very small common white onions, snap beans, gherkins, hard white cabbage quartered, plums, peaches, pears, lemons, green tomatoes and anything else you may wish. When ready, take them out of the brine and simmer in pure water until tender enough to stick a straw through—if still too salt, soak in clear water; drain thoroughly and lay them in vinegar in which is dissolved one ounce of turmeric to the gallon. For five gallons of pickle, take two ounces of mace, two of cloves, two of cinnamon, two of allspice, two of celery seed, a quarter of a pound of white race ginger, cracked fine, half a pound of white mustard seed, half a pint of small red peppers, quarter of a pound of grated horse-radish, half a pint of flour mustard, two ounces of turmeric, half a pint of garlic, if you like; soak in two gallons of cider vinegar for two weeks, stirring daily. After the pickles have lain in the turmeric vinegar for a week, take them out and put in jars or casks, one layer of pickle and one of spice out of the vinegar, till all is used. If the turmeric vinegar is still good and strong, add it and the spiced vinegar. If the turmeric vinegar be much diluted, do not use it, but add enough fresh to the spiced to cover the pickles; put it on the fire with a pound of brown sugar to each gallon; when boiling, pour over the pickle. Repeat this two or three times as your taste may direct.

MIXED PICKLES.

Scald in salt water until tender, cauliflower heads, small onions, peppers, cucumbers cut in dice, nasturtiums and green beans; then drain until dry, and pack into wide-mouthed bottles. Boil in each pint of cider vinegar one tablespoonful of sugar, half a teaspoonful of salt and two tablespoonfuls of mustard; pour over the pickle and seal carefully. Other spices may be added if liked.

BLUE-BERRY PICKLES.

For blue-berry pickles, old jars which have lost their covers, or whose edges have been broken so that the covers will not fit tightly, serve an excellent purpose, as these pickles *must not* be kept air-tight.

Pick over your berries, using only sound ones; fill your jars or wide-mouthed bottles to within an inch of the top, then pour in molasses enough to settle down into *all* the spaces; this cannot be done in a moment, as molasses does not *run* very freely. Only lazy people will feel obliged to stand by and watch its progress. As it settles, pour in more until the berries are covered. Then tie over the top a piece of cotton cloth to keep the flies and other insects out, and set away in the preserve closet. Cheap molasses is good enough, and your pickles will soon be "sharp." Wild grapes may be pickled in the same manner.

PICKLED BUTTERNUTS AND WALNUTS.

These nuts are in the best state for pickling when the outside shell can be penetrated by the head of a pin. Scald them, and rub off the outside skin, put them in a strong brine for six days, changing the water every other day, keeping them closely covered from the air. Then drain and wipe them, (piercing each nut through in several places with a large needle,) and prepare the pickle as follows:—For a hundred large nuts, take of black pepper and ginger root each an ounce; and of cloves, mace and nutmeg each a half ounce. Pound all the spices to powder, and mix them well together, adding two large spoonfuls of mustard seed. Put the nuts into jars, (having first stuck each of them through in several places with a large needle,) strewing the powdered seasoning between every layer of nuts. Boil for five minutes a gallon of the very best cider vinegar, and pour it boiling hot upon the nuts. Secure the jars closely with corks. You may begin to eat the nuts in a fortnight.

WATERMELON PICKLE.

Ten pounds of watermelon rind boiled in pure water until tender; drain the water off, and make a syrup of two pounds of white sugar, one quart of vinegar, half an ounce of cloves, one ounce of cinnamon. The syrup to be poured over the rind boiling hot three days in succession.

SWEET PICKLE FOR FRUIT.

Most of the recipes for making a sweet pickle for fruit, such as cling-stone peaches, damsons, plums, cherries, apricots, etc., are so similar, that we give that which is the most successfully used.

To every quart of fruit, allow a cup of white sugar and a large pint of good cider vinegar, adding half an ounce of *stick* cinnamon, one tablespoonful of *whole* cloves, the same of whole allspice. Let it come to a boil, and pour it hot over the fruit; repeat this two or three days in succession; then seal hot in glass jars if you wish to keep it for a long time

The *fruit,* not the liquor, is to be eaten, and used the same as any pickle. Some confound this with "Spiced Fruit," which is not treated the same, one being a pickle, the other a spiced preserve boiled down thick.

Damsons and plums should be pricked with a needle, and peaches washed with a weak lye, and then rubbed with a coarse cloth to remove the fur.

PEAR PICKLE.

Select small, sound ones, remove the blossom end, stick them with a fork, allow to each quart of pears one pint of cider vinegar and one cup of sugar, put in a teaspoonful allspice, cinnamon and cloves to boil with the vinegar; then add the pears and boil, and seal in jars.

SPICED CURRANTS.

Seven pounds of fruit, four pounds of sugar, one pint of good cider vinegar, one tablespoonful of ground cinnamon, one teaspoonful of cloves. Put into a kettle and boil until the fruit is soft; then skim out the fruit, putting it on dishes until the syrup is boiled down thick. Turn the fruit back into the syrup again, so as to heat it all through; then seal it hot in glass jars, and set it in a cool, dark place.

Any tart fruit may be put up in this way, and is considered a very good embellishment for cold meats.

SPICED PLUMS.

Seven pounds of plums, one pint of *cider* vinegar, four pounds of sugar, two tablespoonfuls of broken cinnamon bark, half as much of whole cloves and the same of broken nutmeg; place these in a muslin bag and simmer them in a little vinegar and water for half an hour; then add it all to the vinegar and sugar, and bring to a boil; add the plums, and boil carefully until they are cooked tender. Before cooking the plums they should be pierced with a darning needle several times; this will prevent the skins bursting while cooking.

SPICED GRAPES.

Take the pulp from the grapes, preserving the skins. Boil the pulp and rub through a colander to get out the seeds; then add the skins to the strained pulp and boil with the sugar, vinegar and spices. To every seven pounds of grapes use four and one-half pounds of sugar, one pint of good vinegar. Spice quite highly with ground cloves and allspice, with a little cinnamon.

PICKLED CHERRIES.

Select sound, large cherries, as large as you can get them; to every quart of cherries allow a large cupful of vinegar, two tablespoonfuls of sugar, a dozen whole cloves, and half a dozen blades of mace; put the vinegar and sugar on to heat with the spices; boil five minutes, turn out into a covered stoneware vessel; cover and let it get perfectly cold; pack the cherries into jars, and pour the vinegar over them when cold; cork tightly and set away; they are fit for use almost immediately.

VEGETABLES.

Vegetables of all kinds should be thoroughly picked over, throwing out all decayed or unripe parts, then well washed in several waters. Most vegetables, when peeled, are better when laid in cold water a short time before cooking. When partly cooked a little salt should be thrown into the water in which they are boiled, and they should cook steadily after they are put on, not allowed to stop boiling or simmering until they are thoroughly done. Every sort of culinary vegetable is much better when freshly gathered and cooked as soon as possible, and, when done, thoroughly drained, and served immediately while hot.

Onions, cabbage, carrots and turnips should be cooked in a great deal of water, boiled only long enough to sufficiently cook them, and immediately drained. Longer boiling makes them insipid in taste, and with *too little* water they turn a dark color.

Potatoes rank first in importance in the vegetable line, and consequently should be properly served. It requires some little intelligence to cook even so simple and common a dish as boiled potatoes. In the first place, all defective or green ones should be cast out; a bad one will flavor a whole dish. If they are not uniform in size, they should be made so by cutting after they are peeled. The best part of a potato, or the most nutritious, is next to the skin, therefore they should be pared very thinly, if at all; then, if old, the cores should be cut out, thrown into *cold* water salted a little, and boiled until soft enough for a fork to pierce through easily; drain immediately, and replace the kettle on the fire with the cover partly removed, until they are completely dried. New potatoes should be put into boiling water, and when partly done salted a little. They should be prepared just in time for cooking, by scraping off the thin outside skin. They require about twenty minutes to boil.

TO BOIL NEW POTATOES.

Do not have the potatoes dug long before they are dressed, as they are never good when they have been out of the ground some time. Well wash them, rub off the skins with a coarse cloth, and put them in *boiling* water salted. Let them boil until tender; try them with a fork, and when done pour the water away from them; let them stand by the side of the fire with the lid of the sauce-pan partially removed, and when the potatoes are thoroughly dry, put them in a hot vegetable dish, with a piece of butter the size of a walnut; pile the potatoes over this, and serve. If the potatoes are too old to have the skins rubbed off, boil them in their jackets; drain, peel and serve them as above, with a piece of butter placed in the midst of them. They require twenty to thirty minutes to cook. Serve them hot and plain, or with melted butter over them.

MASHED POTATOES.

Take the quantity needed, pare off the skins, and lay them in cold water half an hour; then put them into a sauce-pan, with a little salt; cover with water and boil them until done. Drain off the water and mash them fine with a potato-masher. Have ready a piece of butter the size of an egg, melted in half a cup of boiling hot milk, and a good pinch of salt; mix it well with the mashed potatoes until they are a smooth paste, taking care that they are not too wet. Put them into a vegetable dish, heap them up and smooth over the top, put a small piece of butter on the top in the centre, and have dots of pepper here and there on the surface as large as a half dime.

Some prefer using a heavy fork or wire-beater, instead of a potato-masher, beating the potatoes quite light, and heaping them up in the dish without smoothing over the top.

BROWNED POTATOES.

Mash them the same as the above, put them into a dish that they are to be served in, smooth over the top, and brush over with the yolk of an egg, or spread on a bountiful supply of butter and dust well with flour. Set in the oven to brown; it will brown in fifteen minutes with a quick fire.

MASHED POTATOES, (Warmed Over.)

To two cupfuls of cold mashed potatoes, add a half cupful of milk, a pinch of salt, a tablespoonful of butter, two tablespoonfuls of flour, and two eggs beaten to a froth. Mix the whole until thoroughly light; then put into a pudding or vegetable dish, spread a little butter over the top, and bake a golden brown. The quality depends upon very thoroughly beating the eggs before adding them, so that the potato will remain light and porous after baking, similar to sponge-cake.

POTATO PUFFS.

Prepare the potatoes as directed for mashed potato. While *hot*, shape in balls about the size of an egg. Have a tin sheet well buttered, and place the balls on it. As soon as all are done, brush over with beaten egg. Brown in the oven. When done, slip a knife under them and slide them upon a hot platter. Garnish with parsley, and serve immediately.

POTATOES Á LA CRÊME.

Heat a cupful of milk; stir in a heaping tablespoonful of butter cut up in as much flour. Stir until smooth and thick; pepper and salt, and add two cupfuls of cold boiled potatoes, sliced, and a little very finely chopped parsley. Shake over the fire until the potatoes are hot all through, and pour into a deep dish.

NEW POTATOES AND CREAM.

Wash and rub new potatoes with a coarse cloth or scrubbing-brush; drop into boiling water and boil briskly until done, and no more; press a potato against the side of the kettle with a fork; if done, it will yield to a gentle pressure; in a sauce-pan have ready some butter and cream, hot, but not boiling, a little green parsley, pepper and salt; drain the potatoes, add the mixture, put over hot water for a minute or two, and serve.

SARATOGA CHIPS.

Peel good-sized potatoes, and slice them as evenly as possible. Drop them into ice-water; have a kettle of very hot lard, as for cakes; put a few at a time into a towel and shake, to dry the moisture out of them, and then drop them into the boiling lard. Stir them occasionally, and when of a light brown take them out with a skimmer, and they will be crisp and not greasy. Sprinkle salt over them while hot.

FRIED RAW POTATOES.

Peel half a dozen medium-sized potatoes very evenly, cut them in slices as thin as an egg-shell, and be sure to cut them from the *breadth*, not the length, of the potato. Put a tablespoonful each of butter and sweet lard into the frying-pan, and as soon as it boils add the sliced potatoes, sprinkling over them salt and pepper to season them. Cover them with a tight-fitting lid, and let the steam partly cook them; then remove it, and let them fry a bright gold color, shaking and turning them carefully, so as to brown equally. Serve very hot.

Fried, cold, cooked potatoes may be fried by the same recipe, only slice them a little thicker.

Remark.—Boiled or steamed potatoes chopped up or sliced while they are yet warm never fry so successfully as when cold.

SCALLOPED POTATOES, (Kentucky Style.)

Peel and slice raw potatoes thin, the same as for frying. Butter an earthen dish, put in a layer of potatoes, and season with salt, pepper, butter, a bit of onion chopped fine, if liked; sprinkle a little flour. Now put another layer of potatoes and the seasoning. Continue in this way till the dish is filled. Just before putting into the oven, pour a quart of hot milk over. Bake three quarters of an hour.

Cold boiled potatoes may be cooked the same. It requires less time to bake them; they are delicious either way. If the onion is disliked, it can be omitted.

STEAMED POTATOES.

This mode of cooking potatoes is now much in vogue, particularly where they are wanted on a large scale, it being so very convenient. Pare the potatoes, throw them into cold water as they are peeled, then put them in a steamer. Place the steamer over a sauce-pan of boiling water, and steam the potatoes from twenty to forty minutes, according to the size and sort. When the fork goes easily through them, they are done; then take them up, dish, and serve very quickly.

POTATO SNOW.

Choose some mealy potatoes that will boil exceedingly white; pare them, and cook them well, but not so as to be watery; drain them, and mash and season them well. Put in the sauce-pan in which they were dressed, so as to keep them as hot as possible; then press them through a wire sieve into the dish in which they are to be served; strew a little fine salt upon them previous to sending them to table. French cooks also add a small quantity of pounded loaf sugar while they are being mashed.

HASTY COOKED POTATOES.

Wash and peel some potatoes; cut them into slices of about a quarter of an inch in thickness; throw them into *boiling* salted water, and, if of good quality, they will be done in about ten minutes.

Strain off the water, put the potatoes into a hot dish, chop them slightly, add pepper, salt, and a few small pieces of fresh butter, and serve without loss of time.

FAVORITE WARMED POTATOES.

The potatoes should be boiled *whole with the skins on* in plenty of water, well *salted*, and are much better for being boiled the day before needed. Care should be taken that they are not over cooked. Strip off the skins (not pare them with a knife), and slice them nearly a quarter of an inch thick. Place them in a chopping-bowl and sprinkle over them sufficient salt and pepper to season them well; chop them all one way, then turn the chopping-bowl half way around, and chop across them, cutting them into little square pieces, the shape of dice. About twenty-five minutes before serving time, place on the stove a sauce-pan (or any suitable dish) containing a piece of butter the size of an egg; when it begins to melt and run over the bottom of the dish, put in a cup of rich sweet milk. When this boils up, put in the chopped potatoes; there should be about a quart of them; stir them a little so that they become moistened through with the milk; then cover and place them on the back of the stove, or in a moderate oven, where they will heat through gradually. When heated through stir carefully from the bottom with a spoon, and cover tightly again. Keep hot until ready to serve. Baked potatoes are very good warmed in this manner.

CRISP POTATOES.

Cut cold raw potatoes into shavings, cubes, or any small shape; throw them, a few at a time, into boiling fat, and toss them about with a knife until they are a uniform light brown; drain and season with salt and pepper. Fat is never hot enough while bubbling—when it is ready it is still and smoking, but should never burn.

LYONNAISE POTATOES.

Take eight or ten good-sized cold boiled potatoes, slice them endwise, then crosswise, making them like dice in small squares. When you are ready to cook them, heat some butter or good drippings in a frying-pan; fry in it one small onion (chopped fine) until it begins to change color, and look yellow. Now put in your potatoes, sprinkle well with salt and pepper, stir well and cook about five minutes, taking care that you do not break them. *They must not brown.* Just before taking up, stir in a tablespoonful of minced parsley. Drain dry by shaking in a heated colander. Serve *very hot.*

—Delmonico.

POTATO FILLETS.

Pare and slice the potatoes thin; cut them if you like in small fillets, about a quarter of an inch square, and as long as the potato will admit; keep them in cold water until wanted, then drop them into boiling lard; when nearly done, take them out with a skimmer and drain them, boil up the lard again, drop the potatoes back and fry till done; this operation causes the fillets to swell up and puff.

POTATO CROQUETTES. No. 1.

Wash, peel and put four large potatoes in cold water, with a pinch of salt, and set them over a brisk fire; when they are done pour off all the water and mash them. Take another sauce-pan, and put in it ten tablespoonfuls of milk and a lump of butter half the size of an egg; put it over a brisk fire; as soon as the milk comes to a boil, pour the potatoes into it, and stir them very fast with a wooden spoon; when thoroughly mixed, take them from the fire and put them on a dish. Take a tablespoonful and roll it in a clean towel, making it oval in shape; dip it in a well-beaten egg, and then in bread-crumbs, and drop it in hot drippings or lard. Proceed in this manner till all the potato is used, four potatoes making six croquettes. Fry them a light brown all over, turning them gently as may be necessary. When they are done, lay them on brown paper or a hair sieve, to drain all fat off; then serve on a napkin.

POTATO CROQUETTES. No. 2.

Take two cups of cold mashed potato, season with a pinch of salt, pepper and a tablespoonful of butter. Beat up the whites of two eggs, and work all together thoroughly; make it into small balls slightly flattened, dip them in the beaten yolks of the eggs, then roll either in flour or cracker-crumbs; fry the same as fish-balls.

—Delmonico's.

POTATOES Á LA DELMONICO.

Cut the potatoes with a vegetable cutter into small balls about the size of a marble; put them into a stew-pan with plenty of butter, and a good sprinkling of salt; keep the sauce-pan covered, and shake occasionally until they are quite done, which will be in about an hour.

FRIED POTATOES WITH EGGS.

Slice cold boiled potatoes, and fry in good butter until brown; beat up one or two eggs, and stir into them just as you dish them for the table; do not leave them a moment on the fire after the eggs are in, for if they harden they are not half so nice; one egg is enough for three or four persons, unless they are very fond of potatoes; if they are, have plenty, and put in two.

BAKED POTATOES.

Potatoes are either baked in their jackets or peeled; in either case they should not be exposed to a fierce heat, which is wasteful, inasmuch as thereby a great deal of vegetable is scorched and rendered uneatable. They should be frequently turned while being baked, and kept from touching each other in the oven or dish. When done in their skins, be particular to wash and brush them before baking them. If convenient, they may be baked in wood-ashes, or in a Dutch oven in front of the fire. When pared they should be baked in a dish, and fat of some kind added to prevent their outsides from becoming burnt; they are ordinarily baked thus as an accessory to baked meat.

Never serve potatoes, boiled or baked whole, in a closely covered dish. They become sodden and clammy. Cover with a folded napkin that allows the steam to escape, or absorbs the moisture. They should be served promptly when done, and require about three-quarters of an hour to one hour to bake them, if of a good size.

BROWNED POTATOES WITH A ROAST. No. 1.

About three quarters of an hour before taking up your roasts, peel middling-sized potatoes, boil them until partly done, then arrange them in the roasting-pan around the roast, basting them with the drippings at the same time you do the meat, browning then evenly. Serve hot with the meat. Many cooks partly boil the potatoes before putting around the roast. New potatoes are very good cooked around a roast.

BROWNED POTATOES WITH A ROAST. No. 2.

Peel, cook and mash the required quantity, adding while hot a little chopped onion, pepper and salt; form it into small oval balls and dredge them with flour; then place around the meat, about twenty minutes before it is taken from the oven. When nicely browned, drain dry and serve hot with the meat.

SWEET POTATOES.

Boiled, steamed and baked the same as Irish potatoes; generally cooked with their jackets on. Cold sweet potatoes may be cut in slices across or lengthwise, and fried as common potatoes; or may be cut in half and served cold.

Boiled sweet potatoes are very nice. Boil until partly done, peel them and bake brown, basting them with butter or beef drippings several times. Served hot. They should be a nice brown.

BAKED SWEET POTATOES.

Wash and scrape them, split them lengthwise. Steam or boil them until nearly done. Drain, and put them in a baking-dish, placing over them lumps of butter, pepper and salt; sprinkle thickly with sugar, and bake in the oven to a nice brown.

Hubbard squash is nice cooked in the same manner.

ONIONS BOILED.

The white silver-skins are the best species. To boil them peel off the outside, cut off the ends, put them into cold water and into a stew-pan, and let them scald two minutes; then turn off that water, pour on cold water, salted a little, and boil slowly till tender, which will be in thirty or forty minutes, according to their size; when done drain them quite dry, pour a little melted butter over them, sprinkle them with pepper and salt and serve hot.

An excellent way to peel onions so as not to affect the eyes is to take a pan *full* of water, and hold and peel them under the water.

ONIONS STEWED.

Cook the same as boiled onions, and when quite done turn off all the water; add a teacupful of milk, a piece of butter the size of an egg, pepper and salt to taste, a tablespoonful of flour stirred to a cream; let all boil up once and serve in a vegetable dish, hot.

ONIONS BAKED.

Use the large Spanish onion, as best for this purpose; wash them clean, but do not peel, and put into a sauce-pan, with slightly salted water; boil an hour, replacing the water with more boiling hot as it evaporates; turn off the water, and lay the onions on a cloth to dry them well; roll each one in a piece of buttered tissue paper, twisting it at the top to keep it on, and bake in a slow oven about an hour, or until tender all through; peel them; place in a deep dish, and brown slightly, basting well with butter for fifteen minutes; season with salt and pepper, and pour some melted butter over them.

FRIED ONIONS.

Peel, slice, and fry them brown in equal quantities of butter and lard or nice drippings; cover until partly soft, remove the cover and brown them; salt and pepper.

SCALLOPED ONIONS.

Take eight or ten onions of good size, slice them, and boil until tender. Lay them in a baking-dish, put in bread-crumbs, butter in small bits, pepper and salt, between each layer until the dish is full, putting bread-crumbs last; add milk or cream until full. Bake twenty minutes or half an hour

A little onion is not an injurious article of food, as many believe. A judicious use of plants of the onion family is quite as important a factor in successful cookery as salt and pepper. When carefully concealed by manipulation in food, it affords zest and enjoyment to many who could not otherwise taste of it were its presence known. A great many successful compounds derive their excellence from the partly concealed flavor of the onion, which imparts a delicate appetizing aroma highly prized by epicures.

CAULIFLOWER.

When cleaned and washed, drop them into boiling water, into which you have put salt and a teaspoonful of flour, or a slice of bread; boil till tender; take off, drain, and dish them; serve with a sauce spread over, and made with melted butter, salt, pepper, grated nutmeg, chopped parsley, and vinegar.

Another way is to make a white sauce (see Sauces), and when the cauliflowers are dished as above, turn the white sauce over, and serve warm. They may also be served in the same way with a milk, cream, or tomato sauce, or with brown butter.

It is a very good plan to loosen the leaves of a head of cauliflower, and let lie, the top downward in a pan of cold salt water, to remove any insects that might be hidden between them.

FRIED CAULIFLOWER.

Boil the cauliflowers till about half done. Mix two tablespoonfuls of flour with two yolks of eggs, then add water enough to make a rather thin paste; add salt to taste; the two whites are beaten till stiff, and then mixed with the yolks, flour and water. Dip each branch of the cauliflowers into the mixture, and fry them in hot fat. When done, take them off with a skimmer, turn into a colander, dust salt all over, and serve warm. Asparagus, celery, egg-plant, oyster plant are all fine when fried in this manner.

CABBAGE, BOILED.

Great care is requisite in cleaning a cabbage for boiling, as it frequently harbors numerous insects. The large drum-head cabbage requires an hour to boil; the green savory cabbage will boil in twenty minutes. Add considerable salt to the water when boiling. Do not let a cabbage boil too long,—by a long boiling it becomes watery. Remove it from the water into a colander to drain, and serve with drawn butter, or butter poured over it.

Red cabbage is used for slaw, as is also the white winter cabbage. For directions to prepare these varieties, see articles Slaw and Sour-Crout.

CABBAGE WITH CREAM.

Remove the outer leaves from a solid, small-sized head of cabbage, and cut the remainder as fine as for slaw. Have on the fire a spider or deep skillet, and when it is hot put in the cut cabbage, pouring over it right away a pint of boiling water. Cover closely, and allow it to cook rapidly for ten minutes. Drain off the water, and add half a pint of new milk, or part milk and cream; when it boils, stir in a large teaspoonful of either wheat or rice flour, moistened with milk; add salt and pepper, and as soon as it comes to a boil, serve. Those who find slaw and other dishes prepared from cabbage indigestible, will not complain of this.

STEAMED CABBAGE.

Take a sound, solid cabbage, and with a large sharp knife shave it *very finely*. Put it in a sauce-pan, pour in half a teacupful of water or just enough to keep it from burning; cover it very tightly, so as to confine the steam; watch it closely, add a little water now and then, until it begins to be tender; then put into it a large tablespoonful of butter; salt and pepper to taste, dish it hot. If you prefer to give it a tart taste, just before taking from the fire add a third of a cup of good vinegar.

LADIES' CABBAGE.

Boil a firm white cabbage fifteen minutes, changing the water then for more from the boiling tea-kettle. When tender, drain and set aside until perfectly cold. Chop fine and add two beaten eggs, a tablespoonful of butter, pepper, salt, three tablespoonfuls of rich milk or cream. Stir all well together, and bake in a buttered pudding-dish until brown. Serve very hot. This dish resembles cauliflower and is very digestible and palatable.

FRIED CABBAGE.

Place in a frying-pan an ounce of butter and heat it boiling hot. Then take cold boiled cabbage chopped fine, or cabbage hot, cooked the same as steamed cabbage, put it into the hot butter and fry a light brown, adding two tablespoonfuls of vinegar. Very good.

FRENCH WAY OF COOKING CABBAGE.

Chop cold boiled white cabbage and let it drain till perfectly dry; stir in some melted butter to taste; pepper, salt and four tablespoonfuls of cream; after it is heated through add two well-beaten eggs; then turn the mixture into a buttered frying-pan, stirring until it is very hot and becomes a delicate brown on the under side. Place a hot dish over the pan, which must be reversed when turned out to be served.

SOUR-CROUT.

Barrels having held wine or vinegar are used to prepare sour-crout in. It is better, however, to have a special barrel for the purpose. Strasburg, as well as all Alsace, has a well-acquired fame for preparing the cabbages. They slice very white and firm cabbages in fine shreds with a machine made for the purpose. At the bottom of a small barrel they place a layer of coarse salt, and alternately layers of cabbage and salt, being careful to have one of salt on the top. As each layer of cabbage is added, it must be pressed down by a large and heavy pestle, and fresh layers are added as soon as the juice floats on the surface. The cabbage must be seasoned with a few grains of coriander, juniper berries, etc. When the barrel is full it must be put in a dry cellar, covered with a cloth, under a p'ank, and on this heavy weights are placed. At the end of a few days it will begin to ferment, during which time the pickle must be drawn off and replaced by fresh, until the liquor becomes clear. This should be done every day. Renew the cloth and wash the cover, put the weights back, and let stand for a month. By that time the sour-crout will be ready for use. Care must be taken to let the least possible air enter the sour-crout, and to have the cover perfectly clean. Each time the barrel has to be opened it must be properly closed again. These precautions must not be neglected.

This is often fried in the same manner as fried cabbage, excepting it is first boiled until soft in just water enough to cook it, then fry and add vinegar.

TO BOIL RICE.

Pick over the rice carefully, wash it in warm water, rubbing it between the hands, rinsing it in several waters, then let it remain in cold water until ready to be cooked. Have a sauce-pan of water slightly salted; when it is boiling hard, pour off the cold water from the rice, and sprinkle it in the boiling water by degrees, so as to keep the particles separated. Boil it steadily for twenty minutes, then take it off from the fire, and drain off all the water. Place the sauce-pan with the lid partly off, on the back part of the stove, where it is only moderately warm, to allow the rice to dry. The moisture will pass off and each grain of rice will be separated, so that if shaken the grains will fall apart. This is the true way of serving rice as a vegetable, and is the mode of cooking it in the southern States where it is raised.

PARSNIPS, BOILED.

Wash, scrape and split them. Put them into a pot of boiling water; add a little salt, and boil them till quite tender, which will be in from two to three hours according to their size. Dry them in a cloth when done and pour melted butter or white sauce (see Sauces) over them in the dish. Serve them up with any sort of boiled meat or with salt cod.

Parsnips are very good baked or stewed with meat.

FRIED PARSNIPS.

Boil tender in a little hot water salted; scrape, cut into long slices, dredge with flour; fry in hot lard or dripping, or in butter and lard mixed; fry quite brown. Drain off fat and serve.

Parsnips may be boiled and mashed the same as potatoes.

STEWED PARSNIPS.

After washing and scraping the parsnips slice them about half of an inch thick. Put them in a sauce-pan of boiling water containing just enough to barely cook them; add a tablespoonful of butter, season with salt and pepper, then cover closely. Stew them until the water has cooked away, watching carefully and stirring often to prevent burning, until they are soft. When they are done they will be of a creamy light straw color and deliciously sweet, retaining all the goodness of the vegetable.

PARSNIP FRITTERS.

Boil four or five parsnips; when tender take off the skin and mash them fine; add to them a teaspoonful of wheat flour and a beaten egg; put a tablespoonful of lard or beef drippings in a frying-pan over the fire, add to it a saltspoonful of salt; when boiling hot put in the parsnips; make it in small cakes with a spoon; when one side is a delicate brown turn the other; when both are done take them on a dish, put a very little of the fat in which they were fried over and serve hot. These resemble very nearly the taste of the salsify or oyster plant, and will generally be preferred.

CREAMED PARSNIPS.

Boil tender, scrape, and slice lengthwise. Put over the fire with two tablespoonfuls of butter, pepper and salt, and a little minced parsley. Shake until the mixture boils. Dish the parsnips, add to the sauce three tablespoonfuls of cream or milk, in which has been stirred a quarter of a spoonful of flour. Boil once, and pour over the parsnips.

STEWED TOMATOES.

Pour boiling water over a dozen sound ripe tomatoes; let them remain for a few moments; then peel off the skins, slice them, and put them over the fire in a well-lined tin or granite ware sauce-pan. Stew them about twenty minutes, then add a tablespoonful of butter, salt and pepper to taste; let them stew fifteen minutes longer; and serve hot. Some prefer to thicken tomatoes with a little grated bread, adding a teaspoonful of sugar; and others who like the flavor of onion chop up one and add while stewing; then again some add as much green corn as there are tomatoes.

TO PEEL TOMATOES.

Put the tomatoes into a frying-basket, and plunge them into hot water for three or four minutes. Drain and peel. Another way is to place them in a flat baking-tin and set them in a hot oven about five minutes; this loosens the skins so that they readily slip off.

SCALLOPED TOMATOES.

Butter the sides and bottom of a pudding-dish. Put a layer of bread-crumbs in the bottom; on them put a layer of sliced tomatoes; sprinkle with salt, pepper and some bits of butter, and a very *little* white sugar. Then repeat with another layer of crumbs, another of tomato, and seasoning until full, having the top layer of slices of tomato, with bits of butter on each. Bake covered until well cooked through; remove the cover and brown quickly.

STUFFED BAKED TOMATOES.

From the blossom-end of a dozen tomatoes—smooth, ripe and solid—cut a thin slice, and with a small spoon scoop out the pulp without breaking the rind surrounding it; chop a small head of cabbage and a good-sized onion finely, and mix with them fine bread-crumbs and the pulp; season with pepper, salt and sugar, and add a cup of sweet cream; when all is well mixed, fill the tomato shells, replace the slices, and place the tomatoes in a buttered baking dish, cut ends up, and put in the pan just enough water to keep from burning; drop a small lump of butter on each tomato, and bake half an hour or so, till well done; place another bit of butter on each, and serve in same dish. Very fine.

Another stuffing which is considered quite fine. Cut a slice from the stem of each and scoop out the soft pulp. Mince one small onion and fry it slightly: add a gill of hot water, the tomato pulp, and two ounces of cold veal or chicken chopped fine, simmer slowly, and season with salt and pepper. Stir into the pan cracker-dust or bread-crumbs enough to absorb the moisture; take off from the fire and let it cool; stuff the tomatoes with this mass, sprinkle dry crumbs over the top; add a small piece of butter to the top of each and bake until slightly browned on top.

BAKED TOMATOES, (Plain.)

Peel and slice quarter of an inch thick ; place in layers in a pudding dish, seasoning each layer with salt, pepper, butter, and a very little white sugar. Cover with a lid or large plate, and bake half an hour. Remove the lid and brown for fifteen minutes. Just before taking from the oven, pour over the top three or four tablespoonfuls of whipped cream with melted butter.

TO PREPARE TOMATOES, (Raw.)

Carefully remove the peelings. Only perfectly ripe tomatoes should ever be eaten raw, and if ripe the skins easily peel off. Scalding injures the flavor. Slice thin, and sprinkle generously with salt, more sparingly with black pepper, and to a dish holding one quart, add a light tablespoonful of sugar to give a piquant zest to the whole. Lastly, add a gill of best cider vinegar; although, if you would have a dish yet better suited to please an epicurean palate, you may add a teaspoonful of made mustard and two tablespoonfuls of rich sweet cream.

FRIED AND BROILED TOMATOES.

Cut firm, large, ripe tomatoes into thick slices, rather more than a quarter of an inch thick. Season with salt and pepper, dredge well with flour, or roll in egg and crumbs, and fry them brown on both sides evenly, in hot butter and lard mixed. Or, prepare them the same as for frying, broiling on a well-greased gridiron, seasoning afterward the same as beefsteak. A good accompaniment to steak. Or, having prepared the following sauce, a pint of milk, a tablespoonful of flour and one beaten egg, salt, pepper and a very little mace; cream an ounce of butter, whisk into it the milk and let it simmer until it thickens; pour the sauce on a hot side-dish and arrange the tomatoes in the centre.

SCRAMBLED TOMATOES.

Remove the skins from a dozen tomatoes; cut them up in a sauce-pan; add a little butter pepper and salt; when sufficiently boiled, beat up five or six eggs,

A. ADAMS.

MARTHA JEFFERSON RANDOLPH.

MARTHA WASHINGTON.

Mrs. JAMES MONROE.

D. P. MADISON.

and just before you serve turn them into the sauce-pan with the tomatoes, and stir one way for two minutes, allowing them time to be done thoroughly.

CUCUMBER Á LA CRÊME.

Peel and cut into slices (lengthwise) some fine cucumbers. Boil them until soft, salt to taste, and serve with delicate cream sauce.

For Tomato Salad, see "Salads," also for Raw Cucumbers.

FRIED CUCUMBERS.

Pare them and cut lengthwise in very thick slices; wipe them dry with a cloth; sprinkle with salt and pepper, dredge with flour, and fry in lard and butter, a tablespoonful of each, mixed. Brown both sides and serve warm.

GREEN CORN, BOILED.

This should be cooked on the same day it is gathered; it loses its sweetness in a few hours and must be artificially supplied. Strip off the husks, pick out all the silk and put it in boiling water; if not entirely fresh, add a tablespoonful of sugar to the water, but *no salt;* boil twenty minutes, fast, and serve; or you may cut it from the cob, put in plenty of butter and a little salt, and serve in a covered vegetable dish. The corn is much sweeter when cooked with the husks on, but requires longer time to boil. Will generally boil in twenty minutes.

Green corn left over from dinner makes a nice breakfast dish, prepared as follows: Cut the corn from the cob, and put into a bowl with a cup of milk to every cup of corn, a half cup of flour, one egg, a pinch of salt, and a little butter. Mix well into a thick batter, and fry in small cakes in very hot butter. Serve with plenty of butter and powdered sugar.

CORN PUDDING.

This is a Virginia dish. Scrape the substance out of twelve ears of tender, green, uncooked corn (it is better scraped than grated, as you do not get those husky particles which you cannot avoid with a grater); add yolks and whites, beaten separately, of four eggs, a teaspoonful of sugar, the same of flour mixed in a tablespoonful of butter, a small quantity of salt and pepper, and one pint of milk. Bake about half or three quarters of an hour.

STEWED CORN.

Take a dozen ears of green sweet corn, very tender and juicy; cut off the kernels, cutting with a large sharp knife from the top of the cob down; then scrape the cob. Put the corn into a sauce-pan over the fire, with just enough water to make it cook without burning; boil about twenty minutes, then add a teacupful of milk or cream, a tablespoonful of cold butter, and season with pepper and salt. Boil ten minutes longer, and dish up hot, in a vegetable dish. The corn would be much sweeter if the scraped cobs were boiled first in the water that the corn is cooked in.

Many like corn cooked in this manner, putting half corn and half tomatoes; either way is very good.

FRIED CORN.

Cut the corn off the cob, taking care not to bring off any of the husk with it, and to have the grains as separate as possible. Fry in a little butter—just enough to keep it from sticking to the pan; stir very often. When nicely browned, add salt and pepper, and a little rich cream. Do not set it near the stove after the cream is added, as it will be apt to turn. This makes a nice dinner or breakfast dish.

ROASTED GREEN CORN.

Strip off all the husk from green corn, and roast it on a gridiron over a bright fire of coals, turning it as one side is done. Or, if a wood fire is used, make a place clean in front of the fire, lay the corn down, turn it when one side is done; serve with salt and butter

SUCCOTASH.

Take a pint of fresh shelled Lima beans, or any large fresh beans, put them in a pot with cold water, rather more than will cover them. Scrape the kernels from twelve ears of young sweet corn; put the cobs in with the beans, boiling from half to three-quarters of an hour. Now take out the cobs and put in the scraped corn; boil again fifteen minutes, then season with salt and pepper to taste, a piece of butter the size of an egg, and half a cup of cream. Serve hot.

FRIED EGG-PLANT.

Take fresh, purple egg-plants of a middling size; cut them in slices a quarter of an inch thick, and soak them for half an hour in cold water, with a teaspoonful of salt in it. Have ready some cracker or bread-crumbs and one beaten egg; drain off the water from the slices, lay them on a napkin, dip them in the crumbs and then in the egg, put another coat of crumbs on them, and fry them in butter to a light brown. The frying-pan must be hot before the slices are put in,—they will fry in ten minutes.

You may pare them before you put them into the frying-pan, or you may pull the skins off when you take them up. You must not remove them from the water until you are ready to cook them, as the air will turn them black.

STUFFED EGG-PLANT.

Cut the egg-plant in two; scrape out all the inside and put it in a sauce-pan with a little minced ham; cover with water and boil until soft; drain off the water; add two tablespoonfuls of grated crumbs, a tablespoonful of butter, half a minced onion, salt and pepper; stuff each half of the hull with the mixture; add a small lump of butter to each, and bake fifteen minutes

Minced veal or chicken in the place of ham, is equally as good, and many prefer it.

STRING BEANS.

Break off the end that grew to the vine, drawing off at the same time the string upon the edge; repeat the same process from the other end; cut them with a sharp knife into pieces half an inch long, and boil them in *just enough* water to *cover* them. They usually require one hour's boiling; but this depends upon their age and freshness. After they have boiled until tender, and the water *boiled nearly out*, add pepper and salt, a tablespoonful of butter, and a half a cup of cream; if you have not the cream, add more butter.

Many prefer to drain them before adding the seasoning; in that case they lose the real goodness of the vegetable.

LIMA AND KIDNEY BEANS.

These beans should be put into boiling water, a little more than enough to cover them, and boiled till tender—from half an hour to two hours; serve with butter and salt upon them.

These beans are in season from the last of July to the last of September. There are several other varieties of beans, used as summer vegetables, which are cooked as above.

For Baked Beans, see " Pork and Beans."

CELERY.

This is stewed the same as green corn, by boiling, adding cream, butter, salt and·pepper.

STEWED SALSIFY OR OYSTER PLANT.

Wash the roots and scrape off their skins, throwing them, as you do so, into cold water, for exposure to the air causes them to immediately turn dark. Then cut crosswise into little thin slices; throw into fresh water, enough to cover; add a little salt, and stew in a covered vessel until tender, or about one hour. Pour off a little of the water, add a small lump of butter, a little pepper, and a gill of sweet cream, and a teaspoonful of flour stirred to a paste. Boil up and serve hot.

Salsify may be simply boiled, and melted butter turned over them.

FRIED SALSIFY.

Stew the salsify as usual till very tender; then with the back of a spoon or a potato jammer, mash it very fine. Beat up an egg, add a teacupful of milk, a little flour, butter and seasoning of pepper and salt. Make into little cakes, and fry a light brown in boiling lard, first rolling in beaten egg and then flour.

BEETS BOILED.

Select small-sized, smooth roots. They should be carefully washed, but not cut before boiling, as the juice will escape and the sweetness of the vegetable be impaired, leaving it white and hard. Put them into boiling water, and boil them until tender; which requires often from one to two hours. Do not probe them, but press them with the finger to ascertain if they are sufficiently done. When satisfied of this, take them up, and put them into a pan of cold water, and slip off the outside. Cut them into thin slices, and while hot season with butter, salt, a little pepper and very sharp vinegar.

BAKED BEETS.

Beets retain their sugary, delicate flavor to perfection if they are baked instead of boiled. Turn them frequently while in the oven, using a knife, as the fork allows the juice to run out. When done remove the skin, and serve, with butter, salt and pepper on the slices.

STEWED BEETS.

Boil them first, and then scrape and slice them. Put them into a stew-pan with a piece of butter rolled in flour, some boiled onion and parsley chopped fine, and a little vinegar, salt and pepper. Set the pan on the fire, and let the beets stew for a quarter of an hour.

OKRA.

This grows in the shape of pods, and is of a gelatinous character, much used for soup, and is also pickled; it may be boiled as follows. Put the young and tender pods of long white okra in salted boiling water in granite, porcelain or a tin-lined saucepan—as contact with iron will discolor it; boil fifteen minutes; remove the stems, and serve with butter, pepper, salt and vinegar if preferred.

ASPARAGUS.

Scrape the stems of the asparagus lightly, but very clean; throw them into cold water, and when they are all scraped and very clean, tie them in bunches of equal size; cut the large ends evenly, that the stems may be all of the same length, and put the asparagus into plenty of boiling water, well salted. While it is boiling, cut several slices of bread half an inch thick, pare off the crust, and toast it a delicate brown on both sides. When the stalks of the asparagus are tender, (it will usually cook in twenty to forty minutes), lift it out directly, or it will lose both its color and flavor, and will also be liable to break; dip the toast quickly into the liquor in which it was boiled, and dish the vegetable upon it, the heads all lying one way. Pour over white sauce, or melted butter.

ASPARAGUS WITH EGGS.

Boil a bunch of asparagus twenty minutes; cut off the tender tops and lay them in a deep pie plate, buttering, salting and peppering well. Beat up four eggs, the yolks and whites separately, to a stiff froth; add two tablespoonfuls of milk or cream, a tablespoonful of warm butter, pepper and salt to taste. Pour evenly over the asparagus mixture. Bake eight minutes or until the eggs are set. Very good.

GREEN PEAS.

Shell the peas and wash in cold water. Put in boiling water just enough to cover them well, and keep them from burning; boil from twenty minutes to half an hour, when the liquor should be nearly boiled out; season with pepper and salt, and a good allowance of butter; serve very hot.

This is a very much better way than cooking in a larger quantity of water, and draining off the liquor, as that diminishes the sweetness, and much of the fine flavor of the peas is lost. The salt should never be put in the peas before they are tender, unless very young, as it tends to harden them

STEWED GREEN PEAS.

Into a sauce-pan of boiling water put two or three pints of young green peas, and when nearly done and tender, drain in a colander dry; then melt two ounces of butter in two of flour; stir well, and boil five minutes longer; should the pods be quite clean and fresh, boil them first in the water, remove, and put in the peas. The Germans prepare a very palatable dish of sweet young pods alone, by simply stirring in a little butter with some savory herbs.

SQUASHES, OR CYMBLINGS.

The green or summer squash is best when the outside is beginning to turn yellow, as it is then less watery and insipid than when younger. Wash them, cut them into pieces, and take out the seeds. Boil them about three-quarters of an hour, or till quite tender. When done, drain and squeeze them well till you have pressed out all the water; mash them with a little butter, pepper and salt. Then put the squash thus prepared into a stew-pan, set it on hot coals, and stir it very frequently till it becomes dry. Take care not to let it burn.

Summer squash is very nice steamed, then prepared the same as boiled.

BOILED WINTER SQUASH.

This is much finer than the summer squash. It is fit to eat in August, and, in a dry warm place, can be kept well all winter. The color is a very bright yellow. Pare it, take out the seeds, cut it in pieces, and stew it slowly till quite soft, in a very little water. Afterwards drain, squeeze, and press it well; then mash it with a very little butter, pepper and salt. They will boil in from twenty to forty minutes.

BAKED WINTER SQUASH.

Cut open the squash, take out the seeds, and without paring cut it up into large pieces; put the pieces on tins or a dripping-pan, place in a moderately hot oven, .and bake about an hour. When done, peel and mash like mashed potatoes, or serve the pieces hot on a dish, to be eaten warm with butter like sweet potatoes. It retains its sweetness much better baked this way than when boiled.

VEGETABLE HASH.

Chop rather coarsely the remains of vegetables left from a boiled dinner, such as cabbage, parsnips, potatoes, etc., sprinkle over them a little pepper; place in a saucepan or frying-pan over the fire; put in a piece of butter the size of a hickory nut; when it begins to melt, tip the dish so as to oil the bottom, and around the sides; then put in the chopped vegetables; pour in a spoonful or two of hot water from the tea-kettle; cover quickly so as to keep in the steam. When heated thoroughly take off the cover and stir occasionally until well cooked. Serve hot. Persons fond of vegetables will relish this dish very much.

SPINACH.

It should be cooked so as to retain its bright-green color, and not sent to table, as it so often is, of a dull-brown or olive color; to retain its fresh appearance, do not cover the vessel while it is cooking.

Spinach requires close examination and picking, as insects are frequently found among it, and it is often gritty. Wash it through three or four waters. Then drain it and put it in boiling water. Fifteen to twenty minutes is generally sufficient time to boil spinach. Be careful to remove the scum. When it is quite tender, take it up, and drain and squeeze it well. Chop it fine, and put it into a sauce-pan with a piece of butter and a little pepper and salt. Set it on the fire and let it stew five minutes, stirring it all the time, until quite dry. Turn it into a vegetable dish, shape it into a mound, slice some hard-boiled eggs and lay around the top.

GREENS.

About a peck of greens are enough for a mess for a family of six, such as dandelions, cowslips, burdock, chiccory and other greens. All greens should be carefully examined, the tough ones thrown out, then be thoroughly washed through several waters until they are entirely free from sand. The addition of a handful of salt to each pan of water used in washing the greens will free them from insects and worms, especially, if, after the last watering, they are allowed to stand in salted water for a half hour or longer. When ready to boil the greens, put them into a large pot half full of boiling water, with a handful of salt, and boil them steadily until the stalks are tender; this will be in from five to twenty minutes, according to the maturity of the greens; but remember that long-continued boiling wastes the tender substances of the leaves, and so diminishes both the bulk and the nourishment of the dish; for this reason it is best to cut away any tough stalks before beginning to cook the greens. As soon as they are tender, drain them in a colander, chop them a little and return them to the fire long enough to season them with salt, pepper and butter; vinegar may be added if it is liked; the greens should be served as soon as they are hot.

All kinds of greens can be cooked in this manner.

STEWED CARROTS.

Wash and scrape the carrots, and divide them into strips; put them into a stew-pan with water enough to cover them; add a spoonful of salt, and let them boil slowly until tender; then drain and replace them in the pan, with two table-spoonfuls of butter rolled in flour, shake over a little pepper and salt, then add enough cream or milk to moisten the whole; let it come to a boil and serve hot.

CARROTS MASHED.

Scrape and wash them; cook them tender in boiling water salted slightly. Drain well and mash them. Work in a good piece of butter and season with pepper and salt. Heap up on a vegetable dish and serve hot.

Carrots are also good simply boiled in salted water and dished up hot with melted butter over them.

TURNIPS.

Turnips are boiled plain with or without meat, also mashed like potatoes, and stewed like parsnips. They should always be served hot. They require from forty minutes to an hour to cook.

STEWED PUMPKIN.

See "Stewed Pumpkin for Pie." Cook the same, then after stewing, season the same as mashed potatoes. Pumpkin is good baked in the same manner as baked winter squash.

STEWED ENDIVE.

Ingredients.—Six heads of endive, salt and water, one pint of broth, thickening of butter and flour, one tablespoonful of lemon juice, a small lump of sugar.

Mode.—Wash and free the endive thoroughly from insects, remove the green part of the leaves, and put it into boiling water, slightly salted. Let it remain for ten minutes; then take it out, drain it till there is no water remaining, and chop it very fine. Put it into a stew-pan with the broth; add a little salt and a lump of sugar, and boil until the endive is perfectly tender. When done, which may be ascertained by squeezing a piece between the thumb and finger, add a thickening of butter and flour and the lemon juice; let the sauce boil up, and serve.

Time.—Ten minutes to boil, five minutes to simmer in the broth.

BAKED MUSHROOMS.

Prepare them the same as for stewing. Place them in a baking-pan, in a moderate oven. Season with salt, pepper, lemon juice, and chopped parsley. Cook in the oven fifteen minutes, baste with butter. Arrange on a dish and pour the gravy over them. Serve with sauce made by beating a cup of cream, two ounces of butter, a tablespoonful of chopped parsley, a little cayenne pepper, salt, a tablespoonful of white sauce, and two tablespoonfuls of lemon juice. Put in a sauce-pan and set on the fire. Stir until thick, but do not let boil. Mushrooms are very nice placed on slices of well-buttered toast when set into the oven to bake. They cook in about fifteen minutes.

STEWED MUSHROOMS.

Time, twenty-one minutes. Button mushrooms; salt to taste; a little butter rolled in flour; two tablespoonfuls of cream or the yolk of one egg. Choose buttons of uniform size. Wipe them clean and white with a wet flannel; put them in a stew-pan with a little water, and let them stew very gently for a quarter of an hour. Add salt to taste, work in a little flour and butter, to make the liquor about as thick as cream, and let it boil for five minutes. When you are ready to dish it up, stir in two tablespoonfuls of cream or the yolk of an egg; stir it over the fire for a minute, but do not let it boil, and serve. Stewed button mushrooms are very nice, either in fish stews or ragouts, or served apart to eat with fish. Another way of doing them is to stew them in milk and water (after they are rubbed white), add to them a little veal gravy, mace and salt, and thicken the gravy with cream or the yolks of eggs.

Mushrooms can be cooked in the same manner as the recipes for oysters, either stewed, fried, broiled, or as a soup. They are also used to flavor sauces, catsups, meat gravies, game and soups.

CANNED MUSHROOMS.

Canned mushrooms may be served with good effect with game and even with beefsteak if prepared in this way: Open the can and pour off every drop of the liquid found there; let the mushrooms drain, then put them in a sauce-pan with a little cream, and butter, pepper, and salt; let them simmer gently for from five to ten minutes, and when the meat is on the platter pour the mushrooms over it. If served with steak, that should be very tender, and be broiled, never in any case fried.

MUSHROOMS FOR WINTER USE.

Wash and wipe free from grit the small fresh button mushrooms. Put into a frying-pan a quarter of a pound of the very best butter. Add to it two whole cloves, a saltspoonful of salt, and a tablespoonful of lemon juice. When hot, add a quart of the small mushrooms, toss them about in the butter for a moment only, then put them in jars; fill the top of each jar with an inch or two of the butter and let it cool. Keep the jars in a cool place, and when the butter is quite firm, add a top layer of salt. Cover to keep out dust.

The best mushrooms grow on uplands, or in high, open fields, where the air is pure.

TRUFFLES.

The truffle belongs to the family of the mushrooms; they are used principally in this country as a condiment for boned turkey and chicken, scrambled eggs, fillets of beef, game and fish. When mixed in due proportion, they add a peculiar zest and flavor to sauces, that cannot be found in any other plant in the vegetable kingdom.

ITALIAN STYLE OF DRESSING TRUFFLES.

Ten truffles, a quarter of a pint of salad-oil, pepper and salt to taste, one tablespoonful of minced parsley, a very little finely minced garlic, two blades of pounded mace, one tablespoonful of lemon-juice.

After cleansing and brushing the truffles, cut them into thin slices, and put them in a baking-dish, on a seasoning of oil or butter, pepper, salt, parsley, garlic and mace, in the above proportion. Bake them for nearly an hour, and just before serving, add the lemon juice and send them to table very hot.

TRUFFLES AU NATUREL.

Select some fine truffles; cleanse them, by washing them in several waters with a brush, until not a particle of sand or grit remains on them; wrap each truffle in buttered paper, and bake in a hot oven for quite an hour; take off the paper, wipe the truffles, and serve them in a hot napkin.

Maccaroni.

MACCARONI Á LA ITALIENNE.

Divide a quarter of a pound of maccaroni into four-inch pieces. Simmer fifteen minutes in plenty of boiling water, salted. Drain. Put the maccaroni into a sauce-pan and turn over it a strong soup stock, enough to prevent burning. Strew over it an ounce of grated cheese; when the cheese is melted, dish. Put alternate layers of maccaroni and cheese; then turn over the soup stock and bake half an hour.

MACCARONI AND CHEESE.

Break half a pound of maccaroni into pieces an inch or two long; cook it in boiling water enough to cover it well; put in a good teaspoonful of salt; let it boil about twenty minutes. Drain it well, and then put a layer in the bottom of a well-buttered pudding-dish, upon this some grated cheese, and small pieces of butter, a bit of salt, then more maccaroni, and so on, filling the dish; sprinkle the top layer with a thick layer of cracker-crumbs. Pour over the whole a teacupful of cream or milk. Set it in the oven and bake half an hour. It should be nicely browned on top. Serve in the same dish in which it was baked, with a clean napkin pinned around it.

TIMBALE OF MACCARONI.

Break in very short lengths small maccaroni (vermicelli, spaghetti, tagliarini). Let it be rather overdone; dress it with butter and grated cheese; then work into it one or two eggs, according to quantity. Butter and bread-crumb a plain mold, and when the maccaroni is nearly cold fill the mold with it, pressing it well down and leaving a hollow in the centre, into which place a well-flavored mince of meat, poultry or game; then fill up the mold with more maccaroni, pressed well down. Bake in a moderately heated oven, turn out and serve.

MACCARONI A LA CRÊME.

Boil one-quarter of a pound of maccaroni in plenty of hot water, salted, until tender; put half a pint of milk in a double boiler, and when it boils stir into it a mixture of two tablespoonfuls of butter and one of flour. Add two tablespoonfuls of cream, a little white and cayenne pepper; salt to taste, and from one-quarter to one-half a pound of grated cheese according to taste. Drain and dish the maccaroni; pour the boiling sauce over it, and serve immediately.

MACCARONI AND TOMATO SAUCE.

Divide half a pound of maccaroni into four-inch pieces, put it into boiling salted water enough to cover it; boil from fifteen to twenty minutes; then drain; arrange it neatly on a hot dish, and pour tomato sauce over it, and serve immediately while hot. See "Sauces" for tomato sauce.

BUTTER AND CHEESE.

TO MAKE BUTTER.

Thoroughly scald the churn, then cool well with ice or spring water. Now pour in the thick cream; churn fast at first, then, as the butter forms, more slowly; always with perfect regularity; in warm weather, pour a little cold water into the churn, should the butter form slowly; in winter, if the cream is too cold, add a little warm water to bring it to the proper temperature. When the butter has "come," rinse the sides of the churn down with cold water, and take the butter up with the perforated dasher or a wooden ladle, turning it dexterously just below the surface of the buttermilk to catch every stray bit; have ready some very cold water, in a deep wooden tray; and into this plunge the dasher when you draw it from the churn; the butter will float off, leaving the dasher free. When you have collected all the butter, gather behind a wooden butter ladle, and drain off the water, squeezing and pressing the butter with the ladle; then pour on more cold water, and work the butter with the ladle to get the milk out, drain off the water, sprinkle salt over the butter,—a tablespoonful to a pound; work it in a little, and set in a cool place for an hour to harden, then work and knead it until not another drop of water exudes, and the butter is perfectly smooth and close in texture and polish; then with the ladle make up into rolls, little balls, stamped pats, etc.

The churn, dasher, tray and ladle, should be well scalded before using, so that the butter will not stick to them, and then cooled with very cold water.

When you skim cream into your cream jar, stir it well into what is already there, so that it may all sour alike; and no *fresh cream should be put with it* within twelve hours before churning, or the butter will not come quickly; and perhaps, not at all.

Butter is indispensable in almost all culinary preparations. Good, fresh butter, used in moderation, is easily digested; it is softening, nutritious, and fattening, and is far more easily digested than any other of the oleaginous substances sometimes used in its place.

TO MAKE BUTTER QUICKLY.

Immediately after the cow is milked, strain into clean pans, and set it over a moderate fire until it is scalding hot; do not let it boil; then set it aside; when it is cold, skim off the cream; the milk will still be fit for any ordinary use; when you have enough cream, put it into a clean earthen basin; beat it with a wooden spoon until the butter is made, which will not be long; then take it from the milk and work it with a little cold water, until it is free from milk; then drain off the water, put a small tablespoonful of fine salt to each pound of butter, and work it in. A small teaspoonful of fine white sugar, worked in with the salt, will be found an improvement—sugar is a great preservative. Make the butter in a roll; cover it with a bit of muslin, and keep it in a cool place. A reliable recipe.

A BRINE TO PRESERVE BUTTER.

First work your butter into small rolls, wrapping each one carefully in a clean muslin cloth, tying them up with a string. Make a brine, say three gallons, having it strong enough of salt to bear up an egg; add half a teacupful of pure, white sugar, and one tablespoonful of saltpetre; boil the brine, and when cold strain it carefully. Pour it over the rolls so as to more than cover them, as this excludes the air. Place a weight over all to keep the rolls under the surface.

PUTTING UP BUTTER TO KEEP.

Take of the best pure, common salt two quarts, one ounce of white sugar and one of saltpetre; pulverize them together completely. Work the butter well, then thoroughly work in an ounce of this mixture to every pound of butter. The butter to be made into half-pound rolls, and put into the following brine—to three gallons of brine strong enough to bear an egg, add a quarter of a pound of white sugar.

—Orange Co., N. Y., style.

CURDS AND CREAM.

One gallon of milk will make a moderate dish. Put one spoonful of prepared rennet to each quart of milk, and when you find that it has become curd, tie it loosely in a thin cloth and hang it to drain; do not wring or press the cloth; when drained, put the curd into a mug and set in cool water, which must be frequently changed (a refrigerator saves this trouble.) When you dish it, if there is whey in the mug, ladle it gently out without pressing the curd; lay it on a deep dish, and pour fresh cream over it; have powdered loaf-sugar to eat with it; also hand the nutmeg grater.

Prepared rennet can be had at almost any druggist's, and at a reasonable price. Call for Crosse & Blackwell's Prepared Rennet.

NEW JERSEY CREAM CHEESE.

First scald the quantity of milk desired; let it cool a little, then add the rennet; the directions for quantity are given on the packages of "Prepared Rennet." When the curd is formed, take it out on a ladle without breaking it; lay it on a thin cloth held by two persons; dash a ladleful of water over each ladleful of curd, to separate the curd; hang it up to drain the water off, and then put it under a light press for one hour; cut the curd with a thread into small pieces; lay a cloth between each two, and press for an hour; take them out, rub them with fine salt, let them lie on a board for an hour, and wash them in cold water; let them lie to drain, and in a day or two the skin will look dry; put some sweet grass under and over them, and they will soon ripen.

COTTAGE CHEESE.

Put a pan of sour or loppered milk on the stove or range, where it is not too hot; let it scald until the whey rises to the top (be careful that it does not boil, or the curd will become hard and tough). Place a clean cloth or towel over a sieve, and pour this whey and curd into it, leaving it covered to drain two to three hours; then put it into a dish and chop it fine with a spoon, adding a teaspoonful of salt, a tablespoonful of butter and enough sweet cream to make the cheese the consistency of putty. With your hands make it into little balls flattened. Keep it in a cool place. Many like it made rather thin with cream, serving it in a deep dish. You may make this cheese of sweet milk, by forming the curd with prepared rennet.

SLIP.

Slip is bonny-clabber without its acidity, and so delicate is its flavor that many persons like it just as well as ice-cream. It is prepared thus: Make a quart of milk moderately warm; then stir into it one large spoonful of the preparation called rennet; set it by, and when cool again it will be as stiff as jelly. It should be made only a few hours before it is to be used, or it will be tough and watery; in summer set the dish on ice after it has jellied. It must be served with powdered sugar, nutmeg and cream.

CHEESE FONDU.

Melt an ounce of butter, and whisk into it a pint of boiled milk. Dissolve two tablespoonfuls of flour in a gill of cold milk, add it to the boiled milk and let it cool. Beat the yolks of four eggs with a heaping teaspoonful of salt, half a teaspoonful of pepper, and five ounces of grated cheese. Whip the whites of the eggs and add them, pour the mixture into a deep tin lined with buttered paper, and allow for the rising, say four inches. Bake twenty minutes and serve the moment it leaves the oven.

CHEESE SOUFFLÉ.

Melt an ounce of butter in a sauce-pan;. mix smoothly with it one ounce of flour, a pinch of salt and cayenne and a quarter of a pint of milk; simmer the mixture gently over the fire, stirring it all the time, till it is as thick as melted butter; stir into it about three ounces of finely-grated parmesan, or any good cheese. Turn it into a basin, and mix with it the yolks of two well-beaten eggs. Whisk three whites to a solid froth, and just before the soufflé is baked put them into it, and pour the mixture into a small round tin. It should be only half filled, as the fondu will rise very high. Pin a napkin around the dish in which it is baked, and serve the moment it is baked. It would be well to have a metal cover strongly heated. Time twenty minutes. Sufficient for six persons.

SCALLOPED CHEESE.

Any person who is fond of cheese could not fail to favor this recipe.

Take three slices of bread, well-buttered, first cutting off the brown outside crust. Grate fine a quarter of a pound of any kind of good cheese; lay the bread in layers in a buttered baking-dish, sprinkle over it the grated cheese, some salt and pepper to taste. Mix four well-beaten eggs with three cups of milk; pour it over the bread and cheese. Bake it in a hot oven as you would cook a bread pudding. This makes an ample dish for four people.

PASTRY RAMAKINS.

Take the remains or odd pieces of any light puff-paste left from pies or tarts; gather up the pieces of paste, roll it out evenly, and sprinkle it with grated cheese of a nice flavor. Fold the paste in three, roll it out again, and sprinkle more cheese over; fold the paste, roll it out, and with a paste-cutter shape it in any way that may be desired. Bake the ramakins in a brisk oven from ten to fifteen minutes. dish them on a hot napkin, and serve quickly. The appearance of this dish may be very much improved by brushing the ramakins over with yolk of egg before they are placed in the oven. Where expense is not objected to, parmesan is the best kind of cheese to use for making this dish.

Very nice with a cup of coffee for a lunch.

CAYENNE CHEESE STRAWS.

A quarter of a pound of flour, 2 oz. butter, 2 oz. grated parmesan cheese, a pinch of salt, and a few grains of cayenne pepper. Mix into a paste with the yolk of an egg. Roll out to the thickness of a silver quarter, about four or five inches long; cut into strips about a third of an inch wide, twist them as you would a paper spill, and lay them on a baking-sheet slightly floured. Bake in a moderate oven until crisp, but they must not be the least brown. If put away in a tin, these cheese straws will keep a long time. Serve cold, piled tastefully on a glass dish. You can make the straws of remnants of puff-pastry, rolling in the grated cheese.

CHEESE CREAM TOAST.

Stale bread may be served as follows: Toast the slices and cover them slightly with grated cheese; make a cream for ten slices out of a pint of milk and two tablespoonfuls of plain flour. The milk should be boiling, and the flour mixed in a little cold water before stirring in. When the cream is nicely cooked, season with salt and butter; set the toast and cheese in the oven for three or four minutes, and then pour the cream over them.

WELSH RAREBIT.

Grate three ounces of dry cheese, and mix it with the yolks of two eggs, put four ounces of grated bread, and three of butter; beat the whole together in a mortar with a dessertspoonful of made mustard, a little salt and some pepper; toast some slices of bread, cut off the outside crust, cut it in shapes and spread the paste thick upon them, and put them in the oven, let them become hot and slightly browned, serve hot as possible.

Eggs.

There are so many ways of cooking and dressing eggs, that it seems unnecessary for the ordinary family to use only those that are the most practical.

To ascertain the freshness of an egg, hold it between your thumb and forefinger in a horizontal position, with a strong light in front of you. The fresh egg will have a clear appearance, both upper and lower sides being the same. The stale egg will have a clear appearance at the lower side, while the upper side will exhibit a dark or cloudy appearance.

Another test is to put them in a pan of cold water; those that are the first to sink are the freshest; the stale will rise and float on top; or, if the large end turns up in the water, they are not fresh. The best time for preserving eggs is from July to September.

TO PRESERVE EGGS.

There are several recipes for preserving eggs, and we give first one which we know to be effectual, keeping them fresh from August until Spring. Take a piece of quick-lime as large as a good-sized lemon, and two teacupfuls of salt; put it into a large vessel and slack it with a gallon of boiling water. It will boil and bubble until thick as cream; when it is cold, pour off the top, which will be perfectly clear. Drain off this liquor, and pour it over your eggs; see that the liquor more than covers them. A stone jar is the most convenient;—one that holds about six quarts.

Another manner of preserving eggs is to pack them in a jar with layers of salt between, the large end of the egg downward, with a thick layer of salt at the top; cover tightly, and set in a cool place.

Some put them in a wire basket or a piece of mosquito net, and dip them in boiling water half a minute; then pack in saw-dust. Still another manner is to dissolve a cheap article of gum arabic, about as thin as mucilage, and brush over each egg with it; then pack in powdered charcoal; set in a cool, dark place.

Eggs can be kept for some time by smearing the shells with butter or lard; then packed in plenty of bran or sawdust, the eggs not allowed to touch one another; or coat the eggs with melted paraffine.

BOILED EGGS.

Eggs for boiling cannot be too fresh, or boiled too soon after they are laid; but rather a longer time should be allowed for boiling a new-laid egg than for one that is three or four days old. Have ready a sauce-pan of boiling water; put the eggs into it gently with a spoon, letting the spoon touch the bottom of the sauce-pan before it is withdrawn, that the egg may not fall, and consequently crack. For those who like eggs lightly boiled, three minutes will be found sufficient; three and three-quarters to four minutes will be ample time to set the white nicely; and if liked hard, six or seven minutes will not be found too long. Should the eggs be unusually large, as those of black Spanish fowls sometimes are, allow an extra half minute for them. Eggs for salad should be boiled for ten or fifteen minutes, and should be placed in a basin of cold water for a few minutes, to shrink the meat from the shell; they should then be rolled on the table with the hand, and the shell will peel off easily.

SOFT BOILED EGGS.

When properly cooked, eggs are done evenly through, like any other food. This result may be obtained by putting the egg into a dish with a cover, or a tin pail, and then pouring upon them *boiling* water—two quarts or more to a dozen of eggs—and cover and set them away where they will keep *hot* and *not* boil, for ten to twelve minutes. The heat of the water cooks the eggs slowly, evenly and sufficiently, leaving the centre, or yolk, harder than the white, and the egg tastes as much richer and nicer as a fresh egg is nicer than a stale egg.

SCALLOPED EGGS.

Hard-boil twelve eggs; slice them thin in rings; in the bottom of a large well-buttered baking-dish place a layer of grated bread-crumbs, then one of eggs; cover with bits of butter, and sprinkle with pepper and salt. Continue thus to blend these ingredients until the dish is full; be sure, though, that the crumbs cover the eggs upon top. Over the whole pour a large teacupful of sweet cream or milk, and brown nicely in a moderately heated oven.

SHIRRED EGGS.

Set into the oven until quite hot a common white dish, large enough to hold the number of eggs to be cooked, allowing plenty of room for each. Melt in it a small piece of butter, and breaking the eggs carefully in a saucer, one at a time, slip them into the hot dish; sprinkle over them a small quantity of pepper and salt, and allow them to cook four or five minutes. Adding a tablespoonful of cream for every two eggs, when the eggs are first slipped in, is a great improve- ment.

This is far more delicate than fried eggs.

Or prepare the eggs the same, and set them in a steamer, over boiling water.

They are usually served in hotels baked in individual dishes, about two in a dish, and in the same dish they were baked in.

SCRAMBLED EGGS.

Put a tablespoonful of butter into a hot frying-pan; tip around so that it will touch all sides of the pan. Having ready half a dozen eggs broken in a dish, salted and peppered, turn them (without beating) into the hot butter; stir them one way briskly for five or six minutes or until they are mixed. Be careful that they do not get too hard. Turn over toast or dish up without.

POACHED OR DROPPED EGGS.

Have one quart of *boiling* water, and one tablespoonful of salt, in a frying-pan. Break the eggs, one by one, into a saucer, and slide carefully into the salted water. Dash with a spoon a little water over the egg, to keep the top white.

The beauty of a poached egg is for the yolk to be seen blushing through the white, which should only be just sufficiently hardened to form a transparent veil for the egg.

Cook until the white is firm, and lift out with a griddle-cake turner, and place on toasted bread. Serve immediately.

A tablespoonful of vinegar put into the water, keeps the eggs from spreading.

Open gem rings are nice placed in the water and an egg dropped into each ring.

FRIED EGGS.

Break the eggs, one at a time, into a saucer, and then slide them carefully off into a frying-pan of lard and butter mixed, dipping over the eggs the hot grease in spoonfuls, or turn them over-frying both sides without breaking them. They require about three minutes' cooking.

Eggs can be fried round like balls, by dropping one at a time into a quantity of hot lard, the same as for fried cakes, first stirring the hot lard with a stick until it runs round like a whirlpool; this will make the eggs look like balls. Take out with a skimmer. Eggs can be poached the same in boiling water.

EGGS AUX FINES HERBES.

Roll an ounce of butter in a good teaspoonful of flour; season with pepper, salt and nutmeg; put it into a coffeecupful of fresh milk, together with two tea- spoonfuls of chopped parsley; stir and simmer it for fifteen minutes, add a teacupful of thick cream. Hard-boil five eggs, and halve them; arrange them in a dish with the ends upwards, pour the sauce over them, and decorate with little heaps of fried bread-crumbs round the margin of the dish.

POACHED EGGS Á LA CRÊME.

Put a quart of hot water, a tablespoonful of vinegar and a teaspoonful of salt into a frying-pan, and break each egg separately into a saucer; slip the egg care- fully into the hot water, simmer three or four minutes until the white is set, then with a skimmer lift them out into a hot dish. Empty the pan of its contents, put in half a cup of cream, or rich milk; if milk, a large spoonful of butter; pepper and salt to taste, thicken with a very little cornstarch; let it boil up once, and turn it over the dish of poached eggs. It can be served on toast or without.

It is a better plan to warm the cream and butter in a separate dish, that the eggs may not have to stand.

EGGS IN CASES.

Make little paper cases of buttered writing paper; put a small piece of butter in each, and a little chopped parsley or onion; pepper and salt. Place the cases upon a gridiron over a moderate fire of bright coals, and when the butter melts, break a fresh egg into each case. Strew in upon them a few seasoned bread- crumbs, and when nearly done, glaze the tops with a hot shovel. Serve in the paper cases.

MINCED EGGS.

Chop up four or five hard-boiled eggs; do not mince them too fine. Put over the fire in a suitable dish a cupful of milk, a tablespoonful of butter, salt and pepper, and some savory chopped small. When this comes to a boil, stir into it a tablespoonful of flour, dissolved in a little cold milk. When it cooks thick like cream, put in the minced eggs. Stir it gently around and around for a few moments, and serve, garnished with sippets of toast. Any particular flavor may be given to this dish, such as that of mushrooms, truffles, catsup, essence of shrimps, etc., or some shred anchovy may be added to the mince.

MIXED EGGS AND BACON.

Take a nice rasher of mild bacon; cut it into squares no larger than dice; fry it quickly until nicely browned, but on no account burn it. Break half a dozen eggs into a basin, strain and season them with pepper, add them to the bacon, stir the whole about, and, when sufficiently firm, turn it out into a dish. Decorate with hot pickles.

MIXED EGGS GENERALLY.—SAVORY OR SWEET.

Much the same method is followed in mixed eggs generally, whatever may be added to them; really it is nothing more than an omelet which is stirred about in the pan while it is being dressed, instead of being allowed to set as a pancake. Chopped tongue, oysters, shrimps, sardines, dried salmon, anchovies, herbs, may be used.

COLD EGGS FOR A PICNIC.

This novel way of preparing cold egg for the lunch-basket fully repays one for the extra time required. Boil hard several eggs, halve them lengthwise; remove the yolks and chop them fine with cold chicken, lamb, veal or any tender, roasted meat; or with bread soaked in milk, and any salad, as parsley, onion, celery, the bread being half of the whole; or with grated cheese, a little olive oil, drawn butter, flavored. Fill the cavity in the egg with either of these mixtures, or any similar preparation. Press the halves together, roll twice in beaten egg and bread-crumbs, and dip into boiling lard. When the color rises delicately, drain them and they are ready for use.

OMELETS.

In making an omelet, care should be taken that the omelet pan is hot and dry. To ensure this, put a small quantity of lard or suet into a clean frying-pan, let it simmer a few minutes, then remove it; wipe the pan dry with a towel, and then put in a tablespoonful of butter. The smoothness of the pan is most essential, as the least particle of roughness will cause the omelet to stick. As a general rule, a small omelet can be made more successfully than a large one, it being much better to make two small ones of four eggs each, than to try double the number of eggs in one omelet and fail. Allow one egg to a person in making an omelet and one tablespoonful of milk; this makes an omelet more puffy and tender than one made without milk. Many prefer them without milk.

Omelets are called by the name of what is added to give them flavor, as minced ham, salmon, onions, oysters, etc., beaten up in the eggs in due quantity, which gives as many different kinds of omelets.

They are also served over many kinds of thick sauces or purèes, such as tomatoes, spinach, endive, lettuce, celery, etc.

If vegetables are to be added, they should be already cooked, seasoned and hot; place in the centre of the omelet, just before turning; so with mushroom, shrimps, or any cooked ingredients. All omelets should be served the moment they are done, as they harden by standing, and care taken that they do not *cook too much.*

Sweet omelets are generally used for breakfast or plain desserts.

PLAIN OMELET.

Put a smooth, clean, iron frying-pan on the fire to heat; meanwhile, beat four eggs, very light, the whites to a stiff froth, and the yolks to a thick batter. Add to the yolks four tablespoonfuls of milk, pepper and salt; and lastly stir in the whites lightly. Put a piece of butter nearly half the size of an egg into the heated pan; turn it so that it will moisten the entire bottom, taking care that it does not scorch. Just as it begins to boil, pour in the eggs. Hold the frying-pan handle in your left hand, and, as the eggs whiten, carefully, with a spoon, draw up lightly from the bottom, letting the raw part run out on the pan, till all be equally cooked; shake with your left hand, till the omelet be free from the pan, then turn with a spoon one half of the omelet over the other; let it remain a moment, but continue shaking, lest it adhere; toss to a warm platter held in the right hand, or lift with a flat, broad shovel; the omelet will be firm around the edge, but creamy and light inside.

MEAT OR FISH OMELETS.

Take cold meat, fish, game or poultry of any kind; remove all skin, sinew, etc., and either cut it small or pound it to a paste in a mortar, together with a proper proportion of spices and salt; then either toss it in a buttered frying-pan over a clear fire till it begins to brown, and pour beaten eggs upon it, or beat it up with the eggs, or spread it upon them after they have begun to set in the pan. In any case serve hot, with or without a sauce; but garnished with crisp herbs in branches, pickles, or sliced lemon. The right proportion is one tablespoonful of meat to four eggs. A little milk, gravy, water, or white wine, may be advantageously added to the eggs while they are being beaten.

Potted meats make admirable omelets in the above manner.

VEGETABLE OMELET.

Make a purée by mashing up ready-dressed vegetables, together with a little milk, cream or gravy, and some seasoning. The most suitable vegetables are cucumbers, artichokes, onions, sorrel, green peas, tomatoes, lentils, mushrooms, asparagus tops, potatoes, truffles or turnips. Prepare some eggs by beating them very light. Pour them into a nice hot frying-pan, containing a spoonful of butter; spread the purée upon the upper side; and when perfectly hot, turn or fold the omelet together and serve. Or cold vegetables may be merely chopped small, then tossed in a little butter, and some beaten and seasoned eggs poured over.

OMELET OF HERBS.

Parsley, thyme, and sweet marjoram mixed gives the famous *omelette aux fines herbes* so popular at every wayside inn in the most remote corner of sunny France. An omelet "jardiniere" is two tablespoonfuls of mixed parsley, onion, chives, shalots and a few leaves each of sorrel and chevril, minced fine and stirred into the beaten eggs before cooking. It will take a little more butter to fry it than a plain one.

CHEESE OMELET.

Beat up three eggs, and add to them a tablespoonful of milk and a table-spoonful of grated cheese; add a little more cheese before folding; turn it out on a hot dish; grate a little cheese over it before serving.

ASPARAGUS OMELET.

Boil with a little salt, and until about half cooked, eight or ten stalks of asparagus, and cut the eatable part into rather small pieces; beat the eggs, and mix the asparagus with them. Make the omelet as above directed.

Omelet with parsley is made by adding a little chopped parsley.

TOMATO OMELET. No. 1.

Peel a couple of tomatoes, which split into four pieces; remove the seeds, and cut them into small dice; then fry them with a little butter until nearly done, adding salt and pepper. Beat the eggs and mix the tomatoes with them, and make the omelet as usual. Or. stew a few tomatoes in the usual way and spread over before folding.

TOMATO OMELET. No. 2.

Cut in slices and place in a stew-pan six peeled tomatoes; add a tablespoonful of cold water, a little pepper, and salt. When they begin to simmer, break in six eggs, stir well, stirring one way, until the eggs are cooked, but not too hard. Serve warm.

RICE OMELET.

Take a cupful of cold boiled rice, turn over it a cupful of warm milk, add a tablespoonful of butter melted, a level teaspoonful of salt, a dash of pepper; mix well, then add three well-beaten eggs. Put a tablespoonful of butter in a hot frying-pan, and when it begins to boil pour in the omelet and set the pan in a hot oven. As soon as it is cooked through, fold it double, turn it out on a hot dish, and serve at once. Very good.

HAM OMELET.

Cut raw ham into dice, fry with butter, and when cooked enough, turn the beaten egg over it, and cook as a plain omelet.

If boiled ham is used, mince it, and mix with the eggs after they are beaten. Bacon may be used instead of raw ham.

CHICKEN OMELET.

Mince rather fine one cupful of cooked chicken, warm in a teacupful of cream or rich milk, a tablespoonful of butter, salt and pepper; thicken with a large tablespoonful of flour. Make a plain omelet, then add this mixture, just before turning it over. This is much better than the dry minced chicken. Tongue is equally good.

MUSHROOM OMELET.

Clean a cupful of large button mushrooms, canned ones may be used; cut them into bits. Put into a stew-pan an ounce of butter and let it melt; add the mushrooms, a teaspoonful of salt, half a teaspoonful of pepper, and half a cupful of cream or milk. Stir in a teaspoonful of flour, dissolved in a little milk or water to thicken, if needed. Boil ten minutes, and set aside until the omelet is ready.

Make a plain omelet the usual way, and just before doubling it, turn the mushrooms over the centre and serve hot.

OYSTER OMELET.

Parboil a dozen oysters in their own liquor, skim them out, and let them cool; add them to the beaten eggs, either whole or minced. Cook the same as a plain omelet.

Thicken the liquid with butter rolled in flour; season with salt, cayenne pepper and a teaspoonful of chopped parsley. Chop up the oysters and add to the sauce. Put a few spoonfuls in the centre of the omelet before folding; when dished, pour the remainder of the sauce around it.

FISH OMELET.

Make a plain omelet, and when ready to fold, spread over it fish prepared as follows: Add to a cupful of any kind of cold fish, broken fine, cream enough to moisten it, seasoned with a tablespoonful of butter; then pepper and salt to taste. Warm together.

ONION OMELET.

Make a plain omelet, and when ready to turn spread over it a teaspoonful each of chopped onion and minced parsley; then fold, or, if prepared, mix the minces into the eggs before cooking.

JELLY OMELET.

Make a plain omelet, and just before folding together, spread with some kind of jelly. Turn out on a warm platter. Dust it with powdered sugar.

BREAD OMELET. No. 1.

Break four eggs into a basin and carefully remove the treadles; have ready a tablespoonful of grated and sifted bread; soak it in either milk, water, cream, white wine, gravy, lemon-juice, brandy or rum, according as the omelet is intended to be sweet or savory. Well beat the eggs together with a little nut-meg, pepper and salt; add the bread, and, beating constantly (or the omelet will be crumbly), get ready a frying-pan, buttered and made thoroughly hot; put in the omelet; do it on one side only; turn it upon a dish, and fold it double to prevent the steam from condensing. Stale sponge-cake, grated biscuit, or pound cake, may replace the bread for a sweet omelet, when pounded loaf sugar should be sifted over it, and the dish decorated with lumps of currant jelly. This makes a nice dessert.

BREAD OMELET. No. 2.

Let one teacup of milk come to a boil, pour it over one teacupful of bread-crumbs and let it stand a few minutes. Break six eggs into a bowl, stir (not beat) till well mixed; then add the milk and bread, season with pepper and salt, mix all well together and turn into a hot frying-pan, containing a large spoonful of butter boiling hot. Fry the omelet slowly, and when brown on the bottom cut in squares and turn again, fry to a delicate brown and serve hot.

Cracker omelet may be made by substituting three or four rolled crackers in place of bread.

BAKED OMELET.

Beat the whites and yolks of four or six eggs separately; add to the yolks a small cup of milk, a tablespoonful of flour or cornstarch, a teaspoonful of baking powder, one-half teaspoonful of salt, and lastly, the stiff-beaten whites. Bake in a well buttered pie-tin or plate, about half an hour in a steady oven.

It should be served the moment it is taken from the oven, as it is liable to fall.

OMELET SOUFFLÉ.

Break six eggs into separate cups; beat four of the yolks, mix with them one teaspoonful of flour, three tablespoonfuls of powdered sugar, very little salt. Flavor with extract lemon or any other of the flavors that may be preferred. Whisk the whites of six eggs to a firm froth; mix them lightly with the yolks; pour the mixture into a greased pan or dish; bake in a quick oven. When well-risen and lightly browned on the top, it is done; roll out in warm dish, sift pulverized sugar over, and send to table.

RUM OMELET.

Put a small quantity of lard into the pan; let it simmer a few minutes, and remove it; wipe the pan dry with a towel, and put in a little fresh lard in which the omelet may be fried. Care should be taken that the lard does not burn, which would spoil the color of the omelet. Break three eggs separately; put them into a bowl and whisk them thoroughly with a fork. The longer they are beaten, the lighter will the omelet be. Beat up a teaspoonful of milk with the eggs and continue to beat until the last moment before pouring into the pan, which should be over a hot fire. As soon as the omelet sets, remove the pan from the hottest part of the fire. Slip a knife under it to prevent sticking to the pan. When the centre is almost firm, slant the pan, work the omelet in shape to fold easily and neatly, and when slightly browned, hold a platter against the edge of the pan and deftly turn it out on to the hot dish. Dust a liberal quantity of powdered sugar over it, and singe the sugar into neat stripes with a hot iron rod, heated in the coals; pour a glass of warm Jamaica rum around it, and when it is placed on the table set fire to the rum. With a tablespoon dash the burning rum over the omelet, put out the fire and serve. Salt *mixed* with the eggs prevents them from rising, and when it is so used the omelet will look flabby, yet without salt it will taste insipid. Add a little salt to it just before folding it and turning out on the dish.

—*"The Cook."*

SANDWICHES.

HAM SANDWICHES.

Make a dressing of half a cup of butter, one tablespoonful of mixed mustard, one of salad oil, a little red or white pepper, a pinch of salt and the yolk of an egg; rub the butter to a cream, add the other ingredients and mix thoroughly; then stir in as much chopped ham as will make it consistent, and spread between thin slices of bread. Omit salad oil and substitute melted butter, if preferred.

HAM SANDWICHES, PLAIN.

Trim the crusts from thin slices of bread; butter them, and lay between every two some thin slices of cold, boiled ham. Spread the meat with a little mustard, if liked.

CHICKEN SANDWICHES.

Mince up fine any cold boiled or roasted chicken; put it into a sauce-pan with gravy, water or cream enough to soften it; add a good piece of butter, a pinch of pepper; work it very smooth while it is heating until it looks almost like a paste. Then spread it on a plate to cool. Spread it between slices of buttered bread.

SARDINE SANDWICHES.

Take two boxes of sardines, and throw the contents into hot water, having first drained away all the oil. A few minutes will free the sardines from grease. Pour away the water and dry the fish in a cloth; then scrape away the skins, and pound the sardines in a mortar till reduced to paste; add pepper, salt, and some tiny pieces of lettuce, and spread on the sandwiches, which have been previously cut as above. The lettuce adds very much to the flavor of the sardines.

Or chop the sardines up fine and squeeze a few drops of lemon-juice into them and spread between buttered bread or cold biscuits.

WATERCRESS SANDWICHES.

Wash well some watercress, and then dry them in a cloth, pressing out every atom of moisture, as far as possible; then mix with the cresses hard-boiled eggs chopped fine, and seasoned with salt and pepper. Have a stale loaf and some fresh butter, and with a sharp knife, cut as many thin slices as will be required for two dozen sandwiches; then cut the cress into small pieces, removing the stems; place it between each slice of bread and butter, with a slight sprinkling of lemon-juice; press down the slices hard, and cut them sharply on a board into small squares, leaving no crust.

—Nantasket Beach.

EGG SANDWICHES.

Hard boil some very fresh eggs, and when cold, cut them into moderately thin slices, and lay them between some bread and butter cut as thin as possible; season them with pepper, salt and nutmeg. For picnic parties, or when one is travelling, these sandwiches are far preferable to hard-boiled eggs *au naturel.*

MUSHROOM SANDWICHES.

Mince beef tongue and boiled mushrooms together, add French mustard, and spread between buttered bread.

CHEESE SANDWICHES.

These are extremely nice, and are very easily made. Take one hard-boiled egg, a quarter of a pound of common cheese grated, half a teaspoonful of salt, half a teaspoonful of pepper, half a teaspoonful of mustard, one tablespoonful of melted butter, and one tablespoonful of vinegar or cold water. Take the yolk of the egg and put it into a small bowl and crumble it down, put into it the butter and mix it smooth with a spoon, then add the salt, pepper, mustard, and the cheese, mixing each well. Then put in the tablespoonful of vinegar, which will make it the proper thickness. If vinegar is not relished, then use cold water instead. Spread this between two biscuits or pieces of oat-cake, and you could not require a better sandwich. Some people will prefer the sandwiches less highly seasoned. In that case, season to taste.

BREAD.

Among all civilized people bread has become an article of food of the first necessity; and properly so, for it constitutes of itself a complete life sustainer, the gluten, starch and sugar which it contains representing ozotized and hydro-carbonated nutrients, and combining the sustaining powers of the animal and vegetable kingdoms in one product. As there is no one article of food that enters so largely into our daily fare as bread, so no degree of skill in preparing other articles can compensate for lack of knowledge in the art of making good, palatable and nutritious bread. A little earnest attention to the subject will enable any one to comprehend the theory, and then ordinary care in practice will make one familiar with the process.

GENERAL DIRECTIONS.

The first thing required for making wholesome bread is the utmost cleanliness; the next is the soundness and sweetness of all the ingredients used for it; and, in addition to these, there must be attention and care through the whole process.

Salt is always used in bread-making, not only on account of its flavor, which destroys the insipid raw state of the flour, but because it makes the dough rise better.

In mixing with milk, the milk should be boiled—not simply scalded, but heated to boiling over hot water—then set aside to cool before mixing. Simple heating will not prevent bread from turning sour in the rising, while boiling will act as a preventive. So the milk should be thoroughly scalded, and should be used when it is just blood warm.

Too small a proportion of yeast, or insufficient time allowed for the dough to rise, will cause the bread to be heavy.

The yeast must be good and fresh if the bread is to be digestible and nice. Stale yeast produces, instead of vinous fermentation, an acetous fermentation, which flavors the bread and makes it disagreeable. A poor, thin yeast produces an imperfect fermentation, the result being a heavy unwholesome loaf.

If either the sponge or the dough be permitted to overwork itself—that is to say, if the mixing and kneading be neglected when it has reached the proper point for either—sour bread will probably be the consequence in warm weather, and bad bread in any. The goodness will also be endangered by placing it so near a fire as to make any part of it hot, instead of maintaining the gentle and equal degree of heat required for its due fermentation.

Heavy bread will also most likely be the result of making the dough very hard, and letting it become quite cold, particularly in winter.

An almost certain way of spoiling dough is to leave it half-made, and to allow it to become cold before it is finished. The other most common causes of failure are using yeast which is no longer sweet, or which has been frozen, or has had hot liquid poured over it.

As a general rule, the oven for baking bread should be rather quick, and the heat so regulated as to penetrate the dough without hardening the outside. The oven-door should not be opened after the bread is put in until the dough is set or has become firm, as the cool air admitted will have an unfavorable effect on it.

The dough should rise and the bread begin to brown after about fifteen minutes, but only slightly. Bake from fifty to sixty minutes, and have it brown, not black or whitey brown, but brown all over when well baked.

When the bread is baked, remove the loaves immediately from the pans, and place them where the air will circulate freely around them and thus carry off the gas which has been formed, but is no longer needed.

Never leave the bread in the pan or on a pine table to absorb the odor of the wood. If you like crusts that are crisp do not cover the loaves; but to give the soft, tender, wafer-like consistency which many prefer, wrap them, while still hot, in several thicknesses of bread-cloth. When cold put them in a stone jar, removing the cloth, as that absorbs the moisture and gives the bread an unpleasant taste and odor. Keep the jar well covered, and carefully cleansed from crumbs and stale pieces. Scald and dry it thoroughly every two or three days. A yard and a half square of coarse table linen makes the best bread-cloth. Keep in good supply; use them for no other purpose.

Some people use scalding water in making wheat bread; in that case the flour must be scalded and allowed to cool before the yeast is added,—then proceed as above. Bread made in this manner keeps moist in summer, much longer than when made in the usual mode.

Home-made yeast is generally preferred to any other. Compressed yeast, as now sold in most grocery stores, makes fine light, sweet bread, and is a much quicker process, and can always be had fresh, being made fresh every day.

WHEAT BREAD.

Sift the flour into a large bread-pan or bowl; make a hole in the middle of it, and pour in the yeast in the ratio of half a teacupful of yeast to two quarts of flour; stir the yeast lightly, then pour in your "wetting," either milk or water, as you choose,—which use warm in winter, and cold in summer; if you use water as "wetting," dissolve in it a bit of butter of the size of an egg,—if you use milk, no butter is necessary; stir in the "wetting" very lightly, but do not mix all the flour into it; then cover the pan with a thick blanket or towel, and set it, in winter, in a warm place to rise,—this is called "*putting the bread in sponge.*" In summer the bread should not be wet over night. In the morning add a teaspoonful of salt and mix all the flour in the pan with the sponge, kneading it well; then let it stand two hours or more until it has risen quite light; then remove the dough to the molding-board and mold it for a long time, cutting it in pieces and molding them together again and again, until the dough is elastic under the pressure of your hand, using as little flour as possible; then make it into loaves, put the loaves into baking-tins. The loaves should come half-way up the pan, and they should be allowed to rise until the bulk is doubled. When the loaves are ready to be put into the oven, the oven should be ready to receive them. It should be hot enough to brown a teaspoonful of flour in five minutes. The heat should be greater at the bottom than at the top of the oven, and the fire so arranged as to give sufficient strength of heat through the baking without being replenished. Let them stand ten or fifteen minutes, prick them three or four times with a fork, bake in a quick oven from forty-five to sixty minutes.

If these directions are followed, you will obtain sweet, tender and wholesome bread. If by any mistake the dough becomes sour before you are ready to bake it, you can rectify it by adding a little dry supercarbonate of soda, molding the dough a long time to distribute the soda equally throughout the mass. All bread is better, if naturally sweet, without the soda; but *sour bread* you should never eat, if you desire good health.

Keep well covered in a tin box or large stone crock, which should be wiped out every day or two, and scalded and dried thoroughly in the sun once a week.

COMPRESSED YEAST BREAD.

Use for two loaves of bread three quarts of sifted flour, nearly a quart of warm water, a level tablespoonful of salt, and an ounce of compressed yeast.

Dissolve the yeast in a pint of lukewarm water; then stir into it enough flour to make a thick batter. Cover the bowl containing the batter or sponge with a thick folded cloth, and set it in a warm place to rise; if the temperature of heat is properly attended to, the sponge will be foamy and light in half an hour. Now stir into this sponge the salt dissolved in a little warm water, add the rest of the flour and sufficient warm water to make the dough stiff enough to knead; then knead it from five to ten minutes, divide it into loaves, knead again each loaf and put them into buttered baking-tins; cover them with a doubled thick cloth, and set again in a warm place to rise twice their height, then bake the same as any bread. This bread has the advantage of that made of home-made yeast as it is made inside of three hours, whereas the other requires from twelve to fourteen hours.

HOME-MADE YEAST.

Boil six large potatoes in three pints of water. Tie a handful of hops in a small muslin bag and boil with the potatoes; when thoroughly cooked drain the water on enough flour to make a thin batter; set this on the stove or range and scald it enough to cook the flour, (this makes the yeast keep longer); remove it from the fire, and when cool enough, add the potatoes mashed, also half a cup of sugar, half a tablespoonful of ginger, two of salt and a teacupful of yeast. Let it stand in a warm place until it has thoroughly risen, then put it in a large mouthed jug, and cork tightly; set away in a cool place. The jug should be scalded before putting in the yeast.

Two-thirds of a coffeecupful of this yeast will make four loaves.

UNRIVALED YEAST.

On one morning boil two ounces of the best hops in four quarts of water half an hour; strain it, and let the liquor cool to the consistency of new milk; then put it in an earthen bowl, and add half a cupful of salt, and half a cupful of brown sugar; beat up one quart of flour with some of the liquor; then mix all well together, and let it stand till the third day after; then add six medium-sized potatoes, boiled and mashed through a colander; let it stand a day, then strain and bottle, and it is fit for use. It must be stirred frequently while it is making, and kept near a fire. One advantage of this yeast is its spontaneous fermentation, requiring the help of no old yeast; if care be taken to let it ferment well in the bowl, it may immediately be corked tightly. Be careful to keep it in a cool place. Before using it shake the bottle up well. It will keep in a cool place two months, and is best the latter part of the time. Use about the same quantity as of other yeast.

DRIED YEAST OR YEAST CAKES.

Make a pan of yeast the same as "Home-made Yeast;" mix in with it corn-meal that has been sifted and dried, kneading it well until it is thick enough to roll out, when it can be cut into cakes or crumble up. Spread out and dry thoroughly in the shade; keep in a dry place.

When it is convenient to get compressed yeast, it is much better and cheaper than to make your own, a saving of time and trouble. Almost all groceries keep it, delivered to them fresh made daily.

SALT-RAISING BREAD.

While getting breakfast in the morning, as soon as the tea-kettle has boiled, take a quart tin cup or an earthen quart milk pitcher, scald it, then fill one-third full of water about as warm as the finger could be held in; then to this add a teaspoonful of salt, a pinch of brown sugar and coarse flour enough to make a batter of about the right consistency for griddle-cakes. Set the cup, with the spoon in it, in a closed vessel half-filled with water, moderately hot, but not scalding. Keep the temperature as nearly even as possible, and add a teaspoonful of flour once or twice during the process of fermentation. The yeast ought to reach to the top of the bowl in about five hours. Sift your flour into a pan, make an opening in the centre, and pour in your yeast. Have ready a pitcher of warm milk, salted, or milk and water, (not too hot, or you will scald the yeast germs,) and stir rapidly into a pulpy mass with a spoon. Cover this sponge closely, and keep warm for an hour, then knead into loaves, adding flour to make the proper consistency. Place in warm, well-greased pans, cover closely, and leave till it is light. Bake in a steady oven, and when done let all the hot steam escape. Wrap closely in damp towels, and keep in closed earthen jars until it is wanted.

This in our grandmothers' time used to be considered the prize bread, on account of its being sweet and wholesome, and required no prepared yeast to make it. Nowadays yeast-bread is made with very little trouble, as the yeast can be procured at almost any grocery.

BREAD FROM MILK YEAST.

At noon the day before baking, take half a cup of corn-meal, and pour over it enough sweet milk boiling hot to make it the thickness of batter-cakes. In the winter place it where it will keep warm. The next morning before breakfast pour into a pitcher a pint of boiling water; add one teaspoonful of soda and one of salt. When cool enough so that it will not scald the flour, add enough to make a stiff batter; then add the cup of meal set the day before. This will be full of little bubbles. Then place the pitcher in a kettle of warm water, cover the top with a folded towel and put it where it will keep warm, and you will be surprised to find how soon the yeast will be at the top of the pitcher. Then pour the yeast into a bread-pan; add a pint and a half of warm water, or half water and half milk, and flour enough to knead into loaves. Knead but little harder than for biscuit, and bake as soon as it rises to the top of the tin. This recipe makes five large loaves. Do not allow it to get too light before baking, for it will make the bread dry and crumbling. A cup of this milk yeast is excellent to raise buckwheat cakes.

GRAHAM BREAD.

One teacupful of wheat flour, one-half teacupful of Porto Rico molasses, one half cupful of good yeast, one teaspoonful of salt, one pint of warm water; add sufficient Graham flour to make the dough as stiff as can be stirred with a strong spoon; this is to be mixed at night; in the morning, add one teaspoonful of soda, dissolved in a little water; mix well, and pour into two medium-sized pans; they will be about half full; let it stand in a warm place until it rises to the top of the pans, then bake one hour in a pretty hot oven.

This should be covered about twenty minutes when first put into the oven with a thick brown paper, or an old tin cover; it prevents the upper crust hardening before the loaf is well-risen. If these directions are correctly followed the bread will not be heavy or sodden, as it has been tried for years and never failed.

GRAHAM BREAD. (Unfermented.)

Stir together three heaping teaspoonfuls of baking powder, three cups of Graham flour, and one cup of white flour; then add a large teaspoonful of salt and half a cup of sugar. Mix all thoroughly with milk or water into as stiff a batter as can be stirred with a spoon. If water is used, a lump of butter as large as a walnut may be melted and stirred into it. Bake immediately in well-greased pans.

BOSTON BROWN BREAD.

One pint of rye flour, one quart of corn-meal, one teacupful of Graham flour, all fresh; half a teacupful of molasses or brown sugar, a teaspoonful of salt, and two-thirds of a teacupful of home-made yeast. Mix into as stiff a dough as can be stirred with a spoon, using warm water for wetting. Let it rise several hours, or over night; in the morning, or when light, add a teaspoonful of soda dissolved in a spoonful of warm water; beat it well and turn it into well-greased, deep, bread-pans, and let it rise again. Bake in a *moderate* oven from three to four hours.

—*Palmer House, Chicago.*

BOSTON BROWN BREAD. (Unfermented).

One cupful of rye flour, two cupfuls of corn-meal, one cupful of white flour, half a teacupful of molasses or sugar, a teaspoonful of salt. Stir all together *thoroughly*, and wet up with sour milk; then add a level teaspoonful of soda dissolved in a tablespoonful of water. The same can be made of sweet milk, by substituting baking-powder for soda. The batter to be stirred as thick as can be with a spoon, and turned into well-greased pans.

VIRGINIA BROWN BREAD.

One pint of corn-meal, pour over enough boiling water to thoroughly scald it; when cool, add one pint of light, white bread sponge, mix well together, add one cupful of molasses, and Graham flour enough to mold; this will make two loaves; when light, bake in a moderate oven one and a half hours.

RHODE ISLAND BROWN BREAD.

Two and one-half cupfuls of corn-meal, one and one-half cupfuls of rye-meal, one egg, one cup of molasses, two teaspoonfuls of cream of tartar, one teaspoonful of soda, a little salt and one quart of milk. Bake in a covered dish, either earthen or iron, in a moderately hot oven three hours.

STEAMED BROWN BREAD.

One cup of white flour, two of Graham flour, two of Indian meal, one teaspoonful of soda, one cup of molasses, three and a half cups of milk, a little salt. Beat well and steam for four hours. This is for sour milk; when sweet milk is used, use baking powder in place of soda.

This is improved by setting it into the oven fifteen minutes after it is slipped from the mold. To be eaten warm with butter. Most excellent.

RYE BREAD.

To a quart of warm water stir as much wheat flour as will make a smooth batter; stir into it half a gill of home-made yeast, and set it in a warm place to rise; this is called setting a sponge; let it be mixed in some vessel which will contain twice the quantity; in the morning, put three pounds and a half of rye flour into a bowl or tray, make a hollow in the centre, pour in the sponge, add a dessertspoonful of salt, and half a small teaspoonful of soda, dissolved in a little water; make the whole into a smooth dough, with as much warm water as may be necessary; knead it well, cover it, and let it set in a warm place for three hours; then knead it again, and make it into two or three loaves; bake in a quick oven one hour, if made in two loaves, or less if the loaves are smaller.

RYE AND CORN BREAD.

One quart of rye meal or rye flour, two quarts of Indian meal, scalded (by placing in a pan and pouring over it just enough *boiling* water to merely wet it, but not enough to make it into a batter, stirring constantly with a spoon), one-half cup of molasses, two teaspoonfuls salt, one teacup yeast; make it as stiff as can be stirred with a spoon, mixing with warm water, and let rise all night. In the morning add a level teaspoonful of soda dissolved in a little water; then put it in a large pan, smooth the top with the hand dipped in cold water; let it stand a short time, and bake five or six hours. If put in the oven late in the day, let it remain all night.

Graham may be used instead of rye, and baked as above.

This is similar to the " Rye and Injun " of our grandmothers' days, but that was placed in a kettle, allowed to rise, then placed in a covered iron pan upon the hearth before the fire, with coals heaped upon the lid, to bake all night.

FRENCH BREAD.

Beat together one pint of milk, four tablespoonfuls of melted butter, or half butter and half lard, half a cupful of yeast, one teaspoonful of salt and two eggs. Stir into this two quarts of flour. When this dough is risen, make into two large rolls, and bake as any bread. Cut across the top diagonal gashes just before putting into the oven.

TWIST BREAD.

Let the bread be made as directed for wheat bread, then take three pieces as large as a pint bowl each; strew a little flour over the paste-board or table, roll each piece under your hands, to twelve inches length, making it smaller in circumference at the ends than in the middle; having rolled the three in this way, take a baking-tin, lay one part on it, join one end of each of the other two to it, and braid them together the length of the rolls, and join the ends by pressing them together; dip a brush in milk, and pass it over the top of the loaf; after ten minutes or so, set it in a quick oven, and bake for nearly an hour.

NEW ENGLAND CORN CAKE.

One quart of milk, one pint of corn-meal, one teacupful of wheat flour, a tea-spoonful of salt, two tablespoonfuls of melted butter. Scald the milk, and gradually pour it on the meal; when cool, add the butter and salt, also a half cup of yeast. Do this at night; in the morning beat thoroughly and add two well-beaten eggs, and a half teaspoonful of soda, dissolved in a spoonful of water. Pour the mixture into buttered deep earthen plates, let it stand fifteen minutes to rise again, then bake from twenty to thirty minutes.

GERMAN BREAD.

One pint of milk well-boiled, one teacupful of sugar, two tablespoonfuls of nice lard or butter, two-thirds of a teacupful of baker's yeast. Make a rising with the milk and yeast; when light, mix in the sugar and shortening, with flour enough to make as soft a dough as can be handled. Flour the paste-board well, roll out about one-half inch thick; put this quantity into two large pans; make about a dozen indentures with the finger on the top; put a small piece of butter in each, and sift over the whole one tablespoonful of sugar mixed with one teaspoonful of cinnamon. Let this stand for a second rising; when perfectly light, bake in a quick oven fifteen or twenty minutes.

CORN BREAD.

Two cups of sifted meal, half a cup of flour, two cups of sour milk, two well-beaten eggs, half a cup of molasses or sugar, a teaspoonful of salt, two table-spoonfuls of melted butter. Mix the meal and flour smoothly and gradually with the milk, then the butter, molasses, and salt, then the beaten eggs, and lastly dissolve a level teaspoonful of baking-soda in a little milk and beat thoroughly all together. Bake nearly an hour in well-buttered tins, not very shallow. This recipe can be made with sweet milk by using baking-powder in place of soda.

—*St. Charles Hotel, New Orleans.*

VIRGINIA CORN BREAD.

Three cups of white corn-meal, one cup of flour, one tablespoonful of sugar, one teaspoonful of salt, two heaping teaspoonfuls of baking-powder, one table-spoonful of lard, three cups of milk and three eggs. Sift together the flour, corn, meal, sugar, salt and baking-powder; rub in the lard cold, add the eggs well-beaten and then the milk. Mix into a moderately stiff batter; pour it into well-greased, shallow baking-pans, (pie-tins are suitable). Bake from thirty to forty minutes.

BOSTON CORN BREAD.

One cup of sweet milk, two of sour milk, two-thirds of a cup of molasses, one of wheat flour, four of corn-meal and one teaspoonful of soda; steam for three hours, and brown a few minutes in the oven. The same made of sweet milk and baking-powder is equally as good.

INDIAN LOAF CAKE.

Mix a teacupful of powdered white sugar with a quart of rich milk, and cut up in the milk two ounces of butter, adding a saltspoonful of salt. Put this mixture into a covered pan or skillet, and set it on the fire till it is scalding hot. Then take it off, and scald with it as much yellow Indian meal (previously sifted) as will make it of the consistence of thick boiled mush. Beat the whole very hard for a quarter of an hour, and then set it away to cool.

While it is cooling, beat three eggs very light, and stir them gradually into the mixture when it is about as warm as new milk. Add a teacupful of good strong yeast, and beat the whole another quarter of an hour, for much of the goodness of this cake depends on its being long and well-beaten. Then have ready a tin mold or earthen pan with a pipe in the centre, (to diffuse the heat through the middle of the cake). The pan must be very well-buttered, as Indian meal is apt to stick. Put in the mixture, cover it, and set it in a warm place to rise. It should be light in about four hours. Then bake it two hours in a moderate oven. When done, turn it out with the broad surface downwards, and send it to table hot and whole. Cut it into slices and eat it with butter.

This will be found an excellent cake. If wanted for breakfast, mix it, and set it to rise the night before. If properly made, standing all night will not injure it. Like all Indian cakes, (of which this is one of the best), it should be eaten warm.

—*St. Charles Hotel, New Orleans.*

JOHNNIE CAKE.

Sift one quart of Indian meal into a pan; make a hole in the middle and pour in a pint of warm water, adding one teaspoonful of salt; with a spoon mix the meal and water gradually into a soft dough; stir it very briskly for a quarter of an hour or more, till it becomes light and spongy; then spread the dough smooth and evenly on a straight, flat board (a piece of the head of a flour-barrel will serve for this purpose); place the board nearly upright before an open fire, and put an iron against the back to support it; bake it well; when done, cut it in squares; send it hot to table, split and buttered.

—*Old Plantation Style.*

SPIDER CORN-CAKE.

Beat two eggs and one-fourth cup sugar together. Then add one cup sweet milk, and one cup of sour milk in which you have dissolved one teaspoonful soda. Add a teaspoonful of salt. Then mix one and two-thirds cups of granulated corn-meal and one-third cup flour with this. Put a spider or skillet on the range, and when it is hot melt in two tablespoonfuls of butter. Turn the spider so that the butter can run up on the sides of the pan. Pour in the corn-cake mixture and add one more cup of sweet milk, but do not stir afterwards. Put this in the oven and bake from twenty to thirty-five minutes. When done, there should be a streak of custard through it.

SOUTHERN CORN-MEAL PONE OR CORN DODGERS.

Mix with cold water into a soft dough one quart of southern corn-meal, sifted, a teaspoonful of salt, a tablespoonful of butter or lard melted. Mold into oval cakes with the hands and bake in a very hot oven, in well-greased pans. To be eaten hot. The crust should be brown.

RAISED POTATO-CAKE.

Potato-cakes, to be served with roast lamb or with game, are made of equal quantities of mashed potatoes and of flour, say one quart of each, two tablespoonfuls of butter, a little salt, and milk enough to make a batter as for griddle-cakes; to this allow half a teacupful of fresh yeast; let it rise till it is light and bubbles of air form; then dissolve half a teaspoonful of soda in a spoonful of warm water and add to the batter; bake in muffin tins. These are good also with fricasseed chicken; take them from the tins and drop in the gravy just before sending to the table.

Biscuits, Rolls, Muffins, Etc.

GENERAL SUGGESTIONS.

In making batter-cakes, the ingredients should be put together over night to rise, and the eggs and butter added in the morning; the butter melted and eggs well-beaten. If the batter appears sour in the least, dissolve a little soda and stir into it; this should be done early enough to rise some time before baking.

Water can be used in place of milk in all raised dough, and the dough should be thoroughly light before making into loaves or biscuits; then when molding them, use as little flour as possible; the kneading to be done when first made from the sponge, and should be done well and for some length of time, as this makes the pores fine, the bread cut smooth and tender.   Care should be taken not to get the dough too stiff.

Where any recipe calls for baking-powder, and you do not have it, you can use cream-tartar and soda, in the proportion of one level teaspoonful of soda to two of cream-tartar.

When the recipe calls for sweet milk or cream, and you do not have it, you may use in place of it sour milk or cream, and, in that case, baking-powder or cream of tartar *must not* be used, but baking-soda, using a *level* teaspoonful to a quart of sour milk; the milk is always best when just turned, so that it is solid, and not sour enough to whey or to be watery.

When making biscuits or bread with baking-powder or soda and cream tartar, the oven should be prepared first; the dough handled quickly and put into the oven immediately, as soon as it becomes the proper lightness, to ensure good success.   If the oven is *too slow*, the article baked will be heavy and hard.

As in beating cake, never *stir* ingredients into batter, but beat them in, by beating down from the bottom, and up, and over again.   This laps the air into the batter, which produces little air-cells and causes the dough to puff and swell as it comes in contact with the heat while cooking.

TO RENEW STALE ROLLS.

To freshen stale biscuits or rolls, put them into a steamer for ten minutes, then dry them off in a hot oven; or dip each roll for an instant in cold water and heat them crisp in the oven.

WARM BREAD FOR BREAKFAST.

Dough, after it has become once sufficiently raised and perfectly light, cannot afterwards be injured by setting aside in any cold place where it cannot *freeze;* therefore, biscuits, rolls, etc., can be made late the day before wanted for breakfast.   Prepare them ready for baking by molding them out late in the evening; lay them a little apart on buttered tins; cover the tins with a cloth, then fold around that a newspaper, so as to exclude the air, as that has a tendency to cause the crust to be hard and thick when baked.   The best place in summer is to place them in the ice-box, then all you have to do in the morning (an hour before breakfast time, and while the oven is heating) is to bring them from the ice-box, take off the cloth and warm it, and place it over them again; then set the tins in a warm place near the fire.   This will give them time to rise and bake when needed. If these directions are followed rightly, you will find it makes no difference with their lightness and goodness, and you can always be sure of warm raised biscuits for breakfast in one hour's time.

Stale rolls may be made light and flakey by dipping for a moment in cold water, and placing immediately in a very hot oven to be made crisp and hot.

SODA BISCUIT.

One quart of sifted flour, one teaspoonful of soda, two teaspoonfuls of cream tartar, one teaspoonful of salt; mix thoroughly, and rub in two tablespoonfuls of butter, and wet with one pint of sweet milk. Bake in a quick oven.

BAKING-POWDER BISCUIT.

Two pints of flour, butter the size of an egg, three heaping teaspoonfuls of baking-powder, and one teaspoonful of salt; make a soft dough of sweet milk or water, knead as little as possible, cut out with the usual biscuit-cutter and bake in rather a quick oven.

SOUR MILK BISCUIT.

Rub into a quart of sifted flour a piece of butter the size of an egg, one teaspoonful of salt; stir into this a pint of sour milk, dissolve one teaspoonful of soda, and stir into the milk just as you add it to the flour; knead it up quickly, roll it out nearly half an inch thick, and cut out with a biscuit-cutter; bake immediately in a quick oven.

Very nice biscuit may be made with sour cream without the butter by the same process.

RAISED BISCUIT.

Sift two quarts of flour in a mixing-pan, make a hole in the middle of the flour, pour into this one pint of warm water or new milk, one teaspoonful of salt, half a cup of melted lard or butter, stir in a little flour, then add half a cupful of yeast, after which stir in as much flour as you can conveniently with your hand, let it rise over night; in the morning add nearly a teaspoonful of soda, and more flour as is needed to make a rather soft dough; then mold fifteen to twenty minutes, the longer the better; let it rise until light again, roll this out about half an inch thick, and cut out with a biscuit-cutter, or make it into little balls with your hands; cover and set in a warm place to rise. When light, bake a light brown in a moderate oven. Rub a little warm butter or sweet lard on the sides of the biscuits when you place them on the tins, to prevent their sticking together when baked.

LIGHT BISCUIT. No. 1.

Take a piece of bread dough that will make about as many biscuits as you wish; lay it out rather flat in a bowl; break into it two eggs; half a cup of sugar, half a cup of butter; mix this thoroughly with enough flour to keep it from sticking to the hands and board. Knead it well for about fifteen or twenty minutes, make into small biscuits, place in a greased pan, and let them rise until about even with the top of the pan. Bake in a quick oven for about half an hour.

These can be made in the form of rolls, which some prefer.

LIGHT BISCUIT. No. 2.

When you bake take a pint of sponge, one tablespoonful of melted butter, one tablespoonful of sugar, the white of one egg beaten to a foam. Let rise until light, mold into biscuits, and when light bake.

GRAHAM BISCUITS, WITH YEAST.

Take one pint of water or milk, one large tablespoonful of butter, two tablespoonfuls of sugar, a half cup of yeast, and a pinch of salt; take enough wheat flour to use up the water, making it the consistency of batter-cakes; add the rest of the ingredients and as much Graham flour as can be stirred in with a spoon; set it away till morning; in the morning, grease a pan, flour your hands, take a lump of dough the size of an egg, roll it lightly between the palms of your hands, let them rise twenty minutes, and bake in a tolerably hot oven.

EGG BISCUIT.

Sift together a quart of dry flour and three heaping teaspoonfuls of baking-powder. Rub into this thoroughly a piece of butter the size of an egg; add two well-beaten eggs, a tablespoonful of sugar, a teaspoonful of salt. Mix all together quickly into a soft dough, with one cup of milk, or more if needed. Roll out nearly half of an inch thick. Cut into biscuits, and bake immediately in a quick oven from fifteen to twenty minutes.

PARKER HOUSE ROLLS.

One pint of milk, boiled and cooled; a piece of butter the size of an egg; one-half cupful of fresh yeast; one tablespoonful of sugar, one pinch of salt, and two quarts of sifted flour.

Melt the butter in the warm milk, then add the sugar, salt and flour, and let it rise over night. Mix rather soft. In the morning, add to this half of a teaspoonful of soda dissolved in a spoonful of water. Mix in enough flour to make the same stiffness as any biscuit dough; roll out not more than a quarter of an inch thick. Cut with a large round cutter; spread soft butter over the tops and fold one-half over the other by doubling it. Place them apart a little so that there will be room to rise. Cover, and place them near the fire for fifteen or twenty minutes before baking. Bake in rather a quick oven.

PARKER HOUSE ROLLS.　(Unfermented.)

These rolls are made with baking-powder, and are much sooner made, although the preceding recipe is the old original one from the "Parker House." Stir into a quart of sifted flour three large teaspoonfuls of baking-powder, a tablespoonful of cold butter, a teaspoonful of salt and one of sugar, and a well-beaten egg; rub all well into the flour, pour in a pint of cold milk, mix up quickly into a smooth dough, roll it out less than half an inch thick, cut with a large biscuit-cutter, spread soft butter over the top of each, fold one half over the other by doubling it, lay them a little apart on greased tins. Set them immediately in a pretty hot oven. Rub over the tops with sweet milk before putting in the oven, to give them a glaze.

FRENCH ROLLS.

Three cups of sweet milk, one cup of butter and lard, mixed in equal proportions, one-half cup of good yeast, or half a cake of compressed yeast, and a teaspoonful of salt. Add flour enough to make a stiff dough. Let it rise over night; in the morning, add two well-beaten eggs; knead thoroughly, and let it rise again. With the hands, make it into balls as large as an egg; then roll between the hands to make *long rolls*, (about three inches.) Place close together in even rows on well-buttered pans. Cover and let them rise again, then bake in a quick oven to a delicate brown.

BEATEN BISCUIT.

Two quarts of sifted flour, a teaspoonful of salt, a tablespoonful of sweet lard, one egg; make up with half a pint of milk, or, if milk is not to be had, plain water will answer; beat well until the dough blisters and cracks; pull off a two-inch square of the dough; roll it into a ball with the hand; flatten, stick with a fork, and bake in a quick oven.

It is not beating hard that makes the biscuit nice, but the regularity of the motion. Beating hard, the old cooks say, *kills* the dough. *An old-fashioned Southern recipe.*

POTATO BISCUIT.

Boil six good-sized potatoes with their jackets on; take them out with a skimmer, drain and squeeze with a towel to ensure being dry; then remove the skin, mash them perfectly free from lumps, add a tablespoonful of butter, one egg, and a pint of sweet milk. When cool, beat in half a cup of yeast. Put in just enough flour to make a stiff dough. When this rises, make into small cakes. Let them rise the same as biscuit and bake a delicate brown.

This dough is very fine, dropped into meat soups for pot-pie.

VINEGAR BISCUITS.

Take two quarts of flour, one large tablespoonful of lard or butter, one table-spoonful and a half of vinegar and one teaspoonful of soda; put the soda in the vinegar and stir it well; stir in the flour; beat two eggs very light and add to it; make a dough with warm water stiff enough to roll out, and cut with a biscuit-cutter one inch thick, and bake in a *quick* oven.

GRAFTON MILK BISCUITS.

Boil and mash two white potatoes; add two teaspoonfuls of brown sugar; pour boiling water over these, enough to soften them. When tepid, add one small teacupful of yeast; when light, warm three ounces of butter in one pint of milk, a little salt, a third of a teaspoonful of soda, and flour enough to make stiff sponge; when risen, work it on the board; put it back in the tray to rise again; when risen, roll into cakes, and let them stand half an hour. Bake in a *quick* oven. These biscuits are fine.

SALLY LUNN.

Warm one-half cupful of butter in a pint of milk; add a teaspoonful of salt, a tablespoonful of sugar, and seven cupfuls of *sifted* flour; beat thoroughly, and when the mixture is blood warm, add four beaten eggs, and last of all, half a cup of good lively yeast. Beat hard until the batter breaks in blisters. Set it to rise over night. In the morning, dissolve half a teaspoonful of soda, stir it into the batter and turn it into a well-buttered, shallow dish to rise again about fifteen or twenty minutes. Bake about fifteen to twenty minutes.

The cake should be torn apart, not cut; cutting with a knife makes warm bread heavy. Bake a light brown. This cake is frequently seen on Southern tables.

SALLY LUNN. (Unfermented.)

Rub a piece of butter as large as an egg into a quart of flour; add a tumbler of milk, two eggs, three tablespoonfuls of sugar, three teaspoonfuls of baking powder, and a teaspoonful of salt. Scatter the baking-powder, salt and sugar into the flour; add the eggs, the butter, melted, the milk. Stir all together, and bake in well-greased round pans. Eat warm with butter.

LONDON HOT-CROSS BUNS.

Three cups of milk, one cup of yeast, or one cake of compressed yeast dissolved in a cup of tepid water, and flour enough to make a thick batter; set this as a sponge over night. In the morning, add half a cup of melted butter, one cup of sugar, half a nutmeg grated, one saltspoonful of salt, half a teaspoonful of soda, and flour enough to roll out like biscuit. Knead well and set to rise for five hours. Roll the dough half an inch thick; cut in round cakes, and lay in rows in a buttered baking-pan, and let the cakes stand half an hour; or until light; then put them in the oven, having first made a deep cross on each with a knife. Bake a light brown, and brush over with white of egg beaten stiff with powdered sugar.

RUSKS, WITH YEAST.

In one large coffee-cup of warm milk, dissolve half a cake of compressed yeast, or three tablespoonfuls of home-made yeast; to this add three well-beaten eggs, a small cup of sugar, and a teaspoonful of salt; beat these together. Use flour enough to make a smooth, light dough, let it stand until very light, then knead it in the form of biscuits; place them on buttered tins, and let them rise until they are almost up to the edge of the tins; pierce the top of each one, and bake in a quick oven. Glaze the tops of each with sugar and milk, or the white of an egg, before baking. Some add dried currants, well-washed and dried in the oven.

RUSKS.

Two cups of raised dough, one of sugar, half a cup of butter, two well-beaten eggs, flour enough to make a stiff dough; set to rise, and when light, mold into high biscuit, and let rise again; rub damp sugar and cinnamon over the top and place in the oven. Bake about twenty minutes.

RUSKS. (Unfermented.)

Three cups of flour sifted, three teaspoonfuls of baking-powder, one teaspoonful of salt, three tablespoonfuls of sugar, two tablespoonfuls of butter, three eggs, half a nutmeg grated and a teaspoonful of ground cinnamon, two small cups of milk; sift together salt, flour, sugar and baking-powder; rub in the butter cold; add the milk, beaten eggs and spices; mix into a soft dough, break off pieces about as large as an egg, roll them under the hands into round balls, rub the tops with sugar and water mixed, and then sprinkle dry sugar over them. Bake immediately.

SCOTCH SCONES

Thoroughly mix, while dry, one quart of sifted flour, loosely measured, with two heaping teaspoonfuls of baking-powder; then rub into it a tablespoonful of cold butter, and a teaspoonful of salt. Be sure that the butter is well worked m. Add sweet milk enough to make a *very* soft paste. Roll out the paste about a quarter of an inch thick, using plenty of flour on the paste-board, and rolling-pin. Cut it into triangular pieces, each side about four inches long. Flour the sides and bottom of a biscuit-tin, and place the pieces on it. Bake immediately in a quick oven from twenty to thirty minutes. When half done, brush over with sweet milk. Some cooks prefer to bake them on a floured griddle, and cut them a round shape the size of a saucer, then scarred across to form four quarters.

CRACKNELS.

Two cups of rich milk, four tablespoonfuls of butter and a gill of yeast, a teaspoonful of salt; mix warm, add flour enough to make a light dough. When light, roll thin, and cut in long pieces three inches wide, prick well with a fork, and bake in a slow oven. They are to be mixed rather hard, and rolled very thin, like soda crackers.

RAISED MUFFINS. No. 1.

Make a batter of one pint of sweet milk, one teaspoonful of sugar, one of salt, a tablespoonful of butter or sweet lard, and a half cup of yeast; add flour enough to make it moderately thick; keep it in a warm, *not hot*, place, until it is quite light, then stir in one or two well-beaten eggs, and half a teaspoonful of soda, dissolved in a little warm water. Let the batter stand twenty-five or thirty minutes longer to rise a little, turn into well-greased muffin-rings or gem-pans, and bake in a quick oven.

To be served hot, and torn open, instead of cut with a knife.

RAISED MUFFINS. No. 2.

Three pints of flour, three eggs, a piece of butter the size of an egg, two heaping teaspoonfuls of white sugar, one-half cake of compressed yeast, and a quart of milk; warm the milk with the butter in it; cool a little, stir in the sugar and add a little salt; stir this gradually into the flour, then add the eggs well-beaten; dissolve the yeast in half a cup of luke-warm water and add to the other ingredients; if the muffins are wanted for luncheon, mix them about eight o'clock in the morning; if for breakfast, set them at ten o'clock at night; when ready for baking, stir in half a teaspoonful of soda, dissolved in a teaspoonful of hot water; butter the muffin-ring or gem-irons, and bake in a quick oven.

EGG MUFFINS. (Fine.)

One quart of flour, sifted twice; three eggs, the whites and yolks beaten separately, three teacups of sweet milk, a teaspoonful of salt, a tablespoonful of sugar, a large tablespoonful of lard or butter, and two heaping teaspoonfuls of baking-powder. Sift together flour, sugar, salt and baking-powder; rub in the lard cold, add the beaten eggs and milk; mix quickly into a smooth batter, a little firmer than for griddle-cakes. Grease well some muffin-pans, and fill them two-thirds full. Bake in a hot oven fifteen or twenty minutes. These, made of cream, omitting the butter, are excellent.

PLAIN MUFFINS.

One egg, well-beaten, a tablespoonful of butter and a tablespoonful of sugar, with a teaspoonful of salt, all beaten until very light. One cup of milk, three of sifted flour, and three teaspoonfuls of baking-powder. One-half Graham and one-half rye meal may be used instead of wheat flour, or two cups of corn-meal and one of flour.

Drop on well-greased patty-pans and bake twenty minutes in a rather quick oven, or bake on a griddle in muffin-rings.

MUFFINS WITHOUT EGGS.

One quart of buttermilk, a teaspoonful of soda dissolved in the milk, a little salt, and flour enough to make a stiff batter. Drop in hot gem-pans and bake in a quick oven. Two or three tablespoonfuls of sour cream will make them a little richer.

TENNESSEE MUFFINS.

One pint of corn-meal, one pint of flour, one tablespoonful of sugar, one teaspoonful of salt, three of baking-powder, one tablespoonful of lard or butter, two eggs, and a pint of milk. Sift together corn-meal, flour, sugar, salt, and powder; rub in lard or butter cold, and eggs beaten and milk; mix into batter of consistence of cup-cake; muffin-rings to be cold and well-greased, then fill two-thirds full. Bake in hot oven fifteen minutes.

LOUISA CATHERINE ADAMS.

Mrs. MARTIN VAN BUREN.

Mrs. ANDREW JACKSON

Mrs. LETITIA CHRISTIAN TYLER.

Mrs. PRESIDENT HARRISON.

CORN-MEAL MUFFINS. (Without Eggs.)

One cup of flour, one cup of corn-meal, two tablespoonfuls of sugar, water to make a thick batter, or sour milk is better; mix at night; in the morning, add two tablespoonfuls melted butter, and one teaspoonful of soda; bake in cake rounds

HOMINY MUFFINS.

Two cups of boiled hominy; beat it smooth, stir in three cups of sour milk, half a cup of melted butter, two teaspoonfuls of salt, two tablespoonfuls of sugar; add three eggs well-beaten; one teaspoonful of soda, dissolved in hot water; two cups of flour. Bake quickly.

Rice muffins may be made in the same manner.

GRAHAM GEMS. No. 1.

Two cupfuls of Graham flour, one cupful of wheat flour, two teaspoonfuls of baking-powder, a tablespoonful of sugar, one of salt, and one well-beaten egg.

Mix with sweet milk to make a thin batter; beat it well. Bake in gem-irons; have the irons well-greased; fill two-thirds full, and bake in a hot oven. Will bake in from fifteen to twenty minutes.

GRAHAM GEMS. No. 2.

Three cups of sour milk, one teaspoonful of soda, one of salt, one tablespoon-ful of brown sugar, one of melted lard or butter, one or two beaten eggs; to the egg add the milk, then the sugar and salt, then the Graham flour (with the soda mixed in), together with the lard or butter; make a stiff batter, so that it will *drop*, not pour, from the spoon. Have the gem-pans very hot, fill and bake fif teen minutes in a hot oven.

The same can be made of sweet milk, using three teaspoonfuls of baking powder instead of soda, and if you use sweet milk, put in no shortening. Ex cellent.

Muffins of all kinds should only be cut just around the edge, then pulled open with the fingers.

PLAIN GRAHAM GEMS.

Two cupfuls of the best Graham meal, two of water, fresh and cold, or milk and water, and a little salt. Stir briskly for a minute or two. Have the gem-pan, hot and well-greased, on the top of the stove while pouring in the batter. Then place in a very hot oven and bake forty minutes. It is best to check the heat a little when they are nearly done. As the best-prepared gems may be spoiled if the heat is not sufficient, care and judgment must be used in order to secure this most healthful as well as delicious bread.

WAFFLES.

Take a quart of flour and wet it with a little sweet milk that has been boiled and cooled, then stir in enough of the milk to form a thick batter. Add a tablespoonful of melted butter, a teaspoonful of salt, and yeast to raise it. When light, add two well-beaten eggs, heat your waffle-iron, grease it well, and fill it with the batter. Two or three minutes will suffice to bake on one side; then turn the iron over; and when brown on both sides, the cake is done. Serve immediately.

CONTINENTAL HOTEL WAFFLES.

Put into one quart of sifted flour three teaspoonfuls of baking-powder, one teaspoonful of salt, one of sugar, all thoroughly stirred and sifted together; add a tablespoonful of melted butter, six well-beaten eggs, and a pint of sweet milk; cook in waffle-irons, heated and well-greased. Serve hot.

NEWPORT WAFFLES.

Make one pint of Indian meal into mush in the usual way. While hot, put in a small lump of butter, and a dessertspoonful of salt. Set the mush aside to cool. Meanwhile, beat separately till very light the whites and yolks of four eggs. Add the eggs to the mush, and cream in gradually one quart of wheaten flour. Add half a pint of buttermilk or sour cream, in which has been dissolved half a teaspoonful of carbonate of soda. Lastly, bring to the consistency of thin batter, by the addition of sweet milk. Waffle-irons should be put on to heat an hour in advance, that they may be in the proper condition for baking as soon as the batter is ready. Have a brisk fire, butter the irons thoroughly, but with nicety, and bake quickly. Fill the irons only half full of batter, that the waffles may have room to rise.

CREAM WAFFLES.

One pint of sour cream, two eggs, one pint of flour, one tablespoonful of corn-meal, one teaspoonful of soda, half a teaspoonful of salt. Beat the eggs separately, mix the cream with the beaten yolks, stir in the flour, corn-meal and salt; add the soda dissolved in a little sweet milk, and, last, the whites beaten to a stiff froth.

RICE WAFFLES. No. 1.

One quart of flour, half a teaspoonful of salt, one teaspoonful of sugar, two teaspoonfuls of baking-powder, one large tablespoonful of butter, two eggs, one and a half pints of milk, one cupful of hot boiled rice. Sift the flour, salt, sugar, and baking-powder well together; rub the butter into the flour; beat the eggs well, separately, and add the stiff whites last of all.

RICE WAFFLES. No. 2.

Rub through a sieve one pint of boiled rice, add it to a tablespoonful of dry flour, two-thirds of a teaspoonful of salt, two teaspoonfuls of baking-powder. Beat separately the yolks and whites of three eggs; add to the yolks a cup and a half of milk, work it into the flour, then add an ounce of melted butter; beat the white of eggs thoroughly; mix the whole together. Heat the waffle-iron and grease it evenly; pour the batter into the half of the iron over the range until nearly two-thirds full, cover, allow to cook a moment, then turn and brown slightly on the other side.

GERMAN RICE WAFFLES.

Boil a half-pound of rice in milk until it becomes thoroughly soft. Then remove it from the fire, stirring it constantly, and adding, a little at a time, one quart of sifted flour, five beaten eggs, two spoonfuls of yeast, a half-pound of melted butter, a little salt, and a teacupful of warm milk. Set the batter in a warm place, and when risen, bake in the ordinary way.

BERRY TEA-CAKES.

Nice little tea-cakes to be baked in muffin-rings are made of one cup of sugar, two eggs, one and a half cups of milk, one heaping teaspoonful of baking-powder, a piece of butter the size of an egg and flour sufficient to make a stiff batter. In this batter stir a pint bowl of fruit—any fresh are nice—or canned berries with the juice poured off. Serve while warm and they are a dainty addition to the tea-table. Eaten with butter.

RYE DROP-CAKES.

One pint of warm milk, with half a teaspoonful of soda dissolved in it, a little salt, four eggs, well-beaten, and rye flour enough to make a thin batter; bake in small cups, buttered, and in a hot oven, or in small cakes upon a hot griddle.

WHEAT DROP-CAKES.

One pint of cream, six eggs well-beaten, a little salt, and wheat flour enough to make a thin batter; bake in little cups buttered, and in a hot oven fifteen minutes.

POP-OVERS.

Two cups of flour, two cups of sweet milk, two eggs, one teaspoonful of butter, one teaspoonful of salt, bake in cups in a quick oven fifteen minutes. Serve hot with a sweet sauce.

FLANNEL CAKES.   (With Yeast.)

Heat a pint of sweet milk, and into it put two heaping tablespoonfuls of butter, let it melt, then add a pint of cold milk and the well-beaten yolks of four eggs—placing the whites in a cool place; also, a teaspoonful of salt, four table-spoonfuls of home-made yeast, and sufficient flour to make a stiff batter; set it in a warm place to rise; let it stand three hours or over night; before baking add the beaten whites; bake like any other griddle-cakes.   Be sure to make the batter stiff enough, for flour must not be added after it has risen, unless it is allowed to rise again.   These, half corn-meal and half wheat, are very nice.

FEATHER GRIDDLE-CAKES.   (With Yeast.)

Make a batter, at night, of a pint of water or milk, a teaspoonful of salt, and half a teacupful of yeast; in the morning, add to it one teacupful of thick, sour milk, two eggs well-beaten, a level tablespoonful of melted butter, a level tea-spoonful of soda, and flour enough to make the consistency of pan-cake batter; let stand twenty minutes, then bake.

This is a convenient way, when making sponge for bread over night, using some of the sponge.

WHEAT GRIDDLE-CAKES.

Three cups of flour, one teaspoonful of salt, three teaspoonfuls of baking-powder sifted together; beat three eggs and add to three cupfuls of sweet milk, also a tablespoonful of melted butter; mix all into a smooth batter, as thick as will run in a stream from the lips of a pitcher.   Bake on a well-greased, hot griddle, a nice, light brown.   Very good.

SOUR MILK GRIDDLE-CAKES.

Make a batter of a quart of sour milk and as much sifted flour as is needed to thicken so that it will run from the dish; add two well-beaten eggs, a teaspoonful of salt, a tablespoonful of melted butter, and a level teaspoonful of soda dissolved in a little milk or cold water, added last; then bake on a hot griddle, well greased, brown on both sides.

CORN-MEAL GRIDDLE-CÀKES. (With Yeast.)

Stir into one quart of boiling milk three cups of corn-meal; after it cools, add one cup of white flour, a teaspoonful of salt, and three tablespoonfuls of home-made yeast. Mix this over night. In the morning, add one tablespoonful of melted butter or lard, two beaten eggs, and a teaspoonful of soda, dissolved in a little water.

This batter should stand a few minutes, after adding the butter and soda, that it should have time to rise a little; in the meantime, the griddle could be heating. Take a small stick like a good-sized skewer, wind a bit of cloth around the end of it, fasten it by winding a piece of thread around that and tying it firm. Melt together a tablespoonful of butter and lard. Grease the griddle with this. Between each batch of cakes, wipe the griddle off with a clean paper or cloth, and grease afresh. Put the cakes on by spoonfuls, or pour them carefully from a pitcher, trying to get them as near the same size as possible. As soon as they begin to bubble all over turn them, and cook on the other side till they stop puffing. The second lot always cooks better than the first, as the griddle becomes evenly heated.

CORN-MEAL GRIDDLE-CAKES.

Scald two cups of sifted meal, mix with a cup of wheat flour, and a teaspoonful of salt. Add three well-beaten eggs; thin the whole with sour milk enough to make it the right consistency. Beat the whole till very light, and add a teaspoonful of baking-soda dissolved in a little water. If you use sweet milk, use two large teaspoonfuls of baking-powder instead of soda.

GRIDDLE-CAKES. (Very Good.)

One quart of Graham flour, half a pint of Indian meal, one gill of yeast, a teaspoonful of salt; mix the flour and meal, pour on enough warm water to make batter rather thicker than that for buckwheat cakes; add the yeast, and when light bake on griddle not too hot.

GRAHAM GRIDDLE-CAKES.

Mix together dry two cups of Graham flour, one cup wheat flour, two heaping teaspoonfuls of baking-powder, and one teaspoonful of salt. Then add three eggs well-beaten, one tablespoonful of lard or butter melted, and three cups of sweet milk. Cook immediately on a hot griddle.

BREAD GRIDDLE-CAKES.

One quart of milk, boiling hot; two cups fine bread-crumbs, three eggs, one tablespoonful melted butter, one-half teaspoonful salt, one-half teaspoonful soda, dissolved in warm water; break the bread into the boiling milk, and let stand for ten minutes in a covered bowl, then beat to a smooth paste; add the yolks of the eggs well-whipped, the butter, salt, soda, and finally the whites of the eggs previously whipped stiff, and add half of a cupful of flour. These can also be made of sour milk, soaking the bread in it over night, and using a little more soda.

RICE GRIDDLE-CAKES.

Two cupfuls of cold boiled rice, one pint of flour, one teaspoonful sugar, one-half teaspoonful salt, one and one-half teaspoonfuls baking-powder, one egg, a little more than half a pint of milk. Sift together flour, sugar, salt and powder; add rice free from lumps, diluted with beaten egg and milk; mix into smooth batter. Have griddle well-heated, make cakes large, bake nicely brown, and serve with maple syrup.

POTATO GRIDDLE-CAKES.

Twelve large potatoes, three heaping tablespoonfuls of flour, one teaspoonful of baking-powder, one-half teaspoonful of salt, one or two eggs, two teacupfuls of boiling milk. The potatoes are peeled, washed and grated into a little cold water, (which keeps them white), then strain off water and pour on boiling milk, stir in eggs, salt and flour, mixed with the baking-powder; if agreeable, flavor with a little fine chopped onion; bake like any other pan-cakes, allowing a little more lard or butter. Serve with stewed or preserved fruit, especially with huckleberries.

GREEN CORN GRIDDLE-CAKES.

One pint of milk, two cups grated green corn, a little salt, two eggs, a teaspoonful of baking-powder, flour sufficient to make a batter to fry on the griddle. Butter them hot and serve.

HUCKLEBERRY GRIDDLE-CAKES.

Made the same as above, leaving out one cup of milk, adding one tablespoonful of sugar, and a pint of huckleberries, rolled in flour. Blackberries or raspberries can be used in the same manner.

FRENCH GRIDDLE-CAKES.

Beat together, until smooth, six eggs and a pint sifted flour; melt one ounce of butter, and add to the batter, with one ounce of sugar and a cup of milk;

beat until smooth; put a tablespoonful at a time into a frying-pan, slightly greased, spreading the batter evenly over the surface by tipping the pan about; fry to a light brown; spread with jelly, roll up, dust with powdered sugar and serve hot.

RAISED BUCKWHEAT CAKES.

Take a small crock or large earthen pitcher, put into it a quart of warm water or half water and milk, one heaping teaspoonful of salt; then stir in as much buckwheat flour as will thicken it to rather a stiff batter; lastly add half a cup of yeast; make it smooth, cover it up warm to rise over night; in the morning, add a small, level teaspoonful of soda, dissolved in a little warm water; this will remove any sour taste, if any, and increase the lightness.

Not a few object to eating buckwheat, as its tendency is to thicken the blood, and also to produce constipation; this can be remedied by making the batter one-third corn-meal and two-thirds buckwheat, which makes the cakes equally as good. Many prefer them in this way.

BUCKWHEAT CAKES WITHOUT YEAST.

Two cups of buckwheat flour, one of wheat flour, a little salt, three teaspoonfuls baking-powder; mix thoroughly, and add about equal parts of milk and water until the batter is of the right consistency, then stir until free from lumps. If they do not brown well, add a little molasses.

BUCKWHEAT CAKES.

Half a pint of buckwheat flour, a quarter of a pint of corn-meal, a quarter of a pint of wheat flour, a little salt, two eggs beaten very light, one quart of new milk (made a little warm, and mixed with the eggs before the flour is put in), one tablespoonful of butter or sweet lard, two large tablespoonfuls of yeast. Set it to rise at night for the morning. If in the least sour, stir in before baking just enough soda to correct the acidity. A very nice, but more expensive recipe.

SWEDISH GRIDDLE-CAKES.

One pint of white flour, sifted; six eggs, whites and yolks beaten separately to the utmost; one saltspoonful of salt; one saltspoonful of soda dissolved in vinegar; milk to make a thin batter.

Beat the yolks light, add the salt, soda, two cupfuls of milk, then the flour, and beaten whites alternately; thin with more milk if necessary

CORN-MEAL FRITTERS.

One pint of sour milk, one teaspoonful of salt, three eggs, one tablespoonful of molasses or sugar, one handful of flour, and corn-meal enough to make a stiff batter; lastly, stir in a small teaspoonful of soda, dissolved in a little warm water.

This recipe is very nice made of rye flour.

CREAM FRITTERS.

One cup of cream; five eggs—the whites only; two full cups prepared flour; one saltspoonful of nutmeg; a pinch of salt. Stir the whites into the cream in turn with the flour, put in nutmeg and salt, beat all up hard for two minutes. The batter should be rather thick. Fry in plenty of hot, sweet lard, a spoonful of batter for each fritter. Drain, and serve upon a hot, clean napkin. Eat with jelly sauce. Pull, not cut, them open. Very nice.

CURRANT FRITTERS.

Two cupfuls dry, fine, bread-crumbs, two tablespoonfuls of prepared flour, two cups of milk, one-half pound currants, washed and well-dried, five eggs whipped very light, one-half cup powdered sugar, one tablespoonful butter, one half teaspoonful mixed cinnamon and nutmeg. Boil the milk and pour over the bread. Mix and put in the butter. Let it get cold. Beat in next the yolks and sugar, the seasoning, flour, and stiff whites; finally, the currants dredged whitely with flour. The batter should be thick. Drop in great spoonfuls into the hot lard and fry. Drain them and send hot to table. Eat with a mixture of wine and powdered sugar.

WHEAT FRITTERS.

Three eggs, one and a half cups of milk, three teaspoonfuls baking-powder, salt, and flour enough to make quite stiff, thicker than batter-cakes. Drop into hot lard and fry like doughnuts.

A good Sauce for the Above.—One cup of sugar, two tablespoonfuls of butter, one teaspoonful of flour beaten together; half a cup boiling water; flavor with extract lemon and boil until clear. Or serve with maple syrup.

APPLE FRITTERS.

Make a batter in the proportion of one cup sweet milk to two cups flour, a heaping teaspoonful of baking-powder, two eggs beaten separately, one table-spoonful of sugar and a saltspoon of salt; heat the milk a little more than milk-warm; add it slowly to the beaten yolks and sugar; then add flour and whites of the eggs; stir all together and throw in thin slices of good sour apples, dipping the batter up over them; drop into boiling hot lard in large spoonfuls with pieces of apple in each, and fry to a light brown. Serve with maple syrup, or a nice syrup made with clarified sugar.

Bananas, peaches, sliced oranges and other fruits can be used in the same batter.

PINE-APPLE FRITTERS.

Make a batter as for apple fritters; then pare one large pine-apple, cut it in slices a quarter of an inch thick, cut the slices in halves, dip them into the batter and fry them, and serve them as above.

PEACH FRITTERS.

Peel the peaches, split each in two and take out the stones; dust a little powdered sugar over them; dip each piece in the batter, and fry in hot fat. A sauce to be served with them may be made as follows: Put an ounce of butter in a sauce-pan, and whisk it to a cream; add four ounces of sugar gradually. Beat the yolks of two eggs; add to them a dash of nutmeg and a gill each of cold water and rum; stir this into the luke-warm batter, and allow it to heat gradually. Stir constantly until of a smooth, creamy consistency, and serve. The batter is made as follows: Beat the yolks of three eggs; add to them a gill of milk, or half of a cupful, a saltspoonful of salt, four ounces of flour; mix. If old flour is used, a little more milk may be found necessary.

GOLDEN-BALL FRITTERS.

Put into a stew-pan a pint of water, a piece of butter as large as an egg, and a tablespoonful of sugar. When it boils, stir into it one pint of sifted flour, stirring briskly and thoroughly. Remove from the fire, and when nearly cooled, beat into it six eggs, each one beaten separately, and added, one at a time, beating the batter between each. Drop the stiff dough into boiling lard by teaspoonfuls. Eat with syrup, or melted sugar and butter flavored.

Stirring the boiling lard around and around, so that it whirls when you drop in the fritters, causes them to assume a round shape like balls.

CANNELONS, OR FRIED PUFFS.

Half a pound of puff paste; apricot, or any kind of preserve that may be preferred; hot lard.

Cannelons, which are made of puff-paste, rolled very thin, with jam enclosed, and cut out in long, narrow rolls or puffs, make a very pretty and elegant dish. Make some good puff paste, roll it out very thin, and cut it into pieces of an equal size, about two inches wide and eight inches long; place upon each piece a spoonful of jam, wet the edges with the white of egg; and fold the paste over *twice;* slightly press the edges together, that the jam may not escape in the frying; and when all are prepared, fry them in boiling lard until of a nice brown, letting them remain by the side of the fire after they are colored, that the paste may be thoroughly done. Drain them before the fire, dish on a d'oyley, sprinkle over them sifted sugar, and serve. These cannelons are very delicious made with fresh, instead of preserved fruit, such as strawberries, raspberries, or currants; they should be laid in the paste, plenty of pounded sugar sprinkled over, and folded and fried in the same manner as stated above.

GERMAN FRITTERS.

Take slices of stale bread cut in rounds, or stale cake; fry them in hot lard, like crullers, to a *light* brown. Dip each slice when fried in boiling milk, to remove the grease; drain quickly, dust with powdered sugar, or spread with preserves. Pile on a hot plate, and serve. Sweet wine sauce poured over them is very nice.

HOMINY FRITTERS.

Take one pint of hot boiled hominy, two eggs, half a teaspoonful of salt, and a tablespoonful of flour; thin it a little with cold milk; when cold, add a teaspoonful of baking-powder, mix thoroughly, drop tablespoonfuls of it into hot fat and fry to a delicate brown.

PARSNIP FRITTERS.

Take three or four good-sized parsnips. Boil them until tender. Mash and season with a little butter, a pinch of salt and a slight sprinkling of pepper. Have ready a plate with some sifted flour on it. Drop a tablespoonful of the parsnip in the flour and roll it about until well-coated and formed into a ball. When you have a sufficient number ready, drop them into boiling drippings or lard, as you would a fritter; fry a delicate brown, and serve hot. Do not put them in a covered dish, for that would steam them and deprive them of their crispness, which is one of their great charms.

These are also very good fried in a frying-pan with a small quantity of lard and butter mixed, turning them over so as to fry both sides brown.

GREEN-CORN FRITTERS.

One pint of grated, young and tender, green corn, three eggs, two tablespoonfuls of milk or cream, one tablespoonful of melted butter, if milk is used, a teaspoonful of salt. Beat the eggs well, add the corn by degrees, also the milk and butter; thicken with just enough flour to hold them together, adding a teaspoonful of baking-powder to the flour. Have ready a kettle of hot lard, drop the corn from the spoon into the fat and fry a light brown. They are also nice fried in butter and lard mixed, the same as fried eggs.

CREAM SHORT-CAKE.

Sift one quart of fine white flour, rub into it three tablespoonfuls of cold butter, a teaspoonful of salt, a tablespoonful of white sugar. Add a beaten egg to a cup of sour cream, turn it into the other ingredients, dissolve a teaspoonful of soda in a spoonful of water, mix all together, handling as little as possible; roll lightly into two round sheets, place on pie-tins, and bake from twenty to twenty-five minutes in a quick oven.

This crust is delicious for fruit short-cakes.

STRAWBERRY SHORT-CAKE.

Make a rule of baking-powder biscuit, with the exception of a little more shortening; divide the dough in half; lay one-half on the molding-board, (half the dough makes one short-cake), divide this half again, and roll each piece large enough to cover a biscuit-tin, or a large-sized pie-tin; spread soft butter over the lower one, and place the other on top of that; proceed with the other lump of dough the same, by cutting it in halves, and putting on another tin. Set them in the oven; when sufficiently baked take them out, separate each one by running a large knife through where the cold soft butter was spread. Then butter plentifully each crust, lay the bottom of each on earthern platters or dining-plates; cover thickly with a quart of strawberries that have been previously prepared with sugar, lay the top crusts on the fruit. If there is any juice left, pour it around the cake. This makes a delicious short-cake.

Peaches, raspberries, blackberries, and huckleberries can be substituted for strawberries. Always send to the table with a pitcher of sweet cream.

ORANGE SHORT-CAKE.

Peel two large oranges, chop them fine, remove the seeds, add half a peeled lemon, and one cup of sugar. Spread between the layers of short-cake while it is hot.

LEMON SHORT-CAKE.

Make a rich biscuit dough, same as above recipe. While baking, take a cup and a quarter of water, a cup and a half of sugar, and two lemons, peel, juice and pulp, throwing away the tough part of the rind; boil this for some little time; then stir in three crackers rolled fine; split the short-cakes while hot, spread with butter, then with the mixture. To be eaten warm.

HUCKLEBERRY SHORT-CAKE.

Two cupfuls of sugar, half a cupful of butter, one pint of sweet milk, one tablespoonful of salt, two heaping teaspoonfuls of baking-powder, sifted into a quart of flour, or enough to form a thick batter; add a quart of the huckleberries; to be baked in a dripper; cut into squares for the table, and served hot with butter. Blackberries may be used the same.

FRIED DINNER-ROLLS.

When making light raised bread, save out a piece of dough nearly the size of a small loaf, roll it out on the board, spread a tablespoonful of melted butter over it; dissolve a quarter of a teaspoonful of soda in a tablespoonful of water, and pour that also over it; work it all well into the dough, roll it out into a sheet not quite half an inch thick. Cut it in strips three inches long and one inch wide. Lay them on buttered tins, cover with a cloth, and set away in a cool place until an hour before dinner-time; then set them by the fire where they will become light. While they are rising, put into a frying-pan a tablespoonful of cold butter and one of lard; when it boils clear and is *hot*, lay as many of the rolls in as will fry nicely. As soon as they brown on one side, turn them over and brown the other; then turn them on the edges and brown the sides. Add fresh grease as is needed. Eat them warm in place of bread. Nice with warm meat dinner.

NEWPORT BREAKFAST-CAKES.

Take one quart of dough from the bread, at an early hour in the morning; break three eggs, separating yolks and whites, both to be whipped to a light froth; mix them into the dough, and gradually add two tablespoonfuls of melted butter, one of sugar, one teaspoonful of soda, and enough warm milk with it until it is a batter the consistency of buckwheat cakes; beat it well, and let it rise until breakfast-time. Have the griddle hot and nicely greased, pour on the batter in small round cakes, and bake a light brown, the same as any griddle-cake.

PUFF BALLS.

A piece of butter as large as an egg, stirred until soft; add three well-beaten eggs, a pinch of salt, and half a teacupful of sour cream. Stir well together, then add enough flour to make a very thick batter. Drop a spoonful of this into boiling water. Cook until the puffs rise to the surface. Dish them hot with melted butter turned over them. Nice accompaniment to a meat dinner, as a side-dish—similar to plain maccaroni.

BREAKFAST PUFFS.

Two cups of sour milk, one teaspoonful of soda, one teaspoonful of salt, one egg, and flour enough to roll out like biscuit dough. Cut into narrow strips, an inch wide, and three inches long; fry brown in hot lard, like doughnuts. Serve hot; excellent with coffee. Or, fry in a spider with an ounce each of lard and butter, turning and browning all four of the sides.

ENGLISH CRUMPETS.

One quart of warm milk, half a cup of yeast, one teaspoonful of salt, flour enough to make a stiff batter; when light, add half a cupful of melted butter, a teaspoonful of soda, dissolved in a little water, and a very little more flour; let it stand twenty minutes or until light. Grease some muffin rings, place them on a hot griddle, and fill them half full of the batter; when done on one side, turn and bake the other side. Butter them while hot; pile one on another, and serve immediately.

PLAIN CRUMPETS.

Mix together thoroughly, while dry, one quart of sifted flour, loosely measured, two heaping teaspoonfuls baking-powder, and a little salt; then add two table-spoonfuls of melted butter, and sweet milk enough to make a thin dough. Bake quickly in muffin-rings or patty-pans.

PREPARED BREAD-CRUMBS.

Take pieces of stale bread, break them in small bits, put them on a baking-pan and place them in a moderate oven, watching closely that they do not scorch; then take them while hot and crisp and roll them, crushing them. Sift them, using the fine crumbs for breading cutlets, fish, croquettes, etc. The coarse ones may be used for puddings, pan-cakes, etc.

CRACKERS.

Sift into a pint of flour a heaping teaspoonful of baking-powder, four table-spoonfuls of melted butter, half a teaspoonful salt and the white of an egg beaten, and one cup of milk; mix it with more flour, enough to make a very stiff dough, as stiff as can be rolled out; pounded and kneaded a long time. Roll very thin, like pie-crust, and cut out either round or square. Bake a light brown.

Stale crackers are made crisp and better by placing them in the oven a few moments before they are needed for the table.

FRENCH CRACKERS.

Six eggs, twelve tablespoonfuls of sweet milk, six tablespoonfuls of butter, half a teaspoonful of soda; mold with flour, pounding and working half an hour; roll it thin. Bake with rather quick fire.

CORN-MEAL MUSH OR HASTY PUDDING.

Put two quarts of water into a clean dinner-pot or stew-pan, cover it, and let it become boiling hot over the fire; then add a tablespoonful of salt, take off the light scum from the top, have sweet, fresh yellow or white corn-meal; take a handful of the meal with the left hand, and a pudding-stick in the right, then with the stick, stir the water around, and by degrees let fall the meal; when one handful is exhausted, refill it; continue to stir and add meal until it is as thick as you can stir easily, or until the stick will stand in it; stir it a while longer; let the fire be gentle; when it is sufficiently cooked, which will be in half an hour, it will bubble or puff up; turn it into a deep basin. This is eaten cold or hot, with milk or with butter, and syrup or sugar, or with meat and gravy, the same as potatoes or rice.

FRIED MUSH.

Make it like the above recipe, turn it into bread-tins, and when cold slice it, dip each piece in flour and fry it in lard and butter mixed in the frying-pan, turning to brown well both sides. Must be served hot.

GRAHAM MUSH.

Sift Graham meal slowly into boiling salted water, stirring briskly until thick as can be stirred with one hand; serve with milk or cream and sugar, or butter and syrup. It will be improved by removing from the kettle to a pan, as soon as thoroughly mixed, and steaming three or four hours. It may also be eaten cold, or sliced and fried, like corn-meal mush.

OATMEAL.

Soak one cup of oatmeal in a quart of water over night, boil half an hour in the morning, salted to taste. It is better to cook it in a dish set into a dish of boiling water.

RICE CROQUETTES.

Boil for thirty minutes one cup of well-washed rice, in a pint of milk; whip into the hot rice the following ingredients: Two ounces of butter, two ounces of sugar, some salt, and when slightly cool add the yolks of two eggs well beaten; if too stiff pour in a little more milk; when cold, roll into small balls and dip in beaten eggs, roll in fine cracker or bread-crumbs, and fry same as doughnuts. Or they may be fried in the frying-pan, with a tablespoonful each of butter and lard mixed, turning and frying both sides brown. Serve very hot.

HOMINY

This form of cereal is very little known and consequently little appreciated in most Northern households. "Big hominy" and "little hominy," as they are called in the South, are staple dishes there and generally take the place of oatmeal, which is apt to be too heating for the climate. The former is called "samp" here. It must be boiled for at least eight hours to be properly cooked, and may then be kept on hand for two or three days and warmed over, made into croquettes or balls, or fried in cakes. The fine hominy takes two or three hours for proper cooking, and should be cooked in a dish set into another of boiling water, and kept steadily boiling until thoroughly soft.

HOMINY CROQUETTES.

To a cupful of cold boiled hominy, add a teaspoonful of melted butter, and stir it well, adding by degrees a cupful of milk, till all is made into a soft, light paste; add a teaspoonful of white sugar, a pinch of salt, and one well-beaten egg. Roll it into oval balls with floured hands, dipped in beaten egg, then rolled in cracker-crumbs, and fry in hot lard.

The hominy is best boiled the day or morning before using.

BOILED RICE.

Take half or quarter of a pound of the best quality of rice; wash it in a strainer, and put it in a sauce-pan, with a quart of clean water and a pinch of salt; let it boil slowly till the water is all evaporated—see that it does not burn —then pour in a teacupful of new milk; stir carefully from the bottom of the sauce-pan, so that the upper grain may go under, but do not smash it; close the lid on your sauce-pan carefully down, and set it on a cooler part of the fire, where it will not boil; as soon as it has absorbed the added milk, serve it up with fresh new milk, adding fruit and sugar for those who like them.

Another nice way to cook rice is to take one teacupful of rice and one quart of milk, place in a steamer, and steam from two to three hours; when nearly done, stir in a piece of butter as large as the yolk of an egg, and a pinch of salt. You can use sugar if you like. The difference in the time of cooking depends on your rice—the older the rice, the longer time it takes to cook.

SAMP, OR HULLED CORN.

An old-fashioned way of preparing hulled corn was to put a peck of old, dry, ripe corn into a pot filled with water, and with it a bag of hard-wood ashes, say a quart. After soaking awhile it was boiled until the skins or hulls came off easily. The corn was then washed in cold water to get rid of the taste of potash, and then boiled until the kernels were soft. Another way was to take the lye from the leaches where potash was made, dilute it, and boil the corn in this until the skin or hull came off. It makes a delicious dish, eaten with milk or cream.

CKACKED WHEAT.

Soak the wheat over night in cold water, about a quart of water to a cup of wheat; cook it as directed for oatmeal; should be thoroughly done. Eaten with sugar and cream.

OAT FLAKES.

This healthful oat preparation may be procured from the leading grocers, and is prepared as follows: Put into a double sauce-pan or porcelain-lined pan a quart of boiling water, add a saltspoonful of salt, and when it is boiling, add, or rather stir in gradually, three ounces of flakes. Keep stirring to prevent burning. Let it boil from fifteen to twenty minutes, and serve with cream and sugar.

Ordinary oatmeal requires two hours' steady cooking to make it palatable and digestible. Wheaten grits and hominy, one hour, but a half hour longer cooking will not injure them, and makes them easier of digestion. Never be afraid of cooking cereals or preparations from cereals too long, no matter what the directions on the package may be.

STEAMED OATMEAL.

To one teacupful oatmeal add a quart of cold water, a teaspoonful of salt; put in a steamer over a kettle of cold water, gradually heat and steam an hour and a half after it begins to cook.

HOMINY.

Hominy is a preparation of Indian corn, broken or ground, either large or small, and is an excellent breakfast dish in winter or summer. Wash the hominy thoroughly in one or two waters, then cover it with twice its depth of cold water, and let it come to a boil slowly. If it be the large hominy, simmer six hours; if the small hominy, simmer two hours. When the water evaporates, add hot water; when done, it may be eaten with cream, or allowed to become cold and warmed up in the frying-pan, using a little butter to prevent burning.

Toast.

Toast should be made of stale bread, or at least of bread that has been baked a day. Cut smoothly in slices, not more than half an inch thick; if the crust is baked very hard, trim the edges and brown very evenly, but if it happens to burn, that should be scraped off. Toast that is to be served with anything turned over it, should have the slices first dipped quickly in a dish of hot water turned from the boiling tea-kettle, with a little salt thrown in. Cold biscuits cut in halves, and the under crust sliced off, then browned evenly on both sides, make equally as good toast. The following preparations of toast are almost all of them very nice dishes, served with a family breakfast.

MILK TOAST.

Put over the fire a quart of milk, put into it a tablespoonful of cold butter, stir a heaping teaspoonful of flour into half a gill of milk; as soon as the milk on the fire boils, stir in the flour, add a teaspoonful of salt; let all boil up once, remove from the fire, and dip in this slices of toasted bread. When all are used up, pour what is left of the scalded milk over the toast. Cover, and send to the table hot.

CREAM TOAST.

Heat a pint of milk to boiling, and add a piece of butter the size of an egg; stir a tablespoonful of flour smoothly into a cup of rich cream, and add some of the boiling milk to this; heat it gradually and prevent the flour from lumping; then stir into the boiling milk, and let it cook a few moments: salt to taste. After taking from the fire stir in a beaten egg; strain the mixture on to toast lightly buttered.

AMERICAN TOAST.

To one egg thoroughly beaten, put one cup of sweet milk, and a little salt. Slice light bread and dip into the mixture, allowing each slice to absorb some of the milk; then brown on a hot, buttered griddle or thick-bottom frying-pan; spread with butter, and serve hot.

NUNS' TOAST.

Cut four or five hard-boiled eggs into slices. Put a piece of butter half the size of an egg into a sauce-pan, and when it begins to bubble add a finely chopped onion. Let the onion cook a little without taking color, then stir in a teaspoonful of flour. Add a cupful of milk, and stir until it becomes smooth;

then put in the slices of eggs and let them get hot. Pour over neatly trimmed slices of hot buttered toast. The sauce must be seasoned to taste with pepper and salt.

CHEESE TOAST. No. 1.

Toast thin slices of bread an even, crisp brown. Place on a warm plate, allowing one small slice to each person, and pour on enough melted cheese to cover them. Rich new cheese is best. Serve while warm. Many prefer a little prepared mustard spread over the toast before putting on the cheese.

CHEESE TOAST. No. 2.

Put half an ounce of butter in a frying-pan; when hot, add gradually four ounces of mild American cheese. Whisk it thoroughly until melted. Beat together half a pint of cream and two eggs; whisk into the cheese, add a little salt, pour over the crisp toast, and serve.

The two above recipes are usually called " Welsh Rarebit."

OYSTER TOAST.

Select the large ones, used for frying, and first dip them in beaten egg, then in either cracker or bread-crumbs, and cook upon a fine wire gridiron, over a quick fire. Toast should be made ready in advance, and a rich cream sauce poured over the whole. After pouring on the sauce, finely cut celery strewn over the top adds to their delicacy.

Or, wash oysters in the shell, and put them on hot coals, or upon the top of a hot stove, or bake them in a hot oven; open the shells with an oyster-knife, taking care to lose none of the liquor. Dip the toast into hot, salted water quickly, and turn out the oyster and liquor over the toast; season with salt and pepper, and a teaspoonful of melted butter over each.

Oysters steamed in the shell are equally as good.

MUSHROOMS ON TOAST.

Peel a quart of mushrooms, and cut off a little of the root end. Melt an ounce of butter in the frying pan, and fry in it half a pound of raw minced steak; add two saltspoonfuls of salt, a pinch of cayenne, and a gill of hot water; fry until the juices are extracted from the meat; tilt the pan and squeeze the meat with the back of the spoon until there is nothing left but dry meat, then remove it; add the mushrooms to the liquid, and if there is not enough of it, add more butter; toss them about a moment and pour out on hot toast.

Some add a little sherry to the dish before removing from the fire.

TOMATO TOAST.

Pare and stew a quart of ripe tomatoes until smooth. Season with salt, pepper and a tablespoonful of butter. When done, add one cup sweet cream and a little flour. Let it scald but not boil; remove at once. Pour over slices of dipped toast, well-buttered.

EGGS ON TOAST.

Various preparations of eggs can be served on toast, first dipping slices of well-toasted bread quickly in hot salted water, then turning over them scrambled, poached or creamed eggs, all found in the recipes among "Eggs."

BAKED EGGS ON TOAST.

Toast six slices of stale bread, dip them in hot salted water and butter them lightly. After arranging them on a platter or deep plate, break enough eggs to cover them, breaking one at a time, and slip over the toast so that they do not break; sprinkle over them salt and pepper, and turn over all some kind of thickened gravy—either chicken or lamb, cream or a cream sauce made the same as "White Sauce"; turn this over the toast and eggs, and bake in a hot oven until the eggs are set, or about five minutes. Serve at once.

HAM TOAST.

Take a quarter of a pound of either boiled or fried ham, chop it fine, mix it with the yolks of two eggs, well-beaten, a tablespoonful of butter, and enough cream or rich milk to make it soft, a dash of pepper. Stir it over the fire until it thickens. Dip the toast for an instant in hot, salted water; spread over some melted butter, then turn over the ham mixture. Serve hot.

REED BIRDS ON TOAST.

Remove the feathers and legs of a dozen reed birds, split them down the back, remove the entrails, and place them on a double broiler; brush a little melted butter over them, and broil the inner side thoroughly first; then lightly broil the other side. Melt one-quarter of a pound of butter, season it nicely with salt end pepper, dip the birds in it, and arrange them nicely on slices of toast.

MINCED FOWLS ON TOAST.

Remove from the bones all the meat of either cold roast or boiled fowls. Clean it from the skin, and keep covered from the air, until ready for use. Boil the bones and skin with three-fourths of a pint of water until reduced quite half. Strain the gravy and let it cool. Next, having skimmed off the fat, put it into a clean sauce-pan with half a cup of cream, three tablespoonfuls of butter, well-mixed with a tablespoonful of flour. Keep these stirred until they boil. Then put in the fowl finely minced, with three hard-boiled eggs, chopped, and sufficient salt and pepper to season. Shake the mince over the fire until just ready to serve. Dish it over hot toast and serve.

HASHED BEEF ON TOAST.

Chop a quantity of cold roast beef rather fine, and season it well with pepper and salt. For each pint of meat add a level tablespooful of flour. Stir well, and add a small teacupful of soup-stock or water. Put the mixture into a small stew-pan, and, after covering it, simmer for twenty minutes. Meanwhile, toast half a dozen slices of bread nicely, and at the end of the twenty minutes spread the meat upon them. Serve at once on a hot dish. In case water be used instead of soup-stock, add a tablespoonful of butter just before spreading the beef upon the toast. Any kind of cold meat may be prepared in a similar manner.

—Maria Parloa.

VEAL HASH ON TOAST.

Take a teacupful of boiling water in a sauce-pan, stir in an even teaspoonful of flour, wet in a tablespoonful of cold water, and let it boil five minutes; add one-half teaspoonful of black pepper, as much salt, and two tablespoonfuls of butter, and let it keep hot, but not boil. Chop the veal fine, and mix with it half as much stale bread-crumbs. Put it in a pan, and pour the gravy over it, then let it simmer ten minutes. Serve this on buttered toast.

CODFISH ON TOAST. (Cuban Style.)

Take a teacupful of freshened codfish, picked up fine. Fry a sliced onion in a tablespoonful of butter; when it has turned a light brown, put in the fish with water enough to cover it; add half a can of tomatoes, or half a dozen of fresh ones. Cook all nearly an hour, seasoning with a little pepper. Serve on slices of dipped toast, hot. Very fine.

Plain creamed codfish is very nice turned over dipped toast.

HALIBUT ON TOAST.

Put into boiling, salted water, one pound of fresh halibut; cook slowly for fifteen minutes, or until done; remove from the water and chop it fine; then add half a cup of melted butter, and eight eggs well beaten. Season with salt and pepper.

Place over the fire a thick-bottomed frying-pan containing a tablespoonful of cold butter; when it begins to melt, tip the pan so as to grease the sides; then put in the fish and eggs and stir one way until the eggs are cooked, but not *too* hard. Turn over toast, dipped in hot, salted water.

CHICKEN HASH WITH RICE TOAST.

Boil a cup of rice the night before; put it into a square, narrow bread-pan, set it in the ice-box. Next morning, cut it into half-inch slices, rub over each slice a little warm butter, and toast them on a broiler to a delicate brown. Arrange the toast on a warm platter and turn over the whole a chicken hash, made from the remains of cold fowl, the meat picked from the bones, chopped fine, put into the frying-pan, with butter, and a little water to moisten it, adding pepper and salt. Heat hot all through. Serve immediately.

APPLE TOAST.

Cut six apples into quarters, take the core out, peel and cut them in slices; put in the sauce-pan an ounce of butter, then throw over the apples about two ounces of white powdered sugar and two tablespoonfuls of water; put the sauce-pan on the fire, let it stew quickly, toss them up, or stir with a spoon; a few minutes will do them. When tender, cut two or three slices of bread half an inch thick; put in a frying-pan two ounces of butter, put on the fire; when the butter is melted, put in your bread, which fry of a nice yellowish color; when nice and crisp, take them out, place them on a dish, a little white sugar over, the apples about an inch thick. Serve hot.

SUGGESTIONS IN REGARD TO CAKE MAKING.

Use none but the best materials, and all the ingredients should be properly prepared before commencing to mix any of them. Eggs beat up much lighter and sooner by being placed in a cold place some time before using them; a small pinch of soda sometimes has the same effect. Flour should always be sifted before using it. Cream of tartar or baking-powder should be thoroughly mixed with the flour; butter be placed where it will become moderately soft, but *not* melted in the least, or the cake will be sodden and heavy. Sugar should be rolled and sifted; spices ground or pounded; raisins or any other fruit looked over and prepared; currants, especially, should be nicely washed, picked, dried in a cloth, and then carefully examined, that no pieces of grit or stone may be left amongst them. They should then be laid on a dish before the fire to become thoroughly dry; as, if added damp to the other ingredients, cakes will be liable to be heavy.

Eggs should be well-beaten, the whites and yolks separately, the yolks to a thick cream, the whites until they are a stiff froth. Always stir the butter and sugar to a cream, then add the beaten yolks, then the milk, the flavoring, then the beaten whites, and lastly the flour. If fruit is to be used, measure and dredge with a little sifted flour, stir in gradually and thoroughly.

Pour all in well-buttered cake-pans. While the cake is baking, care should be taken that no cold air enters the oven, only when necessary to see that the cake is baking properly; the oven should be an even, moderate heat, not too cold or too hot; much depends on this for success.

Cake is often spoiled for being looked at too often when first put into the oven. The heat should be tested before the cake is put in, which can be done by throwing on the floor of the oven a tablespoonful of new flour. If the flour takes fire, or assumes a dark-brown color, the temperature is too high, and the oven must be allowed to cool; if the flour remains white after the lapse of a few seconds, the temperature is too low. When the oven is of the proper temperature, the flour will slightly brown and look slightly scorched.

Another good way to test the heat, is to drop a few spoonfuls of the cake, batter on a small piece of buttered letter-paper, and place it in the oven during the finishing of the cake, so that the piece will be baked before putting in the whole cake ; if the little drop of cake-batter bakes evenly without burning around the edge, it will be safe to put the whole cake in the oven. Then again if the oven seems too hot, fold a thick brown paper double, and lay on the bottom of the oven; then after the cake has risen, put a thick brown paper over the top, or butter well a thick white paper and lay carefully over the top.

If, after the cake is put in, it seems to bake too fast, put a brown paper loosely over the top of the pan, care being taken that it does not touch the cake, and do not open the door for five minutes at least; the cake should then be quickly examined, and the door shut carefully, or the rush of cold air will cause it to fall. Setting a *small dish* of hot water in the oven, will also prevent the cake from scorching.

To ascertain when the cake is done, run a broom straw into the middle of it; if it comes out clean and smooth, the cake will do to take out.

Where the recipe calls for baking powder, and you have none, you can use cream tartar and soda in proportion to one level teaspoonful of soda, two heaping teaspoonfuls of cream tartar.

When sour milk is called for in the recipe, use only soda. Cakes made with molasses burn much more easily than those made with sugar.

Never stir cake after the butter and sugar is creamed, but beat it down from the bottom, up, and over; this laps air into the cake-batter, and produces little air cells, which causes the dough to puff and swell when it comes in contact with the heat while cooking.

When making most cakes, especially sponge cake, the flour should be added by degrees, stirred very slowly and lightly, for if stirred hard and fast it will make it porous and tough.

Cakes should be kept in tight tin cake-cans, or earthern jars, in a cool, dry place.

Cookies, jumbles, ginger-snaps, etc., require a quick oven; if they become moist or soft by keeping, put again into the oven a few minutes.

To remove a cake from a tin after it is baked, so that it will not crack, break or fall, first butter the tin well all around the sides and bottom; then cut a piece of letter-paper to exactly fit the tin, butter that on both sides, placing it smoothly on the bottom and sides of the tin. When the cake is baked, let it remain in the tin until it is *cold*; then set it in the oven a minute, or just long enough to warm the tin through. Remove it from the oven; turn it upside down on your hand, tap the edge of the tin on the table and it will slip out with ease, leaving it whole.

If a cake-pan is too shallow for holding the quantity of cake to be baked, for fear of its being so light as to rise above the pan, that can be remedied by thoroughly greasing a piece of thick glazed letter-paper with soft butter. Place or fit it around the sides of the buttered tin, allowing it to reach an inch or more above the top. If the oven heat is moderate, the butter will preserve the paper from burning.

FROSTING OR ICING.

In the first place, the eggs should be cold, and the platter on which they are to be beaten also cold. Allow, for the white of one egg, one small teacupful of powdered sugar. Break the eggs and throw a small handful of the sugar on them as soon as you begin beating; keep adding it at intervals until it is all used up. The eggs must *not* be beaten until the sugar has been added in this way, which gives a smooth, tender frosting, and one that will dry much sooner than the old way.

Spread with a broad knife evenly over the cake, and if it seems too thin, beat in a little more sugar. Cover the cake with two coats, the second after the first has become dry, or nearly so. If the icing gets too dry or stiff before the last coat is needed, it can be thinned sufficiently with a little water, enough to make it work smoothly.

A little lemon-juice, or half a teaspoonful of tartaric acid, added to the frosting while being beaten, makes it white and more frothy.

The flavors mostly used are lemon, vanilla, almond, rose, chocolate, and orange. If you wish to ornament with figures or flowers, make up rather more icing, keep about one-third out until that on the cake is dried; then, with a clean glass syringe, apply it in such forms as you desire and dry as before; what you keep out to ornament with may be tinted pink with cochineal, blue with indigo, yellow with saffron or the grated rind of an orange strained through a cloth, green with spinach juice, and brown with chocolate, purple with cochineal and indigo. Strawberry, or currant and cranberry juices color a delicate pink.

Set the cake in a cool oven with the door open, to dry, or in a draught in an open window.

ALMOND FROSTING.

The whites of three eggs, beaten up with three cups of fine, white sugar. Blanch a pound of sweet almonds, pound them in a mortar with a little sugar, until a fine paste, then add the whites of eggs, sugar and vanilla extract. Pound a few minutes to thoroughly mix. Cover the cake with a very thick coating of this, set in a cool oven to dry, afterwards cover with a plain icing.

CHOCOLATE FROSTING.

The whites of four eggs, three cups of powdered sugar, and nearly a cup of grated chocolate. Beat the whites a very little, they must not become white: stir in the chocolate, then put in the sugar gradually, beating to mix it well.

PLAIN CHOCOLATE ICING.

Put into a shallow pan four tablespoonfuls of scraped chocolate, and place it where it will melt gradually, but not scorch; when melted, stir in three table-spoonfuls of milk or cream, and one of water; mix all well together, and add one scant teacupful of sugar; boil about five minutes, and while hot, and when the cakes are nearly cold, spread some evenly over the surface of one of the cakes; put a second one on top, alternating the mixture and cakes; then cover top and sides, and set in a warm oven to harden. All who have tried recipe after recipe, vainly hoping to find one where the chocolate sticks to the cake and not to the fingers, will appreciate the above. In making those most palatable of cakes, "Chocolate Eclairs," the recipe just given will be found very satisfactory.

TUTTI FRUTTI ICING.

Mix with boiled icing one ounce each of chopped citron, candied cherries, seedless raisins, candied pineapple, and blanched almonds.

SUGAR ICING.

To one pound of extra refined sugar, add one ounce of fine white starch; pound finely together, and then sift them through gauze; then beat the whites of three eggs to a froth. The secret of success is to beat the eggs long enough, and always one way; add the powdered sugar by degrees, or it will spoil the froth of the eggs. When all the sugar is stirred in, continue the whipping for half an hour longer, adding more sugar if the ice is too thin. Take a little of the icing and lay it aside for ornamenting afterward. When the cake comes out of the oven, spread the sugar icing smoothly over it with a knife, and dry it at once in a cool oven. For ornamenting the cake, the icing may be tinged any color preferred. For pink, use a few drops of cochineal; for yellow a pinch of saffron, dissolved; for green, the juice of some chopped spinach. Whichever is chosen, let the coloring be first mixed with a little colorless spirit, and then stirred into the white icing until the tint is deep enough. To ornament the cake with it, make a cone of stiff writing paper, and squeeze the colored icing through it, so as to form leaves, beading or letters, as the case may be. It requires nicety and care to do it with success.

BOILED FROSTING.

To one pound of finest pulverised sugar, add three wine-glassfuls of clear water. Let it stand until it dissolves; then boil it until it is perfectly clear and threads from the spoon. Beat well the whites of four eggs. Pour the sugar into the dish with the eggs, but do not mix them until the syrup is luke-warm; then beat all well together for one half hour.

Season to your taste with vanilla, rose-water, or lemon-juice. The first coating may be put on the cake as soon as it is well mixed. Rub the cake with a little flour before you apply the icing. While the first coat is drying, continue to beat the remainder; you will not have to wait long if the cake is set in a warm place near the fire. This is said to be a most excellent recipe for icing.

FROSTING WITHOUT EGGS.

An excellent frosting may be made without eggs or gelatine, which will keep longer, and cut more easily, causing no breakage or crumbling, and withal is very economical.

Take one cup of granulated sugar; dampen it with one-fourth of a cup of milk, or five tablespoonfuls; place it on the fire in a suitable dish, and stir it until it boils; then let it boil for five minutes without stirring; remove it from the fire and set the dish in another of cold water; add flavoring. While it is cooling, stir or beat it constantly, and it will become a thick, creamy frosting.

GELATINE FROSTING.

Soak one teaspoonful of gelatine in one tablespoonful of cold water half an hour, dissolve in two tablespoonfuls of hot water; add one cup of powdered sugar and stir until smooth.

GOLDEN FROSTING.

A very delicious and handsome frosting can be made by using the yolks of eggs instead of the whites. Proceed exactly as for ordinary frosting. It will harden just as nicely as that does. This is particularly good for orange cake, harmonizing with the color of the cake in a way to please those who love rich coloring.

BREAD OR RAISED CAKE.

Two cupfuls of raised dough; beat into it two-thirds of a cup of butter and two cups of sugar creamed together, three eggs, well beaten, one even teaspoonful of soda, dissolved in two tablespoonfuls of milk, half a nutmeg grated, one tablespoonful of cinnamon, a teaspoonful of cloves, one cup of raisins. Mix all well together, put in the beaten whites of eggs and raisins last; beat all hard for several minutes; put in buttered pans, and let it stand half an hour to rise again before baking. Bake in a *moderate* oven. Half a glass of brandy is an improvement, if you have it convenient.

FRUIT CAKE. (Superior.)

Three pounds dry flour, one pound sweet butter, one pound sugar, three pounds stoned raisins, two pounds currants, three-quarters of a pound sweet almonds blanched, one pound citron, twelve eggs, one tablespoonful allspice, one teaspoonful cloves, two tablespoonfuls cinnamon, two nutmegs, one wine-glass of wine, one wine-glass of brandy, one coffee-cupful molasses with the spices in it; steep this gently twenty or thirty minutes, not boiling hot; beat the eggs very lightly; put the fruit in last, stirring it gradually, also a teaspoonful of soda dissolved in a tablespoonful of water; the fruit should be well floured; if necessary add flour after the fruit is in; butter a sheet of paper and lay it in the pan. Lay in some slices of citron, then a layer of the mixture, then of citron again, etc., till the pan is nearly full. Bake three or four hours, according to the thickness of the loaves, in a tolerably hot oven, and with steady heat. Let it cool in the oven gradually. Ice when cold. It improves this cake very much to add three teaspoonfuls of baking-powder to the flour. A fine wedding-cake recipe.

FRUIT CAKE BY MEASURE. (Excellent.)

Two scant teacupfuls of butter, three cupfuls of dark-brown sugar, six eggs, whites and yolks beaten separately, one pound of raisins, seeded, one of currants, washed and dried, and half a pound of citron cut in thin strips; also half a cupful of cooking molasses, and half a cupful of sour milk. Stir the butter and sugar to a cream, add to that half a grated nutmeg, one tablespoonful of ground cinnamon, one teaspoonful of cloves, one teaspoonful of mace, add the molasses and sour milk. Stir all well; then put in the beaten yolks of egg, a wine-glass of brandy; stir again all thoroughly, and then add four cupfuls of sifted flour, alternately with the beaten whites of egg. Now dissolve a level teaspoonful of soda, and stir in thoroughly. Mix the fruit together, and stir into it two heaping tablespoonfuls of flour; then stir it in the cake. Butter two common-sized baking-tins carefully, line them with letter-paper well buttered, and bake in a moderate oven two hours. After it is baked, let it cool in the pan. Afterward put it into a tight can, or let it remain in the pans and cover tightly. Best recipe of all.

—Mrs. S. A. Camp, *Grand Rapids, Mich.*

WHITE FRUIT CAKE.

One cup of butter, two cups of sugar, one cup of sweet milk, two and one-half cups of flour, the whites of seven eggs, two even teaspoonfuls of baking-powder, one pound each of seeded raisins, figs, and blanched almonds, and one-quarter of a pound of citron, all chopped fine. Mix all thoroughly before adding the fruit; add a teaspoonful of lemon extract. Put baking-powder in the flour, and mix it well before adding it to the other ingredients. Sift a little flour over the fruit before stirring it in. Bake slowly two hours and try with a splint to see when it is done. A cup of grated cocoanut is a nice addition to this cake.

MOLASSES FRUIT CAKE.

One teacupful of butter, one teacupful of brown sugar, worked well together; next two teacupfuls of cooking molasses, one cupful of milk with a teaspoonful of soda dissolved in it; one tablespoonful of ginger, one tablespoonful of cinnamon, and one teaspoonful of cloves; a little grated nutmeg. Now add four eggs well-beaten, and five cups of sifted flour, or enough to make a stiff batter. Flour a cup of raisins, and one of currants; add last. Bake in a very *moderate* oven, one hour. If well covered will keep six months.

SPONGE CAKE.

Separate the whites and yolks of six eggs. Beat the yolks to a cream, to which add two teacupfuls of powdered sugar, beating again from five to ten minutes, then add two tablespoonfuls of milk or water, a pinch of salt, and flavoring. Now add part of the beaten whites; then two cups of flour in which you have sifted two teaspoonfuls of baking-powder; mix gradually into the above ingredients, stirring slowly and lightly, only enough to mix them well; lastly add the remainder of the whites of the eggs. Line the tins with buttered paper and fill two-thirds full.

WHITE SPONGE CAKE.

Whites of five eggs, one cup flour, one cup sugar, one teaspoonful baking-powder; flavor with vanilla. Bake in a quick oven.

ALMOND SPONGE CAKE.

The addition of almonds makes this cake very superior to the usual sponge-cake. Sift one pint of fine flour; blanch in scalding water two ounces of sweet and two ounces of bitter almonds, renewing the hot water when expedient; when the skins are all off wash the almonds in cold water (mixing the sweet and bitter), and wipe them dry; pound them to a fine, smooth paste (one at a time), adding, as you proceed, water or white of egg to prevent their boiling. Set them in a cool place; beat ten eggs, the whites and yolks separately, till very smooth and thick, and then beat into them gradually two cups powdered sugar in turn with the pounded almonds; lastly add the flour, stirring it round slowly and lightly on the surface of the mixture, as in common sponge-cake; have ready buttered a *deep* square pan; put the mixture carefully into it, set into the oven, and bake till thoroughly done and risen very high; when cool, cover it with plain white icing flavored with rose-water or with almond icing. With sweet almonds always use a small portion of bitter; without them, *sweet* almonds have little or no taste, though they add to the richness of the cake.

Use two heaping teaspoonfuls of baking-powder in the flour.

OLD-FASHIONED SPONGE CAKE.

Two cups of sifted white sugar, two cups of flour measured before sifting, ten eggs. Stir the yolks and sugar together until perfectly light; add a pinch of salt; beat the whites of the eggs to a very stiff froth, and add them with the flour, after beating together lightly; flavor with lemon. Bake in a *moderate* oven about forty-five minutes. Baking-powder is an improvement to this cake, using two large teaspoonfuls.

LEMON SPONGE CAKE.

Into one level cup of flour put a level teaspoonful of baking-powder and sift it. Grate off the yellow rind of a lemon. Separate the whites from the yolks of four eggs. Measure a scant cup of white granulated sugar and beat it to a cream with the yolks, then add the grated rind and a tablespoonful of the juice of the lemon. Stir together until thick and creamy; now beat the whites to a stiff froth; then quickly and lightly mix *without beating* a third of the flour with the yolks; then a third of the whites; then more flour and whites until all are used. The mode of mixing must be very light, rather cutting down through the cake-batter than beating it; beating the eggs makes them light, but beating the batter makes the cake tough. Bake immediately until a straw run into it can be withdrawn clean.

This recipe is especially nice for Charlotte Russe, being so light and porous.

PLAIN SPONGE CAKE.

Beat the yolks of four eggs together with two cups of fine powdered sugar. Stir in gradually one cup of sifted flour, and the whites of four eggs beaten to a stiff froth, then a cup of sifted flour in which two teaspoonfuls of baking-powder have been stirred, and lastly, a scant teacupful of boiling water, stirred in a little at a time. Flavor, add salt, and, however thin the mixture may seem, do not add any more flour. Bake in shallow tins.

BRIDE'S CAKE.

Cream together one scant cup of butter and three cups of sugar, add one cup of milk, then the beaten whites of twelve eggs; sift three teaspoonfuls of baking-powder into one cup of corn-starch mixed with three cups of sifted flour, and beat in gradually with the rest; flavor to taste. Beat all thoroughly, then put in buttered tins lined with letter-paper well-buttered; bake slowly in a *moderate* oven. A beautiful white cake. Ice the top. Double the recipe if more is required.

ENGLISH POUND CAKE.

One pound of butter, one and one-quarter pounds of flour, one pound of pounded loaf sugar, one pound of currants, nine eggs, two ounces of candied peel, one-half ounce of citron, one-half ounce of sweet almonds; when liked, a little pounded mace. Work the butter to a cream; add the sugar, then the well-beaten yolks of eggs, next the flour, currants, candied peel, which should be cut into neat slices, and the almonds, which should be blanched and chopped, and mix all these well together; whisk the whites of eggs, and let them be thoroughly blended with the other ingredients. Beat the cake well for twenty minutes, and put it into a round tin, lined at the bottom and sides with strips of white buttered paper. Bake it from two hours to two and a half, and let the oven be well-heated when the cake is first put in, as, if this is not the case, the currants will all sink to the bottom of it. A glass of wine is usually added to the mixture; but this is scarcely necessary, as the cake will be found quite rich enough without it.

PLAIN POUND CAKE.

This is the old-fashioned recipe that our mothers used to make, and it can be kept for weeks in an earthen jar, closely covered, first dipping letter-paper in brandy and placing over the top of the cake before covering the jar

Beat to a cream one pound of butter with one pound of sugar, after mixing well with the beaten yolks of twelve eggs, one grated nutmeg, one glass of wine, one glass of rose-water. Then stir in one pound of sifted flour, and the well beaten whites of the eggs. Bake a nice light brown.

COCOANUT POUND CAKE.

One-half cupful of butter, two cupfuls of sugar, one cupful of milk, and five eggs, beaten to a stiff froth; one teaspoonful of soda, and two of cream of tartar, stirred into four cups of sifted flour. Beat the butter and sugar until very light; to which add the beaten yolks, then the milk, the beaten whites of eggs, then the flour by degrees. After beating all well together, add a small cocoanut grated. Line the cake-pans with paper well buttered, and fill rather more than half full, and bake in a *moderate* oven. Spread over the top a thin frosting, sprinkled thickly with grated cocoanut.

CITRON POUND CAKE.

Stir two cups of butter to a cream, then beat in the following ingredients each one in succession: one pint of powdered sugar, one quart of flour, a teaspoonful of salt, eight eggs, the yolks and whites beaten separately, and a wineglass of brandy; then last of all add a quarter of a pound of citron cut into thin slices and floured. Line two cake-pans with buttered paper and turn the cake-batter in. Bake in a *moderate* oven about three quarters of an hour.

CITRON CAKE.

Three cups of white sugar and one cup of butter creamed together; one cup of sweet milk, six eggs, whites and yolks beaten separately; one teaspoonful of vanilla or lemon extract, two heaping teaspoonfuls of baking-powder, sifted with four cups and a half of flour. One cup and a half of citron, sliced thin and dredged with flour. Divide into two cakes and bake in tins lined with buttered letter-paper.

LEMON CAKE.

Three teacupfuls of sugar, one cupful of butter, five eggs, a level teaspoonful of soda dissolved in a cup of sweet milk, four full cups of sifted flour, and lastly, the grated peel and juice of a lemon, the juice to be added the very last. Bake in two shallow tins. When cold, ice with lemon icing, and cut into squares.

DELICATE CAKE.

One cup of corn-starch, one of butter, two of sugar, one of sweet milk, two of flour, the whites of seven eggs; rub butter and sugar to a cream; mix one teaspoonful cream tartar with the flour and corn-starch; one half teaspoonful soda with the sweet milk; add the milk and soda to the sugar and butter, then add flour, then the whites of eggs; flavor to taste. Never fails to be good.

SILVER, OR DELICATE CAKE.

Whites of six eggs, one cupful of sweet milk, two cupfuls of sugar, four cupfuls of sifted flour, two-thirds of a cup of butter, flavoring, and two teaspoonfuls of baking-powder. Stir the sugar and butter to a cream, then add the milk and flavoring, part of the flour, the beaten whites of eggs, then the rest of the flour. Bake carefully in tins lined with buttered white paper.

When using the whites of eggs for nice cake, the yolks need not be wasted; keep them in a cool place and scramble them. Serve on toast or with chipped beef.

GOLD CAKE.

After beating to a cream one cup and a half of butter and two cups of white sugar, stir in the well-whipped yolks of one dozen eggs; four cupfuls of sifted flour, one teaspoonful of baking-powder. Flavor with lemon. Line the bake-pans with buttered paper, and bake in a moderate oven for one hour.

GOLD OR LEMON CAKE.

Two cups of sugar, half a cup of butter, the yolks of six eggs, and one whole one; the grated rind and juice of a lemon or orange; half a teaspoonful of soda, dissolved in half a cup of sweet milk; four cups of sifted flour, sifted twice; cream the butter and sugar, then add the beaten yolks and the flour, beating hard for several minutes. Last add the lemon or orange, and bake, frosting if liked. This makes a more suitable *lemon* cake than if made with the white parts of eggs added.

SNOW CAKE. (Delicious.)

One pound of arrowroot, quarter of a pound of pounded white sugar, half a pound of butter, the whites of six eggs, flavoring to taste of essence of almonds or vanilla, or lemon; beat the butter to a cream; stir in the sugar and arrowroot gradually, at the same time beating the mixture; whisk the whites of the eggs to a stiff froth; add them to the other ingredients, and beat well for twenty minutes; put in whichever of the above flavorings may be preferred; pour the cake into a buttered mold or tin, and bake it in a *moderate* oven from one to one and a half hours. *This is a genuine Scotch recipe.*

MARBLE CAKE.

White part.—Whites of four eggs, one cup of white sugar, half a cup of butter, half a cup of sweet milk, two teaspoonfuls of baking-powder, one teaspoonful of vanilla or lemon, and two and a half cups of sifted flour.

Dark part.—Yolks of four eggs, one cup of brown sugar, half a cup of cooking molasses, half a cup of butter, half a cup of sour milk, one teaspoonful of ground cloves, one teaspoonful of cinnamon, one teaspoonful of mace, one nutmeg grated, one teaspoonful of soda, the soda to be dissolved in a little milk and added after part of the flour is stirred in; one and a half cups of sifted flour.

Drop a spoonful of each kind in a well-buttered cake-dish, first the light part then the dark, alternately. Try to drop it so that the cake shall be well-streaked through, so that it has the appearance of marble.

SUPERIOR LOAF CAKE.

Two cups of butter, three cups of sugar, two small cups of milk, seven cups of sifted flour; four eggs, the whites and yolks separately beaten; one teacupful of seeded raisins, one teacupful of well-washed and dried currants, one teacupful of sliced citron, one tablespoonful of powdered cinnamon, one teaspoonful of mace, one teaspoonful of soda; and one teacupful of home-made yeast.

Take part of the butter and warm it with the milk; stir in part of the flour, and the yeast, and let it rise; then add the other ingredients with a wine-glass of wine or brandy. Turn all into well-buttered cake-tins, and let rise again. Bake slowly in a *moderate* oven, for two hours.

FRENCH CHOCOLATE CAKE.

The whites of seven eggs, two cups of sugar, two-thirds of a cup of butter, one cup of milk and three of flour, and three teaspoonfuls of baking-powder. The chocolate part of the cake is made just the same, only use the yolks of the eggs with a cup of grated chocolate stirred into it. Bake it in layers—the layers being light and dark; then spread a custard between them, which is made with two eggs, one pint of milk, one-half cup of sugar, one tablespoonful of flour or corn-starch; when cool, flavor with vanilla, two teaspoonfuls. Fine.

CHOCOLATE CAKE. No. 1.

One cup of butter and two cups of sugar stirred to a cream, with the yolks of five eggs added after they have been well-beaten. Then stir into that one cup of milk, beat the whites of two of the eggs to a stiff froth, and add that also; now put in three cups and a half of sifted flour, two heaping teaspoonfuls of baking-powder having been stirred into it. Bake in jelly-cake tins.

Mixture for filling.—Take the remaining three whites of the eggs beaten *very* stiff; two cupfuls of sugar boiled to almost candy or until it becomes stringy or almost brittle; take it hot from the fire, and pour it very slowly on the beaten whites of egg, beating quite fast; add one-half cake of grated chocolate, a teaspoonful of vanilla extract. Stir it all until cool, then spread between each cake, and over the top and sides. This, when well-made, is the *premium* cake of its kind.

CHOCOLATE CAKE. No. 2.

One-half cup butter, two cups sugar, three-quarters of a cup sweet milk, two and one-half cups flour, whites of eight eggs, one teaspoonful of cream tartar, one-half teaspoonful soda; bake in shallow pans.

For the frosting.—Take the whites of three eggs, three tablespoonfuls of sugar and one tablespoonful of grated chocolate (confectioners') to one egg; put the cake together with the frosting, then frost the top of the cake with the same.

CHOCOLATE CAKE. No. 3.

Two cups sugar, one cup butter, yolks of five eggs and whites of two, and one cup milk. Thoroughly mix two teaspoonfuls baking-powder with three and one-half cups flour, while dry; then mix all together. Bake in jelly tins.

Mixture for filling.—Whites of three eggs, one and one-half cups of sugar, three tablespoonfuls of grated chocolate, one teaspoonful of vanilla. Beat together, and spread between the layers and on top of the cake.

COCOANUT CAKE.

Cream together three quarters of a cup of butter and two of white sugar; then add one cup of sweet milk, four eggs, whites and yolks separately beaten, the yolks added first to the butter and sugar, then the whites; flavor with lemon or vanilla; mix three heaping teaspoonfuls of baking-powder in three cups of sifted flour and add last; bake in jelly-pans.

For filling.—Make an icing by beating the whites of three eggs and a cup of powdered sugar to a stiff froth. When the cake is cooled, spread a thick layer of this frosting over each cake, and sprinkle very thickly with grated cocoanut.

COCOANUT AND ALMOND CAKE.

Two and one-half cups powdered sugar, one cup butter, four full cups prepared flour, whites of seven eggs, whisked stiff; one small cup of milk, with a mere pinch of soda; one grated cocoanut, one-half teaspoonful nutmeg, the juice and half the grated peel of one lemon; cream, butter and sugar; stir in lemon and nutmeg; mix well; add the milk and whites and flour alternately. Lastly, stir in the grated cocoanut swiftly and lightly. Bake in four jelly-cake tins.

Filling.—One pound sweet almonds, whites of four eggs, whisked stiff; one heaping cup powdered sugar, two teaspoonfuls rose-water. Blanch the almonds.

Let them get cold and dry; then pound in a Wedgewood mortar, adding rose-water as you go. Save about two dozen to shred for the top. Stir the paste into the icing after it is made; spread between the cooled cakes; make that for the top a trifle thicker and lay it on heavily. When it has stiffened somewhat, stick the shred almonds closely over it. Set in the oven to harden, but do not let it scorch.

COFFEE CAKE.

One cup of brown sugar, one cup of butter, two eggs, one-half cup of molasses, one cup of strong, cold coffee, one teaspoonful of soda, two teaspoonfuls of cinnamon, one teaspoonful of cloves, one cup of raisins or currants, and five cups of sifted flour. Add the fruit last, rubbed in a little of the flour. Bake about one hour.

FEATHER CAKE.

One egg, one cup of sugar, one tablespoonful of cold butter, half a cup of milk; one and one-half cups of flour; one teaspoonful of cream tartar; half a teaspoonful of soda. A nice plain cake—to be eaten while it is fresh. A spoonful of dried apple sauce or of peach sauce, a spoonful of jelly, the same of lemon extract, nutmeg, cinnamon, cloves and spice—ground—or half a cupful of raisins might be added for a change.

ELECTION CAKE.

Three cups milk, two cups sugar, one cup yeast; stir to a batter, and let stand over night; in the morning add two cups sugar, two cups butter, three eggs, half a nutmeg, one tablespoonful cinnamon, one pound raisins, a gill of brandy.

Brown sugar is much better than white for this kind of cake, and it is improved by dissolving a half-teaspoonful of soda in a tablespoonful of milk in the morning. It should stand in the greased pans and rise some time until quite light before baking.

CREAM CAKE.

Four eggs, whites and yolks beaten separately, two teacups of sugar, one cup of sweet cream, two heaping cupfuls of flour, one teaspoonful of soda; mix two teaspoonfuls of cream of tartar in the flour before sifting. Add the whites the last thing before the flour, and stir that in gently without beating.

GOLDEN CREAM-CAKE.

Yolks of eight eggs beaten to the lightest possible cream, two cupfuls of sugar, a pinch of salt, three teaspoonfuls of baking-powder sifted well with flour. Bake in three jelly-cake pans. Make an icing of the whites of three eggs and one pound of sugar. Spread it between the cakes and sprinkle grated cocoanut thickly over each layer. It is delicious when properly made.

DRIED APPLE FRUIT-CAKE.

Soak three cupfuls of dried apples over night in cold water enough to swell them; chop them in the morning, and put them on the fire with three cups of molasses; stew until almost soft; add a cupful of nice raisins (seedless, if possible), and stew a few moments; when cold, add three cupfuls of flour, one cupful of butter, three eggs, and a teaspoonful of soda; bake in a steady oven. This will make two good-sized panfuls of splendid cake; the apples will cook like citron and taste deliciously. Raisins may be omitted; also spices to taste may be added. This is not a dear, but a delicious cake.

CAKE WITHOUT EGGS.

Beat together one teacupful of butter, and three teacupfuls of sugar, and when quite light stir in one pint of sifted flour. Add to this, one pound of raisins, seeded and chopped, then mixed with a cup of sifted flour, one teaspoonful of nutmeg, one teaspoonful of powdered cinnamon, and lastly, one pint of thick sour cream or milk, in which a teaspoonful of soda is dissolved. Bake immediately in buttered tins one hour in a *moderate* oven.

WHITE MOUNTAIN CAKE. No. 1.

Two cups of sugar, two-thirds cup of butter, the whites of seven eggs, well-beaten, two-thirds cup of sweet milk, two cups of flour, one cup of corn-starch, two teaspoonfuls baking-powder. Bake in jelly-cake tins.

Frosting.—Whites of three eggs and some sugar beaten together not quite as stiff as usual for frosting; spread over the cake; add some grated cocoanut; then put your cakes together; put cocoanut and frosting on top.

WHITE MOUNTAIN CAKE. No. 2.

Cream three cupfuls of sugar and one of butter, making it very light, then add a cupful of milk. Beat the whites of eight eggs very stiff, add half of those to the other ingredients. Mix well into four cups of sifted flour one tablespoonful of baking-powder; stir this into the cake, add flavoring, then the remaining beaten whites of egg. Bake in layers like jelly-cake. Make an icing for the filling, using the whites of four eggs beaten to a very stiff froth, with two cups of fine white sugar, and the juice of half a lemon. Spread each layer of the cake thickly with this icing, place one on another, then ice all over the top and sides. The yolks left from this cake may be used to make a spice-cake from the recipe of "Golden Spice-Cake."

QUEEN'S CAKE.

Beat well together one cupful of butter, and three cupfuls of white sugar; add the yolks of six eggs and one cupful of milk, two teaspoonfuls of vanilla or lemon extract. Mix all thoroughly. To four cupfuls of flour, add two heaping teaspoonfuls of cream of tartar, and sift gently over the cake, stirring all the time. To this add one even teaspoonful of soda, dissolved in one tablespoonful of warm water. Mix it well. Stir in gently the whites of six eggs beaten to a stiff foam. Bake slowly. It should be put in the oven as soon as possible after putting in the soda and whites of eggs.

This is the same recipe as the one for "Citron Cake," only omitting the citron.

ANGEL CAKE.

Put into one tumbler of flour one teaspoonful of cream of tartar, then sift it five times. Sift also one glass and a half of white powdered sugar. Beat to a stiff froth the whites of eleven eggs; stir the sugar into the eggs by degrees, very lightly and carefully, adding three teaspoonfuls of vanilla extract. After this, add the flour, stirring quickly and lightly. Pour it into a clean, bright tin cake-dish, which should *not* be buttered or lined. Bake at once in a moderate oven about forty minutes, testing it with a broom splint. When done, let it remain in the cake-tin, turning it upside down, with the sides resting on the top of two saucers, so that a current of air will pass under and over it.

This is the best recipe found after trying several. A perfection cake.

WASHINGTON LOAF-CAKE.

Three cups of sugar, two scant cups of butter, one cup of sour milk, five eggs, and one teaspoonful of soda, three tablespoonfuls of cinnamon, half a nutmeg, grated, and two cups of raisins, one of currants, and four cups of sifted flour.

Mix as usual, and stir the fruit in at the last, dredged in flour. Line the cake-pans with paper well buttered. This cake will take longer to bake than plain; the heat of the oven must be kept at an even temperature.

RIBBON CAKE.

This cake is made from the same recipe as marble cake, only make double the quantity of the white part, and divide it in one half; put into it a very little cochineal. It will be a delicate pink. Bake in jelly-cake tins, and lay first the white, then the dark, then the pink one on top of the others; put together with frosting between. It makes quite a fancy cake. Frost the top when cool.

GOLDEN SPICE-CAKE.

This cake can be made to advantage when you have the yolks of eggs left, after having used the whites in making white cake.

Take the yolks of seven eggs, and one whole egg, two cupfuls of brown sugar, one cupful of molasses, one cupful of butter, one large coffee-cupful of sour milk, one teaspoonful of soda, (just even full), and five cupfuls of flour, one teaspoonful of ground cloves, two teaspoonfuls of cinnamon, two teaspoonfuls of ginger, one nutmeg, and a small pinch of Cayenne pepper; beat eggs, sugar and butter to a light batter before putting in the molasses; then add the molasses, flour and milk; beat it well together, and bake in a *moderate* oven; if fruit is used, take two cupfuls of raisins, flour them well and put them in last.

ALMOND CAKE.

One-half cupful butter, two cupfuls sugar, four eggs, one-half cupful almonds, blanched—by pouring water on them until skins easily slip off—and cut in fine shreds, one-half teaspoonful extract bitter almonds, one pint flour, one and one-half teaspoonful baking-powder, one glass brandy, one-half cupful milk. Rub butter and sugar to a smooth white cream; add eggs, one at a time, beating three or four minutes between each. Sift flour and powder together, add to the butter, etc., with almonds, extract of bitter almonds, brandy, and milk; mix into a smooth, medium batter; bake carefully in rather a hot oven twenty minutes.

ROCHESTER JELLY CAKE.

One and one-half cups sugar, two eggs, one-half cup butter, three-fourths cup milk, two heaping cups flour with one teaspoonful cream tartar, one-half teaspoonful of soda, dissolved in the milk. Put half the above mixture in a small shallow tin, and to the remainder add one teaspoonful molasses, one-half cup raisins (chopped) or currants, one-half teaspoonful cinnamon, cloves, allspice, and a little nutmeg, and one tablespoonful flour. Bake this in same kind of tins. Put the sheets of cake together while warm, with jelly between.

FRUIT LAYER CAKE.

This is a delicious novelty in cake-making. Take one cup of sugar, half a cup of butter, one cup and a half of flour, half a cup of wine, one cup of raisins, two eggs and half a teaspoonful of soda; put these ingredients together with care, just as if it were a very rich cake; bake it in three layers, and put frosting between—the frosting to be made of the whites of two eggs with enough powdered sugar to make it thick. The top of the cake may be frosted if you choose.

WHIPPED CREAM CAKE.

One cup of sugar and two tablespoonfuls of soft butter stirred together; add the yolks of two eggs well-beaten, then add four tablespoonfuls of milk, some flavoring, then the beaten whites of the eggs. Mix a teaspoonful of cream tartar and half a teaspoon of soda in a cup of flour, sift it into the cake batter, and stir in lightly. Bake in a small dripping-pan. When the cake is cool, have ready half of a pint of sweet cream sweetened and whipped to a stiff froth, also flavored. Spread it over the cake while fresh. To whip the cream easily, set it on ice before whipping.

ROLLED JELLY CAKE.

Three eggs, one teacup of fine sugar, one teacup of flour; beat the yolks until light, then add the sugar, then add two tablespoonfuls of water, a pinch of salt; lastly stir in the flour, in which there should be a heaping teaspoonful of baking-powder. The flour added gradually. Bake in long, shallow biscuit-tins, well-greased. Turn out on a damp towel on a bread-board, and cover the top with jelly, and roll up while warm.

TO CUT LAYER CAKE.

When cutting Layer-Cakes, it is better to first make a round hole in the cake, with a knife or tin tube, about an inch and a quarter in diameter. This prevents the edge of the cake from crumbling when cutting it.

When making custard filling for Layer-Cake, always set the dish containing the custard in another dish of boiling water over the fire; this prevents its burning, which would destroy its flavor.

LAYER JELLY CAKE.

Almost any soft cake recipe can be used for jelly-cake. The following is excellent: One cup of sugar, half a cup of butter, three eggs, half a cup of sweet milk, two cups of flour, two heaping teaspoonfuls of baking-powder, flavoring.

For white, delicate cake, the rule for "Silver Cake" is fine; care should be taken, however, that the oven is just right for this cake, as it browns very easily. To be baked in jelly-cake tins, in layers, with filling put between when done.

Any of the following cake-filling recipes may be used with these cake recipes.

Fillings for Layer Cakes.

No. 1. CREAM FILLING.

Cream filling is made with one pint of new milk, two eggs, three tablespoon-fuls of sifted flour (or half cup of corn starch), one cup of sugar. Put two-thirds of the milk on the stove to boil, stir the sugar, flour and eggs in what is left. When the milk boils, put into it the whole, and cook it until it is as thick as custard; when cool, add vanilla extract. This custard is nice with a cup of hickory nuts, kernels chopped fine, and stirred into it. Spread between the layers of cake. This custard can be made of the yolks of the eggs only, saving the whites for the cake part.

No. 2. ANOTHER CREAM FILLING.

One cup powdered sugar, one-fourth cup hot water. Let them simmer. Beat white of an egg and mix with the above; when cold, add one-half cup chopped raisins, one-half cup chopped walnuts, one tablespoonful of grated cocoanut.

No. 3. ICE-CREAM FILLING.

Make an icing as follows: Three cups of sugar, one of water; boil to a thick, clear syrup, or until it begins to be brittle; pour this, boiling hot, over the *well-beaten* whites of three eggs; stir the mixture very briskly, and pour the sugar in slowly; beat it when all in, until cool. Flavor with lemon or vanilla extract. This, spread between any white cake layers, answers for "Ice-Cream Cake."

No. 4. APPLE FILLING.

Peel, and slice green, tart apples; put them on the fire with sugar to suit; when tender, remove, rub them through a fine sieve, and add a small piece of butter. When cold, use to spread between the layers; cover the cake with plenty of sugar.

No. 5. ANOTHER APPLE FILLING.

One coffee-cup of sugar, one egg, three large apples grated, one lemon grated, juice and outside of the rind; beat together and cook till quite thick. To be cooled before putting on the cake. Spread between layers of cake.

No. 6. CREAM FROSTING.

A cup of sweet thick cream whipped, sweetened and flavored with vanilla, cut a loaf of cake in two, spread the frosting between and on the top; this tastes like Charlotte Russe,

No. 7. PEACH-CREAM FILLING.

Cut peaches into thin slices, or chop them and prepare cream by whipping and sweetening. Put a layer of peaches between the layers of cake and pour cream over each layer and over the top. Bananas, strawberries or other fruits may be used in the same way, mashing strawberries, and stewing thick with powdered sugar.

No. 8. CHOCOLATE CREAM FOR FILLING.

Five tablespoonfuls of grated chocolate, enough cream or milk to wet it, one cupful of sugar, one egg, one teaspoonful vanilla flavoring. Stir the ingredients over the fire until thoroughly mixed, having beaten the egg well before adding it; then add the vanilla flavoring after it is removed from the fire.

No. 9. ANOTHER CHOCOLATE FILLING.

The whites of three eggs beaten stiff, one cup of sugar, and one cup of grated chocolate, put between the layers and on top.

No. 10. BANANA FILLING.

Make an icing of the whites of two eggs, and one cup and a half of powdered sugar. Spread this on the layers, and then cover thickly and entirely with bananas sliced thin or chopped fine. This cake may be flavored with vanilla. The top should be simply frosted.

No. 11. LEMON-JELLY FILLING.

Grate the yellow from the rind of two lemons and squeeze out the juice; two cupfuls of sugar, the yolks and whites of two eggs beaten separately. Mix the sugar and yolks, then add the whites, and then the lemons. Now, pour on a cupful of boiling water; stir into this two tablespoonfuls of sifted flour, rubbed smooth in half a cup of water; then add a tablespoonful of melted butter; cook until it thickens. When cold, spread between the layers of cake. Oranges can be used in place of lemons.

Another filling of lemon (without cooking) is made of the grated rind and juice of two lemons, and the whites of two eggs beaten with one cup of sugar.

No. 12. ORANGE-CAKE FILLING.

Peel two large oranges, remove the seeds, chop them fine, add half a peeled lemon, one cup of sugar, and the well-beaten white of an egg. Spread between the layers of "Silver Cake" recipe.

No. 13. FIG FILLING.

Take a pound of figs, chop fine, and put into a stew-pan on the stove; pour over them a teacupful of water, and add a half cup of sugar. Cook all together until soft and smooth. When cold, spread between layers of cake.

No. 14. FRUIT FILLING.

Four tablespoonfuls of *very fine* chopped citron, four tablespoonfuls of finely chopped seeded raisins; half of a cupful of blanched almonds chopped fine; also a quarter of a pound of finely chopped figs. Beat the whites of three eggs to a stiff froth, adding half of a cupful of sugar; then mix thoroughly into this the whole of the chopped ingredients. Put it between the layers of cake when the cake is *hot*, so that it will cook the egg a little. This will be found delicious.

CUSTARD OR CREAM CAKE.

Cream together two cups of sugar and half a cup of butter; add half a cup of sweet milk in which is dissolved half a teaspoonful of soda. Beat the whites of six eggs to a stiff froth, and add to the mixture. Have one heaping teaspoonful of cream tartar stirred thoroughly into three cups of sifted flour, and add quickly. Bake in a moderate oven, in layers like jelly-cake, and when done, spread custard between.

For the Custard.—Take two cups of sweet milk, put it into a clean suitable dish, set it in a dish of *boiling* water on the range or stove. When the milk comes to a boil, add two tablespoonfuls of corn-starch or flour stirred into half a cup of sugar, adding the yolks of four eggs, and a little cold milk. Stir this into the boiling milk, and when cooked thick enough, set aside to cool; afterwards add the flavoring, either vanilla or lemon. It is best to make the custard first, before making the cake part.

HICKORY NUT OR WALNUT CAKE.

Two cups of fine, white sugar, creamed with half a cup of butter, three eggs, two-thirds of a cup of sweet milk, three cups of sifted flour, one heaping teaspoonful of baking powder sifted through the flour. A tablespoonful (level) of powdered mace, a coffee-cup of hickory nut or walnut meats, chopped a little. Fill the cake-pans with a layer of the cake, then a layer of raisins upon that, then strew over these a handful of nuts, and so on, until the pan is two-thirds full. Line the tins with well-buttered paper, and bake in a steady but not quick oven. This is most excellent.

CHEAP CREAM CAKE.

One cup of sugar, one egg, one cup sweet milk, two cups flour, one table-spoonful butter, two heaping teaspoonfuls of baking-powder; flavor to taste. Divide into three parts, and bake in round shallow pans.

Cream.—Beat one egg and one half cup sugar together, then add one quarter cup flour, wet with a very little milk, and stir this mixture into one half pint of boiling milk, until thick; flavor to taste. Spread the cream when cool between the cakes.

SOFT GINGER CAKE.

Stir to a cream one cupful of butter and half a cupful of brown sugar; add to this two cupfuls of cooking molasses, a cupful of sweet milk, a tablespoonful of ginger, a teaspoonful of ground cinnamon; beat all thoroughly together, then add three eggs, the whites and yolks beaten separately; beat into this two cups of sifted flour, then a teaspoonful of soda, dissolved in a spoonful of water, and last, two more cupfuls of sifted flour. Butter and paper two common square bread-pans, divide the mixture and pour half into each. Bake in a moderate oven. This cake requires long and slow baking, from forty to sixty minutes. I find that if sour milk is used, the cakes are much lighter, but either sweet or sour is most excellent.

HARD GINGERBREAD.

Made the same as "Soft Gingerbread," omitting the eggs, and mixing hard enough to roll out like biscuit; rolled nearly half an inch thick, and cut out like small biscuits, or it can be baked in a sheet or on a biscuit-tin; cut slits a quarter of an inch deep across the top of the tin from side to side. When baked and while hot, rub over the top with molasses, and let it dry on.

These two above recipes are the best I have ever found among a large variety that I have tried, the ingredients giving the best proportion for flavor and excellence.

PLAIN GINGERBREAD.

One cup of *dark* cooking molasses, one cup of sour cream, one egg, one tea-spoonful of soda, dissolved in a little warm water, a teaspoonful of salt, and one heaping teaspoonful of ginger; make about as thick as cup-cake. To be eaten warm.

WHITE GINGER BISCUIT.

One cup of butter, two cups of sugar, one cup of sour cream or milk, three eggs, one teaspoonful of soda, dissolved in a tablespoonful of warm water, one tablespoonful of ginger, one teaspoonful of ground cinnamon, and five cups of sifted flour, or enough to roll out *soft*. Cut out rather thick, like biscuits; brush over the tops while hot, with the white of an egg, or sprinkle with sugar while hot.

The grated rind and the juice of an orange add much to the flavor of ginger cake.

GOLD AND SILVER CAKE.

This cake is baked in layers like jelly-cake. Divide the silver-cake batter, and color it pink with a little cochineal; this gives you pink, white and yellow layers. Put together with frosting. Frost the top.

This can be put together like marble cake, first a spoonful of one kind, then another, until the dish is full.

BOSTON CREAM CAKES.

Put into a large-sized sauce-pan half a cup of butter, and one cup of hot water; set it on the fire; when the mixture begins to boil, turn in a pint of sifted flour at once, beat and work it well with a vegetable-masher until it is very smooth. Remove from the fire, and when cool enough add five eggs that have been well beaten, first the yolks and then the whites, also half a teaspoonful of soda and a teaspoonful of salt. Drop on buttered tins in large spoonfuls, about two inches apart. Bake in a quick oven about fifteen minutes. When done and quite cold, open them on the side with a knife or scissors, and put in as much of the custard as possible.

Cream for filling.—Made of two eggs, three tablespoonfuls of sifted flour (or half cup of corn-starch), and one cup of sugar. Put two-thirds of a pint of mik over the fire in a double boiler, in a third of a pint of milk; stir the sugar, flour and beaten eggs. As soon as the milk looks like boiling, pour in the mixture, and stir briskly for three minutes, until it thickens; then remove from the fire and add a teaspoonful of butter; when cool, flavor with vanilla or lemon, and fill your cakes.

CHOCOLATE ECLAIRS.

Make the mixture exactly like the recipe for "Boston Cream Cakes." Spread it on buttered pans in oblong pieces about four inches long and one and a half wide, to be laid about two inches apart; they must be baked in a rather quick oven, about twenty-five minutes. As soon as baked, ice with chocolate icing, and when this is cold, split them on one side, and fill with the same cream as "Boston Cream Cakes."

HUCKLEBERRY CAKE.

Beat a cup of butter and two cups of sugar toegther until light, then add a half cup of milk, four eggs, beaten separately, the yolks to a cream, and the whites to a stiff froth, one teaspoonful of grated nutmeg, the same of cinnamon, and two teaspoonfuls of baking-powder. The baking-powder to be rubbed into the flour. Rub one quart of huckleberries well with some flour, and add them last, but do not mash them. Pour into buttered pans, about an inch thick; dust the tops with sugar and bake. It is better the day after baking.

SWEET STRAWBERRY CAKE.

Three eggs, one cupful of sugar, two of flour, one tablespoonful of butter, a teaspoonful, heaped, of baking-powder. Beat the butter and sugar together, and add the eggs well beaten. Stir in the flour and baking-powder well sifted together. Bake in deep tin plate. This quantity will fill four plates. With three pints of strawberries, mix a cupful of sugar and mash them a little. Spread the fruit between the layers of cake. The top layer of strawberries may be covered with a meringue made with the white of an egg and a tablespoonful of powdered sugar.

Save out the largest berries, and arrange them around in circles on the top in the white frosting. Makes a very fancy dish, as well as a most delicious cake.

MOLASSES CUP CAKES.

One cupful of butter, one of sugar, six eggs, five cupfuls of sifted flour, one tablespoonful of cinnamon, two tablespoonfuls of ginger, three teacupfuls of cooking molasses, and one heaping teaspoonful of soda. Stir the butter and sugar to a cream; beat the eggs very light, the yolks and whites separately, and add to it; after which put in the spices; then the molasses and flour in rotation, stirring the mixture all the time; beat the whole *well* before adding the soda, and but little afterwards. Put into well-buttered patty-pan tins, and bake in a *very moderate* oven. A baker's recipe.

BAKERS' GINGER SNAPS.

Boil all together the following ingredients: Two cups of brown sugar, two cups of cooking molasses, one cup of shortening, which should be part butter, one *large* tablespoonful of ginger, one tablespoonful of ground cinnamon, one teaspoonful of cloves; remove from the fire and let it cool. In the meantime, sift four cups of flour and stir part of it into the above mixture. Now dissolve a teaspoonful of soda in a tablespoonful of warm water and beat into this mixture, stir in the remainder of the flour, and make stiff enough to roll into long rolls about one inch in diameter, and cut off from the end into half-inch pieces. Place them on well-buttered tins, giving plenty of room to spread. Bake in a moderate oven. Let them cool before taking out of the tins.

GINGER COOKIES.

One cup sugar, one cup molasses, one cup butter, one egg, one tablespoonful vinegar, one tablespoonful ginger, one teaspoonful soda, dissolved in boiling water, mix like cookey dough, rather soft.

GINGER SNAPS.

One cup brown sugar, two cups molasses, one large cup butter, two teaspoonfuls soda, two teaspoonfuls ginger, three pints flour to commence with; rub shortening and sugar together into the flour; add enough more flour to roll very smooth, very thin, and bake in a quick oven. The dough can be kept for days by putting it in the flour-barrel under the flour, and bake a few at a time. The more flour that can be worked in and the smoother they can be rolled, the better and more brittle they will be. Should be rolled out to wafer-like thinness. Bake quickly without burning. They should become perfectly cold before putting aside.

DOMINOES.

Have a plain cake baked in rather thin sheets, and cut into small oblong pieces the size and shape of a domino, a trifle larger. Frost the top and sides. When the frosting is hard, draw the black lines and make the dots, with a small brush dipped in melted chocolate. These are very nice for children's parties.

FANCY CAKES.

These delicious little fancy cakes may be made by making a rich jumble-paste—rolling out in any desired shape; cut some paste in thick, narrow strips and lay around your cakes, so as to form a deep, cup-like edge; place on a well-buttered tin and bake. When done, fill with iced fruit, prepared as follows: Take rich, ripe peaches (canned nes will do, if fine and well-drained from all juice), cut in halves; plums, strawberries, pineapples cut in squares, or small triangles, or any other available fruit, and dip in the white of an egg that has been very slightly beaten and then in pulverized sugar, and lay in the centre of your cakes.

WAFERS.

Dissolve four ounces of butter in half a teacup of milk; stir together four ounces of white sugar, eight ounces of sifted flour, and the yolk of one egg, adding gradually the butter and milk, a tablespoonful of orange-flower water, and a pinch of salt; mix it well. Heat the wafer-irons, butter their inner surfaces, put in a tablespoonful of the batter, and close the irons immediately; put the irons over the fire, and turn them occasionally, until the wafer is cooked; when the wafers are all cooked, roll them on a small round stick, stand them upon a sieve, and dry them; serve with ices.

PEACH CAKES.

Take the yolks and whites of five eggs and beat them separately (the whites to a stiff froth). Then mix the beaten yolks with half a pound of pulverized and sifted loaf or crushed sugar, and beat the two together thoroughly. Fifteen minutes will be none too long for the latter operation if you would have excellence with your cakes.

Now add half a pound of fine flour, dredging it in a little at a time, and then put in the whites of the eggs, beating the whole together for four or five minutes. Then with a large spoon, drop the batter upon a baking-tin, which has been buttered and floured, being careful to have the cakes as nearly the same size as possible, and resembling in shape the half of a peach. Have a quick oven ready, and bake the cakes about ten minutes, watching them closely so that they may only come to a light brown color. Then take them out, spread the flat side of each with peach jam, and stick them together in pairs, covering the outside with a thin coat of icing, which when dry can be brushed over on one side of the cake, with a little cochineal water.

CUP CAKES.

Two cups of sugar, one cup of butter, one cup of milk, three cups and a half of flour, and four eggs, half a teaspoonful of soda, large spoon cream tartar; stir butter and sugar together, and add the beaten yolks of the eggs, then the milk, then flavoring, and the whites. Put cream tartar in flour and add last. Bake in buttered gem-pans, or drop the batter, a teaspoonful at a time, in rows, on flat buttered tins.

To this recipe may be added a cup of English currants or chopped raisins; and also another variety of cakes may be made by adding a half cup of citron sliced and floured. a half-cupful of chopped almonds, and lemon extract.

THE FAMOUS EAST ROOM.

THE RED ROOM.

THE BLUE ROOM.

VARIEGATED CAKES.

One cup powdered sugar, one-half cup of butter creamed with the sugar, one-half cup of milk, four eggs, the whites only, whipped light, two and one-half cups of prepared flour. Bitter almond flavoring, spinach juice and cochineal. Cream, the butter and sugar; .add the milk, flavoring, the whites and flour. Divide the batter into three parts. Bruise and pound a few leaves of spinach in a thin muslin bag until you can express the juice. Put a few drops of this into one portion of the batter, color another with cochineal, leaving the third white. Put a little of each into small, round pans or cups, giving a light stir to each color as you add the next. This will vein the cakes prettily. Put the white between the pink and green, that the tints may show better. If you can get pistachio nuts to pound up for the green, the cakes will be much nicer. Ice on sides and top.

CORN STARCH CAKES.

One cupful each of butter and sweet milk, and half a cup of corn-starch, two cupfuls each of sugar and flour, the whites of five eggs beaten to a stiff froth, two teaspoonfuls of cream of tartar and one of soda; flavor to taste. Bake in gem-tins or patty-pans.

SPONGE DROPS.

Beat to a froth three eggs and one teacup of sugar; stir into this one heaping coffee-cup of flour, in which one teaspoonful of cream of tartar and half a teaspoonful of saleratus are thoroughly mixed. Flavor with lemon. Butter tin sheets with washed butter, and drop in teaspoonfuls about three inches apart. Bake instantly in a very quick oven. Watch closely as they will burn easily. Serve with ice cream.

SAVORY BISCUITS OR LADY FINGERS.

Put nine tablespoonfuls of fine white sugar into a bowl, and put the bowl into hot water to heat the sugar; when the sugar is thoroughly heated, break nine eggs into the bowl and beat them quickly until they become a little warm and rather thick; then take the bowl from the water, and continue beating until it is nearly or quite cold; now stir in lightly nine tablespoonfuls of sifted flour; then with a paper-funnel, or something of the kind, lay this mixture out upon papers, in biscuits three inches long and half an inch thick, in the form of fingers; sift sugar over the biscuits, and bake them upon tins to a light brown; when they are done and cold, remove them from the papers, by wetting them on the back; dry them, and they are ready for use. They are often used in making Charlotte Russe.

PASTRY SANDWICHES.

Puff-paste, jam of any kind, the white of an egg, sifted sugar.

Roll the paste out thin; put half of it on a baking-sheet or tin, and spread equally over it apricot, greengage, or any preserve that may be preferred. Lay over this preserve another thin paste, press the edges together all round, and mark the paste in lines with a knife on the surface, to show where to cut it when baked. Bake from twenty minutes to half an hour; and, a short time before being done, take the pastry out of the oven, brush it over with the white of an egg, sift over pounded sugar, and put it back in the oven to color. When cold, cut it into strips; pile these on a dish pyramidically, and serve.

This may be made of jelly-cake dough, and, after baking, allowed to cool before spreading with the preserve; either way is good, as well as fanciful.

NEAPOLITAINES.

One cup of powdered sugar, half a cup of butter, two tablespoonfuls of lemon-juice, three whole eggs, and three yolks, beaten separately; three cups of sifted flour. Put this all together with half a teaspoonful of soda, dissolved in a table-spoonful of milk. If it is too stiff to roll out, add just enough more milk. Roll it out a quarter of an inch thick, and cut it out with any tin cutter. Place the cakes in a pan slightly greased, and color the tops with beaten egg and milk, with some chopped almonds over them. Bake in a rather quick oven.

BRUNSWICK JELLY CAKES.

Stir one cup of powdered white sugar, and one half cup of butter together, till perfectly light; beat the yolks of three eggs till very thick and smooth; sift three cups of flour, and stir it into the beaten eggs with the butter and sugar; add a teaspoonful of mixed spice (nutmeg, mace and cinnamon) and half a glass of rose-water or wine; stir the whole well, and lay it on your paste-board, which must first be sprinkled with flour; if you find it so moist as to be unmanageable, throw in a little more flour; spread the dough into a sheet about half an inch thick, and cut it out in round cakes with a biscuit-cutter; lay them in buttered pans and bake about five or six minutes; when cold, spread over the surface of each cake a liquor of fruit-jelly or marmalade; then beat the whites of three or four eggs till it stands alone; beat into the froth, by degrees, a sufficiency of powdered loaf-sugar to make it as thick as icing; flavor with a few drops of strong essence of lemon, and with a spoon heap it up on each cake, making it high in the centre; put the cakes into a coal oven, and as soon as the tops are colored a pale brown, take them out.

LITTLE PLUM CAKES.

One cup of sugar and half a cup of butter, beaten to a smooth cream; add three well-beaten eggs, a teaspoonful of vanilla extract, four cups of sifted flour, one cup of raisins, and one of currants, half of a teaspoonful of baking-soda, dissolved in a little water, and milk enough to make a stiff batter; drop this batter in drops on well-buttered tins, and bake in a *quick* oven.

JUMBLES.

Cream together two cups of sugar and one of butter, add three well-beaten eggs and six tablespoonfuls of sweet milk, two teaspoonfuls of baking-powder, flavor to taste; flour enough to make into a soft dough; do not roll it on the paste-board, but break off pieces of dough the size of a walnut and make into rings by rolling out rolls as large as your finger, and joining the ends; lay them on tins to bake, an inch apart, as it rises and spreads; bake in a *moderate* oven. These jumbles are very delicate, will keep a long time.

WINE JUMBLES.

One cup of butter, two of sugar, three eggs, one wine-glass of wine, one spoonful of vanilla, and flour enough to roll out. Roll as thin as the blade of a knife, and cut with an oval cutter. Bake on tin-sheets, in a quick oven, until a dark brown. These will keep a year if kept in a tin box and in a dry place.

COCOANUT JUMBLES.

Grate one large cupful of cocoanut; rub one cupful of butter with one and a half cupfuls of sugar; add three beaten eggs, whites and yolks separately, two tablespoonfuls of milk, and five cupfuls of sifted flour; then add by degrees the grated nut, so as to make a stiff dough, rolled thin, and cut with a round cutter, having a hole in the middle. Bake in a quick oven from five to ten minutes.

PHILADELPHIA JUMBLES.

Two cups of sugar, one cup of butter, eight eggs, beaten light; essence of bitter almond or rose to taste; enough flour to enable you to roll them out.

Stir the sugar and butter to a light cream, then add the well-whipped eggs, the flavoring and flour; mix well together, roll out in powdered sugar, roll in a sheet a quarter of an inch thick; cut into rings with a jagging-iron, and bake in a quick oven on buttered tins.

ALMOND JUMBLES.

Three cupfuls of soft sugar, two cupfuls of flour, half a cupful of butter, one teacupful of loppered milk, five eggs, well-beaten, two tablespoonfuls of rose-water, three-quarters of a pound of almonds, blanched and chopped *very* fine; one teaspoonful of soda, dissolved in boiling water.

Cream, butter and sugar; stir in the beaten yolks the milk, flour, rose-water, almonds, and, lastly, the beaten whites very lightly, and quickly; drop in rings on buttered paper, and bake at once.

FRUIT JUMBLES.

Two cups of sugar, one cup of butter, five cupfuls of flour, five eggs, one small teacupful of milk, in which dissolve half a teaspoonful of soda; cream the butter; add the sugar; cream again; then add yolks of eggs, the milk, beaten whites and flour; a little cinnamon, nutmeg, allspice, and ground cloves, and one-quarter of a pound of currants, rolled in flour.

COOKIES.

One cup of butter, two cups of sugar, a *small* teacupful of sweet milk, half a grated nutmeg, and five cups of sifted flour, in which there has been sifted with it two teaspoonfuls of baking-powder ; mix into a soft dough, and cut into round cakes; roll the dough as thin as pie-crust. Bake in a quick oven a light-brown. These can be made of sour milk and a teaspoonful of soda dissolved in it, or sour or sweet cream can be used in place of butter.

Water cookies made the same as above, using water in place of milk. Water cookies keep longer than milk cookies.

FAVORITE COOKIES.

One cup of butter, one and a half cups of sugar, one half cup of sour milk, one level teaspoonful of soda, a teaspoonful of grated nutmeg. Flour enough to roll; make quite soft. Put a tablespoonful of fine sugar on a plate and dip the tops of each as you cut them out. Place on buttered tins and bake in a quick oven, a light brown.

FRUIT COOKIES.

One cupful and a half of sugar, one cupful of butter, one-half cup of sweet milk, one egg, two teaspoonfuls of baking-powder, a teaspoonful of grated nutmeg, three tablespoonfuls of English currants or chopped raisins. Mix soft, and roll out, using just enough flour to stiffen sufficiently. Cut out with a large cutter, wet the tops with milk, and sprinkle sugar over them. Bake on buttered tins in a quick oven.

CRISP COOKIES. (Very Nice.)

One cup of butter, two cups of sugar, three eggs well-beaten, a teaspoonful of soda and two of cream tartar, spoonful of milk, one teaspoonful of nutmeg, and one of cinnamon. Flour enough to make a soft dough just stiff enough to roll out. Try a pint of sifted flour to begin with, working it in gradually. Spread a little sweet milk over each, and sprinkle with sugar. Bake in a quick oven a light brown.

LEMON COOKIES.

Four cups of sifted flour, or enough for a stiff dough; one teacupful of butter, two cups of sugar, the juice of one lemon, and the grated peel from the outside, three eggs, whipped very light. Beat thoroughly each ingredient, adding after all is in a half teaspoonful of soda, dissolved in a tablespoonful of milk. Roll out as any cookies, and bake a light brown. Use no other wetting.

COCOANUT COOKIES.

One cup grated cocoanut, one and one-half cups sugar, three-fourths cup butter, one-half cup milk, two eggs, one large teaspoonful baking-powder, one-half teaspoonful extract of vanilla, and flour enough to roll out.

DOUGHNUTS OR FRIED CAKES.

Success in making good fried cakes depends as much on the *cooking* as the mixing. In the first place, there should be boiling lard enough to free them from the bottom of the kettle, so that they swim on the top, and the lard should never be so hot as to smoke or so cool as not to be at the boiling point; if it is, they soak grease, and are spoiled. If it is at the right heat, the doughnuts will in about ten minutes be of a delicate brown outside and nicely cooked inside. Five or six minutes will cook a cruller. Try the fat by dropping a bit of the dough in first; if it is right, the fat will boil up when it is dropped in. They should be turned over almost constantly, which causes them to rise and brown evenly. When they are sufficiently cooked, raise them from the hot fat, and drain them until every drop ceases dripping.

CRULLERS OR FRIED CAKES.

One and a half cupfuls of sugar, one cupful of sour milk, two eggs, two scant tablespoonfuls of melted butter, half a nutmeg grated, a large teaspoonful of cinnamon, a teaspoonful of salt, and one of soda; make a little stiffer than biscuit dough, roll out a quarter of an inch thick, and cut with a fried-cake cutter, with a hole in the centre. Fry in hot lard.

These can be made with sweet milk and baking-powder, using two heaping teaspoonfuls of the baking-powder in place of soda.

RAISED DOUGHNUTS.

Old-fashioned "raised doughnuts," are seldom seen, now-a-days, but are easily made. Make a sponge as for bread, using a pint of warm water or milk, and a large half cupful of yeast; when the sponge is very light, add half a cupful of butter or sweet lard, a coffee-cupful of sugar, a teaspoonful of salt and one small teaspoonful of soda, dissolved in a little water, one tablespoonful of cinnamon, a little grated nutmeg; stir in now two well-beaten eggs, add sifted flour until it is the consistency of biscuit-dough, knead it well, cover and let rise; then roll the dough out into a sheet half an inch thick, cut out with a very small biscuit-cutter, or in strips half an inch wide and three inches long, place them on greased tins, cover them well, and let them rise before frying them. Drop them in very hot lard. Raised cakes require longer time than cakes made with baking-powder. Sift powdered sugar over them as fast as they are fried, while warm. Our grandmothers put allspice into these cakes; that, however, is a matter of taste.

BAKERS' RAISED DOUGHNUTS.

Warm a teacupful of lard in a pint of milk; when nearly cool, add enough flour to make a thick batter, and add a small cupful of yeast; beat it well, and set it to rise; when light, work in gradually and carefully three cupfuls of sugar, the whipped whites of six eggs, half a teaspoonful of soda, dissolved in a spoonful of milk; one teaspoonful of salt, a teaspoonful of ground cinnamon, and half of a nutmeg grated; then work in gradually enough flour to make it stiff enough to roll out; let it rise again, and when very light, roll it out in a sheet an inch thick; cut into rounds; put into the centre of each round a large Sultana raisin, seeded, and mold into perfectly round balls ; flatten a little; let them stand a few minutes before boiling them; have plenty of lard in the pot, and when it boils drop in the cakes; when they are a light brown, take them out with a perforated skimmer; drain on soft white paper, and roll, while warm, in fine powdered sugar.

—Pursell's Bakery, New York City.

CRULLERS OR WONDERS.

Three eggs, three tablespoonfuls of melted lard or butter, three tablespoonfuls of sugar, mix very hard with sifted flour, as hard as can be rolled, and to be rolled very thin like pie-crust; cut in squares three inches long and two wide, then cut several slits or lines lengthwise, to within a quarter of an inch of the edges of the ends; run your two forefingers through every other slit; lay them down on the board edgewise, and dent them. These are very dainty when fried. Fry in hot lard a light brown.

GERMAN DOUGHNUTS.

One pint of milk, four eggs, one small tablespoonful of melted butter, flavoring, salt to taste; first boil the milk and pour it, while hot, over a pint of flour; beat it very smooth, and when it is cool, have ready the yolks of the eggs well-beaten; add them to the milk and flour, beaten well into it, then add the well-beaten whites, then lastly add the salt and as much more flour as will make the whole into a soft dough; flour your board, turn your dough upon it, roll it in pieces as thick as your finger and turn them in the form of a ring; cook in plenty of boiling lard. A nice breakfast cake with coffee.

NUT CAKES (Fried.)

Beat two eggs well, add to them one ounce of sifted sugar, two ounces of warmed butter, two tablespoonfuls of yeast, a teacupful of luke-warm milk and a little salt. Whip all well together, then stir in by degrees one pound of flour, and, if requisite, more milk, making thin dough. Beat it until it falls from the spoon, then set it to rise. When it has risen, make butter or lard hot in a frying-pan; cut from the light dough little pieces the size of a walnut, and without molding or kneading, fry them pale brown. As they are done, lay them on a napkin to absorb any of the fat.

TRIFLES.

Work one egg and a tablespoonful of sugar to as much flour as will make a stiff paste; roll it as thin as a dollar piece, and cut it into small round or square cakes; drop two or three at a time into the boiling lard; when they rise to the surface and turn over they are done; take them out with a skimmer and lay them on an inverted sieve to drain. When served for dessert or supper, put a spoonful of jelly on each.

PUFF-BALL DOUGHNUTS.

These doughnuts, eaten fresh and warm, are a delicious breakfast dish, and are quickly made. Three eggs, one cupful of sugar, a pint of sweet milk, salt, nutmeg, and flour enough to permit the spoon to stand upright in the mixture; add two heaping teaspoonfuls of baking-powder to the flour; beat all until very light. Drop by the dessertspoonful into boiling lard. These will not absorb a bit of fat, and are not at all rich, and consequently are the least injurious of this kind of cakes.

PASTRY, PIES AND TARTS.

GENERAL REMARKS.

Use the very best materials in making pastry; the shortening should be fresh, sweet, and hard; the water cold (ice water is best), the paste rolled on a cold board, and all handled as little as possible.

When the crust is made, it makes it much more flakey and puff much more to put it in a dish covered with a cloth, and set in a very cold place for half an hour, or even an hour; in summer, it could be placed in the ice box.

A great improvement is made in pie-crust by the addition of about a heaping teaspoonful of baking-powder to a quart of flour, also brushing the paste as often as rolled out, and the pieces of butter placed thereon, with the white of an egg, assists it to rise in *leaves* or *flakes*. As this is the great beauty of puff-paste, it is as well to try this method.

If currants are to be used in pies, they should be carefully picked over, and washed in several waters, dried in a towel, and dredged with flour before they are suitable for use.

Raisins, and all dried fruits for pies and cakes, should be seeded, stoned, and dredged with flour, before using.

Almonds should be blanched by pouring boiling water upon them, and then slipping the skin off with the fingers. In pounding them, always add a little rose or orange water, with fine sugar, to prevent their becoming oily.

Great care is requisite in heating an oven for baking pastry. If you can hold your hand in the heated oven while you count twenty, the oven has just the proper temperature, and it should be kept at this temperature as long as the pastry is in; this heat will bake to a light brown, and will give the pastry a fresh and flakey appearance. If you suffer the heat to abate, the under crust will become heavy and clammy, and the upper crust will fall in.

Another good way to ascertain when the oven is heated to the proper degree for puff-paste: put a small piece of the paste in previous to baking the whole, and then the heat can thus be judged of.

Pie-crust can be kept a week, and the last be better than the first, if put in a tightly covered dish, and set in the ice-chest in summer, and in a cool place in winter, and thus you can make a fresh pie every day with little trouble.

In baking custard, pumpkin or squash pies, it is well, in order that the mixture may not be absorbed by the paste, to first partly bake the paste before adding it, and when stewed fruit is used the filling should be perfectly cool when put in, or it will make the bottom crust sodden.

HOW TO MAKE A PIE.

After making the crust, take a portion of it, roll it out and fit it to a buttered pie-plate by cutting it off evenly around the edge; gather up the scraps left from cutting and make into another sheet for the top crust; roll it a little thinner than the under crust; lap one half over the other and cut three or four slits about a quarter of an inch from the folded edge, (this prevents the steam from escaping through the rim of the pie, and causing the juices to run out from the edges). Now fill your pie-plate with your prepared filling, wet the top edge of the rim, lay the upper crust across the centre of the pie, turn back the half that is lapped over, seal the two edges together by slightly pressing down with your thumb, then notch evenly and regularly with a three-tined fork, dipping occasionally in flour to prevent sticking. Bake in a rather quick oven a light brown, and until the filling boils up through the slits in the upper crust.

To prevent the juice soaking through into the crust, making it soggy, wet the under crust with the white of an egg, just before you put in the pie mixture. If the top of the pie is brushed over with the egg, it gives it a beautiful glaze.

FOR ICING PASTRY.

To ice pastry, which is the usual method adopted for fruit tarts and sweet dishes of pastry, put the white of an egg on a plate, and with the blade of a knife beat it to a stiff froth. When the pastry is nearly baked, brush it over with this, and sift over some pounded sugar; put it back into the oven to set the glaze, and in a few minutes it will be done. Great care should be taken that the paste does not catch or burn in the oven, which it is very liable to do after the icing is laid on.

Or make a meringue by adding a tablespoonful of white sugar to the beaten white of one egg. Spread over the top, and slightly brown in the oven.

FINE PUFF-PASTE.

Into one quart of sifted flour, mix two teaspoonfuls of baking-powder, and a teaspoonful of salt; *then sift again.* Measure out one teacupful of butter and one of lard, hard and cold. Take the lard and rub into the flour until a very fine, smooth paste. Then put in just enough *ice-water*, say half a cupful, containing a beaten white of egg, to mix a very stiff dough. Roll it out into a thin sheet, spread with one-fourth of the butter, sprinkle over with a little flour, then roll up closely in a long roll, like a scroll, double the ends towards the centre, flatten and reroll, then spread again with another quarter of the butter. Repeat this operation until the butter is used up. Put it on an earthen dish, cover it with a cloth and set it in a cold place, in the ice-box in summer; let it remain until *cold;* an hour or more before making out the crust. Tarts made with this paste cannot be cut with a knife when fresh; they go into flakes at the touch.

You may roll this pastry in any direction, from you, towards you, sideways, anyway, it matters not, but you must have nice flour, *ice-water*, and very *little* of it, and strength to roll it, if you would succeed.

This recipe I purchased from a colored cook on one of the Lake Michigan steamers many years ago, and it is, without exception, the finest puff-paste I have ever seen.

PUFF-PASTE FOR PIES.

One quart of pastry flour, one pint of butter, one tablespoonful of salt, one of sugar, one and a quarter cupfuls of ice-water. Wash the hands with soap and water, and dip them first in very hot, and then in cold water. Rinse a large bowl or pan with boiling water, and then with cold. Half fill it with cold water. Wash the butter in this, working it with the hands until it is light and waxy. This frees it from the salt and buttermilk, and lightens it, so that the pastry is more delicate. Shape the butter into two thin cakes, and put in a pan of ice-water to harden. Mix the salt and sugar with the flour. With the hands, rub one-third of the butter into the flour. Add the water, stirring with a knife. Stir quickly and vigorously, until the paste is a smooth ball. Sprinkle the board *lightly* with flour. Turn the paste on this and pound quickly and lightly with the rolling-pin. Do not break the paste. Roll from you, and to one side; or, if easier to roll from you all the time, turn the paste around. When it is about one-fourth of an inch thick, wipe the remaining butter, break it in bits, and spread these on the paste. Sprinkle lightly with flour. Fold the paste, one-third from each side, so that the edges meet. Now fold from the ends, but do not have these meet. Double the paste, pound lightly, and roll down to about one-third of an inch in thickness. Fold as before, and roll down again. Repeat this three times, if for pies, and six times if for *vol-au-vents*, patties, tarts, etc. Place on the ice, to harden, when it has been rolled the last time. It should be in the ice-chest at least an hour before being used. In hot weather, if the paste sticks when being rolled down, put it on a tin sheet, and place on ice. As soon as it is chilled, it will roll easily. The less flour you use in rolling out the paste, the tenderer it will be. No matter how carefully every part of the work may be done, the paste will not be good if much flour is used.

—Maria Parloa.

SOYER'S RECIPE FOR PUFF-PASTE.

To every pound of flour allow the yolk of one egg, the juice of one lemon, half a saltspoonful of salt, cold water, one pound of fresh butter.

Put the flour on to the paste-board; make a hole in the centre, into which put the yolk of the egg, the lemon-juice, and salt; mix the whole with cold water (this should be iced in summer, if convenient) into a soft, flexible paste with the right hand, and handle it as little as possible; then squeeze all the buttermilk from the butter, wring it in a cloth, and roll out the paste; place the butter on this, and fold the edges of the paste over, so as to hide it; roll it out again to the thickness of a quarter of an inch; fold over one-third, over which again pass the rolling-pin; then fold over the other third, thus forming a square; place it with the ends, top, and bottom before you, shaking a little flour both under and over, and repeat the rolls and turns twice again, as before. Flour a baking sheet, put the paste on this, and let it remain on ice or in some cool place for half an hour; then roll twice more, turning it as before; place it again upon the ice for a quarter of an hour, give it two more rolls, making seven in all, and it is ready for use when required.

RULE FOR UNDER CRUST.

A good rule for pie-crust for a pie requiring only an under crust,—as a custard or pumpkin pie,—is: Three *large* tablespoonfuls of flour sifted; rubbing into it a *large* tablespoonful of cold butter, or part butter and part lard, and a pinch of salt, mixing with *cold* water enough to form a smooth, stiff paste, and rolled quite thin.

PLAIN PIE-CRUST.

Two and a half cupfuls of sifted flour, one cupful of shortening, half butter and half lard, cold; a pinch of salt, a heaping teaspoonful of baking-powder, sifted through the flour. Rub thoroughly the shortening into the flour. Mix together with half a teacupful of *cold* water, or enough to form a rather stiff dough; mix as little as possible, just enough to get it into shape to roll out; it must be handled very lightly. This rule is for two pies.

When you have a little pie-crust left, do not throw it away; roll it thin, cut it in small squares and bake. Just before tea, put a spoonful of raspberry jelly on each square.

PUFF-PASTE OF SUET.

Two cupfuls of flour, one-half teaspoonful of salt, one teaspoonful of baking-powder, one cup of chopped suet, freed of skin, and chopped very fine, one cupful of water. Place the flour, sifted with the powder, in a bowl, add suet and water; mix into smooth, rather firm dough.

This paste is excellent for fruit puddings, and dumplings that are boiled; if it is well made, it will be light and flaky, and the suet imperceptible. It is also excellent for meat pies, baked or boiled. All the ingredients should be very cold when mixing, and the suet dredged with flour after it is chopped, to prevent the particles from adhering to each other.

POTATO CRUST.

Boil and mash a dozen medium-sized potatoes, add one good teaspoonful of salt, two tablespoonfuls of cold butter, and half a cupful of milk or cream. Stiffen with flour sufficient to roll out. Nice for the tops of meat pies.

TO MAKE PIE-CRUST FLAKY

In making a pie, after you have rolled out your top crust, cut it about the right size, spread it over with butter, then shake sifted flour over the butter, enough to cover it well. Cut a slit in the middle, place it over the top of your pie, and fasten the edges as any pie. Now take the pie on your left hand, and a dipper of cold water in your right hand; tip the pie slanting a little, pour over the water sufficiently to rinse off the flour. Enough flour will stick to the butter to fry into the crust, to give it a fine, blistered, flaky look, which many cooks think is much better than rolling the butter into the crust.

TARTLETS.

Tarts of strawberry or any other kind of preserves are generally made of the trimmings of puff-paste rolled a little thicker than for ordinary pies; then cut out with a round cutter, first dipped in hot water, to make the edges smooth, and placed in small tart-pans, first pricking a few holes at the bottom with a fork before placing them in the oven. Bake from ten to fifteen minutes. Let the paste cool a little; then fill it with preserve. By this manner, both the flavor and color of the jam are preserved, which would be lost were it baked in the oven on the paste; and, besides, so much jam is not required

PATTIES, OR SHELLS FOR TARTS.

Roll out a nice puff-paste thin; cut out with a glass or cookey-cutter, and with a wine-glass or smaller cutter, cut out the centre of two out of three; lay the rings thus made on the third, and bake at once. May be used for veal or oyster patties, or filled with jelly, jam or preserves, as tarts. Or shells may be made by lining patty-pans with paste. If the paste is light, the shells will be fine. Filled with jelly and covered with meringue (tablespoonful of sugar to the white of one egg), and browned in oven, they are very nice to serve for tea.

If the cutters are dipped in *hot water*, the edges of the tartlets will rise much higher and smoother when baking.

TARTLETS.

Tartlets are nice made in this manner: Roll some good puff-paste out thin, and cut it into two and a half inch squares; brush each square over with the white of an egg, then fold down the corners, so that they all meet in the middle of each piece of paste; slightly press the two pieces together, brush them over with the egg, sift over sugar, and bake in a nice quick oven for about a quarter of an hour. When they are done, make a little hole in the middle of the paste, and fill it up with apricot jam, marmalade, or red-currant jelly. Pile them high in the centre of a dish, on a napkin, and garnish with the same preserve the tartlets are filled with.

TARTS.

Larger pans are required for tarts proper, the size of small, shallow pie-tins; then after the paste is baked and cooled and filled with the jam or preserve, a few stars or leaves are placed on the top, or strips of paste, criss-crossed on the top, all of which have been previously baked on a tin by themselves.

Dried fruit, stewed until thick, makes fine tart pies, also cranberries, stewed and well sweetened.

GREEN APPLE PIE.

Peel, core and slice tart apples enough for a pie; sprinkle over about three tablespoonfuls of sugar, a teaspoonful of cinnamon, a small level tablespoonful of sifted flour, two tablespoonfuls of water, a few bits of butter; stir all together with a spoon; put it into a pie-tin lined with pie-paste; cover with a top crust and bake about forty minutes.

The result will be a delicious, juicy pie.

APPLE CUSTARD PIE. No. 1.

Three cupfuls of milk, four eggs, and one cupful of sugar, two cupfuls of thick stewed apples, strained through a colander. Beat the whites and yolks of the eggs lightly, and mix the yolks well with the apples, flavoring with nutmeg. Then beat into this the milk, and lastly the whites. Let the crust partly bake before turning in this filling. To be baked with only the one crust, like all custard pies.

APPLE CUSTARD PIE. No. 2.

Select fair sweet apples, pare and grate them, and to every teacupful of the apple add two eggs well beaten, two tablespoonfuls of fine sugar, one of melted butter, the grated rind and half the juice of one lemon, half a wine-glass of brandy, and one teacupful of milk; mix all well, and pour into a deep plate lined with paste; put a strip of the paste around the edge of the dish and bake thirty minutes.

APPLE CUSTARD PIE. No. 3.

Lay a crust in your plates; slice apples thin, and half fill your plates; pour over them a custard made of four eggs and one quart of milk, sweetened and seasoned to your taste.

APPLE CUSTARD PIE. No. 4.

Peel sour apples and stew until soft, and not much water left in them; then rub through a colander; beat three eggs for each pie to be baked, and put in at the rate of one cupful of butter and one of sugar for three pies; season with nutmeg.

IRISH APPLE PIE.

Pare and take out the cores of the apples, cutting each apple into four or eight pieces, according to their size. Lay them neatly in a baking dish, seasoning them with brown sugar, and any spice, such as pounded cloves and cinnamon, or grated lemon-peel. A little quince marmalade gives a fine flavor to the pie. Add a little water, and cover with puff-paste. Bake for an hour.

MOCK APPLE PIE.

Crush finely, with a rolling-pin, one large Boston cracker; put it into a bowl, and pour upon it one teacupful of cold water; add one teacupful of fine white sugar, the juice and pulp of one lemon, half a lemon-rind grated, and a little nutmeg; line the pie-plate with half puff-paste, pour in the mixture, cover with the paste, and bake half an hour.

These are proportions for one pie.

APPLE AND PEACH MERINGUE PIE.

Stew the apples or peaches and sweeten to taste. Mash smooth and season with nutmeg. Fill the crusts and bake until just done. Put on no top crust. Take the whites of three eggs for each pie, and whip to a stiff froth, and sweeten with three tablespoonfuls of powdered sugar. Flavor with rose-water or vanilla; beat until it will stand alone; then spread it on the pie one-half to one inch thick; set it back into the oven until the meringue is well "set." Eat cold.

COCOANUT PIE. No. 1.

One-half cup dessicated cocoanut, soaked in one cupful of milk, two eggs, one small cupful of sugar, butter the size of an egg. This is for one small-sized pie. Nice with a meringue on top.

COCOANUT PIE. No. 2.

Cut off the brown part of the cocoanut, grate the white part, mix it with milk, and set it on the fire and let it boil slowly eight or ten minutes. To a pound of the grated cocoanut, allow a quart of milk, eight eggs, four tablespoonfuls of sifted white sugar, a glass of wine, a small cracker, pounded fine, two spoonfuls of melted butter, and half a nutmeg. The eggs and sugar should be beaten together to a froth, then the wine stirred in. Put them into the milk and cocoanut, which should be first allowed to get quite cool; add the cracker and nutmeg, turn the whole into deep pie-plates, with a lining and rim of puff-paste. Bake them as soon as turned into the plates.

CHOCOLATE CUSTARD PIE. No. 1.

One quarter cake of Baker's chocolate, grated; one pint of boiling water, six eggs, one quart of milk, one-half cupful of white sugar, two teaspoonfuls of vanilla. Dissolve the chocolate in a very little milk, stir into the boiling water, and boil three minutes. When nearly cold, beat up with this the yolks of all the eggs and the whites of three. Stir this mixture into the milk, season and pour into shells of good paste. When the custard is "set"—but not more than half done—spread over it the whites whipped to a froth, with two tablespoonfuls of sugar. You may bake these custards without paste, in a pudding-dish or cups set in boiling water.

CHOCOLATE PIE. No. 2.

Put some grated chocolate into a basin and place on the back of the stove and let it melt (do not add any water to it); beat one egg and some sugar in it; when melted, spread this on the top of a custard pie. Lovers of chocolate will like this.

LEMON PIE. (Superior.)

Take a deep dish, grate into it the outside of the rind of two lemons; add to that a cup and a half of white sugar, two heaping tablespoonfuls of unsifted flour, or one of corn-starch; stir it well together, then add the yolks of three well-beaten eggs, beat this thoroughly, then add the juice of the lemons, two cups of water, and a piece of butter the size of a walnut. Set this on the fire in another dish containing boiling water and cook it until it thickens, and will dip up on the spoon like cold honey. Remove it from the fire, and when cooled, pour it into a deep pie-tin, lined with pastry; bake, and when done, have ready the whites, beaten stiff, with three small tablespoonfuls of sugar. Spread this over the top and return to the oven to set and brown slightly. This makes a deep, large-sized pie, and very superior.

—Ebbitt House, Washington.

LEMON PIE. No. 2.

One coffee-cupful of sugar, three eggs, one cupful of water, one tablespoonful of melted butter, one heaping tablespoonful of flour, the juice and a little of the rind of one lemon. Reserve the whites of the eggs, and after the pie is baked, spread them over the top, beaten lightly, with a spoonful of sugar, and return to the oven until it is a light brown.

This may be cooked before it is put into the crust or not, but is rather better to cook it first in a double boiler or dish. It makes a medium-sized pie. Bake from thirty-five to forty minutes.

LEMON PIE. No. 3.

Moisten a heaping tablespoonful of corn-starch with a little cold water, then add a cupful of boiling water; stir over the fire till it boils and cook the corn-starch, say two or three minutes; add a teaspoonful of butter, and a cupful of sugar; take off the fire, and when slightly cooled, add an egg well beaten, and the juice and grated rind of a fresh lemon. Bake with a crust. This makes one small pie.

LEMON PIE. No. 4.

Two large, fresh lemons, grate off the rind, if not bitter reserve it for the filling of the pie; pare off every bit of the white skin of the lemon, (as it toughens while cooking); then cut the lemon into very thin slices with a sharp knife, and take out the seeds; two cupfuls of sugar, three tablespoonfuls of water, and two of sifted flour. Put into the pie a layer of lemon, then one of sugar, then one of the grated rind, and, lastly, of flour, and so on till the ingredients are used; sprinkle the water over all, and cover with upper crust. Be sure to have the under crust lap over the upper, and pinch it well, as the syrup will cook all out if care is not taken when finishing the edge of crust. This quantity makes one medium-sized pie.

ORANGE PIE.

Grate the rind of one and use the juice of two large oranges. Stir together a large cupful of sugar and a heaping tablespoonful of flour; add to this the well-beaten yolks of three eggs, two tablespoonfuls of melted butter. Reserve the whites for frosting. Turn this into a pie-pan lined with pie-paste, and bake in a quick oven. When done so as to resemble a finely baked custard, spread on the top of it the beaten whites, which must be sweetened with two tablespoonfuls of sugar; spread evenly, and return to the oven and brown slightly.

The addition of the juice of half a lemon improves it, if convenient to have it.

BAKERS' CUSTARD PIE.

Beat up the yolks of three eggs to a cream. Stir thoroughly a tablespoonful of sifted flour into three tablespoonfuls of sugar; this separates the particles of flour so that there will be no lumps; then add it to the beaten yolks, put in a pinch of salt, a teaspoonful of vanilla, and a little grated nutmeg; next the well-beaten whites of the eggs; and lastly, a pint of scalded milk (not boiled) which has been cooled; mix this in by degrees, and turn all into a deep pie-pan, lined with puff-paste, and bake from twenty-five to thirty minutes.

I received this recipe from a celebrated cook in one of our best New York bakeries. I inquired of him "why it was that their custard pies had that look of solidity and smoothness that our home-made pies have not." He replied, "The secret is the addition of this *bit of flour*—not that it thickens the custard any to speak of, but prevents the custard from breaking or wheying, and gives that smooth appearance when cut."

CREAM PIE.

Pour a pint of cream upon one and a half cupfuls of sugar; let it stand until the whites of three eggs have been beaten to a stiff froth; add this to the cream, and beat up thoroughly; grate a little nutmeg over the mixture, and bake without an upper crust. If a tablespoonful of sifted flour is added to it, as the above Custard Pie recipe, it would improve it.

WHIPPED CREAM PIE.

Line a pie-plate with a rich crust, and bake quickly in a hot oven. When done, spread with a thin layer of jelly or jam, then whip one cupful of thick sweet cream until it is as light as possible; sweeten with powdered sugar and flavor with vanilla; spread over the jelly or jam; set the cream where it will get very cold before whipping.

CUSTARD PIE.

Beat together until very light the yolks of four eggs and four tablespoonfuls of sugar, flavor with nutmeg or vanilla; then add the four beaten whites, a pinch of salt and, lastly, a quart of sweet milk; mix well and pour into tins lined with paste. Bake until firm.

BOSTON CREAM PIE.

Cream part.—Put on a pint of milk to boil. Break two eggs into a dish, and add one cup of sugar and half a cup of flour previously mixed; after beating well, stir it into the milk just as the milk commences to boil; add an ounce of butter and keep on stirring one way until it thickens; flavor with vanilla or lemon.

Crust part.—Three eggs, beaten separately, one cup of granulated sugar, one and a half cups of sifted flour, one large teaspoonful of baking-powder, and two tablespoonfuls of milk or water. Divide the batter in half and bake on two medium-sized pie-tins. Bake in a rather quick oven to a straw color. When done and cool, split each one in half with a sharp broad-bladed knife, and spread half the cream between each. Serve cold.

The cake part should be flavored the same as the custard.

MOCK CREAM PIE.

Take three eggs, one pint of milk, a cupful of sugar, two tablespoonfuls of corn-starch, or three of flour; beat the sugar, corn-starch, and yolks of the eggs together; after the milk has come to a boil, stir in the mixture, and add a pinch of salt and about a teaspoonful of butter. Make crust the same as any pie; bake, then fill with the custard, grate over a little nutmeg and bake again. Take the whites of the eggs and beat to a stiff froth with two tablespoonfuls of sugar, spread over the top and brown in a quick oven.

FRUIT CUSTARD PIE.

Any fruit custard, such as pineapple, banana, can be readily made after the recipe of "Apple Custard Pie."

CHERRY PIE.

Line your pie-plate with good crust, fill half full with ripe cherries; sprinkle over them about a cupful of sugar, a teaspoonful of sifted flour, dot a few bits of butter over that. Now fill the crust full to the top. Cover with the upper crust, and bake.

This is one of the best of pies, if made correctly, and the cherries in any case should be stoned.

CURRANT PIE. No. 1.

Make in just the same way as the Cherry Pie, unless they are somewhat green, then they should be stewed a little

RIPE CURRANT PIE. No. 2.

One cupful of mashed ripe currants, one of sugar, two tablespoonfuls of water, one of flour, beaten with the yolks of two eggs. Bake; frost the top with the beaten whites of the eggs and two tablespoonfuls powdered sugar. and brown in oven.

GREEN TOMATO PIE.

Take medium-sized tomatoes, pare, and cut out the stem end. Having your pie-pan lined with paste made as biscuit dough, slice the tomatoes *very thin*, filling the pan somewhat heaping, then grate over it a nutmeg, put in half a cup of butter, and a medium cup of sugar, if the pan is rather deep. Sprinkle a small handful of flour over all, pouring in half a cup of vinegar before adding the top crust. Bake half an hour, in a moderately hot oven, serving hot. Is good; try it.

APRICOT MERINGUE PIE.

A canned apricot meringue pie is made by cutting the apricots fine and mixing them with a half cup of sugar and the beaten yolk of an egg; fill the crust and bake. Take from the oven, let it stand for two or three minutes, cover with a meringue made of the beaten white of an egg and one tablespoonful of sugar. Set back in a slow oven until it turns a golden brown. The above pie can be made into a tart without the addition of the meringue by adding crisscross strips of pastry when the pie is first put into the oven.

All of the above are good if made from the dried and stewed apricots instead of the canned, and are much cheaper.

Stewed dried apricots are a delicious addition to mince-meat. They may be use in connection with minced apples, or to the exclusion of the latter.

HUCKLEBERRY PIE.

Put a quart of picked huckleberries into a basin of water; take off whatever floats; take up the berries by the handful, pick out all the stems and unripe berries, and put them into a dish; line a buttered pie-dish with a pie-paste, put in the berries half an inch deep, and to a quart of berries, put half of a teacupful of brown sugar; dredge a teaspoonful of flour over, strew a saltspoonful of salt, and a little nutmeg grated over; cover the pie, cut a slit in the centre, or make several small incisions on either side of it; press the two crusts together around the edge, trim it off neatly with a sharp knife, and bake in a quick oven for thre-equarters of an hour.

BLACKBERRY PIE.

Pick the berries clean, rinse them in cold water, and finish as directed for huckleberries.

MOLASSES PIE.

Two teacupfuls of molasses, one of sugar, three eggs, one tablespoonful of melted butter, one lemon, nutmeg; beat and bake in pastry.

LEMON RAISIN PIE.

One cup of chopped raisins, seeded, the juice and grated rind of one lemon, one cupful of cold water, one tablespoonful of flour, one cupful of sugar, two tablespoonfuls of butter. Stir lightly together and bake with upper and under crust.

RHUBARB PIE.

Cut the large stalks off where the leaves commence, strip off the outside skin, then cut the stalks in pieces half an inch long; line a pie-dish with paste rolled rather thicker than a dollar piece, put a layer of the rhubarb nearly an inch deep; to a quart bowl of cut rhubarb put a large teacupful of sugar; strew it over with a saltspoonful of salt and a little nutmeg grated; shake over a little flour; cover with a rich pie-crust, cut a slit in the centre, trim off the edge with a sharp knife, and bake in a quick oven until the pie loosens from the dish. Rhubarb pies made in this way are altogether superior to those made of the fruit stewed.

RHUBARB PIE, COOKED.

Skin the stalks, cut them into small pieces, wash, and put them in a stew-pan with no more water than what adheres to them; when cooked, mash them fine. and put in a small piece of butter; when cool, sweeten to taste; if liked add a little lemon-peel, cinnamon or nutmeg; line your plate with thin crust, put in the filling, cover with crust, and bake in a *quick* oven; sift sugar over it when served.

PINEAPPLE PIE.

A grated pineapple; its weight in sugar; half its weight in butter; one cupful of cream; five eggs; beat the butter to a creamy froth; add the sugar and yolks of the eggs; continue beating till very light; add the cream, the pineapple grated, and the whites of the eggs beaten to a stiff froth. Bake with an under crust. Eat cold.

GRAPE PIE.

Pop the pulps out of the skins into one dish, and put the skins into another. Then simmer the pulp a little over the fire to soften it; remove it and rub it through a colander to separate it from the seeds. Then put the skins and pulp together, and they are ready for pies or for canning or putting in jugs for further use. Fine for pies.

DAMSON OR PLUM PIE.

Stew the damsons whole in water only sufficient to prevent their burning; when tender, and while hot, sweeten them with sugar, and let them stand until they become cold; then pour them into pie-dishes lined with paste, dredge flour upon them, cover them with the same paste, wet and pinch together the edges of the paste, cut a slit in the centre of the cover through which the vapor may escape, and bake twenty minutes.

PEACH PIE.

Peel, stone, and slice the peaches. Line a pie-plate with crust, and lay in your fruit, sprinkling sugar liberally over them in proportion to their sweetness. Allow three peach kernels, chopped fine, to each pie; pour in a very little water, and bake with an upper crust, or with cross-bars of paste across the top.

DRIED FRUIT PIES.

Wash the fruit thoroughly, soak over night in water enough to cover. In the morning, stew slowly, until nearly done, in the same water. Sweeten to taste. The crust, both upper and under, should be rolled thin; a thick crust to a fruit pie is undesirable.

RIPE BERRY PIES.

All made the same as Cherry Pie. Line your pie-tin with crust, fill half full of berries, shake over a tablespoonful of sifted flour, (if very juicy), and as much sugar as is necessary to sweeten sufficiently. Now fill up the crust to the top, making quite full. Cover with crust, and bake about forty minutes.

Huckleberry and blackberry pies are improved by putting into them a little ginger and cinnamon.

JELLY AND PRESERVED FRUIT PIES.

Preserved fruit requires no baking; hence, always bake the shell, and put in the sweetmeats afterwards; you can cover with whipped cream, or bake a top crust shell; the former is preferable for delicacy.

CRANBERRY PIE.

Take fine, sound, ripe cranberries, and with a sharp knife split each one until you have a heaping coffee-cupful; put them in a vegetable dish or basin; put over them one cup of white sugar, half a cup of water, a tablespoon *full* of sifted flour; stir it all together and put into your crust. Cover with an upper crust and bake slowly in a moderate oven. You will find this the true way of making a cranberry pie.

—Newport style.

CRANBERRY TART PIE.

After having washed and picked over the berries, stew them well in a little water, just enough to cover them; when they burst open, and become soft, sweeten them with plenty of sugar, mash them smooth (some prefer them not mashed); line your pie-plates with thin puff-paste, fill them, and lay strips of paste across the top. Bake in a moderate oven. Or you may rub them through a colander to free them from the skins.

GOOSEBERRY PIE.

Can be made the same as Cranberry Tart Pie, or an upper crust can be put on before baking. Serve with boiled custard, or a pitcher of good, sweet cream.

STEWED PUMPKIN OR SQUASH FOR PIES.

Deep-colored pumpkins are generally the best. Cut a pumpkin or squash in half, take out the seeds, then cut it up in thick slices, pare the outside and cut again in small pieces. Put it into a large pot or sauce-pan, with a very little water; let it cook slowly until tender. Now set the pot on the back of the stove, where it will not burn, and cook slowly, stirring often until the moisture is dried out and the pumpkin looks dark and red. It requires cooking a long time, at least half a day, to have it dry and rich. When cool, press through a colander.

BAKED PUMPKIN OR SQUASH FOR PIES.

Cut up in several pieces, do not pare it; place them on baking-tins and set them in the oven; bake slowly until soft, then take them out, scrape all the pumpkin from the shell, rub it through a colander. It will be fine and light and free from lumps.

PUMPKIN PIE. No. 1.

For three pies: One quart of milk, three cupfuls of boiled and strained pumpkin, one and one-half cupfuls of sugar, one-half cupful of molasses, the yolks and whites of four eggs beaten separately, a little salt, one tablespoonful each of ginger and cinnamon. Beat all together and bake with an under crust.

Boston marrow or Hubbard squash may be substituted for pumpkin, and are much preferred by many, as possessing a less strong flavor.

PUMPKIN PIE. No. 2.

One quart of stewed pumpkin, pressed through a sieve; nine eggs, whites and yolks beaten separately; two scant quarts of milk, one teaspoonful of mace, one teaspoonful of cinnamon, and the same of nutmeg; one and one-half cupfuls of white sugar, or very light brown. Beat all well together, and bake in crust without cover.

A tablespoonful of brandy is a great improvement to pumpkin or squash pies.

PUMPKIN PIE, WITHOUT EGGS.

One quart of properly stewed pumpkin, pressed through a colander; to this add enough good, rich milk, sufficient to moisten it enough to fill two good-sized earthen pie plates, a teaspoonful of salt, half a cupful of molasses, or brown sugar, a tablespoonful of ginger, one teaspoonful of cinnamon, or nutmeg. Bake in a moderately slow oven three-quarters of an hour.

SQUASH PIE.

One pint of boiled dry squash, one cupful of brown sugar, three eggs, two tablespoonfuls of molasses, one tablespoonful of melted butter, one tablespoonful of ginger, one teaspoonful of cinnamon, a pinch of salt, and one pint of milk. This makes two pies, or one large deep one.

SWEET POTATO PIE.

One pound of steamed sweet potatoes finely mashed, two cups sugar, one cup cream, one-half cup butter, three well-beaten eggs, flavor with lemon or nutmeg, and bake in pastry shell. Fine.

COOKED MEAT FOR MINCE PIES.

In order to succeed in having good mince pie, it is quite essential to cook the meat properly, so as to retain its juices and strength of flavor.

Select four pounds of lean beef, the neck piece is as good as any; wash it, and put it into a kettle with just water enough to cover it; take off the scum as it reaches the boiling point, add hot water from time to time, until it is tender, then season with salt and pepper; take off the cover and let it boil until almost dry, or until the juice has boiled back into the meat. When it looks as though it was beginning to fry in its own juice, it is time to take up, and set aside to get cold, which should be done the day before needed. Next day, when making the mince-meat, the bones, gristle and stringy bits should be well picked out before chopping.

MINCE PIES. No. 1.

The "Astor House," some years ago, was *famous* for its "mince pies." The chief pastry cook at that time, by request, published the recipe. I find that those who partake of it never fail to speak in laudable terms of the superior excellence of this recipe, when strictly followed.

Four pounds of lean boiled beef, chopped fine, twice as much of chopped green tart apples, one pound of chopped suet, three pounds of raisins, seeded, two pounds of currants picked over, washed and dried, half a pound of citron, cut up fine, one pound of brown sugar, one quart of cooking molasses, two quarts of sweet cider, one pint of boiled cider, one tablespoonful of salt, one tablespoonful of pepper, one tablespoonful of mace, one tablespoonful of allspice, and four tablespoonfuls of cinnamon, two grated nutmegs, one tablespoonful of cloves; mix thoroughly and warm it on the range, until heated through. Remove from the fire and when nearly cool, stir in a pint of good brandy, and one pint of Madeira wine. Put into a crock, cover it tightly, and set it in a cold place where it will not freeze, but keep perfectly cold. Will keep good all winter.

—Chef de Cuisine, Astor House, N. Y.

MINCE PIES. No. 2.

Two pounds of lean fresh beef, boiled, and when cold, chopped fine. One pound of beef suet, cleared of strings and minced to powder. Five pounds of apples, pared and chopped; two pounds of raisins, seeded and chopped; one pound of Sultana raisins, washed and picked over. Two pounds of currants, washed and *carefully* picked over. Three-quarters of a pound of citron cut up fine. Two tablespoonfuls cinnamon, one of powdered nutmeg, two of mace, one of cloves, one of allspice, one of fine salt; two and a quarter pounds of brown sugar, one quart brown sherry, one pint best brandy.

Mince-meat made by this recipe will keep all winter. Cover closely in a jar, and set in a cool place.

—Common Sense in the Household.

For preserving mince-meat, look for " Canned Mince-Meat."

MOCK MINCE-MEAT, WITHOUT MEAT.

One cupful of cold water, half a cupful of molasses, half a cupful of brown sugar, half a cupful of cider vinegar, two-thirds of a cupful of melted butter, one cupful of raisins, seeded and chopped, one egg beaten light, half a cupful of rolled cracker-crumbs, a tablespoonful of cinnamon, a teaspoonful each of cloves, allspice, nutmeg, salt, and black pepper.

Put the sauce-pan on the fire with the water and raisins; let them cook a few minutes, then add the sugar and molasses, then the vinegar, then the other ingredients; lastly, add a wine-glassful of brandy. Very fine.

FRUIT TURNOVER. (Suitable for Picnics.)

Make a nice puff-paste; roll it out the usual thickness, as for pies; then cut it out into circular pieces about the size of a small tea saucer; pile the fruit on half of the paste, sprinkle over some sugar, wet the edges, and turn the paste over. Press the edges together, ornament them, and brush the turnovers over with the white of an egg; sprinkle over sifted sugar, and bake on tins, in a brisk oven, for about twenty minutes. Instead of putting the fruit in raw, it may be boiled down with a little sugar first, and then enclosed in the crust; or jam of any kind may be substituted for fresh fruit.

PLUM CUSTARD TARTLETS.

One pint of greengage plums, after being rubbed through a sieve; one large cup of sugar, the yolks of two eggs well beaten. Whisk all together until light and foamy; then bake in small patty-pans shells of puff-paste, a light brown. Then fill with the plum paste, beat the two whites until stiff; add two table-spoonfuls of powdered sugar, spread over the plum paste and set the shells into a moderate oven for a few moments.

These are much more easily handled than pieces of pie or even pies whole, and can be packed nicely for carrying.

LEMON TARTLETS. No. 1.

Put a quart of milk into a sauce-pan over the fire. When it comes to the boiling point, put into it the following mixture: Into a bowl put a heaping tablespoonful of flour, half a cupful of sugar, and a pinch of salt. Stir this all together thoroughly; then add the beaten yolks of six eggs; stir this one way into the boiling milk, until cooked to a thick cream; remove from the fire, and stir into it the grated rind and juice of one large lemon. Have ready baked and hot, some puff-paste tart shells. Fill them with the custard, and cover each with a meringue, made of the whites of the eggs, sweetened with four table-spoonfuls of sugar. Put into the oven and bake a light straw-color.

LEMON TARTLETS. No. 2.

Mix well together the juice and grated rind of two lemons, two cupfuls of sugar, two eggs, and the crumbs of sponge cake; beat it all together until smooth; put into twelve patty-pans lined with puff-paste and bake until the crust is done.

ORANGE TARTLETS.

Take the juice of two large oranges, and the grated peel of one, three-fourths of a cup of sugar, a tablespoonful of butter; stir in a good teaspoonful of corn-starch into the juice of half a lemon. and add to the mixture. Beat all well together, and bake in tart shells without cover.

MERINGUE CUSTARD TARTLETS.

Select deep individual pie-tins; fluted tartlet pans are suitable for custard tarts, but they should be about six inches in diameter and from two to three inches deep. Butter the pan and line it with ordinary puff-paste, then fill it with a custard made as follows: Stir gradually into the beaten yolks of six eggs two tablespoonfuls of flour, a saltspoonful of salt and half a pint of cream. Stir until free from lumps and add two tablespoonfuls of sugar; put the sauce-pan on the range and stir until the custard coats the spoon. Do not let it boil or it will curdle. Pour it in a bowl, add a few drops of vanilla flavoring and stir until the custard becomes cold; fill the lined mold with this and bake in a moderate oven. In the meantime, put the white of the eggs in a bright copper vessel and beat thoroughly, using a baker's wire egg-beater for this purpose. While beating, sprinkle in lightly half a pound of sugar and a dash of salt. When the paste is quite firm, spread a thin layer of it over the tart and decorate the top with the remainder by squeezing it through a paper funnel. Strew a little powdered sugar over the top, return to the oven, and when a delicate yellow tinge remove from the oven, and when cold, serve.

BERRY TARTS.

Line small pie-tins with pie-crust, and bake. Just before ready to use, fill the tarts with strawberries, blackberries, raspberries, or whatever berries are in season. Sprinkle over each tart a little sugar; after adding berries add also to each tart a tablespoonful of sweet cream. They form a delicious addition to the breakfast table.

CREAM STRAWBERRY TARTS.

After picking over the berries carefully, arrange them in layers in a deep pie-tin lined with puff-paste, sprinkling sugar thickly between each layer; fill the pie-tin pretty full, pouring in a quantity of the juice; cover with a thick crust, with a slit in the top, and bake. When the pie is baked, pour into the slit in the top of the pie the following cream mixture: Take a small cupful of the cream from the top of the morning's milk, heat it until it comes to a boil, then stir into it the whites of two eggs beaten light, also a tablespoonful of white sugar and a teaspoonful of corn-starch wet in cold milk. Boil all together a few moments until quite smooth; set it aside, and when cool, pour it into the pie through the slit in the crust. Serve it cold with powdered sugar sifted over it.

Raspberry, blackberry, and whortleberry may be made the same.

GREEN GOOSEBERRY TART.

Top and tail the gooseberries. Put into a porcelain kettle with enough water to prevent burning, and stew slowly until they break. Take them off, sweeten *well*, and set aside to cool. When cold pour into pastry shells, and bake with a top crust of puff-paste. Brush all over with beaten egg while hot, set back in the oven to glaze for three minutes. Eat cold.

—*Common Sense in the Household.*

COCOANUT TARTS.

Take three cocoanuts, the meats grated, the yolks of five eggs, half a cupful of white sugar, season, a wine-glass of milk; put the butter in cold, and bake in a nice puff-paste.

CHOCOLATE TARTS.

Four eggs, whites and yolks; one half cake of Baker's chocolate, grated; one tablespoonful of corn-starch, dissolved in water; three tablespoonfuls of milk, four of white sugar, two teaspoonfuls of vanilla, one saltspoonful of salt, one-half teaspoonful of cinnamon, one teaspoonful of butter, melted; rub the chocolate smooth in the milk, and heat to boiling over the fire, then stir in the corn-starch. Stir five minutes until well thickened, remove from the fire, and pour into a bowl.　Beat all the yolks and the whites of two eggs well with the sugar, and when the chocolate mixture is almost cold, put all together with the flavoring, and stir until light.　Bake in open shells of pastry.　When done, cover with a meringue made of the whites of two eggs and two tablespoonfuls of sugar flavored with a teaspoonful of lemon-juice.　Eat cold.

These are nice for tea, baked in patty-pans.

—Common Sense in the Household.

MAIDS OF HONOR.

Take one cupful of sour milk, one of sweet milk, a tablespoonful of melted butter, the yolk of four eggs, juice and rind of one lemon, and small cupful of white pounded sugar.　Put both kinds of milk together in a vessel, which is set in another, and let it become sufficiently heated to set the curd, then strain off the milk, rub the curd through a strainer, add butter to the curd, the sugar, well-beaten eggs, and lemon.　Line the little pans with the richest of puff-paste, and fill with the mixture; bake until firm in the centre, from ten to fifteen minutes.

GERMAN FRUIT PIE.

Sift together a heaping teaspoonful of baking-powder and a pint of flour; add a piece of butter as large as a walnut, a pinch of salt, one beaten egg, and sweet milk enough to make a soft dough.　Roll it out half an inch thick; butter a square biscuit tin, and cover the bottom and sides with the dough; fill the pan with quartered juicy apples, sprinkle with a little cinnamon and molasses.　Bake in rather quick oven until the crust and apples are cooked a light brown.　Sprinkle a little sugar over the top five minutes before removing from the oven.

Ripe peaches are fine, used in the same manner.

APPLE TARTS.

Pare, quarter, core and boil in half a cupful of water until quite soft, ten large, tart apples; beat until very smooth and add the yolks of six eggs, or three whole ones, the juice and grated outside rind of two lemons, half a cup butter, one and a half of sugar (or more, if not sufficiently sweet); beat all thoroughly, line patty-pans with a puff-paste, and fill; bake five minutes in a hot oven.

Meringue.—If desired very nice, cover them when removed from the oven with a meringue made of the whites of three eggs remaining, mixed with three tablespoonfuls sugar; return to the oven and delicately brown.

CREAM TARTS.

Make a rich, brittle crust, with which cover your patty-pans, smoothing off the edges nicely, and bake well.　While these "shells" are cooling, take one teacupful (more or less according to the number of tarts you want) of perfectly sweet and fresh cream, skimmed free of milk; put this into a large bowl or other deep dish, and with your egg-beater whip it to a thick, stiff froth; add a heaping tablespoonful of fine, white sugar, with a teaspoonful (a small one) of lemon or vanilla. Fill the cold shells with this and set in a cool place till tea is ready.

OPEN JAM TARTS.

Time to bake until paste loosens from the dish. Line shallow tin dish with puff-paste, put in the jam roll out some of the paste, wet it lightly with the yolk of an egg beaten with a little milk, and a tablespoonful of powdered sugar. Cut it in very narrow strips, then lay them across the tart, lay another strip around the edge, trim off outside, and bake in a quick oven.

CHESS CAKES.

Peel and grate one cocoanut; boil one pound of sugar fifteen minutes in two-thirds of a pint of water; stir in the grated cocoanut and boil fifteen minutes longer. While warm, stir in a quarter of a pound of butter; add the yolks of seven eggs well beaten. Bake in patty-pans with rich paste. If prepared cocoanut is used, take one and a half coffee-cupfuls. Fine.

Custards, Creams and Desserts.

The usual rule for custards is, eight eggs to a quart of milk; but a very good custard can be made of six, or even less, especially with the addition of a level tablespoonful of sifted flour, thoroughly blended in the sugar first, before adding the other ingredients. They may be baked, boiled or steamed, either in cups or one large dish. It improves custards to first boil the milk and then cool it before being used; also a little salt adds to the flavor. A very small lump of butter may also be added, if one wants something especially rich.

To make custards look and taste better, duck's eggs should be used when obtainable; they add very much to the flavor and richness, and so many are not required as of ordinary eggs, four duck's eggs to the pint of milk making a delicious custard. When desired extremely rich and good, cream should be substituted for the milk, and double the quantity of eggs used to those mentioned, omitting the whites.

When making boiled custard, set the dish containing the custard into another and larger dish, partly filled with boiling water, placed over the fire. Let the cream or milk come almost to a boil before adding the eggs or thickening, then stir it briskly one way every moment until smooth and well cooked; it must *not* boil or it will curdle.

To bake a custard, the fire should be moderate, and the dish well buttered.

Everything in baked custard depends upon the *regularly heated slow* oven. If made with nicety, it is the most delicate of all sweets; if cooked till it wheys, it is hardly eatable.

Frozen eggs can be made quite as good as fresh ones if used as soon as thawed soft. Drop them into boiling water, letting them remain until the water is cold. They will be soft all through and beat up equal to those that have not been touched with the frost.

Eggs should always be thoroughly well-beaten, separately, the yolks first, then the sugar added, beat again, then add the beaten whites with the flavoring, then the cooled scalded milk. The lighter the eggs are beaten, the thicker and richer the custard.

Eggs should always be broken into a cup, the whites and yolks separated, and they should always be strained. Breaking the eggs thus, the bad ones may be easily rejected without spoiling the others, and so cause no waste.

A meringue, or frosting for the top, requires about a tablespoonful of fine sugar to the beaten white of one egg; to be placed on the top after the custard or pudding is baked; smoothed over with a broad-bladed knife dipped in cold water, and replaced in the oven to brown slightly.

SOFT CARAMEL CUSTARD.

One quart of milk, half a cupful of sugar, six eggs, half a teaspoonful of salt. Put the milk on to boil, reserving a cupful. Beat the eggs and add the cold milk to them. Stir the sugar in a small frying-pan until it becomes liquid and just begins to smoke. Stir it into the boiling milk; then add the beaten eggs and cold milk, and stir constantly until the mixture begins to thicken. Set away to cool. Serve in glasses.

BAKED CUSTARD.

Beat five fresh eggs, the whites and yolks separately, the yolks with half a cup of sugar, the whites to a stiff froth; then stir them gradually into a quart of sweet, rich milk, previously boiled and cooled; flavor with extract of lemon or vanilla, and half a teaspoonful of salt. Rub butter over the bottom and sides of a baking-dish or tin basin; pour in the custard, grate a little nutmeg over, and bake in a quick oven. It is better to set the dish in a shallow pan of hot water, reaching nearly to the top, the water to be kept boiling until the custard is baked; three-quarters of an hour is generally enough. Run a teaspoon handle into the middle of it; if it comes out clean it is baked sufficiently.

CUP CUSTARD.

Six eggs, half a cupful of sugar, one quart of new milk. Beat the eggs, and the sugar and milk, and any extract or flavoring you like. Fill your custard cups, sift a little nutmeg or cinnamon over the tops, set them in a moderate oven in a shallow pan half filled with hot water. In about twenty minutes try them with the handle of a teaspoon to see if they are firm. Judgment and great care are needed to attain skill in baking custard; for if left in the oven a minute too long, or if the fire is too hot, the milk will certainly whey.

Serve cold, with fresh fruit sugared and placed on top of each. Strawberries, peaches or raspberries, as preferred.

BOILED CUSTARD.

Beat seven eggs very light, omitting the whites of two; mix them gradually with a quart of milk and half a cupful of sugar; boil in a dish set into another of boiling water; add flavoring. As soon as it comes to the boiling point, remove it or it will be liable to curdle and become lumpy. Whip the whites of the two eggs that remain, adding two heaping tablespoonfuls of sugar. When the custard is cold, heap this on top; if in cups put on a strawberry, or a bit of red jelly on each. Set in a cold place till wanted.

—Common Sense in the Household.

BOILED CUSTARD, OR MOCK CREAM.

Take two even tablespoonfuls of corn-starch, one quart of milk, three eggs, half a teaspoonful of salt and a small piece of butter; heat the milk to nearly boiling, and add the starch, previously dissolved in a little cold milk; then add the eggs, well beaten, with four tablespoonfuls of powdered sugar; let it boil up once or twice, stirring it briskly, and it is done. Flavor with lemon, or vanilla, or raspberry, or to suit your taste.

A good substitute for ice cream, served *very* cold.

FRENCH CUSTARD.

One quart of milk, eight eggs, sugar and cinnamon to taste; separate the eggs, beat the yolks until thick, to which add the milk, a little vanilla, and sweeten to taste; put it into a pan or farina kettle, place it over a slow fire and stir it all the time until it becomes custard; then pour it into a pudding-dish to get cold; whisk the whites until stiff and dry; have ready a pan of boiling water, on the top of which place the whites; cover and place them where the water will keep sufficiently hot to cause a steam to pass through and cook them; place in a dish (suitable for the table) a layer of custard and white alternately; on each layer of custard grate a little nutmeg with a teaspoonful of wine; reserve a layer of white for the cover, over which grate nutmeg; then send to table, and eat cold.

GERMAN CUSTARD.

Add to a pint of good, rich, boiled custard an ounce of sweet almonds, blanched, roasted, and pounded to a paste, and half an ounce of pine-nuts or peanuts, blanched, roasted and pounded; also a small quantity of candied citron cut into the thinnest possible slips; cook the custard as usual, and set it on the ice for some hours before using.

APPLE CUSTARD.

Pare, core and quarter a dozen large juicy pippins. Stew among them the yellow peel of a large lemon grated very fine; and stew them till tender in a very small portion of water. When done, mash them smooth with the back of a spoon (you must have a pint and a half of the stewed apple); mix a half-cupful of sugar with them, and set them away till cold. Beat six eggs very light, and stir them gradually into a quart of rich milk, alternately with the stewed apple. Put the mixture into cups, or into a deep dish, and bake it about twenty minutes. Send it to table cold, with nutmeg grated over the top.

ALMOND CUSTARD. No. 1.

Scald and blanch half a pound of shelled sweet almonds, and three ounces of bitter almonds, throwing them, as you do them, into a large bowl of cold water. Then pound them, one at a time, into a paste, adding a few drops of wine or rose-water to them. Beat eight eggs very light, with two-thirds of a cup of sugar, then mix altogether with a quart of rich milk, or part milk and part cream; put the mixture into a sauce-pan and set it over the fire. Stir it one way until it begins to thicken, but not till it curdles; remove from the fire, and when it is cooled, put in a glass dish. Having reserved part of the whites of the eggs, beat them to a stiff froth, season with three tablespoonfuls of sugar, and a teaspoonful of lemon extract; spread over the top of the custard. Serve cold.

ALMOND CUSTARD. No. 2.

Blanch a quarter of a pound of sweet almonds, pound them as in No. 1 above, with six ounces of fine white sugar, and mix them well with the yolks of four eggs; then dissolve one ounce of patent gelatine in one quart of boiling milk, strain it through a sieve, and pour into it the other mixture; stir the whole over the fire until it thickens and is smooth; then pour it into your mold, and keep it upon ice, or in a cool place, until wanted; when ready to serve, dip the mold into warm water, rub it with a cloth, and turn out the cream carefully upon your dish.

SNOWBALL CUSTARD.

Soak half a package of Coxe's gelatine in a teacupful of cold water one hour, to which add a pint of boiling water, stir it until the gelatine is thoroughly dissolved. Then beat the whites of four eggs to a stiff froth, put two teacupfuls of sugar in the gelatine water first, then the beaten whites of egg, and one teaspoonful of vanilla extract, or the grated rind and the juice of a lemon. Whip it some time until it is all quite stiff and cold. Dip some teacups or wine-glasses in cold water and fill them; set in a cold place.

In the meantime, make a boiled custard of the yolks of three of the eggs, with half of a cupful of sugar, and a pint of milk; flavor with vanilla extract. Now after the meringue in the cups has stood four or five hours, turn them out of the molds, place them in a glass dish, and pour this custard around the base.

BAKED COCOANUT CUSTARD.

Grate as much cocoanut as will weigh a pound. Mix half a pound of powdered white sugar with the milk of the cocoanut, or with a pint of cream, adding two tablespoonfuls of rose water. Then stir in gradually a pint of rich milk. Beat to a stiff froth the whites of eight eggs, and stir them into the milk and sugar, a little at a time, alternately with the grated cocoanut; add a teaspoonful of powdered nutmeg and cinnamon. Then put the mixture into cups, and bake them twenty minutes in a moderate oven, set in a pan half filled with boiling water. When cold, grate loaf sugar over them.

WHIPPED CREAM. No. 1.

To the whites of three eggs beaten to a stiff froth, add a pint of thick, sweet cream (previously set where it is very cold), and four tablespoonfuls of sweet wine, with three of fine white sugar, and a teaspoonful of the extract of lemon or vanilla. Mix all the ingredients together on a broad platter or pan, and whip it to a standing froth; as the froth rises, take it off lightly with a spoon, and lay it on an inverted sieve with a dish under it to catch what will drain through; and what drains through can be beaten over again.

Serve in a glass dish with jelly or jam, and sliced sponge cake. This should be whipped in a cool place, and set in the ice-box.

WHIPPED CREAM. No. 2.

Three coffee-cupfuls of good thick sweet cream, half of a cup of powdered sugar, three teaspoonfuls of vanilla; whip it to a stiff froth. Dissolve three-fourths of an ounce of best gelatine in a teacup of hot water, and when cool pour it in the cream and stir it gently from the bottom upward, cutting the cream into it, until it thickens. The dish which contains the cream should be set in another dish containing ice water, or cracked ice. When finished, pour in molds and set on ice or in a very cold place.

SPANISH CREAM.

Take one quart of milk and soak half a box of gelatine in it for an hour; place it on the fire and stir often. Beat the yolks of three eggs very light with a cupful of sugar, stir into the scalding milk, and heat until it begins to thicken, (it should not boil, or it will curdle); remove from the fire, and strain through thin muslin or tarletan, and when nearly cold, flavor with vanilla or lemon; then wet a dish or mold in cold water and set aside to stiffen.

BAVARIAN CREAM.

One quart of sweet cream, the yolks of four eggs, beaten together with a cupful of sugar. Dissolve half an ounce of gelatine or isinglass in half a teacup-ful of warm water; when it is dissolved, stir in a pint of boiling hot cream; add the beaten yolks and sugar; cook all together until it begins to thicken, then remove from the fire and add the other pint of cold cream, whipped to a stiff froth; adding a little at a time, and beating hard. Season with vanilla or lemon. Whip the whites of the eggs for the top. Dip the mold in cold water before filling; set it in a cold place. To this could be added almonds, pounded; grated chocolate, peaches, pineapples, strawberries, raspberries or any seasonable fruit.

STRAWBERRY BAVARIAN CREAM.

Pick off the hulls of a box of strawberries, bruise them in a basin with a cup of powdered sugar; rub this through a sieve, and mix with it a pint of whipped cream and one ounce and a half of clarified isinglass or gelatine; pour the cream into a mold, previously oiled. Set it in rough ice, and when it has become firm turn out on a dish

Raspberries or currants may be substituted for strawberries.

GOLDEN CREAM.

Boil a quart of milk; when boiling, stir into it the well-beaten yolks of six eggs; add six tablespoonfuls of sugar and one tablespoonful of sifted flour, which have been well-beaten together; when boiled, turn it into a dish, and pour over it the whites beaten to a stiff froth, mixing with them six tablespoonfuls of powdered sugar. Set all in the oven, and brown slightly. Flavor the top with vanilla, and the bottom with lemon. Serve cold.

CHOCOLATE CREAM. No. 1.

Three ounces of grated chocolate, one-quarter pound of sugar, one and one-half pints of cream, one and one-half ounces of clarified isinglass, or gelatine, the yolks of six eggs.

Beat the yolks of the eggs well; put them into a basin with the grated chocolate, the sugar, and one pint of the cream; stir these ingredients well together, pour them into a basin, and set this basin in a sauce-pan of boiling water; stir it one way until the mixture thickens, but *do not allow it to boil,* or it will curdle. Strain the cream through a sieve into a basin, stir in the isinglass and the other one-half pint of cream, which should be well whipped; mix all well together, and pour it into a mold which has been previously oiled with the purest salad-oil, and, if at hand, set it in ice until wanted for table.

CHOCOLATE CREAM OR CUSTARD. No. 2.

Take one quart of milk, and when nearly boiling stir in two ounces of grated chocolate; let it warm on the fire for a few moments, and then remove and cool; beat the yolks of eight eggs and two whites with eight tablespoonfuls of sugar, then pour the milk over them; flavor and bake as any custard, either in cups or a large dish. Make a meringue of the remaining whites.

LEMON CREAM. No. 1.

One pint of cream, the yolks of two eggs, one quarter of a pound of white sugar, one large lemon, one ounce isinglass or gelatine.

Put the cream into a *lined* sauce-pan, with the sugar, lemon-peel, and isinglass, and simmer these over a gentle fire for about ten minutes, stirring them all the time. Strain the cream into a basin add the yolks of eggs, which should be well-beaten, and put the basin into a sauce-pan of boiling water; stir the mixture one way until it thickens, *but do not allow it to boil;* take it off the fire, and keep stirring it until nearly cold. Strain the lemon-juice into a basin, gradually pour on it the cream, and *stir it well* until the juice is well mixed with it. Have ready a well-oiled mold, pour the cream into it, and let it remain until perfectly set. When required for table, loosen the edges with a small blunt knife, put a dish on the top of the mold, turn it over quickly, and the cream should easily slip away.

LEMON CREAM. No. 2.

Pare into one quart of boiling water the peels of four large lemons, the yellow outside only; let it stand for four hours; then take them out and add to the water the juice of the four lemons, and one cupful of white, fine sugar. Beat the yolks of ten eggs, and mix all together; strain it through a piece of lawn or lace into a porcelain lined stew-pan; set it over a slow fire; stir it one way until it is as thick as good cream, *but do not let it boil;* then take it from the fire, and when cool, serve in custard cups.

LEMON CREAM. No. 3.

Peel three lemons, and squeeze out the juice into one quart of milk. Add the peel; cut in pieces and cover the mixture for a few hours; then add six eggs, well-beaten, and one pint of water, well-sweetened. Strain and simmer over a gentle fire till it thickens; *do not let it boil.* Serve very cold.

ORANGE CREAM.

Whip a pint of cream so long that there will be but one-half the quantity left when skimmed off. Soak in half a cupful of cold water a half package of gelatine, and then grate over it the rind of two oranges. Strain the juice of six oranges, and add to it a cupful of sugar; now put the half pint of unwhipped cream into a double boiler, pour into it the well-beaten yolks of six eggs, stirring until it begins to thicken, then add the gelatine. Remove from the fire, let it stand for two minutes and add the orange juice and sugar; beat all together until about the consistency of soft custard, and add the whipped cream. Mix well, and turn into moulds to harden. To be served with sweetened cream. Fine.

SOLID CREAM.

Four tablespoonfuls of pounded sugar, one quart of cream, two tablespoonfuls of brandy, the juice of one large lemon.

Strain the lemon-juice over the sugar, and add the brandy, then stir in the cream, put the mixture into a pitcher and continue pouring from one pitcher to another, until it is quite thick, or it may be whisked until the desired consistency is obtained. It should be served in jelly-glasses.

BANANA CREAM.

After peeling the bananas, mash them with an iron or wooden spoon; allow equal quantities of bananas and sweet cream; to one quart of the mixture, allow one-quarter of a pound of sugar. Beat them all together until the cream is light.

TAPIOCA CREAM CUSTARD.

Soak three heaping tablespoonfuls of tapioca in a teacupful of water over night. Place over the fire a quart of milk; let it come to a boil, then stir in the tapioca; a good pinch of salt; stir until it thickens; then add a cupful of sugar, and the beaten yolks of three eggs. Stir it quickly and pour it into a dish and stir gently into the mixture the whites beaten stiff, the flavoring, and set it on ice, or in an ice-chest.

PEACH CREAM. No. 1.

Mash very smooth two cupfuls of canned peaches, rub them through a sieve, and cook for three minutes in a syrup made by boiling together one cupful of sugar, and stirring all the time. Place the pan containing the syrup and peaches into another of boiling water and add one-half packet of gelatine, prepared the same as in previous recipes, and stir for five minutes to thoroughly dissolve the gelatine; then take it from the fire, place in a pan of ice-water, beat until nearly cool, and then add the well-frothed whites of six eggs. Beat this whole mixture until it commences to harden. Then pour into a mould, set away to cool, and serve with cream and sugar. It should be placed on the ice to cool for two or three hours before serving.

PEACH CREAM. No. 2.

A quart of fine peacnes, pare and stone the fruit and cut in quarters. Beat the whites of three eggs with a half cupful of powdered sugar until it is stiff enough to cut with a knife. Take the yolks and mix with half a cupful of granulated sugar and a pint of milk. Put the peaches into the mixture, place in a pudding-dish and bake until almost firm; then put in the whites, mixing all thoroughly again, and bake a light brown. Eat ice-cold.

ITALIAN CREAM.

Put two pints of cream into two bowls; with one bowl mix six ounces of powdered loaf sugar, the juice of two large lemons and two glassfuls of white wine; then add the other pint of cream, and stir the whole very hard; boil two ounces of isinglass or gelatine with four small teacupfuls of water till reduced to one-half; then stir the mixture lukewarm into the other ingredients; put them in a glass dish to congeal.

SNOW CREAM.

Heat a quart of thick, sweet cream; when ready to boil, stir into it quickly three tablespoonfuls of corn-starch flour, blended with some cold cream; sweeten to taste, and allow it to boil gently, stirring for two or three minutes; add quickly the whites of six eggs, beaten to a stiff froth; do not allow it to boil up more than once after adding the egg; flavor with lemon, vanilla, bitter almond or grated lemon peel; lay the snow thus formed quickly in rocky heaps on silver or glass dishes, or in shapes. Iced, it will turn out well.

If the recipe is closely followed, any family may enjoy it at a trifling expense, and it is really worthy the table of an epicure. It can be made the day before it is to be eaten; kept cold.

MOCK ICE.

Take about three tablespoonfuls of some good preserve; rub it through a sieve with as much cream as will fill a quart mould; dissolve three-quarters of an ounce of isinglass or gelatine in half a pint of water; when almost cold, mix it well with the cream; put it into a mold; set it in a cool place, and turn out next day.

PEACH MERINGUE.

Pare and quarter (removing stones) a quart of sound, ripe peaches; place them all in a dish that it will not injure to set in the oven, and yet be suitable to place on the table. Sprinkle the peaches with sugar, and cover them well with the beaten whites of three eggs. Stand the dish in the oven, until the eggs have become a delicate brown, then remove, and, when cool enough, set the dish on ice, or in a very cool place. Take the yolks of the eggs, add to them a pint of milk, sweeten and flavor, and boil same in a custard kettle, being careful to keep the eggs from curdling. When cool, pour into a glass pitcher and serve with the meringue when ready to use.

APPLE FLOAT.

One dozen apples, pared and cored, one pound and a half of sugar. Put the apples on with water enough to cover them, and let them stew until they look as if they would break; then take them out and put the sugar into the same water; let the syrup come to a boil; put in the apples, and let them stew until done through and clear; then take them out, slice into the syrup one large lemon, and add an ounce of gelatine dissolved in a pint of cold water. Let the whole mix well and come to a boil; then pour upon the apples. The syrup will congeal. It is to be eaten cold with cream.

Or you may change the dish by making a soft custard with the yolk of four eggs, three tablespoonfuls of powdered sugar, and a scant quart of milk. When cold, spread it over the apples. Whip the whites of the eggs, flavor with lemon, and place on the custard. Color in the oven.

SYLLABUB.

One quart of rich milk or cream, a cupful of wine, half a cupful of sugar; put the sugar and wine into a bowl, and the milk lukewarm in a separate vessel. When the sugar is dissolved in the wine, pour the milk in, holding it high; pour it back and forth until it is frothy. Grate nutmeg over it.

CREAM FOR FRUIT.

This recipe is an excellent substitute for pure cream, to be eaten on fresh berries and fruit.

One cupful of sweet milk; heat it until boiling. Beat together the whites of two eggs, a tablespoonful of white sugar, and a piece of butter the size of a nutmeg. Now add half a cupful of cold milk and a teaspoonful of corn-starch; stir well together until very light and smooth, then add it to the boiling milk; cook it until it thickens; it must not boil. Set it aside to cool. It should be of the consistence of real fresh cream. Serve in a creamer.

STRAWBERRY SPONGE.

One quart of strawberries, half a package of gelatine, one cupful and a half of water, one cupful of sugar, the juice of a lemon, the whites of four eggs. Soak the gelatine for two hours in half a cupful of the water. Mash the strawberries, and add half the sugar to them. Boil the remainder of the sugar and the water gently twenty minutes. Rub the strawberries through a sieve. Add the gelatine to the boiling syrup and take from the fire immediately; then add the strawberries. Place in a pan of ice water, and beat five minutes. Add the whites of eggs, and beat until the mixture begins to thicken. Pour in the molds and set away to harden. Serve with sugar and cream. Raspberry and black-berry sponges are made in the same way.

LEMON SPONGE.

Lemon sponge is made from the juice of four lemons, four eggs, a cupful of sugar, half a package of gelatine, and one pint of water. Strain lemon juice on the sugar; beat the yolks of the eggs, and mix with the remainder of the water, having used a half cupful of the pint in which to soak the gelatine. Add the sugar and lemon to this and cook until it begins to thicken, then add the gelatine. Strain this into a basin, which place in a pan of water to cool. Beat with a whisk until it has cooled but not hardened; now add the white of the eggs until it begins to thicken, turn into a mold and set to harden.

Remember, the sponge 'hardens very rapidly when it commences to cool, so have your molds all ready. Serve with powdered sugar and cream.

APPLE SNOW.

Stew some fine-flavored sour apples tender, sweeten to taste, strain them through a fine wire sieve, and break into one pint of strained apples the white of an egg; whisk the apple and egg very briskly till quite stiff, and it will be as white as snow; eaten with a nice boiled custard it makes a very desirable dessert. More eggs may be used, if liked.

QUINCE SNOW.

Quarter five fair-looking quinces, and boil them till they are tender in water, then peel them and push them through a coarse sieve. Sweeten to the taste and add the whites of three or four eggs. Then with an egg-whisk beat all to a stiff froth and pile with a spoon upon a glass dish and set away in the ice-box, unless it is to be served immediately.

ORANGE TRIFLE.

Take the thin parings from the outside of a dozen oranges and put to steep in a wide-mouthed bottle; cover it with good cognac, and let it stand twenty-four hours; skin and seed the oranges, and reduce to a pulp; press this through a sieve, sugar to taste, arrange in a dish, and heap with whipped cream flavored with the orange brandy; ice two hours before serving.

LEMON TRIFLE.

The juice of two lemons and grated peel of one, one pint of cream, well-sweetened and whipped stiff, one cupful of sherry, a little nutmeg. Let sugar, lemon-juice, and peel lie together two hours before you add wine and nutmeg. Strain through double tarlatan, and whip gradually into the frothed cream. Serve very soon heaped in small glasses. Nice with cake.

FRUIT TRIFLE.

Whites of four eggs beaten to a stiff froth, two tablespoonfuls each of sugar, currant jelly and raspberry jam. Eaten with sponge cakes, it is a delicious dessert.

GRAPE TRIFLE.

Pulp through a sieve two pounds of ripe grapes, enough to keep back the stones, add sugar to taste. Put into a trifle dish, and cover with whipped cream, nicely flavored. Serve very cold.

APPLE TRIFLE.

Peel, core and quarter some good tart apples of nice flavor, and stew them with a strip of orange and a strip of quince-peel, sufficient water to cover the bottom of the stew-pan, and sugar in the proportion of half a pound to one pound of fruit; when cooked, press the pulp through a sieve; and when cold, dish, and cover with one pint of whipped cream, flavored with lemon-peel.

Quinces prepared in the same manner are equally as good.

PEACH TRIFLE.

Select perfect, fresh peaches, peel and core and cut in quarters; they should be *well sugared*, arranged in a trifle dish with a few of their own blanched kernels among them, then heaped with whipped cream as above; the cream should not be flavored; this trifle should be set on the ice for at least an hour before serving; home-made sponge cakes should be served with it.

GOOSEBERRY TRIFLE.

One quart of gooseberries, sugar to taste, one pint of custard, a plateful of whipped cream.

Put the gooseberries into a jar, with sufficient moist sugar to sweeten them, and boil them until reduced to a pulp. Put this pulp at the bottom of a trifle dish; pour over it a pint of custard, and, when cold, cover with whipped cream. The cream should be whipped the day before it is wanted for table, as it will then be so much firmer and more solid. This dish may be garnished as fancy dictates.

LEMON HONEY.

One coffee-cupful of white sugar, the grated rind and juice of one large lemon, the yolk of three eggs, and the white of one, a tablespoonful of butter. Put into a basin the sugar and butter, set it in a dish of boiling water over the fire; while this is melting, beat up the eggs, and add to them the grated rind from the outside of the lemon; then add this to the sugar and butter, cooking and stirring it until it is thick and clear like honey.

This will keep for some days, put into a tight preserve jar, and is nice for flavoring pies, etc.

FLOATING ISLANDS.

Beat the yolks of five eggs and the whites of two very light; sweeten with five tablespoonfuls of sugar and flavor to taste; stir them into a quart of scalded milk and cook it until it thickens. When cool, pour it into a glass dish. Now whip the whites of the three remaining eggs to a *stiff* froth; adding three table-spoonfuls of sugar, and a little flavoring. Pour this froth over a shallow dish of boiling water; the steam passing through it cooks it; when sufficiently cooked, take a tablespoon and drop spoonfuls of this over the top of the custard, far enough apart so that the "little white islands" will not touch each other. By dropping a teaspoonful of bright jelly on the top or centre of each island, is produced a pleasing effect; also by filling wine-glasses and arranging them around a standard adds much to the appearance of the table.

FLOATING ISLAND.

One quart of milk, five eggs, and five tablespoonfuls of sugar. Scald the milk, then add the beaten yolks and one of the whites together with the sugar. First stir into them a little of the scalded milk to prevent curdling, then all of the milk. Cook it the proper thickness; remove from the fire, and when cool, flavor; then pour it into a glass dish and let it become very cold. Before it is served, beat up the remaining four whites of the eggs to a *stiff* froth, and beat into them three tablespoonfuls of sugar and two tablespoonfuls of currant jelly. Dip this over the top of the custard.

TAPIOCA BLANC MANGE.

Half a pound of tapioca, soaked an hour in one pint of milk, and boiled till tender; add a pinch of salt, sweeten to taste, and put into a mold; when cold, turn it out, and serve with strawberry or raspberry jam around it and a little cream. Flavor with lemon or vanilla.

BLANC MANGE. No. 1.

In one teacupful of water boil until dissolved one ounce of clarified isinglass, or of patent gelatine, (which is better); stir it continually while boiling. Then squeeze the juice of a lemon upon a cupful of fine, white sugar; stir the sugar into a quart of rich cream, and half a pint of Madeira or Sherry wine; when it is well mixed, add the dissolved isinglass or gelatine, stir all well together, pour it into molds previously wet with cold water; set the molds upon ice, let them stand until their contents are hard and cold, then serve with sugar and cream or custard sauce.

BLANC MANGE. No. 2.

Dissolve two ounces of patent gelatine in cold water; when it is dissolved, stir it into two quarts of rich milk, with a teacupful of fine white sugar; season it to your taste with lemon, or vanilla, or peach water; place it over the fire and boil it, stirring it continually; let it boil five minutes; then strain it through a cloth, pour it into molds previously wet with cold water, and salt; let it stand on ice, or in any cool place, until it becomes hard and cold; turn it out carefully upon dishes and serve; or, half fill your mold; when this has set, cover with cherries, peaches in halves, strawberries or sliced bananas, and add the remainder.

CHOCOLATE BLANC MANGE.

Half a box of gelatine soaked in a cupful of water for an hour, half a cupful of grated chocolate, rubbed smooth in a little milk. Boil two cupfuls of milk, then add the gelatine and chocolate, and one cupful of sugar; boil all together eight or ten minutes. Remove from the fire, and when nearly cold beat into this the whipped whites of three eggs, flavored with vanilla. Should be served cold with custard made of the yolks, or sugar and cream. Set the molds in a cold place.

CORN-STARCH BLANC MANGE.

Take one quart of sweet milk, and put one pint upon the stove to heat; in the other pint mix four heaping tablespoonfuls of corn-starch and half a cupful of sugar; when the milk is hot, pour in the cold milk with the corn-starch and sugar thoroughly mixed in it, and stir all together until there are no lumps and it is thick; flavor with lemon; take from the stove, and add the whites of three eggs beaten to a stiff froth.

A Custard for the above.—One pint of milk boiled with a little salt in it; beat the yolks of three eggs with half a cupful of sugar, and add to the boiling milk; stir well, but do not let it boil until the eggs are put in; flavor to taste.

FRUIT BLANC MANGE.

Stew nice, fresh fruit (cherries, raspberries, and strawberries being the best), or canned ones will do; strain off the juice, and sweeten to taste; place it over the fire in a double kettle until it boils; while boiling, stir in corn-starch wet with a little cold water, allowing two tablespoonfuls of corn-starch to each pint of juice; continue stirring until sufficiently cooked; then pour into molds wet in cold water, and set away to cool. Served with cream and sugar.

ORANGE CHARLOTTE.

For two molds of medium size, soak half a box of gelatine in half a cupful of water for two hours. Add one and a half cupful of boiling water, and strain. Then add two cupfuls of sugar, one of orange juice and pulp, and the juice of one lemon. Stir until the mixture begins to cool, or about five minutes; then add the whites of six eggs, beaten to a stiff froth. Beat the whole until so stiff that it will only just pour into molds lined with sections of orange. Set away to cool.

STRAWBERRY CHARLOTTE.

Make a boiled custard of one quart of milk, the yolks of six eggs, and three-quarters of a cupful of sugar; flavor to taste. Line a glass fruit dish with slices of sponge cake, dipped in sweet cream; lay upon this ripe strawberries sweetened to taste; then a layer of cake and strawberries as before. When the custard is cold, pour over the whole. Now beat the whites of the eggs to a stiff froth, add a tablespoonful of sugar to each egg, and put over the top. Decorate the top with the largest berries saved out at the commencement.

Raspberry Charlotte may be made the same way.

CHARLOTTE RUSSE. (Fine.)

Whip one quart of rich cream to a stiff froth, and drain well on a nice sieve. To one scant pint of milk add six eggs beaten very light; make very sweet; flavor high with vanilla. Cook over hot water till it is a thick custard. Soak one full ounce of Cox's gelatine in a very little water, and warm over hot water. When the custard is very cold, beat in lightly the gelatine and the whipped cream. Line the bottom of your mold with buttered paper, the side with sponge cake or lady-fingers fastened together with the white of an egg. Fill with the cream, put in a cold place, or in summer on ice. To turn out, dip the mold for a moment in hot water. In draining the whipped cream, all that drips through can be re-whipped.

CHARLOTTE RUSSE.

Cut stale sponge cake into slices about half an inch thick and line three molds with them, leaving a space of half an inch between each slice; set the molds where they will not be disturbed until the filling is ready. Take a deep tin pan and fill about one-third full of either snow or pounded ice, and into this set another pan that will hold at least four quarts. Into a deep bowl or pail (a whip churn is better) put one and a half pints of cream (if the cream is very thick take one pint of cream and a half pint of milk); whip it to a froth, and when the bowl is full, skim the froth into the pan which is standing on the ice, and repeat this until the cream is all froth; then with a spoon draw the froth to one side, and you will find that some of the cream has gone back to milk; turn this into the bowl again, and whip as before; when the cream is all whipped, stir into it two-thirds of a cup of powdered sugar, one teaspoonful of vanilla and half of a box of gelatine, which has been soaked in cold water enough to cover it for one hour, and then dissolved in boiling water enough to dissolve it (about half a cup); stir from the bottom of the pan until it begins to grow stiff; fill the molds and set them on ice in the pan for one hour, or until they are sent to the table. When ready to dish them, loosen lightly at the sides and turn out on a flat dish. Have the cream ice-cold when you begin to whip it; and it is a good plan to put a lump of ice into the cream while whipping it.

—Maria Parloa.

ANOTHER CHARLOTTE RUSSE.

Two tablespoonfuls of gelatine soaked in a little cold milk two hours; two coffeecupfuls of rich cream; one teacupful of milk. Whip the cream stiff in a large bowl or dish; set on ice. Boil the milk and pour gradually over the gelatine until dissolved, then strain; when nearly cold, add the whipped cream, a spoonful at a time. Sweeten with powdered sugar, flavor with extract of vanilla. Line a dish with lady-fingers or sponge cake; pour in cream, and set in a cool place to harden. This is about the same recipe as M. Parloa's, but is not as explicit in detail.

PLAIN CHARLOTTE RUSSE.

Make a rule of white sponge cake; bake in narrow, shallow pans. Then make a custard of the yolks, after this recipe. Wet a sauce-pan with cold water to prevent the milk that will be scalded in it from burning. Pour out the water and put in a quart of milk; boil and partly cool. Beat up the yolks of six eggs, and add three ounces of sugar and a saltspoonful of salt; mix thoroughly and add the luke-warm milk. Stir and pour the custard into a porcelain or double sauce-pan, and stir while on the range until of the consistency of cream; do not allow it to boil, as that would curdle it; strain, and when almost cold, add two teaspoonfuls of vanilla. Now having arranged your cake (cut into inch slices) around the sides and on the bottom of a glass dish, pour over the custard. If you wish a meringue on the top, beat up the whites of four eggs with four table-spoonfuls of sugar; flavor with lemon or vanilla, spread over the top, and brown slightly in the oven.

PLAIN CHARLOTTE RUSSE. No. 2.

Put some thin slices of sponge cake in the bottom of a glass sauce-dish; pour in wine enough to soak it; beat up the whites of three eggs until very light; add to it three tablespoonfuls of finely powdered sugar, a glass of sweet wine, and one pint of thick, sweet cream; beat it well, and pour over the cake. Set it in a cold place until served.

NAPLE BISCUITS, OR CHARLOTTE RUSSE.

Make a double rule of sponge cake; bake it in round, deep patty-pans; when cold, cut out the inside about one quarter of an inch from the edge and bottom, leaving the shell. Replace the inside with a custard made of the yolks of four eggs, beaten with a pint of boiling milk, sweetened and flavored; lay on the top of this some jelly or jam; beat the whites of three eggs with three heaping tablespoonfuls of powdered sugar until it will stand in a heap; flavor it a little; place this on the jelly. Set them aside in a cold place until time to serve.

ECONOMICAL CHARLOTTE RUSSE.

Make a quart of nicely flavored mock custard, put it into a large glass fruit dish, which is partly filled with stale cake (of any kind) cut up into small pieces about an inch square, stir it a little, then beat the whites of two or more eggs stiff, sweetened with white sugar; spread over the top, set in a refrigerator to become cold.

Or, to be still more economical: To make the cream, take a pint and a half of milk, set it on the stove to boil; mix together in a bowl the following named articles: large half cup of sugar, one moderately heaped teaspoonful of corn-starch, two tablespoonfuls of grated chocolate, one egg, a small half cup of milk and a pinch of salt. Pour into the boiling milk, remove to top of the stove and let simmer a minute or two. When the cream is cold pour over the cake just before setting it on the table. Serve in saucers. If you do not have plenty of eggs you can use all corn-starch, about two heaping teaspoonfuls; but be careful and not get the cream too thick, and have it free from lumps.

The cream should be flavored, either with vanilla or lemon extract. Nutmeg might answer.

TIPSY CHARLOTTE.

Take a stale sponge cake, cut the bottom and sides of it, so as to make it stand even in a glass fruit dish; make a few deep gashes through it with a sharp knife, pour over it a pint of good wine, let it stand and soak into the cake. In the meantime, blanch, peel and slice lengthwise half a pound of sweet almonds; stick them all over the top of the cake. Have ready a pint of good boiled custard, well flavored, and pour over the whole. To be dished with a spoon. This is equally as good as any Charlotte.

ORANGE CHARLOTTE.

One-third of a box of gelatine, one-third of a cupful of cold water, one-third of a cupful of boiling water, and one cup of sugar, the juice of one lemon, and one cupful of orange-juice and pulp, a little grated orange-peel and the whites of four eggs. Soak the gelatine in the cold water one hour. Pour the boiling water over the lemon and orange juice, cover it and let stand half an hour; then add the sugar, let it come to a boil on the fire, stir in the gelatine, and when it is thoroughly dissolved, take from the fire. When cool enough, beat into it the four beaten whites of egg, turn into the mold and set in a cold place to stiffen, first placing pieces of sponge cake all around the mold.

BURNT ALMOND CHARLOTTE.

One cupful of sweet almonds, blanched and chopped fine, half a box of gelatine soaked two hours in half a cupful of cold water; when the gelatine is sufficiently soaked, put three tablespoonfuls of sugar into a sauce-pan over the fire and stir until it becomes liquid and looks dark; then add the chopped almonds to it, and stir two minutes more; turn it out on a platter and set aside to get cool. After they become cool enough, break them up in a mortar, put them in a cup and a half of milk, and cook again for ten minutes. Now beat together the yolk of two eggs with a cupful of sugar, and add to the cooking mixture; add also the gelatine; stir until smooth and well dissolved; take from the fire and set in a basin of ice-water and beat it until it begins to thicken; then add to that two quarts of whipped cream, and turn the whole carefully into molds, set away on the ice to become firm. Sponge cake can be placed around the mold or not, as desired.

CHARLOTTE RUSSE, WITH PINEAPPLE.

Peel and cut a pineapple in slices, put the slices into a stew-pan with half a pound of fine white sugar, half an ounce of isinglass, or of patent gelatine, (which is better), and half a teacupful of water; stew it until it is quite tender, then rub it through a sieve, place it upon ice, and stir it well; when it is upon the point of setting, add a pint of cream well whipped, mix it well, and pour it into a mold lined with sponge cake, or prepared in any other way you prefer.

Mrs. JAMES K. POLK.

Mrs. ABIGAIL FILLMORE.

Mrs. ABRAHAM LINCOLN.

HARRIET LANE JOHNSTON.

Mrs. FRANKLIN PIERCE.

PHOTO-ELECTROTYPE ENG CO N.Y.

COUNTRY PLUM CHARLOTTE.

Stone a quart of ripe plums; first stew, and then sweeten them. Cut slices of bread and butter, and lay them in the bottom and around the sides of a large bowl or deep dish. Pour in the plums boiling hot, cover the bowl, and set it away to cool gradually. When quite cold, send it to table, and eat it with cream.

VELVET CREAM, WITH STRAWBERRIES.

Dissolve half an ounce of gelatine in a gill of water; add to it half a pint of light sherry, grated lemon-peel and the juice of one lemon and five ounces of sugar. Stir over the fire until the sugar is thoroughly dissolved. Then strain and cool. Before it sets beat into it a pint of cream; pour into molds and keep on ice until wanted. Half fill the small molds with fine strawberries, pour the mixture on top, and place on ice until wanted.

CORN-STARCH MERINGUE.

Heat a quart of milk until it boils, add four heaping teaspoonfuls of corn-starch which has previously been dissolved in a little cold milk. Stir constantly while boiling, for fifteen minutes. Remove from the fire, and gradually add while hot the yolks of five eggs, beaten together with three-fourths of a cupful of sugar, and flavored with lemon, vanilla or bitter almond. Bake this mixture for fifteen minutes in a well-buttered pudding-dish or until it begins to "set."

Make a meringue of the whites of five eggs, whipped stiff with a half cupful of jelly, and spread evenly over the custard, without removing the same farther than the edge of the oven.

Use currant jelly if vanilla is used in the custard, crab-apple for bitter almond, and strawberry for lemon. Cover and bake for five minutes, after which take off the lid and brown the meringue a very little. Sift powdered sugar thickly over the top. To be eaten cold.

WASHINGTON PIE.

This recipe is the same as "Boston Cream Pie," (adding half an ounce of butter,) which may be found under the head of "Pastry, Pies and Tarts." In summer time, it is a good plan to bake the pie the day before wanted; then when cool, wrap around it a paper and place it in the ice-box so as to have it get *very cold;* then serve it with a dish of fresh strawberries, or raspberries. A delicious dessert.

CREAM PIE. No. 2.

Make two cakes as for Washington pie, then take one cup of sweet cream and three tablespoonfuls of white sugar. Beat with egg-beater or fork till it is stiff enough to put on without running off, and flavor with vanilla.   If you beat it after it is stiff it will come to butter.   Put between the cakes and on top.

DESSERT PUFFS.

Puffs for dessert are delicate and nice; take one pint of milk and cream each, the white of four eggs beaten to a stiff froth, one heaping cupful of sifted flour, one scant cupful of powdered sugar, add a little grated lemon-peel, and a little salt; beat these all together till very light, bake in gem-pans, sift pulverized sugar over them, and eat with sauce flavored with lemon.

PEACH CAKE FOR DESSERT.

Bake three sheets of sponge-cake, as for jelly-cake; cut nice ripe peaches in thin slices, or chop them; prepare cream by whipping, sweetening and adding flavor of vanilla, if desired; put layers of peaches between the sheets of cake; pour cream over each layer and over the top.   To be eaten soon after it is prepared.

FRUIT SHORT-CAKES.

For the recipes of strawberry, peach and other fruit short-cakes, look under the head of "Biscuits, Rolls and Muffins."   They all make a very delicious dessert when served with a pitcher of fresh, sweet cream, when obtainable.

SALTED OR ROASTED ALMONDS.

Blanch half a pound of almonds.   Put with them a tablespoonful of melted butter and one of salt.   Stir them till well mixed, then spread them over a baking-pan and bake fifteen minutes, or till crisp, stirring often.   They must be bright yellow-brown when done.   They are a fashionable appetizer, and should be placed in ornamental dishes at the beginning of dinner, and are used by some in place of olives, which, however, should also be on the table, or some fine pickles may take their place.

ROAST CHESTNUTS.

Peel the raw chestnuts and scald them to remove the inner skin; put them in a frying-pan with a little butter and toss them about a few moments; add a sprinkle of salt and a suspicion of cayenne.   Serve them after the cheese.

Peanuts may be blanched and roasted the same.

AFTER-DINNER CROUTONS.

These crispy *croutons* answer as a substitute for hard-water crackers, and are also relished by most people.

Cut sandwich-bread into slices one-quarter of an inch thick; cut each slice

into four small triangles; dry them in the oven slowly until they assume a delicate brownish tint, then serve, either hot or cold. A nice way to serve them is
to spread a paste of part butter and part rich, creamy cheese, to which may be
added a very little minced parsley.

ORANGE FLOAT.

To make orange float, take one quart of water, the juice and pulp of two
lemons, one coffee-cupful of sugar. When boiling hot, add four tablespoonfuls
of corn-starch. Let it boil fifteen minutes, stirring all the time. When cold,
pour it over four or five oranges that have been sliced into a glass dish, and over
the top spread the beaten whites of three eggs, sweetened and flavored with
vanilla. A nice dessert.

LEMON TOAST.

This dessert can be made very conveniently without much preparation.

Take the yolks of six eggs, beat them well, and add three cupfuls of sweet
milk; take baker's bread, not too stale and cut into slices; dip them into the
milk and eggs, and lay the slices into a spider, with sufficient melted butter, hot,
to fry a delicate brown. Take the whites of the six eggs, and beat them to a
froth, adding a large cupful of white sugar; add the juice of two lemons, heating
well, and adding two cupfuls of boiling water. Serve over the toast as a sauce,
and you will find it a very delicious dish.

SWEET OMELET. No. 1.

One tablespoonful of butter, two of sugar, one cupful of milk, four eggs
Let the milk come to a boil. Beat the flour and butter together ; add to them
gradually the boiling milk, and cook eight minutes, stirring often; beat the sugar and the yolks of the eggs together; add to the cooked mixture, and set away
to cool. When cool, beat the whites of the eggs to a stiff froth, and add to the
mixture. Bake in a buttered pudding-dish for twenty minutes in a moderate
oven. Serve *immediately*, with creamy sauce.

SWEET OMELET. No. 2.

Four eggs, two tablespoonfuls of sugar, a pinch of salt, half a teaspoonful of
vanilla extract, one cupful of whipped cream. Beat the whites of the eggs to a
stiff froth, and gradually beat the flavoring and sugar into them. When well
beaten add the yolks, and lastly, the whipped cream. Have a dish holding
about one quart slightly buttered. Pour the mixture into this and bake just
twelve minutes. Serve the moment it is taken from the oven.

SALAD OF MIXED FRUITS.

Put in the centre of a dish a pineapple properly pared, cored and sliced, yet retaining as near as practicable its original shape. Peel, quarter and remove the seeds from four sweet oranges; arrange them in a border around the pineapple. Select four fine bananas, peel and cut into slices lengthwise; arrange these zigzag-fence fashion around the border of the dish. In the V-shaped spaces around the dish put tiny mounds of grapes of mixed colors. When complete, the dish should look very appetizing. To half a pint of clear sugar syrup add half an ounce of good brandy, pour over the fruit and serve.

ORANGE COCOANUT SALAD.

Peel and slice a dozen oranges, grate a cocoanut, and slice a pineapple. Put alternate layers of each until the dish is full. Then pour over them sweetened wine. Served with small cakes.

When oranges are served whole, they should be peeled and prettily arranged in a fruit dish. A small knife is best for this purpose. Break the skin from the stem into six or eight even parts, peel each section down half way, and tuck the point in next to the orange.

CRYSTALLIZED FRUIT.

Pick out the finest of any kind of fruit, leave on their stalks, beat the whites of three eggs to a stiff froth, lay the fruit in the beaten egg with the stalks upward, drain them and beat the part that drips off again; select them out, one by one, and dip them into a cup of finely powdered sugar; cover a pan with a sheet of fine paper, place the fruit inside of it, and put it in an oven that is cooling; when the icing on the fruit becomes firm, pile them on a dish and set them in a cool place. For this purpose, oranges or lemons should be carefully pared, and all the white inner skin removed that is possible, to prevent bitterness; then cut either in thin horizontal slices if lemons, or in quarters if oranges. For cherries, strawberries, currants, etc., choose the largest and finest, leaving stems out. Peaches should be pared and cut in halves, and sweet juicy pears may be treated in the same way, or look nicely when pared, leaving on the stems, and iced. Pineapples should be cut in thin slices, and these, again, divided into quarters.

PEACHES AND CREAM.

Pare and slice the peaches just before sending to table. Cover the glass dish containing them to exclude the air as much as possible, as they soon change color. Do not sugar them in the dish—they then become preserves, not fresh fruit. Pass the powdered sugar and cream with them.

SNOW PYRAMID.

Beat to a stiff foam the whites of half a dozen eggs, add a small teacupful of currant jelly, and whip all together again. Fill half full of cream as many saucers as you have guests, dropping in the centre of each saucer a tablespoonful of the beaten eggs and jelly in the shape of a pyramid.

JELLY FRITTERS.

Make a batter of three eggs, a pint of milk, and a pint bowl of wheat flour or more, beat it light; put a tablespoonful of lard or beef fat in a frying or omelet pan, add a saltspoonful of salt, making it boiling hot, put in the batter by the large spoonful, not too close; when one side is a delicate brown, turn the other; when done, take them on to a dish with a d'oyley over it; put a dessertspoonful of firm jelly or jam on each, and serve. A very nice dessert.

STEWED APPLES. No. 1.

Take a dozen green, tart apples, core and slice them, put into a sauce-pan with just enough water to cover them, cover the sauce-pan closely, and stew the apples until they are tender and clear; then take them out, put them into a deep dish and cover them; add to the juice in the sauce-pan a cupful of loaf sugar for every twelve apples, and boil it half an hour, adding to the syrup a pinch of mace and a dozen whole cloves just ten minutes before taking from the fire; pour scalding hot over the apple, and set them in a cold place; eat ice cold with cream or boiled custard.

STEWED APPLES. No. 2.

Apples cooked in the following way look very pretty on a tea-table and are appreciated by the palate. Select firm round greenings, pare neatly and cut in halves; place in a shallow stew-pan with sufficient boiling water to cover them and a cup of sugar to every six apples. Each half should cook on the bottom of the pan and be removed from the others so as not to injure its shape. Stew slowly until the pieces are very tender, remove to a glass dish carefully, boil the syrup a half hour longer, pour it over the apples and eat cold. A few pieces of lemon boiled in the syrup adds to the flavor.

BAKED PEARS.

Pare and core the pears, without dividing; place them in a pan, and fill up the orifice with brown sugar; add a little water, and let them bake until perfectly tender. Nice with sweet cream or boiled custard.

STEWED PEARS.

Stewed pears with a thick syrup make a fine dessert dish accompanied with cake.

Peel and cut them in halves, leaving the stems on, and scoop out the cores. Put them into a sauce-pan, placing them close together, with the stems upper-most. Pour over sufficient water, a cup of sugar, a few whole cloves, and some sticks of cinnamon, a tablespoonful of lemon juice. Cover the stew-pan closely. to stew gently till the fruit is done, which will depend on the quality of the fruit. Then take out the fruit carefully, and arrange it on a dish for serving. Boil down the syrup until quite thick; strain it and allow it to cool enough to set it; then pour it over the fruit.

The juice could be colored by a few drops of liquid cochineal, or a few slices of beets, while boiling. A teaspoonful of brandy adds much to the flavor. Serve with cream or boiled custard.

BAKED QUINCES.

Take ripe quinces, pare and quarter them, cut out the seeds; then stew them in clear water until a straw will pierce them; put into a baking dish with half a cupful of loaf sugar to every eight quinces; pour over them the liquor in which they were boiled, cover closely, and bake in the oven one hour; then take out the quinces and put them into a covered dish; return the syrup to the sauce-pan and boil twenty minutes; then pour over the quinces, and set them away to cool.

GOOSEBERRY FOOL.

Stew a quart of ripe gooseberries in just enough water to cover them, when soft, rub them through a colander to remove the skins and seeds; while hot stir into them a tablespoonful of melted butter, and a cupful of sugar. Beat the yolks of three eggs, and add that; whip all together until light. Fill a large glass fruit dish, and spread on the top of the beaten whites mixed with three tablespoonfuls of sugar. Apples or any tart fruit is nice made in this manner.

MERINGUES OR KISSES.

A coffee-cupful of fine, white sugar, the whites of six eggs; whisk the whites of the eggs to a stiff froth, and with a wooden spoon stir in *quickly* the pounded sugar; and have some boards put in the oven thick enough to prevent the bottom of the meringues from acquiring too much color. Cut some strips of paper about two inches wide; place this paper on the board and drop a tablespoonful at a time of the mixture on the paper, taking care to let all the meringues be the same size. In dropping it from the spoon, give the mixture the form of an egg, and keep the meringues about two inches apart from each other on the paper. Strew over them some sifted sugar, and bake in a moderate oven for half an hour. As soon as they begin to color, remove them from the oven; take each slip of paper by the two ends, and turn it gently on the table, and, with a small spoon take out the soft part of each meringue. Spread some clean paper on the board, turn the meringues upside down, and put them into the oven to harden, and brown on the other side. When required for table, fill them with whipped cream, flavored with liquor or vanilla, and sweeten with pounded sugar. Join two of the meringues together, and pile them high in the dish. To vary their appearance, finely chopped almonds or currants may be strewn over them before the sugar is sprinkled over; and they may be garnished with any bright-colored preserve. Great expedition is necessary in making this sweet dish, as, if the meringues are not put into the oven as soon as the sugar and eggs are mixed, the former melts, and the mixture would run on the paper instead of keeping its egg-shape. The sweeter the meringues are made the crisper will they be; but if there is not sufficient sugar mixed with them, they will most likely be tough. They are sometimes colored with cochineal; and, if kept well-covered in a dry place, will remain good for a month or six weeks.

JELLY KISSES.

Kisses, to be served for dessert at a large dinner, with other suitable confectionary, may be varied in this way: Having made the kisses, heap them in the shape of half an egg, placed upon stiff letter-paper lining the bottom of a thick baking-pan; put them in a moderate oven until the outside is a little hardened; then take one off carefully, take out the soft inside with the handle of a spoon, and put it back with the mixture, to make more; then lay the shell down. Take another and prepare it likewise; fill the shells with currant jelly or jam; join two together, cementing them with some of the mixture; so continue until you have enough. Make kisses, cocoanut drops, and such like, the day before they are wanted.

This recipe will make a fair-sized cake-basket full. It adds much to their beauty when served up to tint half of them pale pink, then unite white and pink. Serve on a high glass dish.

COCOANUT MACAROONS.

Make a "kiss" mixture, add to it the white meat, grated, and finish as directed for "Kisses."

ALMOND MACAROONS.

Half a pound of sweet almonds, a coffee-cupful of white sugar, the whites of two eggs; blanch the almonds and pound them to a paste; add to them the sugar and the beaten whites of eggs; work the whole together with the back of a spoon, then roll the mixture in your hands in balls about the size of a nutmeg, dust sugar over the top, lay them on a sheet of paper at least an inch apart. Bake in a cool oven a light brown.

CHOCOLATE MACAROONS.

Put three ounces of plain chocolate in a pan and melt on a slow fire; then work it to a thick paste with one pound of powdered sugar and the whites of three eggs; roll the mixture down to the thickness of about one-quarter of an inch; cut it in small, round pieces with a paste-cutter, either plain or scalloped; butter a pan slightly, and dust it with flour and sugar in equal quantities; place in it the pieces of paste or mixture, and bake in a hot but not too quick oven.

LEMON JELLY. No. 1.

Wash and prepare four calf's feet, place them in four quarts of water, and let them simmer gently five hours. At the expiration of this time take them out and pour the liquid into a vessel to cool; there should be nearly a quart. When cold, remove every particle of fat, replace the jelly into the preserving-kettle, and add one pound of loaf sugar, the rind and juice of two lemons; when the sugar has dissolved, beat two eggs with their shells in one gill of water, which pour into the kettle, and boil five minutes, or until perfectly clear; then add one gill of Madeira wine, and strain through a flannel bag into any form you like.

LEMON JELLY. No. 2.

To a package of gelatine add a pint of cold water, the juice of four lemons and the rind of one; let it stand one hour, then add one pint of boiling water, a pinch of cinnamon, three cups of sugar; let it all come to a boil; strain through a napkin into molds; set away to get cold. Nice poured over sliced bananas and oranges.

WINE JELLY.

One package of gelatine, one cupful of cold water soaked together two hours; add to this three cupfuls of sugar, the juice of three lemons and the grated rind of one. Now pour over this a quart of boiling water, and stir until dissolved, then add a pint of sherry wine. Strain through a napkin, turn into molds dipped in cold water, and placed in the ice-box for several hours.

One good way to mold this jelly is to pour some of it into the mold, harden it a little, put in a layer of strawberries or raspberries, or any fresh fruit in season, pour in jelly to set them; after they have set, another layer of jelly, then another of berries, and so fill each mold, alternating with jelly and berries.

CIDER JELLY.

This can be made the same, by substituting clear, sweet cider in place of the wine.

ORANGE JELLY.

Orange jelly is a great delicacy, and not expensive. To make a large dish, get six oranges, two lemons, a two-ounce package of gelatine. Put the gelatine to soak in a pint of water, squeeze the orange-juice into a bowl, also the lemon juice, and grate one of the lemon skins in with it. Put about two cupfuls of sugar with the gelatine, then stir in the orange-juice, and pour over all three pints of boiling water, stirring constantly. When the gelatine is entirely dissolved, strain through a napkin into molds or bowls wet with cold water, and set aside to harden. In three or four hours it will be ready for use, and will last several days.

VARIEGATED JELLY.

After dividing a box of Cox's gelatine into halves, put each half into a bowl with half a cupful of cold water. Put three-quarters of an ounce or six sheets of pink gelatine into a third bowl containing three-fourths of a cupful of cold water. Cover the bowls to keep out the dust, and set them away for two hours. At the end of that time, add a pint of boiling water, a cupful of sugar, half a pint of wine, and the juice of lemon to the pink gelatine, and, after stirring till the gelatine is dissolved, strain the liquid through a napkin. Treat one of the other portions of the gelatine in the same way. Beat together the yolks of four eggs and half a cupful of sugar, and, after adding this mixture to the third portion of gelatine, stir the new mixture into a pint and a third of boiling milk, contained in a double boiler. Stir on the fire for three minutes, then strain through a fine sieve, and flavor with a teaspoonful of vanilla extract. Place in a deep pan two molds, each holding about three pints, and surround them with ice and water. Pour into these molds, in equal parts, the wine jelly which was made with the clear gelatine, and set it away to harden. When it has become set, pour in the pink gelatine, which should have been set away in a place not cold enough to make it harden. After it has been transferred and has become hard, pour into the molds the mixture of eggs, sugar and gelatine, which should be in a liquid state. Set the molds in an ice-chest for three or four hours. At serving time, dip them into tepid water to loosen the contents, and gently turn the jelly out upon flat dishes.

The clear jelly may be made first and poured into molds, then the pink jelly, and finally the egg jelly.

STRAWBERRY JELLY.

Strawberries, pounded sugar; to every pint of juice allow half a package of Cox's gelatine.

Pick the strawberries, put them into a pan, squeeze them well with a wooden spoon, add sufficient pounded sugar to sweeten them nicely, and let them remain for one hour, that the juice may be extracted; then add half a pint of water to every pint of juice. Strain the strawberry juice and water through a napkin; measure it, and to every pint allow half a package of Cox's gelatine, dissolved in a teacupful of water. Mix this with the juice; put the jelly into a mold, and set the mold on ice. A little lemon juice added to the strawberry juice improves the flavor of the jelly, if the fruit is very ripe; but it must be well strained before it is put with the other ingredients, or it will make the jelly muddy. Delicious and beautiful.

ICE-CREAM.

One pint of milk, the yolks of two eggs, six ounces of sugar, and one table-spoonful of corn-starch. Scald, but do not boil. Then put the whites of the two eggs into a pint of cream; whip it. Mix the milk and cream, flavor and freeze. One teaspoonful of vanilla or lemon is generally sufficient.

The quantity, of course, can be increased to any amount desired, so long as the relative proportions of the different ingredients are observed.

PURE ICE-CREAM.

Genuine ice-cream is made of the pure sweet cream in this proportion: Two quarts of cream, one pound of sugar; beat up, flavor, and freeze.

For family use, select one of the new patent freezers, as being more rapid and less laborious for small quantities than the old style turned entirely by hand. All conditions being perfect, those with crank and revolving dashers effect freezing in eight to fifteen minutes.

FRUIT ICE-CREAM.

Ingredients.—To every pint of fruit-juice allow one pint of cream; sugar to taste.

Let the fruit be well ripened; pick it off the stalks, and put it into a large earthen pan. Stir it about with a wooden spoon, breaking it until it is well-mashed; then, with the back of the spoon, rub it through a hair-sieve. Sweeten it nicely with pounded sugar; whip the cream for a few minutes, add it to the fruit, and whisk the whole again for another five minutes. Put the mixture into the freezer and freeze. Raspberry, strawberry, currant, and all fruit ice-creams, are made in the same manner. A little pounded sugar sprinkled over the fruit before it is mashed assists to extract the juice. In winter, when fresh fruit is not obtainable, a little jam may be substituted for it; it should be melted and worked through a sieve before being added to the whipped cream; and if the color should not be good, a little prepared cochineal may be put in to improve its appearance.

In making berry flavoring for ice-cream, the milk should never be heated; the juice of the berries added to *cold* cream, or fresh, rich milk, mixed with *cold* cream, the juice put in just before freezing, or when partly frozen.

CHOCOLATE ICE-CREAM. No. 1. (Very fine.)

Add four ounces of grated chocolate to a cupful of sweet milk, then mix it thoroughly to a quart of thick, sweet cream; no flavoring is required but vanilla. Sweeten with a cupful of sugar; beat again and freeze.

CHOCOLATE ICE-CREAM. No. 2.

Beat two eggs very light, and cream them with two cupfuls of sugar. Scald a pint of milk and turn on by degrees, mixing well with the sugar and eggs. Stir in this half a cupful of grated chocolate; return to the fire, and heat until it thickens, stirring briskly; take off, and set aside to cool. When thoroughly cold, freeze.

COCOANUT ICE-CREAM.

One quart of cream, one pint of milk, three eggs, one cupful and a half of sugar and one of prepared cocoanut, the rind and juice of a lemon. Beat together the eggs and grated lemon-rind, and put with the milk in the double boiler. Stir until the mixture begins to thicken. Add the cocoanut and put away to cool. When cool, add the sugar, lemon-juice and cream. Freeze.

CUSTARD ICE-CREAM.

Sweeten one quart of cream or rich milk with half a pound of sugar, and flavor to taste; put it over the fire in a farina-kettle; as soon as it begins to boil, stir into it a tablespoonful of corn-starch or rice flour which has been previously mixed smooth with a little milk; after it has boiled a few minutes, take it off the fire and stir in very gradually six eggs which have been beaten until thick; when quite cold, freeze it as ice-cream.

STRAWBERRY ICE-CREAM.

Mix a cupful of sugar with a quart of ripe strawberries, let them stand half a day, then mash and strain them through a coarse towel, then add to the juice a full cupful of sugar, and when dissolved, beat in a quart of fresh, thick cream. Raspberries, pineapple and other fruits made the same.

FRUIT CREAM.

Make a rich, boiled custard; flavor with wine and vanilla; pour into a freezer. When half frozen, add pounded almonds, chopped citron and brandy, peaches or chopped raisins. Have the freezer half full of custard and fill up with the fruit. Mix well, and freeze again. Almost any kind of fruits that are preferred may be substituted for the above.

TUTTI FRUTTI ICE-CREAM.

Take two quarts of the richest cream, and add to it one pound of pulverized sugar, and four whole eggs; mix well together; place on the fire, stirring constantly, and just bring to boiling point; now remove immediately and continue to stir until nearly cold; flavor with a tablespoonful of extract of vanilla; place in freezer and when half frozen, mix thoroughly into it one pound of preserved fruits, in equal parts of peaches, apricots, gages, cherries, pineapples, etc.; all of these fruits are to be cut up into small pieces, and mixed well with the frozen cream. If you desire to *mold* this ice, sprinkle it with a little carmine, dissolved in a teaspoonful of water, with two drops of spirits of ammonia; mix in this color, so that it will be streaky, or in veins like marble.

ICE-CREAM WITHOUT A FREEZER.

Beat the yolks of eight eggs very light, and add thereto four cupfuls of sugar, and stir well. Add to this, little by little, one quart of rich milk that has been heated almost to boiling, beating all the while; then put in the whites of eight eggs beaten to a stiff froth. Then boil the mixture in a pail set inside another containing hot water. Boil about fifteen minutes, or until it is as thick as a boiled custard, stirring steadily meanwhile. Pour into a bowl to cool. When quite cold, beat into it three pints of rich sweet cream and five teaspoonfuls of vanilla, or such other flavoring as you prefer. Put it into a pail having a close-fitting cover, and pack in pounded ice and salt—*rock salt*, not the common kind, —about three-fourths ice and one-fourth salt. When packed, before putting the ice on top of the cover, beat the custard as you would batter, for five minutes steady; then put on the cover and put the ice and salt over it, and cover the whole with a thick mat, blanket or carpet, and let it stand for an hour. Then carefully uncover and scrape from the bottom and sides of the pail the thick coating of frozen custard, making every particle clear, and beat again very hard, until the custard is a smooth, half-congealed paste. Do this thoroughly. Put on the cover, ice, salt and blanket, and leave it for five or six hours, replenishing the ice and salt if necessary.

—Common Sense in the Household.

FROZEN PEACHES.

One can or twelve large peaches, two coffee-cupfuls of sugar, one pint of water, and the whites of three eggs beaten to a stiff froth; break the peaches rather fine and stir all the ingredients together; freeze the whole into form.

Frozen fruits of any kind can be made the same way; the fruit should be mashed to a smooth pulp, but not thinned too much. In freezing, care should be taken to prevent its getting lumpy.

FROZEN FRUITS.

The above recipe, increasing the quantity of peaches, raspberries or whatever fruit you may use, and adding a small amount of rich cream, make fine frozen fruits. In freezing, you must be especially careful to prevent its getting lumpy.

LEMON ICE.

The juice of six lemons and the grated rind of three, a large sweet orange, juice and rind; squeeze out all the juice, and steep in it the rind of orange and lemons a couple of hours; then squeeze and strain through a towel, add a pint of water and two cupfuls of sugar. Stir until dissolved, turn into a freezer, then proceed as for ice-cream, letting it stand longer, two or three hours.

When fruit jellies are used, gently heat the water sufficiently to melt them; then cool and freeze. Other flavors may be made in this manner, varying the flavoring to taste.

PINEAPPLE SHERBET.

Grate two pineapples and mix with two quarts of water, and a pint of sugar; add the juice of two lemons, and the beaten whites of four eggs. Place in a freezer and freeze.

RASPBERRY SHERBET.

Two quarts of raspberries, one cupful of sugar, one pint and a half of water, the juice of a large lemon, one tablespoonful of gelatine. Mash the berries and sugar together and let them stand two hours. Soak the gelatine in cold water to cover. Add one pint of the water to the berries, and strain. Dissolve the gelatine in half a pint of boiling water, add this to the strained mixture and freeze.

ORANGE-WATER ICE.

Add a tablespoonful of gelatine to one gill of water; let it stand twenty minutes and add half a pint of boiling water; stir until dissolved and add four ounces of powdered sugar, the strained juice of six oranges, and cold water enough to make a full quart in all. Stir until the sugar is dissolved; pour into the freezing can and freeze (see "Lemon Ice.")

ALMOND ICE.

Two pints of milk, eight ounces of cream, two ounces of orange-flower water, eight ounces of sweet almonds, four ounces of bitter almonds; pound all in a marble mortar, pouring, in, from time to time, a few drops of water; when thoroughly pounded add the orange-flower water and half of the milk; pass this, tightly squeezed, through a cloth; boil the rest of the milk with the cream, and keep stirring it with a wooden spoon; as soon as it is thick enough, pour in the almond milk; give it one boiling, take it off and let it cool in a bowl or pitcher, before pouring it into the mold for freezing.

CURRANT ICE.

A refreshing ice is made of currants or raspberries, or equal portions of each. Squeeze enough fruit in a jelly-bag to make a pint of juice; add a pint each of the water and sugar; pour the whole, boiling hot, on to three whites of eggs, beaten to a stiff froth, and whip the mixture thoroughly. When cool, freeze in the usual manner. Part red raspberry juice is a much finer flavor.

Any juicy fruit may be prepared in this manner.

DUMPLINGS AND PUDDINGS

It depends as much upon the judgment of the cook as on the materials used to make a good pudding. Everything should be the best in the way of materials, and a proper attention to the rules, with some practice, will ensure success.

Puddings are either boiled, baked, or steamed; if boiled, the materials should be well worked together, put into a thick cloth bag, previously dipped in hot water, wringing it slightly, and dredging the inside *thickly* with flour; tie it firmly, allowing room for it to swell; drop it into a kettle of *boiling* water, with a small plate or saucer in the bottom to keep it from sticking to the kettle. It should not cease boiling one moment from the time it is put in until taken out, and the pot must be tightly covered, and the cover not removed except when necessary to add water from the *boiling* tea-kettle when the water is getting low. When done, dip immediately in cold water and turn out. This should be done just before placing on the table.

Or, butter a tin pudding-mold or an earthen bowl; close it tight so that water cannot penetrate; drop it into boiling water and boil steadily the required time. If a bowl is used it should be well buttered, and not quite filled with the pudding, allowing room for it to swell; then a cloth wet in hot water, slightly wringing it, then floured on the inner side, and tied over the bowl, meeting under the bottom.

To steam a pudding, put it into a tin pan or earthen dish; tie a cloth over the top, first dredging it in flour, and set it into a steamer. Cover the steamer closely; allow a little longer time than you do for boiling.

Molds or basins for baking, steaming or boiling should be well buttered before the mixture is put into them. Allow a little longer time for steaming than for boiling.

Dumplings boiled the same way, put into little separate cloths.

Batter puddings should be smoothly mixed and free from lumps. To ensure this, first mix the flour with a very small proportion of milk, the yolks of the eggs and sugar thoroughly beaten together, and added to this; then add the remainder of the milk by degrees, then the seasoning, then the beaten whites of eggs last. Much success in making this kind of pudding depends upon a strict observance of this rule; for, although the materials may be good, if the eggs are put into the milk before they are mixed with the flour, there will be a custard at the top and a soft dough at the bottom of your dish.

All sweet puddings require a *little* salt to prevent insipidity and to draw out the flavor of the several ingredients, but a grain too much will spoil any pudding.

In puddings where wine, brandy, cider, lemon-juice or any acid is used, it should be stirred in last, and gradually, or it is apt to curdle the milk or eggs.

In making *custard puddings* (puddings made with eggs and milk), the yolk of the eggs and sugar should be thoroughly beaten together before any of the milk or seasoning is added, and the beaten whites of egg last.

In making puddings of bread, rice, sago, tapioca, etc., the eggs should be beaten very light, and mixed with a portion of the milk, before adding them to the other ingredients. If the eggs are mixed with the milk, without having been thus beaten, the milk will be absorbed by the bread, rice, sago, tapioca, etc., without rendering them light.

The freshness of all pudding ingredients is of much importance, as one bad article will taint the whole mixture.

When the *freshness* of eggs is *doubtful*, break each one separately in a cup, before mixing them all together. Should there be a bad one amongst them, it can be thrown away; whereas, if mixed with the good ones, the entire quantity would be spoiled. The yolks and whites beaten separately make the articles they are put into much lighter.

Raisins and dried fruits for puddings should be carefully picked, and, in many cases, stoned. Currants should be well-washed, pressed in a cloth, and placed on a dish before the fire to get thoroughly dry; they should then be picked carefully over, and *every piece of grit or stone* removed from amongst them. To plump them, some cooks pour boiling water over them, and then dry them before the fire.

Many baked-pudding recipes are quite as good boiled. As a safe rule, boil the pudding *twice as long* as you would require to bake it; and remember that a boiling pudding should never be touched after it is once put on the stove; a jar of the kettle destroys the lightness of the pudding. If the water boils down and more must be added, it must be done so carefully that the mold will not hit the side of the kettle, and it must not be allowed to stop boiling for an instant.

Batter should never stick to the knife when it is sent to the table; it will do this both when a less than sufficient number of eggs is mixed with it and when it is not enough cooked; about four eggs to the half pound of flour will make it firm enough to cut smoothly.

When baked or boiled puddings are sufficiently solid, turn them out of the dish they were baked in, bottom uppermost, and strew over them finely sifted sugar.

When pastry or baked puddings are not done through, and yet the outside is sufficiently brown, cover them over with a piece of white paper until thoroughly cooked; this prevents them from getting burnt.

TO CLEAN CURRANTS.

Put them in a sieve or colander, and sprinkle them thickly with flour; rub them well until they are separated, and the flour, grit and fine stems have passed through the strainer. Place the strainer and currants in a pan of water and wash thoroughly; then lift the strainer and currants together, and change the water until it is clear. Dry the currants between clean towels. It hardens them to dry in an oven.

TO CHOP SUET.

Break or cut in small pieces, sprinkle with sifted flour, and chop in a cold place to keep it from becoming sticky and soft.

TO STONE RAISINS.

Put them in a dish and pour *boiling* water over them; cover and let them remain in it ten minutes; it will soften so that by rubbing each raisin between the thumb and finger, the seeds will come out clean; then they are ready for cutting or chopping if required.

APPLE DUMPLINGS.

Make a rich biscuit dough, the same as soda or baking-powder biscuit, only adding a little more shortening. Take a piece of dough out on the molding-board, roll out almost as thin as pie-crust; then cut into square pieces large enough to cover an apple. Put into the middle of each piece two apple halves that have been pared and cored; sprinkle on a spoonful of sugar and a pinch of ground cinnamon, turn the ends of the dough over the apple, and lap them tight. Lay the dumplings in a dripping-pan well buttered, the smooth side upward. When the pans are filled, put a small piece of butter on the top of each, sprinkle over a large handful of sugar, turn in a cupful of boiling water, then place in a moderate oven for three-quarters of an hour. Baste with the liquor once while baking. Serve with pudding-sauce or cream and sugar.

BOILED APPLE DUMPLINGS.

The same recipe as the above, with the exception that they are put into a small coarse cloth well-floured after being dipped in hot water. Each cloth to be tied securely, but leaving room enough for the dumpling to swell. Put them in a pot of boiling water and boil three-quarters of an hour. Serve with sweet sauce. Peaches and other fruits used in the same manner.

BOILED RICE DUMPLINGS, CUSTARD SAUCE.

Boil half a pound of rice; drain, and mash it moderately fine. Add to it two ounces of butter, three ounces of sugar, half a saltspoonful of mixed ground spice, salt and the yolks of two eggs. Moisten a trifle with a tablespoonful or two of cream. With floured hands shape the mixture into balls, and tie them in floured pudding-cloths. Steam or boil forty minutes, and send to table with a custard sauce made as follows:

Mix together four ounces of sugar and two ounces of butter (slightly warmed). Beat together the yolks of two eggs and a gill of cream; mix and pour the sauce in a double sauce-pan; set this in a pan of hot water, and whisk thoroughly three minutes. Set the sauce-pan in cold water and whisk until the sauce is cooled.

SUET DUMPLINGS. No. 1.

One pint bowl of fine bread-crumbs, one-half cupful of beef suet chopped fine, the whites and yolks of four eggs beaten separately and very light, one tea-spoonful of cream tartar sifted into half a cupful of flour, half a teaspoonful of soda dissolved in a little water, and a teaspoonful of salt. Wet it all together with milk enough to make a stiff paste. Flour your hands and make into balls. Tie up in separate cloths that have been wrung out in hot water, and floured inside; leave room, when tying, for them to swell. Drop them into *boiling* water and boil about three-quarters of an hour. Serve *hot*, with wine sauce, or syrup and butter.

SUET DUMPLINGS. No. 2.

One cupful of suet chopped fine, one cupful of grated English muffins or bread, one cupful of flour, half a teaspoonful of baking-powder, half a cupful of sugar, two eggs, one pint of milk, a large pinch of salt. Sift together powder and flour, add the beaten eggs, grated muffins, sugar, suet and milk; form into smooth batter, which drop by tablespoonfuls into a pint of boiling milk, three or four at a time; when done, dish, and pour over them the milk they were boiled in. A Danish dish; very good.

PRESERVE DUMPLINGS.

Preserved peaches, plums, quinces, cherries or any other sweetmeat; make a light crust, and roll a small piece of moderate thickness and fill with the fruit in quantity to make the size of a peach dumpling; tie each one in a dumpling cloth, well floured inside, drop them into hot water, and boil half an hour; when done, remove the cloth, send to table hot, and eat with cream.

OXFORD DUMPLINGS.

Beat until quite light one tablespoonful of sugar and the yolks of three eggs, add half a cupful of finely chopped suet, half a cupful of English currants, one cupful of sifted flour, in which there has been sifted a heaping teaspoonful of baking-powder, a little nutmeg, one teaspoonful of salt, and lastly, the beaten whites of the eggs; flour your hands and make it into balls the size of an egg; boil in separate cloths one hour or more.   Serve with wine sauce.

LEMON DUMPLINGS.

Mix together a pint of grated bread-crumbs, half a cupful of chopped suet, half a cupful of moist sugar, a little salt, and a small tablespoonful of flour, adding the grated rind of a lemon.   Moisten it all with the whites and yolks of two eggs, *well* beaten, and the juice of the lemon, strained.   Stir it all well together, and put the mixture into small cups well buttered; tie them down with a cloth dipped in flour, and boil three-quarters of an hour.   Turn them out on a dish, strew sifted sugar over them, and serve with wine sauce.

BOILED APPLE PUFFETS.

Three eggs, one pint of milk, a little salt, sufficient flour to thicken as waffle-batter; one and one-half teaspoonfuls of baking-powder.   Fill teacups alternately with a layer of batter, and then of apples chopped fine.   Steam one hour.   Serve hot with flavored cream and sugar.   You can substitute any fresh fruit or jams your taste prefers.

COMMON BATTER,

For boiled pudding, fritters, etc., is made with one cupful of milk, a pinch of salt, two eggs, one tablespoonful of melted butter, one cupful of flour, and a small teaspoonful of baking-powder.   Sift the flour, powder and salt together, add the melted butter, the eggs, well beaten, and the milk; mix into a very smooth batter, a little thicker than for griddle-cakes.

ALMOND PUDDING.

Turn boiling water on to three-fourths of a pound of sweet almonds; let it remain until the skin comes off easily; rub with a dry cloth; when dry, pound fine with one large spoonful of rose-water; beat six eggs to a stiff froth with three spoonfuls of fine white sugar; mix with one quart of milk, three spoonfuls of pounded crackers, four ounces of melted butter, and the same of citron cut into bits; add almonds, stir all together, and bake in a small pudding-dish with a lining and rim of pastry. This pudding is best when cold. It will bake in half an hour in a quick oven.

APPLE PUDDING, BAKED.

Stir two tablespoonfuls of butter and half a cupful of sugar to a cream; stir into this the yolks of four eggs, well beaten, the juice and grated rind of one lemon, and half a dozen sound, green, tart apples, grated. Now stir in the four beaten whites of the eggs, season with cinnamon or nutmeg; bake. To be served cold with cream.

BOILED APPLE PUDDING.

Take three eggs, three apples, a quarter of a pound of bread-crumbs, one lemon, three ounces of sugar, three ounces of currants, half a wine-glassful of wine, nutmeg, butter and sugar for sauce. Pare, core and mince the apple and mix with the bread-crumbs, nutmeg grated, sugar, currants, the juice of the lemon, and half the rind grated. Beat the eggs well, moisten the mixture with these and beat all together, adding the wine last; put the pudding in a buttered mold, tie it down with a cloth; boil one hour and a half, and serve with sweet sauce.

BIRDS' NEST PUDDING.

Core and peel eight apples, put in a dish, fill the places from which the cores have been taken with sugar and a little grated nutmeg; cover and bake. Beat the yolks of four eggs light, add two teacupfuls of flour, with three even teaspoonfuls of baking-powder sifted with it, one pint of milk with a teaspoonful of salt; then add the whites of the eggs well beaten, pour over the apples, and bake one hour in a moderate oven. Serve with sauce.

BREAD AND BUTTER PUDDING. NO. 1.

Butter the sides and bottom of a deep pudding-dish, then butter thin slices of bread, sprinkle thickly with sugar, a little cinnamon, chopped apple, or any fruit you prefer between each slice, until your dish is full. Beat up two eggs, add a tablespoonful of sifted flour; stir with this three cupfuls of milk and a little salt; pour this over the bread, let it stand one hour and then bake slowly, with a cover on, three-quarters of an hour; then take the cover off and brown. Serve with wine and lemon sauce.

Pie-plant, cut up in small pieces with plenty of sugar, is fine made in this manner.

BREAD AND BUTTER PUDDING. No. 2.

Place a layer of stale bread, rolled fine, in the bottom of a pudding dish, then a layer of any kind of fruit; sprinkle on a little sugar, then another layer of bread-crumbs and of fruit; and so on until the dish is full, the top layer being crumbs. Make a custard as for pies, add a pint of milk, and mix. Pour it over the top of the pudding, and bake until the fruit is cooked.

Stale cake, crumbed fine, in place of bread, is an improvement.

COLD BERRY PUDDING.

Take rather stale bread—baker's bread or light home-made—cut in thin slices, and spread with butter. Add a very little water and a little sugar to one quart or more of huckleberries and blackberries, or the former alone. Stew a few minutes until juicy; put a layer of buttered bread in your buttered pudding-dish, then a layer of stewed berries while hot, and so on until full; lastly, a covering of stewed berries. It may be improved with a rather soft frosting over the top. To be eaten cold with thick cream and sugar.

APPLE TAPIOCA PUDDING.

Put one teacupful of tapioca and one teaspoonful of salt into one pint and a half of water, and let it stand several hours where it will be quite warm, but not cook; peel six tart apples, take out the cores, fill them with sugar, in which is grated a little nutmeg and lemon-peel, and put them in a pudding-dish; over these pour the tapioca, first mixing with it one teaspoonful of melted butter and a cupful of cold milk, and half a cupful of sugar; bake one hour; eat with sauce.

When fresh fruits are in season, this pudding is exceedingly nice, with damsons, plums, red currants, gooseberries, or apples; when made with these, the pudding must be thickly sprinkled over with sifted sugar.

Canned or fresh peaches may be used in place of apples in the same manner, moistening the tapioca with the juice of the canned peaches in place of the cold milk. Very nice when quite cool to serve with sugar and cream.

APPLE AND BROWN-BREAD PUDDING.

Take a pint of brown bread-crumbs, a pint bowl of chopped apples, mix; add two-thirds of a cupful of finely chopped suet, a cupful of raisins, one egg, a tablespoonful of flour, half a teaspoonful of salt. Mix with half a pint of milk, and boil in buttered molds about two hours. Serve with sauce flavored with lemon.

APPLE-PUFF PUDDING.

Put half a pound of flour into a basin, sprinkle in a little salt, stir in gradually a pint of milk; when quite smooth add three eggs; butter a pie-dish, pour in the batter; take three-quarters of a pound of apples, seed and cut in slices, and put in the batter; place bits of butter over the top; bake three-quarters of an hour; when done, sprinkle sugar over the top and serve hot.

PLAIN BREAD PUDDING, BAKED.

Break up about a pint of stale bread after cutting off the crust ; pour over it a quart of boiling milk; add to this a piece of butter the size of a small egg; cover the dish tight and let it stand until cool; then with a spoon mash it until fine, adding a teaspoonful of cinnamon, and one of nutmeg grated, half a cupful of sugar, and one quarter of a teaspoonful of soda, dissolved in a little hot water. Beat up four eggs very light, and add last. Turn all into a well-buttered pudding-dish, and bake three-quarters of an hour. Serve it warm with hard sauce.

This recipe may be steamed or boiled; very nice either way.

SUPERIOR BREAD PUDDINGS.

One and one-half cupfuls of white sugar; two cupfuls of fine, dry bread-crumbs, five eggs, one tablespoonful of butter, vanilla, rose-water or lemon flavoring, one quart of fresh, rich milk, and half a cupful of jelly or jam. Rub the butter into a cupful of sugar; beat the yolks very light, and stir these together to a cream. The bread-crumbs soaked in milk come next, then the flavoring. Bake in a buttered pudding-dish—a large one, and but two-thirds full—until the custard is "set." Draw to the mouth of the oven, spread over with jam or other nice fruit conserve. Cover this with a meringue made of the whipped whites and half a cupful of sugar. Shut the oven, and bake until the meringue begins to color. Eat cold, with cream. In strawberry season, substitute a pint of fresh fruit for preserves. It is then delicious. Serve with any warm sauce.

BOILED BREAD PUDDING.

To one quart of bread-crumbs, soaked soft in a cup of hot milk, add one cupful of molasses, one cupful of fruit, or chopped raisins, one teaspoonful each of spices, one tablespoonful of butter, a teaspoonful of salt, one teaspoonful of soda, about a cupful of flour sifted; boil or steam three hours. Serve with sweet sauce.

ALMOND PUDDING. No. 1.

Put two quarts of milk into a double boiler; stir into it two heaping table-spoonfuls of sifted flour that has been stirred to a cream, with a little of the milk. When it boils, care should be taken that it does not burn; when cooked, take from the fire, and let it cool. Take the skins off from two pounds of sweet almonds, pound them fine, stir them into the milk; add a teaspoonful of salt, a cupful of sugar, flavoring, and six well-beaten eggs, the yolks and whites beaten separately. Put bits of butter over the top. Bake one hour. A gill of brandy or wine improves it.

ALMOND PUDDING. No. 2.

Steep four ounces of crumbs of bread, sliced, in one and one-half pints of cream, or grate the bread; then beat half a pound of blanched almonds very fine till they become a paste, with two teaspoonfuls of orange-flower water; beat up the yolks of eight eggs and the whites of four; mix all well together; put in a quarter of a pound of loaf sugar, and stir in three or four ounces of melted butter; put it over the fire, stirring it until it is thick; lay a sheet of paper at the bottom of a dish, and pour in the ingredients; bake half an hour. Use the remaining four whites of egg for a meringue for the top.

BATTER PUDDING, BAKED.

Four eggs, the yolks and whites beaten separately, one pint of milk, one teaspoonful of salt, one teaspoonful of baking-powder, two cupfuls of sifted flour. Put the whites of the eggs in last. Bake in an earthen dish that can be set on the table. Bake forty-five minutes; serve with rich sauce.

BOILED BATTER PUDDING.

Sift together a pint of flour and a teaspoonful of baking-powder into a deep dish, sprinkle in a little salt, adding also a tablespoonful of melted butter. Stir into this gradually a pint of milk; when quite smooth, add four eggs, yolks and whites beaten separately. Now add enough more flour to make a *very stiff* batter. If liked, any kind of fruit may be stirred into this; a pint of berries or sliced fruit. Boil two hours. Serve with cream and sugar, wine sauce, or any sweet sauce.

CUSTARD PUDDING. No. 1.

Take five tablespoonfuls out of a quart of cream or rich milk, and mix them with two large spoonfuls of fine flour. Set the rest of the milk to boil, flavoring it with bitter almonds broken up. When it has boiled hard, take it off, strain it, and stir it in the cold milk and flour. Set it away to cool, and beat well eight yolks and four whites of eggs; add them to the milk, and stir in, at the last, a glass of brandy or white wine, a teaspoonful of powdered nutmeg, and half a cupful of sugar. Butter a large bowl or mold; pour in the mixture; tie a cloth tightly over it; put it into a pot of boiling water, and boil it two hours, replenishing the pot with hot water from a tea-kettle. When the pudding is done, let it get cool before you turn it out. Eat it with butter and sugar stirred together to a cream and flavored with lemon-juice or orange.

CUSTARD PUDDING. No. 2.

Pour one quart of milk in a deep pan, and let the pan stand in a kettle of boiling water, while you beat to a cream eight eggs and six tablespoonfuls of fine sugar and a teaspoon of flour; then stir the eggs and sugar into the milk, and continue stirring until it begins to thicken; then remove the pan from the boiling water, scrape down the sides, stir to the bottom until it begins to cool, add a tablespoonful of peach water, or any other flavor you may prefer, pour into little cups, and when cold, serve.

CUSTARD PUDDINGS.

The recipe for "Common Custard," with the addition of chocolate, grated banana, or pineapple or cocoanut, makes successfully those different kinds of puddings.

APPLE CUSTARD PUDDINGS.

Put a quart of pared and quartered apples into a stew-pan, with half a cupful of water, and cook them until they are soft. Remove from the fire, and add half a cupful of sugar, two tablespoonfuls of butter and the grated rind and the juice of a lemon. Have ready mixed two cupfuls of grated bread-crumbs, and two tablespoonfuls of flour; add this also to the apple mixture, after which, stir in two well-beaten eggs. Turn all into a well-buttered pudding-dish, and bake forty-five minutes in a moderate oven. Serve with sugar and cream or hard sweet sauce.

CREAM PUDDING.

Beat the yolks and whites of six eggs well, and stir them into one pint of flour, one pint of milk, a little salt, and a bit of soda, dissolved in a little water, the grated rind of a lemon, and three spoonfuls of sugar; just before baking, stir in one pint of cream, and bake in a buttered dish. Eat with cream.

CREAM MERINGUE PUDDING.

Stir to a cream half a cupful of sugar with the white of one egg and the yolks of four. Add one quart of milk and mix thoroughly. Put four tablespoonfuls of flour and a teaspoonful of salt into another dish, and pour half a cupful of the milk and egg mixture upon them, and beat very smooth, gradually adding the rest of the milk and egg mixture. Turn this all into a double boiler surrounded by boiling water; stir this until smooth and thick like cream, or about fifteen minutes; then add vanilla or other extract. Rub all through a strainer into a well-buttered pudding-dish. Now beat the remaining three whites of eggs to a stiff froth, and gradually add three tablespoonfuls of powdered sugar, and spread roughly over the pudding. Cook for twenty minutes in a *moderate* oven. Serve cold.

CORN-STARCH PUDDING.

Reserve half a cupful of milk from a quart, and put the remainder on the stove in a double boiler. Mix four large tablespoonfuls of corn-starch, and a teaspoonful of salt, with the half-cupful of milk; then stir the mixture into the boiling milk, and beat well for two minutes. Cover the boiler and cook the pudding for twelve minutes; then pour it into a pudding-dish, and set in a cool place for half an hour. When the time for serving comes, make a sauce in this manner: Beat the whites of two eggs to a stiff, dry froth, and beat into this two tablespoonfuls of powdered sugar. As soon as the sugar has been well mixed with the whites, add half of a large tumbler of currant jelly, or any other bright jelly, or any kind of preserved fruit may be used. If you prefer, serve sugar and cream with the pudding instead of a sauce.

COLD FRUIT PUDDING.

Throw into a pint of new milk the thin rind of a lemon, heat it slowly by the side of the fire, and keep at the boiling point until strongly flavored. Sprinkle in a small pinch of salt, and three-quarters of an ounce of the finest isinglass or gelatine. When dissolved, strain through muslin into a clean sauce-pan with five ounces of powdered sugar and half a pint of rich cream. Give the whole one boil, stir it briskly and add by degrees the well-beaten yolks of five eggs. Next thicken the mixture as a custard over a slow fire, taking care not to keep it over the fire a moment longer than necessary; pour it into a basin and flavor with orange-flower water or vanilla. Stir until nearly cold, then add two ounces of citron cut in thin strips and two ounces of candied cherries. Pour into a buttered mold. For sauce use any kind of fruit syrup.

CUBAN PUDDING.

Crumble a pound of sponge cakes, an equal quantity, or less if preferred, of cocoanut, grated in a basin. Pour over two pints of rich cream previously sweetened with a quarter of a pound of loaf sugar and brought to the boiling point. Cover the basin, and when the cream is soaked up stir in it eight well-beaten eggs. Butter a mold, arrange four or five ounces of preserved ginger around it, pour in the pudding carefully, and tie it down with a cloth. Steam or boil slowly for an hour and a half; serve with the syrup from the ginger, which should be warmed and poured over the pudding.

CRACKER PUDDING

Of raspberries, may be made of one large teacupful of cracker-crumbs, one quart of milk, one spoonful of flour, a pinch of salt, the yolks of three eggs, one whole egg and half a cupful of sugar. Flavor with vanilla, adding a little pinch of salt. Bake in a moderate oven. When done, spread over the top, while hot, a pint of well-sugared raspberries. Then beat the whites of the three eggs very stiff, with two tablespoonfuls of sugar, a little lemon extract, or whatever one prefers. Spread this over the berries, and bake a light brown. Serve with fruit sauce made of raspberries.

BAKED CORN-MEAL PUDDING, WITHOUT EGGS.

Take a large cupful of yellow meal, and a teacupful of cooking molasses, and beat them well together; then add to them a quart of boiling milk, some salt and a large tablespoonful of powdered ginger, add a cupful of finely chopped suet or a piece of butter the size of an egg. Butter a brown earthen pan, and turn the pudding in, let it stand until it thickens; then as you put it into the oven, turn over it a pint of cold milk, but do not stir it, as this makes the jelly. Bake three hours. Serve warm with hard sauce.

This recipe has been handed down from mother to daughter for many years back in a New England family.

BAKED CORN-MEAL PUDDING, WITH EGGS.

One small cupful of Indian meal, one-half cupful of wheat flour stirred together with cold milk.   Scald one pint of milk, and stir the mixture in it and cook until thick; then thin with cold milk to the consistency of batter, not very thick; add half a cupful of sugar, half a cupful of molasses, two eggs, two tablespoonfuls of butter, a little salt, a tablespoonful of mixed cinnamon and nutmeg, two-thirds of a teaspoonful of soda added just before putting it into the oven.   Bake two hours.   After baking it half an hour, stir it up thoroughly, then finish baking.

Serve it up hot, eat it with wine sauce, or with butter and syrup.

BOILED CORN-MEAL PUDDING.

Warm a pint of molasses and a pint of milk, stir well together; beat four eggs, and stir gradually into molasses and milk; add a cupful of beef suet chopped fine, or half a cupful of butter, and corn-meal sufficient to make a thick batter; add a teaspoonful of pulverized cinnamon, the same of nutmeg, a teaspoonful of soda, one of salt, and stir all together thoroughly; dip a cloth into boiling water, shake, flour a little, turn in the mixture, tie up, leaving room for the pudding to swell, and boil three hours; serve hot with sauce made of drawn butter, wine and nutmeg.

BOILED CORN-MEAL PUDDING, WITHOUT EGGS.

To one quart of boiling milk, stir in a pint and a half of Indian meal, well-sifted, a teaspoonful of salt, a cupful of molasses, half a cupful of chopped suet, and a teaspoonful of dissolved soda; tie it up tight in a cloth, allowing room for it to swell, and boil four hours.   Serve with sweet sauce.

CORN-MEAL PUFFS.

Into one quart of boiling milk stir eight tablespoonfuls of Indian meal, four tablespoonfuls of powdered sugar, and a teaspoonful of nutmeg; let the whole boil five minutes, stirring constantly to prevent its adhering to the sauce-pan; then remove it from the fire, and when it has become cool stir into it six eggs, beaten as light as possible; mix well, and pour the mixture into buttered teacups, nearly filling them; bake in a moderate oven half an hour; serve with lemon sauce.

DELICATE INDIAN PUDDING.

One quart milk, two heaping tablespoonfuls of Indian meal, four of sugar, one of butter, three eggs, one teaspoonful of salt.   Boil milk in double boiler sprinkle the meal into it, stirring all the while; cook twelve minutes, stirring often. Beat together the eggs, salt, sugar and one-half teaspoonful of ginger. Stir the butter into the meal and milk. Pour this gradually over the egg mixture. Bake slowly one hour. Serve with sauce of heated syrup and butter.

—Maria Parloa.

COTTAGE PUDDING.

One heaping pint of flour, half a cupful of sugar, one cupful of milk, one teaspoonful of soda dissolved in the milk, one tablespoonful of butter, two teaspoonfuls of cream of tartar rubbed dry in the flour; flavor with nutmeg; bake in a *moderate* oven; cut in slices and serve warm with wine or brandy sauce, or sweet sugar sauce.

FRENCH COCOANUT PUDDING. No. 1.

One quart of milk, three tablespoonfuls of corn-starch, the yolks of four eggs, half a cupful of sugar and a little salt; put part of the milk, salt and sugar on the stove and let it boil; dissolve the corn-starch in the rest of the milk; stir into the milk, and while boiling add the yolks and a cupful of grated chocolate. Flavor with vanilla.

Frosting.—The whites of four eggs beaten to a stiff froth, half a cupful of sugar; flavor with lemon; spread it on the pudding, and put it into the oven to brown, saving a little of the frosting to moisten the top; then put on grated cocoanut to give it the appearance of snow-flake.

COCOANUT PUDDING. No. 2.

Half a pound of grated cocoanut. Then mix with it half a cupful of stale sponge-cake, crumbled fine. Stir together until very light half a cupful of butter and one of sugar, add a *coffee*-cupful of rich milk or cream. Beat six eggs very light, and stir them gradually into the butter and sugar in turn, with the grated cocoanut. Having stirred the whole very hard, add two teaspoonfuls of vanilla; stir again, put into a buttered dish and bake until set, or about three-quarters of an hour. Three of the whites of the eggs could be left out for a meringue on the top of the pudding. Most excellent.

COCOANUT PUDDING. No. 3.

A cup of grated cocoanut put into the recipes of "Cracker Pudding" and "Bread Pudding," makes good cocoanut pudding.

CHERRY PUDDING, BOILED OR STEAMED.

Two eggs, well-beaten, one cupful of sweet milk, sifted flour enough to make a *stiff* batter, two large teaspoonfuls of baking-powder, a pinch of salt, and as many cherries as can be stirred in. Boil one hour, or steam, and serve with liquid sauce.

Cranberries, currants, peaches, cherries, or any tart fruit is nice used with this recipe. Serve with sweet sauce.

CHERRY PUDDING. No. 2.

Make a crust or paste of two cupfuls of flour, two teaspoonfuls of baking-powder, a teaspoonful of salt; wet up with milk or water; roll out a quarter of an inch thick, butter a large common bowl and line it with this paste, leaving it large enough to lap over the top; fill it with stoned cherries and half a cupful of sugar. Gather the paste closely over the top, sprinkle a little with dry flour, and cover the whole with a linen cloth, fastening it with a string. Put it into a pot of boiling water, and cook for an hour and a half. Serve with sweet sauce.

ENGLISH PLUM PUDDING. (The Genuine.)

Soak one pound of stale bread in a pint of hot milk, and let it stand and cool. When cold, add to it one-half pound of sugar and the yolks of eight eggs beaten to a cream, one pound of raisins, stoned and floured, one pound of Zante currants, washed and floured, a quarter of a pound of citron, cut in slips and dredged with flour, one pound of beef suet, chopped finely, and *salted*, one glass of wine, one glass of brandy, one nutmeg, and a tablespoonful of mace, cinnamon and cloves mixed; beat the whole well together, and, as the last thing, add the whites of the eight eggs, beaten to a stiff froth; pour into a cloth, previously scalded and dredged with flour, tie the cloth firmly, leaving room for the pudding to swell, and boil six hours. Serve with wine or brandy sauce.

It is best to prepare the ingredients the day before, and cover closely.

CHRISTMAS PLUM-PUDDING. (By Measure.)

One cupful of finely chopped beef suet, two cupfuls of fine bread-crumbs, one heaping cupful of sugar, one cupful of seeded raisins, one cupful of well-washed currants, one cupful of chopped blanched almonds, half a cupful of citron, sliced thin, a teaspoonful of salt, one of cloves, two of cinnamon, half a grated nutmeg, and four well-beaten eggs. Dissolve a level teaspoonful of soda in a tablespoonful of warm water. Flour the fruit thoroughly from a pint of flour; then mix the remainder as follows: In a large bowl put the well-beaten eggs, sugar, spices, and salt in one cupful of milk. Stir in the fruit, chopped nuts, bread-crumbs, and suet, one after the other, until all are used, putting in the dissolved soda last, and adding enough flour to make the fruit stick together, which will take all the pint. Boil or steam four hours. Serve with wine or brandy or any well-flavored sauce.

BAKED PLUM-PUDDING.

It will be found best to prepare the ingredients the day before and cover closely. Grate a stale loaf of bread, or enough for a pint of crumbs; boil one quart of milk, and turn boiling hot over the grated bread; cover and let steep an hour; in the meantime pick, soak and dry half a pound of currants, half a pound of raisins, a quarter of a pound of citron cut in large slips, one nutmeg, one tablespoonful of mace and cinnamon, mixed, one cupful of sugar, with half of a cupful of butter; when the bread is ready, mix with it the butter, sugar, spice and citron, adding a glassful of white wine; beat eight eggs very light, and when the mixture is quite cold, stir them gradually in; then add by degrees the raisins and currants dredged with flour; stir the whole very hard; put it into a buttered dish; bake two hours, send to the table warm. Eat with wine sauce, or wine and sugar. Most excellent.

PLUM-PUDDING, WITHOUT EGGS.

This delicious, light pudding is made by stirring thoroughly together the following ingredients: One cupful of finely chopped beef suet, two cupfuls of fine bread-crumbs, one cupful of molasses, one of chopped raisins, one of well-washed currants, one spoonful of salt, one teaspoonful each of cloves, cinnamon, allspice, and carbonate of soda, one cupful of milk, and flour enough to make a stiff batter. Put into a well-greased pudding mold, or a three-quart pail, and cover closely. Set this pail into a larger kettle, close covered, and half full of boiling water, adding boiling water as it boils away. Steam not less than four hours. This pudding is sure to be a success, and is quite rich for one containing neither eggs nor butter. One-half of the above amount is more than eight persons would be able to eat, but it is equally good some days later, steamed again for an hour, if kept closely covered meantime. Serve with wine sauce or common sweet sauce.

CABINET PUDDING.

Butter well the inside of a pudding-mold. Have ready a cupful of chopped citron, raisins and currants. Sprinkle some of this fruit on the bottom of the mold, then slices of stale sponge cake; shake over this some spices, cinnamon, cloves and nutmeg, then fruit again and cake, until the mold is nearly full. Make a custard of a quart of milk, four eggs, a pinch of salt, two tablespoonfuls of melted butter; pour this over the cake, without cooking it; let it stand and soak one hour; then steam one hour and a half. Serve with wine sauce or a custard. Seasoned with wine.

—Manhattan Beach Hotel.

BAKED CRANBERRY PUDDING.

Pour boiling water on a pint of bread-crumbs; melt a tablespoonful of butter and stir in. When the bread is softened, add two eggs and beat thoroughly with the bread. Then put in a pint of the stewed fruit and sweeten to your taste. Fresh fruit of many kinds can be used instead of cranberries. Slices of peaches put in layers are delicious. Serve with sweet sugar sauce.

ORANGE PUDDING. No. 1.

One pint of milk; the juice of six oranges and the rind of three, eight eggs; half a cupful of butter, half a cupful of granulated sugar, one tablespoonful of ground rice, paste to line the pudding-dish. Mix the ground rice with a little of the cold milk. Put the remainder of the milk in the double boiler, and when it boils stir in the mixed rice. Stir for five minutes; then add the butter, and set away to cool. Beat together the sugar, the yolks of eight eggs, and whites of four. Grate the rind and squeeze the juice of the oranges into this. Stir all into the cooked mixture. Have a pudding-dish holding about three quarts lined with paste. Pour the preparation into this, and bake in a moderate oven for forty minutes. Beat the remaining four whites of the eggs to a stiff froth, and gradually beat in the powdered sugar. Cover the pudding with this. Return to the oven and cook ten minutes, leaving the door open. Set away to cool. It must be ice cold when served.

—Maria Parloa.

ORANGE PUDDING. No. 2.

Five sweet oranges, one coffee-cupful of white sugar, one pint of milk, the yolks of three eggs, one tablespoonful of corn-starch. Peel and cut the oranges into thin slices, taking out the seeds; pour over them the sugar and let them stand while you make the rest. Now set the milk in a suitable dish into another of boiling water, let the milk get boiling hot, add a piece of butter as large as a nutmeg, the corn-starch made smooth with a little cold milk, and the well-beaten yolks of the eggs, and a little flavoring. Stir it all well together until it is smooth and cooked. Set it off and pour it over the oranges. Beat the whites to a stiff froth, adding two tablespoonfuls of sugar, spread over the top for frosting. Set into the oven a few minutes to brown. Eat cold. Berries, peaches and other fruits may be substituted.

BAKED LEMON PUDDING. (Queen of Puddings.)

Ingredients.—One quart of milk, two cupfuls of bread-crumbs, four eggs, whites and yolks beaten separately, butter the size of an egg, one cupful of white sugar, one large lemon—juice and grated rind. Heat the milk and pour over the bread-crumbs, add the butter, cover and let it get soft. When cool, beat the sugar and yolks, and add to the mixture, also the grated rind. Bake in a buttered dish until firm and slightly brown, from a half to three-quarters of an hour. When done, draw it to the door of the oven, and cover with a meringue made of the whites of the eggs, whipped to a froth with four table-spoonfuls of powdered sugar, and the lemon-juice; put it back in the oven and brown a light straw color. Eat warm, with lemon sauce.

LEMON PUDDING.

A *small* cupful of butter, the grated peel of two large lemons, and the juice of one; the yolks of ten eggs and whites of five; a cupful and a half of white sugar. Beat all together, and, lining a deep pudding-dish with puff paste, bake the lemon pudding in it; while baking, beat the whites of the remaining five eggs to a stiff froth, whip in fine white sugar to taste, cover the top of the pudding (when baked) with the meringue, and return to the oven for a moment to brown; eat cold, it requires no sauce.

BOILED LEMON PUDDING.

Half a cupful of chopped suet, one pint of bread-crumbs, one lemon, one cupful of sugar, one of flour, a teaspoonful of salt and two eggs, milk. First mix the suet, bread-crumbs, sugar and flour well together, adding the lemon-peel, which should be the yellow grated from the outside, and the juice, which should be strained. When these ingredients are well mixed, moisten with the eggs and sufficient milk to make the pudding of the consistency of thick batter; put it into a well-buttered mold, and boil for three and a half hours; turn it out, strew sifted sugar over and serve warm with lemon sauce, or not, at pleasure.

LEMON PUDDING, COLD.

One cupful of sugar, four eggs, the whites and yolks beaten separately, two tablespoonfuls of corn-starch, one pint of milk, one tablespoonful of butter and the juice and rind of two lemons. Wet the corn-starch in some of the milk, then stir it into the remainder of the milk, which should be boiling on the stove, stirring constantly and briskly for five minutes. Take it from the stove, stir in the butter and let it cool. Beat the yolks and sugar together, then stir them thoroughly into the milk and corn-starch. Now stir in the lemon-juice and grated rind, doing it very gradually, making it very smooth. Bake in a well-buttered dish. To be eaten cold. Oranges may be used in place of lemons. This also may be turned while *hot* into several small cups or forms previously dipped in cold water, place them aside; in one hour they will be fit to turn out. Serve with cream and sugar. Should be boiled all together not baked.

ROYAL SAGO PUDDING.

Three-quarters of a cupful of sago, washed and put into one quart of milk; put it into a sauce-pan, let it stand in boiling water on the stove or range until the sago has well-swelled. While hot, put in two tablespoonfuls of butter with one cupful of white sugar, and flavoring. When cool, add the well-beaten yolks of four eggs, put in a buttered pudding-dish, and bake from half to three-quarters of an hour; then remove it from the oven and place it to cool. Beat the whites of the eggs with three tablespoonfuls of powdered white sugar, till they are a mass of froth; spread the pudding with either raspberry or strawberry jam, and then spread on the frosting; put in the oven for two minutes to slightly brown. If made in summer, be sure and keep the whites of the eggs on ice until ready for use, and beat them in the coolest place you can find, as it will make a much richer frosting.

The small white sago called pearl is the best. The large brown kind has an earthy taste. It should always be kept in a covered jar or box.

This pudding, made with tapioca, is equally as good. Serve with any sweet sauce.

SAGO APPLE PUDDING.

One cupful of sago in a quart of tepid water, with a pinch of salt, soaked for one hour; six or eight apples, pared and cored, or quartered, and steamed tender, and put in the pudding dish; boil and stir the sago until clear, adding water to make it thin, and pour it over the apples; bake one hour. This is good hot, with butter and sugar, or cold with cream and sugar.

PLAIN SAGO PUDDING.

Make the same as "Tapioca Pudding," substituting sago for tapioca.

CHOCOLATE PUDDING. No. 1.

Make a corn-starch pudding with a quart of milk, three tablespoonfuls of corn-starch, and three tablespoonfuls of sugar. When done, remove about half and flavor to taste, and then to that remaining in the kettle add an egg beaten very light, and four tablespoonfuls of vanilla chocolate, grated and dissolved in a little milk. Put in a mold, alternating the dark and light. Serve with whipped cream or boiled custard. This is more of a blanc-mange than a pudding.

CHOCOLATE PUDDING. No. 2.

One quart of sweet milk, three-quarters of a cupful of grated chocolate; scald the milk and chocolate together; when *cool*, add the yolks of five eggs, one cupful of sugar; flavor with vanilla. Bake about twenty-five minutes. Beat the five whites of eggs to a stiff froth, adding four tablespoonfuls of fine sugar, spread evenly over the top and brown slightly in the oven.

CHOCOLATE PUDDING. No. 3.

One quart of milk, fourteen even tablespoonfuls of grated bread-crumbs, twelve tablespoonfuls grated chocolate, six eggs, one tablespoonful vanilla, sugar to make very sweet. Se arate the yolks and whites of four eggs, beat up the four yolks and two whole eggs together very light with the sugar. Put the milk on the range, and when it comes to a perfect boil pour it over the bread and chocolate; add the beaten eggs and sugar and vanilla; be sure it is sweet enough; pour into a buttered dish; bake one hour in a moderate oven. When cold, and just before it is served, have the four whites beaten with a little powdered sugar, and flavor with vanilla, and use as a meringue.

CHOCOLATE PUDDING. No. 4.

Half a cake of chocolate broken in one quart of milk and put on the range until it reaches boiling point; remove the mixture from the range; add four teaspoonfuls of corn-starch mixed with the yolks of three eggs and one cup and a half of sugar; stir constantly until thick; remove from the fire and flavor with vanilla; pour the mixture in a dish; beat the whites of the three eggs to a stiff froth, and add a little sugar; cover the top of the pudding with a meringue, and set in the oven until a light brown. Serve cold.

TAPIOCA PUDDING.

Five tablespoonfuls of tapioca, one quart of milk, two ounces of butter, a cupful of sugar, four eggs, flavoring of vanilla or bitter almonds. Wash the tapioca, and let it stew gently in the milk on the back part of the stove for a quarter of an hour, occasionally stirring it; then let it cool; mix with it the butter, sugar and eggs, which should be well beaten, and flavor with either of the above ingredients. Butter a dish, put in the pudding, and bake in a moderate oven for an hour. If the pudding is boiled, add a little more tapioca, and boil it in a buttered basin one and a half hours.

STRAWBERRY TAPIOCA.

This makes a most delightful dessert. Soak over night a large teacupful of tapioca in cold water; in the morning, put half of it in a buttered yellow-ware baking-dish, or any suitable pudding-dish. Sprinkle sugar over the tapioca; then on this put a quart of berries, sugar, and the rest of the tapioca. Fill the dish with water, which should cover the tapioca about a quarter of an inch. Bake in a moderately hot oven until it looks clear. Eat cold, with cream or custard. If not sweet enough, add more sugar at table; and in baking, if it seems too dry, more water is needed.

A similar dish may be made, using peaches, either fresh or canned.

RASPBERRY PUDDING.

One-quarter cupful of butter, one-half cupful of sugar, two cupfuls of jam, six cupfuls of soft bread-crumbs, four eggs. Rub the butter and sugar together; beat the eggs, yolks and whites separately; mash the raspberries, add the whites beaten to a stiff froth; stir all together to a smooth paste; butter a pudding-dish, cover the bottom with a layer of the crumbs, then a layer of the mixture; continue the alternate layers until the dish is full, making the last layer of crumbs; bake one hour in a moderate oven. Serve in the dish in which it is baked, and serve with fruit sauce made with raspberries. This pudding may be made the same with other kinds of berries.

PEAR, PEACH AND APPLE PUDDING.

Pare some nice, ripe pears (to weigh about three-fourths of a pound); put them in a sauce-pan with a few cloves, some lemon or orange peel, and stew about a quarter of an hour in two cupfuls of water; put them in your pudding-dish, and having made the following custard, one pint of cream, or milk, four eggs, sugar to taste, a pinch of salt and a tablespoonful of flour; beat eggs and sugar well, add the flour, grate some nutmeg, add the cream by degrees, stirring all the time,—pour this over the pears, and bake in a *quick* oven. Apples or peaches may be substituted.

Serve cold with sweetened cream.

FIG PUDDINGS.

Half a pound of good, dried figs, washed, wiped and minced; two cupfuls of fine, dry bread-crumbs, three eggs, half a cupful of beef suet, powdered, two scant cupfuls of sweet milk, half a cupful of white sugar, a little salt, half a teaspoonful of baking-powder, stirred in half a cupful of sifted flour. Soak the crumbs in milk, add the eggs, beaten light, with sugar, salt, suet, flour and figs. Beat three minutes, put in buttered molds with tight top, set in boiling water with weight on cover to prevent mold from upsetting, and boil three hours. Eat hot with hard sauce or butter, powdered sugar, one teaspoonful of extract of nutmeg.

FRUIT PUDDING, CORN-MEAL.

Take a pint of hot milk, and stir in sifted Indian meal till the batter is stiff; add a teaspoonful of salt and half of a cup of molasses, adding a teaspoonful of soda dissolved; then stir in a pint of whortleberries or chopped sweet apple; tie in a cloth that has been wet, and leave room for it to swell, or put it in a pudding-pan, and tie a cloth over; boil three hours; the water must boil when it is put in; you can use cranberries and sweet sauce.

APPLE CORN-MEAL PUDDING.

Pare and core twelve pippen apples; slice them very thin; then stir into one quart of new milk one quart of sifted corn-meal; add a little salt, then the apples, four spoonfuls of chopped suet and a teacupful of good molasses, adding a teaspoonful of soda dissolved; mix these well together; pour into a buttered dish, and bake four hours; serve hot, with sugar and wine sauce. This is the most simple, cheap and luxuriant fruit pudding that can be made.

RHUBARB, OR PIE-PLANT PUDDING.

Chop rhubarb pretty fine, put in a pudding-dish, and sprinkle sugar over it; make a batter of one cupful of sour milk, two eggs, a piece of butter the size of an egg, half a teaspoonful of soda, and enough flour to make batter about as thick as for cake. Spread it over the rhubarb, and bake till done. Turn out on a platter upside down, so that the rhubarb will be on top. Serve with sugar and cream.

FRUIT PUDDINGS.

Fruit puddings, such as green gooseberry, are very nice made in a basin, the basin to be buttered and lined with a paste, rolling it round to the thickness of half an inch; then get a pint of gooseberries and three ounces of sugar; after having made your paste, take half the fruit, and lay it at the bottom of your basin; then add half your sugar, then put the remainder of the gooseberries in, and the remainder of the sugar; on that, draw your paste to the centre, join the edges well together, put the cloth over the whole, tying it at the bottom, and boil in plenty of water. Fruit puddings of this kind, such as apples and rhubarb, should be done in this manner.

Boil for an hour, take out of the sauce-pan, untie the cloth, turn out on a dish, or let it remain in the basin, and serve with sugar over. A thin cover of the paste may be rolled round and put over the pudding.

Ripe cherries, currants, raspberries, greengages, plums and such like fruit, will not require so much sugar, or so long boiling. These puddings are also very good steamed.

SNOW PUDDING.

One half a package of Cox's gelatine; pour over it a cupful of cold water, and add one and a half cupfuls of sugar; when soft, add one cupful of boiling water and the juice of one lemon; then the whites of four well-beaten eggs; beat all together until it is light and frothy, or until the gelatine will not settle clear in the bottom of the dish after standing a few minutes; put it on a glass dish. Serve with a custard made of one pint of milk, the yolks of four eggs, four tablespoonfuls of sugar, and the grated rind of a lemon; boil.

DELMONICO PUDDING.

Three tablespoonfuls of corn-starch, the yolks of five eggs, six tablespoonfuls of sugar; beat the eggs light; then add the sugar and beat again till very light; mix the corn-starch with a little cold milk; mix all together and stir into one quart of milk just as it is about to boil, having added a little salt; stir it until it has thickened well; pour it into a dish for the table and place it in the oven until it will bear icing; place over the top a layer of canned peaches or other fruit (and it improves it to mix the syrup of the fruit with the custard part); beat the whites to a stiff froth with two tablespoonfuls of white sugar to an egg; then put it into the oven until it is a light brown.

This is a very delicate and delicious pudding.

SAUCER PUDDINGS.

Two tablespoonfuls of flour, two tablespoonfuls of powdered sugar, three eggs, a teacupful of milk, butter, preserve of any kind. Mix the flour and sugar, beat the eggs, add them to the milk, and beat up with the flour and sugar. Butter well three saucers, half fill them, and bake in a quick oven about twenty minutes. Remove them from the saucers when cool enough, cut in half, and spread a thin layer of preserve between each half; close them again, and serve with cream.

NANTUCKET PUDDING.

One quart of berries or any small fruit; two tablespoonfuls of flour, two tablespoonfuls of sugar; simmer together and turn into molds; cover with frosting as for cake, or with whipped eggs and sugar, browning lightly in the oven; serve with cream.

TOAST PUDDING.

Toast several thin slices of stale bread, removing the crust, butter them well, and pour over them hot stewed fruit in alternate layers. Serve warm with rich hot sauce.

PLAIN RICE PUDDING.

Pick over, wash and boil, a teacupful of rice; when soft, drain off the water; while warm, add to it a tablespoonful of cold butter. When cool, mix with it a cupful of sugar, a teaspoonful of grated nutmeg, and one of ground cinnamon. Beat up four eggs very light, whites and yolks separately; add them to the rice; then stir in a quart of sweet milk gradually. Butter a pudding dish, turn in the mixture, and bake one hour in a moderate oven. Serve warm, with sweet wine sauce.

If you have cold cooked rice, first soak it in the milk, and proceed as above.

RICE PUDDING. (Fine.)

Wash a teacupful of rice, and boil it in two teacupfuls of water; then add, while the rice is hot, three tablespoonfuls of butter, five tablespoonfuls of sugar, five eggs well-beaten, one tablespoonful of powdered nutmeg, a little salt, one glass of wine, a quarter of a pound of raisins, stoned and cut in halves, a quarter of a pound of Zante currants, a quarter of a pound of citron cut in slips, and one quart of cream; mix well, pour into a buttered dish and bake an hour in a moderate oven.

—Astor House, New York City.

RICE MERINGUE.

One cupful of carefully sorted rice, boiled in water until it is soft; when done, drain it so as to remove all the water; cool it, and add one quart of new milk, the well-beaten yolks of three eggs, three tablespoonfuls of white sugar, and a little nutmeg, or flavor with lemon or vanilla; pour into a baking dish, and bake about half an hour. Let it get cold; beat the whites of the eggs, add two tablespoonfuls of sugar, flavor with lemon or vanilla; drop or spread it over the pudding, and slightly brown it in the oven

RICE LEMON PUDDING.

Put on to boil one quart of milk, and when it simmers stir in four table-spoonfuls of rice flour that has been moistened in a little milk; let it come to a boil, and remove from the fire; add one-quarter of a pound of butter, and when cool, the grated peel, with the juice of two lemons, and the yolks and beaten whites of four eggs; sweeten to taste; one wine-glassful of wine, put in the last thing, is also an improvement.

RICE PUDDING WITHOUT EGGS.

Two quarts of milk, two-thirds of a cupful of rice, a cupful of sugar, a piece of butter as large as a walnut, a teaspoonful of cinnamon, a little nutmeg and a pinch of salt. Put into a deep pudding-dish, well-buttered, set into a moderate oven; stir it once or twice until it begins to cook, let it remain in the oven about two hours (until it is the consistency of cream). Eat cold.

FRUIT RICE PUDDING.

One large teacupful of rice, a little water to cook it partially; dry, line an earthen basin with part of it; fill nearly full with pared, cored and quartered apples, or any fruit you choose; cover with the balance of your rice; tie a cloth tightly over the top, and steam one hour. To be eaten with sweet sauce. Do not butter your dish.

BOILED RICE PUDDING. No. 1.

One cupful of cold, boiled rice, one cupful of sugar, four eggs, a pinch of soda, and a pinch of salt. Put it all in a bowl, and beat it up until it is very light and white. Beat four ounces of butter to a cream, put it into the pudding, and ten drops of essence of lemon. Beat altogether for five minutes. Butter a mold, pour the pudding into it, and boil for two hours. Serve with sweet fruit sauce.

BOILED RICE PUDDING. No. 2.

Wash two teacupfuls of rice, and soak it in water for half an hour; then turn off the water, and mix the rice with half a pound of raisins stoned and cut in halves; add a little salt, tie the whole in a cloth, leaving room for the rice to swell to twice its natural size, and boil two hours in plenty of water; serve with wine sauce.

RICE SNOW-BALLS.

Wash two teacupfuls of rice, and boil it in one teacupful of water and one of milk, with a little salt; if the rice is not tender when the milk and water are absorbed, add a little more milk and water; when the rice is tender, flavor with vanilla, form it into balls, or mold it into a compact form with little cups; place these rice balls around the inside of a deep dish, fill the dish with a rich soft custard, and serve either hot or cold. The custard and balls should be flavored with the same.

PRUNE PUDDING.

Heat a little more than a pint of sweet milk to the boiling point, then stir in gradually a little cold milk in which you have rubbed smooth a heaping table-spoonful of corn-starch; add sugar to suit your taste; three well-beaten eggs, about a teaspoonful of butter, and a little grated nutmeg. Let this come to a boil, then pour it in a buttered pudding-dish, first adding a cupful of stewed prunes, with the stones taken out. Bake for from fifteen to twenty minutes, according to the state of the oven. Serve with or without sauce. A little cream improves it if poured over it when placed in saucers.

BLACKBERRY OR WHORTLEBERRY PUDDING.

Three cupfuls of flour, one cupful of molasses, half a cupful of milk, a tea-spoonful of salt, a little cloves and cinnamon, a teaspoonful of soda, dissolved in a little of the milk. Stir in a quart of huckleberries, floured. Boil in a well-buttered mold two hours. Serve with brandy sauce.

BAKED HUCKLEBERRY PUDDING.

One quart of ripe, fresh huckleberries or blueberries; half a teaspoonful of mace or nutmeg, three eggs well beaten, separately; two cupfuls of sugar; one tablespoonful of cold butter; one cupful of sweet milk, one pint of flour, two teaspoonfuls of baking-powder. Roll the berries well in the flour, and add them last of all. Bake half an hour and serve with sauce. There is no more delicate and delicious pudding than this.

FRUIT PUDDING.

This pudding is made without cooking and is nice prepared the day before used.

Stew currants or any small fruits, either fresh or dried, sweeten with sugar to taste, and pour hot over *thin* slices of bread with the crust cut off, placed in a suitable dish, first a layer of bread, then the hot stewed fruit, then bread and fruit, then bread, leaving the fruit last. Put a plate over the top and when cool, set it on ice. Serve with sugar and cream.

This pudding is very fine made with Boston crackers split open, and placed in layers with stewed peaches.

BOILED CURRANT PUDDING.

Five cupfuls of sifted flour in which two teaspoonfuls of baking-powder have been sifted. One-half a cupful of chopped suet; half a pound of currants, milk, a pinch of salt. Wash the currants, dry them thoroughly, and pick away any stalks or grit; chop the suet finely; mix all the ingredients together and moisten with sufficient milk to make the pudding into a stiff batter; tie it up in a floured cloth, put it into boiling water, and boil for three hours and a half. Serve with jelly sauce made very sweet.

TRANSPARENT PUDDING.

A small cupful of fresh butter warmed, but not melted, one cupful of sifted sugar creamed with the butter, a teaspoonful of nutmeg, grated, eight eggs, yolks and whites beaten separately. Beat the butter and sugar light, and then add the nutmeg and the beaten eggs, which should be stirred in gradually; flavor with vanilla, almond, peach or rosewater; stir *hard;* butter a deep dish, line with puff-paste, and bake half an hour. Then make a meringue for the top, and brown. Serve cold.

SWEET-POTATO PUDDING.

To a large sweet potato, weighing two pounds, allow half a pound of sugar, half a pound of butter, one gill of sweet cream, one gill of strong wine or brandy, one grated nutmeg, a little lemon peel, and four eggs. Boil the potato until thoroughly done, mash up fine, and while hot add the sugar and butter. Set aside to cool while you beat the eggs light, and add the seasoning last. Line tin plates with puff-paste, and pour in the mixture. Bake in a moderate but regularly heated oven. When the puddings are drawn from the fire, cover the top with thinly sliced bits of preserved citron or quince marmalade. Strew the top thickly with granulated white sugar, and serve, with the addition of a glass of rich milk for each person at table.

PINEAPPLE PUDDING.

Butter a pudding-dish and line the bottom and sides with slices of stale cake (sponge cake is best); pare and slice thin a large pineapple; place in the dish first a layer of pineapple, then strew with sugar, then more pineapple, and so on until all is used. Pour over a small teacupful of water, and cover with slices of cake which have been dipped in cold water; cover the whole with a buttered plate, and bake slowly for two hours.

ORANGE ROLEY POLEY.

Make a light dough the same as for apple dumplings, roll it out into a narrow long sheet, about quarter of an inch thick. Spread thickly over it peeled and sliced oranges, sprinkle it plentifully with white sugar; scatter over all a teaspoonful or two of grated orange-peel, then roll it up. Fold the edges well together, to keep the juices from running out. Boil it in a floured cloth one hour and a half. Serve it with lemon sauce. Fine.

ROLEY POLEY PUDDING. (Apple.)

Peel, core and slice sour apples; make a rich biscuit dough, or raised biscuit dough may be used if rolled thinner; roll not quite half an inch thick, lay the slices on the paste, roll up, tuck in the ends, prick deeply with a fork, lay it in a steamer, and steam hard for an hour and three-quarters. Or, wrap it in a pudding-cloth well floured ; tie the ends, baste up the sides, plunge into boiling water, and boil continually an hour and a half, perhaps more. Stoned cherries, dried fruits, or any kind of berries, fresh or dried, may be used.

FRUIT PUFF PUDDING.

Into one pint of flour stir two teaspoonfuls baking-powder and a little salt; then sift and stir the mixture into milk, until very soft. Place well-greased cups in a steamer, put in each a spoonful of the above batter, then add one of berries or steamed apples, cover with another spoonful of batter, and steam twenty minutes. This pudding is delicious made with strawberries, and eaten with a sauce made of two eggs, half a cup butter, a cup of sugar beaten thoroughly with a cup of boiling milk, and one cup of strawberries.

SPONGE CAKE PUDDING. No. 1.

Bake a common sponge cake in a flat-bottomed pudding-dish; when ready to use, cut in six or eight pieces; split and spread with butter, and return them to the dish. Make a custard with four eggs to a quart of milk; flavor and sweeten to taste; pour over the cake, and bake one-half hour. The cake will swell and fill the custard. Serve with or without sauce.

SPONGE CAKE PUDDING. No. 2.

Butter a pudding-mold: fill the mold with small sponge cakes or slices of stale plain cake, that have been soaked in a liquid made by dissolving one-half pint of jelly in a pint of hot water. This will be of as fine a flavor and much better for all than if the cake had been soaked in wine. Make a sufficient quantity of custard to fill the mold, and leave as much more to be boiled in a dish by itself. Set the mold, after being tightly covered, into a kettle, and boil one hour. Turn out of the mold, and serve with some of the other custard poured over it.

GRAHAM PUDDING.

Mix well together one half a coffee-cupful of molasses, one-quarter of a cupful of butter, one egg, one-half a cupful of milk, one-half a teaspoonful of pure soda, one and one half cupfuls of good Graham flour, one small teacupful of raisins, spices to taste. Steam four hours, and serve with brandy or wine sauce, or any sauce that may be preferred. This makes a showy as well as a light and wholesome dessert, and has the merit of simplicity and cheapness.

BANANA PUDDING.

Cut sponge cake in slices, and, in a glass dish, put alternately a layer of cake and a layer of bananas sliced. Make a soft custard, flavor with a little wine, and pour over it. Beat the whites of the eggs to a stiff froth and heap over the whole.

Peaches cut up, left a few hours in sugar and then scalded, and added when cold to thick boiled custard, made rather sweet, are a delicious dessert.

DRIED PEACH PUDDING.

Boil one pint of milk and while hot turn it over a pint of bread-crumbs. Stir into it a tablespoonful of butter, one pint of dried peaches stewed soft. When all is cool, add two well-beaten eggs, half of a cupful of sugar and a pinch of salt; flavor to taste. Put into a well-buttered pudding-dish and bake half an hour.

SUET PUDDING, PLAIN.

One cupful of chopped suet, one cupful of milk, two eggs beaten, half a tea-spoonful of salt, and enough flour to make a stiff batter, but thin enough to pour from a spoon. Put into a bowl, cover with a cloth, and boil three hours. The same, made a little thinner, with a few raisins added, and baked in a well-greased dish is excellent. Two teaspoonfuls of baking-powder in the flour improves this pudding. Or if made with sour milk and soda it is equally as good.

SUET PLUM PUDDING.

One cupful of suet, chopped fine, one cupful of cooking molasses, one cupful of milk, one cupful of raisins, three and one-half cupfuls of flour, one egg, one teaspoonful of cloves, two of cinnamon, and one of nutmeg, a little salt, one tea-spoonful of soda; boil three hours in a pudding-mold set into a kettle of water; eat with common sweet sauce. If sour milk is used in place of sweet, the pudding will be much lighter.

PEACH COBBLER.

Line a deep dish with rich thick crust; pare and cut into halves or quarters some juicy, rather tart peaches; put in sugar, spices and flavoring to taste; stew it slightly, and put it in the lined dish; cover with thick crust of rich puff-paste, and bake a rich brown; when done, break up the top crust into small pieces, and stir it into the fruit; serve hot or cold; very palatable without sauce, but more so with plain, rich cream or cream sauce, or with a rich brandy or wine. Other fruits can be used in place of peaches. Currants are best made in this manner:

Press the currants through a sieve to free it from pips; to each pint of the pulp put two ounces of crumbed bread and four ounces of sugar; bake with a rim of puff-paste; serve with cream. White currants may be used instead of red.

HOMINY PUDDING.

Two-thirds of a cupful of hominy, one and a half pints of milk, two eggs, one tablespoonful of butter, one teaspoonful of extract of lemon or vanilla, one cupful of sugar. Boil hominy in milk one hour; then pour it on the eggs, extract and sugar, beaten together; add butter, pour in buttered pudding-dish, bake in hot oven for twenty minutes.

BAKED BERRY ROLLS.

Roll rich biscuit-dough thin, cut it into little squares four inches wide and seven inches long. Spread over with berries. Roll up the crust, and put the rolls in a dripping-pan just a little apart; put a piece of butter on each roll, spices if you like. Strew over a large handful of sugar, a little hot water. Set in the oven and bake like dumplings. Served with sweet sauce.

GREEN-CORN PUDDING.

Take two dozen full ears of sweet green corn, score the kernels and cut them from the cob. Scrape off what remains on the cob with a knife. Add a pint and a half or one quart of milk, according to the youngness and juiciness of the corn. Add four eggs well beaten, a half teacupful of flour, a half teacupful of butter, a tablespoonful of sugar, and salt to taste. Bake in a well-greased earthen dish, in a hot oven, two hours. Place it on the table browned and smoking hot, eat it with plenty of fresh butter. This can be used as a dessert, by serving a sweet sauce with it. If eaten plainly with butter, it answers as a side vegetable.

GENEVA WAFERS.

Two eggs, three ounces of butter, three ounces of flour, three ounces of pounded sugar. Well whisk the eggs, put them into a basin, and stir to them the butter, which should be beaten to a cream; add the flour and sifted sugar gradually, and then mix all well together. Butter a baking-sheet, and drop on it a teaspoonful of the mixture at a time, leaving a space between each. Bake in a cool oven; watch the pieces of paste, and, when half done, roll them up like wafers, and put in a small wedge of bread or piece of wood, to keep them in shape. Return them to the oven until crisp. Before serving, remove the bread, put a spoonful of preserve in the widest end, and fill up with whipped cream. This is a very pretty and ornamental dish for the supper-table, and is very nice, and very easily made.

MINUTE PUDDING. No. 1.

Set a sauce-pan or deep frying-pan on the stove, the bottom and sides well buttered, put into it a quart of sweet milk, a pinch of salt, and a piece of butter as large as half an egg; when it boils have ready a dish of sifted flour, stir it into the boiling milk, sifting it through your fingers, a handful at a time, until it becomes smooth and quite thick. Turn it into a dish that has been dipped in water. Make a sauce very sweet to serve with it. Maple molasses is *fine* with it. This pudding is much improved by adding canned berries or fresh ones just before taking from the stove.

MINUTE PUDDING. No. 2.

One quart of milk, salt, two eggs, about a pint of flour. Beat the eggs well; add the flour and enough milk to make it smooth. Butter the sauce-pan and put in the remainder of the milk well salted; when it boils, stir in the flour, eggs, etc., lightly; let it cook well. It should be of the consistency of thick corn mush. Serve immediately with the following simple sauce, *viz:* Rich milk or cream sweetened to taste, and flavored with grated nutmeg.

SUNDERLAND PUDDING.

One cupful of sugar, half a cupful of cold butter, a pint of milk, two cupfuls of sifted flour, and five eggs. Make the milk hot; stir in the butter, and let it cool before the other ingredients are added to it; then stir in the sugar, flour, and eggs, which should be well whisked, and omit the whites of two; flavor with a little grated lemon-rind, and beat the mixture well. Butter some small cups, rather more than half fill them; bake from twenty minutes to half an hour, according to the size of the puddings, and serve with fruit, custard or wine sauce, a little of which may be poured over them. They may be dropped by spoonfuls on buttered tins, and baked, if cups are not convenient.

JELLY PUDDINGS.

Two cupfuls of *very* fine, stale biscuit or bread-crumbs; one cupful of rich milk—half cream, if you can get it; five eggs, beaten very light; half a teaspoonful of soda, stirred in boiling water; one cupful of sweet jelly, jam or marmalade. Scald the milk and pour over the crumbs. Beat until half cold, and stir in the beaten yolks, then whites, finally the soda. Fill large cups half full with the batter; set in a quick oven and bake half an hour. When done, turn out quickly, and dexterously; with a sharp knife make an incision in the side of each; pull partly open, and put a liberal spoonful of the conserve within. Close the slit by pinching the edges with your fingers. Eat warm with sweetened cream.

QUICK PUDDING.

Soak and split some crackers; lay the surface over with raisins and citron; put the halves together, tie them in a bag, and boil fifteen minutes in milk and water: delicious with rich sauce.

READY PUDDING.

Make a batter of one quart of milk, and about one pound of flour; add six eggs, the yolks and whites separately beaten, a teaspoonful of salt and four tablespoonfuls of sugar. It should be as stiff as can possibly be stirred with a spoon. Dip a spoonful at a time into quick boiling water, boil from five to ten minutes, take out. Serve hot with sauce or syrup.

A ROYAL DESSERT.

Cut a stale cake into slices an inch and a half in thickness; pour over them a little good, sweet cream; then fry *lightly* in fresh butter in a smooth frying-pan; when done, place over each slice of cake a layer of preserves; or, you may make a rich sauce to be served with it.

Another dish equally as good, is to dip thin slices of bread into fresh milk; have ready two eggs well-beaten; dip the slices in the egg, and fry them in butter to a light brown; when fried, pour over them a syrup, any kind that you choose, and serve hot.

HUCKLEBERRIES WITH CRACKERS AND CREAM.

Pick over carefully one quart of blueberries, and keep them on ice until wanted. Put into each bowl, for each guest, two soda-crackers, broken in not too small pieces; add a few tablespoonfuls of berries, a teaspoonful of powdered sugar, and fill the bowl with the richest of cold, sweet cream. This is an old-fashioned New England breakfast dish. It also answers for a dessert.

Mrs. ANDREW JOHNSON.

Mrs. ULYSSES S. GRANT.

LUCY WEBB HAYES.

LUCRETIA RUDOLPH GARFIELD.

MARY ARTHUR McELROY.

ROSE ELIZABETH CLEVELAND.

SAUCES FOR PUDDINGS.

BRANDY SAUCE, COLD.

Two cupfuls of powdered sugar, half a cupful of butter, one wine-glassful of brandy, cinnamon and nutmeg, a teaspoonful of each. Warm the butter slightly, and work it to a light cream with the sugar, then add the brandy and spices; beat it hard and set aside until wanted. Should be put into a mold to look nicely, and serve on a flat dish.

BRANDY OR WINE SAUCE. No. 1.

Stir a heaping teaspoonful of corn-starch in a little cold water to a smooth paste (or instead use a tablespoonful of sifted flour); add to it a cupful of boiling water, with one cupful of sugar, a piece of butter as large as an egg, boil all together ten minutes. Remove from the fire, and when cool, stir into it half of a cupful of brandy or wine. It should be about as thick as thin syrup.

RICH WINE SAUCE. No. 2.

One cupful of butter, two of powdered sugar, half a cupful of wine. Beat the butter to a cream. Add the sugar gradually, and when very light add the wine, which has been made hot, a little at a time, a teaspoonful of grated nutmeg. Place the bowl in a basin of hot water, and stir for two minutes. The sauce should be smooth and foamy.

BRANDY OR WINE SAUCE. No. 3

Take one cupful of butter, two of powdered sugar, the whites of two eggs, five tablespoonfuls of sherry wine or brandy, and a quarter of a cupful of boiling water. Beat butter and sugar to a cream, add the whites of the eggs, one at a time, unbeaten, and then the wine or brandy. Place the bowl in hot water, and stir till smooth and frothy.

379

SAUCE FOR PLUM-PUDDING. (Superior.)

Cream together a cupful of sugar and half a cupful of butter; when light and creamy, add the well-beaten yolks of four eggs. Stir into this one wine-glass of wine or one of brandy, a pinch of salt and one large cupful of hot cream or rich milk. Beat this mixture well; place it in a sauce-pan over the fire, stir it until it cooks sufficiently to thicken like cream. Be sure and not let it boil. Delicious.

LIQUID BRANDY SAUCE.

Brown over the fire three tablespoonfuls of sugar; add a cupful of water, six whole cloves and a piece of stick cinnamon, the yellow rind of a lemon cut very thin; let the sauce boil, strain while hot, then pour it into a sauce bowl containing the juice of the lemon and a cup of brandy. Serve warm.

GRANDMOTHER'S SAUCE.

Cream together a cupful of sifted sugar and half a cupful of butter, add a teaspoonful of ground cinnamon and an egg well beaten. Boil a teacupful of milk and turn it, boiling hot, over the mixture slowly, stirring all the time; this will cook the egg smoothly. It may be served cold or hot.

SUGAR SAUCE.

One coffee-cupful of granulated sugar, half of a cupful of water, a piece of butter the size of a walnut. Boil all together until it becomes the consistency of syrup. Flavor with lemon or vanilla extract. A tablespoonful of lemon-juice is an improvement. Nice with cottage pudding.

LEMON SAUCE.

One cupful of sugar, half a cupful of butter, one egg beaten light, one lemon, juice and grated rind, half a cupful of boiling water; put in a tin basin and thicken over steam.

LEMON CREAM SAUCE, HOT.

Put half a pint of new milk on the fire, and when it boils stir into it one teaspoonful of wheat flour, four ounces of sugar and the well-beaten yolks of three eggs; remove it from the fire and add the grated rind and the juice of one lemon; stir it well, and serve hot in a sauce tureen.

ORANGE CREAM SAUCE, HOT.

This is made as "Lemon Cream Sauce," substituting orange for lemon.

Creams for puddings, pies and fritters, may be made in the same manner with any other flavoring; if flour is used in making them, it should boil in the milk three or four minutes.

COLD LEMON SAUCE.

Beat to a cream one teacupful of butter and two teacupfuls of fine white sugar; then stir in the juice and grated rind of one lemon; grate nutmeg upon the sauce, and serve on a flat dish.

COLD ORANGE SAUCE.

Beat to a cream one teacupful of butter and two teacupfuls of fine white sugar; then stir in the grated rind of one orange and the juice of two; stir until all the orange-juice is absorbed; grate nutmeg upon the sauce, and serve on a flat dish.

COLD CREAM SAUCE.

Stir to a cream one cupful of sugar, half a cupful of butter, then add a cupful of sweet, thick, cold cream, flavor to taste. Stir well, and set it in a cool place.

CREAM SAUCE, WARM.

Heat a pint of cream slowly in a double boiler; when nearly boiling, set it off from the fire, put into it half a cupful of sugar, a little nutmeg or vanilla extract; stir it thoroughly, and add, when cool, the whites of two well-beaten eggs. Set it on the fire in a dish containing hot water to keep it warm until needed, stirring once or more.

CARAMEL SAUCE.

Place over the fire a sauce-pan; when it begins to be hot, put into it four tablespoonfuls of white sugar, and one tablespoonful of water. Stir it continually for three or four minutes, until all the water evaporates; then watch it carefully until it becomes a delicate brown color. Have ready a pint of cold water and cup of sugar mixed with some flavoring; turn it into the sauce-pan with the browned sugar, and let it simmer for ten minutes; then add half a glass of brandy or a glass of wine. The wine or brandy may be omitted if preferred.

A GOOD, PLAIN SAUCE.

A good sauce to go with plain fruit puddings is made by mixing one cupful of brown sugar, one cupful of best molasses, half a cupful of butter, one large teaspoonful of flour; add the juice and grated rind of one lemon, half a nutmeg, grated, half a teaspoonful of cloves and cinnamon. When these are all stirred together, add a teacupful of boiling water; stir it constantly, put into a sauce-pan and let it boil until clear; then strain.

OLD-STYLE SAUCE.

One pint of sour cream, the juice and finely grated rind of a large lemon; sugar to taste. Beat hard and long until the sauce is very light. This is delicious with cold " Brown Betty "—a form of cold farina, corn-starch, blanc-mange, and the like.

PLAIN COLD, HARD SAUCE.

Stir together one cupful of white sugar, and half a cupful of butter, until it is creamy and light; add flavoring to taste. This is very nice, flavored with the juice of raspberries or strawberries, or beat into it a cupful of ripe strawberries or raspberries and the white of an egg, beaten stiff.

CUSTARD SAUCE.

One cupful of sugar, two beaten eggs, one pint of milk, flavoring to taste, brandy or wine, if preferred.

Heat the milk to boiling, add by degrees the beaten eggs and sugar, put in the flavoring, and set within a pan of boiling water; stir until it begins to thicken; then take it off, and stir in the brandy or wine gradually; set, until wanted, within a pan of boiling water.

MILK SAUCE. No. 1.

Dissolve a tablespoonful of flour in cold milk; see that it is free from lumps. Whisk an ounce of butter and a cupful of sugar to a cream, and add to it a pinch of salt. Mix together half a pint of milk, one egg, and the flour; stir this into the butter, and add a dash of nutmeg, or any flavor; heat until near the boiling point, and serve. Very nice in place of cold cream.

MILK OR CREAM SAUCE.

Cream or rich milk, simply sweetened with plenty of white sugar and flavored, answers the purpose of some kinds of pudding, and can be made very quickly.

FRUIT SAUCE.

Two thirds of a cupful of sugar, a pint of raspberries or strawberries, a tablespoonful of melted butter and a cupful of hot water. Boil all together slowly, removing the scum as fast as it rises; then strain through a sieve. This is very good served with dumplings or apple puddings.

JELLY SAUCE.

Melt two tablespoonfuls of sugar and half a cupful of jelly over the fire in a cupful of boiling water, adding also two tablespoonfuls of butter; then stir into it a teaspoonful of corn-starch, dissolved in half a cupful of water or wine; add it to the jelly, and let it come to a boil. Set it in a dish of hot water to keep it warm until time to serve; stir occasionally. Any fruit jelly can be used.

COMMON SWEET SAUCE.

Into a pint of water stir a paste made of a tablespooonful of corn-starch or flour (rubbed smooth with a little cold water); add a cupful of sugar and a tablespoonful of vinegar. Cook well for three minutes. Take from the fire and add a piece of butter as large as a small egg; when cool, flavor with a tablespoonful of vanilla or lemon extract.

SYRUP FOR FRUIT SAUCE.

An excellent syrup for fruit sauce is made of Morello cherries (red, sour cherries). For each pound of cherry juice, allow half a pound of sugar and six cherry kernels; seed the cherries and let them stand in a bowl over night; in the morning, press them through a fine cloth which has been dipped in boiling water; weigh the juice, add the sugar, boil fifteen minutes, removing all the scum. Fill small bottles that are perfectly dry with the syrup; when it is cold, cork the bottles tightly, seal them and keep them in a cool place, standing upright.

Most excellent to put into pudding sauces.

ROSE BRANDY. (For Cakes and Puddings.)

Gather the leaves of roses while the dew is on them, and as soon as they open, put them into a wide-mouthed bottle, and when the bottle is full, pour in the best of fourth proof French brandy.

It will be fit for use in three or four weeks, and may be frequently replenished. It is sometimes considered preferable to wine as a flavoring to pastries and pudding sauces.

LEMON BRANDY. (For Cakes and Puddings.)

When you use lemons for punch or lemonade, do not throw away the peels, but cut them in small pieces—the thin yellow outside (the thick part is not good), and put them in a glass jar or bottle of brandy. You will find this brandy useful for many purposes.

In the same way keep for use the kernels of peach and plum stones, pounding them slightly before you put them into the brandy.

PRESERVES, JELLIES, ETC.

Fruit for preserving should be sound and free from all defects, using white sugar, and also that which is dry, which produces the nicest syrup; dark sugar can be used by being clarified, which is done by dissolving two pounds of sugar in a pint of water; add to it the white of an egg, and beat it well, put it into a preserving kettle on the fire, and stir with a wooden spoon. As soon as it begins to swell and boil up, throw in a little cold water; let it boil up again, take it off, and remove the scum; boil it again, throw in more cold water, and remove the scum; repeat until it is clear and pours like oil from the spoon.

In the old way of preserving, we used pound for pound, when they were kept in stone jars or crocks; now, as most preserves are put up in sealed jars or cans, less sugar seems sufficient; three-quarters of a pound of sugar is generally all that is required for a pound of fruit.

Fruit should be boiled in a porcelain-lined or granite-ware dish, if possible; but other utensils, copper or metal, if made bright and clean, answer as well.

Any of the fruits that have been preserved in syrup may be converted into dry preserves, by first draining them from the syrup, and then drying them in a stove or very moderate oven, adding to them a quantity of powdered loaf sugar, which will gradually penetrate the fruit, while the fluid parts of the syrup gently evaporate. They should be dried in the stove or oven on a sieve, and turned every six or eight hours, fresh powdered sugar being sifted over them every time they are turned. Afterwards, they are to be kept in a dry situation, in drawers or boxes. Currants and cherries preserved whole in this manner, in bunches, are extremely elegant, and have a fine flavor. In this way it is, also, that orange and lemon chips are preserved.

Mold can be prevented from forming on fruit jellies by pouring a little melted paraffine over the top. When cool, it will harden to a solid cake, which can be easily removed when the jelly is used, and saved to use over again another year. It is perfectly harmless and tasteless.

Large glass tumblers are the best for keeping jellies, much better than large vessels, for by being opened frequently they soon spoil; a paper should be cut to fit, and placed over the jelly; then put on the lid or cover, with thick paper rubbed over on the inside with the white of an egg.

There cannot be too much care taken in selecting fruit for jellies, for if the fruit is over ripe, any amount of time in boiling will never make it jelly,—there is where so many fail in making good jelly; and another important matter is overlooked—that of carefully skimming off the juice after it begins to boil and a scum rises from the bottom to the top; the juice should not be stirred, but the scum carefully taken off: if allowed to boil under, the jelly will not be clear.

When either preserves or canned fruits show any indications of fermentation, they should be immediately reboiled with more sugar, to save them. It is much better to be generous with the sugar at first, than to have any losses afterwards. Keep all preserves in a cool, dry closet.

PRESERVED CHERRIES.

Take large, ripe Morella cherries; weigh them, and to each pound allow a pound of loaf sugar. Stone the cherries, (opening them with a sharp quill,) and save the juice that comes from them in the process. As you stone them, throw them into a large pan or tureen, and strew about half the sugar over them, and let them lie in it an hour or two after they are all stoned. Then put them into a preserving-kettle with the remainder of the sugar, and boil and skim them till the fruit is clear and the syrup thick.

PRESERVED CRANBERRIES.

The cranberries must be large and ripe. Wash them, and to six quarts of cranberries allow nine pounds of the best loaf sugar. Take three quarts of the cranberries, and put them into a stew-pan with a pint and a half of water. Cover the pan, and boil or stew them till they are all to pieces. Then squeeze the juice through a jelly bag. Put the sugar into a preserving kettle, pour the cranberry juice over it, and let it stand until it is all melted, stirring it up frequently. Then place the kettle over the fire, and put in the remaining three quarts of whole cranberries. Let them boil till they are tender, clear, and of a bright color, skimming them frequently. When done, put them warm into jars with the syrup, which should be like a thick jelly.

PRESERVED STRAWBERRIES.

For every pound of fruit weigh a pound of refined sugar, put them with the sugar over the fire in a porcelain kettle, bring to a boil slowly about twenty minutes. Take them out carefully with a perforated skimmer, and fill your *hot* jars nearly full; boil the juice a few minutes longer, and fill up the jars; seal them *hot*. Keep in a cool, dry place.

TO PRESERVE BERRIES WHOLE. (Excellent.)

Buy the fruit when not *too ripe*, pick over immediately, wash if absolutely necessary, and put in glass jars, filling each one about two-thirds full.

Put in the preserving kettle a pound of sugar and one cupful of water for every two pounds of fruit, and let it come slowly to a boil. Pour this syrup into the jars over the berries, filling them up to the brim; then set the jars in a pot of *cold* water on the stove, and let the water boil and the fruit become scalding hot. Now take them out and seal perfectly tight. If this process is followed thoroughly, the fruit will keep for several years.

PRESERVED EGG PLUMS.

Use a pound of sugar for a pound of plums; wash the plums, and wipe dry; put the sugar on a slow fire in the preserving-kettle, with as much water as will melt the sugar, and let it simmer slowly; then prick each plum thoroughly with a needle, or a fork with fine prongs, and place a layer of them in the syrup; let them cook until they lose their color a little and the skins begin to break; then lift them out with a perforated skimmer, and place them singly in a large dish to cool; then put another layer of plums in the syrup, and let them cook and cool in the same manner, until the whole are done; as they cool, carefully replace the broken skins so as not to spoil the appearance of the plums; when the last layer is finished, return the first to the kettle, and boil until transparent; do the same with each layer; while the latest cooked are cooling, place the first in glass jars; when all are done, pour the hot syrup over them; when they are cold, close as usual; the jelly should be of the color and consistency of rich wine jelly.

PRESERVED PEACHES.

Peaches for preserving may be ripe but not soft; cut them in halves, take out the stones, and pare them neatly; take as many pounds of white sugar as of fruit, put to each pound of sugar a teacupful of water; stir it until it is dissolved; set it over a moderate fire; when it is boiling hot, put in the peaches; let them boil gently until a pure, clear, uniform color; turn those at the bottom to the top carefully with a skimmer several times; do not hurry them. When they are clear, take each half up with a spoon, and spread the halves on flat dishes to become cold. When all are done, let the syrup boil until it is quite thick; pour it into a large pitcher, and let it set to cool and settle. When the peaches are cold put them carefully into jars, and pour the syrup over them, leaving any sediment which has settled at the bottom, or strain the syrup. Some of the kernels from the peach-stones may be put in with the peaches while boiling. Let them remain open one night, then cover.

In like manner quince, plum, apricot, apple, cherry, greengage and other fruit preserves are made; in every case fine large fruit should be taken, free from imperfections, and the slightest bruises or other fault should be removed.

PRESERVED GREEN TOMATOES.

Take one peck of green tomatoes. Slice six fresh lemons without removing the skins, but taking out the seeds; put to this quantity six pounds of sugar, common white, and boil until transparent and the syrup thick. Ginger root may be added, if liked.

PRESERVED APPLES. (Whole.)

Peel and core large firm apples (pippins are best). Throw them into water as you pare them. Boil the parings in water for fifteen minutes, allowing a pint to one pound of fruit. Then strain, and, adding three-quarters of a pound of sugar to each pint of water, as measured at first, with enough lemon-peel, orange-peel or mace, to impart a pleasant flavor, return to the kettle. When the syrup has been well-skimmed and is clear, pour it boiling hot over the apples, which must be drained from the water in which they have hitherto stood. Let them remain in the syrup until both are perfectly cold. Then, covering closely, let them simmer over a slow fire until transparent. When all the minutiæ of these directions are attended to, the fruit will remain unbroken, and present a beautiful and inviting appearance.

PRESERVED QUINCES.

Pare, core and quarter your fruit, then weigh it and allow an equal quantity of white sugar. Take the parings and cores, and put in a preserving-kettle; cover them with water and boil for half an hour; then strain through a hair sieve, and put the juice back into the kettle and boil the quinces in it a little at a time until they are tender; lift out as they are done with a drainer and lay on a dish; if the liquid seems scarce add more water. When all are cooked, throw into this liquor the sugar, and allow it to boil ten minutes before putting in the quinces; let them boil until they change color, say one hour and a quarter, on a slow fire; while they are boiling occasionally slip a silver spoon under them to see that they do not burn, but on no account stir them. Have two fresh lemons cut in thin slices, and when the fruit is being put in jars lay a slice or two in each. Quinces may be steamed until tender.

PRESERVED PEARS.

One pound of fruit, one pound of sugar; pare off the peeling thin. Make a nice syrup of nearly one cupful of water and one pound of sugar, and when clarified by boiling and skimming put in the pears and stew gently until clear. Choose rather pears like the Seckle for preserving, both on account of the flavor and size. A nice way is to stick a clove in the blossom end of each pear, for this fruit seems to require some extraneous flavor to bring out its own piquancy. Another acceptable addition to pear preserves may be found instead, by adding the juice and thinly pared rind of one lemon to each five pounds of fruit. If the pears are hard and tough, parboil them until tender before beginning to preserve, and from the same water take what you need for making their syrup.

If you can procure only large pears to preserve, cut them into halves, or even slices, so that they can get done more quickly, and lose nothing in appearance, either.

PINEAPPLE PRESERVES.

Twist off the top and bottom, and pare off the rough outside of pineapples; then weigh them and cut them in slices, chips or quarters, or cut them in four or six, and shape each piece like a whole pineapple; to each pound of fruit, put a teacupful of water; put it in a preserving kettle, cover it and set it over the fire, and let them boil gently until they are tender and clear; then take them from the water, by sticking a fork in the centre of each slice, or with a skimmer, into a dish.

Put to the water white sugar, a pound for each pound of fruit; stir it until it is all dissolved; then put in the pineapple, cover the kettle, and let them boil gently until transparent thoughout; when it is so, take it out, let it cool, and put it in glass jars; let the syrup boil or simmer gently until it is thick and rich, and when nearly cool, pour it over the fruit. The next day secure the jars, as before directed.

Pineapple done in this way is a beautiful and delicious preserve. The usual manner of preserving it, by putting it into the syrup without first boiling it, makes it little better than sweetened leather.

TO PRESERVE WATERMELON RIND AND CITRON.

Pare off the green skin, cut the watermelon rind into pieces. Weigh the pieces, and allow to each pound a pound and a half of loaf sugar. Line your kettle with green vine-leaves, and put in the pieces *without* the sugar. A layer of vine-leaves must cover each layer of melon rind. Pour in water to cover the whole, and place a thick cloth over the kettle. Simmer the fruit for two hours, after scattering a few bits of alum amongst it. Spread the melon rind on a dish to cool. Melt the sugar, using a pint of water to a pound and a half of sugar, and mix with it some beaten white of egg. Boil and skim the sugar. When quite clear, put in the rind, and let it boil two hours; take out the rind, boil the syrup again, pour it over the rind, and let it remain all night. The next morning, boil the syrup with lemon-juice, allowing one lemon to a quart of syrup. When it is thick enough to hang in a drop from the point of a spoon, it is done. Put the rind in jars, and pour over it the syrup. It is not fit for use immediately.

Citrons may be preserved in the same manner, first paring off the outer skin, and cutting them into quarters. Also green limes.

TO PRESERVE AND DRY GREENGAGES.

To every pound of sugar allow one pound of fruit, one quarter pint of water.

For this purpose, the fruit must be used before it is quite ripe, and part of the stalk must be left on. Weigh the fruit, rejecting all that is in the least degree blemished, and put it into a lined sauce-pan with the sugar and water, which should have been previously boiled together to a rich syrup. Boil the fruit in this for ten minutes, remove it from the fire, and drain the greengages. The next day boil up the syrup and put in the fruit again, let it simmer for three minutes, and drain the syrup away. Continue this process for five or six days, and the last time place the greengages, when drained, on a hair-sieve, and put them in an oven or warm spot to dry; keep them in a box, with paper between each layer, in a place free from damp.

PRESERVED PUMPKINS.

To each pound of pumpkin allow one pound of roughly pounded loaf sugar, one gill of lemon-juice.

Obtain a good, sweet pumpkin; halve it, take out the seeds, and pare off the rind; cut it into neat slices. Weigh the pumpkin, put the slices in a pan or deep dish in layers, with the sugar sprinkled between them; pour the lemon-juice over the top, and let the whole remain for two or three days. Boil all together, adding half a pint of water to every three pounds of sugar used until the pumpkin becomes tender; then turn the whole into a pan, where let it remain for a week; then drain off the syrup, boil it until it is quite thick; skim, and pour it boiling over the pumpkin. A little bruised ginger, and lemon-rind, thinly pared, may be boiled in the syrup to flavor the pumpkin.

—A Southern recipe.

PRESERVING FRUIT. (New Mode.)

Housekeepers who dislike the tedious, old-time fashion of clarifying sugar and boiling the fruit, will appreciate the following two recipes, no fire being needed in their preparation. The first is for "tutti frutti," and has been repeatedly tested with unvarying success.

Put one quart of white, preserving, fine Batavia brandy into a two-gallon stone jar that has a tightly fitting top. Then for every pound of fruit, in prime condition and perfectly dry, which you put in the brandy, use three-quarters of a pound of granulated sugar; stir every day so that the sugar will be dissolved, using a clean, wooden spoon kept for the purpose. Every sort of fruit may be used, beginning with strawberries and ending with plums. Be sure and have at least one pound of black cherries, as they make the color of the preserve very rich. Strawberries, raspberries, blackberries, apricots, cherries (sweet and sour), peaches, plums, are all used, and, if you like, currants and grapes. Plums and grapes should be peeled and seeded, apricots and peaches peeled and cut in quarters or eighths or dice; cherries also must be seeded: quinces may be steamed until tender. The jar must be kept in a cool, dry place, and the daily stirring must never be forgotten, for that is the secret of success. You may use as much of one sort of fruit as you like, and it may be put in from day to day, just as you happen to have it. Half the quantity of spirits may be used. The preserve will be ready for use within a week after the last fruit is put in, and will keep for a number of months. We have found it good eight months after making.

The second is as follows: Take some pure white vinegar and mix with it granulated sugar until a syrup is formed quite free from acidity. Pour this syrup into earthen jars and put in it good, perfectly ripe fruit, gathered in dry weather. Cover the jars tight, and put them in a dry place. The contents will keep for six or eight months, and the flavor of the fruit will be excellent.

TO PRESERVE FRUIT WITHOUT SUGAR.

Cherries, strawberries, sliced pineapple, plums, apricots, gooseberries, etc., may be preserved in the following manner—to be used the same as fresh fruit.

Gather the fruit before it is very ripe; put it in wide-mouthed bottles made for the purpose; fill them as full as they will hold, and cork them tight; seal the corks; put some hay in a large sauce-pan, set in the bottles, with hay between them to prevent their touching; then fill the sauce-pan with water to the necks of the bottles, and set it over the fire until the water is nearly boiling, then take it off; let it stand until the bottles are cold. Keep them in a cool place until wanted, when the fruit will be found equal to fresh.

NEW METHOD OF PRESERVING FRUIT.

A new method of preserving fruit is practiced in England. Pears, apples and other fruits are reduced to a paste by jamming, which is then pressed into cakes and gently dried. When required for use it is only necessary to pour four times their weight of boiling water over them, and allow them to soak for twenty minutes, and then add sugar to suit the taste. The fine flavor of the fruit is said to be retained to perfection. The cost of the prepared product is scarcely greater than that of the original fruit, differing with the supply and price of the latter; the keeping qualities are excellent, so that it may be had at any time of the year, and bears long sea-voyages without detriment. No peeling or coring is require l. so there is no waste.

FRUIT JELLIES.

Take a stone jar and put in the fruit, place this in a kettle of tepid water, and set on the fire; let it boil closely covered, until the fruit is broken to pieces; strain, pressing the bag, a stout, coarse one, hard, putting in a few handfuls each time, and between each squeezing turning it inside out to scald off the pulp and skins; to each pint of juice allow a pound of loaf sugar; set the juice on alone to boil, and while it is boiling, put the sugar into shallow dishes or pans, and heat it in the oven, watching and stirring the sugar to prevent burning; boil the juice just twenty minutes from the time it begins fairly to boil; by this time the sugar should be *very* hot; throw the sugar into the boiling juice, stirring rapidly all the time; withdraw the spoon when all is thoroughly dissolved; let the jelly come to a boil to make all certain; withdraw the kettle instantly from the fire; roll your glasses and cups in hot water, and fill with the scalding liquid; the jelly will form within an hour; when cold, close and tie up as you do preserves.

CURRANT JELLY.

Currants for jelly should be perfectly ripe and gathered the *first* week of the season; they lose their jelly property if they hang on the bushes too long, and become too juicy—the juice will not be apt to congeal. Strip them from the stalks, put them into a stone jar, and set it in a vessel of hot water over the fire; keep the water around it boiling until the currants are all broken, stirring them up occasionally. Then squeeze them through a coarse cloth or towel. To each pint of juice allow a pound and a quarter of refined sugar. **Put** the sugar into a porcelain kettle, pour the juice over it, stirring frequently. Skim it before it boils; boil about twenty minutes, or until it congeals in the spoon when held in the air. Pour it into hot jelly glasses and seal when cool.

Wild frost grape jelly is nice made after this recipe.

CURRANT JELLY. (New Method.)

This recipe for making superior jelly without heat is given in a Parisian journal of chemistry, which may be worth trying by some of our readers. The currants are to be washed and squeezed in the usual way, and the juice placed in a stone or earthen vessel, and set away in a cool place in the cellar. In about twenty-four hours a considerable amount of froth will cover the surface, produced by fermentation, and this must be removed, and the whole strained again through the jelly bag, then weighed, and an equal weight of powdered white sugar is to be added. This is to be stirred constantly until entirely dissolved, and then put into jars, tied up tightly, and set away. At the end of another twenty-four hours a perfectly transparent jelly of the most satisfactory flavor will be formed, which will keep as long as if it had been cooked.

QUINCE JELLY.

Quinces for jelly should not be quite ripe, they should be a fine yellow; rub off the down from them, core them, and cut them small; put them in a preserving kettle with a teacupful of water for each pound; let them stew gently until soft, without mashing; put them in a thin muslin bag with the liquor; press them very lightly; to each pint of the liquor put a pound of sugar; stir it until it is all dissolved, then set it over the fire, and let it boil gently, until by cooling some on a plate you find it a good jelly; then turn it into pots or tumblers, and when cold, secure as directed for jellies.

RASPBERRY JELLY.

To each pint of juice allow one pound of sugar. Let the raspberries be freshly gathered, quite ripe, picked from the stalks; put them into a large jar after breaking the fruit a little with a wooden spoon, and place this jar, covered, in a sauce-pan of boiling water. When the juice is well drawn, which will be in from three-quarters to one hour, strain the fruit through a fine hair sieve or cloth; measure the juice, and to every pint allow the above proportion of white sugar. Put the juice and sugar into a preserving-pan, place it over the fire, and boil gently until the jelly thickens, when a little is poured on a plate; carefully remove all the scum as it rises, pour the jelly into small pots, cover down, and keep in a dry place. This jelly answers for making raspberry cream, and for flavoring various sweet dishes, when, in winter, the fresh fruit is not obtainable.

APPLE JELLY.

Select apples that are rather tart and highly flavored; slice them without paring; place in a porcelain preserving-kettle, cover with water, and let them cook slowly until the apples look red. Pour into a colander, drain off the juice, and let this run through a jelly-bag; return to the kettle, which must be carefully washed, and boil half an hour; measure it and allow to every pint of juice a pound of sugar and half the juice of a lemon; boil quickly for ten minutes.

The juice of apples, boiled in shallow vessels, without a particle of sugar, makes the most sparkling, delicious jelly imaginable. Red apples will give jelly the color and clearness of claret, while that from light fruit is like amber. Take the cider just as it is made, not allowing it to ferment at all, and, if possible, boil it in a pan, flat, very large, and shallow.

GRAPE JELLY.

Mash well the berries so as to remove the skins; pour all into a preserving-kettle, and cook slowly for a few minutes to extract the juice; strain through a colander, and then through a flannel jelly-bag, keeping as hot as possible, for if not allowed to cool before putting again on the stove the jelly comes much stiffer; a few quince seeds boiled with the berries the first time tend to stiffen it; measure the juice, allowing a pound of loaf sugar to every pint of juice, and boil fast for at least half an hour. Try a little, and if it seems done, remove and put into glasses.

FLORIDA ORANGE JELLY.

Grate the yellow rind of two Florida oranges and two lemons, and squeeze the juice into a porcelain-lined preserving-kettle, adding the juice of two more oranges, and removing all the seeds; put in the grated rind a quarter of a pound of sugar, or more if the fruit is sour, and a gill of water, and boil these ingredients together until a rich syrup is formed; meantime, dissolve two ounces of gelatine in a quart of warm water, stirring it over the fire until it is entirely dissolved; then add the syrup, strain the jelly, and cool it in molds wet in cold water.

CRAB-APPLE JELLY.

The apples should be juicy and ripe. The fruit is then quartered, the black spots in the cores removed, afterward put into a preserving-kettle over the fire, with a teacupful of water in the bottom to prevent burning; more water is added as it evaporates while cooking. When boiled to a pulp, strain the apples through a coarse flannel, then proceed as for currant jelly.

PEACH JELLY.

Pare the peaches, take out the stones, then slice them; add to them about a quarter of the kernels. Place them in a kettle with enough water to cover them. Stir them often until the fruit is well cooked, then strain, and to every pint of the juice add the juice of a lemon; measure again, allowing a pound of sugar to each pint of juice; heat the sugar very hot, and add when the juice has boiled twenty minutes; let it come to a boil, and take instantly from the fire.

ORANGE SYRUP.

Pare the oranges, squeeze and strain the juice from the pulp. To one pint of juice allow one pound and three-quarters of loaf sugar. Put the juice and sugar together, boil and skim it until it is cream; then strain it through a flannel bag, and let it stand until it becomes cool, then put in bottles and cork tight.

Lemon syrup is made in the same way, except that you scald the lemons, and squeeze out the juice, allowing rather more sugar.

ORANGE MARMALADE.

Allow pound for pound. Pare half the oranges, and cut the rind into shreds. Boil in three waters until tender, and set aside. Grate the rind of the remaining oranges; take off, and throw away every bit of the thick white inner skin; quarter all the oranges and take out the seeds. Chop, or cut them into small pieces; drain all the juice that will come away, without pressing them, over the sugar; heat this, stirring until the sugar is dissolved, adding a *very* little water, unless the oranges are very juicy. Boil and skim five or six minutes; put in the boiled shreds, and cook ten minutes; then the chopped fruit and grated peel, and boil twenty minutes longer. When cold, put into small jars, tied up with bladder or paper next the fruit, cloths dipped in wax over all. A nicer way still is to put away in tumblers with self-adjusting metal tops. Press brandied tissue paper down closely to the fruit.

LEMON MARMALADE

Is made as you would prepare orange—allowing a pound and a quarter of sugar to a pound of the fruit, and using but half the grated peel.

RAISINS. (A French Marmalade.)

This recipe is particularly valuable at seasons when fruit is scarce. Take six fine large cooking apples, peel them, put them over a slow fire, together with a wineglassful of Madeira wine, and half a pound of sugar. When well stewed, split and stone two and a half pounds of raisins, and put them to stew with the apples, and enough water to prevent their burning. When all appears well dissolved, beat it through a strainer bowl, and lastly through a sieve. Mold, if you like, or put away in small preserve jars, to cut in thin slices for the ornamentation of pastry, or to dish up for eating with cream.

STRAWBERRY JAM.

To each pound of fine, and not too ripe berries, allow three-quarters of a pound of sugar. Put them into a preserving pan, and stir gently, not to break up the fruit; simmer for one-half hour, and put into pots air-tight. An excellent way to seal jellies and jams is as the German women do: Cut round covers from writing paper a half-inch too large for the tops, smear the inside with the unbeaten white of an egg, tie over with a cord, and it will dry quickly and be absolutely preservative. A circular paper dipped in brandy, and laid over the toothsome contents before covering, will prevent any dampness from affecting the flavor. I have removed these covers heavy with mold, to find the preserve intact.

GOOSEBERRY JAM.

Pick the gooseberries just as they begin to turn. Stem, wash and weigh. To four pounds of fruit add half a teacupful of water; boil until soft and add four pounds of sugar and boil until clear. If picked at the right stage the jam will be amber-colored and firm, and very much nicer than if the fruit is preserved when ripe.

BRANDIED PEACHES OR PEARS.

Four pounds of fruit, four pounds of sugar, one pint of best white brandy. Make a syrup of the sugar and enough water to dissolve it. Let this come to a boil; put the fruit in and boil five minutes. Having removed the fruit carefully, let the syrup boil fifteen minutes longer, or until it thickens well; add the brandy, and take the kettle at once from the fire; pour the hot syrup over the fruit, and seal. If, after the fruit is taken from the fire, a reddish liquor oozes from it, drain this off before adding the clear syrup. Put up in glass jars. Peaches and pears should be peeled for brandying. Plums should be pricked and watched carefully for fear of bursting.

RASPBERRY JAM.

To five or six pounds of fine red raspberries (not too ripe) add an equal quantity of the finest quality of white sugar. Mash the whole well in a preserving kettle; add about one quart of currant juice (a little less will do), and boil gently until it jellies upon a cold plate; then put into small jars; cover with brandied paper, and tie a thick white paper over them.   Keep in a dark, dry and cool place.

Blackberry or strawberry jam is made the same way, leaving out the curran juice.

A NEW WAY OF KEEPING FRUIT.

It is stated that experiments have been made in keeping fruit in jars covered only with cotton batting, and at the end of two years the fruit was sound.   The following directions are given for the process: Use crocks, stone butter-jars on any other convenient dishes.   Prepare and cook the fruit precisely as for canning in glass jars; fill your dishes with fruit while hot; and immediately cover with cotton batting, securely tied on.   Remember that all putrefaction is caused by the invisible creatures in the air.   Cooking the fruit expels all these, and they cannot pass through the cotton batting.   The fruit thus protected will keep an indefinite period.   It will be remembered that Tyndall has proved that the atmospheric germs cannot pass through a layer of cotton.

MACEDOINES.

Suspend in the centre of the jelly mold a bunch of grapes, cherries, berries, or currants on their stems, sections of oranges, pineapples, or brandied fruits, and pour in a little jelly when quite cold, but not set.   It makes a very agreeable effect.   By a little ingenuity you can imbed first one fruit and then another, arranging in circles, and pour a little jelly successively over each.   Do not re-heat the jelly, but keep it in a warm place, while the mold is on ice and the first layers are hardening.

CANNED FRUITS.

Berries and all ripe, mellow fruit require but little cooking, only long enough for the sugar to penetrate. Strew sugar over them, allow them to stand a few hours, then merely scald with the sugar; half to three-quarters of a pound is considered sufficient. Harder fruits like pears, quinces, etc., require longer boiling.

The great secret of canning is to make the fruit or vegetable perfectly air-tight. It must be put up boiling hot, and the vessel filled to the brim.

Have your jars conveniently placed near your boiling fruit, in a tin pan of hot water on the stove, roll them in the hot water, then fill immediately with the hot, scalding fruit, fill to the top, and seal quickly with the tops, which should also be heated; occasionally screw down the tops tighter, as the fruit shrinks as it cools, and the glass contracts, and allows the air to enter the cans. They must be perfectly air-tight. The jars to be kept in a dark, cool, dry place.

Use glass jars for fruit always, and the fruit should be cooked in a porcelain or granite-iron kettle. If you are obliged to use common large-mouthed bottles with corks, steam the corks and pare them to a close fit, driving them in with a mallet. Use the following wax for sealing: one pound of resin, three ounces of beeswax, one and one-half ounces of tallow. Use a brush in covering the corks, and as they cool, dip the mouth into the melted wax. Place in a basin of cool water. Pack in a cool, dark, and dry cellar. After one week, examine for flaws, cracks or signs of ferment.

The rubber rings used to assist in keeping the air from the fruit cans sometimes become so dry and brittle as to be almost useless. They can be restored to normal condition usually by letting them lie in water in which you have put a little ammonia. Mix in this proportion: One part of ammonia and two parts water. Sometimes they do not need to lie in this more than five minutes, but frequently a half-hour is needed to restore their elasticity.

CANNED PEACHES.

To one pound of peaches allow half a pound of sugar; to six pounds of sugar, add half a tumbler of water; put in the kettle a layer of sugar and one of peaches until the whole of both are in. Wash about eight peach-leaves, tie them up and put into the kettle, remembering to take them out when you begin to fill up the jars. Let the sugared fruit remain on the range, but away from the fire, until upon tipping the vessel to one side you can see some liquid; then fill the jars, taking them out of hot water into which they were put when cold, remaining until it was made to boil around them. In this way you will find out if the glass has been properly annealed; for we consider glass jars with stoppers screwing down upon India-rubber rings as the best for canning fruit in families. They should be kept in a dark closet; and although somewhat more expensive than tin in the first instance, are much nicer, and keep for years with careful usage.

Fruit must be of fine flavor, and *ripe*, though not *soft*, to make nice canned fruit.

Peaches should be thrown into cold water as they are peeled, to prevent a yellowish crust.

CANNED GRAPES.

There is no fruit so difficult to can nicely as the grape; by observing the following instructions you will find the grapes rich and tender a year from putting up. Squeeze the pulp from the skin, as the seeds are objectionable; boil the pulp until the seeds begin to loosen, in one kettle, having the skins boiling in a little water, hard, in another kettle, as they are tough. When the pulp seems tender, put it through the sieve; then add the skins, if tender, with the water they boil in, if not too much. We use a large coffee-cupful of sugar for a quart can; boil until thick, and can in the usual way.

CANNED STRAWBERRIES.

After the berries are picked over, let as many as can be put carefully in the preserve kettle at once be placed on a platter. To each pound of fruit add three-fourths of a pound of sugar; let them stand two or three hours, till the juice is drawn from them; pour it into the kettle and let it come to a boil, and remove the scum which rises; then put in the berries very carefully. As soon as they come thoroughly to a boil put them in warm jars, and seal while boiling hot.

TO CAN QUINCES.

Cut the quinces into thin slices like apples for pies. To one quart jarful of quince, take a coffee-saucer and a half of sugar, and a coffee-cupful of water; put the sugar and water on the fire, and when boiling put in the quinces; have ready the jars with their fastenings, stand the jars in a pan of boiling water on the stove, and when the quince is clear and tender put rapidly into the jars, fruit and syrup together. The jars must be filled so that the syrup overflows, and fastened up tight as quickly as possible.

CANNED PINEAPPLE.

For six pounds of fruit, when cut and ready to can, make syrup with two and a half pounds of sugar and nearly three pints of water; boil syrup five minutes and skim or strain if necessary; then add the fruit, and let it boil up; have cans hot, fill and shut up as soon as possible. Use the best white sugar. As the cans cool, keep tightening them up. Cut the fruit half an inch thick.

CANNED FRUIT JUICES.

Canned fruit juices are an excellent substitute for brandy or wine in all puddings and sauces, etc.

It is a good plan to can the pure juices of fruit in the summer time, putting it by for this purpose.

Select clean ripe fruit, press out the juice and strain it through a flannel cloth. To each pint of juice add one cupful of white granulated sugar. Put it in a porcelain kettle, bring it to the boiling point, and bottle while hot in small bottles. It must be sealed very tight while it is *hot*. Will keep a long time, the same as canned fruit.

CANNED TOMATOES.

Canning tomatoes is quite a simple process. A large or small quantity may be done at a time, and they should be put in glass jars in preference to those of tin, which are apt to injure the flavor. Very ripe tomatoes are the best for the purpose. They are first put into a large pan and covered with boiling water. This loosens the skin, which is easily removed, and the tomatoes are then put into the preserving kettle, set over a moderate fire without the addition of water or any seasoning, and brought to a boil. After boiling slowly one-half hour, they are put into the jars while boiling hot and sealed tightly. They will keep two or three years in this way. The jars should be filled to the brim to prevent air from getting in, and set in a cool, dark closet.

TO CAN CORN.

Split the kernels lengthwise with a knife, then scrape with the back of the knife, thus leaving the hulls upon the cob. Fill cans full of cut corn, pressing it in very hard. To press the corn in the can, use the small end of a potato masher, as this will enter the can easily. It will take from ten to a dozen large ears of corn to fill a one-quart can. When the cans are full, screw cover on with thumb and first finger; this will be tight enough, then place a cloth in the bottom of a wash boiler to prevent breakage. On this put a layer of cans in any position you prefer, over the cans put a layer of cloth, then a layer of cans. Fill the boiler in this manner, then cover the cans well with cold water, place the boiler on the fire, and *boil* three hours without ceasing. On steady boiling, depends much of your success. After boiling three hours, lift the boiler from the fire, let the water cool, then take the cans from the boiler and tighten, let them remain until cold, then tighten again. Wrap each can in brown paper to exclude the light, and keep in a cool dry cellar and be very sure the rubber rings are not hardened by use. The rings should be renewed every two years. I would advise the beginner to use new rings entirely, for poor rings cause the loss of canned fruit and vegetables in many cases. You will observe that in canning corn the cans are not wrapped in a cloth nor heated; merely filled with the cut corn. The corn in the cans will shrink considerably in boiling, but on no account open them after canning.

TO CAN PEAS.

Fill the can full of peas, shake the can so they can be filled well. You cannot press the peas in the can as you did the corn, but by shaking the cans they may be filled quite full. Pour into the cans enough cold water to fill to overflowing, then screw the cover tight as you can with your thumb and first finger and proceed exactly as in canning corn.

String beans are cut as for cooking and canned in the same manner. No seasoning of salt, pepper or sugar should be added.

—Mary Currier Parsons.

CANNED PLUMS.

To every pound of plums allow a quarter of a pound of sugar. Put the sugar and plums alternately into the preserving-kettle, first pricking the plums to prevent their breaking. Let them stand on the back of the stove for an hour or two, then put them over a moderate fire, and allow to come to a boil; skim and pour at once into jars, running a silver spoon handle around the inside of the jar to break the air-bubbles; cover and screw down the tops.

CANNED MINCE-MEAT.

Mince-meat for pies can be preserved for years if canned the same as fruit while *hot*, and put into glass jars and sealed perfectly tight, and set in a cool, dark place. One glass quart jar will hold enough to make two ordinary-sized pies, and in this way "mince pies" can be had in the middle of summer as well as in winter, and if the cans are sealed properly, the meat will be just as fine when opened as when first canned.

CANNED BOILED CIDER.

Boiled cider, in our grandmothers' time, was indispensable to the making of a good "mince pie," adding the proper flavor and richness, which cannot be substituted by any other ingredient, and a gill of which being added to a rule of "fruit cake" makes it more moist, keeps longer, and is far superior to fruit cake made without it. Boiled cider is an article rarely found in the market, now-a-days, but can be made by any one, with but little trouble and expense, using *sweet* cider, shortly after it is made, and before fermentation takes place. Place five quarts of *sweet* cider in a porcelain-lined kettle over the fire, boil it slowly until reduced to one quart, carefully watching it that it does not burn; turn into glass jars while hot, and seal tightly, the same as canned fruit. It is then ready to use any time of the year.

CANNED PUMPKIN.

Pumpkins or squash canned are far more convenient for ready use than those dried in the old-fashioned way.

Cut up pumpkin or squash into small pieces, first cutting off the peel; stew them until tender, add no seasoning; then mash them very fine with a potato-masher. Have ready your cans, made hot, and then fill them with the hot pumpkin or squash, seal tight; place in a dark, cool closet.

PEACH BUTTER.

Pare ripe peaches and put them in a preserving-kettle, with sufficient water to boil them soft; then sift through a colander, removing the stones. To each quart of peach put one and one-half pound of sugar, and boil very slowly one hour. Stir often, and do not let them burn. Put in stone or glass jars, and keep in a cool place

PEACHES DRIED WITH SUGAR.

Peel yellow peaches, cut them from the stone in one piece; allow two pounds of sugar to six pounds of fruit; make a syrup of three-quarters of a pound of sugar, and a little water; put in the peaches, a few at a time, and let them cook gently until quite clear. Take them up carefully on a dish and set them in the sun to dry. Strew powdered sugar over them on all sides, a little at a time; if any syrup is left, remove to fresh dishes. When they are quite dry, lay them lightly in a jar with a little sugar sifted between the layers.

COLORING FOR FRUIT, ETC.

RED OR PINK COLORING.

Take two cents' worth of cochineal. Lay it on a flat plate, and bruise it with the blade of a knife. Put it into half a teacupful of alcohol. Let it stand a quarter of an hour, and then filter it through fine muslin. Always ready for immediate use. Cork the bottle tight.

Strawberry or cranberry juice makes a fine coloring for frosting sweet puddings and confectionery.

DEEP RED COLORING.

Take twenty grains of cochineal, and fifteen grains of cream of tartar finely powdered; add to them a piece of alum the size of a cherry stone, and boil them with a gill of soft water, in an earthen vessel, slowly, for half an hour. Then strain it through muslin, and keep it tightly corked in a phial. If a little alcohol is added, it will keep any length of time.

YELLOW COLORING.

Take a little saffron, put it into an earthen vessel with a very small quantity of cold, soft water, and let it steep till the color of the infusion is a bright yellow. Then strain it, add half alcohol to it. To color fruit yellow, boil the fruit with fresh skin lemons in water to cover them until it is tender; then take it up, spread it on dishes to cool, and finish as may be directed.

To color icing, put the grated peel of a lemon or orange in a thin muslin bag, squeezing a little juice through it, then mixing with the sugar.

GREEN COLORING.

Take fresh spinach or beet leaves, and pound them in a marble mortar. If you want it for immediate use, take off the green froth as it rises, and mix it with the article you intend to color. If you wish to keep it a few days, take the juice when you have pressed out a teacupful, and adding to it a piece of alum the size of a pea, give it a boil in a sauce-pan. Or make the juice very strong and add a quart of alcohol. Bottle it air-tight.

SUGAR GRAINS.

These are made by pounding white lump sugar in a mortar and shaking it through sieves of different degrees of coarseness, thus accumulating grains of different sizes. They are used in ornamenting cake.

SUGAR GRAINS, COLORED.

Stir a little coloring—as the essence of spinach, or prepared cochineal, or liquid carmine, or indigo, rouge, saffron, etc.,—into the sugar grains made as above, un-til each grain is stained, then spread them on a baking-sheet, and dry them in a warm place. They are used in ornamenting cake.

CARAMEL OR BURNT SUGAR.

Put one cupful of sugar and two teaspoonfuls of water in a sauce-pan on the fire; stir constantly until it is quite a dark color, then add a half cupful of water, and a pinch of salt; let it boil a few minutes, and when cold, bottle.

For coloring soups, sauces or gravies.

TO CLARIFY JELLY.

The white of eggs is, perhaps, the best substance that can be employed in clarifying jelly, as well as some other fluids, for the reason that when albumen (and the white of eggs is nearly pure albumen) is put into a liquid that is muddy, from substances suspended in it, on boiling the liquid the albumen coagulates in a flocculent manner, and, entangling with the impurities, rises with them to the surface as a scum, or sinks to the bottom, according to their weight.

CONFECTIONERY.

In the making of confections, the best *granulated* or *loaf* sugar should be used. (Beware of glucose mixed with sugar.) Sugar is boiled more or less, according to the kind of candy to be made, and it is necessary to understand the proper degree of sugar boiling to operate it successfully.

Occasionally sugar made into candies, "creams" or syrups, will need clarifying. The process is as follows: Beat up well the white of an egg with a cupful of cold water and pour it into a very clean iron or thick new tin sauce-pan, then put into the pan four cupfuls of sugar, mixed with a cupful of warm water. Put on the stove, and heat *moderately* until the scum rises. Remove the pan, and skim off the top, then place on the fire again until the scum rises again. Then remove as before, and so continue until no scum rises.

This recipe is for good brown or yellowish sugar; for soft, white sugars, half the white of an egg will do, and for refined or loaf sugar a quarter will do.

The quantities of sugar and water are the same in all cases. Loaf sugar will generally do for all candy-making without further clarification. Brown or yellow sugars are used for caramels, dark-colored cocoanut, taffy, and pulled molasses candies generally.

Havana is the cheapest grade of white sugar and a shade or two lighter than the brown.

Confectioners' A is superior in color and grain to the Havana. It is a centrifugal sugar—that is, it is not re-boiled to procure its white color, but is moistened with water and then put into rapidly revolving cylinders. The uncrystalized syrup or molasses is whirled out of it, and the sugar comes out with a dry, white grain.

Icing or Powdered Sugars. This is powdered loaf sugar. Icing can only be made with powdered sugar, which is produced by grinding or crushing loaf sugar as fine as flour nearly.

Granulated Sugar This is a coarse-grained sugar, generally very clean and sparkling, and fit for use as a colored sugar in crystalized goods, and other superior uses.

This same syrup answers for most candies, and should be boiled to such a degree, that when a fork or splinter is dipped into it the liquid will run off and form a thick drop on the end, and long, silk-like threads hang from them when exposed to the air. The syrup never to be stirred while hot, or else it will grain, but if intended for soft, French candies, should be removed, and, when nearly cold, stirred to a cream. For hard, brittle candies, the syrup should be boiled until, when a little is dropped in *cold* water, it will crack and break when biting it.

The hands should be buttered when handling it, or it will stick to them.

The top of the inside of the dish that the sugar or molasses is to be cooked in, should be buttered a few inches around the inside; it prevents the syrup from rising and swelling any higher than where it reaches the buttered edge.

For common crack candies, the sugar can be kept from graining by adding a teaspoonful of vinegar or cream tartar.

Colorings for candies should be harmless, and those used for fruit and confectionery, on page 395, will be most suitable.

Essences and extracts should be bought at the druggist's, not the poor kind usually sold at the grocer's.

FRENCH CREAM CANDY.

Put four cupfuls of white sugar and one cupful of water into a bright tin pan on the range, and let it boil without stirring for ten minutes. If it looks somewhat thick, test it by letting some drop from the spoon, and if it threads, remove the pan to the table. Take out a small spoonful, and rub it against the side of a cake-bowl; if it becomes creamy, and will roll into a ball between the fingers, pour the whole into the bowl. When cool enough to bear your finger in it, take it in your lap, stir or beat it with a large spoon, or pudding-stick. It will soon begin to look like cream, and then grow stiffer until you find it necessary to take your hands and work it like bread dough. If it is not boiled enough to cream, set it back upon the range, and let it remain one or two minutes, or as long as is necessary, taking care not to cook it too much. Add the flavoring as soon as it begins to cool. This is the foundation of all French creams. It can be made into rolls, and sliced off, or packed in plates and cut into small cubes, or made into any shape imitating French candies. A pretty form is made by coloring some of the cream pink, taking a piece about as large as a hazel nut, and crowding an almond meat half way into one side, till it looks like a bursting kernel. In working, should the cream get too cold, warm it.

To be successful in making this cream, several points are to be remembered; when the boiled sugar is cool enough to beat, if it looks rough and has turned to sugar it is because it has been boiled *too much*, or has been *stirred*. If, after it is beaten, it does not look like lard or thick cream, and is sandy or sugary instead, it is because you did not let it get cool enough before beating.

It is not boiled enough if it does not harden so as to work like dough, and should not stick to the hands; in this case put it back into the pan with an ounce of hot water, and cook over just enough, by testing in water as above. After it is turned into the bowl to cool, it should look clear as jelly. Practice and patience will make perfect.

FRUIT CREAMS.

Add to "French Cream," raisins, currants, figs, a little citron, chopped and mixed thoroughly through the cream while quite warm. Make into bars or flat cakes.

WALNUT CREAMS.

Take a piece of "French Cream" the size of a walnut. Having cracked some English walnuts, using care not to break the meats, place one-half of each nut upon each side of the ball, pressing them into the ball.

Walnut creams can be made by another method: First take a piece of "French Cream," put it into a cup, and setting the cup into a vessel of boiling water, heating it until it turns like thick cream; drop the walnut meats into it, one at a time, taking it out on the end of a fork, and placing it on buttered paper; continue to dip them until all are used, then go over again, giving them a second coat of candy. They look nicely colored pink, and flavored with vanilla.

CHOCOLATE CREAMS.

Use "French Cream," and form it into small cone-shaped balls with the fingers. Lay them upon paper to harden until all are formed. Melt one cake of bakers' chocolate in an earthen dish or small basin; by setting it in the oven it will soon melt; do not let it cook, but it *must* be kept *hot*.

Take the balls of cream, one at a time, on the tines of a fork, pour the melted chocolate over them with a teaspoon, and when well covered, slip them from the fork upon oiled paper.

COCOANUT CREAMS.

Take two tablespoonfuls of grated cocoanut and half as much "French candy;" work them both together with your hand till the cocoanut is all well mixed in it. If you choose, you can add a drop of vanilla. If too soft to work into balls, add confectioners' sugar to stiffen; make into balls the size of hazelnuts, and dip twice, as in the foregoing recipes, flavoring the melted "French Cream" with vanilla.

VARIEGATED CREAMS.

Make the "French Cream" recipe, and divide into three parts, leaving one part white, color one pink with cochineal syrup, and the third part color brown with chocolate, which is done by just letting the cream soften and stirring in a little finely grated chocolate. The pink is colored by dropping on a few drops of cochineal syrup while the cream is warm, and beating it in. Take the white cream, make a flat ball of it, and lay it upon a buttered dish, and pat it out flat until about half an inch thick. If it does not work easily, dip the hand in alcohol. Take the pink cream, work in the same way as the white and lay it upon the white; then the chocolate in the same manner, and lay upon the pink, pressing all together. Trim the edges off smooth, leaving it in a nice, square cake, then cut into slices or small cubes, as you prefer. It is necessary to work it all up as rapidly as possible.

RASPBERRY CREAMS.

Stir enough confectioners' sugar into a teaspoonful of raspberry jam to form a thick paste; roll it into balls between the palms of your hands. Put a lump of "French Cream" into a teacup, and set it into a basin of boiling water, stirring it until it has melted; then drop a few drops of cochineal coloring to make it a pale pink, or a few drops of raspberry juice, being careful not to add enough to prevent its hardening. Now dip these little balls into the sugar cream, giving them two coats. Lay aside to harden.

Remember to *keep stirring* the melted cream, or if not it will *turn back to clear syrup.*

NUT CREAMS.

Chop almonds, hickory nuts, butternuts or English walnuts quite fine. Make the "French Cream," and before adding all the sugar, while the cream is quite soft, stir into it the nuts, and then form into balls, bars or squares. Several kinds of nuts may be mixed together.

MAPLE SUGAR CREAMS.

Grate fine maple sugar and mix in quantity to suit the taste, with "French Cream;" make any shape desired. Walnut creams are sometimes made with maple sugar and are very fine.

STICK CANDY.

One pound of granulated sugar, one cupful of water, a quarter of a cupful of vinegar, or half a teaspoonful of cream tartar, one small tablespoonful of glycerine. Flavor with vanilla, rose or lemon. Boil all except the flavoring, without stirring, twenty minutes or half an hour, or until crisp when dropped in water. Just before pouring upon greased platters to cool, add half a teaspoonful of soda. After pouring upon platters to cool, pour two teaspoonfuls of flavoring over the top. When partly cool, pull it until very white. Draw it into sticks the size you wish, and cut off with shears into sticks or kiss-shaped drops. It may be colored if desired. (See page 395, for coloring.)

CHOCOLATE CARAMELS.

One cupful of grated chocolate, two cupfuls of brown sugar, one cupful of West India molasses, one cupful of milk or cream, butter the size of an egg, boil until thick, *almost* brittle, stirring constantly. Turn it out on to buttered plates, and when it begins to stiffen, mark it in small squares so that it will break easily when cold. Some like it flavored with a tablespoonful of vanilla.

GRILLED ALMONDS.

These are a very delicious candy seldom met with out of France. They are rather more trouble to make than other kinds, but well repay it from their novel flavor. Blanch a cupful of almonds; dry them thoroughly. Boil a cupful of sugar and a quarter of a cupful of water till it "hairs," then throw in the almonds; let them fry, as it were, in this syrup, stirring them occasionally; they will turn a faint yellow brown before the sugar changes color; do not wait an instant once this change of color begins, or they will lose flavor; remove them from the fire, and stir them until the syrup has turned back to sugar and clings irregularly to the nuts.

These are grilled almonds. You will find them delicious, as they are to alternate at dinner with the salted almonds now so fashionable.

PEPPERMINT DROPS.

One cupful of sugar, crushed fine, and just moistened with boiling water, then boiled five minutes; then take from the fire and add cream of tartar the size of a pea; mix well and add four or five drops of oil of peppermint. Beat briskly until the mixture whitens, then drop quickly upon white paper. Have the cream of tartar and oil of peppermint measured while the sugar is boiling. If it sugars before it is all dropped, add a little water and boil a minute or two.

CURRANT DROPS.

Use currant-juice, instead of water, to moisten a quantity of sugar. Put it in a pan and heat, stirring constantly; be sure not to let it boil; then mix a very little more sugar, let it warm with the rest a moment; then, with a smooth stick, drop on paper.

LEMON DROPS.

Upon a coffee-cupful of finely powdered sugar, pour just enough lemon-juice to dissolve it, and boil it to the consistency of thick syrup, and so that it appears brittle when dropped in cold water. Drop this on buttered plates in drops; set away to cool and harden.

NUT MOLASSES CANDY.

When making molasses candy, add any kind of nuts you fancy; put them in after the syrup has thickened, and is ready to take from the fire; pour out on buttered tins. Mark it off in squares before it gets too cool. Peanuts should be fresh roasted and then tossed in a sieve, to free them of their inner skins.

SUGAR NUT CANDY.

Three pounds of white sugar; half a pint of water; half a pint of vinegar; a quarter of a pound of butter; one pound of hickory-nut kernels. Put the sugar, butter, vinegar and water together into a thick sauce-pan. When it begins to thicken, add the nuts. To test it, take up a very small quantity as quickly as possible directly from the centre, taking care not to disturb it any more than is necessary. Drop it into cold water, and remove from the fire the moment the little particles are brittle. Pour into buttered plates. Use any nuts with this recipe.

COCOANUT CANDY.

One cocoanut, one and one-half pounds of granulated sugar. Put sugar and milk of cocoanut together, heat slowly until the sugar is melted, then boil five minutes; add cocoanut (finely grated), boil ten minutes longer, stir constantly to keep from burning. Pour on buttered plates, cut in squares. Will take about two days to harden. Use prepared cocoanut when other cannot be had.

BUTTER-SCOTCH.

Three cupfuls of white sugar, half a cupful of water, half a cupful of vinegar, or half a teaspoonful of cream tartar; a tablespoonful of butter and eight drops of extract of lemon. Boil *without stirring*, till it will snap and break. Just before taking from the fire, add a quarter of a teaspoonful of soda; pour into well-buttered biscuit tins, a quarter of an inch thick. Mark off into inch squares when partly cold.

EVERTON TAFFY, OR BUTTER-SCOTCH.

Two cupfuls of sugar, two cupfuls of dark molasses, one cupful of cold butter, grated rind of half a lemon. Boil over a slow fire until it hardens when dropped in cold water. Pour thinly into tins well-buttered, and mark into little inch squares, before it cools.

MAPLE WALNUTS.

Beat the white of one egg to a stiff froth, stir in enough powdered sugar to make it like hard frosting, dip the walnut meats (which you have taken care to remove from the shells without breaking) in a syrup made by boiling for two or three minutes two tablespoonfuls of maple sugar in one of water, or in this proportion. Press some of the hard frosting between the two halves of the walnut, and let it harden. Dates may be prepared in this way, and butternuts and English walnuts also.

POP-CORN CANDY. No. 1.

Put into an iron kettle one tablespoonful of butter, three tablespoonfuls of water and one cupful of white sugar; boil until ready to candy, then throw in three quarts nicely popped corn; stir vigorously until the sugar is evenly distributed over the corn; take the kettle from the fire and stir until it cools a little, and in this way you may have each kernel separate and all coated with the sugar. Of course it must have your undivided attention from the first, to prevent scorching. Almonds, English walnuts, or, in fact, any nuts are delicious prepared in this way.

POP-CORN CANDY, No. 2.

Having popped your corn, salt it and keep it warm, sprinkle over with a whisk broom a mixture composed of an ounce of gum arabic, and a half pound of sugar, dissolved in two quarts of water; boil all a few minutes. Stir the corn with the hands or large spoon thoroughly; then mold into balls with the hands.

POP-CORN BALLS. No. 3.

Take three large ears of pop-corn (rice is best). After popping, shake it down in pan so the unpopped corn will settle at the bottom; put the nice white popped in a greased pan. For the candy, take one cup of molasses, one cup of light brown or white sugar, one tablespoonful of vinegar. Boil until it will harden in water. Pour on the corn. Stir with a spoon until thoroughly mixed; then mold into balls with the hand.

No flavor should be added to this mixture, as the excellence of this commodity depends entirely upon the united flavor of the corn, salt and the sugar or molasses.

HOARHOUND CANDY.

Boil two ounces of dried hoarhound in a pint and a half of water for about half an hour; strain, and add three and a half pounds of brown sugar; boil over a hot fire until sufficiently hard; pour out in flat, well-greased tins and marked into sticks or small squares with a knife as soon as cool enough to retain its shape.

JUJUBE PASTE.

Two cupfuls of sugar, one-quarter of a pound of gum arabic, one pint of water. Flavor with the essence of lemon, and a grain of cochineal. Let the mixture stand, until the gum is dissolved, in a warm place on the back of the stove, then draw forward and cook until thick; try in cold water; it should be limber and bend when cold. Pour in buttered pans, an eighth of an inch thick; when cool, roll up in a scroll.

CANDIED ORANGES.

Candied orange is a great delicacy, which is easily made: Peel and quarter the oranges; make a syrup in the proportion of one pound of sugar to one pint of water; let it boil until it will harden in water; then take it from the fire and dip the quarters of orange in the syrup; let them drain on a fine sieve placed over a platter, so that the syrup will not be wasted; let them drain this until cool, when the sugar will crystalize. These are nice served with the last course of dinner. Any fruit the same.

FIG CANDY.

One cup of sugar, one-third cup of water, one-fourth teaspoonful cream of tartar. Do not stir while boiling. Boil to amber color, stir in the cream of tartar just before taking from the fire. Wash the figs, open and lay in a tin pan and pour the candy over them. Or you may dip them in the syrup the same as "Candied Oranges."

CANDY ROLEY POLEY.

Take half a pint of citron, half a pint of raisins, half a pound of figs, a quarter of a pound of shelled almonds, one pint of peanuts before they are hulled; cut up the citron, stone the raisins, blanch the almonds, and hull the peanuts; cut up the figs into small bits. Take two pounds of coffee-sugar, and moisten with vinegar; put in a piece of butter as large as a walnut; stew till it hardens, but take off before it gets to the brittle stage; beat it with a spoon six or eight times; then stir in the mixed fruits and nuts. Pour into a wet cloth and roll it up like a pudding, twisting the ends of the cloth to mold it. Let it get cold, and slice off pieces as it may be wanted for eating.

MOLASSES CANDY.

Put one quart of West India molasses, one cupful of brown sugar, a piece of butter the size of half an egg, into a six-quart kettle. Let it boil over a slack fire until it begins to look thick, stirring it often to prevent burning. Test it by taking some out and dropping a few drops in a cup of cold water. If it hardens quickly and breaks short between the teeth it is boiled enough. Now put in half a teaspoonful of baking soda, and stir it well; then pour it out into well-buttered, flat tins. When partly cooled, take up the candy with your hands well buttered, then pull and double, and so on, until the candy is a whitish yellow. It may be cut in strips and rolled or twisted.

If flavoring is desired, drop the flavoring on the top as it begins to cool, and when it is pulled, the whole will be flavored.

STRAWBERRY CONSERVE.

Prepare the fruit as for preserving, allowing half a pound of loaf sugar to one pound of fruit. Sprinkle the sugar over the fruit at night; in the morning, put it on the fire in a kettle, and boil until the berries are clear. Spread on dishes, and put in the sun until dry; after which, roll the fruit in sugar, and pack in jars.

PEACH CONSERVE.

Halve the peaches and take out the stones; pare. Have ready some powdered white sugar on a plate or dish. Roll the peaches in it several times, until they will not take up any more. Place them singly on a plate, with the cup or hollow side up, that the juices may not run out. Lay them in the sun. The next morning roll them again. As soon as the juice seems set in the peaches, turn the other side to the sun. When they are thoroughly dry, pack them in glass jars, or, what is still nicer, fig-drums. They make an excellent sweetmeat just as they are; or, if wanted for table use, put over the fire in porcelain, with a very little water, and stew a few minutes.

PEACH LEATHER.

Stew as many peaches as you choose, allowing a quarter of a pound of sugar to one of fruit; mash it up smooth as it cooks, and when it is dry enough to spread in a thin sheet on a board greased with butter, set it out in the sun to dry; when dry it can be rolled up like leather, wrapped up in a cloth, and will keep perfectly from season to season. School-children regard it as a delightful addition to their lunch of biscuit or cold bread. Apple and quince leather are made in the same fashion, only a little flavoring or spice is added to them.

COCOANUT CARAMELS.

Two cupfuls of grated cocoanut, one cupful of sugar, two tablespoonfuls of flour, the whites of three eggs, beaten stiff. Soak the cocoanut, if dessicated, in milk enough to cover it; then beat the whites of the eggs, add gradually the sugar, cocoanut, and flour; with your fingers make, by rolling the mixture, into cone shapes. Place them on buttered sheets of tin, covered with buttered letter-paper, and bake in a moderate heat about fifteen or twenty minutes. They should cool before removing from the tins.

DRIED PRESERVES.

Any of the fruits that have been preserved in syrup may be converted into dry preserves, by first draining them from the syrup and then drying them slowly on the stove, strewing them thickly with powdered sugar. They should be turned every few hours, sifting over them more sugar.

CANDIES WITHOUT COOKING.

Very many candies made by confectioners are made without boiling, which makes them very desirable, and they are equal to the best "French Creams." The secret lies in the sugar used, which is the XXX powdered or confectioners' sugar. Ordinary powdered sugar, when rubbed between the thumb and finger has a decided grain, but the confectioners' sugar is fine as flour. The candies made after this process are better the day after.

FRENCH VANILLA CREAM.

Break into a bowl the white of one or more eggs, as the quantity you wish to make will require; add to it an equal quantity of cold water, then stir in XXX powdered or confectioners' sugar until you have it stiff enough to mold into shape with the fingers. Flavor with vanilla to taste. After it is formed in balls, cubes or lozenge shapes, lay them upon plates or waxed paper, and set them aside to dry. This cream can be worked in candies similar to the French cooked cream.

CHOCOLATE CREAM DROPS.

These are made or molded into cone-shape forms with the fingers, from the uncooked "French Cream," similar to that which is cooked. After forming into these little balls or cones, lay them on oiled paper until the next day, to harden, or make them in the morning and leave them until afternoon. Then melt some chocolate (the best confectioners') in a basin set in another basin of boiling water; when melted, and the creams are hard enough to handle, take one at a time on a fork, and drop into the melted chocolate, roll it until well covered, then slip from the fork upon oiled or waxed paper, and set them aside to harden.

FRUIT AND NUT CREAMS.

Raisins seeded, currants, figs and citron, chopped fine, and mixed with the uncooked "French Cream," while soft, before the sugar is all mixed in, makes a delicious variety. Nuts also may be mixed with this cream, stirring into it chopped almonds, hickory nuts, butternuts, or English walnuts, then forming them into balls, bars or squares. Several kinds of nuts may be mixed together.

ORANGE DROPS.

Grate the rind of one orange and squeeze the juice, taking care to reject the seeds; add to this a pinch of tartaric acid; then stir in confectioners' sugar until it is stiff enough to form into small balls the size of a small marble. This is delicious candy.

The same process for lemon drops, using lemons in place of orange. Color a faint yellow

COCOANUT CREAMS.

Make the uncooked cream as in the foregoing recipe. Take the cream while soft, add fresh grated cocoanut to taste; add sufficient confectioners' sugar to mold into balls and then roll the balls in the fresh grated cocoanut. These may be colored pink with a few drops of cochineal syrup, also brown by adding a few spoonfuls of grated chocolate; then rolling them in grated cocoanut; the three colors are very pretty together. The cocoanut cream may be made into a flat cake and cut into squares or strips.

With this uncooked cream, all the recipes given for the cooked "French Cream," may be used:—English walnut creams, variegated creams, etc., etc

COFFEE, TEA, BEVERAGES.

Boiling water is a very important desideratum in the making of a good cup of coffee or tea, but the average housewife is very apt to overlook this fact. Do not boil the water more than three or four minutes; longer boiling ruins the water for coffee or tea-making, as most of its natural properties escape by evaporation, leaving a very insipid liquid, composed mostly of lime and iron, that would ruin the best coffee, and give the tea a dark, dead look, which ought to be the reverse.

Water left in the tea-kettle over night *must never be used for preparing the breakfast coffee*; no matter how excellent your coffee or tea may be, it will be ruined by the addition of water that has been boiled more than once.

THE HEALING PROPERTIES OF TEA AND COFFEE.

The medical properties of these two beverages are considerable. Tea is used advantageously in inflammatory diseases and as a cure for the headache. Coffee is supposed to act as a preventive of gravel and gout, and to its influence is ascribed the rarity of those diseases in France and Turkey. Both tea and coffee powerfully counteract the effects of opium and intoxicating liquors; though, when taken in excess, and without nourishing food, they themselves produce, temporarily at least, some of the more disagreeable consequences incident to the use of ardent spirits. In general, however, none but persons possessing great mobility of the nervous system, or enfeebled or effeminate constitutions, are injuriously affected by the moderate use of tea and coffee in connection with food.

COFFEE.

One full coffee-cupful of ground coffee, stirred with one egg and part of the shell, adding a half cupful of *cold* water. Put it into the coffee boiler, and pour on to it a quart of boiling water; as it rises and begins to boil, stir it down with a silver spoon or fork. Boil hard for ten or twelve minutes. Remove from the fire, and pour out a cupful of coffee, then pour back into the coffee-pot. Place it on the back of the stove or range, where it will keep hot, (and not boil); it will settle in about five minutes. Send to the table *hot*. Serve with good cream and lump sugar. Three-quarters of a pound of Java and a quarter of a pound of Mocha make the best mixture of coffee.

VIENNA COFFEE.

Equal parts of Mocha and Java coffee; allow one heaping tablespoonful of coffee to each person, and two extra to make good strength. Mix one egg with grounds; pour on coffee half as much boiling water as will be needed; let coffee froth, then stir down grounds, and let boil five minutes; then let coffee stand where it will keep hot, but not boil, for five or ten minutes, and add rest of water. To one pint of cream add the white of an egg, well-beaten; this is to be put in cups with sugar, and hot coffee added.

FILTERED OR DRIP COFFEE.

For each person allow a large tablespoonful of finely ground coffee, and to every tablespoonful allow a cupful of boiling water; the coffee to be one part Mocha to two of Java.

Have a small iron ring made to fit the top of the coffee-pot inside, and to this ring sew a small muslin bag (the muslin for the purpose must not be too thin). Fit the bag into the pot, pour some boiling water in it, and, when the pot is well-warmed, put the ground coffee into the bag; pour over as much boiling water as is required, close the lid, and, when all the water has filtered through, remove the bag, and send the coffee to table. Making it in this manner prevents the necessity of pouring the coffee from one vessel to another, which cools and spoils it. The water should be poured on the coffee gradually so that the infusion may be stronger; and the bag must be well made that none of the grounds may escape through the seams and so make the coffee thick and muddy.

Patented coffee-pots on this principle can be purchased at most house-furnishing stores.

ICED COFFEE.

Make more coffee than usual at breakfast time and stronger. When cold put on ice. Serve with cracked ice in each tumbler.

SUBSTITUTE FOR CREAM IN COFFEE.

Beat the white of an egg put to it a small lump of butter and pour the coffee into it gradually, stirring it so that it will not curdle. It is difficult to distinguish this from fresh cream.

Many drop a tiny piece of sweet butter into their cup of hot coffee as a substitute for cream.

TO MAKE TEA.

Allow two teaspoonfuls of tea to one large cupful of boiling water. Scald the teapot, put in the tea, pour on about a cupful of *boiling* water, set it on the fire in a warm place where it will not boil, but keep very hot, to almost boiling; let it steep or "draw" ten or twelve minutes. Now fill up with as much boiling water as is required. Send *hot* to the table. It is better to use a china or porcelain teapot, but if you do use metal let it be tin, new, bright and clean; never use it when the tin is worn off and the iron exposed. If you do you are drinking tea-ate of iron.

To make tea to perfection, boiling water must be poured on the leaves directly it boils. Water which has been boiling more than five minutes, or which has previously boiled, should on no account be used. If the water does not boil, or if it be allowed to overboil, the leaves of the tea will be only half-opened and the tea itself will be quite spoiled. The water should be allowed to remain on the leaves from ten to fifteen minutes.

A Chinese being interviewed for the *Cook* says: Drink your tea plain. Don't add milk or sugar. Tea-brokers and tea-tasters never do; epicures never do; the Chinese never do. Milk contains fibrin, albumen or some other stuff, and the tea a delicate amount of tannin. Mixing the two makes the liquid turbid. This turbidity, if I remember the cylopædia aright, is tannate of fibrin, or leather. People who put milk in tea are therefore drinking boots and shoes in mild disguise.

ICED TEA.

Is now served to a considerable extent during the summer months. It is of course used without milk, and the addition of sugar serves only to destroy the finer tea flavor. It may be prepared some hours in advance, and should be made stronger than when served hot. It is bottled and placed in the ice-chest till required. Use the black or green teas, or both, mixed, as fancied.

CHOCOLATE.

Allow half a cupful of grated chocolate to a pint of water and a pint of milk. Rub the chocolate smooth in a little cold water, and stir into the boiling water. Boil twenty minutes, add the milk and boil ten minutes more, stirring it often. Sweeten to your taste.

The French put two cupfuls of boiling water to each cupful of chocolate.

They throw in the chocolate just as the water commences to boil. Stir it with a spoon as soon as it boils up, add two cupfuls of good milk, and when it has boiled sufficiently, serve with a spoonful of thick whipped cream with each cup.

COCOA.

Six tablespoonfuls of cocoa to each pint of water, as much milk as water, sugar to taste. Rub cocoa smooth in a little cold water; have ready on the fire a pint of boiling water; stir in grated cocoa paste. Boil twenty minutes, add milk and boil five minutes more, stirring often. Sweeten in cups so as to suit different tastes.

BUTTERMILK AS A DRINK.

Buttermilk, so generally regarded as a waste product, has latterly been coming somewhat into vogue, not only as a nutrient, but as a therapeutic agent, and in an editorial article the *Canada Lancet*, some time ago, highly extolled its virtues. Buttermilk may be roughly described as milk which has lost most of its fat and a small percentage of casein, and which has become sour by fermentation. Long experience has demonstrated it to be an agent of superior digestibility. It is, indeed, a true milk peptone—that is, milk already partially digested, the coagulation of the coagulable portion being loose and flaky, and not of that firm indigestible nature which is the result of the action of the gastric juice upon sweet cow's milk. It resembles koumiss in its nature, and, with the exception of that article, it is the most grateful, refreshing, and digestible of the products of milk. It is a decided laxative to the bowels, a fact which must be borne in mind in the treatment of typhoid fever, and which may be turned to advantage in the treatment of habitual constipation. It is a diuretic, and may be prescribed with advantage in some kidney troubles. Owing to its acidity, combined with its laxative properties, it is believed to exercise a general impression on the liver. It is well adapted to many cases where it is customary to recommend lime water and milk. It is invaluable in the treatment of diabetes, either exclusively, or alternating with skimmed milk. In some cases of gastric ulcer and cancer of the stomach, it is the only food that can be retained.

—Medical Journal.

CURRANT WINE. No. 1.

The currants should be quite ripe. Stem, mash and strain them, adding a half pint of water and less than a pound of sugar to a quart of the mashed fruit. Stir well up together, and pour into a clean cask, leaving the bung-hole open, or covered with a piece of lace. It should stand for a month to ferment, when it will be ready for bottling; just before bottling you may add a small quantity of brandy or whiskey.

CURRANT WINE. No. 2.

To each quart of currant juice, add two quarts of soft water and three pounds of brown sugar. Put into a jug or small keg, leaving the top open until fermentation ceases, and it looks clear. Draw off and cork tightly.   .

—Long Island recipe.

BLACKBERRY WINE. No. 1.

Cover your blackberries with cold water; crush the berries well with a wooden masher; let them stand twenty-four hours; then strain, and to one gallon of juice put three pounds of common brown sugar; put into wide-mouthed jars for several days, carefully skimming off the scum that will rise to the top; put in several sheets of brown paper, and let them remain in it three days; then skim again, and pour through a funnel into your cask. There let it remain undisturbed till March; then strain again, and bottle. These directions, if carefully followed out, will insure you excellent wine.

—Orange County recipe.

BLACKBERRY WINE. No. 2.

Berries should be ripe and plump. Put into a large wood or stone vessel with a tap; pour on sufficient boiling water to cover them; when cool enough to bear your hand, bruise well until all the berries are broken; cover up, let stand until berries begin to rise to top, which will occur in three or four days. Then draw off the clear juice in another vessel, and add one pound of sugar to every ten quarts of the liquor, and stir thoroughly. Let stand six to ten days in first vessel with top; then draw off through a jelly bag. Steep four ounces of isinglass in a pint of wine for twelve hours; boil it over a slow fire till all dissolved, then place dissolved isinglass in a gallon of blackberry juice, give them a boil together, and pour all into the vessel. Let stand a few days to ferment and settle, draw off and keep in a cool place. Other berry wines may be made in the same manner.

GRAPE WINE.

Mash the grapes and strain them through a cloth; put the skins in a tub after squeezing them, with barely enough water to cover them; strain the juice thus obtained into the first portion; put three pounds of sugar to one gallon of the mixture; let it stand in an open tub to ferment, covered with a cloth, for a period of from three to seven days; skim off what rises every morning. Put the juice in a cask, and leave it open for twenty-four hours; then bung it up, and put clay over the bung to keep the air out. Let your wine remain in the cask until March, when it should be drawn off and bottled.

FLORIDA ORANGE WINE.

Wipe the oranges with a wet cloth, peel off the yellow rind very thin, squeeze the oranges, and strain the juice through a hair sieve; measure the juice after it is strained, and for each gallon allow three pounds of granulated sugar, the white and shell of one egg, and one-third of a gallon of cold water; put the sugar, the white and shell of the egg (crushed small) and the water over the fire, and stir them every two minutes until the eggs begins to harden; then boil the syrup until it looks clear under the froth of egg which will form on the surface; strain the syrup, pour it upon the orange rind, and let it stand over night; then next add the orange-juice and again let it stand over night; strain it the second day, and put it into a tight cask with a small cake of compressed yeast to about ten gallons of wine, and leave the bung out of the cask until the wine ceases to ferment; the hissing noise continues as long as fermentation is in progress; when fermentation ceases, close the cask by driving in the bung, and let the wine stand about nine months before bottling it; three months after it is bottled, it can be used. A glass of brandy added to each gallon of wine after fermentation ceases is generally considered an improvement.

There are seasons of the year when Florida oranges by the box are very cheap, and this fine wine can be made at a small expense.

METHELIN, OR HONEY WINE.

This is a very ancient and popular drink in the north of Europe. To some new honey, strained, add spring water; put a whole egg into it; boil this liquor till the egg swims above the liquor; strain, pour it in a cask. To every fifteen gallons add two ounces of white Jamaica ginger, bruised, one ounce of cloves and mace, one and a half ounces of cinnamon, all bruised together, and tied up in a muslin bag; accelerate the fermentation with yeast; when worked sufficiently, bung up; in six weeks draw off into bottles.

Another Mead.—Boil the combs, from which the honey has been drained, with sufficient water to make a tolerably sweet liquor; ferment this with yeast, and proceed as per previous formula.

Sack Mead is made by adding a handful of hops and sufficient brandy to the comb liquor.

BLACK CURRANT WINE.

Four quarts of whiskey, four quarts of black currants; four pounds of brown or white sugar, one tablespoonful of cloves; one tablespoonful of cinnamon.

Crush the currants, and let them stand in the whiskey with the spices for three weeks; then strain and add the sugar; set away again for three weeks longer; then strain and bottle.

RAISIN WINE.

Take two pounds of raisins, seed and chop them, a lemon, a pound of white sugar, and about two gallons of boiling water. Pour into a stone jar, and stir daily for six or eight days. Strain, bottle, and put in a cool place for ten days or so, when the wine will be ready for use.

CHERRY BOUNCE.

To one gallon of wild cherries add enough good whiskey to cover the fruit. Let soak two or three weeks and then drain off the liquor. Mash the cherries without breaking the stones and strain through a jelly-bag; add this liquor to that already drained off. Make a syrup with a gill of water and a pound of white sugar to every two quarts of liquor thus prepared; stir in well and bottle, and tightly cork. A common way of making cherry bounce is to put wild cherries and whiskey together in a jug and use the liquor as wanted.

BLACKBERRY CORDIAL.

Warm and squeeze the berries; add to one pint of juice one pound of white sugar, one-half ounce of powdered cinnamon, one-fourth ounce of mace, two teaspoonfuls of cloves. Boil all together for one-fourth of an hour; strain the syrup, and to each pint add a glass of French brandy. Two or three doses of a tablespoonful or less will check any slight diarrhoea. When the attack is violent, give a tablespoonful after each discharge, until the complaint is in subjection. It will arrest dysentery if given in season, and is a pleasant and safe remedy. Excellent for children when teething.

HOP BEER.

Take five quarts of water, six ounces of hops, boil it three hours; then strain the liquor, add to it five quarts of water, four ounces of bruised ginger root, boil this again twenty minutes, strain and add four pounds of sugar. When luke-warm, put in a pint of yeast. Let it ferment; in twenty-four hours it will be ready for bottling.

GINGER BEER.

Put into a kettle two ounces of powdered ginger root (or more if it is not very strong), half an ounce of cream of tartar, two large lemons, cut in slices, two pounds of broken loaf sugar, and two gallons of soft boiling water. Simmer them over a slow fire for half an hour. When the liquor is nearly cold, stir into it a large tablespoonful of the best yeast. After it has fermented, which will be in about twenty-four hours, bottle for use.

SPRUCE BEER.

Allow an ounce of hops and a spoonful of ginger to a gallon of water. When well boiled, strain it, and put in a pint of molasses, or a pound of brown sugar, and half an ounce or less of the essence of spruce; when cool, add a teacupful of yeast, and put into a clean, tight cask, and let it ferment for a day or two, then bottle it for use. You can boil the sprigs of spruce fir in place of the essence.

ROMAN PUNCH. No. 1.

Grate the yellow rind of four lemons and two oranges upon two pounds of loaf sugar. Squeeze the juice of the lemons and oranges; cover the juice and let it stand until the next day. Strain it through a sieve, mix with the sugar; add a bottle of champagne and the whites of eight eggs beaten to a stiff froth. It may be frozen or not, as desired. For winter use snow instead of ice.

ROMAN PUNCH. No. 2.

Make two quarts of lemonade, rich with pure juice lemon fruit; add one tablespoonful of extract of lemon. Work well, and freeze; just before serving, add for each quart of ice half a pint of brandy and half a pint of Jamaica rum. Mix well and serve in high glasses, as this makes what is called a semi or half-ice. It is usually served at dinners as a *coup de milieu.*

DELICIOUS JUNKET.

Take two quarts of new milk, warm it on the stove to about blood-heat; pour it into a glass or china bowl, and stir into it two tablespoonfuls of Grosse & Blackwell's prepared rennet, two tablespoonfuls of powdered loaf sugar, and a small wine-glassful of pale brandy. Let it stand till cold and eat with sugar and rich cream. Half the quantity can be made.

RASPBERRY SHRUB.

One quart of raspberry juice, half a pound of loaf sugar, dissolved, a pint of Jamaica rum, or part rum and brandy. Mix thoroughly. Bottle for use.

SASSAFRAS MEAD.

Mix gradually with two quarts of boiling water three pounds and a half of the best brown sugar, a pint and a half of good West India molasses, and a quarter of a pound of tartaric acid. Stir it well, and when cool, strain it into a large jug or pan, then mix in a teaspoonful (not more) of essence of sassafras. Transfer it to clean bottles, (it will fill about half a dozen,) cork it tightly, and keep it in a cool place. It will be fit for use next day. Put into a box or boxes a quarter of a pound of carbonate of soda, to use with it. To prepare a glass of sassafras mead for drinking, put a large tablespoonful of the mead into a half tumbler full of ice-water, stir into it a half teaspoonful of the soda, and it will immediately foam up to the top.

Sassafras mead will be found a cheap, wholesome, and pleasant beverage for warm weather. The essence of sassafras, tartaric acid and carbonate of soda, can, of course, all be obtained at the druggist's.

CREAM SODA WITHOUT THE FOUNTAIN.

Coffee-sugar, four pounds; three pints of water, three nutmegs, grated, the whites of ten eggs, well-beaten, gum arabic, one ounce; twenty drops of oil of lemon, or extract equal to that amount. By using oils of other fruits, you can make as many flavors from this as you desire. Mix all, and place over a gentle fire, and stir well about thirty minutes; remove from the fire and strain, and divide into two parts; into one-half put eight ounces of bi-carbonate of soda, into the other half put six ounces of tartaric acid. Shake well, and when cold they are ready for use by pouring three or four spoonfuls from both parts into separate glasses, each one-third full of water. Stir each and pour together, and you have a nice glass of cream soda which you can drink at your leisure, as the gum and eggs hold the gas.

WINE WHEY.

Sweeten one pint of milk to taste, and when boiling, throw in two wine-glasses of sherry; when the curd forms, strain the whey through a muslin bag into tumblers.

LEMON SYRUP.

Take the juice of twelve lemons; grate the rind of six in it, let it stand over night; then take six pounds of white sugar, and make a thick syrup. When it is quite cool, strain the juice into it, and squeeze as much oil from the grated rind as will suit the taste. Put in bottles, securely corked, for future use. A tablespoonful in a goblet of water will make a delicious drink on a hot day.

FOR A SUMMER DRAUGHT.

The juice of one lemon, a tumblerful of cold water, pounded sugar to taste, half a small teaspoonful of carbonate of soda. Squeeze the juice from the lemon; strain, and add it to the water, with sufficient pounded sugar to sweeten the whole nicely. When well-mixed, put in the soda, stir well, and drink while the mixture is in an effervescing state.

NOYEAU CORDIAL.

To one gallon of proof spirit add three pounds of loaf sugar and a table-spoonful of extract of almonds. Mix well together, and allow to stand forty-eight hours, covered closely; now strain through thick flannel, and bottle. This liquor will be much improved by adding half a pint of apricot or peach juice.

EGG NOGG.

Beat the yellows of twelve eggs very light, stir in as much white sugar as they will dissolve, pour in gradually one glass of brandy to cook the eggs, one glass of old whiskey, one grated nutmeg, and three pints of rich milk. Beat the whites to a froth and stir in last.

EGG FLIP, OR MULLED ALE.

Boil one quart of good ale, with some nutmeg; beat up six eggs, and mix them with a little cold ale; then pour the hot ale to it, and pour it back and forth several times to prevent its curdling; warm, and stir it till sufficiently thick; add a piece of butter or a glass of brandy, and serve it with dry toast.

MILK PUNCH.

One pint of milk made very sweet; a wine-glassful of brandy or rum, well-stirred together; grate a little nutmeg over the top of the glasses. Serve with a straw in each glass.

FINE MILK PUNCH.

Pare off the yellow rind of four large lemons, and steep it for twenty-four hours in a quart of brandy or rum. Then mix with it the juice of the lemons, a pound and a half of loaf-sugar, two grated nutmegs, and a quart of water. Add a quart of rich unskimmed milk, made boiling hot, and strain the whole through a jelly bag. You may either use it as soon as it is cold, or make a larger quantity (in the above proportions), and bottle it. It will keep several months.

THE FAMILY DINING ROOM.

REAR VIEW OF THE WHITE HOUSE.

TO MAKE HOT PUNCH.

Half a pint of rum, half a pint of brandy, quarter of a pound of sugar, one large lemon, half a teaspoonful of nutmeg, one pint of boiling water.

Rub the sugar over the lemon until it has absorbed all the yellow part of the skin, then put the sugar into a punch-bowl; add the lemon-juice (free from pips), and mix these two ingredients, well together. Pour over them the boiling water, stir well together, add the rum, brandy, and nutmeg; mix thoroughly and the punch will be ready to serve. It is very important in making good punch that all the ingredients are thoroughly incorporated; and to insure success, the processes of mixing must be diligently attended to. (This is an old-style punch.)

LEMONADE.

Three lemons to a pint of water makes strong lemonade; sweeten to your taste.

STRAWBERRY WATER.

Take one cupful of ripe hulled berries; crush with a wooden spoon, mixing with the mass a quarter of a pound of pulverized sugar and half a pint of cold water. Pour the mixture into a fine sieve, rub through and filter till clear; add the strained juice of one lemon and one and a half pints of cold water, mix thoroughly, and set in ice-chest till wanted.

This makes a nice, cool drink on a warm day, and easily to be made in strawberry season.

STRAWBERRY AND RASPBERRY SYRUP.

Mash the fresh fruit, express the juice, and to each quart add three and a half pounds of granulated sugar. The juice, heated to 180° Fahrenheit, and strained or filtered previous to dissolving the sugar, will keep for an indefinite time, canned hot in glass jars.

The juice of soft fruits is best when allowed to drop therefrom by its own weight, lightly mash the fruit and then suspend in a cloth, allowing the juice to drop in a vessel beneath. Many housekeepers, after the bottles and jars are thoroughly washed and dried, smoke them with sulphur in this way: Take a piece of wire and bend it around a small piece of brimstone the size of a bean; set the brimstone on fire, put it in the jar or bottle, bending the other end over the mouth of the vessel, and cover with a cork; after the brimstone has burned away, fill the vessel with the syrup or preserves and cover tightly. There is no sulphurous taste left by the process.

KOUMISS.

Koumiss is prepared by dissolving four ounces of white sugar in one gallon of skimmed milk, and placing in bottles of the capacity of one quart; add two ounces of bakers' yeast, or a cake of compressed yeast to each bottle. Cork and tie securely, set in a warm place until fermentation is well under way, and lay the bottles on their sides in a cool cellar. In three days, fermentation will have progressed sufficiently to permit the koumiss to be in good condition.

PINEAPPLE VINEGAR.

Cover sliced pine-apples with pure cider vinegar; let them stand three or four days, then mash and strain through a cloth as long as it runs clear; to every three quarts of juice add five pounds of sugar.

Boil it all together about ten minutes, skim carefully until nothing rises to the surface, take from the fire; when cool, bottle it. Blackberries and raspberries, and, in fact, any kind of highly flavored fruit, is fine; a tablespoonful in a glass of ice-cold water, to drink in warm weather.

RASPBERRY VINEGAR. No. 1.

Put a quart of raspberries into a suitable dish, pour over them a quart of good vinegar, let it stand twenty-four hours, then strain through a flannel bag, and pour this liquor on another quart of berries; do this for three or four days successively, and strain it; make it very sweet with loaf sugar; bottle, and seal it.

RASPBERRY VINEGAR. No. 2.

Turn over a quart of ripe raspberries, mashed, a quart of good cider vinegar, add one pound of white sugar, mix well, then let stand in the sun four hours. Strain it, squeeze out the juice, and put in a pint of good brandy. Seal it up in bottles, air tight, and lay them on their sides in the cellar; cover them with sawdust. When used, pour two tablespoonfuls to a tumblerful of ice-water. Fine.

HOME-MADE TABLE VINEGAR.

Put in an open cask four gallons of warm rain-water, one gallon of common molasses, and two quarts of yeast; cover the top with thin muslin and leave it in the sun, covering it up at night and when it rains. In three or four weeks it will be good vinegar. If cider can be used in place of rain-water the vinegar will make much sooner—will not take over a week to make a very sharp vinegar. Excellent, for pickling purposes.

VERY STRONG TABLE VINEGAR.

Take two gallons of good cider and thoroughly mix it with two pounds of new honey, pour into your cask or bottle, and let it stand from four to six months, when you will have vinegar so strong that it cannot be used at table without diluting with water. It is the best ever procured for pickling purposes.

PINEAPPLE-ADE.

Pare and slice some very ripe pineapples; then cut the slices into small pieces. Put them with all their juice into a large pitcher, and sprinkle among them plenty of powdered white sugar. Pour on boiling water, allowing a small half pint to each pineapple. Cover the pitcher, and let it stand till quite cool, occasionally pressing down the pineapple with a spoon. Then set the pitcher for a while in ice. Lastly, strain the infusion into another vessel, and transfer it to tumblers, putting into each glass some more sugar and a bit of ice. This beverage will be found delicious.

SEIDLITZ POWDERS.

Fold in a white paper a mixture of one drachm of Rochelle salts and twenty-five grains of carbonate of soda, in a blue·paper twenty grains of tartaric acid. They should all be pulverized very finely. Put the contents of the white paper into a tumbler, not quite half full of cold water, and stir it till dissolved. Then put the mixture from the blue paper into another tumbler with the same quantity of water, and stir that also. When the powders are dissolved in both tumblers, pour the first into the other, and it will effervesce immediately. Drink it quickly, while foaming.

INEXPENSIVE DRINK.

A very nice, cheap drink which may take the place of lemonade, and be found fully as healthful, is made with one cupful of pure cider vinegar, half a cupful of good molasses, put into one quart pitcher of ice-water. A tablespoonful of ground ginger added makes a healthful beverage.

THE
VARIETIES OF SEASONABLE FOOD

TO BE OBTAINED IN OUR MARKETS DURING THE YEAR.

JANUARY.

MEATS.

Beef, mutton, pork, lamb.

POULTRY AND GAME.

Rabbits, hares, partridges, woodcocks, grouse or prairie chickens, snipes, antelope, quails, swans, geese, chickens, capons, tame pigeons, wild ducks, the canvas-back duck being the most popular and highly prized; turkeys.

FISH.

Haddock, fresh codfish, halibut, flounders, bass, fresh salmon, turbot. Frozen fresh mackerel is found in our large cities during this month; also frozen salmon, red-snapper, shad, frozen bluefish, pickerel, smelts, green turtle, diamond-back terrapin, prawns, oysters, scallops, hard crabs, white bait, finnan haddie, smoked halibut, smoked salmon.

VEGETABLES.

Cabbage, carrots, turnips, parsnips, beets, pumpkins, chives, celery, winter squash, onions, white and sweet potatoes, Jerusalem artichokes, chiccory, Brussels-sprouts, kale-sprouts, oyster plant, leeks, cress, cauliflower. Garden herbs, both dry and green, being chiefly used in stuffing and soups, and for flavoring and garnishing certain dishes, are always in season, such as sage, thyme, sweet basil, borage, dill, mint, parsley, lavender, summer savory, etc., may be procured green in the summer and dried in the winter.

FEBRUARY.

MEATS.

Beef, mutton, pork, lamb, antelope.

430

POULTRY AND GAME.

Partridges, hares, rabbits, snipes, capons, pheasants, fowls, pullets, geese, ducks, turkeys, wild ducks, swan, geese and pigeons.

FISH.

Halibut, haddock, fresh codfish, striped bass, eels, fresh salmon, live lobsters, pompano, sheep's-head, red-snapper, white perch, a panfish, smelts—green and frozen; shad, herring, salmon-trout, whitefish, pickerel, green turtle, flounders, scallops, prawns, oysters, soft-shell crabs—which are in excellent condition this month; hard crabs, white bait, boneless dried codfish, finnan haddie, smoked halibut, smoked salmon.

VEGETABLES.

White potatoes, sweet potatoes, cabbage, onions, parsnips, oyster plant, okra, celery, chiccory, carrots, turnips, Jerusalem artichokes, French artichokes, Brussels-sprouts, beets, mushrooms raised in hot-houses, pumpkin, winter squash, dry shallots and garden herbs for seasoning put up in the dried state.

MARCH.

MEATS.

Beef, veal, mutton, lamb, pork.

POULTRY AND GAME.

Chickens, turkeys, ducks, rabbits, snipes, wild pigeons, capons.

FISH.

Striped bass, halibut, salmon, live codfish, chicken halibut, live lobster, Spanish mackerel, flounders, sheep's-head, pompano, grouper, red-snapper. Shad are plentiful this month. Herring, salmon-trout, sturgeon, whitefish, pickerel, yellow perch, catfish, green turtle, terrapin, scallops, soft-shell clams, oysters, prawns, smoked salmon, smoked halibut, smoked haddock, salt codfish.

VEGETABLES.

Cabbages, turnips, carrots, parsnips, artichokes, white potatoes, sweet potatoes, onions, leeks, radishes, Brussels-sprouts, celery, mushrooms, salsify-chives, cress, parsley and other garden herbs, greens, rhubarb and cucumbers raised in hot-beds.

APRIL.

MEATS.

Beef, veal, pork, mutton, lamb.

POULTRY AND GAME.

Chickens, fowls, green geese, young ducks, capons, golden plover, squabs, wild ducks.

FISH.

Haddock, fresh cod, striped bass, halibut, eels, chicken halibut, live lobsters, salmon, white perch, flounders, fresh mackerel, sheep's-head, smelts, red-snapper, bluefish, skate or ray fish, shad, whitefish, brook trout, salmon-trout, pickerel, catfish, prawns, crayfish, green turtle, oysters, scallops, frogs' legs, clams, hard crabs, white bait, smoked halibut, smoked salmon, smoked haddock, salt mackerel, salt codfish.

VEGETABLES.

Onions, white and sweet potatoes, kale-sprouts, rhubarb, artichokes, turnips, radishes, Brussels-sprouts, okra, cabbage, parsnips, mushrooms, cress, carrots, beets, dandelion, egg-plant, leeks, lettuce, cucumbers, asparagus, string beans, peas, chives.

MAY.

MEATS.

Beef, veal, mutton, lamb, pork.

POULTRY AND GAME.

Fowls, pigeons, spring chickens, young ducks, chickens, green geese, young turkeys.

FISH.

Halibut, haddock, striped bass, salmon, flounders, fresh mackerel, Spanish mackerel, blackfish, pompano, butterfish, weakfish, kingfish, porgies, shad, bluefish, clams, brook-trout, whitefish, carp, crayfish, prawns, green turtle, soft crabs, frogs' legs, smoked fish.

VEGETABLES.

New potatoes, sweet potatoes, cabbage, young onions, asparagus, beets, carrots, kidney beans, string beans, lettuce, tomatoes, cauliflower, peas, turnips, squash, rhubarb, spinach, radishes, artichokes, sorrel, egg-plant, cucumbers, salads generally.

JUNE.

MEATS.

Beef, veal, mutton, lamb.

POULTRY AND GAME.

Chickens, geese, ducks, young turkeys, plovers, pigeons.

FISH.

Fresh salmon, striped bass, halibut, fresh mackerel, flounders, kingfish, black-fish, weakfish, butterfish, pompano, Spanish mackerel, porgies, sheep's-head, sturgeon, sea bass, bluefish, skate or rayfish, carp, black bass, crayfish, lobsters, eels, white bait, frogs' legs, soft crabs, clams.

VEGETABLES.

Potatoes, spinach, cauliflower, string beans, peas, tomatoes, asparagus, carrots, artichokes, parsnips, onions, cucumbers, lettuce, radishes, cress, oyster plant, egg plant, rhubarb and all kinds of garden herbs, sorrel, horse-radish.

JULY.

MEATS.

Beef, veal, mutton, lamb, pork.

POULTRY AND GAME.

Fowls, chickens, pigeons, plovers, young geese, turkey-plouts, squabs, doe-birds, tame rabbits.

FISH.

Spanish mackerel, striped bass, fresh mackerel, blackfish, kingfish, flounders, salmon, cod, haddock, halibut, pompano, butterfish, a sweet panfish, sheep's-head, porgies, sea bass, weakfish, swordfish, tantog, bluefish, skate, brook trout, crayfish, blask bass, moonfish—a fine baking or boiling fish; pickerel, perch, eels, green turtle, frogs' legs, soft crabs, white bait, prawns, lobsters, clams.

VEGETABLES.

Potatoes, asparagus, peas, green string beans, butter beans, artichokes, celery, lettuce, carrots, salsify, tomatoes, spinach, mushrooms, cabbage, onions, endive, radishes, turnips, mint, various kinds of greens and salads.

AUGUST.

MEATS.

Beef, veal, mutton, lamb, pork.

POULTRY AND GAME.

Venison, young ducks, green geese, snipe, plover, turkeys, guinea-fowls, squabs, wild pigeons, woodcock, fowls.

FISH.

Striped bass, cod, halibut, haddock, salmon, flounders, fresh mackerel, ponito, butterfish, sea bass, kingfish, sheep's-head, porgies, bluefish, moonfish, brook-trout, eels, black bass, crayfish, skate or rayfish, catfish, green turtle, white bait, squid, frogs' legs, soft crabs, prawns, clams.

VEGETABLES.

Carrots, artichokes, onions, string beans, lima beans, cauliflower, Irish potatoes, sweet potatoes, green corn, tomatoes, peas, summer squash, cucumbers, radishes, lettuce, celery, rhubarb, beets, greens, mushrooms, chives.

SEPTEMBER.

MEATS.

Beef, veal, mutton, lamb, pork, venison.

POULTRY AND GAME.

Larks, woodcock, snipe, wild pigeons, squabs, young geese, young turkeys, plover, wild ducks, wild geese, swans and brant fowls, reed-birds, grouse, doe-birds, partridges.

FISH.

Salmon, halibut, codfish, pompano, striped bass, haddock, cero, a large fish similar to the Spanish mackerel; flounders, fresh mackerel, blackfish, Spanish mackerel, butterfish, whitefish, weakfish, smelts, porgies, squids, pickerel, crayfish, catfish, bluefish, wall-eyed pike, sea bass, skate, carp, prawns, white bait, frog's legs, hard crabs, moonfish, soft crabs, herrings, lobsters, clams.

VEGETABLES.

Potatoes, cabbages, turnips, artichokes, peas, beans, carrots, onions, salsify, mushrooms, lettuce, sorrel, celery, cauliflower, Brussels-sprouts, sweet potatoes, squash, rhubarb, green-peppers, parsnips, beets, green corn, tomatoes, cress.

OCTOBER.

MEATS.

Beef, veal, mutton, lamb, pork, venison, antelope.

POULTRY AND GAME.

Turkeys, geese, fowls, pullets, chickens, wild ducks, the canvas-back duck being the most highly prized, for its delicate flavor; woodcock, grouse, pheasants, pigeons, partridges, snipes, reed-birds, golden plover, gray plover, squabs.

FISH.

Striped bass, fresh cod, halibut, haddock, Spanish mackerel, fresh mackerel, cero, flounders, pompano, weakfish, white perch, grouper, sheep's-head, whitefish, bluefish, pickerel, red-snapper, yellow perch; smelts, sea bass, black bass, cisco, wall-eyed pike, crayfish, carp, salmon-trout, spotted bass, terrapin, frogs' legs, hard crabs, soft crabs, white bait, green turtle, scallops, eels, lobsters, oysters.

VEGETABLES.

Potatoes, cabbages, turnips, carrots, cauliflowers, parsnips, string beans, peas, lima beans, corn, tomatoes, onions, spinach, salsify, egg-plant, beets, pumpkins, endive, celery, parsley squash, cucumbers, mushrooms, sweet herbs of all kinds, salads of all kinds, garlic, shallots.

NOVEMBER.

MEATS.

Beef, veal, mutton, pork, venison, antelope.

POULTRY AND GAME.

Rabbits, hares, pheasants, woodcock, partridges, quails, snipe, grouse, wild ducks, wild geese, fowls, turkeys, pigeons.

FISH.

Striped bass, fresh cod, halibut, haddock, salmon, fresh mackerel, blackfish, whitefish, bluefish, catfish, redfish or spotted bass, black bass, yellow perch, skate, red-snapper, salmon-trout, pickerel, shad, wall-eyed pike, cisco, crayfish, terrapin, green turtle, scallops, prawns, white bait, frogs' legs, hard crabs, oysters.

VEGETABLES.

Potatoes, carrots, parsnips, turnips, onions, dried beans, artichokes, cabbages, beets, winter squash, celery parsley, pumpkins, shallots, mushrooms, chiccory, all sorts of salads and sweet herbs.

DECEMBER.

MEATS.

Beef, veal, mutton, pork, venison.

POULTRY AND GAME.

Rabbits, hares, grouse, pheasants, woodcock, snipe, partridges, turkey, fowls, chickens, pullets, geese, wild geese, ducks, wild duck, tame duck, canvas-back duck, quails.

FISH.

Turbot, sturgeon, haddock, halibut, eels, striped bass, flounders, salmon, fresh cod, blackfish, whitefish, grouper, cusk, shad, mullet, a sweet panfish, black bass, yellow perch, salmon-trout, pickerel, cisco, skate, wall-eyed pike, terrapin, crayfish, green turtle, prawns, hard crabs, soft crabs, scallops, frogs' legs, oysters.

VEGETABLES.

Potatoes, cabbages, onions, winter squash, beets, turnips, pumpkins, carrots, parsnips, dried beans, dried peas, mushrooms, parsley, shallots, Brussels-sprouts, leeks, horse-radish, garlic, mint, sage and small salads. Garden herbs which are mostly used for stuffings and for flavoring dishes, soups, etc., or for garnishing, may be found either green or dried the year round, always in season.

Melons can be had at most of our markets from July 1st until the 15th of October; they are received from the South in the early part of the season, and are not as fresh and good as those ripened in our own vicinity.

MENUS.

.·.

BREAKFAST, LUNCHEON AND DINNER

FOR THE HOLIDAYS

AND FOR

A WEEK IN EACH MONTH IN THE YEAR.

.·.

JANUARY.

New Year's Day.

Breakfast.

Baked Apples 425.
Hominy 244.
Broiled White Fish 51.   Ham Omelet 206.
Potatoes a la Creme 171.   Parker House Rolls 224.
Crullers 281.   Toast 246.
Coffee 408.

Supper.

Cold Roast Turkey 71.
Boston Oyster Pie 66.   Celery Salad 154.
Baked Sweet Potatoes 175.
Rusks 227.   Fruit Cake 256.
Sliced Oranges.
Tea 410.

Dinner.

Oysters on Half Shell.
Julienne Soup 26.
Baked Pickerel 43.
Roast Turkey 71, Oyster Stuffing 72.
Mashed Potatoes 170.   Boiled Onions 176.
Baked Winter Squash 188.
Cranberry Sauce 144.   Chicken Pie 77.
Plain Celery 155.   Lobster Salad 151.
Olives.   Spiced Currants 168.
English Plum Pudding 353, Wine Sauce 371.
Mince Pie 300.   Orange Water Ice 337.
Fancy Cakes 275.   Cheese.   Fruits.
Nuts.   Raisins.   Confectionery.
Coffee 408.

Sunday.

Breakfast.

Oranges.
Oatmeal, with Cream 243.
Broiled Mutton Chops 122.   Tomato Sauce 140.
Favorite Warmed Potatoes 173.
Eggs on Toast 248.   Graham Gems 230.
Wheat Bread 213.   Coffee 408.

Supper.

Potted Ham 134.
Cheese Cream Toast 198.   Celery Salad 154·
Cold Raised Biscuit 223.
Gooseberry Jam 387.   Citron Cake 260.
Tea 410.

Dinner.

Oysters on Half Shell.
Mock Turtle Soup 32.
Boiled Halibut 48, Sauce Maitre d'Hotel 142.
Roast Haunch of Venison 91, Currant Jelly 383.
Potato Croquettes No. 1 174.
Creamed Parsnips 180.   Celery.
Pickled White Cabbage 162.
Chicken Patties 77.
Baked Lemon Pudding 355.   Jelly Kisses 330.
Raisins.   Nuts.   Fruit.
Coffee 408.

Monday.

Breakfast.

Baked Apples 425.
Boiled Rice 244.   Pork Cutlets 130.
Waffles 231, with Maple Syrup.
Potato Fillets 173.
Toast 246.   Coffee 408.

Luncheon.

Cold Roast Venison 91.
Broiled Oysters 63.   Potato Salad 155
Rye Drop Cakes 232.
Canned Peaches 390.   Tea 410.

Dinner.

Macaroni Soup 33.
Boiled Leg of Mutton 121, Caper Sauce 140.
Potatoes a la Delmonico 174.
Steamed Cabbage 178.   Cheese Fondu 197.
Cucumber Pickles 159.
Boston Cream Pie 294.   Sliced Oranges.
Crackers.   Cheese.
Coffee 408.

Tuesday.

Breakfast.

Raspberry Jam 387.
Hominy 244.   Saratoga Chips 171.
Porterhouse Steak 97.
French Griddle Cakes 235.
Brown Bread 216.   Coffee 408.

Luncheon.

Scrambled Mutton 125.
Welsh Rarebit 198.   Olives.
Hominy Croquettes 244.
Currant Jelly 383.   Molasses Cup Cake 274.
Chocolate 410.

Dinner.

Oyster Soup 33.
Roast Loin of Pork 128, Apple Sauce 143.
Boiled Sweet Potatoes 175.
Scalloped Onions 177.   Stewed Carrots 189.
Pickled Green Peppers 162.
Royal Sago Pudding 357, Sweet Sauce 375.
Crullers 281.
Fruit.   Cheese.
Coffee 408.

Wednesday.

Breakfast.

Old-fashioned Apple Sauce 143.
Fried Mush 243.
Pork Tenderloins 129. Fried Sweet Potatoes 175.
Parker House Rolls 224. Omelet 208.
Wheat Bread 213.
Coffee 408.

Luncheon.

Cold Roast Pork 128. Stewed Codfish 55.
Green Tomato Pickles 161.
Rusks 227. Strawberry Jam 387.
Tea 410.

Dinner.

Beef Soup 25.
Roast Fillet of Veal 112, Tomato Sauce 140.
Browned Potatoes 175.
Macaroni a la Creme 193. Parsnip Fritters 180.
Piccalili 165.
Lemon Pie 292. Cocoanut Tarts 303.
Cheese.
Coffee 408.

Thursday.

Breakfast.

Stewed Peaches.
Corn Meal Mush 243.
Stewed Beef Kidney 109. Crisp Potatoes 173.
Egg Muffins 229. Ham Toast 248.
Coffee 408

Luncheon.

Veal Croquettes 114.
Sardines.
Cold Slaw 153. Cheese Toast 247.
Canned Plums 392. Soft Ginger Cake 272.
Cocoa 411.

Dinner.

Chicken Cream Soup 27.
Boiled Corned Beef 104.
Boiled Potatoes 104. Boiled Turnips 104.
Boiled Cabbage 104. Beets Boiled 186.
Charlotte Russe 320.
Preserved Strawberries 377.
Fruit Jumbles 280. Fruit.
Coffee 408.

Friday.

Breakfast.

Orange Marmalade 386.
Oat Flakes 245.
Codfish Balls 54. Baked Eggs on Toast 248.
Lyonnaise Potatoes 173.
Sally Lunn 226. Raised Doughnuts 282.
Coffee 408.

Luncheon.

Cold Corned Beef 104.
Vegetable Hash 188. Deviled Lobster 59.
Graham Bread 216. Peach Butter 393.
Golden Spice Cake 267.
Tea 410.

Dinner.

Celery Soup 35.
Baked Halibut 49, Hollandaise Sauce 142.
Browned Potatoes 170.
Scalloped Oysters 66. Stewed Tomatoes 181.
Fried Salsify 186.
Suet Plum Pudding 367, Brandy Sauce 371.
Sponge Drops 277. Fruit.
Coffee 408.

Saturday.

Breakfast.

Apple Sauce 143.
Cracked Wheat 245.
Beef Hash 108.   Fried Raw Potatoes 171.
Buckwheat Cakes with Maple Syrup 236.
Wheat Bread 213
Coffee 408.

Luncheon.

Scalloped Fish 55.   Head Cheese 136.
Celery 155.   Grafton Milk Biscuits 226.
Grape Jelly 385.   Cream Cake 264.
Chocolate 410.

Dinner.

Tomato Soup 31.
Fricassee Chicken 75.
Mashed Potatoes 170.   Ladies' Cabbage 178.
Boiled Rice 179.   Cold Slaw 153.
Apple Pie 289.   Mock Ice 314.
Cookies 280.   Cheese.
Coffee 408.

.·.

FEBRUARY.

Washington's Birthday.

Breakfast.

Oranges.
Oatmeal with Cream 243.
Country Sausage 135.   Baked Omelet 208.
Lyonnaise Potatoes 173.   Clam Fritters 68.
Egg Muffins 229.   Wheat Bread 213.
Coffee 408.

Supper.

Cold Boiled Turkey 73.
Potatoe Croquettes 174.   Lobster Salad 151
Soda Biscuit 223.
English Pound Cake 259.
Pineapple Preserves 380.
Tea 410.

Dinner.

Oysters on Half Shell.
Mock Turtle Soup 32.
Baked White Fish 50, Bechamel Sauce 141.
Boiled Turkey 73, Oyster Sauce 138.
Boiled Sweet Potatoes 175.
Steamed Potatoes 172.   Stewed Tomatoes 181.
Scalloped Onions 177.
Salmi of Game 90.
Olives.   Chicken Salad 151.
Washington Pie 324.   Bavarian Cream 310.
Variegated Jelly 332.   Marble Cake 261.
Candied Fruits.   Raisins and Nuts.
Coffee 408.

Sunday.

Breakfast.

Old-fashioned Apple Sauce 143.
Graham Mush 243.
Broiled Ham 134.   Potatoe Croquettes 174
Fried Eggs 201.
Virginia Corn Bread 219.
German Doughnuts 283.   Wheat Bread 213.
Coffee 408.

Supper.

Boston Oyster Pie 66.
Cold Boiled Tongue 110.
Sliced Cucumber Pickle 160.
Orange Short Cake 240.   Ginger Snaps 275.
Tea 410.

Dinner.

Oxtail Soup 28.
Baked White Fish (Bordeaux Sauce) 50.
Braised Ducks with Turnips 84.
Mashed Potatoes 170.   Stewed Tomatoes 181.
Timbale of Macaroni 193.
Celery Salad 154.   Fried Sweetbreads 119.
Sago Apple Pudding 357.
Lemon Jelly 331.   Fruit.
Almond Macaroons 331.
Coffee 408.

Monday.

Breakfast.

Stewed Apricots.
Steamed Oatmeal 245.
Fried Chicken 78.   Potato Puffs 171.
Flannel Cakes 233.   Milk Toast 246.
Coffee 408.

Luncheon.

Warmed-up Duck 85.
Sliced Bologna Sausage 135.
Celery 155.   Potato Biscuit 226.
Canned Grapes 390.
Chocolate 410.

Dinner.

Vermicelli Soup 35.
Stewed Brisket of Beef 106.
Scalloped Potatoes 172.
Stewed Parsnips 180.
French Cabbage 179.   Mixed Pickles 166.
Cranberry Pie 298.
Spanish Cream 310.
Fruit.   Cheese.
Coffee 408.

Tuesday.

Breakfast.

Sliced Oranges.
Hominy 244.
Hamburger Steak 109.   Grilled Pork 132.
Saratoga Chips 171.   Tennessee Muffins 229.
Puff Ball Doughnuts 283.
Wheat Bread 213.
Coffee 408.

Luncheon.

Cold Sliced Beef 106.
Potato Puffs 171.   Tomato Catsup 156.
Light Biscuit 224.   Jelly Fritters 328.
Tea 410.

Dinner.

Scotch Mutton Broth 25.
Baked Ham 133.
Potato Snow 172.
Scalloped Tomatoes 181.
Veal Croquettes 114.   Stewed Beets 186.
Sunderland Pudding 369, Custard Sauce 374.
Lemon Cookies 281.
Fruit.
Coffee 408.

Wednesday.

Breakfast.

Fried Apples 130.
Corn Meal Mush 243.
Fried Pork Chops 130.   Newport Waffles 231.
Favorite Warmed Potatoes 173.
Brown Bread 216.   Coffee 408.

Luncheon.

Sliced Ham 133.   Scalloped Oysters 66.
Fried Sweet Potatoes 175.
Sweet Pickle 167.   Lemon Toast 326.
Tea 410.

Dinner.

Mullagatawny Soup 31.
Boned Leg of Mutton, Roasted, 120.
Boiled Potatoes 169.   Stewed Onions 176.
Mashed Turnips 190.
Hot Slaw 153.
Tapioca Blanc Mange 318,
                with Raspberry Jam 387.
Neapolitaines 278.   Fruit.
Coffee 408.

Thursday.

Breakfast.

Bananas.
Samp 245.
Broiled Veal Cutlets 114.   Tomato Sauce 140.
Fried Potatoes 171.   French Rolls 225.
Wonders 282.   Wheat Bread 213.
Coffee 408.

Luncheon.

Hashed Mutton on Toast 122.
Potato Croquettes 174.   Pickled Oysters 164.
Preserved Cherries 377.   Feather Cake 264.
Chocolate 410.

Dinner.

Tapioca Cream Soup 34.
Curry Chicken with Rice 81.
Steamed Sweet Potatoes 175.
Stewed Salsify 185.
Boiled Squash 188.   Pickled Onions 163.
Delicate Indian Pudding 351.
Orange Jelly 332.
Crackers.   Cheese.
Coffee 408.

Friday.

Breakfast.

Oranges.
Oatmeal, with Cream 243.
Boiled Salt Mackerel 51.
Veal Hash on Toast 249.
Fried Sweet Potatoes 175.
Corn Meal Griddle Cakes 234.
Coffee 408.

Luncheon.

Lobster Croquettes 60.   French Stew 105.
Cold Slaw 153.   Rusks 227.
Sweet Omelet 326.
Tea 410.

Dinner.

Lobster Soup 38.
Boiled Cod with Oyster Sauce 56.
Potato Puffs 171.   Fried Cabbage 178.
Muttonettes 124.
Olives.
Cocoanut Pudding 352.
Banana Cream 313.
Cup Cakes 276.
Coffee 408.

Saturday.

Breakfast.

Apple Jelly 385.
Boiled Rice 244.
Fried Pickled Pigs' Feet 133.
Baked Potatoes 175.   Fish Omelet 207.
English Crumpets 242.   Wheat Bread 213.
Coffee 408.

Luncheon.

Dried Beef with Cream 106.
Cheese Fondu 197.
Potato Salad 154.   Grafton Milk Biscuit 226.
Corn Meal Puffs 351.
Lemon Sauce 373.
Cocoa 411.

Dinner.

Turtle Bean Soup 30.
Beef a la Mode 99.
Baked Potatoes 175.   Sour-crout 179.
Macaroni a la Italienne 192.
Chowchow 163.
Chocolate Custard Pie 291.
Little Plum Cakes 279.
Fruit.
Coffee 408.

.·.

MARCH.

Sunday.

Breakfast.

Sliced Oranges.
Oat Flakes 245.
Porterhouse Steak 97.
Lyonnaise Potatoes 173.
Oyster Omelet 206.   Raised Biscuit 223.
Sour Milk Griddle Cakes 233.
Coffee 408.

Supper.

Calf's Head Cheese 117.
Lobster Patties 60.   Potato Salad 154.
Warm Soda Biscuits 223.
Honey.
Lemon Cookies 281.
Tea 410.

Dinner.

Swiss White Soup 35.
Boiled Fresh Mackerel 52, Egg Sauce 188.
Roast Beef 96.
Yorkshire Pudding 97.
Browned Potatoes 175.
Spinach with Eggs 188.   Boiled Parsnips 180.
Scalloped Cheese 197.
Chicken Croquettes 78.
Tapioca Cream Custard 313.
Rhubarb Pie 296.
Sponge Drops 277.   Cheese.
Coffee 408.

Monday.

Breakfast.

Baked Apples 425.
Hominy 244.
Fried Ham and Eggs 132.
Crisp Potatoes 173.   Plain Muffins 229.
Brown Bread 216.
Coffee 408.

Luncheon.

Cold Roast Beef 96.   Fish Fritters 56.
Baked Potatoes 175.
Indian Loaf Cake 220.   Plum Preserves 378
Chocolate 410.

Dinner.

Split Pea Soup 29.

Braised Veal 117.

Steamed Potatoes 172.

Cabbage with Cream 178.

Stewed Beets 186.   Mixed Pickles 166.

Superior Bread Pudding 346, Plain Sauce 373.

Orange Tarts 302.   Fruit.

Coffee 408.

Tuesday.

Breakfast.

Bananas.
Fried Mush 243.
Fried Veal Chops 113.
Hasty Cooked Potatoes 172.
Egg Biscuit 224.   Wheat Bread 213.
Coffee 408.

Luncheon.

Oyster Stew 63.   Spiced Beef Relish 105.
Hominy Croquettes 244.
Rusks 227.   Canned Peaches 390.
Tea 410.

Dinner.

Consomme Soup 26.

Roast Chicken 74.

Mashed Potatoes 170.   Stewed Carrots 189.

Tomato Toast 248.

Spiced Currants 168.

Almond Pudding 347.   Lemon Trifle 316.

Angel Cake 266.   Fruit

Coffee 408.

Wednesday.

Breakfast.

Lemon Marmalade 386.
Cracked Wheat 245.
Country Sausages 135.   Potato Puffs 171.
Bread Griddle Cakes 235.
Cream Toast 246.
Coffee 408.

Luncheon.

Chicken Patties 77.   Baked Omelet 208.
Potato Croquettes 174.
East India Pickle 165.
Beaten Biscuit 225.   Apple Pudding 359.
Tea 410.

Dinner.

Vegetable Soup 34.

Baked Calf's Head 117.

Boiled Potatoes 169.   Stewed Onions 176.

Macaroni and Tomato Sauce 193.

Cold Slaw 153.

Apple Custard Pie 290.

Wine Jelly 331.

Cocoanut Cookies 281.

Cheese.

Coffee 408.

Thursday.

Breakfast.

Stewed Prunes.
Steamed Oatmeal 245.
Pork Cutlets 130.   Baked Potatoes 175.
Scrambled Eggs 201.
Corn Meal Fritters 237.
Wheat Bread 213.   Coffee 408.

Luncheon.

Fricasseed Tripe 111.
Hashed Beef on Toast 249.
Chicken Salad 151.   Cream Toast 246.
Crullers 282.   Grape Jelly 385.
Chocolate 410.

Dinner.

Oyster Soup 39.

Spiced Beef 99.

Potato Croquettes 174.

Spinach with Eggs 188.

Scalloped Tomatoes 181.

Olives.

Plain Charlotte Russe 321.

Jam Tarts 305.   Fruit.

Coffee 408.

Friday.

Breakfast.

Peach Jelly 386.   Boiled Rice 244.
Fried Pan Fish 43.
Veal Hash on Toast 249.   Saratoga Chips 171.
Feather Griddle Cakes 233.
Coffee 408.

Luncheon.

Cold Spiced Beef 99.   Stewed Codfish 55.
Fried Potatoes 171.   Brown Bread 217.
Apple Fritters 237.
Tea 410.

Dinner.

Tomato Soup No. 2 31.

Boiled White Fish 50, Maitre d'Hotel Sauce 142.

Potato Snow 172.   Fried Parsnips 180.

Boiled Cabbage 177, and Ham 134.

Cucumber Pickle 159.

Cracker Pudding 350, Fruit Sauce 374.

Lemon Jelly 331.

Delicate Cake 261.   Fruit.

Coffee 408.

Saturday.

Breakfast.

Cider Apple Sauce 143.
Hominy 244.
Calf's Liver and Bacon 118.
Potatoes a la Creme 171.   Egg Muffins 229.
Brown Bread 216.   Coffee 408.

Luncheon.

Ham Omelet 206.   Pan Oysters 64.
Rice Croquettes 243.   Cream Short Cake 240.
Strawberry Preserves 377.
Chocolate 410.

Dinner.

Philadelphia Pepper Pot 30.

Baked Mutton Cutlets 123.

Roast Sweet Potatoes 176.

Mashed Turnips 190.   Stewed Celery 185.

Lobster Salad 152.

Apple Dumplings 341, Sweet Sauce 375.

Baked Custard 306.

Raisins.   Nuts.

Coffee 408.

APRIL.

Sunday.

Breakfast.

Stewed Apples 328.
Oatmeal with Cream 243.
Veal Cutlets Broiled 114.　　Shirred Eggs 200.
Warmed Potatoes 173.
French Rolls 225.　　Wheat Bread 213.
Coffee 408.

Supper.

Cold Roast Chicken 74.
Mayonnaise Fish 54.　　Welsh Rarebit 198.
Baking Powder Biscuit 223.
Layer Cake 268, with Banana Filling 270.
Chocolate 410.

Dinner.

Cream of Spinach Soup 27.
Boiled Shad 46, Sauce Tartare 138.
Leg of Mutton a la Venison 121.
Steamed Potatoes 172.　Creamed Parsnips 180.
Oyster Patties 65.　　Currant Jelly 383.
Lettuce Salad 154.
Delmonico Pudding 361, Pineapple Sherbet 337.
Rolled Jelly Cake 268.　　　Fruit.
Coffee 408.

Monday.

Breakfast.

Sliced Oranges.
Hominy 244.
Broiled Halibut 49.　　Omelet of Herbs 205.
Saratoga Chips 171.　Raised Muffins 228.
Brown Bread 217.
Coffee 408.

Luncheon.

Mutton Pudding 124.
Oyster Roast 64.
Lettuce with Cream Dressing 150.
French Rolls 225.　　Cup Custard 307.
Tea 410.

Dinner.

Mock Turtle Soup 32.
Tenderloin of Beef 100.
Boiled Potatoes 169.　　Steamed Cabbage 178.
Stewed Onions 176.
Radishes.
Snow Pudding 361.
Peach Meringue Pie 291.
Crisp Cookies 281.　　　Fruit.
Coffee 408.

Tuesday.

Breakfast.

Stewed Prunes.
Oat Flakes 245.
Frizzled Beef 104.　　Grilled Salt Pork 132.
Potato Puffs 171.　　Sally Lunn 226.
Toast 246.　　Coffee 408.

Luncheon.

Roast Beef Pie with Potato Crust 103.
Fried Tripe 110.　　Hominy Croquettes 244.
Olives.　　Light Biscuit 224.
Jelly Puddings 369.
Chocolate 410.

Dinner.

Celery Soup 35.
French Stew 105.
Potato Puffs 171.　　Mashed Turnips 190.
Brain Cutlets 118.
Pickled Cabbage 161.
Golden Cream Cake 264.
Orange Cocoanut Salad 329.
Nuts.　　　Raisins.
Coffee 408.

Wednesday.

Breakfast.

Baked Apples 425.
Boiled Rice 244.
Mutton Chops Fried 123.   Lyonnaise Potatoes 173.
Parker House Rolls 224.
Wheat Bread 213.
Coffee 408.

Luncheon.

Chicken Omelet 206.
Fried Eels 47.   Radishes 155.
Steamed Brown Bread 217.
Sponge Cake 257.   Quince Preserves 379.
Tea 410.

Dinner.

Mullagatawny Soup 31.
Boiled Fillet of Veal 112.
Boiled Sweet Potatoes 175.
Stewed Tomatoes 181.   Baked Sweetbreads 119.
Chowchow 163.
Mock Cream Pie 294.   Lemon Jelly 331.
Almond Jumbles 280.   Fruit.
Coffee 408.

Thursday.

Breakfast.

Oranges.
Cracked Wheat 245.
Dried Beef with Cream 106.
Veal Collops 113.   Baked Potatoes 175.
Grafton Milk Biscuits 226.
Dipped Toast 246.   Coffee 408.

Luncheon.

Pressed Beef 105.   Stewed Kidneys 109.
Baked Potatoes 175.   Pickled Peppers 162.
Fried Dinner Rolls 241.
Canned Peaches 390.
Cocoa 411.

Dinner.

Beef Soup 25.
Chicken a la Terrapin 82.
Browned Potatoes 170.   Fried Parsnips 180.
Macaroni and Cheese 192.
Lettuce 156, with French Dressing 150.
Banana Pudding 367.
Jam Tarts 305.   Nuts.   Raisins.
Coffee 408.

Friday.

Breakfast.

Bananas.
Steamed Oatmeal 245.
Stewed Codfish 55.   Bread Omelet 207.
Boiled Potatoes 169.
Hot Cross Buns 227.   Brown Bread 217.
Coffee 408.

Luncheon.

Rissoles of Chicken 76.
Potted Fish 52.   Nun's Toast 246.
Potato Biscuit 226.
Lemon Cake 260.   Peach Jelly 386.
Tea 410.

Dinner.

Vermicelli Soup 35.
Baked Shad with Dressing 46.
Scalloped Potatoes 172.   Spinach with Eggs 188.
Veal Croquettes 114.
Olives.
Fig Pudding 359.
Chocolate Eclairs 273.   Fruit.
Coffee 408.

Saturday.

Breakfast.

Stewed Apricots.
Samp 245.
Broiled Ham 134.   Fried Eggs 201.
Sweet Potatoes Fried 175.
Newport Waffles 231.   Flannel Cakes 233.
Coffee 408.

Luncheon.

Veal Stew 115.   Scalloped Cheese 197.
Potato Croquettes 174.
Radishes 155.
Boston Brown Bread 216.
Ginger Snaps 275.   Canned Grapes 390.
Chocolate 410.

Dinner.

Onion Soup 84.

Pot Roast 98.

Mashed Potatoes 170.   Boiled Onions 176.

Lobster Patties 60.

Lettuce 156, with Mayonnaise 149.

Pineapple Charlotte Russe 323.

Lady Fingers 277.

Nuts.   Raisins.

Coffee 408.

MAY.

Sunday.

Breakfast.

Sliced Pineapple.
Oat Flakes 245.
Fried Chicken 78.   Mushroom Omelet 206.
Saratoga Chips 171.   Sally Lunn 226.
Wheat Bread 213.
Coffee 408.

Supper.

Veal Loaf Sliced 116.
Scalloped Clams 69.   Ham Salad 153.
Rusks 227.   Preserved Pears 380.
Almond Cake 267.
Tea 410.

Dinner.

Cream of Asparagus Soup 29.

Boiled Bass 47, Sauce Tartare 138.

Roast Lamb 125, with Mint Sauce 141.

Boiled New Potatoes 169.

Green Peas 187.   Rice Croquettes 243.

Lobster Salad 152.

Cabinet Pudding 354.

Custard Ice Cream 335.

Jelly Kisses 330.   Fruit.

Coffee 408.

Monday.

Breakfast.

Oranges.
Boiled Rice 244.
Broiled Lamb Chops 122.
Lyonnaise Potatoes 173.
Egg Muffins 229.   Milk Toast 246.
Coffee 408.

Luncheon.

Cold Roast Lamb 125.
Chicken Turnovers 83.
Lettuce 156, with Mayonnaise 149.
French Bread 218.
Layer Cake with Fig Filling 271.
Chocolate 410.

Dinner.

Macaroni Soup 33.

Beef Steak Pie 103.

Mashed Potatoes 170.

String Beans 185.   Ladies' Cabbage 178.

Horse-radish 156.

Rhubarb Pie 296.

Rice Meringue 362.

Nuts.   Cheese.   Raisins.

Coffee 408.

Tuesday.

Breakfast.

Stewed Rhubarb.
Oatmeal with Cream 243.
Broiled Shad 46.   Scrambled Eggs 201.
Browned Potatoes 170.   Brown Bread 217.
Parker House Rolls 224.
Coffee 408.

Luncheon.

Hamburger Steak 109.
Potato Croquettes 174.
Bean Salad 155.   Sour Milk Biscuits 223.
Election Cake 264.   Peach Butter 393.
Tea 410.

Dinner.

Swiss White Soup 35.

Roast Loin of Veal 111.

New Potatoes a la Creme 171.

Baked Onions 176.   Cheese Fondu 197.

Spinach with Egg 188.

Transparent Pudding 365,
          Cold Cream Sauce 373.

Cookies 280.   Fruit.

Coffee 408.

Wednesday.

Breakfast.

Stewed Peaches.
Fried Mush 243.
Frogs' Legs Fried 69, Tomato Sauce 140.
New Boiled Potatoes 769.
French Rolls 225.   Wheat Bread 213.
Coffee 408.

Luncheon.

Veal Pie 115.   Broiled Ham 134.
String Beans 185.   Corn Bread 219.
Pineapple Fritters 238.
Chocolate 410.

Dinner.

Julienne Soup 27.

Boiled Beef Tongue 110.

Potato Snow 172.   Boiled Turnips 190.

Macaroni a la Italienne 192.

Lettuce Salad 154.

Chocolate Pudding 357, Whipped Cream 309.

Nuts.   Raisins.

Coffee 408.

Thursday.

Breakfast.

Sliced Pineapple.
Hominy 244.
Tripe Lyonnaise 111.   Plain Omelet 204.
New Potatoes a la Creme 171.
Plain Crumpets 242.
Wheat Griddle Cakes 233.
Coffee 408.

Luncheon.

Cold Tongue 110.   Beefsteak 97.
Walnut Catsup 157.
Light Biscuit 224.   Cheap Cream Cake 272.
Preserved Apples 379.
Tea 410.

Dinner.

Split Pea Soup 29.

Chicken Pot Pie 81.

Boiled Potatoes 169.   Stewed Tomatoes 181

Fried Sweetbreads 119.

Bean Salad 155.

Burnt Almond Charlotte 323.

Orange Jelly 332.

Corn Starch Cakes 277.   Fruit.

Coffee 408.

Friday.

Breakfast.

Oranges.
Steamed Oatmeal 245.
Fresh Salmon Fried 44.   Boiled Eggs 200.
Warmed Potatoes 173.
Cream Waffles 231.   Brown Bread 217.
Coffee 408.

Luncheon.

Lamb Stew 126.   Asparagus Omelet 205.
Lettuce Salad 154.
German Bread 219.   Canned Peaches 390.
Molasses Cup Cakes 274.
Chocolate 410.

Dinner.

Irish Potato Soup 35.

Steamed Halibut 48, Egg Sauce 138.

Steamed Sweet Potatoes 175.

Green Peas 187.   Veal Olives 113.

Dandelion Greens 189.

Cold Lemon Pudding 356.

Jelly Fritters 328.   Fruit.

Coffee 408.

Saturday.

Breakfast.

Stewed Rhubarb.
Cracked Wheat 245.
Baked Mutton Chops with Potatoes 123.
Eggs aux Fines Herbes 202.
Graham Gems 230.   Dipped Toast 246.
Coffee 408.

Luncheon.

Fried Spring Chicken 78.
Clam Fritters 68.   Sliced Tomatoes.
Wheat Drop Cakes 233.
Coffee Cake 264.   Crab Apple Jelly 385.
Chocolate 410.

Dinner.

Ox-tail Soup 28.

Spiced Beef 99.

Boiled New Potatoes 169.

String Beans 185.   Spinach with Eggs 188.

Radishes 155.

Pineapple Pie 297.

Dessert Puffs 325.   Fruit.

Coffee 408.

JUNE.

Sunday.

Breakfast.
Strawberries and Cream.
Hominy 244.
Fried Brook Trout 49.   Poached **Eggs 201.**
Potatoes a la Creme 171.
Corn Meal Muffins 230.
Mushrooms on Toast 247.
Coffee 408.

Supper.
Scalloped Crabs 52.   Cold Pressed Lamb **126.**
Sliced Tomatoes with Mayonnaise 149.
Buns 227.
Angel Cake 266.   Raspberries.
Tea 410.

Dinner.
Green Pea Soup 29.
Boiled Salmon 43, Bechamel Sauce **141.**
Stewed whole Spring Chicken 76.
Steamed New Potatoes 172.   Beet Greens **189.**
Summer Squash 188.   Raw Cucumbers **155.**
Sweetbread Croquettes 119.
Chocolate Blanc Mange 319.
Strawberry Ice Cream 335.   Queens Cake, **266.**
Coffee 408.

Monday.

Breakfast.
Stewed Apricots.
Graham Mush 243.
Fried Chicken a la Italienne 78
Steamed Potatoes 172.
Continental Hotel Waffles 231.
Wheat Bread 213.   Coffee 408.

Luncheon.
Pickled Salmon 44.
Scalloped Chicken 80.   Hominy Croquettes 244.
Sliced Cucumbers.
Strawberry Short-cake 240, with Cream.
Chocolate 410.

Dinner.
Beef Soup 25, with Noodles **36.**
Veal Pie 115.
New Potatoes 169   Cucumbers a la Creme **183.**
Asparagus 187, White Sauce 138.
Lettuce 156, French Dressing 150.
Green Currant Pie 295.   Boiled Custard **307.**
Brunswick Jelly Cakes 278,
Cheese.   Coffee 408.

Tuesday.

Breakfast.
Raspberries and Cream.
Oat Flakes 245.
Soft Shell Crabs Fried 62.   Ham Omelet 206.
Warmed Potatoes 173   Pop-overs, **233.**
Toast 246.   Coffee 408.

Luncheon.
French Stew 105.
Cold Sliced Tongue 110.
Bean Salad 155.   Milk Biscuits **226.**
Cold Custard Pie 294.
Iced Tea 410.

Dinner.
White Mushroom Soup 26.
Roast Beef 96.
Potatoes a la Creme 171.   Fried Cauliflower **177.**
Spinach with Eggs 188.
Sliced Tomatoes, Mayonnaise 149.
Strawberry Short-cake 240,
with whipped Cream **309.**
Wafers 276.   Cheese.
Coffee 408.

Wednesday.

Breakfast.

Cherries.
Cracked Wheat 245.
Broiled Lamb Chops 122.   Tomato Sauce 140.
Saratoga Chips 171.   Raised Muffins 228.
Brown Bread 217.
Coffee 408.

Luncheon.

Roast Beef Pie 103.
Fried Potatoes with Eggs 174.
Crab Salad 153.   Soda Biscuit 223.
Pineapple Fritters 238.
Tea 410.

Dinner.

Veal Soup 25, with Croutons 37.
Boiled Chicken 75.   Caper Sauce 140.
Steamed New Potatoes 172.
Asparagus on Toast 187.
String Beans 185.   Young Onions.
Green Gooseberry Tart 303.
Golden Cream 311.
Cocoanut Macaroons 330.   Cheese.
Coffee 408.

Thursday.

Breakfast.

Strawberries and Cream.
Oatmeal with Cream 243.
Chicken Omelet 206.   Corned Beef Hash 108.
Potatoe Fillets 173.
Grafton Milk Biscuits 226.
Cream Toast 246.   Coffee 408.

Luncheon.

Smothered Beefsteak 101.
Potato Croquettes 174.
Lettuce with Mayonnaise 149.
Cream Short-cake 240.   Cherry Pudding 352.
Chocolate 410.

Dinner.

Clam Soup, French Style 39.
Broiled Forequarter of Lamb 126,
Tomato Sauce 140.
Potatoes a la Delmonico 174.
String Beans 185.
Cauliflower 177.   Tomato Salad 154.
Strawberry Bavarian Cream 310.
Sliced Pineapple.   Pound Cake 259.
Coffee 408.

Friday.

Breakfast.

Sliced Tomatoes.
Boiled Rice 244.
Broiled Spanish Mackerel 51.
Scalloped Eggs 200.   Lyonnaise Potatoes 173.
French Rolls 225.   Wheat Bread 213.
Coffee 408.

Luncheon.

Clam Chowder 63.   Cold Pressed Beef 105.
Mixed Summer Salad 151.
Buns 227.   Fancy Cakes 295.
Currants.
Tea 410.

Dinner.

Cream of Asparagus 29.
Baked Blue Fish 47, Tomato Sauce 140.
New Potatoes and Cream 171.
Summer Squash 188.
Muttonettes 124.   Sliced Cucumbers 155.
Charlotte Russe 320.
Strawberries and Cream.
Pastry Ramakins 197.
Coffee 408.

Saturday.

Breakfast.

Stewed Green Currants.
Steamed Oatmeal 245.
Porterhouse Steak Broiled with Watercresses 97.
New Boiled Potatoes 169.
Rusks 227.   American Toast 246.
Coffee 408.

Luncheon.

Fricassee Chicken 75.
Rice Croquettes 243.
Dressed Cucumbers 155.   French Bread 218.
Cup Cakes 276.
Srawberries and Cream.
Iced Tea 410.

Dinner.

Tomato Soup 31.
Roast Loin of Mutton 120.
Scalloped New Potatoes 172.
Cauliflower 177.
Beet Greens 189.   Radishes 155.
Cherry Pie 295.   Mock Ice 314.
Variegated Cakes 277.   Cheese.
Coffee 408.

.·.

JULY.

Fourth of July.

Breakfast.

Red Raspberries and Cream.
Fried Chicken 78.
Scrambled Tomatoes 182.
Warmed Potatoes 173.   Tennessee Muffins 229.
Toast 146.   Coffee 408.

Supper.

Cold Sliced Lamb 125.
Crab Pie 61.   Watercress Salad 155.
Cheese Toast 247.
Graham Bread 216.   Sponge Cake 257.
Blackberries.
Tea 410.

Dinner.

Clam Soup 39.
Boiled Cod 56, with Lobster Sauce 139.
Roast Lamb 125, Mint Sauce 141.
New Potatoes Boiled 169.
Green Peas 187.   Spinach with Eggs 188.
Cucumbers Sliced 155.
Chicken Patties 77.
Naples Biscuits 322.   Vanilla Ice Cream 334.
Chocolate Macaroons 331.   Strawberries.
Coffee 408.

Sunday.

Breakfast.

Fresh Cherries.
Hominy 244.
Broiled Chicken 77. Poached Eggs 202.
Saratoga Chips 171.
New England Corn Cake 219.
Wheat Bread 213.
Coffee 408.

Supper.

Spiced Beef Tongue 110.
Lobster Patties 60.
Sliced Tomatoes with Mayonnaise 149.
Crumpets 242. White Fruit Cake 257.
Blackberries. Tea 410.

Dinner.

Cream of Spinach Soup 27.
Boiled Blue Fish 47, Sauce Maitre d'Hotel 142.
Roast Lamb 125, Tomato Sauce 140.
New Potatoes with Cream 171.
Green Corn 183. Cauliflower 177.
White Sauce 138. Crab Salad 153.
Salmon Croquettes 57.
Cottage Pudding 352. Chocolate Ice Cream 335.
Raspberries.
Coffee 408.

Monday.

Breakfast.

Stewed Pears 329.
Oatmeal with Cream 243.
Veal Chops Fried 113. Plain Omelet 204.
Warmed Potatoes 173.
Raised Muffins 228. Dry Toast 246.
Coffee 408.

Luncheon.

Cold Roast Lamb 125. Corn Pudding 183.
Potato Salad 154. French Bread 218.
Currant Fritters 237.
Cocoa 411

Dinner.

Julienne Soup 27.
Beef a la Mode 99.
Boiled Potatoes 169. Green Peas 187.
Stuffed Baked Tomatoes 181.
Lettuce Salad 154.
Blackberry Pudding 364. Floating Islands 318.
Sponge Cake 259.
Coffee 408.

Tuesday.

Breakfast.

Raspberries.
Cracked Wheat 245.
Beefsteak Broiled 97. Cream Toast 246.
Lyonnaise Potatoes 173.
Light Biscuit 224. Brown Bread 217.
Coffee 408.

Luncheon.

Cold Sliced Beef 99.
Cheese Souffle 197.
Tomato Salad 154. Graham Bread 216.
Green Gooseberry Tart 303.
Tea 410.

Dinner.

Vermicelli Soup 35.
Chicken Stewed, with Biscuit 82.
Steamed Potatoes 172. Stewed Corn 183.
Lobster Croquettes 60.
Cucumbers Sliced 155.
Ripe Currant Pie 295. Snow Cream 314.
Ribbon Cake 266. Cheese.
Coffee 408.

Wednesday.

Breakfast.

Blackberries.
Steamed Oatmeal 245.
Fresh Salmon Fried 44.   Beef Hash 108.
Potato Fillets 173.
Tennessee Muffins 229.   Dipped Toast 246.
Coffee 408.

Luncheon.

Beefsteak Pie 103.   Chicken Turnovers 83.
Lettuce with Mayonnaise 149.
Buns 227.
Layer Cake 268, Banana Filling 270.
Chocolate 410.

Dinner.

Spring Vegetable Soup 35.
Scalloped Mutton and Tomatoes 125.
Boiled Potatoes 169.
Spinach with Eggs 188.   Clam Fritters 68.
Young Onions.
Corn Starch Pudding 349.
Raspberries with Cream.   Silver Cake 261.
Coffee 408.

Thursday.

Breakfast.

Red Raspberries.
Graham Mush with Maple Syrup 243.
Broiled Lamb Chops 122.
Fried Tomatoes 182.   Potatoes a la Creme 171.
Raised Biscuit 223.   Dry Toast 246.
Coffee 408.

Luncheon.

Sliced Veal Loaf 116.
Brain Cutlets 118.   Fried Potatoes 171.
Dressed Cucumbers 155.
French Bread 218.   Cherry Pie 295.
Tea 410.

Dinner.

Gumbo Soup 33.
Roast Beef Pie with Potato Crust 103.
Potatoes a la Delmonico 174.
Cauliflower 177.   Stewed Green Peas 187.
Lettuce 156, with Mayonnaise 149.
Cherry Roley Poley 366.   Syllabub 315.
Boston Cream Cakes 273.
Coffee 408.

Friday.

Breakfast.

Fresh Currants.
Boiled Rice 244.
Perch Fried 42.   Scrambled Eggs 201.
Baked Potatoes 175.
Parker House Rolls 224.   Wheat Bread 213.
Coffee 408.

Luncheon.

Broiled Chicken on Toast 80.
Green Corn Fritters 239.
Stewed Tomatoes 181.   Blackberries.
Berry Tea Cakes 232.
Cocoa 411.

Dinner.

Clam Chowder 68.
Salmon 44, and Caper Sauce 140.
New Potatoes Scalloped 172.
Summer Squash 188.   Chicken Turnovers 83.
New Beets Boiled 186.
Rice Pudding 362.   Raspberry Sherbet 337.
Philadelphia Jumbles 279.
Coffee 408.

Saturday.

Breakfast.

Stewed Gooseberries.
Corn Meal Mush 243.
Broiled Ham 134.   Vegetable Omelet 205.
Newport Breakfast Cakes 241.
Crisp Potatoes 173.   Brown Bread 217.
Coffee 408.

Luncheon.

Fricassee Salmon 45.   Beefsteak 97.
Bean Salad 155.   Corn Bread 219.
Transparent Pudding 365.
Iced Tea 410.

Dinner.

Green Pea Soup 29

French Stew 105.

New Potatoes with Cream 171.

Mock Oysters 67.   Scalloped Clams 69.

Tomato Salad 154.

Custard Pie 294.   Sponge Drops 277.

Red Raspberries and Cream.

Coffee 408.

.·.

AUGUST.

Sunday.

Breakfast

Peaches and Cream.
Boiled Rice 244.
Broiled Spanish Mackerel 51.
Eggs aux Fines Herbes 202.
Warmed Potatoes 173.   Rusks 227.
Wheat Bread 213.
Coffee 408.

Supper.

Cold Boiled Chicken 75.
Pickled Salmon 44.   Potato Salad 155.
French Rolls 225.   Raspberries.
White Mountain Cake 265.
Tea 410.

Dinner.

Consomme Soup 26.

Baked Pickerel 43, Egg Sauce 138.

Stewed Ducks 85.

Potatoes a la Delmonico 174.

Cabbage with Cream 178.   Lobster Salad 151.

Stuffed Baked Tomatoes 181.

Lamb Sweetbreads 125.

Custard Pudding 348.   Frozen Peaches 337.

Fruit Jumbles 280.

Coffee 408.

Monday.

Breakfast.

Stewed Plums.
Steamed Oatmeal 245.
Mutton Cutlets 123.   Tomato Toast 248.
Potato Fillets 173.
Egg Muffins 229.   Brown Bread 217.
Coffee 408.

Luncheon.

Veal Pot Pie 114.   Vegetable Omelet 205.
Lettuce with French Dressing 150.
German Bread 219.   Peach Fritters 238.
Chocolate 410.

Dinner.

Tomato Soup 31.
Roast Beef's Heart 109.
Boiled New Potatoes 169.
Cauliflower 177.   String Beans 185.
Cucumbers Sliced 155
Damson Pie 297.   Peach Trifle 317
Sponge Cake 257.   Cheese.
Coffee 408.

Tuesday.

Breakfast.

Blackberries.
Hominy 244.
Frizzled Beef 104.   Boiled Eggs 200.
Saratoga Chips 171.
Breakfast Puffs 242.   Dipped Toast 246.
Coffee 408.

Luncheon.

Sliced Beef Heart 109.   Fried Tripe 110.
Stuffed Baked Tomatoes 182.
Pear Pickle 167.   Buns 227.
Plum Cobbler 367.
Tea 410.

Dinner.

Scotch Mutton Broth 25.
Broiled Fore-quarter of Lamb 126.
New Potatoes and Cream 171.   Green Peas 187.
Lettuce 156, French Dressing 150.
Corn Pudding 183.
Apricot Meringue Pie 295.
Lemon Jelly 331.
Cookies 280.   Fruit.
Coffee 408.

Wednesday.

Breakfast.

Fresh Pears.
Cracked Wheat 245.
Brain Cutlets 118.   Meat Omelet 204.
Lyonnaise Potatoes 173.
Huckleberry Griddle Cakes 235.
Wheat Bread 213.   Coffee 408.

Luncheon.

Broiled Salmon 44.   Sliced Pressed Lamb 126.
Tomatoes with Mayonnaise 149.
French Bread 218.   Sponge Cake 257.
Blackberries and Cream.
Iced Tea 410.

Dinner.

Cream of Spinach Soup 27.
Fried Chicken a la Italienne 78,
Tomato Sauce 140.
Boiled Sweet Potatoes 175.
Stuffed Egg Plant 185.
Green Corn Boiled 183.   Young Onions.
Rice Pudding 363.   Peaches and Cream.
Walnut Cake 271.
Coffee 408.

Thursday.

Breakfast.

Musk Melon.
Oatmeal, with Cream 243.
Calf's Liver and Bacon 118.
Broiled Tomatoes 182.   Crisp Potatoes 173.
New England Corn Cake 219.
Dry Toast 246.   Coffee 408.

Luncheon.

Steamed Chicked 75.   Green Corn Fritters 239.
Fried Sweet Potatoes 175.
Dressed Cucumbers 155.   Light Biscuit 224.
Peaches and Cream.
Chocolate 410.

Dinner.

Green Pea Soup 29.
Stewed Brisket of Beef 106.
New Potatoes Boiled 169.   Lima Beans 185.
Fried Egg Plant 184.
Lettuce Salad 154.
Huckleberry Pudding 364, Rich Wine Sauce 371.
Cream Tarts 304.   Fruit.
Coffee 408.

Friday.

Breakfast.

Whole Peaches.
Corn Meal Mush 243.
Fried Blue Fish 42.   Dried Beef, with Cream 106.
Sweet Potatoes Fried 175.
Raised Muffins 228.
Brown Bread 217.   Coffee 408.

Luncheon.

Beef Croquettes 106.   Scalloped Lobster 59.
Mixed Summer Salad 151.
German Bread 219.
Huckleberry Short-cake 241.
Tea 410.

Dinner.

Corn Soup 28.
Baked Salmon Trout 50, Bechamel Sauce 141.
Potato Croquettes 174.   Spinach with Eggs 188
Hashed Mutton 122.
Tomatoes with Mayonnaise 149.
Grape Pie 297.   Peach Cream 313.
Wafers 276.   Cheese.
Coffee 408.

Saturday.

Breakfast.

Fresh Green Gages.
Oat Flakes 245.
Broiled Chicken 77.   Cream Toast 246.
Boiled Potatoes 169.
Graham Gems 230.   Wheat Bread 213.
Coffee 408.

Luncheon.

Broiled Ham 134.   Tomato Omelet 205.
Dressed Cucumbers 155.
French Bread 218.
Cold Fruit Pudding 349.
Chocolate 410.

Dinner.

Chicken Cream Soup 27.
Irish Stew 124.
Steamed Potatoes 172.   Green Peas 187.
Boiled Corn 183.   Crab Salad 153.
Huckleberry Pie 296.
Peaches and Cream.
Cup Cakes 276.   Cheese.
Coffee 408.

SEPTEMBER.

Sunday.

Breakfast.
Musk Melon.
Corn Meal Mush 243.
Fried Smelts 50.   Veal Hash on Toast 249.
Potatoes a la Creme 171.
Graham Gems 230.   Wheat Bread 213.
Coffee 408.

Supper.
Potted Ham 134.   Small Oyster Pies 67.
Rice Omelet 206.   Cold Slaw 153.
French Bread 218.
Cream Cake 264.   Sliced Peaches.
Tea 410.

Dinner.
Beef Soup 25, with Croutons 37.
Boiled Fresh Mackerel 52, Hollandaise Sauce 142.
Roast Partridges 88.
Mashed Potatoes 170.   Stewed Corn 183.
Stuffed Egg Plant 185.   Tomato Salad 154.
Lobster Croquettes 60.   Peach Meringue Pie 291;
Tutti Frutti Ice Cream 336.
Rochester Jelly Cake 267.   Cheese.
Coffee 408.

Monday.

Breakfast.
Peaches and Cream.
Graham Mush with Maple Syrup 243
Broiled Lamb Chops 122.   Fried Tomatoes 182.
Baked Potatoes 175.   Raised Muffins 228.
Dry Toast 246.   Coffee 408.

Luncheon.
Salmi of Game 90.   Cold Beef Tongue 110.
Potato Croquettes 174.
Watermelon Pickle 167   Egg Biscuit 224.
Layer Cake 268, with Peach Cream Filling 270.
Chocolate 410.

Dinner.
Vegetable Soup 35.
Tenderloin of Beef 100.
Potato Puffs 171.   Lima Beans 185.
Fried Tomatoes 182.
Mixed Summer Salad 151.
Peach Pudding 359, with Whipped Cream 303.
Cocoanut Tarts 303.   Cheese.
Coffee 408.

Tuesday.

Breakfast.
Huckleberries.
Steamed Oatmeal 245.
Veal Collops 113.   Ham Toast 248.
Potato Fillets 173.
Newport Breakfast Cakes 241.
Brown Bread 217.   Coffee 408.

Luncheon.
Cold Roast Warmed, 107.
Cheese Fondu 197.   Fish Salad 152.
Potato Biscuit 226.
Peach Cobbler 367.   Tea 410.

Dinner.
Vermicelli Soup 35.
Baked Mutton Cutlets 123.
Boiled Potatoes 169.   Baked Beets 186.
Corn Pudding 183.   Horseradish 156.
Plum Pie 297.
Floating Island 318   Lemon Cake 260.
Cheese.
Coffee 408.

Wednesday.

Breakfast.

Sliced Tomatoes.
Oat Flakes 245.
Beef Hash 108.   Boiled Eggs 200.
Sweet Potatoes Baked 175.
Parker House Rolls 224.   Wheat Bread 213.
Coffee 408.

Luncheon.

Fried Smelts 50.   Ham Toast 248.
Potato Salad 155.   French Bread 218.
Huckleberry Cake 274.
Chocolate 410.

Dinner.

Split Pea Soup 29.

Roast Tame Duck 84.

Browned Potatoes 170.   String Beans 185.

Baked Tomatoes 182.

Lettuce 156, with Mayonnaise 149.

Boiled Lemon Pudding 356.

Peach Meringue 314.   Feather Cake 264.

Coffee 408.

Thursday.

Breakfast.

Whole Pears.
Hominy 244.
Hamburger Steak 109.   Bread Omelet 207.
Saratoga Chips 171.   Light Biscuit 224.
Dry Toast 246.   Coffee 408.

Luncheon.

Duck Pie 85.   Grilled Bacon 132.
Tomato Salad 154.   Graham Bread 216.
Cold Berry Pudding 345.
Tea 410.

Dinner.

Corn Soup 28.

Steamed Leg of Mutton 122.

Potatoes a la Delmonico 174.

Fried Corn 184.   Stewed Salsify 185.

Currant Jelly 383.

Grape Pie 297.   Tapioca Cream Custard 313.

Watermelon.   Cheese.

Coffee 408.

Friday.

Breakfast.

Musk Melon.
Oatmeal with Cream 243.
Broiled Spanish Mackerel 51.
Scalloped Eggs 200.   Warmed Potatoes 173.
Tennessee Muffins 229.   Wheat Bread 213.
Coffee 408.

Luncheon.

Hashed Mutton 122.   Oyster Fritters 65.
Cold Greens 189.   Corn Bread 219.
Boston Cream Cakes 273.   Grape Jelly 385.
Chocolate 410.

Dinner.

Clam Soup 39.

Fresh Salmon Fried 44, Tomato Sauce 140.

Mashed Potatoes 170.   Cauliflower 177.

White Sauce 138.   Beefsteak Rolls 101.

Cucumbers Sliced 155.

Country Plum Charlotte 324.

German Custard 308.   Jumbles 279.

Fruit.   Coffee 408.

Saturday.

Breakfast.

Fresh Apricots.
Cracked Wheat 245.
Stewed Kidneys 109.   Grilled Salt Pork 132.
Lyonnaise Potatoes 173.   Sally Lunn 226.
Dry Toast 246.   Coffee 408.

Luncheon.

Breaded Chicken 80.   Potato Croquettes 174.
Tomatoes with Mayonnaise 149.
Twist Bread 218.   Sponge Drops 277.
Huckleberries and Cream.
Tea 410.

Dinner.

Gumbo Soup 33.

Roast Loin of Veal 111.

Browned Potatoes 175.

Succotash 184.   Mashed Squash 188.

Bean Salad 155.

Baked Custard 306.   Peaches and Cream.

Almond Cake 267.

Coffee 408.

.∙.

OCTOBER.

Sunday.

Breakfast.

Grapes.
Oatmeal with Cream 243.
Broiled Veal Cutlets 114.   Minced Eggs 202.
Crisp Potatoes 173.   Buckwheat Cakes 236.
Wheat Bread 213.
Coffee 408.

Supper.

Oyster Stew 63.   Cold Pork and Beans 131.
Cold Slaw 153.   Boston Brown Bread 216.
Peach Meringue Pie 291.
Tea 410.

Dinner.

Ox-tail Soup 28.

Broiled Halibut 49, Sauce Tartare 138.

Roast Beef 96, Brown Sauce 142.

Steamed Potatoes 172.   Cauliflower 177.

Boiled Onions 176.   Chicken Salad 151.

Scalloped Tomatoes 181.

French Cocoanut Pudding 352.

Grape Trifle 317.

Fancy Cakes 275.   Fruit.

Coffee 408.

Monday.

Breakfast.

Stewed Quinces.
Lamb 245.
Blue Fish Fried 42.   Milk Toast 246.
Hasty Cooked Potatoes 172.   Pop-overs 233.
Brown Bread 217.   Coffee 408.

Luncheon.

Cold Roast Beef 96.   Onion Omelet 206.
Fried Potatoes 171.   French Bread 218.
Peach Fritters 238.
Chocolate 410.

Dinner.

Julienne Soup 27.
Roast Pheasants 88.
Cabbage with Cream 178.
Boiled Potatoes 169.   Mashed Turnips 190.
Tomato Salad 154.
Apple Custard Pie 290.
Baked Quinces 329.   Chocolate Eclairs 273.
Coffee 408.

Tuesday.

Breakfast.

Baked Pears 328.
Cracked Wheat 245.
Calf's Liver and Bacon 118.   Fried Eggs 201.
Lyonnaise Potatoes 173.   Dry Toast 246.
New England Corn Cake 219.
Coffee 408.

Luncheon.

Cold Roast Pheasant 88.
Potato Croquettes 174.   Lobster Salad 151.
Graham Bread 216.
Country Plum Charlotte 324.
Tea 410.

Dinner.

Game Soup 26.
Braised Leg of Mutton 121.
Mashed Potatoes 170.   Scalloped Oysters 66.
Boiled Sweet Potatoes 175.
Cold Slaw 153.
Peach Cobbler 367.   French Custard 307.
Layer Jelly Cake 268.
Coffee 408.

Wednesday.

Breakfast.

Grapes.
Steamed Oatmeal 245.
Beefsteak Broiled 97.   Tomato Omelet 205.
Warmed Potatoes 173.   English Crumpets 242.
Brown Bread 217.   Coffee 408.

Luncheon.

Scrambled Mutton 125.   Sardines.
Corn Pudding 183.   French Rolls 225.
Ginger Bread 272.
Sliced Oranges   Cocoa 411.

Dinner.

Mock Turtle Soup 32.
Boiled Fillet of Veal 112.
Potatoes a la Delmonico 174.
Fried Egg Plant 184.   Mashed Squash 188.
Olives.
Saucer Puddings 361.
Apple Snow 316.   Crisp Cookies 281.
Coffee 408.

Thursday.

Breakfast.

Baked Quinces 329.
Boiled Rice 244.
Broiled Grouse 88.   Tripe Lyonnaise 111.
Potatoes a la Creme 171.   Raised Muffins 228.
Dry Toast 246.   Coffee 408.

Luncheon.

Veal Croquettes 114.   Cheese Souffle 197
Potato Salad 154.   Buns 227.
Grape Pie 297.
Tea 410.

Dinner.

Swiss White Soup 35.

Pot Roast 98.

Steamed Potatoes 172.

Lima Beans 185.   French Cabbage 179.

Lettuce Salad 154.

Plum Puff Pudding 366.   Blanc Mange 319.

Dominoes 275.   Fruit.

Coffee 408.

Friday.

Breakfast.

Stewed Plums.
Oat Flakes 245.
Eels Fried 47.   Beef Hash 108.
Potato Fillets 173.   Egg Muffins 229.
Wheat Bread 213.   Coffee 408.

Luncheon.

Oyster Pot Pie 66.   Muttonettes 124.
Fried Egg Plant 184.   French Bread 218.
Stewed Crab Apples.
Silver Cake 261.   Chocolate 410.

Dinner.

Onion Soup 34.

Baked Smelts 51.

Potato Snow 172.   Cauliflower 177

Beef Croquettes 106.

Spiced Plums 168.

Plain Charlotte Russe 321.

Quince Jelly 384.   Nuts.   Raisins.

Coffee 408.

Saturday.

Breakfast.

Whole Pears.
Hominy 244.
Mutton Cutlets 123.   Tomato Sauce 140.
Saratoga Chips 171.
Corn Meal Griddle Cakes 234.
Dry Toast 246.   Coffee 408.

Luncheon.

Dried Beef with Cream 106.
Baked Omelet 208.   Tomato Salad 154.
Rusks 227.   Quince Trifle 317.
Tea 410.

Dinner.

Veal Soup 25, with Noodles 36.

Chicken Pot Pie 81.

Mashed Potatoes 170.

Fried Salsify 186.   Baked Onions 176.

Ham Salad 153.

Chocolate Pie 292.   Sliced Oranges.

Hickory Nut Cake 271.

Coffee 408.

NOVEMBER.

Thanksgiving Day.

Breakfast.

Grapes.
Oat Flakes 245.
Broiled Porterhouse Steak 97.
Codfish Balls 54.   Browned Potatoes 170.
Buckwheat Cakes 236, Maple Syrup.
Wheat Bread 213.
Coffee 408.

Supper.

Cold Roast Turkey 71.
Scalloped Oysters 66.   Potato Salad 154.
Cream Short Cake 240.   Eclairs 273.
Preserved Egg Plums 378.
Tea 410.

Dinner.

Oysters on Half Shell.
Cream of Chicken Soup 27.
Fried Smelts 50, Sauce Tartare 138.
Roast Turkey 71, Cranberry Sauce 144.
Mashed Potatoes 170.   Baked Squash 188.
Boiled Onions 176.   Parsnip Fritters 180.
Olives.   Chicken Salad 151.
Venison Pastry 92.
Pumpkin Pie 299.   Mince Pie 300.
Charlotte Russe 320.   Almond Ice Cream 334.
Lemon Jelly 331.   Hickory Nut Cake 271.
Cheese.   Fruits.
Coffee 408.

Sunday.

Breakfast.
Stewed Crab Apples.
Cracked Wheat 245.
White Fish Fried 42.   Jelly Omelet 207.
Hasty Cooked Potatoes 172.
Tennessee Muffins 229.   Crullers 281.
Wheat Bread 213.   Coffee 408.

Supper.
Pickled Pigs' Feet 133.
Scalloped Potatoes 172.   Chicken Salad 151.
Light Biscuit 224.   Golden Spice Cake 267.
Preserved Cherries 377.
Tea 410.

Dinner.

Mullagatawny Soup 31.
Boiled Codfish 56, Oyster Sauce 138.
Roast Wild Duck 85.
Mashed Potatoes 170.   Currant Jelly Sauce 142.
Baked Squash 188.   Boiled Beets 186.
Small Oyster Pies 67.
Baked Plum Pudding 354, Sweet Sauce 375.
Jelly Kisses 330.   Fruit.
Coffee 408.

Monday.

Breakfast.

Grapes.
Hominy 244.
Fricasseed Tripe with Oysters 111.
Baked Potatoes 175.   Breakfast Puffs 242.
Brown Bread 217.   Coffee 408.

Luncheon.

Cold Roast Duck 85.   Welsh Rarebit 198.
Fried Sweet Potatoes 175.
Cold Pickled Beets 186.   French Bread 218.
Cookies 280.   Gooseberry Jam 387.
Cocoa 411.

Dinner.

Vermicelli Soup 35.

Leg of Mutton a la Venison 121.

Steamed Potatoes 172.

Ladies' Cabbage 178.   Stewed Onions 176.

Mixed Pickles 166.

Pumpkin Pie 299.   Orange Jelly 332.

Nut Cakes 283.   Cheese.

Coffee 408.

Tuesday.

Breakfast.

Stewed Prunes.
Oatmeal with Cream 243.
Snipe on Toast 88.   Scrappel 133.
Potato Puffs 171.   Newport Waffles 231.
Wheat Bread 213.   Coffee 408.

Luncheon.

Scalloped Mutton and Tomatoes 125.
Hominy Croquettes 244.   Cold Slaw 153.
Beaten Biscuit 225.
Chocolate Custard Pie 291.
Tea 410.

Dinner.

Oxtail Soup 28.

Roast Leg of Pork 128.

Browned Potatoes 175.

Lima Beans 185.   Mashed Turnips 190.

Celery Salad 154.

Apple Corn Meal Pudding 360, Wine Sauce 371.

Lemon Tartlets 301.   Fruit.

Coffee 408.

Wednesday.

Breakfast.

Oranges.
Graham Mush 243.
Country Sausages 135.   Boiled Eggs 200.
Saratoga Chips 171.
Buckwheat Cakes 236.   Dry Toast 246.
Coffee 408.

Luncheon.

Cold Roast Pork 128.   Lobster Salad 151.
Baked Sweet Potatoes 175.
German Bread 219.   Doughnuts 281.
Apple Sauce 143.   Chocolate 410.

Dinner.

Turtle Soup from Beans 30.

Spiced Beef 99.

Mashed Potatoes 170.

Fried Parsnips 180.   Scalloped Onions 177.

Pickled White Cabbage 162.

Cranberry Tart Pie 298.   Blanc Mange 318.

Crackers.   Cheese.

Coffee 408.

Thursday.

Breakfast.

Stewed Apricots.
Oat Flakes 245.
Broiled Veal Cutlets 114.   Fried Oysters 62.
Warmed Potatoes 173.   Cream Waffles 231.
Brown Bread 217.   Coffee 408.

Luncheon.

Beef Croquettes 107.   Fish Omelet 207.
Celery Salad 154.
Raised Biscuit 223.   Feather Cake 264.
Canned Peaches 390.
Tea 410.

Dinner.

Squirrel Soup 30.
Roast Loin of Mutton 120.
Boiled Potatoes 169.
Mashed Squash 188.   Fried Cabbage 178.
Olives.
Apple Puff Pudding 346,
Grandmother's Sauce 372.
Nuts.   Raisins.   Fruit.
Coffee 408.

Friday.

Breakfast.

Bananas.
Steamed Oatmeal 245.
Striped Bass Fried 42.   Minced Eggs 202.
Lyonnaise Potatoes 173.
Corn Bread 219.   Nut Cakes 283.
Wheat Bread 213.   Coffee 408.

Luncheon.

Cold Roast Mutton 120.
Halibut on Toast 249.
Potato Salad 154.   French Bread 218.
Grape Jelly Pie 298.
Chocolate 410.

Dinner.

Fish Chowder 54.
Baked Pickerel 43.
Steamed Potatoes 172.
Boiled Turnips 190.   Rabbit Pie 90.
Plain Celery.
Apple Custard Pudding 348, Hard Sauce 374.
Savory Biscuits 277.   Fruit.
Coffee 408.

Saturday.

Breakfast.

Baked Sour Apples 425.
Boiled Rice 244.
Porterhouse Steak Broiled 97.
Plain Omelet 204.   Potatoes a la Creme 171.
Wheat Griddle Cakes 233.
Dry Toast 246.   Coffee 408.

Luncheon.

Veal Stew 115.   Potato Puffs 171.
Pickled Mangoes 163.
Grafton Milk Biscuits 226.
Chocolate Eclairs 273.   Lemon Sponge 315.
Tea 410.

Dinner.

Celery Soup 35.
Boiled Ham 134.
Baked Sweet Potatoes 175.
Lima Beans 185.   Stewed Parsnips 180.
Sour-crout 179.
Oxford Dumplings 343, Sweet Sauce 375.
Cream Tarts 304.   Fruit.
Coffee 408.

DECEMBER.

Christmas Day

Breakfast.

Oranges.
Boiled Rice 244.
Broiled Salt Mackerel 44.
Poached Eggs a la Creme 202.
Potato Fillets 173.
Feather Griddle Cakes 233.
Wheat Bread 213.
Coffee 408.

Supper.

Cold Roast Goose 74.
Oyster Patties 65.
Cold Slaw 153.   Buns 227.
Charlotte Russe 323.
Peach Jelly 386.
Tea 410.

Dinner.

Oysters on Half Shell.
Game Soup 26.
Boiled White Fish 50, Sauce Maitre d'Hotel 142.
Roast Goose 74, Apple Sauce 143.
Boiled Potatoes 169.   Mashed Turnips 190.
Creamed Parsnips 180.   Stewed Onions 176.
Boiled Rice 179.   Lobster Salad 152.
Canvas Back Duck 86.
Christmas Plum Pudding 353, Sauce 372.
Vanilla Ice Cream 334.
Mince Pie 300.   Orange Jelly 332.
Delicate Cake 260.   Salted Almonds 325.
Confectionery.   Fruits.
Coffee 408.

Sunday.

Breakfast.

Grapes.
Steamed Oatmeal 245.
Pickled Pigs' Feet Fried 133.
Oyster Toast 247.   Potato Puffs 171.
Egg Muffins 229.   Wheat Bread 213.
Coffee 408.

Supper.

Cold Potted Beef 105.   Panned Oysters 64.
Celery Salad 154.   Saratoga Chips 171.
Rusks 227.   Little Plum Cakes 279.
Quince Jelly 384.
Tea 410.

Dinner.

Chicken Cream Soup 27.
Boiled Halibut 48, Sauce Hollandaise 142.
Roast Goose 74, Apple Sauce 143.
Boiled Potatoes 169.   Stewed Celery 185.
Mashed Turnips 190.   Lobster Salad 151.
Scalloped Clams 69.
Mince Pie 300.   Orange Cream 312.
Citron Cake 260.   Cheese.
Coffee 408.

Monday.

Breakfast.

Sliced Oranges.
Graham Mush 243.
Codfish Steak 57.   Lyonnaise Potatoes 173.
Hashed Beef on Toast 249.
French Rolls 225.   Brown Bread 217.
Coffee 408.

___

Luncheon.

Cold Roast Goose 74.
Scalloped Cheese 197.   Ham Salad 153.
French Bread 218.
Apple Meringue Pie 291.
Chocolate 410.

Dinner.

Onion Soup 34.

Roast Spare Rib 129.   Cranberry Sauce 144.

Browned Potatoes 175.

Stewed Carrots 189.   Boiled Onions 176.

Plain Celery.

Boiled Rice Dumplings with Custard Sauce 342.

Pastry Sandwiches 278.   Fruit.

Coffee 408.

Tuesday.

Breakfast.

Stewed Prunes.
Boiled Rice 244.
Pork Chops and Fried Apples 130.
Warmed Potatoes 173.
Buckwheat Cakes 236.   Wheat Bread 213.
Coffee 408.

___

Luncheon.

Sliced Head Cheese 136.
Bread Omelet 207.   Parsnip Fritters 180.
Cold Slaw 153.
Graham Bread 216.   Mince Pie 300.
Tea 410.

Dinner.

Scotch Mutton Broth 25.

Boiled Turkey 73, Oyster Dressing 72.

Mashed Potatoes 170.

Baked Squash 188.   Boiled Parsnips 180.

Piccalili 165.

Baked Corn Meal Pudding 350, Hard Sauce 374.

Apple Tarts 304.   Cheese.

Coffee 408.

Wednesday.

Breakfast.

Cider Apple Sauce 143.
Hominy 244.
Broiled Rabbits 90.   Codfish Balls 54.
Potato Fillets 173.
Continental Hotel Waffles 231.
Dry Toast 246.   Coffee 408.

Luncheon.

Turkey Hash 73.   Rice Croquettes 243.
Lobster Salad 151.
Raised Biscuits 223.   Almond Custard 308.
Cocoa 411.

Dinner.

Oyster Soup 39.

Sliced Beef Tongue 110, Brown Sauce 142.

Potato Puffs 171.

Steamed Cabbage 178.

Lamb Sweetbreads 125, with Tomato Sauce 140.

Birds' Nest Pudding 344, Plain Sauce 373.

Crackers.   Cheese.

Coffee 408.

Thursday.

Breakfast.

Stewed Peaches.
Cracked Wheat 245.
Mutton Chops Broiled 122, Tomato Sauce **140.**
Saratoga Chips 171.
New England Corn Cake 219.
Bakers' Doughnuts 282. Wheat Bread 213.
Coffee 408.

Luncheon.

Cold Spiced Tongue 110.
Cheese Cream Toast 198. Pickled Onions 163.
Fried Sweet Potatoes 175. Twist Bread 218.
Layer Cake 268, with Apple Filling 269.
Tea 410.

Dinner.

Vegetable Soup 34.
Beef a la Mode 99.
Browned Potatoes 170.
Boiled Turnips 190. Fried Onions **176.**
Oyster Salad 152.
Snow Pudding 361. Squash Pie 299.
Nuts. Raisins.
Coffee 408.

Friday.

Breakfast.

Apple Sauce 143.
Oatmeal with Cream 243.
White Fish Fried 42. Grilled Bacon **132.**
Baked Potatoes 175.
Feather Griddle Cakes 233.
Brown Bread 217. Coffee 408.

Luncheon.

Cold Pork and Beans 131. Beef Croquettes **106.**
Green Tomato Pickles 100.
Milk Biscuits 226. Angel Cake 266.
Preserved Pears 380.
Chocolate 410.

Dinner.

Pea Soup 36, with Croutons **37.**
Codfish Steaks 57.
Potato Snow 172. Baked Beets **186.**
Chicken with Macaroni 84.
Celery Salad 154.
Baked Apple Dumplings 341, Sweet Sauce **375.**
Bakers' Custard Pie 293. Cheese.
Coffee 408.

Saturday.

Breakfast.

Bananas.
Oat Flakes 245.
Pork Cutlets 130. Oyster Fritters 65.
Hasty Cooked Potatoes 172.
Graham Griddle Cakes 234.
Wheat Bread 213. Coffee 408.

Luncheon.

Boiled Tripe 110. Chicken Omelet 206.
Potato Salad 154.
French Bread 218. Ginger Cookies **275.**
Preserved Citron 380.
Tea 410.

Dinner.

Tapioca Cream Soup 34.
Lamb Stew 126.
Mashed Potatoes 170. Creamed Parsnips **180.**
Boston Pork and Beans 131.
Cold Slaw 153.
Apple Fritters 237, Sugar Sauce 372.
Lemon Pie 292.
Nuts. Raisins.
Coffee 408.

Special Menus.

. · .

State Dinner at White House.

———

Blue Points.

Haute Sauterne.
Amontillado.

———

POTAGES.

Potage tortue à l'Anglaise Consommé Printaniére Royale.

HORS D'ŒUVRES.

Canapé à la Russe.   Timbales à la Talleyrand.

Rauenthaler Be~~.

———

POISSONS.

Saumon, Sauce Hollandaise.   Grenadines de Bass.
Pommes de Terre Duchesse.   Cucumber Salade.

Ernest Jeroy.

———

RELEVÉS.

Selle d'Agneau, Sauce Menthe.   Filet de Boeuf à la Richelieu.

Chateau Margause.

———

ENTREES.

Ris de Veau à la Perigneux.   Cotelettes d'Agneau d'or Maison.

Terrapin à la Maryland.

Punch Cardinal.

———

Clas de Vougeot.

RÔTI.

Canvas Back Duck.

———

ENTREMETS.

German Asparagus.   Petite Pois.

Gelée au Champagne.   Plombieré aux Framboise.

———

Pudding Diplomate.
Café.   Liqueurs.
Fruits.   Fromage.

470

Mrs. Cleveland's Wedding Lunch.

JUNE 4TH, '88.

Consommé en tasse.

Soft Shell Crabs.

Coquilles de Ris de Vean.   Chateau Iquem.

Snipes on Toast.

Lettuce and Tomato Salade.

Fancy Ice Cream.   Moet & Chanden.

Cakes.

Tea.   Coffee.

Fruits.   Mottos.

General Grant's Birthday Dinner.

Clams.

Haute Sauterne.

POTAGES.

Consommé Imperatrice Bisque de Crabes.

Amontillado.

VARIES HORS D'ŒUVRE VARIES.

Bouchees à la Regence.

POISSON.

Truites de riviere Hollandaise vert pré.   Pommes de terre à la Parisienne.

Coucombres.

Johannisberger.

RELEVE.

Filet de Boeuf à la Bernardi.

Ernest Jeroy

ENTREES.

Ailes de Poulets à la Perigord.   Petits Pois au Beune.

Caisses de ris de Vean à l'Italienne.

Haricots verts.   Asperges, Sauce Creme.

Sorbet Fantaisie.

RÔTI.

Squabs.   Salade de Laitue.

Nuits.

ENTREMETS SUCRES.

Croute aux Mille Fruits.   Cornets à la Chantilly.

Gelée à la Prunelle.

PIECES MONTEES.

Glace Varietees.

Fruits.   Petits Fours.   Café.

Menu for 4 Covers.

Huitres en Coquille.

———

Potage Julienne aux Quenelles.

———

Paupiettes de Turbots à la Joinville.
Cucumbers.   Pommes d'Auphine.

———

Filets Mignons à la Provencale.
Larded Sweetbread à la Meissoniére.

———

Punch au Kirsh.

———

Quails Bardés sur Cronstade.
Lettuce Salad.

———

German Asparagus.

———

Plombiere aux Fraises.

———

Fruits.   Café.   **Fromage.**

———————

Menu for 6 Covers.

Huitres en Coquilles.
                              Sauterne

———

Purée St. Germain.   Consommé Paté d'Italie.
                                        Amontillado

———

Broiled Blue Fish, Maitre d'Hotel.
Cucumbers.   Pommes Duchesse.
                                        Hochheimer

———

Small Tenderloin Sautés, Marrow Sauce.
Lamb Chops à la Maréchale.
                              Moet & Chandon

———

Croutes aux Champignons à la Parisienne.

———

Sorbet Venetienne.

———

Squabs with Water-cresses.
                              Chateau Latour.
Lettuce and Tomato Salad.

———

Artichauts, Sauce Hollandaise.

———

Créme Bavaroise au Chocolat.

———

Fruits.   Café.   **Fromage.**

Menu for 8 Covers.

Huitres en Coquille.
                              Haute Sauterne.

———

Bisque of Lobster.   Lamb Broth with Vegetables.
Radishes.   Olives.
                                        Amontillado.

———

Timbales à l'Ecossaise.   Bass à la Régence.
                                        Rauenthaler Berg.
Potatoes Windsor.

———

Filet of Beef Larded à la Parisienne.
Saddle of Mutton, Currant Jelly.
                                        Ernest Jeroy.

———

Sweetbreads à la Pompadour.
Terrapin à la Maryland.
                                        Chateau Latour.

———

Cauliflower au Gratin.   Celery au Jus.

———

Punch Maraschino.

———

Canvas Back Duck.

———

Lettuce Salad.

———

Souflé à l'Orange.

———

Fruits.   Café.   **Fromage.**

———————

Menu for 10 Covers.

Consommé de Volaille.
                              Haute Sauterne.

———

Huitres à la Poulette.

———

Radishes.   Olives.
Bouchées à la Bohemienne.
                                        Johannisberger.
Truites Saumoné au Beurre de Montpellier.
Tartelette Potatoes.   Cucumbers.

———

Filets Mignon de Bouef à la Trianon.
Cotelettes de Pigeon, Maréchale.
                                        Moet & Chandon.
Petits Pois Garnis de Fleurous.
Artichauts à la Barigoule.

———

Punch Romaine.

———

Bécassines au Cresson.
                              Chas. de Vougeot
Lettuce Salad.

———

Pouding Nesselrode.

———

Fruits.   Café.   **Fromage.**

Menu for 12 Covers.

Little Neck Clams.

Haute Sauterne.

___

Cream of Asparagus.   Consommé Royal.

___

Radishes.   Olives.

Amontillado.

___

Caviar sur Toast.

Pompano Maitre d'Hotel.   Bass à la Régence.

Pommes Parisienne.

Moselbluemchen.

Cotelettes d'Agneau à la Purée de Célen.

Filet of Boeuf à la Pocahontas.

Moet & Chandon.

___

Terrapin à la Richelieu.

___

Sorbet Dunderberg.

___

Canvas Back Ducks.

Nuits.

___

Celery Mayonnaise.

___

Artichauts Bottoms.   French Peas.

___

Omelette Célestine.

___

Fruits.   Café.   Fromage.

Menu for 24 Covers.

Huitres.

___

POTAGES.

Consommé Francatelli.   Bisque d'Ecrevisses.

___

HORS L'ŒUVRE.

Timbales à la Reyniére.

___

POISSON.

Filet Turbot Portugaise.
Pommes de terre Parisienne
Celery Mayonnaise.

___

RELEVÉ.

Selle d'Agneau à la Colbert
Haricots verts.

___

ENTREES.

Ailes de Poulets à la Hongroise.
Cépes à la Bordelaise.   Asperges Sauce Crème.

___

Sorbet à la Prunelle.

___

Â
ROTI.

Faisan rotes Franqué de Cailles.

___

ENTREMETS DE DOUCEUR

Croutes aux Ananas.   Glaces Fantaisies.
Fruits.   Café.   Petits Fours.

THE GREAT STATE DINING ROOM.

BUFFET FOR 1,000 PEOPLE.

COLD SERVICE.

Consommé en Tasse.

Sandwiches.   Caviar on Toast.   Radishes.   Celery.

Cold Salmon Mayonnaise.   Lobster and Shrimp Salad.

Westphalia Ham à la Gelée.

Boned Turkey.   Galantine of Faison.

Cold Game in Season.

Mayonnaise of Chicken.   Cold Turkey.   Fillet of Beef.   Game Pies.

Saddle of Venison, Currant Jelly.

Russian Salad.

Neapolitaine Ice Cream.   Water Ices.

Nesselrode Puddings.

Claret and Champagne Jellies.

Biscuits Glacée.   Charlottes Glacée.

Assorted Cakes.   Assorted Candies.

Tea.   Coffee.   Lemonade.

MANAGEMENT AND DIRECTIONS

OF

DINNERS AND RECEPTIONS

ON

STATE OCCASIONS AT THE WHITE HOUSE.

Etiquette as observed in European courts is not known at the White House.

The President's Secretary issues invitations by direction of the President, to the distinguished guests.

The Usher in charge of the cloak-room hands to the gentleman on arrival an envelope containing a diagram of the table (as cut shows), whereon the name and

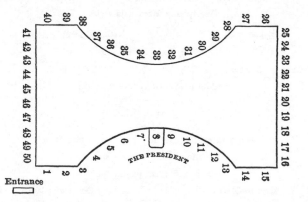

seat of the respective guest, and the lady he is to escort to dinner, are marked.

A card corresponding with his name is placed on the napkin belonging to the cover of the seat he will occupy.

The President's seat is in the middle of the table. The most distinguished guests sit on his right and left. If their wives are present they will occupy these seats, and the gentlemen will be seated next to the President's wife, whose seat is directly opposite the President.

476

Official dinners all over the world are always served after the French fashion, and are divided into three distinct parts. Two of them are served from the kitchen, and the third from the pantry.

The first part of the dinner served French style includes from oysters on the shell to the sherbets.

The second service continues to the sweet dishes.

The third includes ice, cakes, fruits, cheeses, which are all understood as desserts, and are dressed in the pantry.

All principal dishes which are artistically decorated are shown to the President first, then are carried around the table before being carved by the Steward in the pantry.

Fancy folding of the napkins is considered out of fashion; plain square folded, so as to show monogram in the middle, is much preferred.

The following diagram will illustrate the arrangement of the glasses on the table. (See diagram.)

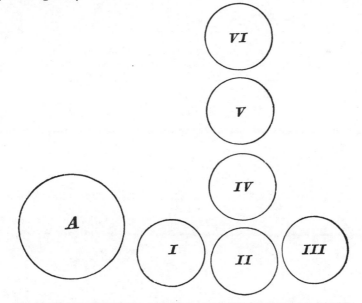

DIAGRAM ILLUSTRATING HOW TO ARRANGE GLASSES ON TABLE.

	I—Glass for Sauterne.	IV—Glass for Water.
A—Plate.	II—Glass for Sherry.	V—Glass for Champagne.
	III—Glass for Rhine Wine.	VI—Glass for Burgundy.

Flower decorations on the table are to be in flat designs, so as not to obscure the view of the guests.

Corsage Bouquets for ladies consist of not more than eight large roses tied together by silk ribbon, with the name of the lady stamped on in gold letters.

Gentlemen's Bouttonieres consist only of one rose bud.

Bouquets for ladies are to be placed on the right side; for gentlemen, on the napkin next to card bearing his name.

Printed Menus are never used on any official occasion.

The private dinners Menus are either printed or written on a plain card and placed on each cover.

Liquors, cordials, cigars are served on a separate table after the ladies have retired to the parlor.

FOR THE SICK.

Dishes for invalids should be served in the daintiest and most attractive way; never send more than a supply for one meal; the same dish too frequently set before an invalid often causes a distaste, when perhaps a change would tempt the appetite.

When preparing dishes where milk is used, the condition of the patient should be considered. Long cooking hardens the albumen and makes the milk very constipating; then, if the patient should be already constipated, care should be taken not to heat the milk above the boiling point.

The seasoning of food for the sick should be varied according to the condition of the patient; one recovering from illness can partake of a little piece of roast mutton, chicken, rabbit, game, fish, simply dressed, and simple puddings are all light food and easily digested. A mutton chop, nicely cut, trimmed and broiled, is a dish that is often inviting to an invalid. As a rule, an invalid will be more likely to enjoy any preparation sent to him if it is served in small, delicate pieces. As there are so many small, dainty dishes that can be made for this purpose, it seems useless to try to more than give a small variety of them. Pudding can be made of prepared barley, or tapioca, well-soaked before boiling, with an egg added, and a change can be made of light puddings by mixing up some stewed fruit with the puddings before baking; a bread pudding from stale bread-crumbs, and a tiny cup-custard, boiled in a small basin or cup; also various drinks, such as milk punch, wine, whey, apple-toddy, and various other nourishing drinks.

BEEFSTEAK AND MUTTON CHOPS.

Select the tenderest cuts, and broil over a clear, hot fire. Let the steak be rare, the chops well done. Salt and pepper; lay between two *hot* plates three minutes, and serve to your patient. If he is very weak, do not let him swallow anything except the juice, when he has chewed the meat well. The essence of rare beef, roasted or broiled, thus expressed, is considered by some physicians to be more strengthening than beef tea prepared in the usual manner.

BEEF TEA.

One pound of *lean* beef, cut into small pieces. Put into a glass canning-jar without a drop of water; cover tightly, and set in a pot of cold water. Heat gradually to a boil, and continue this steadily for three or four hours, until the meat is like white rags, and the juice all drawn out. Season with salt to taste, and when cold, skim.

VEAL OR MUTTON BROTH.

Take a scrag-end of mutton (two pounds), put it in a sauce-pan, with two quarts of cold water, and an ounce of pearl barley or rice. When it is coming to a boil, skim it well, then add half a teaspoonful of salt; let it boil until half reduced, then strain it, and take off all the fat, and it is ready for use. This is excellent for an invalid. If vegetables are liked in this broth, take one turnip, one carrot, and one onion, cut them in shreds, and boil them in the broth half an hour. In that case, the barley may be served with the vegetables in broth.

CHICKEN BROTH.

Make the same as mutton or beef broth. Boil the chicken slowly, putting on just enough water to cover it well, watching it closely that it does not boil down too much. When the chicken is tender, season with salt and a very little pepper. The yolk of an egg beaten light and added, is very nourishing

OATMEAL GRUEL.

Put four tablespoonfuls of the best grits (oatmeal coarsely ground) into a pint of boiling water. Let it boil gently, and stir it often, till it becomes as thick as you wish it. Then strain it, and add to it while warm, butter, wine, nutmeg, or whatever is thought proper to flavor it. Salt to taste.

If you make the gruel of fine oatmeal, sift it, mix it first to a thick batter with a little cold water, and then put it into the sauce-pan of boiling water. Stir it all the time it is boiling, lifting the spoon gently up and down, and letting the gruel fall slowly back again into the pan.

CORN-MEAL GRUEL.

Two tablespoonfuls of fine Indian meal, mixed smooth with cold water and a salt-spoonful of salt; add one quart of boiling water, and cook twenty minutes. Stir it frequently, and if it becomes too thick use boiling water to thin it. If the stomach is not too weak, a tablespoonful of cream may be used to cool it. Some like it sweetened and others like it plain. For very sick persons, let it settle, pour off the top, and give without other seasoning. For convalescents, toast a piece of bread as nicely as possible, and put it in the gruel with a tablespoonful of nice sweet cream, and a little ginger and sugar. This should be used only when a laxative is allowed.

EGG GRUEL.

Beat the yolk of an egg with one tablespoonful of sugar; pour one teacupful of boiling water on it; add the white of an egg, beaten to a froth, with any seasoning or spice desired. Take warm.

MILK PORRIDGE.

The same as arrowroot, excepting it should be all milk, and thickened with a scant tablespoonful of sifted flour; let it boil five minutes, stirring it continually, add a little cold milk, and give it one boil up, and it is ready for use.

ARROWROOT MILK PORRIDGE.

One large cupful of fresh milk, new if you can get it; one cupful of boiling water; one teaspoonful of arrowroot, wet to a paste with cold water; two teaspoonfuls of white sugar; a pinch of salt. Put the sugar into the milk, the salt into the boiling water, which should be poured into a farina-kettle. Add the wet arrowroot, and boil, stirring constantly until it is clear; put in the milk, and cook ten minutes, stirring often. Give while warm, adding hot milk should it be thicker than gruel.

ARROWROOT BLANC MANGE.

One large cupful of boiling milk, one even tablespoonful of arrowroot rubbed to a paste with cold water, two teaspoonfuls of white sugar, a pinch of salt; flavor with rose-water. Proceed as in the foregoing recipes, boiling and stirring eight minutes. Turn into a wet mold, and when firm, serve with cream and powdered sugar.

TAPIOCA JELLY.

Soak a cupful of tapioca in a quart of cold water, after washing it thoroughly two or three times; after soaking three or four hours, simmer it in a stew-pan until it becomes quite clear, stirring often; add the juice of a lemon, and a little of the grated peel, also a pinch of salt. Sweeten to taste. Wine can be substituted for lemon, if liked.

SLIPPERY-ELM BARK TEA.

Break the bark into bits, pour boiling water over it, cover, and let it infuse until cold. Sweeten, ice, and take for summer disorders, or add lemon juice and drink for a bad cold.

FLAX-SEED TEA.

Upon an ounce of unbruised flax-seed and a little pulverized liquorice-root pour a pint of boiling (soft or rain) water; and place the vessel containing these ingredients near, but not on, the fire for four hours. Strain through a linen cloth. Make it fresh every day. An excellent drink in fever accompanied by a cough.

FLAX-SEED LEMONADE.

To a large tablespoonful of flax-seed, allow a tumbler and a half of cold water. Boil them together till the liquid becomes very sticky. Then strain it hot over a quarter of a pound of pulverized sugar, and an ounce of pulverized gum arabic. Stir it till quite dissolved, and squeeze into it the juice of a lemon.

This mixture has frequently been found an efficacious remedy for a cold, taking a wine-glass of it as often as the cough is troublesome.

TAMARIND WATER.

Put tamarinds into a pitcher or tumbler till it is one-third full; then fill up with cold water, cover it, and let it infuse for a quarter of an hour or more.

Currant jelly or cranberry juice mixed with water makes a pleasant drink for an invalid.

SAGO JELLY.

Made the same as tapioca. If seasoning is not advisable, the sago may be boiled in milk, instead of water, and eaten plain.

Rice jelly made the same, using only half as much rice as sago.

ARROWROOT WINE JELLY.

One cupful of boiling water, one scant tablespoonful of arrowroot; mix with a little cold water; one tablespoonful of sugar, a pinch of salt, one tablespoonful of brandy, or three tablespoonfuls of wine. Excellent for a sick person without fever.

HOMINY.

Put to soak one pint of hominy in two and one-half pints of boiling water over night, in a tin vessel with a tight cover; in the morning add one-half pint of sweet milk, and a little salt. Place on a brisk fire in a kettle of boiling water, the tin vessel containing the hominy; let boil one-half hour.

Cracked wheat, oatmeal, mush, are all good food for the sick.

CHICKEN JELLY.

Cook a chicken in enough water to little more than cover it; let it stew gently until the meat drops from the bones, and the broth is reduced to about a pint; season it to taste, with a little salt and pepper. Strain and press, first through a colander, then through a coarse cloth. Set it over the fire again, and cook a few minutes longer. Turn it into an earthen vegetable dish to harden; set it on the ice in the refrigerator. Eat cold in slices. Nice made into sandwiches, with *thin* slices of bread, lightly spread with butter.

BOILED RICE.

Boil half a cupful of rice in just enough water to cover it, with half a teaspoonful of salt; when the water has boiled nearly out and the rice begins to look soft and dry, turn over it a cupful of milk, and let it simmer until the rice is done and nearly dry; take from the fire and beat in a well-beaten egg. Eat it warm with cream and sugar. Flavor to taste.

CUP PUDDING.

Take one tablespoonful of flour, one egg; mix with cold milk and a pinch of salt to a batter. Boil fifteen minutes in a buttered cup. Eat with sauce, fruit, or plain sugar.

TAPIOCA CUP PUDDING.

This is very light and delicate for invalids. An even tablespoonful of tapioca, soaked for two hours in nearly a cup of new milk; stir into this the yolk of a fresh egg, a little sugar, a grain of salt, and bake it in a cup for fifteen minutes. A little jelly may be eaten with it.

BAKED APPLES.

Get nice fruit, a little tart and juicy, but not sour; clean them nicely, and bake in a moderate oven—regulated so as to have them done in about an hour; when the skin cracks and the pulp breaks through in every direction they are done and ready to take out. Serve with white sugar sprinkled over them.

SOFT TOAST.

Toast well, but not too brown, two thin slices of stale bread; put them on a warm plate, sprinkle with a pinch of salt, and pour upon them some boiling water; quickly cover with another dish of the same size, and drain off the water. Put a very small bit of butter on the toast and serve at once while hot.

IRISH MOSS BLANC MANGE.

A small handful of moss (to be purchased at any drug store); wash it very carefully, and put it in one quart of milk on the fire. Let the milk simmer for about twenty minutes, or until the moss begins to dissolve. Then remove from the fire and strain through a fine sieve. Add two tablespoonfuls of sugar and half a teaspoonful of vanilla flavoring. Put away to harden in cups or molds, and serve with sugar and cream.

A delicate dish for an invalid.

EGG TOAST.

Brown a slice of bread nicely over the coals, dip it in hot water slightly salted, butter it, and lay on the top an egg that has been broken into boiling water, and cooked until the white has hardened; season the egg with a bit of butter and a crumb of salt.

The best way to cook eggs for an invalid is to drop them, or else pour boiling water over the egg in the shell and let it stand for a few minutes on the back of the stove.

OYSTER TOAST.

Make a nice slice of dry toast, butter it and lay it on a hot dish. Put six oysters, half a teacupful of their own liquor, and half a cupful of milk, into a tin cup or basin, and boil one minute. Season with a little butter, pepper and salt, then pour over the toast and serve.

MULLED JELLY.

Take one tablespoonful of currant or grape jelly; beat with it the white of one egg and a teaspoonful of sugar; pour on it a teacupful of boiling water, and break in a slice of dry toast or two crackers.

CUP CUSTARD.

Break into a coffee-cup an egg, put in two teaspoonfuls of sugar, beat it up thoroughly, a pinch of salt and a pinch of grated nutmeg; fill up the cup with good sweet milk; turn it into another cup, well buttered, and set it in a pan of boiling water, reaching nearly to the top of the cup. Set in the oven, and when the custard is set, it is done. Eat cold.

CLAM BROTH.

Select twelve small, hardshell clams, drain them, and chop them fine; add half a pint of clam juice or hot water, a pinch of cayenne, and a walnut of butter; simmer thirty minutes; add a gill of boiled milk, strain, and serve. This is an excellent broth for weak stomachs.

MILK OR CREAM CODFISH.

This dish will often relish when a person is recovering from sickness, when nothing else would. Pick up a large tablespoonful of salt codfish very fine; freshen it considerably by placing it over the fire in a basin, covering it with cold water as it comes to a boil; turn off the water and freshen again if very salt, then turn off the water until dry, and pour over half a cupful of milk or thin cream; add a bit of butter, a sprinkle of pepper, and a thickening made of one teaspoonful of flour or corn-starch, wet up with a little milk; when this boils up, turn over a slice of dipped toast.

CRACKER PANADA.

Break in pieces three or four hard crackers that are baked quite brown, and let them boil fifteen minutes in one quart of water; then remove from the fire, let them stand three or four minutes, strain off the liquor through a fine wire sieve, and season it with sugar.

This is a nourishing beverage for infants that are teething, and with the addition of a little wine and nutmeg, is often prescribed for invalids recovering from a fever.

BREAD PANADA

Put three gills of water and one tablespoonful of white sugar on the fire, and just before it boils add two tablespoonfuls of the crumbs of stale white bread; stir it well, and let it boil three or four minutes; then add one glass of white wine, a grated lemon and a little nutmeg; let it boil up once, then remove it from the fire, and keep it closely covered until it is wanted for use.

SLIPPERY-ELM TEA.

Put a teaspoonful of powdered slippery-elm into a tumbler, pour cold water upon it, and season with lemon and sugar.

TOAST WATER, OR CRUST COFFEE.

Take stale pieces of crusts of bread, the end pieces of the loaf; toast them a nice, dark brown, care to be taken that they do not burn in the least, as that affects the flavor. Put the browned crusts into a large milk pitcher, and pour enough boiling water over to cover them; cover the pitcher closely, and let steep until cold. Strain, and sweeten to taste; put a piece of ice in each glass.

This is also good. drank warm with cream and sugar, similar to coffee.

PLAIN MILK TOAST.

Cut a thin slice from a loaf of stale bread, toast it very quickly, sprinkle a little salt over it, and pour upon it three tablespoonfuls of boiling milk or cream. Crackers split and toasted in this manner, are often very grateful to an invalid.

LINSEED TEA.

Put one tablespoonful of linseed into a stew-pan with half a pint of cold water; place the stew-pan over a moderate fire, and, when the water is quite warm, pour it off, and add to the linseed half a pint of fresh cold water; then let the whole boil three or four minutes; season it with lemon and sugar.

POWDERS FOR CHILDREN.

A very excellent carminative powder for flatulent infants may be kept in the house, and employed with advantage whenever the child is in pain or griped, dropping five grains of oil of anise-seed and two of peppermint on half an ounce of lump sugar, and rubbing it in a mortar, with a drachm of magnesia, into a fine powder. A small quantity of this may be given in a little water at any time, and always with benefit.

FOR CHILDREN TEETHING.

Tie a quarter of a pound of wheat flour in a thick cloth, and boil it in one quart of water for three hours; then remove the cloth and expose the flour to the air or heat until it is hard and dry; grate from it, when wanted, one table-spoonful, which put into half a pint of new milk, and stir over the fire until it comes to a boil, when add a pinch of salt and a tablespoonful of cold water, and serve. This gruel is excellent for children afflicted with summer complaint.

Or, brown a tablespoonful of flour in the oven or on top of the stove on a baking-tin; feed a few pinches at a time to a child, and it will often check a diarrhœa. The tincture of "kino"—of which from ten to thirty drops, mixed with a little sugar and water in a spoon, and given every two or three hours, is very efficacious and harmless—can be procured at almost any druggist's. Tablespoon doses of pure cider vinegar, and a pinch of salt, has cured when all else failed.

BLACKBERRY CORDIAL.

This recipe may be found under the head of "Coffee, Tea, Beverages." It will be found an excellent medicine for children teething and summer diseases.

ACID DRINKS.

1. Peel thirty large Malaga grapes, and pour half a pint of boiling water upon them; cover them closely, and let them steep until the water is cold.

2. Pour half a pint of boiling water upon one tablespoonful of currant jelly, and stir until the jelly is dissolved.

3. Cranberries and barberries may be used in the same way to make very refreshing acid drinks for persons recovering from fevers.

DRAUGHTS FOR THE FEET.

Take a large leaf from the horseradish plant, and cut out the hard fibres that run through the leaf; place it on a hot shovel for a moment to soften it, fold it, and fasten it closely in the hollow of the foot by a cloth bandage.

Burdock-leaves, cabbage-leaves, and mullen-leaves, are used in the same manner, to alleviate pain and promote perspiration.

Garlics are also made for draughts by pounding them, placing them on a hot tin plate for a moment to sweat them, and binding them closely to the hollow of the foot by a cloth bandage.

Draughts of onions, for infants, are made by roasting onions in hot ashes, and, when they are quite soft, peeling off the outside, mashing them, and applying them on a cloth as usual.

POULTICES.

A Bread and Milk Poultice.—Put a tablespoonful of the crumbs of stale bread into a gill of milk, and give the whole one boil up. Or, take stale bread-crumbs, pour over them boiling water and boil till soft, stirring well; take from the fire and gradually stir in a little glycerine or sweet oil, so as to render the poultice pliable when applied.

A Hop Poultice.—Boil one handful of dried hops in half a pint of water, until the half pint is reduced to a gill, then stir into it enough Indian meal to thicken it.

A Mustard Poultice.—Into one gill of boiling water stir one tablespoonful of Indian meal; spread the paste thus made upon a cloth, and spread over the paste one teaspoonful of mustard flour. If you wish a mild poultice, use a tea-spoonful of mustard as it is prepared for the table, instead of the mustard flour.

Equal parts of ground mustard and flour made into a paste with warm water, and spread between two pieces of muslin, form the indispensable mustard plaster.

A Ginger Poultice.—This is made like a mustard poultice, using ground ginger instead of mustard. A little vinegar is sometimes added to each of these poultices.

A Stramonium Poultice.—Stir one tablespoonful of Indian meal into a gill of boiling water, and add one tablespoonful of bruised stramonium seeds.

Wormwood and Arnica are sometimes applied in poultices. Steep the herbs in half a pint of cold water, and when all their virtue is extracted stir in a little bran or rye-meal to thicken the liquid; the herbs must not be removed from the liquid.

This is a useful application for sprains and bruises.

Linseed Poultice.—Take four ounces of powdered linseed, and gradually sprinkle it into a half pint of hot water.

A REMEDY FOR BOILS.

An excellent remedy for boils is water of a temperature agreeable to the feelings of the patient. Apply wet linen to the part affected, and frequently renew or moisten it. It is said to be the most effectual remedy known. Take inwardly some good blood purifier.

CURE FOR RINGWORMS.

Yellow dock, root or leaves, steeped in vinegar, will cure the worst case of ringworm.

HOW COLDS ARE CAUGHT.

A great many cannot see why it is they do not take a cold·when exposed to cold winds and rain. The fact is, and ought to be more generally understood, that nearly every cold is contracted indoors, and is not directly due to the cold outside, but to the heat inside. A man will go to bed at night feeling as well as usual and get up in the morning with a royal cold. He goes peeking around in search of cracks and keyholes and tiny drafts. Weather-strips are procured, and the house made as tight as a fruit-can. In a few days more the whole family has colds.

Let a man go home, tired or exhausted, eat a full supper of starchy and vegetable food, occupy his mind intently for a while, go to bed in a warm, close room, and if he doesn't have a cold in the morning it will be a wonder. A drink of whiskey or a glass or two of beer before supper will facilitate matters very much.

People swallow more colds down their throats than they inhale or receive from contact with the air, no matter how cold or chilly it may be. Plain, light suppers are good to go to bed on, and are far more conducive to refreshing sleep than a glass of beer or a dose of chloral. In the estimation of a great many this statement is rank heresy, but in the light of science, common sense and experience it is gospel truth.

Pure air is strictly essential to maintain perfect health. If a person is accustomed to sleeping with the windows open there is but little danger of taking cold winter or summer. Persons that shut up the windows to keep out the "night air" make a mistake, for at night the only air we breathe is "night air," and we need good air while asleep as much or even more than at any other time of day. Ventilation can be accomplished by simply opening the window an inch at the bottom and also at the top, thus letting the pure air in, the bad air going outward at the top.   Close, foul air poisons the blood, brings on disease which often results in death; this poisoning of the blood is only prevented by pure air, which enters the lungs, becomes charged with *waste* particles, then thrown out, and which are poisoning if taken back again.   It is estimated that a grown person corrupts *one gallon of pure air every minute,* or twenty-five barrels full in a single night, in breathing alone.

Clothing that has been worn through the day should be changed for fresh or dry ones to sleep in.   Three pints of moisture, filled with the waste of the body, are given off every twenty-four hours, and this is mostly absorbed by the clothing.   Sunlight and exposure to the air purifies the clothing of the poisons which nature is trying to dispose of, and which would otherwise be brought again into contact with the body.

Colds are often taken by extreme cold and heat, and a sudden exposure to cold by passing from a heated room to the cold outside air.   Old and weak persons, especially, should avoid such extreme change.   In passing from warm crowded rooms to the cold air, the mouth should be kept closed, and all the breathing done through the nostrils only, that the cold air may be warmed before it reaches the lungs, or else the sudden change will drive the blood from the surface of the internal organs, often producing congestions.

Dr. B. I. Kendall writes that " *the temperature of the body* should be evenly and properly maintained to secure perfect health; and to accomplish this purpose requires great care and caution at times.   The human body is, so to speak, the most delicate and intricate piece of machinery that could possibly be conceived of, and to keep this in perfect order requires constant care.   It is a fixed law of Nature that every violation thereof shall be punished; and so we find that he who neglects to care for his body by protecting it from sudden changes of weather, or draughts of cold air upon unprotected parts of the body, suffers the penalty by sickness, which may vary according to the exposure and the habits of the person, which affect the result materially; for what would be an easy day's work for a man who is accustomed to hard labor, would be sufficient to excite the circulation to such an extent in a person unaccustomed to work, that only slight exposure might cause the death of the latter when over-heated in this way; while the same exercise and exposure to the man accustomed to hard labor might not affect him.   So, we say, be careful of your bodies, for it is a duty you owe to yourselves, your friends, and particularly to Him who created you. When your body is over-heated and you are perspiring, be very careful about sitting down to ' cool off,' as the custom of some is, by removing a part of the clothing and sitting in a cool place, and perhaps where there is a draught of air passing over your body. The proper way to 'cool off' when over-heated is to put on more clothing, especially if you are in a cool place; but never remove a part of the clothing you have already on. If possible, get near a fire where there is no wind blowing, and *dry off* gradually, instead of cooling off suddenly, which is always dangerous."

Many colds are taken from the feet being damp or wet. To keep these extremities warm and dry is a great preventative against the almost endless list of disorders which come from a "slight cold." Many imagine if their feet are not thoroughly wet, there will be no harm arising from mere dampness, not knowing that the least dampness is absorbed into the sole, and is attracted nearer the foot itself by its heat, and thus perspiration is dangerously checked.

WATER.

All beings need drink as much as they need food, and it is just as necessary to health as pure air; therefore the water should be boiled or filtered before being drank. Rain-water filtered is probably the best attainable. Boiling the water destroys the vegetable and animal matter, and leaves the mineral matter deposited on the bottom of the vessel containing it; therefore it leaves it clear from poisonous substances.

REGULATION IN DIET.

The food we eat is a very important item, and one which it would be difficult to arrange any rule for which would apply to all persons under different circumstances. In health, it is safer to eat by instinct rather than to follow any definite rules. While there are many who have a scanty living, with a small variety of food, there is a large number who have an abundance and a large variety. The former class, in many cases, live miserable lives, either to hoard up for miserly purposes the money which might make them happy, or in some cases through poverty; while the latter class, as a rule, have better health and have much more enjoyment in this life, unless it be some who are gluttonous, and make themselves miserable by abusing the blessings they should enjoy. Avoid extremes in living too free or scanty; have a good nourishing diet, and a sufficient quantity, and it should always be properly cooked; for if the cooking is poorly done, it affects not only the nutritious qualities, but is not so easily digested; thus making food, which is originally the best kind, of very little value to us; and with very poor cooking it is sometimes a positive injury.

It is very important that the food be taken with regularity at the accustomed time. Be careful not to take too much drink during any meal; but, if thirsty, drink water before meal-time so that you will not care for it until some time after eating, as it is a bad plan to drink much either during or for a little time after the meal is taken. It is a very bad plan to hurry in eating, because by so doing the food is not properly masticated; it is better to be a long time in eating and chew the food well.

—*Dr. B. I. Kindall, Enosburg Falls, Vt.*

HOW TO USE HOT WATER.

One of the simplest and most effectual means of relieving pain is by the use of hot water, externally and internally, the temperature varying according to the feelings of the patient. For bruises, sprains, and similar accidental hurts, it should be applied immediately, as hot as can be borne, by means of a cloth dipped in the water and laid on the wounded part, or by immersion, if convenient, and the treatment kept up until relief is obtained. If applied at once, the use of hot water will generally prevent, nearly, if not entirely, the bruised flesh from turning black. For pains resulting from indigestion, and known as wind colic, etc., a cupful of hot water, taken in sips, will often relieve at once. When that is insufficient, a flannel folded in several thicknesses, large enough to fully cover the painful place, should be wrung out of hot water and laid over the seat of the pain. It should be as hot as the skin can bear without injury, and be renewed every ten minutes or oftener, if it feels cool, until the pain is gone. The remedy is simple, efficient, harmless, and within the reach of every one; and should be more generally used than it is. If used along with common sense, it might save many a doctor's bill, and many a course of drug treatment as well.

GROWING PAINS CURED.

Following in our mother's footsteps, we have been routed night after night from our warm quarters, in the dead of winter, to kindle fires and fill frosty kettles from water-pails thickly crusted with ice, that we might get the writhing pedal extremities of our little heir into a tub of water as quickly as possible. But lately we have learned that all this work and exposure is needless. We simply wring a towel from salted water—a bowl of it standing in our sleeping room, ready for such an emergency—wrap the limb in it from the ankle to knee, without taking the child from his bed, and then swathe with dry flannels, thick and warm, tucking the blankets about him a little closer, and relief is sure.

—*Good Housekeeping.*

HOW TO KEEP WELL.

Don't sleep in a draught.
Don't go to bed with cold feet.
Don't stand over hot-air registers.

Don't eat what you do not need, just to save it.

Don't try to get cool too quickly after exercising.

Don't sleep in a room without ventilation of some kind.

Don't stuff a cold lest you should be next obliged to starve a fever.

Don't sit in a damp or chilly room without a fire.

Don't try to get along without flannel underclothing in winter.

DIPHTHERIA.

A gargle of sulphur and water has been used with much success in cases of diphtheria. Let the patient swallow a little of the mixture. Or, when you discover that your throat is a little sore, bind a strip of flannel around the throat, wet in camphor, and gargle salt and vinegar occasionally.

COLDS AND HOARSENESS.

Borax has proved a most effective remedy in certain forms of colds. In sudden hoarseness or loss of voice in public speakers or singers, from colds, relief for an hour or so may be obtained by slowly dissolving, and partially swallowing, a lump of borax the size of a garden pea, or about three or four grains held in the mouth for ten or fifteen minutes before speaking or singing. This produces a profuse secretion of saliva, or "watering" of the mouth and throat, just as wetting brings back the missing notes to a flute when it is too dry.

A flannel dipped in boiling water, and sprinkled with turpentine, laid on the chest as quickly as possible, will relieve the most severe cold or hoarseness.

Another simple, pleasant remedy is furnished by beating up the white of one egg, adding to it the juice of one lemon, and sweetening with white sugar to taste. Take a teaspoonful from time to time. It has been known to effectually cure the ailment.

Or, bake a lemon or sour orange twenty minutes in a moderate oven. When done, open at one end and take out the inside. Sweeten with sugar or molasses. This is an excellent remedy for hoarseness.

An old time and good way to relieve a cold is to go to bed, and stay there, *drinking nothing,* not even water, for twenty-four hours, and eating as little as possible. Or, go to bed; put your feet in hot mustard and water; put a bran or oatmeal poultice on the chest; take ten grains of Dover's powder, and an hour afterwards a pint of hot gruel; in the morning, rub the body all over with a coarse towel, and take a dose of aperient medicine.

Violet, pennyroyal, or boneset tea, is excellent to promote perspiration in case of sudden chill. Care should be taken next day not to get chilled by exposure to fresh out-door air.

MOLASSES POSSET.

This old-fashioned remedy for a cold is as effectual now as it was in old times. Put into a sauce-pan a pint of the best West India molasses, a teaspoonful of powdered white ginger, and a quarter of a pound of fresh butter. Set it over the fire, and simmer it slowly for half an hour, stirring it frequently. Do not let it come to a boil. Then stir in the juice of two lemons, or two tablespoonfuls of vinegar; cover the pan and let it stand by the fire five minutes longer. This is good for a cold. Some of it may be taken warm at once, and the remainder kept at hand for occasional use.

It is the preparation absurdly called by the common people a *stewed quaker*.

Half a pint of strained honey mixed cold with the juice of a lemon, and a tablespoonful of sweet oil, is another remedy for a cold: a teaspoonful or two to be taken whenever the cough is troublesome.

COUGH SYRUP.

Syrup of squills four ounces, syrup of tolu four ounces, tincture of bloodroot one and one-half ounces, camphorated tincture of opium four ounces. Mix. Dose for an adult, one teaspoonful repeated every two to four hours, or as often as necessary.

LEANNESS

Is caused generally by lack of power in the digestive organs to digest and assimilate the fat-producing elements of food. First restore digestion, take plenty of sleep, drink all the water the stomach will bear in the morning on rising, take moderate exercise in the open air, eat oatmeal cracked wheat, Graham mush, baked sweet apples, roasted and broiled beef; cultivate jolly people, and bathe daily.

FOR TOOTHACHE.

The worst toothache, or neuralgia coming from the teeth, may be speedily and delightfully ended by the application of a bit of clean cotton, saturated in a solution of ammonia, to the defective tooth. Sometimes the late sufferer is prompted to momentary laughter by the application, but the pain will disappear.

Alum reduced to a powder, a teaspoonful of the powder and an equal quantity of fine salt well mixed, applied to the gums by dipping your moistened finger in the mixed powder; put some also in the tooth, and keep rubbing the gums with it; it scarcely ever fails to cure.

TO CURE A STING OF A BEE OR WASP.

Bind on common baking-soda, dampened with water. Or mix common earth with water to about the consistency of mud.

TO CURE EARACHE.

Take a bit of cotton batting, put on it a pinch of black pepper, gather it up and tie it, dip it in sweet oil, and insert it in the ear; put a flannel bandage over the head to keep it warm; it often gives immediate relief.

Tobacco smoke, puffed into the ear, has oftentimes been effectual.

Another remedy: Take equal parts of tincture of opium and glycerine. Mix, and from a warm teaspoon drop two or three drops into the ear, and stop the ear tight with cotton, and repeat every hour or two. If matter should form in the ear, make a suds with castile soap and warm water about 100° F., or a little more than milk warm, and have some person inject it into the ear while you hold that side of the head the lowest. If it does not heal in due time, inject a little carbolic acid and water in the proportion of one drachm of the acid to one pint of warm water each time after using the suds.

CROUP.

Croup, it is said, can be cured in one minute, and the remedy is simply alum and sugar. Take a knife or grater, and shave off in small particles about a teaspoonful of alum; then mix it with twice its amount of sugar, to make it palatable, and administer it as quickly as possible. Almost instantaneous relief will follow. Turpentine is said to be an excellent remedy for croup. Saturate a piece of flannel, and apply it to the chest and throat, and take inwardly three or four drops on a lump of sugar.

Another remedy.—Give a teaspoonful of ipecacuanha wine every few minutes, until free vomiting is excited.

Another recipe said to be most reliable: Take two ounces of the wine of ipecac, hive syrup four ounces, tincture of bloodroot two ounces. Mix it well.

Dose, for a child one year old, five to ten drops; two years, eight to twelve drops; three years, twelve to fifteen drops; four years old, fifteen to twenty drops; five years old twenty to twenty-five drops, and older children in proportion to age. Repeat as often as shall be necessary to procure relief. If it is thought best to produce vomiting, repeat the dose every ten or fifteen minutes for a few doses.

BURNS AND SCALDS.

A piece of cotton wadding, spread with butter or sweet oil, and bound on the burn instantly, will draw out the pain without leaving a scar; also a handful of flour, bound on instantly, will prevent blistering. The object is to entirely exclude the air from the part affected. Some use common baking-soda, dry or wet, often giving instant relief, withdrawing the heat and pain. Another valuable remedy is to beat the yellow of an egg into linseed oil, and apply it with a feather on the injured part frequently. It will afford ready relief, and heals with great rapidity. Some recommend the white part of the egg, which is very cooling and soothing, and soon allays the smarting pain. It is the exposure of the part coming in contact with the air that gives the extreme discomfort experienced from ordinary afflictions of this kind, and anything which excludes air and prevents inflammation is the thing to be at once applied.

TO STOP THE FLOW OF BLOOD.

For a slight cut there is nothing better to control the hemorrhage than common unglazed brown wrapping paper, such as is used by marketmen and grocers; a piece to be bound over the wound. A handful of flour bound on the cut. Cobwebs and brown sugar, pressed on like lint. When the blood ceases to flow, apply arnica or laudanum.

When an artery is cut the red blood spurts out at each pulsation. Press the thumb firmly over the artery near the wound, and on the side towards the heart. Press hard enough to stop the bleeding, and wait till a physician comes. The wounded person is often able to do this himself, if he has the requisite knowledge.

GRAVEL.

Into a pint of water put two ounces of bicarbonate of soda. Take two tablespoonfuls in the early forenoon, and the same towards night; also drink freely of water through the day. Inflammation of the kidneys has been successfully treated with large doses of lime-water.

Persons troubled with kidney difficulties should abstain from sugar and things that are converted into sugar in digestion, such as starchy food and sweet vegetables.

SORE THROAT.

Everybody has a cure for this trouble, but simple remedies appear to be most effectual. Salt and water is used by many as a gargle, but a little alum and honey dissolved in sage tea is better. An application of cloths wrung out of hot water and applied to the neck, changing as often as they begin to cool, has the most potency for removing inflammation of anything we ever tried. It should be kept up for a number of hours; during the evening is usually the most convenient time for applying this remedy.

Cut slices of salt pork or fat bacon, simmer a few moments in hot vinegar, and apply to throat as hot as possible. When this is taken off, as the throat is relieved, put around a bandage of soft flannel. A gargle of equal parts of borax and alum, dissolved in water, is also excellent. To be used frequently.

Camphorated oil is an excellent lotion for sore throat, sore chest, aching limbs, etc. For a gargle for sore throat, put a pinch of chlorate of potash in a glass of water. Gargle the throat with it twice a day, or oftener, if necessary.

WHOOPING COUGH.

Two level tablespoonfuls of powdered alum; two-thirds of a cupful of brown sugar, dissolved in two quarts of water; bottle and put in a dark closet where it is cool.

For a child one year old, a teaspoonful three times a day on an empty stomach. For a child two years old, two teaspoonfuls for a dose. For a child five years old, a tablespoonful. The state of the bowels must be attended to, and the doses repeated accordingly. No other medicine to be taken, except an emetic, at first, if desirable. Except in the case of an infant, a milk diet is to be avoided.

DIARRHŒA.

Take tincture of Jamaica ginger one ounce, tincture of rhubarb one ounce, tincture of opium half ounce, tincture of cardamom one and one-half ounces, tincture of kino one ounce. Mix. Dose for an adult, half to one teaspoonful, repeated every two to four hours; and for children one year old, five drops; two years old, five to ten drops; three years old, ten to twelve drops, and older children in proportion to age.

FOR CONSTIPATION.

One or two figs eaten fasting is sufficient for some, and they are especially good in the case of children, as there is no trouble in getting them to take them. A spoonful of wheaten bran in a glass of water is a simple remedy, and quite effective, taken half an hour before breakfast; fruit eaten raw; partake largely of laxative food; exercise in the open air; drink freely of cold water during the day, etc. It is impossible to give many of the numerous treatments in so short a space, suffice it to say that the general character of our diet and experience is such as to assure us that at least one-quarter of the food that we swallow is intended by nature to be evacuated from the system; and if it is not, it is again absorbed into the system, poisoning the blood and producing much suffering and permanent disease. The evacuation of the bowels *daily*, and above all, *regularly*, is therefore all important to aid this form of disorder.

RELIEF FROM ASTHMA.

Sufferers from asthma should get a muskrat skin and wear it over their lungs, with the fur side next to the body. It will bring certain relief.

Or, soak blotting-paper in saltpetre water, then dry, burning at night in the patient's bedroom.

Another excellent recipe : Take powdered liquorice root, powdered elecampane root, powdered anise-seed, each one drachm, powdered ipecac ten grains, powdered lobelia ten grains; add sufficient amount of tar to form into pills of ordinary size. Take three or four pills on going to bed at night. An excellent remedy for asthma or shortness of breath.

RECIPES FOR FELONS.

Take common rock salt, as used for salting down pork or beef, dry in an oven, then pound it fine and mix with spirits of turpentine in equal parts; put it in a rag and wrap it around the parts affected; as it gets dry put on more, and in twenty-four hours you are cured. The felon will be dead.

Or purchase the herb of stramonium at the druggist's; steep it and bind it on the felon; as soon as cold, put on new, warm herbs. It will soon kill it, in a few hours at least.

Or saturate a bit or grated wild turnip, the size of a bean, with spirits of turpentine, and apply it to the affected part. It relieves the pain at once; in twelve hours there will be a hole to the bone, and the felon destroyed; then apply healing salve, and the finger is well.

Another way to cure a Felon : Fill a tumbler with equal parts of fine salt and ice; mix well. Sink the finger in the centre, allow it to remain until it is nearly frozen and numb; then withdraw it, and when sensation is restored, renew the operation four or five times, when it will be found the disease is destroyed. This must be done before pus is formed.

A simple remedy for felons, relieving pain at once, no poulticing, no cutting, no "holes to the bone," no necessity for healing salve, but simple oil of cedar applied a few times at the commencement of the felon, and the work is done.

REMEDY FOR LOCKJAW.

If any person is threatened or taken with lockjaw from injuries of the arms, legs or feet, do not wait for a doctor, but put the part injured in the following preparation: Put hot wood-ashes into water as warm as can be borne; if the injured part cannot be put into water, then wet thick folded cloths in the water and apply them to the part as soon as possible, at the same time bathe the back-bone from the neck down with some laxative stimulant—say cayenne pepper and water, or mustard and water (good vinegar is better than water); it should be as hot as the patient can bear it. Don't hesitate; go to work and do it, and don't stop until the jaws will come open. No person need die of lockjaw if these directions are followed.

Cure for Lockjaw, said to be positive.—Let any one who has an attack of lockjaw take a small quantity of spirits of turpentine, warm it, and pour it in the wound—no matter where the wound is or what its nature is—and relief will follow in less than one minute. Turpentine is also a sovereign remedy for croup. Saturate a piece of flannel with it, and place the flannel on the throat and chest —and in very severe cases, three to five drops on a lump of sugar may be taken internally.

BLEEDING AT THE NOSE.

Roll up a piece of paper and press it under the upper lip. In obstinate cases, blow a little gum arabic up the nostril through a quill, which will immediately stop the discharge; powdered alum, dissolved in water, is also good. Pressure by the finger over the small artery near the ala (wing) of the nose, on the side where the blood is flowing, is said to arrest the hemorrhage immediately. Some-times by wringing a cloth out of very hot water, and laying it on the back of the neck, gives relief. Napkins wrung out of cold water must be laid across the forehead and nose, the hands dipped in cold water, and a bottle of hot water applied to the feet.

TO TAKE CINDERS FROM THE EYE.

In most cases a simple and effective cure may be found in one or two grains of flax-seed, which can be placed in the eye without pain or injury. As they dissolve, a glutinous substance is formed, which envelops any foreign body that may be under the lid, and the whole is easily washed out. A dozen of these seeds should constitute a part of every traveller's outfit.

Another remedy for removing objects from the eye: Take a horsehair and double it, leaving a loop. If the object can be seen, lay the loop over it, close the eye, and the mote will come out as the hair is withdrawn. If the irritating object cannot be seen, raise the lid of the eye as high as possible and place the loop as far as you can, close the eye and roll the ball around a few times, draw out the hair, and the substance which caused the pain will be sure to come with it. This method is practiced by axemakers and other workers in steel

—Montreal Star.

EYE-WASHES.

The best eye-wash for granulated lids and inflammation of the eyes is composed of camphor, borax and morphine, in the following proportions: To a large wine-glass of camphor water—not spirits—add two grains of morphine and six grains of borax. Pour a few drops into the palm of the hand, and hold the eye in it, opening the lid as much as possible. Do this three or four times in twenty-four hours, and you will receive great relief from pain and smarting soreness. This recipe was received from a celebrated oculist, and has never failed to relieve the most inflamed eyes.

Another remedy said to be reliable: A lump of alum as large as a cranberry boiled in a teacupful of sweet milk, and the curd used as a poultice, is excellent for inflammation of the eyes.

Another wash : A cent's worth of pure, refined white copperas, dissolved in a pint of water, is also a good lotion; but label it *poison*, as it should never go near the mouth. Bathe the eyes with the mixture, either with the hands or a small piece of linen cloth, allowing some of the liquid to get under the lids.

Here is another from an eminent oculist : Take half an ounce of rock salt and one ounce of dry sulphate of zinc ; simmer in a clean, covered porcelain vessel with three pints of water until all are dissolved; strain through thick muslin; add one ounce of rose-water; bottle and cork it tight. To use it, mix one teaspoonful of rain-water with one of the eye-water, and bathe the eyes frequently. If it smarts too much, add more water.

SUNSTROKE.

Wrap a wet cloth bandage over the head; wet another cloth, folded small, square, cover it thickly with salt, and bind it on to the back of the neck; apply dry salt behind the ears. Put mustard plasters to the calves of the legs and soles of the feet. This is an effectual remedy.

TO REMOVE WARTS.

Wash with water saturated with common washing-soda, and let it dry without wiping; repeat frequently until they disappear. Or pass a pin through the wart and hold one end of it over the flame of a candle or lamp until the wart fires by the heat, and it will disappear.

Another treatment of warts is to pare the hard and dry skin from their tops, and then touch them with the smallest drop of strong acetic acid, taking care that the acid does not run off the wart upon the neighboring skin; for if it does, it will occasion inflammation and much pain. If this is continued once or twice daily, with regularity, paring the surface of the wart occasionally when it gets hard and dry, the wart will be soon effectually cured.

SWAIM'S VERMIFUGE.

Worm seed, two ounces; valerian, rhubarb, pink root, white agaric, senna, of each one ounce and a half. Boil in sufficient water to yield three quarts of decoction. Now add to it ten drops of the oil of tansy and forty-five drops of the oil of cloves, dissolved in a quart of rectified spirit. Dose: one tablespoonful at night.

FAINTING. (Syncope.)

Immediately place the person fainting in a lying position, with head lower than body. In this way consciousness returns immediately, while in the erect position it often ends in death.

FOR SEVERE SPRAINS.

The white of an egg, a tablespoonful of vinegar and a tablespoonful of spirits of turpentine. Mix in a bottle, shake thoroughly, and bathe the sprain as soon as possible after the accident. This was published in *Life Secrets*, but it is republished by request on account of its great value. It should be remembered by every one.

An invaluable remedy for a sprain or bruise is wormwood boiled in vinegar and applied hot, with enough cloths wrapped around it to keep the sprain moist.

CAMPHORATED OIL.

Best oil of Lucca; gum camphor. Pound some gum camphor and fill a wide-necked pint bottle one-third full; fill up with olive oil, and set away until the camphor is absorbed. Excellent lotion for sore chest, sore throat, aching limbs, etc.

LINIMENT FOR CHILBLAINS.

Spirits of turpentine, three drachms; camphorated oil, nine drachms.

Mix for a liniment. For an adult four drachms of the former and eight of the latter may be used. If the child be young, or if the skin be tender, the camphorated oil may be used without the turpentine.

32

"THE SUN'S" CHOLERA MIXTURE.

More than forty years ago, when it was found that prevention for the Asiatic cholera was easier than cure, the learned doctors of both hemispheres drew up a prescription, which was published (for working people) in *The New York Sun,* and took the name of "*The Sun Cholera Mixture.*" It is found to be the best remedy for looseness of the bowels ever yet devised. It is to be commended for several reasons. It is not to be mixed with liquor, and therefore will not be used as an alcoholic beverage. Its ingredients are well known among all the common people, and it will have no prejudice to combat; each of the materials is in equal proportions to the others, and it may therefore be compounded without professional skill; and as the dose is so very small, it may be carried in a tiny phial in the waistcoat pocket, and be always at hand. It is:

Take equal parts of tincture of cayenne, tincture of opium, tincture of rhubarb, essence of peppermint, and spirits of camphor. Mix well. Dose fifteen to thirty drops in a wine-glass of water, according to age and violence of the attack. Repeat every fifteen or twenty minutes until relief is obtained. No one who takes it in time will ever have the cholera. Even when no cholera is anticipated, it is a valuable remedy for ordinary summer complaints, and should always be kept in readiness.

COMP. CATHARTIC ELIXIR.

The only pleasant and reliable cathartic in liquid form that can be prescribed.

Each fluid ounce contains: sulph. magnesia one dr., senna two drs., scammony six grs., liquorice one dr., ginger three grs., coriander, five grs., with flavoring ingredients.

Dose.—Child five years old, one or two teaspoonfuls; adult, one or two tablespoonfuls.

This preparation is being used extensively throughout the country. It was originated with the design of furnishing a liquid cathartic remedy that could be prescribed in a palatable form. It will be taken by children with a relish.

GRANDMOTHER'S COUGH SYRUP.

Take half a pound of dry hoarhound herbs, one pod of red pepper, four tablespoonfuls of ginger, boil all in three quarts of water, then strain; and add one teaspoonful of good, fresh tar and a pound of sugar. Boil slowly and stir often, until it is reduced to one quart of syrup. When cool, bottle for use. Take one or two teaspoonfuls four or six times a day.

GRANDMOTHER'S UNIVERSAL LINIMENT.

One pint of alcohol, and as much camphor gum as can be dissolved in it, half an ounce of the oil of cedar, one-half ounce of the oil of sassafras, aqua ammonia, half an ounce, and the same amount of the tincture of morphine. Shake well together, and apply by the fire; the liniment must not be heated, or come in contact with the fire, but the rubbing to be done by the warmth of the fire.

These recipes of Grandmother's are all old, tried medicines, and are more effectual than most of those that are advertised, as they have been thoroughly tried, and proved reliable.

GRANDMOTHER'S FAMILY SPRING BITTERS.

Mandrake root, one ounce; dandelion root, one ounce; burdock root, one ounce; yellow dock root, one ounce; prickly ash berries, two ounces; marsh mallow, one ounce; turkey rhubarb, half an ounce; gentian, one ounce; English camomile flowers, one ounce; red clover tops, two ounces.

Wash the herbs and roots; put them into an earthen vessel, pour over two quarts of water that has been boiled and cooled; let it stand over night and soak; in the morning, set it on the back of the stove, and steep it five hours; it must not boil, but nearly ready to boil. Strain it through a cloth, and add half a pint of good gin. Keep it in a cool place. Half a wine-glass taken as a dose twice a day.

This is better than all the patent blood-medicines that are in the market—a superior blood purifier, and will cure almost any malignant sore, by taking according to direction, and washing the sore with a strong tea of red raspberry leaves steeped, first washing the sore with castile soap, then drying with a soft cloth, and washing it with the strong tea of red raspberry leaves.

GRANDMOTHER'S EYE-WASH.

Take three fresh eggs, and break them into one quart of clear, cold rain-water; stir until thoroughly mixed; bring to a boil on a slow fire, stirring often; then add half an ounce of sulphate of zinc (white vitriol); continue the boiling for two minutes, then set it off the fire. Take the curd that settles at the bottom of this and apply to the eye at night with a bandage. It will speedily draw out all fever and soreness. Strain the liquid through a cloth and use for bathing the eyes occasionally. This is the best eye-water ever made for man or beast. I have used it for twenty years without knowing it to fail.

HUNTER'S PILLS.

These pills can be manufactured at home, and are *truly reliable*, having been sold and used for more than fifty years in Europe. The ingredients may be procured at almost any druggist's. The articles should be all in the powder. Saffron, one grain; rue, one grain; Scot aloes, two grains; savin one grain; cayenne pepper, one grain: Mix all into a very thick mass by adding sufficient syrup. Rub some fine starch on the surface of a platter or large dinner-plate, then with your forefinger and thumb nip off a small piece of the mass the size of a pill and roll it in pill form, first dipping your fingers in the starch. Place them as fast as made on the platter, set where they will dry slowly. Put them into a dry bottle or paper box. Dose, one every night and morning as long as occasion requires.

This recipe is worth *ten times* the price of this book to any female requiring the *need* of these regulating pills.

HINTS IN REGARD TO HEALTH.

It is plainly seen by an inquiring mind that, aside from the selection and preparation of food, there are many little things constantly arising in the experience of every-day life which, in their combined effect, are powerful agents in the formation (or prevention) of perfect health. A careful observance of these little occurrences, an inquiry into the philosophy attending them, lies within the province, and indeed should be considered among the highest duties, of every housekeeper.

That one should be cautious about entering a sick room in a state of perspiration, as the moment you become cool your pores absorb. Do not approach contagious diseases with an empty stomach, nor sit between the sick and the fire, because the heat attracts the vapor.

That the flavor of cod-liver oil may be changed to the delightful one of fresh oyster, if the patient will drink a large glass of water poured from a vessel in which nails have been allowed to rust.

That a bag of hot sand relieves neuralgia.

That warm borax water will remove dandruff.

That salt should be eaten with nuts to aid digestion.

That it rests you, in sewing, to change your position frequently.

That a little soda water will relieve sick headache caused by indigestion.

That a cupful of strong coffee will remove the odor of onions from the breath.

That well-ventilated bedrooms will prevent morning headaches and lassitude.

A cupful of hot water drank before meals will relieve nausea and dyspepsia.

That a fever patient can be made cool and comfortable by frequent sponging off with soda water.

That consumptive night-sweats may be arrested by sponging the body nightly in salt water.

That one in a faint should be laid flat on his back, then loosen his clothes and let him alone.

The best time to bathe is just before going to bed, as any danger of taking cold is thus avoided; and the complexion is improved by keeping warm for several hours after leaving the bath.

To beat the whites of eggs quickly add a pinch of salt. Salt cools, and cold eggs froth rapidly.

Hot, dry flannels, applied as hot as possible, for neuralgia.

Sprains and bruises call for an application of the tincture of arnica.

If an artery is severed, tie a small cord or handkerchief above it.

For bilious colic, soda and ginger in hot water. It may be taken freely.

Tickling in the throat is best relieved by a gargling of salt and water.

Pains in the side are most promptly relieved by the application of mustard.

For cold in the head, nothing is better than powdered borax, sniffed up the nostrils.

A drink of hot, strong lemonade before going to bed will often break up a cold and cure a sore throat.

Nervous spasms are usually relieved by a little salt taken into the mouth and allowed to dissolve.

Whooping-cough paroxysms are relieved by breathing the fumes of turpentine and carbolic acid.

Broken limbs should be placed in natural positions, and the patient kept quiet until the surgeon arrives.

Hemorrhages of the lungs or stomach are promptly checked by small doses of salt. The patient should be kept as quiet as possible.

Sleeplessness caused by too much blood in the head may be overcome by applying a cloth wet with cold water to the back of the neck.

Wind colic is promptly relieved by peppermint essence, taken in a little warm water. For small children it may be sweetened. Paregoric is also good.

For stomach cramps, ginger ale or a teaspoonful of the tincture of ginger in a half glass of water in which a half teaspoonful of soda has been dissolved.

Sickness of the stomach is most promptly relieved by drinking a teacupful of hot soda and water. If it brings the offending matter up, all the better.

A teaspoonful of ground mustard in a cupful of warm water is a prompt and reliable emetic, and should be resorted to in cases of poisoning or cramps in the stomach from over-eating.

Avoid purgatives or strong physic, as they not only do no good, but are positively hurtful. Pills may relieve for the time, but they seldom cure.

Powdered rosin is the best thing to stop bleeding from cuts. After the powder is sprinkled on, wrap the wound with soft cotton cloth. As soon as the wound begins to feel feverish, keep the cloth wet with cold water.

Eggs are considered one of the best remedies for dysentery. Beaten up slightly, with or without sugar, and swallowed, they tend by their emollient qualities to lessen the inflammation of the stomach and intestines, and by forming a transient coating on those organs, enable Nature to resume her healthful sway over the diseased body. Two, or at most, three, eggs per day, would be all that is required in ordinary cases; and, since the egg is not merely medicine, but food as well, the lighter the diet otherwise, and the quieter the patient is kept, the more certain and rapid is the recovery.

Hot water is better than cold for bruises. It relieves pain quickly, and by preventing congestion often keeps off the ugly black and blue mark. "Children cry for it," when they experience the relief it affords their bumps and bruises.

For a sprained ankle, the white of eggs and powdered alum made into a plaster is almost a specific.

MEDICINAL FOOD.

Spinach has a direct effect upon complaints of the kidneys; the common dandelion, used as greens, is excellent for the same trouble; asparagus purifies the blood; celery acts admirably upon the nervous system, and is a cure for rheumatism and neuralgia; tomatoes act upon the liver; beets and turnips are excellent appetizers; lettuce and cucumbers are cooling in their effects upon the system; beans are a very nutritious and strengthening vegetable; while onions, garlic, leeks, chives and shalots, all of which are similar, possess medical virtues of a marked character, stimulating the circulatory system, and the consequent increase of the saliva and the gastric juice promoting digestion. Red onions are an excellent diuretic, and the white ones are recommended raw as a remedy for insomnia. They are tonic, nutritious. A soup made from onions is regarded by the French as an excellent restorative in debility of the digestive organs. We might go through the entire list and find each vegetable possessing its especial mission of cure, and it will be plain to every housekeeper that a vegetable diet should be partly adopted, and will prove of great advantage to the health of the family

HOUSEKEEPER'S TIME-TABLE.

	Mode of Preparation.	Time of Cooking.	Time of Digestion.
		H. M.	H. M.
Apples, sour, hard................................	Raw	......	2 50
Apples, sweet and mellow.....................	Raw	......	1 50
Asparagus..	Boiled	15 to 30	2 30
Beans (pod)......................................	Boiled	1 00	2 30
Beans with green corn.........................	Boiled	45	3 45
Beef...	Roasted	* 25	3 00
Beefsteak...	Broiled	15	3 00
Beefsteak...	Fried	15	4 00
Beef, salted......................................	Boiled	* 35	4 15
Bass, fresh.......................................	Broiled	20	3 00
Beets, young.....................................	Boiled	2 00	3 45
Beets, old..	Boiled	4 30	4 00
Bread, corn......................................	Baked	45	3 15
Bread, wheat.....................................	Baked	1 00	3 30
Butter...	Melted	......	3 30
Cabbage..	Raw	......	2 30
Cabbage and vinegar...........................	Raw	......	2 00
Cabbage..	Boiled	1 00	4 30
Cauliflower.......................................	Boiled	1-2 00	2 30
Cake, sponge....................................	Baked	45	2 30
Carrot, orange...................................	Boiled	1 00	3 15
Cheese, old.......................................	Raw	......	3 30
Chicken...	Fricasseed	1 00	3 45
Codfish, dry and whole........................	Boiled	* 15	2 00
Custard (one quart).............................	Baked	30	2 45
Duck, tame.......................................	Roasted	1 30	4 00
Duck, wild..	Roasted	1 00	4 50
Dumpling, apple................................	Boiled	1 00	3 00
Eggs, hard..	Boiled	10	3 30
Eggs, soft..	Boiled	3	3 00
Eggs...	Fried	5	3 30
Eggs...	Raw	......	2 00
Fowls, domestic, roasted or...................	Boiled	1 00	4 00
Gelatine..	Boiled	......	2 30
Goose, wild.......................................	Roasted	* 20	2 30
Lamb..	Boiled	* 20	2 30
Meat and vegetables...........................	Hashed	30	2 30
Milk...	Raw	......	2 15
Milk...	Boiled	......	2 00
Mutton..	Roast	* 25	3 15
Mutton..	Broiled	20	3 00
Onions..	Boiled	1-2 00	3 00
Oysters...	Roasted	......	3 15
Oysters...	Stewed	5	3 30
Parsnips..	Boiled	1 00	3 00
Pigs' feet...	Soused	......	1 00
Pork...	Roast	* 30	5 15
Pork...	Boiled	* 25	4 30
Pork, raw or......................................	Fried	......	4 15
Pork...	Broiled	20	3 15
Potatoes..	Boiled	30	3 30
Potatoes..	Baked	45	3 30
Potatoes..	Roasted	45	2 30
Rice...	Boiled	20	1 00
Salmon, fresh....................................	Boiled	8	1 45
Sausage...	Fried	25	4 00
Sausage...	Broiled	20	3 30
Soup, vegetable.................................	Boiled	1 00	4 00
Soup, chicken....................................	Boiled	2 00	3 00
Soup, oyster or mutton.........................	Boiled	†3 30	3 30
Spinach...	Boiled	1-2 00	2 30
Tapioca...	Boiled	1 30	2 00
Tomatoes...	Fresh	1 00	2 30
Tomatoes...	Canned	30	2 30
Trout, salmon, fresh, boiled or...............	Fried	30	1 30
Turkey, boiled or................................	Roasted	* 20	2 30
Turnips...	Boiled	45	3 30
Veal...	Broiled	20	4 00
Venison steak....................................	Broiled	20	1 35

* Minutes to the pound.   † Mutton soup.
The time given is the general average; the time will vary slightly with the quality of the article.

USES OF AMMONIA.

All housekeepers should keep a bottle of liquid ammonia, as it is the most powerful and useful agent for cleaning silks, stuffs and hats, in fact cleans everything it touches. A few drops of ammonia in water will take off grease from dishes, pans, etc., does not injure the hands as much as the use of soda and strong chemical soaps. A spoonful in a quart of warm water for cleaning paint, makes it look like new, and so with everything that needs cleaning.

Spots on towels and hosiery will disappear with little trouble if a little ammonia is put into enough water to soak the articles, and they are left in it an hour or two before washing; and if a cupful is put into the water in which clothes are soaked the night before washing, the ease with which the articles can be washed, and their great whiteness and clearness when dried, will be very gratifying. Remembering the small sum paid for three quarts of ammonia of common strength, one can easily see that no bleaching preparation can be more cheaply obtained.

No articles in kitchen use are so likely to be neglected and abused as the dish-cloths and dish-towels; and in washing these, ammonia, if properly used, is a greater comfort than anywhere else. Put a teaspoonful into the water in which these clothes are, or should be washed every day; rub soap on the towels. Put them in the water; let them stand half an hour or so; then rub them out thoroughly, rinse faithfully, and dry out-doors in clear air and sun, and dish-cloths and towels need never look gray and dingy—a perpetual discomfort to all housekeepers.

A dark carpet often looks dusty soon after it has been swept, and you know it does not need sweeping again; so wet a cloth or a sponge, wring it almost dry, and wipe off the dust. A few drops of ammonia in the water will brighten the colors.

For cleaning hair-brushes it is excellent; put a tablespoonful into the water, having it only tepid, and dip up and down until clean; then dry with the brushes down, and they will be like new ones.

When employed in washing anything that is not especially soiled, use the waste water afterward for the house plants that are taken down from their usual position and immersed in the tub of water. Ammonia is a fertilizer, and helps to keep healthy the plants it nourishes. In every way, in fact, ammonia is the housekeeper's friend.

Ammonia is not only useful for cleaning, but as a household medicine. Half a teaspoonful taken in half a tumbler of water is far better for faintness than alcoholic stimulants. In the Temperance Hospital, in London, it is used with the best results. It was used freely by Lieutenant Greely's Artic party for keeping up circulation. It is a relief in nervousness, headache, and heart disturbances.

TO DESTROY INSECTS AND VERMIN.

Dissolve two pounds of alum in three or four quarts of water. Let it remain over night, till all the alum is dissolved. Then, with a brush, apply, boiling hot, to every joint or crevice in the closet or shelves where croton bugs, ants, cockroaches, etc., intrude; also to the joints and crevices of bedsteads, as bed bugs dislike it as much as croton bugs, roaches, or ants. Brush all the cracks in the floor and mopboards. Keep it boiling hot while using.

To keep woolens and furs from moths, be sure that none are in the articles when they are put away; then take a piece of strong brown paper, with not a hole through which even a pin can enter. Put the article in it, with several lumps of gum camphor between the folds. Place this in a close box or trunk. Cover every joint with paper. A piece of cotton cloth, if thick and firm, will answer. Wherever a knitting-needle can pass, the parent moth can enter.

Place pieces of camphor, cedar-wood, Russia leather, tobacco-leaves, whole cloves, or anything strongly aromatic, in the drawers or boxes where furs and other things to be preserved from moths are kept, and they will never be harmed. Mice never get into drawers or trunks where gum camphor is placed.

Another recipe:—Mix half a pint of alcohol, the same quantity of turpentine, and two ounces of camphor. Keep in a stone bottle, and shake well before using. The clothes or furs are to be wrapped in linen, and crumbled-up pieces of blotting-paper dipped in the liquid to be placed in the box with them, so that it smells strong. This requires renewing but once a year.

Another authority says that a positive, sure recipe is this: Mix equal quantities of pulverized borax, camphor gum and saltpetre together, making a powder. Sprinkle it dry under the edges of carpets, in drawers, trunks, etc., etc. It will also keep out all kinds of insects, if plentifully used. If the housekeeper will begin at the top of her house with a powder bellows and a large quantity of this fresh powder, and puff it thoroughly into every crack and crevice, whether or not there are croton bugs in them, to the very bottom of her house, special attention being paid to old furniture, closets, and wherever croton water is introduced, she will be freed from these torments. The operation may require a repetition, but the end is success.

MOTHS IN CARPETS.

If you fear that they are at work at the edge of the carpet, it will sometimes suffice to lay a wet towel, and press a hot flat-iron over it; but the best way is to take the carpet up, and clean it, and give a good deal of attention to the floor. Look in the cracks, and if you discover signs of moths, wash the floor with benzine, and scatter red pepper on it before putting the carpet lining down.

Heavy carpets sometimes do not require taking up every year, unless in constant use. Take out the tacks from these, fold the carpets back, wash the floor in strong suds with a tablespoonful of borax dissolved in them. Dash with insect powder, or lay with tobacco leaves along the edge, and retack. Or use turpentine, the enemy of buffalo moths, carpet worms and other insects that injure and destroy carpets. Mix the turpentine with pure water in the proportion of three tablespoonfuls to three quarts of water, and then after the carpet has been well swept, go over each breadth carefully with a sponge dipped in the solution and wrung nearly dry. Change the water as often as it becomes dirty. The carpet will be nicely cleaned as well as disinfected. All moths can be kept away and the eggs destroyed by this means. Spots may be renovated by the use of ox-gall or ammonia and water.

A good way to brighten a carpet is to put a half tumbler of spirits of turpentine in a basin of water, and dip your broom in it and sweep over the carpet once or twice, and it will restore the color and brighten it up until you would think it new. Another good way to clean old carpets is to rub them over with meal; just dampen it a very little and rub the carpet with it, and when perfectly dry, sweep over with meal. After a carpet is thoroughly swept, rub it with a cloth dipped in water and ammonia: it will brighten the colors and make it look like new.

TO TAKE OUT MACHINE GREASE.

Cold water, a tablespoonful of ammonia, and soap, will take out machine grease where other means would not answer on account of colors running, etc.

TO WASH FLANNELS.

The first thing to consider in washing flannels so that they retain their size, is, that the article be *washed* and *rinsed* in water of the *same temperature*, that is, about as warm as the hands can bear, and not allowed to cool between. The water should be a strong suds. Rub through two soapy waters; wring them out, and put into plenty of clear, clean, warm water to rinse. Then into another of the same temperature, blued a little. Wring, shake them well, and hang up. Do not take out of this warm water and hang out in a freezing air, as that certainly tends to shrink them. It is better to dry them in the house, unless the sun shines. They should dry *quickly*. Colored flannels should never be washed in the same water after white clothes, or they will be covered, when dry, with lint; better be washed in a water for themselves. In washing worsted, such as merino dress goods, pursue the same course, only do not wring them hard; shake, hang them up and let drain. While a little damp, bring in and press smoothly on the wrong side with as hot an iron as can be used without scorching the goods.

Flannels that have become yellow from being badly washed, may be nicely whitened by soaking them two or three hours in a lather made of one-quarter of a pound of soft soap, two tablespoonfuls of powdered borax, and two table-spoonfuls of carbonate of ammonia, dissolved in five or six gallons of water.

TO STARCH, FOLD AND IRON SHIRTS.

To three tablespoonfuls of dry, fine starch allow a quart of water. First wet the starch smooth in a little cold water in a tin pan, put into it a little pinch of salt and a piece of enamel, or shirt polish, the size of a bean, or a piece of clean tallow, or a piece of butter the size of a cranberry; pour over this a quart of *boiling* water, stirring rapidly, placing it over the fire. Cook until clear, then remove it from the fire and set the pan in another of warm water to keep the starch warm.

Turn the shirt wrong side out and dip the bosom in the hot starch as warm as the hands can bear the heat; rub the starch evenly through the linen, saturating it thoroughly; wring hard to make dry as possible. Starch the collar and wristbands the same way; then hang them out to dry. Three hours before ironing them, wet the bosoms and cuffs in cold water, wring out, shake and fold, roll up tightly, wrap in a towel and let remain two or three hours.

The back of the shirt should be ironed first by doubling it lengthwise through the centre, the wristbands may be ironed next, and both sides of the sleeves;

then the collar band; now place a bosom board under the bosom and with a fresh clean napkin dampened a little, rub the bosom from the top towards the bottom, arranging and smoothing each plait neatly; then with a smooth, moderately hot flat-iron, begin ironing from the top downward, pressing hard until the bosom becomes smooth dry and glossy. Remove the bosom board and iron the front, fold both sides of the shirt towards the centre of the back, fold together below the bosom and hang on the bars to air.

CLEANING OIL-CLOTHS.

A dingy oil-cloth may be brightened by washing it with clear water with a little borax dissolved in it; wipe it with a flannel cloth that you have dipped into milk, and then wring as dry as possible.

TO CLEAN BLACK LACE. No. 1.

A teaspoonful of gum arabic, dissolved in one teacupful of boiling water; when cool, add half a teaspoonful of black ink; dip the lace and spread smoothly between the folds of a newspaper and press dry with book or the like. Lace shawls can be dressed over in this way, by pinning a sheet to the carpet, and stretching the shawl upon that; or black lace can be cleaned the same as ribbon and silk. Take an old kid glove (black preferable), no matter how old, and boil it in a pint of water for a short time; then let it cool until the leather can be taken in the hand without burning; use the glove to sponge off the ribbon; if the ribbon is very dirty, dip it into water and draw through the fingers a few times before sponging. After cleaning, lay a piece of paper over the ribbon, and iron; paper is better than cloth. The ribbon will look like new.

TO CLEAN BLACK LACE. No. 2.

Black laces of all kinds may be cleaned by alcohol. Throw them boldly into the liquid; churn them up and down till they foam; if very dusty, use the second dose of alcohol; squeeze them out, " spat " them, pull out the edges, lay them between brown paper, smooth and straight; leave under a heavy weight till dry; do not iron.

TO WASH WHITE LACE. No. 1.

First, the soiled laces should be carefully removed from the garment and folded a number of times, keeping the edges evenly together, then basted with a coarse thread without a knot in the end. Now put them in a basin of luke-warm suds. After soaking a half hour, rub them carefully between the hands, renewing the suds several times; then, after soaping them well, place them in *cold* water and let them come to a scald. Take them from this and rinse them thoroughly in luke-warm water, blued a very little, then dip them into a *very thin*, clear starch, allowing a teaspoonful of starch to a pint of water, so thin that it will be scarcely perceptible. Now roll them in a clean, fresh towel without taking out the bastings; let them lie for an hour or more; iron over several thicknesses of flannel, taking out the bastings of one piece at a time, and ironing on the wrong side, with a moderately hot iron; the laces should be nearly dry, and the edges and points pulled gently with the fingers into shape, before ironing.

TO WASH WHITE THREAD LACE. No. 2.

To wash white lace, cover a bottle with linen, stitched smoothly to fit the shape. Wind the lace about it, basting both edges to the linen. Wash on the bottle, soaping and rinsing well, then boil in soft water. Dry in the sun. Clip the basting threads and do not iron. If carefully done, it will look like new lace.

TO CLEAN SILKS OR RIBBONS.

Half a pint of gin, half a pound of honey, half a pound of soft soap, one-eighth of a pint of water.

Mix the above ingredients together; then lay each breadth of silk upon a clean kitchen table or dresser, and scrub it well on the soiled side with the mixture. Have ready three vessels of cold water; take each piece of silk at two corners, and dip it up and down in each vessel, but do not wring it; and take care that each breadth has one vessel of quite clean water for the last dip. Hang it up dripping for a minute or two, then dab in a cloth, and iron it quickly with a very hot iron.

Where the lace or silk is very much soiled, it is best to pass them through a warm liquor of bullock's gall and water; rinse in cold water; then take a small piece of glue, pour boiling water on it, and pass the veil through it; clap it, and frame to dry. Instead of framing, it may be fastened with drawing-pins closely fixed upon a very clean paste, or drawing-board.

TO CLEAN BLACK DRESS SILKS.

One of the things "not generally known," at least in this country, is the Parisian method of cleaning black silk; the *modus operandi* is very simple, and the result infinitely superior to that achieved in any other manner. The silk must be thoroughly brushed and wiped with a cloth, then laid flat on a board or table, and well-sponged with hot coffee, thoroughly freed from sediment by being strained through muslin. The silk is sponged on the side intended to show;

it is allowed to become partially dry, and then ironed on the wrong side. The coffee removes every particle of grease, and restores the brilliancy of silk, without imparting to it either the shiny appearance or crackly and papery stiffness obtained by beer, or, indeed, any other liquid. The silk really appears thickened by the process, and this good effect is permanent. Our readers who will experimentalize on an apron or cravat, will never again try any other method.

TO WASH FEATHERS.

Wash in warm soap-suds and rinse in water a very little blued; if the feather is white, then let the wind dry it. When the curl has come out by washing the feather or getting it damp, place a hot flat-iron so that you can hold the feather just above it while curling. Take a bone or silver knife, and draw the fibres of the feather between the thumb and the dull edge of the knife, taking not more than three fibres at a time, beginning at the point of the feather and curling one-half the other way. The hot iron makes the curl more durable. After a little practice one can make them look as well as new feathers. Or they can be curled by holding them over the stove or range, not near enough to burn; withdraw, and shake out; then hold them over again, until they curl. When swansdown becomes soiled, it can be washed and look as well as new. Tack strips on a piece of muslin and wash in warm water with white soap, then rinse and hang in the wind to dry. Rip from the muslin, and rub carefully between the fingers to soften the leather.

INCOMBUSTIBLE DRESSES.

By putting an ounce of alum or sal ammoniac in the *last* water in which muslins or cottons are rinsed, or a similar quantity in the starch in which they are stiffened, they will be rendered almost uninflammable; or, at least, will with difficulty take the fire, and if they do, will burn without flame. It is astonishing that this simple precaution is so rarely adopted. Remember this and save the lives of your children.

HOW TO FRESHEN UP FURS.

Furs when taken out in the fall are often found to have a mussed, crushed-out appearance. They can be made to look like new, by following these simple directions: Wet the fur with a hair-brush, brushing up the wrong way of the fur. Leave it to dry in the air for about half an hour, and then give it a good beating on the right side with a rattan. After beating it, comb it with a coarse comb, combing up the right way of the fur.

NOVEL DRESS MENDING.

A novel way of mending a woolen or silk dress in which a round hole has been torn, and where only a patch could remedy matters, is the following: The frayed portions around the tear should be carefully smoothed, and a piece of the material, moistened with very thin mucilage, placed under the hole. A heavy weight should be put upon it until it is dry, when it is only possible to discover the mended place by careful observation.

TO RENEW OLD CRAPE.

Place a little water in a teakettle, and let it boil until there is plenty of steam from the spout; then, holding the crape in both hands, pass it to and fro several times through the steam, and it will be clean and look nearly equal to new.

TO RAISE THE PILE ON VELVET.

To raise the pile on velvet, put on a table two pieces of wood; place between them, bottom side up, three very hot flat-irons, and over them lay a wet cloth; hold the velvet over the cloth, with the wrong side down; when thoroughly steamed, brush the pile with a light wisp, and the velvet will look as good as new.

TO CLEAN KID GLOVES.

Make a thick mucilage by boiling a handful of flax-seed; add a little dissolved toilet soap; then, when the mixture cools, put the glove on the hands and rub them with a piece of white flannel wet with the mixture. Do not wet the gloves through. Or take a fine, clean, soft cloth, dip it into a little sweet milk, then rub it on a cake of soap, and rub the gloves with it; they will look like new.

Another good way to clean any color of kid gloves is to pour a little benzine into a basin and wash the gloves in it, rubbing and squeezing them until clean. If much soiled, they must be washed through clean benzine, and rinsed in a fresh supply. Hang up in the air to dry.

STARCH POLISH.

Take one ounce of spermaceti and one ounce of white wax; melt and run it into a thin cake on a plate. A piece the size of a quarter dollar added to a quart of prepared starch gives a beautiful lustre to the clothes and prevents the iron from sticking.

FOR CLEANING JEWELRY.

For cleaning jewelry there is nothing better than ammonia and water. If very dull or dirty, rub a little soap on a soft brush and brush them in this wash, rinse in cold water, dry first in an old handkerchief, and then rub with buck or chamois skin. Their freshness and brilliancy when thus cleaned cannot be surpassed by any compound used by jewelers.

TO CLEAN SILVER PLATE.

Wash well in strong, warm soap-suds, rinse and wipe dry with a dry, soft cloth; then mix as much hartshorn powder as will be required into a thick paste, with cold water; spread this over the silver, with a soft cloth, and leave it for a little time to dry. When perfectly dry, brush it off with a clean soft cloth, or brush and polish it with a piece of chamois skin. Hartshorn is one of the best possible ingredients for plate powder for daily use. It leaves on the silver a deep, dark polish, and at the same time does not injure it. Whiting, dampened with liquid ammonia, is excellent also.

TO REMOVE STAINS FROM MARBLE.

Mix together one-half pound of soda, one-half pound of soft soap, and one pound of whiting. Boil them until they become as thick as paste, and let it cool. Before it is quite cold, spread it over the surface of the marble and leave it at least a whole day. Use a soft water to wash it off, and rub it well with soft cloths. For a black marble, nothing is better than spirits of turpentine.

Another paste answers the same purpose: Take two parts of soda, one of pumice-stone, and one of finely-powdered chalk. Sift these through a fine sieve, and mix them into a paste with water. Rub this well all over the marble, and the stains will be removed; then wash it with soap and water, and a beautiful bright polish will be produced.

TO WHITEN WALLS.

To whiten walls, scrape off all the old whitewash, and wash the walls with a solution of two ounces of white vitriol to four gallons of water. Soak a quarter of a pound of white glue in water for twelve hours; strain and place in a tin pail in a kettle of boiling water. When melted, stir in the glue eight pounds of whiting and water enough to make it as thick as common whitewash. Apply evenly with a good brush. If the walls are very yellow, blue the water slightly by squeezing in it a flannel blue-bag.

Before kalsomining a wall, all cracks should be plastered over. Use plaster of Paris. Kalsomine may be colored easily by mixing with it yellow ochre, Spanish brown, indigo; squeeze through a bag into the water, etc.

PAPER-HANGERS' PASTE.

To make paper-hangers' paste, beat up four pounds of good, white, wheat flour (well sifted previously) in sufficient cold water to form a stiff batter. Beat it well in order to take out all lumps, and then add enough cold water to make the mixture of the consistency of pudding batter. To this add about two ounces of well-pounded alum. Pour gently and quickly over the batter boiling water, stirring rapidly at the same time, and when it is seen to lose the white color of the flour, it is cooked and ready. Do not use it, however, while hot, but allow it to cool. Pour about a pint of cold water over the top to prevent a skin from forming. Before using, the paste should be thinned by the addition of cold water.

TO WASH COLORED GARMENTS.

Delicately colored socks and stockings are apt to fade in washing. If they are soaked for a night in a pail of tepid water containing a half pint of turpentine, then wrung out and dried, the colors will "set," and they can afterwards be washed without fading.

For calicoes that fade, put a teaspoonful of sugar of lead into a pailful of water and soak the garment fifteen minutes before washing.

THE MARKING SYSTEM.

Mark all your own personal wardrobe which has to be washed. If this were invariably done, a great deal of property would be saved and a great deal of trouble would be spared. For the sake of saving trouble to others, if for no other reason, all of one's handkerchiefs, collars and underclothing should be plainly and permanently marked. A bottle of indelible ink is cheap, a clean pen still cheaper, and a bright, sunny day or a hot flat-iron will complete the business. Always keep on hand a stick of linen tape, written over its whole length with your name, or the names of your family, ready to be cut off and sewed on to stockings and such other articles as do not afford a good surface on which to mark.

Then there are the paper patterns, of which every mother has a store. On the outside of each, as it is tied up, the name of the pattern should be plainly written. There are the rolls of pieces, which may contain a good deal not apparent from the outside. All these hidden mysteries should be indicated. The winter things, which are wrapped up and put away for summer, and the summer things, which are wrapped up and put away for the winter, should all be in labeled packages, and every packing trunk should have on its lid a complete list of its contents.

—Congregationalist.

33

TO REMOVE STAINS AND SPOTS.

Children's clothes, table linens, towels, etc., should be thoroughly examined before wetting, as soap-suds, washing-fluids, etc., will fix almost any stain past removal. Many stains will pass away by being simply washed in pure, soft water; or alcohol will remove, before the article has been in soap-suds, many stains; iron-mold, mildew, or almost any similar spot, can be taken out by dipping in diluted citric acid; then cover with salt and lay in the bright sun till the stain disappears. If of long standing, it may be necessary to repeat the wetting and the sunlight. Be careful to rinse in several waters as soon as the stain is no longer visible. Ink, fruit, wine, and mildew stains must first be washed in clear, cold water, removing as much of the spots as can be; then mix one teaspoonful of oxalic acid, and a half pint of rain water. Dip the stain in this, and wipe off in clear water. Wash at once, if a fabric that will bear washing. A tablespoonful of white currant juice, if any can be had, is even better than lemon. This preparation may be used on the most delicate articles without injury. Shake it up before using it. Mark it "poison," and put it where it will not be meddled with.

OIL STAINS IN SILK AND OTHER FABRICS.

Benzine is most effectual, not only for silk, but for any other material whatever. It can be procured from any druggist. By simply covering both sides of greased silk with magnesia, and allowing it to remain for a few hours, the oil is absorbed by the powder. Should the first application be insufficient, it may be repeated, and even rubbed in with the hand. Should the silk be Tussah or Indian silk, it will wash.

To remove an acid stain on violet silk: Brush the discoloration with tincture of iodine, then saturate the spot well with a solution of hypo-sulphite of soda, and dry gradually. This restores the original color perfectly.

Muriatic acid is successfully used for removing ink stains and iron mold on a number of colors which it does not attack.

Sulphurous acid is only employed for whitening undyed goods, straw hats, etc., and for removing the stains of certain fruits on silks and woolens. Sulphurous gas is also used for this purpose, but the liquid gas is safer.

Oxalic acid is used for removing ink and rust stains, and remnants of mud stains, which do not yield to other deterrents. It may also be used for destroying the stains of fruits and astringent juices, and old stains of urine. However, its use is limited to white goods, as it attacks fugitive colors, and even light shades of those reputed to be fast. The best method of applying it is to dissolve it in cold or lukewarm water, to let it remain a moment upon the spot, and then rub it with the fingers. Wash out in clear, warm water, immediately.

Citric acid serves to revive and brighten certain colors, especially greens and yellows. It restores scarlets which have been turned to a crimson by the action of alkalies. Acetic acid or tartaric acid may be used instead.

Where it is feared that soap may change the color of an article, as, for instance, scarlet hosiery or lilac print, if the garment be not badly soiled, it may be cleansed by washing without soap in water in which pared potatoes have been boiled. This method will also prevent color from running in washing prints.

To prevent blue from running into a white ground, dissolve a teaspoonful of copperas in a pailful of soft water, add a piece of lime the size of an acorn, and soak the garments in this water two hours before washing. To keep colors from running in washing black prints, put a teaspoonful of black pepper in the first water.

Salt or beef's gall in the water helps to set black. A tablespoonful of spirits of turpentine to a gallon of water sets most blues, and alum is very efficacious in setting green. Black or very dark calicoes should be stiffened with gum arabic —five cents worth is enough for a dress. If however, starch is used, the garment should be turned wrong side out.

A simple way to remove grass stains is to spread butter on them, and lay the article in hot sunshine, or wash in alcohol. Fruit stains upon cloth or the hands may be removed by rubbing with the juice of ripe tomatoes. If applied immediately, powdered starch will also take fruit stains out of table linen. Left on the spot for a few hours, it absorbs every trace of the stain.

For mildew stains or iron-rust, mix together soft soap, laundry starch, half as much salt, and the juice of a lemon. Apply to the spots, and spread the garment on the grass. Or wet the linen, rub into it white soap, then finely powdered chalk; lay upon the grass and keep damp. Old mildew stains may be removed by rubbing yellow soap on both sides, and afterwards laying on, very thick, starch which has been dampened. Rub in well, and expose to light and air.

There are several effectual methods of removing grease from cloths. First, wet with a linen cloth dipped in chloroform. Second, mix four tablespoonfuls of alcohol with one tablespoonful of salt; shake together until the salt is dissolved, and apply with a sponge. Third, wet with weak ammonia water; then lay a thin white blotting or tissue paper over it, and iron lightly with an iron not too hot. Fourth, apply a mixture of equal parts of alcohol, gin, and ammonia.

Candle grease yields to a warm iron. Place a piece of blotting or other absorbing paper under the absorbing fabric; put a piece of the paper also on the spot, apply the warm iron to the paper, and as soon as a spot of grease appears, move the paper and press again until the spot disappears. Lard will remove wagon grease. Rub the spot with the lard as if washing it, and when it is well out, wash in the ordinary way with soap and water until thoroughly cleansed.

To make linen beautifully white, prepare the water for washing by putting into every ten gallons a large handful of powdered borax; or boil with the clothes one teaspoonful of spirits of turpentine.

Fruit stains may be taken out by boiling water. Place the material over a basin or other vessel, and pour the boiling water from the kettle over the stains.

Pure water, cold or hot, mixed with acids, serves for rinsing goods in order to remove foreign and neutral bodies which cover the color. Steam softens fatty matters, and thus facilitates their removal by reagents.

Sulphuric acid may be used in certain cases, particularly for brightening and raising greens, reds, yellows, etc., but it must be diluted with at least one hundred times its weight of water and more in cases of delicate shades.

CEMENT FOR CHINA AND GLASS.

To half a pint of milk put an equal quantity of vinegar in order to curdle it; then separate the curd from the whey, and mix the whey with the whites of four or five eggs, beating the whole well together. When it is well-mixed, add a little quick-lime, through a sieve, until it has acquired the consistence of a thick paste. With this cement broken vessels and cracks of all kinds may be mended. It dries quickly, and resists the action of fire and water.

Another: Into a thick solution of gum arabic, stir plaster of Paris until the mixture assumes the consistency of cream, apply with a brush to the broken edges of china and join together. In three days the article cannot be broken in the same place. The whiteness of the cement adds to its value.

CLEANSING SINKS.

To purify greasy sinks and pipes, pour down a pailful of boiling water in which three or four pounds of washing soda have been dissolved. A disinfectant is prepared in the same way, using copperas. Copperas is a poison and should not be left about.

Leaks in waste pipes:—Shut yourself into a room from which the pipe starts. Put two or three ounces of oil of peppermint into a pail of boiling hot water and pour down the pipe. Another person who has not yet inhaled the strong odor should follow the course of the pipe through the house. The peppermint will be pretty sure to discover a break that even an expert plumber might overlook.

—The Examiner.

MANAGEMENT OF STOVES.

If the fire in a stove has plenty of fresh coals on top not yet burned through it will need only a little shaking to start it up; but if the fire looks dying and the coals look white, don't shake it. When it has drawn till it is red again, if there is much ash and little fire, put coals on very carefully. A mere handful of fire can be coaxed back to life by adding another handful or so of new coals on the red spot, and giving plenty of draught, but don't shake a dying fire, or you lose it. This management is often necessary after a warm spell, when the stove has been kept dormant for days, though I hope you will not be so unfortunate as to have a fire to coax up on a cold winter morning. They should be arranged over night, so that all that is required is to open the draughts in order to have a cheery glow in a few minutes.

—Good Housekeeping.

TO REMOVE INK FROM CARPETS.

When freshly spilled, ink can be removed from carpets by wetting in milk. Take cotton batting and soak up all of the ink that it will receive, being careful not to let it spread. Then take fresh cotton, wet in milk, and sop it up carefully. Repeat this operation, changing cotton and milk each time. After most of the ink has been taken up in this way, with fresh cotton and clean, rub the spot. Continue till all disappears; then wash the spot in clean warm water and a little soap; rinse in clear water and rub till nearly dry. If the ink is dried in, we know of no way that will not take the color from the carpet as well as the ink, unless the ink is on a white spot. In that case, salts of lemon, or soft soap, starch, and lemon juice, will remove the ink as easily as if on cotton.

TO TAKE RUST OUT OF STEEL.

If possible, place the article in a bowl containing kerosene oil, or wrap the steel up in a soft cloth well-saturated with kerosene; let it remain twenty-four hours or longer; then scour the rusty spots with brick dust; if badly rusted, use salt wet with hot vinegar; after scouring rinse every particle of brick dust or salt off with boiling hot water; dry thoroughly with flannel cloths, and place near the fire to make sure; then polish off with a clean flannel cloth and a little sweet oil.

TO MAKE A PASTE OR MUCILAGE TO FASTEN LABELS.

Soften good glue in water, then boil it with strong vinegar, and thicken the liquid, during boiling, with fine wheat flour, so that a paste results; or starch paste, with which a little Venice turpentine has been incorporated while it was warm.

A recipe for a transparent cement which possesses great tenacity and has not the slightest yellow tinge: Mix in a well-stoppered bottle ten drachms of chloroform with ten and one-half of non-vulcanized caoutchouc (rubber) cut in small pieces. Solution is readily effected, and when it is completed add two and one-half drachms of mastic. Let the whole macerate from eight to ten days without the application of any heat, and shake the contents of the bottle at intervals. A perfectly white and very adhesive cement is the result.

POSTAGE STAMP MUCILAGE.

Take of gum dextrine, two parts; acetic acid, one part; water, five parts. Dissolve in a water bath and add alcohol one part.

—*Scientific American.*

Gum of great strength, which will also keep for a long time, is prepared by dissolving equal parts of gum arabic and gum tragacanth in vinegar. A little vinegar added to ordinary gum water will make it keep much better.

FAMILY GLUE.

Crack the glue and put it in a bottle; add common whiskey; shake up, cork tight, and in three or four days it can be used. It requires no heating, will keep for almost any length of time, and is at all times ready to use, except in the coldest of weather, when it will require warming. It must be kept tight, so that the whiskey will not evaporate. The usual corks or stoppers should not be used. It will become clogged. A tin stopper covering the bottle, but fitting as closely as possible, must be used.

GLUE.

Glue to resist *heat* and *moisture* is made as follows: Mix a handful of quicklime in four ounces of linseed oil, boil to a good thickness, then spread it on tin plates in the shade, and it will become very hard, but may be easily dissolved over the fire as glue.

A glue which will resist the action of water is made by boiling one pound of common glue in two quarts of skimmed milk.

FURNITURE CREAM.

Shred finely two ounces of beeswax and half an ounce of white wax into half a pint of turpentine; set in a warm place until dissolved, then pour over the mixture the following, boiled together until melted:—Half a pint of water, an ounce of castile soap, and a piece of resin the size of a small nutmeg. Mix thoroughly, and keep in a wide-necked stone bottle for use. This cleans well, and leaves a good polish, and may be made at a fourth of the price it is sold at.

CEMENT CRACKS IN FLOOR.

Cracks in floors may be neatly but permanently filled by thoroughly soaking newspapers in paste made of half a pound of flour, three quarts of water and half a pound of alum mixed and boiled. The mixture will be about as thick as putty, and may be forced into the crevice with a case knife. It will harden like papier-mache.

A POLISH FOR LADIES' KID SHOES.

A fine liquid polish for ladies' kid shoes, satchels, etc., that is easy of application, recommended as containing no ingredients in any manner injurious to leather, is found by digesting in a close vessel at gentle heat, and straining, a solution made as follows: lamplack, one drachm; oil turpentine, four drachms; alcohol, (trymethyl), twelve ounces; shellac, one and one-half ounces; white turpentine, five drachms; saudarac, two drachms.

PASTE FOR SCRAP-BOOKS, ETC.

Paste that will keep.—Dissolve a teaspoonful of alum in a quart of water. When cold, stir in flour, to give it the consistency of thick cream, being particular to beat up all the lumps. Stir in as much powdered resin as will lie on a dime, and throw in half a dozen cloves to give it a pleasant odor. Have on the fire a teacupful of boiling water; pour the flour mixture into it, stirring well all the time. In a few minutes it will be of the consistency of molasses. Pour it into an earthen or china vessel, let it cool, and stir in a small teaspoonful each of oil of cloves and of sassafras; lay a cover on, and put in a cool place. When needed for use, take out a portion and soften it with warm water. This is a fine paste to use to stiffen embroidery.

TO REMOVE INDELIBLE INK.

Most indelible inks contain nitrate of silver, the stain of which may be removed by first soaking in a solution of common salt, and afterward washing with ammonia. Or use solution of ten grains of cyanide of potassium and five grains of iodine to one ounce of water, or a solution of eight parts each bichloride of mercury and chloride of ammonium in one hundred and twenty-five parts of water.

A CEMENT FOR ACIDS.

A cement which is proof against boiling acids may be made by a composition of India rubber, tallow, lime and red lead. The India rubber must first be melted by a gentle heat, and then six to eight per cent. by weight of tallow is added to the mixture while it is kept well-stirred; next day slaked lime is applied, until the fluid mass assumes a consistency similar to that of soft paste; lastly, twenty per cent. of red lead is added, in order to make it harden and dry.

TO KEEP CIDER.

Allow three-fourths of a pound of sugar to the gallon, the whites of six eggs, well beaten, a handful of common salt. Leave it open until fermentation ceases, then bung up. This process a dealer in cider has used for years, and always successfully.

Another recipe:—To keep cider sweet allow it to work until it has reached the state most desirable to the taste, and then add one and a half tumblers of grated horse-radish to each barrel, and shake up well. This arrests further fermentation. After remaining a few weeks, rack off and bung up closely in clean casks.

A gentleman of Denver writes he has a sure preservative: Put eight gallons of cider at a time into a clean barrel; take one ounce of powdered charcoal; and one ounce of powdered sulphur; mix, and put it into some iron vessel that will go down through the bung-hole of the barrel. Now put a piece of red-hot iron into the charcoal and sulphur, and while it is burning, lower it through the bung-hole to within one foot of the cider, and suspend it there by a piece of wire. Bring it up and in twelve hours you can cure another batch. Put the cider in a tight barrel and keep in a cool cellar and it will keep for years.

A Holland recipe:—To one quart of new milk, fresh from the cow (not strained), add one-half pound of ground black mustard seed and six eggs. Beat the whole well together, and pour into a barrel of cider. It will keep cider sweet for one year or more.

TO BLEACH COTTON CLOTH.

Take one large spoonful of sal soda and one pound of chloride lime for thirty yards; dissolve in clean, soft water; rinse the cloth thoroughly in cold, soft water so that it may not rot. This amount of cloth may be bleached in fourteen or fifteen minutes.

A POLISH FOR LEATHER.

Put a half pound of shellac broken up in small pieces into a quart bottle or jug, cover it with alcohol, cork it tight, and put it on the shelf in a warm place; shake it well several times a day, then add a piece of camphor as large as a hen's egg; shake it well, and in a few hours shake it again and add one ounce of lamp-black. If the alcohol is good, it will all be dissolved in two days; then shake and use. If the materials were of the proper kind, the polish correctly prepared, it will dry in about five minutes, giving a gloss equal to patent leather. Using aniline dyes instead of the lampblack, you can have it any desired color, and it can be used on wood or hard paper.

TO SOFTEN WATER.

Add half a pound of the best quick lime dissolved in water to every hundred gallons. Smaller proportions may be more conveniently managed, and if allowed to stand a short time the lime will have united with the carbonate of lime, and been deposited at the bottom of the receptacle. Another way is to put a gallon of lye into a barrelful of water, or two or three shovels full of wood-ashes, let stand over night; it will be clear and soft.

WASHING FLUID.

One gallon of water and four pounds of ordinary washing soda, and a quarter of a pound of soda. Heat the water to boiling hot, put in the soda, boil about five minutes, then pour it over two pounds of unslaked lime, let it bubble and foam until it settles, turn it off and bottle it for use. This is the article that is used in the Chinese laundries for whitening their linen, and is called " Javelle water;" a tablespoonful put into a suds of three gallons, and a little, say a quarter of a cupful, in the boiler when boiling the clothes, makes them very white and clear. Must be well-rinsed afterwards. This preparation will remove tea stains, and almost all ordinary stains of fruit, grass, etc. This fluid brightens the colors of colored clothes, does not rot them, but should not be *left long in any water;* the boiling, sudsing, rinsing and blueing, should be done in quick succession, until the clothes are ready to hang on the line.

HARD SOAP. (Washing.)

Six pounds of washing soda, and three of unslaked lime. Pour on four gallons of boiling water, let it stand until perfectly clear, then drain off, and put in six pounds of clean fat. Boil it until it begins to harden about two hours, stirring most of the time. While boiling, thin it with two gallons of cold water, which you have previously poured on the alkaline mixture, after draining off the four gallons. This must be settled clear before it is drawn off. Add it when there is danger of boiling over. Try the thickness by cooling a little on a plate. Put in a handful of salt just before taking from the fire. Wet a tub to prevent sticking; turn in the soap, and let it stand until solid. Cut into bars, put on a board and let it dry. This makes about forty pounds of soap. It can be flavored just as you turn it out.

SOAP FOR WASHING WITHOUT RUBBING.

A soap to clean clothes without rubbing: Take two pounds of sal soda, two pounds of common bar soap, and ten quarts of water. Cut the soap in thin slices, and boil together two hours; strain, and it will be fit for use. Put the clothes in soak the night before you wash, and to every pailful of water in which you boil them add a pound of soap. They will need no rubbing, but merely rinsing.

TO MAKE SOFT SOAP WITHOUT COOKING.

Pour two pailfuls of boiling water upon twenty pounds of potash, and let it stand two hours. Have ready thirty pounds of clean grease, upon which pour one pailful of the lye, adding another pail of water to the potash; let it stand three or four hours, stir it well; then pour a gallon of the lye upon the grease, stir it well; and in half an hour another gallon of the lye, stir it thoroughly; in half an hour repeat the process, and thus proceed until you have poured off all the lye; then add two pails of boiling hot water to the remainder of the potashes, and let it stand ten hours; then stir the mixture, and if it has become stiff, and the grease has disappeared from the surface, take out a little, and see whether the weak lye will thicken it; if it does, add the lye; if it does not, try water, and if that thickens it, let it stand another day, stirring it well five or six times during the day; if the lye does not separate from the grease you may fill up with water.

OLD-STYLE FAMILY SOFT SOAP.

To *set the leach*, bore several holes in the bottom of a barrel; or use one without a bottom; prepare a board larger than the barrel, then set the barrel on it, and cut a grove around just outside the barrel, making one grove from this to the edge of the board, to carry off the lye as it runs off, with a groove around it, running into one in the centre of the board. Place all two feet from the ground and tip it so that the lye may run easily from the board into the vessel below prepared to receive it. Put half bricks or stones around the edge of the inside of the barrel; place on them one end of some sticks about two inches wide, inclining to the centre; on those place some straw to the depth of two inches, over it scatter two pounds of slaked lime. Put in ashes, about half of a bushel at a time, pack it well, by pounding it down, and continue doing so until the barrel is full, leaving a funnel-shaped hollow in the centre large enough to hold several quarts of water. Use rain water boiling hot. Let the water disappear before adding more. If the ashes are packed very *tightly* it may require two or three days before the lye will begin to run, but it will be the stronger for it, and much better.

To make boiled soft soap. Put in a kettle the grease consisting of all kinds of fat that has accumulated in the kitchen, such as scraps and bones from the soup-kettle, rinds from meat, etc.; fill the kettle half full; if there is too much grease it can be skimmed off after the soap is cold, for another kettle of soap. This is the only true test when enough grease is used, as the lye will consume all that is needed and no more. Make a fire under one side of it. The kettle should be in an out-house or out of doors. Let it heat very hot so as to fry; stir occasionally to prevent burning. Now put in the lye a gallon at a time, watching it closely until it boils, as it sometimes runs over at the beginning. Add lye until the kettle is full enough, but not *too full to boil well.* Soap should boil from the *side* and not the middle, as this would. be more likely to cause it to boil over. To test the soap, to one spoonful of soap add one of rain-water; if it stirs up very thick, the soap is good and will keep; if it becomes thinner, it is not good. This is the result of one of three causes, either it is too weak, or there is a deposit of dirt, or it is too strong. Continue to boil for a few hours, when it should flow from the stick with which it is stirred, like thick molasses; but if after boiling it remains thin, let it stand over night, removing it from the fire, then draining it off very carefully into another vessel, being very particular to prevent any sediment from passing. Wash the kettle, return the soap, and boil again, if dirt was the cause; it will now be thick and good; otherwise, if it·was *too strong*, rain-water added will make it right, adding the water gradually until right and just thick enough.

FACTS WORTH KNOWING.

An agreeable Disinfectant: Sprinkle fresh ground coffee on a shovel of hot coals, or burn sugar on hot coals. Vinegar boiled with myrrh, sprinkled on the floor and furniture of a sick room, are excellent deodorizers.

To prevent Mold: A small quantity of carbolic acid added to paste, mucilage, and ink, will prevent mold. An ounce of the acid to a gallon of white-wash will keep cellars and dairies from the disagreeable odor which often taints milk and meat kept in such places.

To make Tracing-paper:—Dissolve a ball of white bees-wax, one inch in diameter, in half a pint of turpentine. Saturate the paper in this bath and let it dry two or three days before using.

To preserve Brooms: Dip them for a minute or two in a kettle of boiling suds once a week and they will last much longer, making them tough and pliable. A carpet wears much longer swept with a broom cared for in this manner.

To clean Brass-ware, etc.: Mix one ounce of oxalic acid, six ounces of rotten stone, all in powder, one ounce of sweet oil, and sufficient water to make a paste. Apply a small portion, and rub dry with a flannel or leather. The liquid dip most generally used consists of nitric and sulphuric acids; but this is more corrosive.

Polish, or Enamel for Shirt-bosoms, is made by melting together one ounce of white wax, and two ounces of spermaceti; heat gently and turn into a very shallow pan; when cold cut or break in pieces. When making boiled starch the usual way, enough for a dozen bosoms, add to it a piece of the polish the size of a hazel nut.

An Erasive Fluid for the Removal of Spots on Furniture, and all kinds of fabrics, without injuring the color, is made of four ounces of aqua ammonia, one ounce of glycerine, one ounce of castile soap and one of spirits of wine. Dissolve the soap in two quarts of soft water, add the other ingredients. Apply with a soft sponge, and rub out. Very good for cleaning silks.

To remove the Odor of Onion from fish-kettle and sauce-pans in which they have been cooked, put wood-ashes or sal soda, potash or lye; fill with water and let stand on the stove until it boils; then wash in hot suds, and rinse well.

To clean Marble Busts: First free them from all dust, then wash them with very weak hydrochloric acid. Soap injures the color of marble.

To remove old Putty from Window Frames, pass a red-hot poker slowly over it and it will come off easily.

Hanging Pictures: The most safe material and also the best, is copper wire, of the size proportioned to the weight of the picture. When hung the wire is scarcely visible, and its strength is far superior to cord.

To keep Milk Sweet: Put into a panful a spoonful of grated horse-radish, it will keep it sweet for days.

To take Rust from Steel Implements or Knives: Rub them well with kerosene oil, leaving them covered with it a day or so; then rub them hard and well with finely powdered unslaked lime.

Poison Water: Water boiled in galvanized iron becomes poisonous, and cold water passed through zinc-lined iron pipes should never be used for cooking or drinking. Hot water for cooking should never be taken from hot water pipes; keep a supply heated in kettles.

Scouring Soap for Cotton and Silk Goods: Mix one pound of common soap, half of a pound of beef-gall and one ounce and a half of Venetian turpentine

A Paint for Wood or Stone that resists all Moisture: Melt twelve ounces of resin; mix with it, thoroughly, six gallons of fish oil, and one pound of melted sulphur. Rub up some ochre or any other coloring substance with a little linseed oil, enough to give it the right color and thickness. Apply several coats of the hot composition with a brush. The first coat should be very thin.

To Ventilate a Room: Place a pitcher of cold water on a table in your room and it will absorb all the gases with which the room is filled from the respiration of those eating or sleeping in the apartment. Very few realize how important such purification is for the health of the family, or, indeed, understand or realize that there can be any impurity in the rooms; yet in a few hours a pitcher or pail of cold water—the colder the more effective—will make the air of a room pure, but the water will be entirely unfit for use.

To fill Cracks in Plaster: Use vinegar instead of water to mix your plaster of Paris. The resultant mass will be like putty, and will not "set" for twenty or thirty minutes; whereas if you use water the plaster will become hard almost immediately, before you have time to use it. Push it into the cracks and smooth it off nicely with a table-knife.

To take Spots from Wash Goods: Rub them with the yolk of egg before washing.

To take White Spots from Varnished Furniture: Hold a hot stove lid or plate over them and they will soon disappear.

To prevent Oil from becoming Rancid: Drop a few drops of ether into the bottle containing it.

Troublesome Ants: A heavy chalk-mark laid a finger's distance from your sugar-box and all around (there must be no space not covered) will surely prevent ants from troubling.

To make Tough Meat Tender: Lay it a few minutes in a strong vinegar water.

To remove Discoloration from Bruises: Apply a cloth wrung out in very hot water, and renew frequently until the pain ceases. Or apply raw beefsteak.

A Good Polish for removing Stains, Spots, and Mildew from Furniture, is made as follows: Take half a pint of ninety-eight per cent. alcohol; a quarter of an ounce each of pulverized resin and gum shellac; add half a pint of linseed oil; shake well and apply with a brush or sponge.

To remove Finger-marks: Sweet oil will remove finger-marks from varnished furniture, and kerosene from oiled furniture.

To remove Paint from Black Silk: Patient rubbing with chloroform will remove paint from black silk or any other goods, and will not hurt the most delicate color or fabric.

To freshen Gilt Frames: Gilt frames may be revived by carefully dusting them, and then washing with one ounce of soda beaten up with the whites of three eggs. Scraped patches might be touched up with Judson's or any gold paint. Castile soap and water, with proper care, may be used to clean oil paintings; other methods should not be employed without some skill.

To destroy Moths in Furniture: All the baking and steaming are useless, as, although the moths may be killed, their eggs are sure to hatch, and the up-holstery to be well riddled. The naphtha-bath process is effectual. A sofa, chair or lounge may be immersed in the large vats used for the purpose, and all insect life will be absolutely destroyed. No egg ever hatches after passing through the naphtha-bath; all oil, dirt, or grease disappears, and not the slight-est damage is done to the most costly article. Sponging with naphtha will not answer. It is the immersion for two hours or more in the specially prepared vats which is effectual.

Slicing Pine-apples: The knife used for peeling a pine-apple should not be used for slicing it, as the rind contains an acid that is apt to cause a swollen mouth and sore lips. The Cubans use salt as an antidote for the ill effects of the peel.

To clean Iron Sinks: Rub them well with a cloth wet with kerosene oil.

To erase Discoloration on Stone-china: Dishes and cups that are used for baking custards, puddings, etc., that require scouring, may be easily cleaned by rubbing with a damp cloth dipped in whiting or "Sapolio," then washed as usual.

To remove Ink, Wine or Fruit Stains: Saturate well in tomato juice; it is also an excellent thing to remove stains from the hands.

To set Colors in Washable Goods: Soak them previous to washing in a water in which is allowed a tablespoonful of ox-gall to a gallon of water.

To take out Paint: Equal parts of ammonia and turpentine will take paint out of clothing, no matter how dry or hard it may be. Saturate the spot two or three times, then wash out in soap-suds. Ten cents' worth of oxalic acid dis-solved in a pint of hot water will remove paint spots from the windows. Pour a little into a cup, and apply to the spots with a swab, but be sure not to allow the acid to touch the hands. Brasses may be quickly cleaned with it. Great care must be exercised in labelling the bottle, and putting it out of the reach of children, as it is a deadly poison.

To remove Tar from Cloth: Saturate the spot and rub it well with turpen-tine, and every trace of tar will be removed.

To destroy Ants: Ants that frequent houses or gardens may be destroyed by taking flour of brimstone half a pound, and potash four ounces; set them in an iron or earthern pan over the fire until dissolved and united; afterwards beat them to a powder, and infuse a little of this powder in water, and wherever you sprinkle it the ants will fly the place.

Simple Disinfectant: The following is a refreshing disinfectant for a sick room, or any room that has an unpleasant aroma pervading it: Put some fresh ground coffee in a saucer, and in the centre place a small piece of camphor gum, which light with a match. As the gum burns, allow sufficient coffee to consume with it. The perfume is very pleasant and healthful, being far superior to pastiles, and very much cheaper.

Cure for Hiccough: Sit erect and inflate the lungs fully. Then, retaining the breath, bend forward slowly until the chest meets the knees. After slowly rising again to the erect position, slowly exhale the breath. Repeat this process a second time, and the nerves will be found to have received an access of energy that will enable them to perform their natural functions.

To keep out Mosquitos and Rats: If a bottle of the oil of penny-royal is left uncorked in a room at night, not a mosquito, nor any other blood-sucker, will be found there in the morning. Mix potash with powdered meal, and throw it into the rat-holes of a cellar, and the rats will depart. If a rat or a mouse get into your pantry, stuff into its hole a rag saturated with a solution of cayenne pepper, and no rat or mouse will touch the rag for the purpose of opening communication with a depot of supplies.

Salt will Curdle new Milk; hence, in preparing porridge, gravies, etc., the salt should not be added until the dish is prepared.

To prevent Rust on Flat-irons: Bees-wax and salt will make your rusty flat-irons as smooth and clean as glass. Tie a lump of wax in a rag and keep it for that purpose. When the irons are hot, rub them first with the wax rag, then scour with a paper or cloth sprinkled with salt.

To prevent Rust on Knives: Steel knives which are not in general use may be kept from rusting if they are dipped in a strong solution of soda; one part water to four of soda; then wipe dry, roll in flannel, and keep in a dry place.

Flowers may be kept very Fresh over Night if they are excluded from the air. To do this, wet them thoroughly, put in a damp box, and cover with wet raw cotton or wet newspaper, then place in a cool spot.

To sweeten Milk: Milk which is slightly turned or changed may be sweetened and rendered fit for use again by stirring in a little soda.

To scour Knives easily: Mix a small quantity of baking soda with your brick-dust and see if your knives do not polish better.

To soften Boots and Shoes: Kerosene will soften boots and shoes which have been hardened by water, and render them as pliable as new. Kerosene will make tin tea-kettles as bright as new. Saturate a woolen rag and rub with it. It will also remove stains from clean varnished furniture.

Faded Goods: Plush goods and all articles dyed with aniline colors which have faded from exposure to the light will look as bright as new after sponging with chloroform.

Choking: A piece of food lodged in the throat may sometimes be pushed down with the finger, or removed with a hair-pin quickly straightened and hooked at the end, or by two or three vigorous blows on the back between the shoulders.

To prevent Mold on the top of Glasses of Jelly, lay a lump of paraffine on the top of the hot jelly, letting it melt and spread over it. No brandy paper and no other covering is necessary. If preferred the paraffine can be melted and poured over after the jelly is cold.

To preserve Ribbons and Silks: Ribbons and silks should be put away for preservation in brown paper; the chloride of lime in white paper discolors them. A white satin dress should be pinned up in blue paper with brown paper outside sewn together at the edges.

To preserve Bouquets: Put a little saltpetre in the water you use for your bouquets, and the flowers will live for a fortnight.

To destroy Cockroaches: Hellebore sprinkled on the floor at night. They eat it and are poisoned.

To remove Iron Rust: Lemon-juice and salt will remove ordinary iron rust. If the hands are stained there is nothing that will remove the stains as well as lemon. Cut a lemon in halves and apply the cut surface as if it were soap.

To keep Bar Soap: Cut it into pieces and put it into a dry place; it is more economical to use after it has become hard, as it does not waste so readily.

To brighten Carpets: Carpets after the dust has been beaten out may be brightened by scattering upon them corn-meal mixed with salt and then sweeping it off. Mix salt and meal in equal proportions. Carpets should be thoroughly beaten on the wrong side first and then on the right side, after which spots may be removed by the use of ox-gall or ammonia and water.

Silver Tea and Coffee-pot: When putting away those not in use every day lay a little stick across the top under the cover. This will allow fresh air to get in and prevent the mustiness of the contents, familiar to hotel and boarding-house sufferers.

To prevent Creaking of Bedsteads: If a bedstead creaks at each movement of the sleeper, remove the slats, and wrap the ends of each in old newspapers.

To clean Unvarnished Black Walnut: Milk, sour or sweet, well-rubbed in with an old, soft flannel, will make black walnut look new.

To prevent Cracking of Bottles and Fruit-jars: If a bottle or fruit-jar that has been more than once used is placed on a towel thoroughly soaked in hot water, there is little danger of its being cracked by the introduction of a hot liquid.

To prevent Lamp-wicks from Smoking: Soak them in vinegar, and then dry them thoroughly.

Rub the nickel stove-trimmings and the plated handles and hinges of doors with kerosene and whiting, and polish with a dry cloth.

Death to Bugs: Varnish is death to the most persistent bug. It is cheap—ten cents' worth will do for one bedstead—is easily used, is safe, and improves the looks of the furniture to which it is applied. The application must, however, be thorough, the slats, sides, and every crack and corner receiving attention.

That salt should be eaten with nuts to aid digestion.

That milk which stands too long makes bitter butter.

To clean Drain Pipes: Drain pipes, and all places that are sour or impure, may be cleaned with lime-water or carbolic acid.

If oil cloth be occasionally rubbed with a mixture of beeswax and turpentine, it will last longer.

To remove Mildew from Cloth: Put a teaspoonful of chloride of lime into a quart of water, strain it twice, then dip the mildewed places in this weak solution; lay in the sun; if the mildew has not disappeared when dry, repeat the operation. Also soaking the article in sour milk and salt; then lay in the sun; repeat until all the mildew is out.

To take Ink out of Linen: Dip the ink-spot in pure melted tallow, then wash out the tallow and the ink will come out with it. This is said to be unfailing. Milk will remove ink from linen or colored muslins, when acids would be ruinous, by soaking the goods until the spot is very faint and then rubbing and rinsing in cold water.

Ink spots on floors can be extracted by scouring with sand wet in oil of vitriol and water. When ink is removed, rinse with strong pearl-ash water.

To toughen Lamp-chimneys and Glass-ware: Immerse the article in a pot filled with cold water, to which some common salt has been added. Boil the water well then cool slowly. Glass treated in this way, will resist any sudden change of temperature.

To remove Paint from Window-glass: Rub it well with hot sharp vinegar.

To clean Stove-pipe: A piece of zinc put on the live coals in the stove will clean out the stove-pipe.

Packing Bottles: India-rubber bands slipped over them will prevent breakage.

To clean Ivory Ornaments: When ivory ornaments become yellow or dusky, wash them well in soap and water with a small brush, to clean the carvings, and then place them, while wet, in the sunshine. Wet them with soapy water for two or three days, several times a day, still keeping them in the sunshine, then wash them again, and they will be perfectly white.

Stained Brass: Whiting wet with aqua ammonia will cleanse brass from stains, and is excellent for polishing faucets and door-knobs of brass or silver. "Sapolio" is still better.

Hartshorn applied to the stings of poisonous insects will allay the pain and stop the swelling; or apply oil of sassafras, which is better. Bee-stings should be treated in this way.

For Cleaning Glass Bottles: Crush egg-shells into small bits, or a few carpet tacks, or a small quantity of gunshot, put into the bottle; then fill one-half full of strong soap-suds; shake thoroughly; then rinse in clear water. Will look like new.

Cutting off Glass Bottles for Cups or Jars: A simple, practical way is to take a red-hot poker with a pointed end; make a mark with a file to begin the cut; then apply the hot iron and a crack will start, which will follow the iron wherever it is carried. This is, on the whole, simple, and better than the use of strings wet with turpentine, etc.

Cistern Water may be purified by charcoal put in a bag and hung in the water.

Salt will remove the Stain from Silver caused by eggs, when applied dry with a soft cloth.

Opened Fruit, Fish or Vegetable: Never allow opened fruit, fish or vegetables to stand in the tin can. Never stir anything in tin, or, if it is done, use a wooden spoon. In lifting pies or cakes from bright tin pans, use great caution that the knife does not scrape off flecks of bright metal.

Never use water which has stood in a lead pipe over night. *Not less than a wooden bucketful should be allowed to run.*

Never use water from a stone reservoir for cooking purposes.

Never allow fresh meat to remain in paper; it absorbs the juices.

Never keep vinegar or yeast in stone crocks or jugs; their acid attacks the glazing, which is said to be poisonous. Glass for either is better.

Squeaking doors ought to have the hinges oiled by putting on a drop from the sewing machine oil-can.

Plate Glass and Mirrors: A soft cloth, wetted in alcohol, is excellent to wipe off plate glass and mirrors, and prevent their becoming frosty in winter.

A red-hot iron will soften old putty so that it can be easily removed.

To test Nutmegs: Prick them with a pin; if good, the oil will instantly spread around the puncture.

A good Way to clean Mica in a stove that has become blackened with smoke, is to take it out, and thoroughly wash it with vinegar. If the black does not come off at once, let it soak a little.

To banish Rats from the Premises, use pounded glass mixed with dry corn meal, placed within their reach. Sprinkling cayenne pepper in their holes will also banish them. Chloride of lime is an infallible remedy, spread around where they come, and thrown into their holes; it should be renewed once in two weeks. Tar is also a good remedy.

To prevent the Odor of Boiling Ham or Cabbage: Throw red pepper pods or a few bits of charcoal into the pan they are cooking in.

To brighten Gilt Frames: Take sufficient flour of sulphur to give a golden tinge to about one and one-half pints of water, and in this boil four or five bruised onions, or garlic, which will answer the same purpose. Strain off the liquid, and with it, when cold, wash with a soft brush any gilding which requires restoring, and when dry, it will come out as bright as new work.

All cooking utensils, including iron-ware, should be washed outside and inside in hot, soapy water; rinsed in clean hot water, wiped dry with a dry towel; a soapy or greasy dish-cloth should never be used for the purpose.

A cake of sapolio should be kept in every kitchen, to be used freely on all dishes that require scouring and cleansing. All tins that have become discolored can be made as bright and clean as new by the use of sapolio; also shines dishes, and, in fact, almost all articles that require any scouring. Purchased at all groceries. One of the most useful articles ever used in the kitchen.

COLOGNE WATER. (Superior.)

Oil of lavender, two drachms; oil of rosemary, one drachm and a half; orange, lemon and bergamot, one drachm each of the oil; also two drachms of the essence of musk, attar of rose ten drops, and a pint of proof spirit. Shake all together thoroughly three times a day for a week.

JOCKEY CLUB BOUQUET.

Mix one pint extract of rose, one pint extract of tuberose, half a pint of extract of cassia, four ounces extract of jasmine, and three ounces tincture of civet. Filter the mixture.

ROSE-WATER.

Preferable to the distilled for a perfume, or for culinary purposes: Attar of rose, twelve drops; rub it up with half an ounce of white sugar and two drachms carbonate magnesia; then add gradually one quart of water, and two ounces of proof spirit, and filter through paper.

BAY RUM.

French proof spirit one gallon, extract bay, six ounces. Mix and color with caramel· needs no filtering.

LAVENDER WATER.

Oil of lavender, two ounces; orris root, half an ounce; spirits of wine, one pint. Mix and keep two or three weeks. It may then be strained through two thicknesses of blotting-paper and is ready for use.

CREAM OF LILIES.

Best white castor oil; pour in a little strong solution of sal tartar in water, and shake it until it looks thick and white. Perfume with lavender.

CREAM OF ROSES.

Olive oil, one pound; attar of roses, fifty drops; oil of rosemary, twenty-five drops; mix, and color it with alkanet root.

COLD CREAM.

Melt one ounce oil of almonds, half-ounce spermaceti, one drachm white wax, and then add two ounces of rose-water, and stir it constantly until cold.

LIP-SALVE.

Melt one ounce white wax, one ounce sweet oil, one drachm spermaceti, and throw in a piece of alkanet root to color it, and, when cooling, perfume it with oil rose, and then pour it into small white jars or boxes.

FOR DANDRUFF.

Take glycerine four ounces, tincture of cantharides five ounces, bay rum four ounces, water two ounces. Mix, and apply once a day, and rub well down the scalp.

HAIR INVIGORATOR.

Bay rum, two pints; alcohol, one pint; castor oil, one ounce; carb. ammonia, half an ounce; tincture of cantharides, one ounce. Mix them well. This compound will promote the growth of the hair and prevent it from falling out.

MACCASSAR OIL FOR THE HAIR.

Renowned for the past fifty years, is as follows: Take a quarter of an ounce of the chippings of alkanet root, tie this in a bit of coarse muslin, and put it in a bottle containing eight ounces of sweet oil; cover it to keep out the dust; let it stand several days; add to this sixty drops of tincture of cantharides, ten drops of oil of rose, neroli and lemon each sixty drops; let it stand one week and you will have one of the most powerful stimulants for the growth of the hair ever known.

Another:—To a pint of strong sage tea, a pint of bay rum and a quarter of an ounce of the tincture of cantharides, add an ounce of castor oil and a teaspoonful of rose, or other perfume. Shake well before applying to the hair, as the oil will not mix.

PHALON'S INSTANTANEOUS HAIR DYE.

To one ounce of crystallized nitrate of silver, dissolved in one ounce of concentrated aqua ammonia, add one ounce of gum arabic, and six ounces of soft water. Keep in the dark. Remember to remove all grease from the hair before applying the dye.

There is danger in some of the patent hair-dyes, and hence the *Scientific American* offers what is known as the walnut hair-dye. The simplest form is the expressed juice of the bark or shell of green walnuts. To preserve the juice a little alcohol is commonly added to it with a few bruised cloves, and the whole digested together, with occasional agitation for a week or fortnight, when the clear portion is decanted, and, if necessary, filtered. Sometimes a little common salt is added with the same intention. It should be kept in a cool place. The most convenient way of application is by means of a sponge.

DYE FOR WHITE OR LIGHT EYEBROWS.

Boil an ounce of walnut bark in a pint of water for an hour. Add a lump of alum the size of a filbert, and when cold, apply with a camel's-hair brush.

HAIR WASH.

One penny worth of borax, half a pint of olive oil, one pint of boiling water.

Pour the boiling water over the borax and oil; let it cool; then put the mixture into a bottle. Shake it before using, and apply it with a flannel. Camphor and borax, dissolved in boiling water and left to cool, make a very good wash for the hair; as also does rosemary water mixed with a little borax. After using any of these washes, when the hair becomes thoroughly dry, a little pomatum or oil should be rubbed in to make it smooth and glossy—that is, if one prefers oil on the hair.

OX-MARROW POMADE FOR THE HAIR.

One marrow bone, half a pint of oil, ten cents' worth of citronella. Take the marrow out of the bone, place it in warm water, let it get almost to boiling point, then let it cool and pour the water away; repeat this three times until the marrow is thoroughly "fined." Beat the marrow to a cream with a silver fork, stir the oil in, drop by drop, beating all the time; when quite cold add the citronella, pour into jars and cover down.

TO INCREASE THE HAIR IN THE BROWS.

Clip them and anoint with a little sweet oil. Should the hair fall out, having been full, use one of the hair invigorators.

BANDOLINE.

To one quart of rose-water add an ounce and a half of gum tragacanth; let it stand forty-eight hours, frequently straining it, then strain through a coarse linen cloth; let it stand two days, and again strain; add to it a drachm of oil of roses. Used by ladies dressing their hair, to make it lie in any position.

COMPLEXION WASH.

Put in a vial one drachm of benzoin gum in powder, one drachm nutmeg oil, six drops of orange-blossom tea, or apple blossoms put in half pint of rain-water and boiled down to one teaspoonful and strained, one pint of sherry wine. Bathe the face morning and night; will remove all flesh-worms and freckles, and give a beautiful complexion. Or, put one ounce of powdered gum of benzoin in a pint of whiskey; to use, put in water in wash-bowl till it is milky, allowing it to dry without wiping. This is perfectly harmless.

Cream cures sun-burn on some complexions, lemon-juice is best on others, and cold water suits still others best.

BURNET'S CELEBRATED POWDER FOR THE FACE.

Five cents' worth of bay rum, five cents' worth of magnesia snowflake, five cents' worth of bergamot, five cents' worth of oil of lemon; mix in a pint bottle and fill up with rain water. Shake well, and apply on a soft sponge or cloth.

TOILET OR FACE POWDER.

Take a quarter of a pound of wheat starch pounded fine; sift it through a fine sieve, or a piece of lace; add to it eight drops of oil of rose, oil of lemon thirty drops, oil of bergamot fifteen drops. Rub thoroughly together.

The French throw this powder into alcohol, shaking it, letting it settle, then pouring off the alcohol and drying the powder. In that case, the perfume is added lastly.

TO REMOVE FRECKLES.

The following lotion is highly recommended: One ounce of lemon-juice, a quarter of a drachm of powdered borax, and half a drachm of sugar; mix in a bottle, and allow them to stand a few days, when the liquor should be rubbed occasionally on the hands and face. Another application is: Friar's balsam, one part; rose water, twenty parts.

Powdered nitre moistened with water, and applied to the face night and morning, is said to remove freckles without injury to the skin.

Also, a tablespoonful of freshly grated horse-radish, stirred into a cupful of sour milk; let it stand for twelve hours, then strain and apply often. This bleaches the complexion also, and takes off tan.

TO REMOVE MOTH PATCHES.

Into a pint bottle of rum put a tablespoonful of flour of sulphur. Apply this to the patches once a day, and they will disappear in two or three weeks.

CURE FOR PIMPLES.

One teaspoonful of carbolic acid and one pint of rose-water mixed is an excellent remedy for pimples. Bathe the skin thoroughly and often, but do not let the wash get into the eyes.

This wash is soothing to mosquito bites, and irritations of the skin of every nature.

It is advisable, in order to clear the complexion permanently, to cleanse the blood; then the wash would be of advantage.

To obtain a good complexion a person's diet should receive the first attention. Greasy food, highly spiced soups, hot bread and butter, meats or game, rich gravies, alcoholic liquors, coffee—all are injurious to the complexion. Strong tea used daily will after a time give the skin the color and appearance of leather. Coffee affects the nerves more, but the skin less, and a healthy nervous system is necessary to beauty. Eating between meals, late suppers, overeating at meals, eating sweetmeats, candies, etc., all these tend to disorder the blood, producing pimples and blotches.

Washing of the face or skin is another consideration for a good complexion; it should be thoroughly washed in plenty of lukewarm water with some mild soap—then rinsed in clear water *well*; dry with a thick soft towel. If suds is left or wiped off the skin, the action of the air and sun will tan the surface, and permanently deface the complexion; therefore one should be sure to thoroughly rinse off all soap from the skin to avoid the tanning, which will leave a brown or yellow tinge impossible to efface.

PEARL SMELLING SALTS.

Powdered carbonate of ammonia, one ounce; strong solution of ammonia, half a fluid ounce; oil of rosemary, ten drops; oil of bergamot, ten drops. Mix, and while moist put in a wide-mouthed bottle, which is to be well-closed.

PEARL TOOTH POWDER.

Prepared chalk, half a pound; powdered myrrh, two ounces; camphor, two drachms; orris root, powdered, two ounces; moisten the camphor with alcohol and mix well together.

REMOVING TARTAR FROM THE TEETH.

This preparation is used by dentists. Pure muriatic acid, one ounce; water, one ounce; honey, two ounces; mix thoroughly. Take a tooth-brush, and wet it freely with this preparation, and briskly rub the black teeth, and in a moment's time they will be perfectly white; then immediately wash out the mouth well with water, that the acid may not act on the enamel of the teeth. This should be done only occasionally.

BAD BREATH.

Bad breath from catarrh, foul stomach, or bad teeth, may be temporarily relieved by diluting a little bromo chloralum with eight or ten parts of water, and using it as a gargle, and swallowing a few drops before going out. A pint of bromo chloralum costs fifty cents, but a small vial will last a long time.

SHAVING COMPOUND.

Half a pound of plain, white soap, dissolved in a small quantity of alcohol, as little as can be used; add a tablespoonful of pulverized borax. Shave the soap and put it in a small tin basin or cup; place it on the fire in a dish of boiling water; when melted, add the alcohol, and remove from the fire; stir in oil of bergamot sufficient to perfume it.

BARBER'S SHAMPOO MIXTURE.

Dissolve half an ounce of carbonate of ammonia and one ounce of borax in one quart of water; then add two ounces of glycerine in three quarts of New England rum, and one quart of bay rum. Moisten the hair with this liquid, shampoo with the hands until a light lather is formed; then wash off with plenty of clean water.

RAZOR-STROP PASTE.

Wet the strop with a little sweet oil, and apply a little flour of emery evenly over the surface.

CAMPHOR ICE.

Melt together over a water bath white wax and spermaceti each one ounce, camphor two ounces, in sweet almond oil, one pound, then triturate until the mixture has become homogeneous, and allow one pound of rose-water to flow in slowly during the operation. Excellent for chapped lips or hands.

ODORIFEROUS OR SWEET-SCENTING BAGS.

Lavender flowers, one ounce; pulverized orris, two drachms; bruised rosemary leaves, half ounce; musk, five grains; attar of rose, five drops. Mix well, sew up in small flat muslin bags, and cover them with fancy silk or satin.

These are very nice to keep in your bureau drawers or trunk, as the perfume penetrates through the contents of the trunk or drawers. An acceptable present to a single gentleman.

HOW TO KEEP BRUSHES CLEAN.

The best way in which to clean hair-brushes is with spirits of ammonia, as its effect is immediate. No rubbing is required, and cold water can be used just as successfully as warm. Take a tablespoonful of ammonia to a quart of water, dip the hair part of the brush without wetting the ivory, and in a moment the grease is removed; then rinse in cold water, shake well, and dry in the air, but not in the sun. Soda and soap soften the bristles and invariably turn the ivory yellow.

TOILET ITEMS.

Mutton tallow is considered excellent to soften the hands. It may be rubbed on at any time when the hands are perfectly dry, but the best time is when retiring, and an old pair of soft, large gloves thoroughly covered on the inside with the tallow and glycerine in equal parts, melted together, can be worn during the night with the most satisfactory results.

Four parts of glycerine and five parts of yolks of eggs thoroughly mixed, and applied after washing the hands, is also considered excellent.

For chapped hands or face: One ounce of glycerine, one ounce of alcohol mixed, then add eight ounces of rose-water.

Another good rule is to rub well in dry oatmeal after every washing, and be particular regarding the quality of soap. Cheap soap and hard water are the unknown enemies of many people, and the cause of rough skin and chapped hands. Castile soap and rain-water will sometimes cure without any other assistance.

Camphor ice is also excellent, and can be applied with but little inconvenience. Borax dissolved and added to the toilet water is also good.

For chapped lips, beeswax dissolved in a small quantity of sweet oil, by heating carefully. Apply the salve two or three times a day, and avoid wetting the lips as much as possible.

To soften the hands: One can have the hands in soap-suds with soft soap without injury to the skin if the hands are dipped in vinegar or lemon-juice immediately after. The acids destroy the corrosive effects of the alkali, and make the hands soft and white. Indian meal and vinegar or lemon-juice used on hands where roughened by cold or labor will heal and soften them. Rub the hands in this, then wash off thoroughly and rub in glycerine. Those who suffer from chapped hands will find this comforting.

To remove stains, rub a slice of raw potato upon the stains; or wash the hands in lemon-juice or steeped laurel-leaves.

To give a fine color to the nails, the hands and fingers must be well lathered and washed with fine soap; then the nails must be rubbed with equal parts of cinnebar and emery, followed by oil of bitter almonds. To take white spots from the nails, melt equal parts of pitch and turpentine in a small cup; add to it vinegar and powdered sulphur. Rub this on the nails, and the spots will soon disappear.

TOILET SOAP.

One pound of washing soda, one pound of lard or clear tallow, half a pound of unslaked lime, one tablespoonful of salt, three quarts of water. Put the soda and lime in a large dish, and pour over the water, boiling hot; stir until dissolved; let it stand until clear; then pour off the clear liquid, add the grease and salt; boil four hours, then pour into pans to cool. If it should be inclined to curdle or separate, indicating the lime to be too strong, pour in a little more water, and boil again. Perfume as you please, and pour into molds or a shallow dish, and, when cold, cut into bars to dry.

ANTIDOTES FOR POISONS.

The following list gives some of the more common poisons and the remedies most likely to be on hand in case of need:

Acids:—These cause great heat and sensation of burning pain from the mouth down to the stomach. The remedies are: Magnesia, soda, pearl ash, or soap dissolved in water, every two minutes: then use the stomach pump, or an emetic.

Alkali:—Drink freely of water with vinegar or lemon-juice in it, made very strong of the sour.

Ammonia:—Remedy is lemon-juice or vinegar.

Arsenic Remedies:—Give prompt emetic of mustard and salt, a tablespoonful of each, in a coffee cup of *warm* water; then follow with sweet oil, butter made warm, or milk. Also may use the white of an egg in half a cupful of milk or lime water. Chalk and water is good, and the preparation of iron, ten drops in water every half hour; hydrated magnesia.

Alcohol:—First cleanse out the stomach by an emetic, then dash cold water on the head, and give ammonia (spirits of hartshorn).

Laudanum, Morphine, Opium:—First give a strong emetic of mustard and water, then very strong coffee and acid drinks; dash cold water on the head, then keep in motion.

Belladonna:—Give an emetic of mustard, salt and water; then drink plenty of vinegar and water or lemonade.

Charcoal:—In poisons, by carbonic gas, remove the patient to the open air, dash cold water on the head and body, and stimulate the nostrils and lungs with hartshorn, at the same time rubbing the chest briskly.

Corrosive Sublimate, Saltpetre, Blue Vitriol, Bed-bug poison:—Give white of egg, freshly mixed with water, in large quantities; or give wheat flour and water, or soap and water freely, or salt and water, or large draughts of milk.

Lead:—White lead and sugar of lead. Give an emetic, then follow with cathartics, such as castor oil, and epsom salts especially.

Nux Vomica:—First emetics, and then brandy.

Oxalic Acid (frequently taken for epsom salts): First give soap and water, or chalk or magnesia and water. Give every two minutes.

White Vitriol:—Give plenty of milk and water.

Tartar Emetic:—Take large doses of tea made of white oak bark, or peruvian bark. Drink plenty of warm water to encourage vomiting; then, if the vomiting should not stop, give a grain of opium in water.

Nitrate of Silver (lunar caustic):—Give a strong solution of common salt and water, and then an emetic.

Verdigris:—Give plenty of white of egg and water.

Tobacco:—Emetics, frequent draughts of cold water; camphor and brandy.

French Words in Cooking.

Aspic:—Savory jelly for cold dishes.

Au gratin:—Dishes prepared with sauce and crumbs and baked.

Bouchées:—Very thin patties or cakes, as name indicates—mouthfuls.

Baba:—A peculiar, sweet French yeast cake.

Bechamel:—A rich, white sauce made with stock.

Bisque:—A white soup made of shell fish.

To Blanch:—To place any article on the fire till it boils, then plunge it in cold water; to whiten poultry, vegetables, etc. To remove the skin by immersing in boiling water.

Bouillon:—A clear soup, stronger than broth, yet not so strong as *consommé*, which is "reduced" soup

Braisé:—Meat cooked in a closely covered stew-pan, so that it retains its own flavor and those of the vegetables and flavorings put with it.

Brioche:—A very rich, unsweetened, French cake made with yeast.

Cannelon:—Stuffed rolled-up meat.

Consommé:—Clear soup or bouillon boiled down till very rich, *i. e.* consumed.

Croquettes:—A savory mince of fish or fowl, made with sauce into shapes, and fried.

Croustades:—Fried forms of bread to serve minces, or other meats upon.

Entrée:—A small dish, usually served between the courses at dinner.

Fondue:—A light preparation of melted cheese.

Fondant:—Sugar boiled, and beaten to a creamy paste.

Hollandaise Sauce:—A rich sauce, something like hot mayonnaise.

Matelote:—A rich fish stew, with wine.

Mayonnaise:—A rich salad dressing.

Meringue:—Sugar and white of egg beaten to sauce.

Marmade:—A liquor of spices, vinegar, etc. in which fish or meats are steeped before cooking.

Miroton:—Cold meat warmed in various ways, and dished in circular form.

Purse:—This name is given to very thick soups, the ingredients for thickening which have been rubbed through a sieve.

Poulette Sauce:—A bechamel sauce, to which white wine, and sometimes eggs are added.

Ragout:—A rich, brown stew, with mushrooms, vegetables, etc.

Piquante:—A sauce of several flavors, acid predominating.

Quenelles:—Forcemeat with bread, yolk of eggs, highly seasoned, and formed with a spoon to an oval shape; then poached and used either as a dish by them-selves, or to garnish.

Remoulade:—A salad dressing differing from mayonnaise, in that the eggs are hard boiled and rubbed in a mortar with mustard, herbs, etc.

Rissole:—Rich mince of meat or fish, rolled in thin pastry and fried.

Roux:—A cooked mixture of butter and flour, for thickening soups and stews.

Salmi:—A rich stew of game, cut up and dressed, when half roasted.

Sauter:—To toss meat, etc., over the fire, in a little fat.

Souffle:—A very light, much whipped-up pudding or omelette.

Timbale:—A sort of pie in a mold.

Vol au vents:—Patties of very light puff paste, made without a dish or mold, and filled with meat or preserves, etc.

—Catherine Owen, in Good Housekeeping.

Articles Required for the Kitchen.

The following list will show what articles are necessary for the kitchen, and will be quite an aid to young housekeepers when about commencing to furnish the utensils needed in the kitchen department, and may prove useful to many.

2 Sweeping brooms and 1 dust-pan.
1 Whisk broom
1 Bread box.
2 Cake boxes.
1 Large flour box.
1 Dredging box.
1 Large-sized tin pepper box.
1 Spice box containing smaller spice boxes.
2 Cake pans, two sizes.
4 Bread pans.
2 Square biscuit pans.

1 Apple corer.
1 Lemon squeezer.
1 Meat cleaver.
3 Kitchen knives and forks.
1 Large kitchen fork and 4 kitchen spoons, two sizes.
1 Wooden spoon for cake making.
1 Large bread knife.
1 Griddle cake turner, also 1 griddle.
1 Potato masher.
1 Meat board.

1 Dozen patty pans, and the same number of tartlet pans.
1 Large tin pail and 1 wooden pail.
2 Small tin pails.
1 Set of tin basins.
1 Set of tin measures.
1 Wooden butter ladle.
1 Tin skimmer.
1 Tin steamer.
2 Dippers, two sizes.
2 Funnels, two sizes.
1 Set of jelly cake tins.
4 Pie pans.
3 Pudding molds, one for boiling, two for baking, two sizes.
2 Dish pans, two sizes.
2 Cake or biscuit cutters, two sizes.
2 Graters, one large and one small.
1 Coffee canister.
1 Tea canister.
1 Tin or granite-ware teapot.
1 Tin or granite-ware coffee-pot.
1 Griddle cake turner.
4 Milk pans, 1 milk strainer.
1 Dozen iron gem pans or muffin rings.
1 Coarse gravy strainer, 1 fine strainer.
1 Colander.
1 Flour sifter.
2 Scoops, one for flour, one for sugar.
2 Jelly molds, two sizes.
1 Can opener, 1 egg beater.
1 Cork screw.
1 Chopping-knife.
2 Wooden chopping bowls, two sizes.

1 Meat saw.
2 Large earthen bowls.
4 Stone jars.
1 Coffee mill.
1 Candlestick.
2 Market baskets, two sizes.
1 Clock.
1 Ash bucket.
1 Gridiron.
2 Frying pans or spiders, two sizes.
4 Flat-irons, 2 number 8 and 2 number 6.
2 Dripping pans, two sizes.
3 Iron kettles, porcelain lined if possible.
1 Corn beef or fish kettle.
1 Tea kettle.
2 Granite-ware stew pans, two sizes.
1 Wire toaster.
1 Double kettle for cooking custards, grains, etc.
2 Sugar boxes, one for coarse and one for fine sugar.
1 Waffle iron.
1 Step ladder.
1 Stove, 1 coal shovel.
1 Pair of scales.
2 Coal hods or buckets.
1 Kitchen table, 2 kitchen chairs.
1 Large clothes basket.
1 Wash boiler, 1 wash board.
8 Dozen clothes pins.
1 Large nail hammer and one small tack hammer.
1 Bean pot.
1 Clothes wringer.

An ingenious housewife will manage to do with less conveniences, but these articles, if they can be purchased in the commencement of housekeeping, will save time and labor, making the preparation of food more easily—and it is always economy in the end to get the best material in all wares—as, for instance, the double plate tin will last for years, whereas the poor kind has to be replaced in a short time; the low-priced earthenware is soon broken up, whereas the strong stone ware, costing but a trifle more, lasts almost a lifetime.

In relation to the economy and management of the kitchen, I might suggest that the most essential thing is cleanliness in cooking, and also cleanliness with your person as well as in the keeping of the kitchen.

The hands of the cook should be always thoroughly cleansed before touching or handling anything pertaining to the cooking. Next there should never be any wasted or thrown away that can be turned to account, either for your own family or some family in poor circumstances. Bread that has become hard can be used for toasting, or for stuffing and pudding. In warm weather any gravies or soups that are left from the preceding day should be boiled up and poured into clean pans. This is particularly necessary where vegetables have been added to the preparation, as it then so soon turns sour. In cooler weather, every other day will be often enough to warm up these things.

In cooking, clear as you go; that is to say, do not allow a host of basins, plates, spoons, and other utensils, to accumulate on the dressers and tables whilst you are engaged in preparing the dinner. By a little management and forethought, much confusion may be saved in this way. It is as easy to put a thing in its place when it is done with, as it is to keep continually moving it to find room for fresh requisites. For instance, after making a pudding, the flour-tub, paste-board, and rolling-pin, should be put away, and any basins, spoons, etc., should be neatly packed up near the sink, to be washed when the proper time arrives. Neatness, order, and method should be always observed.

Never let your stock of spices, salt, seasonings, herbs, etc., dwindle down so low that some day, in the midst of preparing a large dinner, you find yourself minus a very important ingredient, thereby causing much confusion and annoyance.

After you have washed your sauce-pans, fish-kettle, etc., stand them before the fire for a few minutes to get thoroughly dry inside, before putting them away. They should then be kept in a dry place, in order that they may escape the deteriorating influence of rust, and thereby be quickly destroyed. Never leave sauce-pans dirty from one day's use to be cleaned the next; it is slovenly and untidy.

Do not be afraid of hot water in washing up dishes and dirty cooking utensils. As these are essentially greasy, lukewarm water cannot possibly have the effect of cleansing them effectually. Do not be chary also of changing and renewing the water occasionally. You will thus save yourself much time and labor in the long run.

Keep a cake of sapolio always on hand in the kitchen—always convenient for rubbing off stains, from earthenware, tin, glass, in fact, almost every thing but silver; it is a cheap and valuable article, and can be purchased at nearly every grocery in the United States.

Dyeing or Coloring.

GENERAL REMARKS.

Everything should be clean. The goods should be scoured in soap and the soap rinsed out. They are often steeped in soap lye over night. Dip them into water just before putting them into preparations, to prevent spotting. Soft water should be used, *sufficient to cover the goods well; this is always understood where quantity is not mentioned.* When goods are dyed, air them; then rinse well, and hang up to dry. Do not wring silk or merino dresses when scouring or dyeing them. If cotton goods are to be dyed a light color, they should first be bleached.

SILKS.

Black:—Make a weak lye as for black or woolens; work goods in bichromate of potash a little below boiling heat, then dip in the logwood in the same way; if colored in blue vitriol dye, use about the same heat.

Orange:—For one pound goods, annotto, one pound; soda, one pound; repeat as desired.

Green:—Very Handsome:—For one pound goods, yellow oak bark, eight ounces; boil one-half hour; turn off the liquor from bark and add alum, six ounces; let it stand until cold; while making this, color goods in blue dye-tub a light blue; dry and wash; dip in alum and bark dye. If it does not take well, warm the dye a little.

Purple:—For one pound goods. First obtain a light blue, by dipping in homemade dye-tub; then dry; dip in alum, four ounces; with water to cover, when little warm. If color is not full enough add chemic.

Yellow:—For one pound goods, alum, three ounces; sugar of lead, three-fourths ounce; immerse goods in solution over night; take out; drain, and make a new lye with fustic, one pound; dip until the required color is obtained.

Crimson:—For one pound goods—alum, three ounces; dip at hand heat one hour; take out and drain while making new dye by boiling ten minutes, cochineal, three ounces; bruised nutgalls, two ounces; and cream-tartar, one-fourth ounce, in one pail of water; when little cool, begin to dip, raising heat to boil; dip one hour; wash and dry.

Sky Blue on Silk or Cotton:—Very Beautiful:—Give goods as much color from a solution of blue vitriol, two ounces, to water, one gallon, as it will take up in dipping fifteen minutes; then run it through lime water. This will make a beautiful and durable sky blue.

*Brown on Silk or Cotton:—Very Beautiful:—*After obtaining a blue color as above, run goods through a solution of prussiate of potash, one ounce, to water, one gallon.

*Light Blue:—*For cold water, one gallon, dissolve alum, one-half tablespoonful, in hot water, one teacupful, and add to it; then add chemic, one teaspoonful at a time to obtain the desired color—the more chemic the darker the color.

WOOLEN GOODS.

*Chrome Black:—Best in Use:—*For five pounds of goods, blue vitriol six ounces; boil a few minutes, then dip the goods three-fourths of an hour, airing often; take out the goods, make a dye with three pounds of logwood, boil one-half hour; dip three-fourths of an hour, and air goods, and dip three-fourths of an hour more. Wash in strong suds. This will not fade by exposure to sun.

*Wine Color:—*For five pounds of goods, camwood, two pounds; boil fifteen minutes and dip the goods one-half hour; boil again and dip one-half hour; then darken with blue vitriol, one and one-half ounces; if not dark enough, add copperas, one-half ounce.

*Scarlet:—Very Fine:—*For one pound of goods, cream tartar one-half ounce; cochineal, well-pulverized, one-half ounce; muriate of tin, two and one-half ounces; boil up the dye and enter the goods; work them briskly for ten or fifteen minutes, then boil one and one-half hours, stirring goods slowly while boiling. Wash in clear water and dry in the shade.

*Pink:—*For three pounds of goods, alum three ounces; boil and dip the goods one hour, then add to the dye, cream-tartar, four ounces; cochineal, well-pulverized, one ounce; boil well and dip the goods while boiling until the color suits.

*Blue:—Quick Process:—*For two pounds of goods, alum, five ounces; cream-tartar, three ounces; boil goods in this one hour, then put goods into warm water which has more or less extract of indigo in it, according to the depth of color desired, and boil again until it suits, adding more of the blue if needed.

*Madder Red:—*To each pound of goods, alum, five ounces; red, or cream-tartar, one ounce. Put in the goods and bring the kettle to a boil, for one-half hour; then air them and boil one-half hour longer; empty the kettle and fill with clean water; put in bran, one peck; make it milk-warm, and let it stand until the bran rises; then skim off the bran and put in one-half pound madder; put in the goods and heat slowly until it boils and is done. Wash in strong suds.

*Green:—*For each pound of goods, fustic, one pound; with alum, three and one-half ounces; steep until strength is out, and soak the goods therein until a good yellow is obtained; then remove the chips, and add extract of indigo or chemic, one tablespoonful at a time, until color suits.

Snuff Brown, Dark:—For five pounds of goods, camwood, one pound; boil it fifteen minutes, then dip the goods three-fourths of an hour; take out the goods, and add to the dye two and one-half pounds fustic; boil ten minutes, and dip the goods three-fourths of an hour; then add blue vitriol, one ounce; copperas, four ounces; dip again one-half hour. If not dark enough, add more copperas.

Another Method:—*Any Shade:*—Boil the goods in a mordant of alum, two parts, copperas three parts; then rinse them through a bath of madder. The tint depends on the relative proportions of the copperas and alum; the more copperas, the darker the dye; joint weight of both should not be more than one-eighth of weight of goods. Mixtures of red and yellows with blues and blacks, or simple dyes, will make any shade.

Orange:—For five pounds of goods, muriate of tin, six tablespoonfuls; argal, four ounces; boil and dip one hour, and add again to the dye one teacupful of madder; dip again one-half hour. Cochineal, about two ounces, in place of madder, makes a much brighter color.

Purple:—For each pound of goods, two ounces of cudbear; rinse the goods well in soap-suds, then dissolve cudbear in hot suds—not quite boiling, and soak the goods until of required color. The color is brightened by rinsing in alum water.

Yellow:—*Rich:*—Work five pounds of goods one-half hour in a boiling bath with three ounces bichromate of potassa and two ounces alum; lift and expose till well-cooled and drained; then work one-half hour in another bath with five pounds of fustic. Wash out and dry.

Crimson:—Work for one hour in a bath with one pound cochineal paste; six ounces of dry cochineal; one pound of tartar; one pint of protochloride of tin. Wash out and dry.

Salmon:—For each pound of goods, one-fourth pound of annatto; one-fourth pound of soap; rinse the goods well in warm water, put them into mixture and boil one-half hour. Shade will be according to the amount of annatto.

Dove and Slate Colors of all Shades:—Boil in an iron vessel a teacupful of black tea with a teaspoonful of copperas, and sufficient water. Dilute till you get the shade wanted.

COTTON GOODS.

Black:—For five pounds of goods, boil them in a decoction of three pounds of sumach one-half hour, and steep twelve hours; dip in lime-water one-half hour; take out and let them drip one hour, run them through the lime-water again fifteen minutes. Make a new dye with two and one-half pounds logwood (boiled one hour), and dip again three hours; add bichromate potash, two ounces, to the logwood dye and dip one hour. Wash in clear, cold water and dry in the shade. Only process for permanent black.

Sky Blue:—For three pounds of goods, blue vitriol, four ounces; boil a few minutes, then dip the goods three hours; then pass them through a strong lime-water. *A beautiful* brown can be obtained by next putting the goods through a solution of prussiate of potash.

Green:—Dip the goods in home-made blue; dye until blue enough is obtained to make the green as dark as required; take out, dry and rinse a little. Make a dye with fustic, three pounds, of logwood three ounces, to each pound of goods, by boiling dye one hour; when cooled so as to bear the hand put in the goods, move briskly a few minutes, and let lie one hour; take out and thoroughly drain; dissolve and add to the dye for each pound of cotton, blue vitriol, one-half ounce, and dip another hour. Wring out and let dry in the shade. By adding or diminishing the logwood and fustic, any shade may be had.

Yellow:—For five pounds of goods, seven ounces of sugar of lead; dip the goods two hours; make a new dye with bichromate of potash, four ounces; dip until the color suits; wring out and dry. If not yellow enough, repeat.

Orange:—For five pounds of goods, sugar of lead, four ounces; boil a few minutes; when a little cool, put in the goods; dip for two hours; wring out; make a new dye with bichromate potash, eight ounces, madder two ounces; dip until it suits; if color is too red, take a small sample and dip into lime-water and choose between them.

Red:—Muriate of tin, two-thirds of a teacupful; add water to cover the goods; raise to boiling heat; put in the goods one hour; stir often; take out, empty the kettle, put in clean water with nic-wood, one pound; steep one-half hour at hand heat; then put in the goods and increase the heat one hour—not boiling. Air the goods and dip them one hour as before. Wash without soap.

Small Points on Table Etiquette.

Delicacy of manner at table stamps both man and woman, for one can, at a glance, discern whether a person has been trained to eat well—*i. e.* to hold the knife and fork properly, to eat without the slightest sound of the lips, to drink quietly, to use the napkin rightly, to make no noise with any of the implements of the table, and last, but not least, to eat slowly and masticate the food thoroughly. All these points should be most carefully taught to children, and then they will always feel at their ease at the grandest tables in the land. There is no position where the innate refinement of a person is more fully exhibited than at the table, and nowhere that those who have not been trained in table etiquette feel more keenly their deficiencies. The knife should never be used to carry food to the mouth, but only to cut it up into small mouthfuls; then place it upon the plate at one side, and take the fork in the right hand, and eat all the food with it. When both have been used finally, they should be laid diagonally across the plate, with both handles towards the right hand; this is understood by well-trained waiters, to be the signal for removing them, together with the plate.

Be careful to keep the mouth shut closely while masticating the food. It is the opening of the lips which causes the smacking which seems very disgusting. Chew your food well, but do it silently, and be careful to take small mouthfuls. The knife can be used to cut the meat finely, as large pieces of meat are not healthful, and appears very indelicate. At many tables, two, three or more knives and forks are placed on the table, the knives at the right hand of the plate, the forks at the left,—a knife and a fork for each course, so that there need be no replacing of them after the breakfast or dinner is served. The smaller ones, which are for game, dessert, or for hot cakes at breakfast, can be tucked under the edges of the plate, and the large ones, for the meat and vegetables, are placed outside of them. Be very careful not to clatter your knives and forks upon your plates, but use them without noise. When you are helped to anything, *do not* wait until the rest of the company are provided, it is not considered good breeding. When passing the plate for a second helping, lay them together at one side of the plate, with handles to the right. Soup is always served for the first course, and it should be eaten with dessert spoons, and taken from the sides, not the tips of them, without any sound of the lips, and not sucked into the mouth audibly from the ends of the spoon. Bread should not be broken into soup or gravy. Never ask to be helped to soup a second time. The hostess may ask you to take a second plate, but you will politely decline. Fish chowder, which is served in soup plates, is said to be an exception which proves this rule, and when eating of that it is correct to take a second plateful, if desired.

Another generally neglected obligation is that of spreading butter on one's bread as it lies in one's plate, or but slightly lifted at one end of the plate; it is very frequently buttered in the air, bitten in gouges, and still held in the face and eyes of the table with the marks of the teeth on it. This is certainly not altogether pleasant, and it is better to cut it, a bit at a time, after buttering it, and put piece by piece in the mouth with one's finger and thumb. Never help yourself to butter, or any other food with your own knife or fork. It is not considered good taste to mix food on the same plate. Salt must be left on the side of the plate and never on the table-cloth.

Let us mention a few things concerning the eating of which there is sometimes doubt. A cream-cake and anything of similar nature should be eaten with knife and fork, never bitten. Asparagus—which should be always served on bread or toast, so as to absorb superfluous moisture—may be taken from the finger and thumb; if it is fit to be set before you, the whole of it may be eaten. Pastry should be broken and eaten with a fork, never cut with a knife. Raw oysters should be eaten with a fork, also fish. Peas and beans, as we all know, require the fork only; however, food that cannot be held with a fork should be eaten with a spoon. Potatoes, if mashed, should be mashed with the fork. Green corn should be eaten from the cob; but it must be held with a single hand.

Celery, cresses, olives, radishes, and relishes of that kind are, of course, to be eaten with the fingers; the salt should be laid upon one's plate, not upon the cloth. Fish is to be eaten with the fork, without the assistance of the knife; a bit of bread in the left hand sometimes helps one to master a refractory morsel. Fresh fruit should be eaten with a silver bladed-knife, especially pears, apples, etc.

Berries, of course, are to be eaten with a spoon. In England they are served with their hulls on, and three or four are considered an ample quantity. But then in England they are many times the size of ours; there they take the big berry by the stem, dip into powdered sugar, and eat it as we do the turnip radish. It is not proper to drink with a spoon in the cup; nor should one, by-the-way, ever quite drain a cup or glass.

Don't, when you drink, elevate your glass as if you were going to stand it inverted on your nose. Bring the glass perpendicularly to the lips, and then lift it to a slight angle. Do this easily.

Drink sparingly while eating. It is far better for the digestion not to drink tea or coffee until the meal is finished. Drink gently, and do not pour it down your throat like water turned out of a pitcher.

When seating yourself at the table, unfold your napkin and lay it across your lap in such a manner that it will not slide off upon the floor; a gentleman should place it across his right knee. Do not tuck it into your neck, like a child's bib. For an old person, however, it is well to attach the napkin to a napkin hook and slip it into the vest or dress buttonholes, to protect their garments, or sew a broad tape at two places on the napkin, and pass it over the head. When the soup is eaten, wipe the mouth carefully with the napkin, and use it to wipe the hands after meals. Finger bowls are not a general institution, and yet they seem to be quite as needful as the napkin, for the fingers are also liable to become a little soiled in eating. They can be had quite cheaply, and should be half-filled with water, and placed upon the side table or butler's tray, with the dessert, bread and cheese, etc. They are passed to each person half-filled with water, placed on a parti-colored napkin with a dessert plate underneath, when the dessert is placed upon the table. A leaf or two of sweet verbena, an orange flower, or a small slice of lemon, is usually put into each bowl to rub upon the fingers. The slice of lemon is most commonly used. The finger tips are slightly dipped into the bowl, the lemon juice is squeezed upon them, and then they are dried softly upon the napkin. At dinner parties and luncheons they are indispensable.

Spoons are sometimes used with firm puddings, but forks are the better style. A spoon should never be turned over in the mouth.

Ladies have frequently an affected way of holding the knife half-way down its length, as if it were too big for their little hands; but this is as awkward a way as it is weak; the knife should be grasped freely by the handle only, the fore-finger being the only one to touch the blade, and that only along the back of the blade at its root, and no further down.

At the conclusion of a course, where they have been used, knife and fork should be laid side by side across the middle of the plate—never crossed; the old custom of crossing them was in obedience to an ancient religious formula. The servant should offer everything at the left of the guest, that the guest may be at liberty to use the right hand. If one has been given a napkin ring, it is necessary to fold one's napkin and use the ring; otherwise the napkin should be left unfolded. One's teeth are not to be picked at table; but if it is impossible to hinder it, it should be done behind the napkin. One may pick a bone at the table, but, as with corn, only one hand is allowed to touch it; yet one can usually get enough from it with knife and fork, which is certainly the more elegant way of doing; and to take her teeth to it gives a lady the look of caring a little too much for the pleasures of the table; one is, however, on no account to suck one's finger after it.

Wherever there is any doubt as to the best way to do a thing, it is wise to follow that which is the most rational, and that will almost invariably be found to be proper etiquette. To be at ease is a great step towards enjoying your own dinner; and making yourself agreeable to the company. There is a reason for everything in polite usage; thus the reason why one does not blow a thing to cool it, is not only that it is an inelegant and vulgar action intrinsically, but because it may be offensive to others—can not help being so, indeed; and it, moreover implies haste, which, whether from greediness or a desire to get away, is equally objectionable. Everything else may be as easily traced to its origin in the fit and becoming.

If, to conclude, one seats one's self properly at table, and takes reason into account, one will do tolerably well. One must not pull one's chair too closely to the table, for the natural result of that is the inability to use one's knife and fork without inconveniencing one's neighbors; the elbows are to be held well in and close to one's side, which cannot be done if the chair is too near the board. One must not lie or lean along the table, nor rest one's arms upon it. Nor is one to touch any of the dishes; if a member of the family, one can exercise all the duties of hospitality through servants, and wherever there are servants, neither family nor guests are to pass or help from any dish. Finally, when rising from your chair leave it where it stands.

Dinner=Giving.

THE LAYING OF THE TABLE AND THE TREATMENT OF GUESTS.

In giving "dinners," the apparently trifling details are of great importance when taken as a whole.

We gather around our board agreeable persons, and they pay us and our dinner the courtesy of dressing for the occasion, and this reunion should be a time of profit as well as pleasure. There are certain established laws by which "dinner giving" is regulated in polite society; and it may not be amiss to give a few observances in relation to them. One of the first is that an invited guest should arrive at the house of his host at least a quarter of an hour before the time appointed for dinner. In laying the table for dinner *all* the linen should be a spotless white throughout, and underneath the linen table-cloth should be spread one of thick cotton-flannel or baize, which gives the linen a heavier and finer appearance, also deadening the sound of moving dishes. Large and neatly folded napkins (ironed without starch), with pieces of bread three or four inches long, placed between the folds, but not to completely conceal it, are laid on each plate. An ornamental centre-piece, or a vase filled with a few rare flowers, is put on the centre of the table, in place of the large table-castor, which has gone into disuse, and is rarely seen now on well-appointed tables. A few choice flowers make a charming variety in the appearance of even the most simply laid table, and a pleasing variety at table is quite as essential to the enjoyment of the repast as is a good choice of dishes, for the eye in fact should be gratified as much as the palate.

All dishes should be arranged in harmony with the decorations of the flowers, such as covers, relishes, confectionary, and small sweets. Garnishing of dishes has also a great deal to do with the appearance of a dinner-table, each dish garnished sufficiently to be in good taste without looking absurd.

Beside each plate should be laid as many knives, forks, and spoons as will be required for the several courses, unless the hostess prefers to have them brought on with each change. A glass of water, and when wine is served glasses for it, and individual salt-cellars may be placed at every plate. Water-bottles are now much in vogue with corresponding tumblers to cover them; these, accompanied with dishes of broken ice, may be arranged in suitable places. When butter is served a special knife is used, and that, with all other required service, may be left to the judgment and taste of the hostess, in the proper placing of the various aids to her guests' comfort.

The dessert plates should be set ready, each with a doily and a finger-glass partly filled with water, in which is dropped a slice of lemon; these, with extra knives, forks and spoons, should be on the side-board ready to be placed by the guest, between the courses when required.

If preferred, the "dinner" may all be served from the side-table, thus relieving the host from the task of carving. A plate is set before each guest, and the dish carved is presented by the waiter on the left-hand side of each guest. At the end of each course the plates give way for those of the next. If not served from the side-table, the dishes are brought in ready carved, and placed before the host and hostess, then served and placed upon the waiter's salver, to be laid by that attendant before the guest.

Soup and fish being the first course, plates of soup are usually placed on the table before the dinner is announced; or if the hostess wishes the soup served at the table, the soup-tureen, containing *hot* soup, and the *warm* soup-plates are placed before the seat of the hostess. Soup and fish being disposed of, then come the joints or roasts, *entrées* (made dishes), poultry, etc., also relishes.

After dishes have been passed that are required no more, such as vegetables, hot sauces, etc., the dishes containing them may be set upon the side-board, ready to be taken away.

Jellies and sauces, when not to be eaten as a dessert, should be helped on the dinner-plate, not on a small side dish as was the former usage.

If a dish be on the table, some parts of which are preferred to others, according to the taste of the individuals, all should have the opportunity of choice. The host will simply ask each one if he has any preference for a particular part; if he replies in the negative, you are not to repeat the question, nor insist that he must have a preference.

Do not attempt to eulogize your dishes, or apologize that you cannot recommend them,—this is extreme bad taste; as also is the vaunting of the excellence of your wines, etc., etc.

Do not insist upon your guests partaking of particular dishes. Do not ask persons more than once, and never force a supply upon their plates. It is ill-bred, though common, to press any one to eat; and moreover, it is a great annoyance to many.

In winter, plates should always be warmed, but not made hot. Two kinds of animal food, or two kinds of dessert, should not be eaten off of one plate, and there should never be more than two kinds of vegetables with one course. Asparagus, green corn, cauliflower and raw tomatoes, comprise one course in place of a salad. All meats should be cut across the grain in very thin slices. Fish, at dinner, should be baked or boiled, never fried or broiled. Baked ham may be used in every course after fish, sliced thin and handed after the regular course is disposed of.

The hostess should retain her plate, knife and fork, until her guests have finished.

The crumb-brush is not used, until the preparation for bringing in the dessert; then all the glasses are removed, except the flowers, the water-tumblers, and the glass of wine which the guest wishes to retain with his dessert. The dessert plate containing the finger-bowl, also a dessert knife and fork, should then be set before each guest, who at once removed the finger-bowl and its doily, and the knife and fork to the table, leaving the plate ready to be used for any dessert chosen.

Finely sifted sugar should always be placed upon the table to be used with puddings, pies, fruit, etc., and if cream is required, let it stand by the dish it is to be served with.

To lay a dessert for a small entertainment, and a few guests outside of the family, it may consist simply of two dishes of fresh fruit in season, two of dried fruits and two each of cakes and nuts.

Coffee and tea are served *lastly*, poured into tiny cups and served clear, passed around on a tray to each guest, then the sugar and cream passed, that each person may be allowed to season his black coffee or *café noir* to suit himself.

A *family dinner*, even with a few friends, can be made quite attractive and satisfactory without much display or expense; consisting first of good soup, then fish garnished with suitable additions, followed by a roast; then vegetables and some made dishes, a salad, crackers, cheese and olives, then dessert. This sensible meal, well-cooked and neatly served, is pleasing to almost any one, and is within the means of any housekeeper in ordinary circumstances.

Measures and Weights

IN ORDINARY USE AMONG HOUSEKEEPERS.

---

4 Teaspoonfuls equal 1 tablespoonful liquid.

4 Tablespoonfuls equal 1 wineglass, or half a gill.

2 Wineglasses equal 1 gill, or half a cup.

2 Gills equal 1 coffee-cupful, or 16 tablespoonfuls.

2 Coffee-cupfuls equal 1 pint.

2 Pints equal 1 quart.

4 Quarts equal 1 gallon.

2 Tablespoonfuls equal 1 ounce, liquid.

1 Tablespoonful of salt equals 1 ounce.

16 Ounces equal 1 pound, or a pint of liquid.

4 Coffee-cupfuls of sifted flour equal 1 pound.

1 Quart of unsifted flour equals 1 pound.

8 or 10 ordinary sized eggs equal 1 pound.

1 Pint of sugar equals 1 pound.   (White granulated.)

2 Coffee-cupfuls of powdered sugar equal 1 pound.

1 Coffee-cupful of cold butter, pressed down, is one half pound.

1 Tablespoonful of soft butter, well rounded, equals 1 ounce.

An ordinary tumblerful equals 1 coffee cupful, or half a pint.

About 25 drops of any thin liquid will fill a common-sized teaspoon.

1 Pint of finely chopped meat, packed solidly, equals one pound.

A set of tin measures (with small spouts or lips), from a gallon down to half a gill, will be found very convenient in every kitchen; though common pitchers, bowls, glasses, etc., may be substituted.